Other Useful Constants

Name	Symbol	Value
Planck's constant	h	4.136×10^{-15} eV $\cdot$ s
Boltzmann's constant	k	8.617×10^{-5} eV/K
Coulomb constant	$e^2/4\pi\varepsilon_0$	14.42 eV $\cdot$ Å $= 1.442$ eV $\cdot$ nm
Electron rest energy	mc^2	0.5110 MeV
Proton rest energy	$M_p c^2$	938.3 MeV
Energy equivalent of $1\,u$	Mc^2	931.5 MeV
Electron magnetic moment	$\mu = e\hbar/2m$	0.9273×10^{-23} J $\cdot$ m^2/Wb
Bohr radius	$a = 4\pi\varepsilon_0\hbar^2/me^2$	0.5292×10^{-10} m
Electron Compton wavelength	$\lambda_c = h/mc$	2.426×10^{-12} m
Fine-structure constant	$\alpha = e^2/4\pi\varepsilon_0\hbar c$	$1/137.0$
Classical electron radius	$r_e = e^2/4\pi\varepsilon_0 mc^2$	2.818×10^{-15} m
Rydberg constant	R_∞	1.097×10^7 m^{-1}

Conversion Factors

$$1\ \text{eV} = 1.602 \times 10^{-19}\ \text{J}$$
$$1\ \text{Å} = 10^{-10}\ \text{m} = 10^{-1}\ \text{nm}$$
$$1\,u = 1.661 \times 10^{-27}\ \text{kg} \leftrightarrow 931.5\ \text{MeV}$$

Fundamentals
of Waves,
Optics, and
Modern Physics

SECOND EDITION

FUNDAMENTALS OF WAVES, OPTICS, AND MODERN PHYSICS

HUGH D. YOUNG
Associate Professor of Physics
Carnegie-Mellon University

McGRAW-HILL BOOK COMPANY
New York   St. Louis   San Francisco   Auckland   Düsseldorf
Johannesburg   Kuala Lumpur   London   Mexico   Montreal   New Delhi
Panama   Paris   São Paulo   Singapore   Sydney   Tokyo   Toronto

FUNDAMENTALS
OF WAVES, OPTICS, AND MODERN PHYSICS

5 6 7 8 9 10   KPKP   8321

Library of Congress Cataloging in Publication Data

Young, Hugh D
    Fundamentals of waves, optics, and modern physics.

    (McGraw-Hill series in fundamentals of physics)
    First published in 1968 under title: Fundamen-
tals of optics and modern physics.
    Includes index.
    1. Physics. 2. Waves. 3. Optics. I. Title.
QC21.2.Y66 1976   530   75-15958
ISBN 0-07-072521-7

This book was set in Bodoni Book by York Graphic Services, Inc.
The editors were Robert A. Fry and Douglas J. Marshall;
the cover was designed by Nicholas Krenitsky;
the production supervisor was Dennis J. Conroy.
New drawings were done by Danmark & Michaels, Inc.
Kingsport Press, Inc., was printer and binder.

Contents

Editor's Introduction

This volume in the Introductory Program of the McGraw-Hill Series in Fundamentals of Physics is devoted primarily to the physics of the twentieth century, including relativity, the successes and failures of classical optics, and the fundamentals of quantum mechanics as applied to atomic and molecular structure, nuclear physics, the solid state, and high-energy physics. Although it can be used independently, this textbook was particularly planned to be used in conjunction with the two companion volumes in this series, *Fundamentals of Mechanics and Heat* by Hugh D. Young and *Fundamentals of Electricity and Magnetism* by Arthur F. Kip. The homogeneity of level and viewpoint of these three books makes them an ideal "package" for a high-level calculus-based introductory physics sequence which includes a substantial component of modern physics. However, the present volume may also be used following any of several other popular texts which include mechanics, heat and thermodynamics, and electromagnetism.

Preface
to the Second Edition

The objectives and basic outline of the book, as described in the original Preface, remain unaltered, but several substantial changes have been made to enhance its usefulness. Here are the most significant changes:

1 The two opening chapters provide a self-contained introduction to the special theory of relativity, including simple but complete derivations of the Lorentz transformations and the relativistic energy and momentum expressions.

2 The treatment of mechanical waves has been expanded somewhat, and now includes consideration of energy and normal modes.

3 The material on physical optics has been reorganized and expanded into two chapters; among the additions are a section on circular polarization, material on diffraction from a circular aperture, and a section on holography.

4 The chapter on statistical mechanics now includes an introduction to the elementary kinetic theory of an ideal gas, including a derivation of the equation of state and a discussion of specific heats.

5 The treatment of quantum mechanics and its applications to atomic systems has been simplified somewhat, but no important results from the first edition have been deleted.

6 The chapter on fundamental particles has been updated and expanded, especially the material on classifying particles and interactions and the role of symmetry and conservation principles.

7 Several topics not included in the first edition have been added; there is a new section on lasers and masers, one on nuclear decay rates, and one on the biological effects of radiation.

8 Nearly 200 new problems have been added, bringing the total to over 500 and providing greater variety and broader coverage than in the first edition.

The book may be used in its entirety for a one-semester, four- or five-credit-hour course, following introductory courses in mechanics, thermodynamics, and electromagnetism. For a three-credit-hour course some instructors may wish to shorten it somewhat by the omission of certain topics. Any or all of Chapters 7 and 12 through 16, and numerous sections within the other chapters, may be omitted without interrupting the continuity. Thus courses with a variety of length and emphasis can be constructed. The position of the relativity chapters is somewhat arbitrary; this material can be postponed until after Chapter 7 if desired.

ACKNOWLEDGMENTS

It is a pleasure for the author again to express his gratitude to his colleagues at Carnegie-Mellon and elsewhere for their many valuable comments and suggestions. Their kindness and generosity are greatly appreciated. In particular, John Rayne, D. Allan Bromley, Arthur F. Kip, Daniel Sober, Ray Tipsword, Chia-Wei Woo, James McCarthy, and Albion Kromminga have read the manuscript and have provided many critical but constructive comments. The author also wishes to thank Carnegie-Mellon University for providing a supported leave of absence during which much of the work of this revision was accomplished, and the University of California at Berkeley for its hospitality during this period. Mrs. Linda Billard typed most of the manuscript and did a superb job of deciphering the author's scrawlings.

Finally and most important, the author acknowledges again his great debt to his wife Alice and his children Gretchen and Rebecca for their unending patience, confidence, and moral support throughout the writing and revising of this text.

HUGH D. YOUNG

Preface
to the First Edition

The principal objective of this book is to present in elementary form some of the most important physical theory that has been developed during the current century. Contemporary concepts of atomic and nuclear physics and the structure of matter are presented against a background of classical mechanics, electrodynamics, and optics, and at each stage in the presentation the empirical basis and physical motivation of new developments are exhibited clearly. Analytical techniques such as calculus and vector analysis are used freely wherever they are needed, and a strong attempt is made to exhibit the spirit of scientific inquiry and the empirical basis of natural science.

Specifically, this book is intended for the conclusion of a series of courses with a total length of one to two years, starting in the freshman or sophomore college year, and with a concurrent course in calculus. For the beginning of the sequence, the other volumes in the McGraw-Hill Series in Fundamentals of Physics are particularly suitable because of their uniformity of level and viewpoint, but there are several other suitable combinations.

As the table of Contents shows, the subject of optics is regarded as a natural and useful bridge between classical mechanics and electrodynamics and contemporary quantum theory. The classical theory of optics is a natural outgrowth of classical electrodynamics; in turn, optical phenomena have provided much of the important motivation for the development of quantum mechanics and its many applications, especially to an understanding of the macroscopic behavior of matter on the basis of its microscopic structure, one of the unifying themes of this book.

The table of Contents indicates the scope of the book, but we also wish to point out the following features:

1 The book assumes that the student has taken a thorough course in classical mechanics, electromagnetism, and elementary thermodynamics, including

Maxwell's equations in integral form. However, applications of these equations are spelled out in considerable detail, since for most students they will be new and somewhat unfamiliar. Calculus and vector algebra, including line and surface integrals, are used freely where needed, but no knowledge of the vector differential operations (grad, div, and curl) is assumed. As is customary, vector quantities are denoted by boldface symbols; in addition, boldface **+**, **−**, **Σ**, and **=** signs are used in vector equations to denote vector operations and equality.

2 The book attempts to exhibit the inductive and empirical nature of physics along with its deductive aspects. Care has been taken to distinguish clearly between principles that are generalizations from experience and those that are derived and to indicate the experimental basis of the former. The relative status of each principle in the whole logical structure is thus made clear. The author has made every effort to avoid the two extremes of a dry recitation of experimental results or of a tightly knit body of theory without reference to empirical observations.

3 Throughout the book the importance of *models* is stressed. We rarely deal directly with physical reality but rather with simplified models designed to retain the essential features of a physical situation and eliminate the unessential ones, to facilitate analysis. The student is constantly reminded of the process of constructing models as idealizations of reality as well as of the limitations of analytical results imposed by the limitations of validity of the models.

4 The texture of the book is not entirely even; some sections are more difficult reading than others. This variation is deliberate; some topics are intrinsically more subtle or demanding than others, and in addition not all students have equal abilities. Almost always the most difficult sections are arranged in such a way that they can be omitted without undue interruption of continuity. In addition, several important topics which are likely to cause difficulty, such as the concept of waves, wave pulses, and group velocity, are introduced several different times with a "spiral" approach, in order to help the student attain successively higher levels of sophistication in these important but sometimes elusive concepts. In the latter chapters of the book, some topics which are conceptually most subtle are softened somewhat by including less than the usual amount of analytical detail.

5 The mks system of units is used exclusively. There seems little doubt that it will eventually be used universally in scientific work. In addition, the author feels strongly that the burden of mastering several systems of units simultaneously should not be added to that of mastering new physical concepts.

6 A large collection of over 300 problems is included. A few of them are simple substitution exercises, designed to illustrate definitions, but most require some thought and insight on the part of the student. Many of the problems are literal or algebraic rather than numerical; some are too difficult for all except the best students, and there is plenty of material for "honors" sections. Many problems ask only for an order of magnitude or for a discussion; the author feels strongly that such questions are often at least as instructive as more specific problems having a definite numerical answer. For some problems the student will need to look up additional information in the *Handbook of Chemistry and Physics* or a similar reference; familiarity with such standard reference works is highly recommended.

Although this book is intended primarily as a high-level introductory text, it may also be used for an intermediate-level course following a first general physics course given without calculus. A thorough and detailed exposition of principles and a plentiful supply of challenging problems make it useful for such intermediate courses.

HUGH D. YOUNG

Fundamentals
of Waves,
Optics, and
Modern Physics

PROSPECTUS

"To both the intellect and the emotions the study of physics is exciting, satisfying, and even beautiful, and it is the author's intention to convey these qualities to the student." This remark appears at the beginning of the first volume of the Fundamentals of Physics Series, but it is even more appropriate for the present volume. The subject matter of this book includes some of the most exciting areas of physics, concentrating particularly on the physics that has developed in the twentieth century, some of it even during the lifetime of the reader. These recent years have witnessed many revolutionary changes in our conception of the physical world in which we live and remarkable progress in our understanding of it.

The special theory of relativity is a natural starting point for our study of twentieth-century physics. The concepts of this theory, including the relative nature of space and time and of matter and energy, and the role of the observer in measurements, provide a unifying thread that runs through all of contemporary physics and plays an essential role in our present-day understanding of the nature and structure of the physical world.

From relativity we proceed into optics; this is a logical direction for the continuation of our study, for a variety of reasons. Some branches of optics, especially those concerned with wave phenomena, are a natural outgrowth of classical electrodynamics and provide a beautiful illustration of the great power of Maxwell's electromagnetic field equations in unifying various branches of physical science. Conversely, however, the shortcomings and insufficiencies of this so-called classical branch of optics, especially with problems involving the interaction of matter and radiation, provided the original motivation for the development of quantum mechanics, one of the central themes in this book.

Since the language of waves and wave phenomena occupies a central

1

position in both classical optics and contemporary quantum mechanics, we first undertake a general discussion of waves, using as a prototype problem the propagation of waves in a simple mechanical system. The wave concept, together with Maxwell's electromagnetic field equations, provides the basis for an understanding of a wide variety of optical phenomena such as interference, diffraction, and polarization. We then discuss these, along with the simpler but more specialized subject of geometrical optics.

With Chap. 8 we begin an investigation of the inadequacies of classical optics, and in the process of analyzing them we develop the basic ideas of quantum mechanics, which form the core subject matter for the remainder of the book. A number of phenomena are introduced, concerning the structure of atoms and the interaction of radiation with matter, which cannot be understood on the basis of classical newtonian mechanics (even with relativistic modifications) and classical electromagnetism as formulated in Maxwell's equations. We discuss in some detail the basic modifications in the formal structure of these disciplines which are needed for the foundation of quantum mechanics.

The next several chapters are devoted to applications of quantum mechanics to various systems whose understanding is central to a thorough analysis of the structure and properties of matter. Beginning with the simplest atom, hydrogen, we progress to more complicated atoms, molecules, matter in the solid state, and finally the structure of nuclei and of fundamental particles.

The careful reader will notice several central themes running throughout this book. Among them are the use of idealized models to simplify complex situations, the general concepts of waves and of wave propagation, the relationship of the microscopic structure of matter to its macroscopic properties, and such fundamental concepts as mass, energy, momentum, force, and the associated conservation principles. In these common themes is found much of the great power and beauty of physical science.

The author has tried throughout to exhibit his personal conviction that physics is beautiful, exciting, and satisfying. It is his hope that the reader will enjoy understanding new principles and grasping their power and usefulness and will feel the satisfaction and personal achievement that come from struggling with and solving challenging problems.

Relativity | 1

The special theory of relativity is one of the indispensable cornerstones of the entire structure of twentieth-century physics. It is based on the principle that all inertial frames of reference are completely equivalent with respect to the formulation of physical laws. This requirement can be satisfied for both the laws of mechanics and those of electromagnetism only when certain modifications are made in the familiar relationships between distances and time intervals measured in two different coordinate systems which are moving relative to each other. The modified *kinematic* relations which result also necessitate a reformulation and generalization of the laws of *dynamics*. The resulting principles have greater generality than those based on Newton's laws; newtonian mechanics emerges as a special case of the more general formation, retaining its validity in situations where all speeds are much smaller than the speed of light.

1-1 INVARIANCE OF PHYSICAL LAWS

The concept of *inertial frame of reference* plays an essential role in newtonian mechanics. By definition, a coordinate system in which Newton's laws of motion are found to be valid is called an inertial frame of reference. For many purposes the earth may be taken as an inertial frame, although its rotation and orbital motion make it not precisely an inertial frame. A rotating merry-go-round or an accelerating truck is *not* an inertial frame; when the motion of a body is described using coordinates based on such a system, Newton's laws are *not* obeyed.

Once an inertial frame has been found, any other frame moving relative to it with constant velocity is *also* inertial, because the acceleration of a body is the same when measured in the two frames. Newton's laws of motion are

3

valid *only* in an inertial frame, but they are valid in *all* inertial frames. Any inertial frame is as good as any other in stating the basic principles of mechanics; some may be more *convenient* than others for specific problems, but there is no difference in *principle*.

An observer who drops an object in a moving train may see it drop straight down, while to an observer standing beside the track the object appears to follow a parabolic path. To *each* observer, using velocities and accelerations measured in his own frame of reference, Newton's laws are obeyed. For mechanics, at least, there is no evidence for a single coordinate system that is better than all others for describing motion; all inertial frames of reference are equivalent. To put it another way: *The laws of mechanics are the same (invariant) in every inertial frame of reference.*

Einstein proposed in 1905 that this principle should be extended to *all* the laws of physics. This is a natural suggestion; when a phenomenon is observed in two different inertial frames, it would be very strange if some of the governing physical laws were the same in both systems while others were different. Obvious though Einstein's proposal may seem, it has very subtle and far-reaching consequences.

We first consider wave propagation in matter. This may appear to be extraneous, but the basic ideas are central to our discussion. We consider a source of sound waves that is stationary in a mass of air through which the waves travel out from the source. Experiment shows that to an observer at rest in the frame of reference of the source and the air, the waves travel with a definite speed in all directions. To a moving observer, however, the speed appears different. In Fig. 1-1, observer A is moving away from the source, and the apparent speed in his frame of reference is *less* than in the stationary frame. If the wave speed relative to the air is v and the speed of the observer u, then A measures a wave speed of not v but $v - u$. Similarly, observer B is approaching the source and measures a speed relative to his frame of reference of $v + u$. This asymmetry does not violate our basic premise of equivalence of inertial frames because the air is at rest in only one frame.

Do these considerations apply also to *optical* phenomena? In the early nineteenth century it was known with a fair degree of certainty that light is a wave phenomenon. Physicists of that era liked to picture everything in mechanical terms, and it was commonly thought that light should have some material medium in which to travel, analogous to air or other matter as a medium for sound waves. This hypothetical medium was given the name *the ether*. Its properties had to be strange indeed; its density would have to be immeasurably small, yet it must be extremely rigid to account for the large value of the speed of light.

If the ether existed, one ought to be able to determine our motion relative

Fig. 1-1 The speed of sound emitted by a moving source is different for observer B moving toward the source and for observer A moving away from the source.

to it by measuring the speed of light in various directions, just as with sound waves as discussed above. A great deal of effort was put into experiments to measure this *ether drift*, as it came to be called. The details of these experiments need not concern us; the best known are those of Michelson and Morley, beginning in 1881 and extending over several decades. The results were entirely negative; no evidence for any motion relative to the ether was found, despite the fact that the earth in its orbital motion moves through space in different directions at different times of the year. From these and other experiments it became more and more clear that *there is no ether*. The behavior of light in vacuum cannot be understood on the basis of propagation through a material medium.

In the absence of such a medium, we are forced to conclude that if all inertial frames of reference are to be equivalent for light propagation as well as mechanical phenomena, then *the speed of light in vacuum must be the same in all inertial frames*. It follows that the speed of light is independent of the motion of its source. Once light is emitted by a source, it "forgets" whatever motion the source may have relative to a given observer and travels with a definite speed independent of this motion.

In recent years this conclusion has been confirmed directly by experiment. In 1962 J. G. Fox and collaborators measured the speed of electromagnetic radiation emitted by decay of π^0 mesons moving at high speeds relative to the observer. Their results confirmed the conclusion that the speed of light is independent of the motion of source or observer.

The speed of light, a universal physical constant, is one of the most precisely known of all physical constants. It is usually denoted by c; its value is

$$c = 2.997925 \times 10^8 \text{ m/s} \tag{1-1}$$

with a probable uncertainty of 0.000001 m/s. The approximate value $c = 3.00 \times 10^8$ m/s is in error by less than one part in 1000 and is often used when greater accuracy is not needed.

To make certain the reader is sufficiently impressed by our conclusion concerning the speed of light, we return to Fig. 1-1. If instead of a bell we have a light source emitting radiation with speed c relative to the source and observer A measures the speed of this radiation in *his* frame of reference, he will obtain the value c despite the fact that he is moving away from the source with speed u. This conclusion is the first of several in this chapter which appear at first not to agree with common sense, but it is correct. We must keep in mind that what we call common sense is intuition growing out of everyday experience, and this experience does not include measuring speeds of the magnitude of the speed of light. Thus intuition may often be misleading in domains far-removed from everyday experience.

1-2   GALILEAN TRANSFORMATION

To explore the consequences of the special role of the speed of light in kinematics, we now proceed to a detailed analysis of the relationships between two inertial frames of reference. We consider two coordinate systems, which we call S and S', as shown in Fig. 1-2. Let the x and x' axes coincide, but let S' move along this line relative to S, with constant speed u. The two origins O and O' coincide at time $t = 0$; then at time t the distance between O and O' is ut.

Any point P can be located by its coordinates (x,y,z) in system S or, alternatively, its coordinates (x',y',z') in S'. The figure shows that these coordinates are related by

$$x' = x - ut \qquad y' = y \qquad z' = z \tag{1-2}$$

Fig. 1-2 Position of point P described in two different coordinate systems S and S'. S' moves relative to S with constant velocity u along the x and x' axes; the two origins O and O' coincide at time $t = 0$.

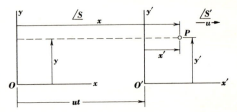

By taking the second derivative of each of Eqs. (1-2), recalling that u is constant, we see immediately that the components of acceleration of P are the same in the two systems; hence Newton's second law is *invariant* under the transformation of coordinates given by Eqs. (1-2). Such a coordinate transformation is called a *galilean transformation.*

The relationship between the *velocities* of a point P measured in the two systems is of particular interest. For example, suppose a rifle bullet is fired in the $+x$ direction with a speed $v = dx/dt$ as observed in S. What is its speed $v' = dx'/dt$ with respect to S'? This question can be answered immediately by taking the time derivative of the first of Eqs. (1-2):

$$\frac{dx'}{dt} = \frac{dx}{dt} - u \qquad \text{or} \qquad v' = v - u \tag{1-3}$$

which says that the speed v' measured in S' is less than the speed v measured in S, the difference u simply being the speed of the system S' with respect to S, as we might have guessed. Comparing this result with our discussion of the speed of light, we see a clear contradiction. If Eq. (1-3) is correct for the motion of light as well as material bodies, then the speed c' in frame S' must be related to the speed c in S by

$$c' = c - u$$

Einstein's postulates and the absence of an ether require instead that $c' = c$. Thus if the equivalence of all inertial frames is to hold for both mechanics and electrodynamics, the formulation of newtonian mechanics is in need of modification. As we shall see, Eqs. (1-2) are correct only in the limit of very small values of u but must be modified when u approaches the speed of light.

There is also direct evidence that at high speeds newtonian mechanics is not precisely correct. One example is an experiment in which the relationship between kinetic energy and speed is examined.[1] The results can be compared with the newtonian relation $E_k = \frac{1}{2}mv^2$. Electrons are accelerated in a vacuum tube by an arrangement similar to that used to produce the electron beam in a TV picture tube. They are then sent down a long evacuated pipe, and their speeds are measured directly by measuring the time of flight down the tube. Their kinetic energies are determined from the electrical potential difference through which they are accelerated.

The result of this experiment, shown graphically in Fig. 1-3, is an empirical determination of the functional relationship between speed and kinetic energy. Two striking features are evident. The empirical result agrees

---

[1] This experiment is beautifully illustrated in a film *The Ultimate Speed*, by W. Bertozzi, Education Development Center, Newton, Mass., 1962.

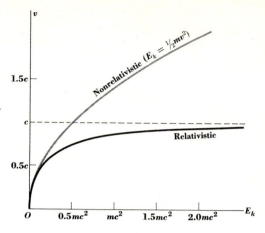

Fig. 1-3 Relation between the speed v of a particle and its kinetic energy E_k. The speed never exceeds c, no matter how great the kinetic energy. At speeds small compared to c, the kinetic energy is approximately $\frac{1}{2}mv^2$, but at larger speeds this expression deviates more and more from the relativistically correct equation.

with the newtonian one at small speeds but departs more and more significantly from it at higher speeds. In addition, the speed appears to be tending toward an asymptotic value c, as though the speed might never exceed c no matter how much the energy is increased. We shall return to this experiment later; for the present we take it as an additional piece of evidence for the conclusion that newtonian mechanics needs to be reexamined carefully and modified wherever necessary.

In beginning this examination, we mention two assumptions which may seem too obvious to require discussion and yet lie at the very heart of the problem. First, in deriving Eqs. (1-2), we assumed that when two observers moving relative to each other measure the distance between two points at a given time, they obtain the same result; rulers do not shrink or expand when moving. We also assumed that the *time scale* is the same for both coordinate systems; $t' = t$. This assumption, in turn, implies that it is possible to observe two clocks moving relative to each other and to determine with certainty that they remain synchronized during their motion.

These assumptions are certainly in accord with intuition based on everyday observation; yet we must consider the possibility that seemingly obvious conclusions may require modification when applied to situations far-removed from everyday experience. It is shown in the next section that *both* assumptions, the invariance of length and the universal time scale, require modification in order to conform to a more general principle of invariance of physical laws under coordinate transformations.

In the experiments on which newtonian mechanics is based, speeds are always small compared with that of light; hence it is essential that the modified mechanical principles reduce to the newtonian principles when the speeds are sufficiently small. Newtonian mechanics must retain its validity for the class of phenomena for which it was originally developed.

1-3 RELATIVITY OF TIME

In developing the consequences of Einstein's postulates, it is often helpful to consider imaginary experiments which illustrate particular points. Such experiments, often called *thought experiments*,[1] are very useful in clarifying new physical theories. In discussing thought experiments, it is necessary to be extremely careful lest assumptions incompatible with the basic postulate of relativity sneak in unnoticed, for we are on ground where intuition can be misleading, and it is essential to proceed with utmost caution.

Frequently thought experiments involve the description of one or more *events* in various frames of reference. A description of an event includes the position and time at which it occurs. An event described in a frame of reference S as (x,y,z,t) may be described in a second frame S' as (x',y',z',t'). One of our goals will be to derive a general transformation which relates these two descriptions; the result, the *Lorentz transformation*, is a generalization of the newtonian relations given by Eqs. (1-2).

We begin by questioning the newtonian assumption that $t = t'$, that is, that there exists a universal time scale for all reference frames. The question is best stated as follows: When two events occur, each observed in two frames of reference S and S', will the time interval between the two events appear the same or different?

In attempting to answer this question qualitatively, we first point out that measuring times and time intervals involves the concept of *simultaneity* of two events. When we say that a bus leaves the station at noon, we mean that the event of the bus passing the end of the platform is simultaneous with the event of the hour hand of the clock arriving at the number 12. The fundamental difficulty with time measurements is that two events that appear simultaneous in one frame of reference do not in general appear simultaneous in a second frame moving relative to the first.

The following thought experiment, devised by Einstein, illustrates this point. Consider a long train moving with uniform velocity, as shown in Fig. 1-4a. Two lightning bolts strike the train, one at each end. Each bolt leaves a mark on the train and on the ground at the same instant. The points on the ground are labeled A and B in the figure and the corresponding points on the train A' and B'. An observer on the ground is located at O, midway between A and B; another observer is at O', moving with the train and midway between A' and B'. Both these observers use the light signals from the lightning to observe the events.

Suppose the two lightning bolts strike at such times that the two light pulses reach the observer at O simultaneously; he concludes that the two

---

Fig. 1-4 (*a*) To the stationary observer *O*, two lightning bolts appear to strike the two ends of the train simultaneously. (*b*) The light pulse from the front of the train arrives at the position of the moving observer *O'* sooner than that from the rear; hence *O'* thinks the front bolt struck first. (*c*) The two light pulses arrive at *O* simultaneously, and this observer thinks the two bolts were simultaneous.

events took place at *A* and *B* simultaneously. But the observer at *O'* is moving with the train, and the light pulse from *B'* reaches him before the light pulse from *A'*; he concludes that the event at the front of the train happened *earlier* than that at the rear. Thus the two events appear simultaneous to one observer but not to the other. More generally, whether or not two events occurring at points distant from an observer are simultaneous depends on the state of motion of the observer. Thus the time interval between two distant events is different for two observers in relative motion.

A reader steeped in the newtonian tradition might argue that in this example the lightning bolts really *are* simultaneous and that if the observer at *O'* could communicate with the distant points without time delay, he would realize this. But the finite speed of information transmission is *not* the problem. If *O'* is really midway between *A'* and *B'*, then in his frame of reference the time for a signal to travel from *A'* to *O'* is the same as from *B'* to *O'*. Two signals arrive simultaneously at *O'* only if they were emitted simultaneously at *A'* and *B'*, and since in this example they do not arrive simultaneously at *O'*, *O'* must conclude that the events at *A'* and *B'* were not simultaneous.

Furthermore, we have no basis for saying that *O* is right and *O'* is wrong, or the reverse, since according to our basic postulate no inertial frame is preferred over any other in the formulation of physical laws. Each observer is correct *in his own frame of reference*, and we have to conclude that *simultaneity is not an absolute concept.* Whether or not two events are simultaneous depends on the frame of reference in which they are observed, and the time *interval* between two events is different for observers in different frames of reference.

To obtain a quantitative relationship between time intervals, we consider another thought experiment. A frame of reference *S'* moves with velocity

u relative to a frame S. An observer O' in S' has a source of light which he directs at a mirror a distance d away, oriented so that the light is reflected back to him as shown in Fig. 1-5. This observer measures the time interval $\Delta t'$ required for a light pulse to make the round trip to the mirror and back. The total distance, as measured in S', is $2d$, the speed is c, and the time required is

$$\Delta t' = \frac{2d}{c} \tag{1-4}$$

Now we consider how this experiment looks to an observer at O, with respect to which O' is moving with speed u. Let the time interval observed by O for the round trip be Δt. During this time, the source moves relative to O a distance $u \, \Delta t$, as shown in Fig. 1-5b. The total round-trip distance as seen by O is not $2d$ but

$$2l = 2\sqrt{d^2 + (\tfrac{1}{2}u \, \Delta t)^2} \tag{1-5}$$

According to the basic postulate of relativity, the speed of light c is the same with respect to both observers, and so the relation in S analogous to Eq. (1-4) is

$$\Delta t = \frac{2l}{c} = \frac{2}{c} \sqrt{d^2 + (\tfrac{1}{2}u \, \Delta t)^2} \tag{1-6}$$

Equations (1-4) and (1-6) can be combined to obtain a relationship between Δt and $\Delta t'$ which does not contain the distance d. We solve Eq. (1-4) for d, substitute the result in Eq. (1-6), and solve for Δt. The result of this algebraic manipulation is

$$\Delta t = \frac{\Delta t'}{\sqrt{1 - u^2/c^2}} \tag{1-7}$$

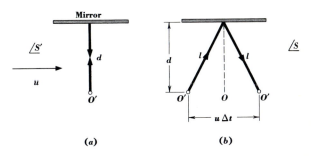

Fig. 1-5 (a) Light pulse emitted at O' and reflected back along the same line, as observed in S'. (b) Path of the same light pulse, as observed in S. The initial and final positions of O' are shown. The light path is longer in S than in S', but the speed of the pulse is the same in both.

We may generalize this important result: If two events occurring at the same space point in a frame of reference S' (in this case, the departure and arrival of light signal at O') are observed to be separated in time by an interval $\Delta t'$, then the time interval Δt between these two events as observed in the frame of reference S is *larger* than $\Delta t'$, and the two are related by Eq. (1-7). Thus a clock moving with S' appears to an observer in S to run at a rate which is *slower* than the rate observed in S'. This effect is called *time dilation.*

Example

The π^+ meson (pion) is an unstable particle with mass about 273 times that of the electron. After it is produced in a high-energy collision between nuclear particles, it lives on the average about 2.6×10^{-8} s before decaying into a muon and a neutrino. This time is measured in a frame of reference in which the particle is at rest (the *rest frame* of the particle). If such a particle is created with a speed $u = 0.99c$, what is its lifetime as measured in the laboratory, and how far does it travel during that time?

Solution

We identify S' with the particle's frame and S with that of the laboratory. Thus $\Delta t' = 2.6 \times 10^{-8}$ s. Using Eq. (1-7), we find

$$\Delta t = \frac{\Delta t'}{\sqrt{1 - u^2/c^2}} = \frac{2.6 \times 10^{-8} \text{ s}}{\sqrt{1 - (0.99c)^2/c^2}} = 18.4 \times 10^{-8} \text{ s}$$

This represents a dilation of the time interval of about a factor of 7. The distance d traveled in S during this interval is

$$d = u\,\Delta t = (0.99)(3.0 \times 10^8 \text{ m/s})(18.4 \times 10^{-8} \text{ s}) = 54.7 \text{ m}$$

Of course, not all the particles live the same time in S'; there is a statistical distribution of decay times. But if all particles have the same velocity, there lifetimes are all dilated by the same factor, so the *average* lifetime in S is increased relative to that in S' by this same factor.

This dependence of apparent lifetime on velocity is a well-established experimental fact. A more dramatic example occurs in the production and decay of hyperons (particles of mass greater than protons and neutrons). For example, the Σ^+ hyperon, produced in high-energy proton-proton collisions, has a lifetime at rest of about 0.8×10^{-10} s. Except for the relativistic time dilation, a Σ^+ with speed close to c could travel less than 3 cm between production and decay. But a Σ^+ with energy 80 GeV has a speed $0.9999c$, corresponding to a time-dilation factor of about 70, and can travel about 2 m in the laboratory, far enough to permit a variety of experiments with a beam of such particles.

The derivation of Eq. (1-7) is not complete without two additional remarks. First, the observer in S who measures the time interval Δt between the departure and arrival of the light pulse cannot make this measurement with only one clock, because the two events occur at different points in S. If he uses a single clock at the point of departure, there arises the question of the time required for the signal to travel to the clock from the point at which the light pulse returns. This difficulty is easily circumvented by using *two* clocks, one where the light pulse departs and one where it returns. Since these two clocks are both stationary in S, it is possible to synchronize them unambiguously. It is of course essential to avoid errors introduced by the finite propagation time for light signals, but this is not difficult. One scheme is to place a light source midway between the clocks and send a light pulse. The operators of both clocks set their clocks at the prearranged time when they receive the signal. Many other schemes are possible. In any event, there is no difficulty in synchronizing two or any number of clocks *in a single frame of reference*, and it is often useful in thought experiments to consider many synchronized clocks distributed in a frame of reference. Only when a clock is moving relative to a frame of reference do synchronization difficulties arise.

Second, we have assumed the distance d in Fig. 1-5 to be the same in S and S'. This assumption, though correct, is not quite as trivial as it may appear. To justify it, we observe that to measure the length of a ruler stationary in S' but moving in S requires simultaneous observation of the positions of the two ends. When the ruler is moving perpendicular to its length, as in the measurement of the distance d in Fig. 1-5, there is no problem; we need only to station observers along the line described by the midpoint of the ruler. All such observers, whether moving or not, agree on the simultaneity of arrival of the ends of the moving ruler at predetermined points and thus on the length measured in the various frames of reference. When the ruler moves *parallel* to its length, the situation is quite different, as we shall see in the next section.

Because a time interval between two events occurring at the same point in a given frame of reference is more fundamental than one between two events at *different* space points, we use the term *proper time* to designate a time interval between two events at the *same point* in a given frame of reference. Equation (1-7) shows that when the relative velocity u of the two observers is small compared with c, the quantity u^2/c^2 is extremely small; then Δt is very nearly equal to $\Delta t'$. Hence, in the limit as $u \to 0$, this relationship approaches the newtonian $\Delta t = \Delta t'$, which assumes an absolute time scale for all frames of reference.

1-4 RELATIVITY OF LENGTH

Because of the relative nature of time intervals and simultaneity, we anticipate that there may be difficulties in comparing length measurements in different frames of reference, especially when the lengths are measured parallel to the direction of motion. To measure the length of a ruler, we must observe the positions of its two ends *simultaneously*, but what is simultaneous in one frame may not be in another. Suppose a ruler is at rest in a coordinate system S' and lies parallel to the x' axis. Both ruler and S' move with uniform velocity u with respect to another frame of reference S. If observers in S and S' measure the length of this ruler, how will their results compare?

One way to measure the length in each coordinate system, at least in principle, is to attach a source of light to one end of the ruler and a mirror to the other end. One can then send a pulse of light toward the mirror and measure the amount of time required for it to be reflected back to the source. This thought experiment is illustrated in Fig. 1-6, which shows the process as it appears both in S' and in S. Denoting by l' the length measured in S', we observe that the time $\Delta t'$ required for the light pulse to travel the length of the ruler twice is given simply by

$$\Delta t' = \frac{2l'}{c} \tag{1-8}$$

This is a *proper* time interval, since it is measured between two events, the departure and arrival of the light pulse, at the same space point in S'.

From the point of view of S, the light pulse leaving the left end must travel farther than l (the ruler length in S) because the ruler is displaced during its travel. We let the total light path from source to mirror be d and the time of travel from source to mirror be Δt_1. Then, during this time, the mirror moves a distance $u \, \Delta t_1$, so the total light path, as shown in Fig. 1-6, is

$$d = l + u \, \Delta t_1 \tag{1-9}$$

It is also true, of course, that $d = c \, \Delta t_1$, since the light pulse travels with constant speed c. Combining this with Eq. (1-9) to eliminate d, we find

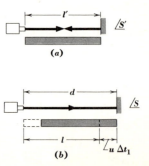

Fig. 1-6 (*a*) Light pulse emitted from a source at one end of a ruler, reflected from a mirror at the opposite end and returning to the source, as seen in S'. (*b*) Same light pulse, viewed from S. The light pulse travels farther than the length of the ruler, since the ruler is moving in S with speed u. The speed of the light pulse in S is the same as in S'.

$$\Delta t_1 = \frac{l}{c - u}$$

In exactly the same way, one can show that the time Δt_2 required for the return trip is given by

$$\Delta t_2 = \frac{l}{c + u}$$

Thus the total time $\Delta t = \Delta t_1 + \Delta t_2$ required for the entire trip, as observed in S, is

$$\Delta t = \frac{l}{c - u} + \frac{l}{c + u} = \frac{2l}{c(1 - u^2/c^2)} \tag{1-10}$$

This relationship differs from Eq. (1-8) by the factor $1 - u^2/c^2$ in the denominator.

We also know that the time intervals Δt and $\Delta t'$ are related by Eq. (1-7) since $\Delta t'$ is a proper time interval in S' and Δt is the interval between the same two events as observed in S. Substituting the expressions for the time intervals, Eqs. (1-8) and (1-10), into Eq. (1-7) and rearranging, we obtain

$$l = l' \sqrt{1 - \frac{u^2}{c^2}} \tag{1-11}$$

This important result shows that the length l measured in S, in which the ruler is moving, is *shorter* than the length l' in S', in which it is at rest. As with time intervals, it is customary to call a length measured in the rest frame of the body a *proper length*. Thus Eq. (1-11) shows that the length observed by a moving observer is always less than the proper length, an effect referred to as *length contraction*. As in the case of time dilation, we note that when $v \ll c$, the length-contraction relation, Eq. (1-11), reduces to the newtonian one, $l = l'$.

Example
In the π^+ meson example in Sec. 1-3, what distance does the pion travel as measured in its rest frame?

Solution
In this case the path d measured in the laboratory is the proper length, and in the pion's rest frame the path length d' appears contracted by the factor given in Eq. (1-11):

$$d' = d \sqrt{1 - \frac{u^2}{c^2}} = (54.7 \text{ m}) \sqrt{1 - \frac{(0.99c)^2}{c^2}} = 7.71 \text{ m}$$

We note that an observer moving with the pion can calculate his speed relative to the laboratory (frame S) from this information:

$$u = \frac{d'}{\Delta t'} = \frac{7.71 \text{ m}}{2.6 \times 10^{-8} \text{ s}} = 2.97 \times 10^8 \text{ m/s}$$

which agrees with the direct measurement.

It is important to note that in discussing length measurements by various observers we always assumed that each observer uses appropriate equipment to determine the positions of two end points *simultaneously* in his frame of reference. In *visual* observation from a single point this is not what happens at all. When a rapidly moving car cuts across our path of vision, we see positions of points on the far side at *earlier* times than for points on the near side because the light signals take longer to reach us. Points on the near side appear to be *ahead* of corresponding points on the far side.

Thus if one could make visual observations of a body moving with a speed approaching c, the effect would be much more complex than a simple foreshortening in the direction of motion. Different points are at different distances from the observers, light signals require different times to travel from these points to the observer, and one sees their positions at different times. The result is a complex change of shape and orientation of the body. An example is shown in Fig. 1-7. Since such observations are impossible in practice, these considerations have only theoretical interest, but in actual

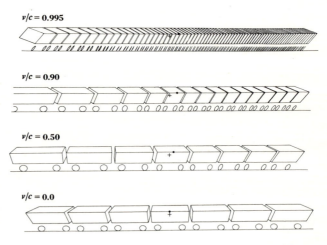

Fig. 1-7 Views of a train of boxcars (each 1 by 1 by 3 units) by an observer 10 units away at an angle 30° above the plane of the tracks. The axis of the observer's camera is directed at the center of the middle car shown by a cross (+). The dot (·) marks the center of the near edge of the middle car in each case. (From G. D. Scott and H. J. van Driel, *Amer. J. Phys.*, **38**, 971 (1970). Used by permission.)

experiments, signal transit time must always be considered carefully in equipment design and data analysis.

1-5   THE LORENTZ TRANSFORMATION

We have seen that the galilean coordinate transformation, Eqs. (1-2), relating the position and time of an event in one coordinate system with those in another system, are inconsistent with the basic postulates of relativity. We have examined two specific problems involving time and length transformations and have obtained results that *are* consistent with those postulates, and we are now in a position to derive a relativistically correct coordinate transformation. Called the *Lorentz transformation,* these equations were actually developed by H. A. Lorentz in 1887, 18 years before Einstein first published the theory of relativity; but not until the work of Einstein was their real significance understood.

Consider, as previously, two inertial frames of reference, S and S', the latter moving in the $+x$ direction with constant speed u relative to the former. Furthermore, suppose that at the instant the two origins O and O' coincide, clocks in the two frames of reference located at the respective origins are synchronized, so that when $x = x'$, $t = t' = 0$. Note that this procedure does not conflict with our previous discussion of simultaneity because we are comparing two clocks at the same point in space. We now ask: If a certain event occurs at point (x',y',z') at time t', as observed in S', at what point and at what time does the event occur as observed in S?

First, as already pointed out, there is no difficulty in comparing lengths measured perpendicular to the direction of motion. Hence we can say immediately that $y = y'$ and $z = z'$. A relation between the two x coordinates can also be obtained quite simply. In S, the distance between O and O' at time t is simply ut. The coordinate x' is a proper length in S', so when viewed from S, it appears foreshortened by the factor given by Eq. (1-11). Then the total x distance in S from O to the point at which the event takes place is

$$x = ut + x' \sqrt{1 - \frac{u^2}{c^2}} \tag{1-12}$$

Rearranging this expression to obtain an equation for x' in terms of x and t gives

$$x' = \frac{x - ut}{\sqrt{1 - u^2/c^2}} \tag{1-13}$$

which differs from the first of Eqs. (1-2) in having an additional factor in the denominator.

Equation (1-13) is half of the Lorentz transformation. The other half is the equation giving t' in terms of x and t. This is obtained most easily by noting first that since S and S' are completely equivalent, the transformation giving x in terms of x' and t' must have exactly the same *form* as Eq. (1-13) for x' in terms of x and t. The only difference is that the sign of u must be reversed, since the velocity of S relative to S' is the negative of that of S' relative to S. Thus we can write immediately

$$x = \frac{x' + ut'}{\sqrt{1 - u^2/c^2}} \tag{1-14}$$

We can now solve this equation for t' as a function of x and x' and then use Eq. (1-13) to eliminate x' in favor of x and t, as follows:

$$ut' = x\sqrt{1 - \frac{u^2}{c^2}} - x'$$

$$= x\sqrt{1 - \frac{u^2}{c^2}} - \frac{x - ut}{\sqrt{1 - u^2/c^2}}$$

Simplifying the right side and dividing by u gives

$$t' = \frac{t - ux/c^2}{\sqrt{1 - u^2/c^2}} \tag{1-15}$$

The form of Eq. (1-15) shows the time-dilation factor derived previously and also shows that the time for an event observed in S' depends on both its time and position in S. This reflects the fact that two clocks that appear synchronized in S are out of synchronization in S' by an amount proportional to the distance between them in S. This equation is the second half of the Lorentz transformation.

Collecting all the transformation equations, we have

$$x' = \frac{x - ut}{\sqrt{1 - u^2/c^2}}$$

$$y' = y$$

$$z' = z \tag{1-16}$$

$$t' = \frac{t - ux/c^2}{\sqrt{1 - u^2/c^2}}$$

These are the Lorentz transformation. In this form, the equations show explicitly that if the relative velocity u of the two frames of reference is much smaller than c, so that $u/c \ll 1$, the transformation reduces to the galilean transformation, Eqs. (1-2).

1-6 VELOCITY TRANSFORMATIONS

One of many useful results which can be obtained from the Lorentz transformation equations is the relation between the velocities of a body observed in two different frames of reference. We have noted that Eq. (1-3) is not consistent with the basic postulate of relativity, and we can now derive the correct relativistic generalization of this relation.

We consider first a body moving with constant velocity parallel to the x axis in each coordinate system. To apply the Lorentz transformations, we may consider as events the arrival of the moving object at two different points. In S', let the object be at position x_1' at time t_1' and at x_2' at time t_2'. The velocity v' observed in S' is then

$$v' = \frac{x_2' - x_1'}{t_2' - t_1'} = \frac{\Delta x'}{\Delta t'} \tag{1-17}$$

We now use Eqs. (1-16) to express the quantities in this equation in terms of quantities measured in S:

$$x_2' - x_1' = \frac{x_2 - x_1 - u(t_2 - t_1)}{\sqrt{1 - u^2/c^2}} = \frac{x - u\,\Delta t}{\sqrt{1 - u^2/c^2}}$$

$$t_2' - t_1' = \frac{t_2 - t_1 - (x_2 - x_1)u/c^2}{\sqrt{1 - u^2/c^2}} = \frac{\Delta t - \Delta x\,u/c^2}{\sqrt{1 - u^2/c^2}}$$

$$v' = \frac{\Delta x - u\,\Delta t}{\Delta t - xu/c^2} \tag{1-18}$$

We note that it would *not* be correct to substitute Eqs. (1-7) and (1-11) directly into Eq. (1-17), since these are valid only when $\Delta t'$ and $\Delta l'$ are proper in S'; this is not the case here because both the locations and times of the two events are different. Hence the general coordinate transformation given by Eqs. (1-16) must be used.

The velocity observed in S, of course, is simply $v = \Delta x/\Delta t$. To relate this to v', we divide numerator and denominator of Eq. (1-18) by Δt:

$$v' = \frac{\Delta x/\Delta t - u}{1 - (\Delta x/\Delta t)(u/c^2)} = \frac{v - u}{1 - vu/c^2} \tag{1-19}$$

This equation can also be rearranged to give v in terms of v'. The details of this calculation are left as an exercise; the result is

$$v = \frac{v' + u}{1 + v'u/c^2} \tag{1-20}$$

which has the same form as Eq. (1-19) except that the terms containing u have signs opposite those in Eq. (1-19), as might be expected.

If both u and v are much smaller than c, the second term in the denominator of Eqs. (1-19) and (1-20) is negligible and these expressions reduce to the newtonian equation (1-3). But if the speeds are comparable to that of light, the results may be quite different. The extreme case occurs when $v' = c$; then no matter what value u has, Eq. (1-20) gives $v = c$, in agreement with the basic postulate of relativity.

Example

Suppose a body moves in S' with a speed $v' = 0.9c$ and S' moves relative to S with a speed $u = 0.9c$. What is the body's speed in S?

Solution

The nonrelativistic velocity relations give $v = 1.8c$. Using Eq. (1-20), we find instead

$$v = \frac{0.9c + 0.9c}{1 + (0.9c)(0.9c)/c^2} = 0.994c$$

We can also derive a velocity transformation for the more general case of a point moving in the $xy(x'y')$ plane with components of velocity v'_x and v'_y in S'. The x-component relation is still given by Eq. (1-20) since the y coordinate is not involved at all in this equation. The y component of velocity in S' is given by

$$v'_y = \frac{y'_2 - y'_1}{t'_2 - t'_1} = \frac{\Delta y'}{\Delta t'}$$

Applying the Lorentz transformation equations (1-16), we obtain

$$v'_y = \frac{(y_2 - y_1)\sqrt{1 - u^2/c^2}}{(t_2 - t_1) - u(x_2 - x_1)/c^2} = \frac{\Delta y \sqrt{1 - u^2/c^2}}{\Delta t - u\,\Delta x/c^2}$$

Again we divide numerator and denominator by Δt and identify $v_x = \Delta x/\Delta t$, $v_y = \Delta y/\Delta t$ to obtain

$$v'_y = \frac{v_y \sqrt{1 - u^2/c^2}}{1 - v_x u/c^2} \tag{1-21}$$

The general velocity transformation can be summarized:

$$v'_x = \frac{v_x - u}{1 - v_x u/c^2} \qquad v'_y = \frac{v_y \sqrt{1 - u^2/c^2}}{1 - v_x u/c^2} \tag{1-22}$$

The inverse transformation is obtained easily by interchanging v_x and v'_x, v_y and v'_y, and changing the sign on u:

$$v_x = \frac{v'_x + u}{1 + v'_x u/c^2} \qquad v_y = \frac{v'_y \sqrt{1 - u^2/c^2}}{1 + v'_x u/c^2} \tag{1-23}$$

A striking feature of these equations is that the y component of velocity in one frame depends on *both* the x and y components in the other, quite unlike the situation with the galilean transformation. These relations are very useful when we consider conservation of momentum in various frames of reference in Chap. 2.

Example
A light source at rest at the origin O' of S' emits a ray of light in the $x'y'$ plane at an angle θ' with the x' axis. What is its direction as seen in S?

Solution
The components of velocity of the light ray in S' are

$$v'_x = c \cos \theta' \qquad v'_y = c \sin \theta'$$

We use Eqs. (1-23) to obtain the components of velocity in S:

$$v_x = \frac{c \cos \theta' + u}{1 + cu \cos \theta'/c^2} \qquad v_y = \frac{c \sin \theta' \sqrt{1 - u^2/c^2}}{1 + cu \cos \theta'/c^2}$$

The direction θ in S, that is, the angle the light ray makes with the x axis in S, is given by

$$\tan \theta = \frac{v_y}{v_x} = \frac{\sin \theta' \sqrt{1 - u^2/c^2}}{\cos \theta' + u/c}$$

We note that when $u = 0$, $\tan \theta = \tan \theta'$, as expected. This formula is useful in the analysis of a phenomenon known as *stellar aberration*, in which the true position of a star differs somewhat from the direction a telescope is aimed if there is relative motion of the two.

We have now completed the development of the coordinate transformations required by Einstein's principle of the invariance of physical laws. The next step is to explore the modifications of *dynamics*, including the relationships between force, momentum, and energy, which are required for consistency with Einstein's principle. These considerations are the topics of the next chapter.

Problems

1-1 A π^+ meson at rest decays on the average approximately 2.6×10^{-8} s after it is produced. This time is called its *lifetime*.

    a A π^+ meson is moving with a speed of $0.8c$ with respect to an observer in a laboratory. He measures the lifetime of the particle; what result does he obtain?

    b What distance (measured in the laboratory) does the particle travel between production and decay?

1-2 The μ mesons (muons) are unstable particles which decay into electrons and neutrinos after an average lifetime (in the rest frame of the mesons) of 2.3×10^{-6} s. For a meson traveling at a speed of $0.99c$ relative to the laboratory, how far does the meson travel on the average before decaying? Compare your result with a nonrelativistic calculation.

1-3 For the train struck by lightning in Sec. 1-3, construct the corresponding argument to show that if the two lightning bolts appear simultaneous to an observer on the train, they do not appear simultaneous to an observer on the ground. What one appears to come first?

1-4 A jet airplane flies from San Francisco to New York, about 4000 km, at a speed of 300 m/s, carrying a clock which was initially synchronized with a clock in San Francisco, also synchronized with a clock in New York. When the plane arrives in New York, will its clock be fast or slow compared to the one in New York, and by how much? Neglect the curvature and rotation of the earth.

1-5 A meter stick is oriented parallel to the x axis of a coordinate system S and moves along this axis. At what speed will its apparent length in S (measured by observing the positions of the ends simultaneously in S) be half its proper length?

1-6 A meter stick is stationary in a frame of reference S' and is oriented at an angle θ' with respect to the x' axis. Frame S' moves with speed u along the common xx' axis relative to frame S.

    a What angle does the meter stick make with the x axis in S?

    b What is its apparent length in S?

1-7 A supercar traveling along a drag strip passes one check point, and 5×10^{-7} s later passes a second check point 100 m away; the time and distance are measured by observers at rest on the ground.

    a What is the car's speed relative to these observers?

    b What is the time interval between the two check points, as measured by the driver of the car?

    c What is the distance between the two check points, as measured by the driver of the car?

    d What is the car's speed, as determined by the driver from the results of (*b*) and (*c*)? Does this agree with the result of (*a*)? Explain.

1-8 Two spaceships, each of which has a length of 100 m in its rest frame, meet in outer space. An observer in the cockpit at the front of one ship observes that a time of 2.0×10^{-6} s elapses while the second moves past him, heading in the opposite direction.

     a   How much time (measured in the first ship) elapses while the front of the second ship moves from front to back of the first?

     b   What is the relative velocity of the ships?

1-9 A race-car driver at Indianapolis passes a timer holding a stopwatch at a speed of 1.0×10^8 m/s. The driver observes that 1.0×10^{-7} s elapses between the times the watch is started and stopped, but he cannot see its face. What does the stopwatch read?

1-10 The Orient Express moves past a small-town station at a speed of 1.5×10^8 m/s. It has mirrors attached to both ends; the (proper) length of the train is 100 m. After it passes, the stationmaster turns on a light. The light travels to both mirrors and is reflected back to him. How much time elapses between the arrivals of the two reflected light beams?

1-11 In Prob. 1-10 describe a method by which the stationmaster can measure the length of the train as it passes. What results does he obtain?

1-12 A Porsche is driving on the Autobahn between Munich and Salzburg at a speed of $0.6c$. One of the fuel injectors has a leak, so a drop of gasoline falls to the pavement 100 times each second, as measured by the driver.

     a   At what rate do the drops fall as measured by an observer beside the road?

     b   What is the distance between adjacent drops, measured in the frame of reference of the road?

     c   Why is the accident rate on the Autobahn so high?

1-13 Solve Eqs. (1-16) for x and t in terms of x' and t', and show directly that the resulting inverse transformations have the same form as the original transformations except that the sign of u is changed.

1-14 In a frame of reference S, consider two events (x_1, t_1) and (x_2, t_2). Using the notation $\Delta x = x_2 - x_1$, $\Delta t = t_2 - t_1$, show that in a frame S' moving just fast enough so that the events occur at the same space point in S', the time interval $\Delta t'$ between the two events is given by

$$\Delta t' = \sqrt{(\Delta t)^2 - \left(\frac{\Delta x}{c}\right)^2}$$

Hence show that if $\Delta x > c \, \Delta t$, there is *no* frame S' in which the two events occur at the same space point. The interval $\Delta t'$ is often called the *proper time* for the two events. Is this term appropriate?

1-15 For the two events in Prob. 1-14, show that if $\Delta x > c \, \Delta t$, and only then, there exists a frame of reference S' in which the two events occur simultaneously.

Find the distance between the two events in S'. Such a distance is often called a *proper length*. Is this term appropriate?

1-16 A light pulse is emitted at the origin O' of frame S' at time $t' = 0$. Its distance x' from the origin after a time t' is given by $x'^2 = c^2 t'^2$. Use the Lorentz transformation equations with this relation to show that in a frame of reference S the pulse motion appears exactly the same; i.e., after a time t its distance x from O is given by $x^2 = c^2 t^2$.

1-17 Two events observed in a frame S occur at points x_1 and x_2, at times t_1 and t_2, respectively. The same events observed in a frame S' moving relative to S along the x axis with velocity u are observed at x_1', x_2', t_1', t_2'. Show that the quantities

$$(x_2 - x_1)^2 - c^2 (t_2 - t_1)^2 \qquad \text{and} \qquad (x_2' - x_1')^2 - c^2 (t_2' - t_1')^2$$

are always equal.

1-18 A rocket ship traveling west at a speed of $0.5c$ meets a ship traveling east with a speed of $0.5c$, both speeds measured by an observer on earth. If they are moving along approximately the same line so that they nearly (but not quite!) collide, what is the speed of the eastbound ship relative to the westbound ship, after they pass?

1-19 A source of light at rest in S' emits light uniformly in all directions.
  a If S' moves with speed $u = 0.6c$ relative to S, and a certain ray makes an angle of $45°$ with the x' axis, what angle does the angle make with the x axis, as seen in S? The discussion in Sec. 1-6 may be useful.
  b Show that in the above situation the angle with the x axis observed in S is always less than in S'. Hence the light from a moving source appears to be concentrated along the line of motion. This is called the *headlight effect*.

1-20 Consider two successive Lorentz transformations, the first from S to S', moving at speed u_1 relative to S, the second from S' to S'', moving at speed u_2 relative to S'. Write the transformations from S to S', giving x' and t' in terms of x and t, and those from S' to S'', giving x'' and t'' in terms of x' and t'. Combine these to obtain x'' and t'' in terms of x and t, and show that the result is equivalent to a single Lorentz transformation from S to S'' with relative speed u given by

$$u = \frac{u_1 + u_2}{1 + u_1 u_2 / c^2}$$

Relativistic Dynamics | 2

The *kinematic* relations of relativity require corresponding modifications of the principles of *dynamics*. For the principle of conservation of momentum of an isolated system to hold in all inertial frames, the definition of momentum must be generalized. The generalized definition points the way to the new equation of motion which is the generalization of Newton's second law. The corresponding modification of the definition of kinetic energy leads naturally to consideration of energy associated with mass of a body, and the principles of conservation of mass and energy emerge as two aspects of a single conservation law. The relation between energy and momentum for a massless particle also emerges naturally from the new definitions. Finally, we look briefly at the behavior of electric and magnetic fields under relativistic coordinate transformations.

2-1 MOMENTUM

The laws of mechanics as formulated by Newton are invariant under the galilean coordinate transformation, Eqs. (1-2), but this transformation is inconsistent with the basic postulates of relativity and must be replaced by the more general Lorentz transformation, Eqs. (1-16). Corresponding modifications are needed in the principles of dynamics if they are to be brought into harmony with relativity theory. For example, we shall see that if conservation of momentum holds in one inertial frame, it *does not* hold in a second inertial frame unless we modify the definition of momentum.

To illustrate, we consider an elastic collision between two bodies of equal mass. We arrange the collision symmetrically as shown in Fig. 2-1*a*. In frame *S* body *B* has no *x* component of velocity either before or after the collision, and the *y* component of velocity of each body is reversed after the collision.

The various velocity components are labeled as shown in the figure. We now view this same collision from a second frame S' moving relative to S just fast enough so that in S' body A has no x component of velocity, as shown in Fig. 2-1b. The velocity u of S' relative to S is then given simply by $u = v_{Ax}$; we shall make use of this fact below in Eq. (2-1).

Using the newtonian definition of momentum $\mathbf{p} = m\mathbf{v}$, we consider conservation of the y component of momentum. Symmetry shows that for the y component of momentum to be conserved in S, $v_{Ay} = v_{By}$, and the *total* y component of momentum in S is zero. In S' the magnitudes of the y components of initial velocity, obtained from Eqs. (1-22), are

$$v'_{Ay} = \frac{v_{Ay}\sqrt{1 - u^2/c^2}}{1 - v_{Ax}u/c^2} = \frac{v_{Ay}}{\sqrt{1 - u^2/c^2}} \qquad v'_{By} = v_{By}\sqrt{1 - \frac{u^2}{c^2}} \qquad (2\text{-}1)$$

The fact that these have different magnitudes shows that the total y component of momentum in S' is *not* zero. Furthermore, since the y velocities in S'

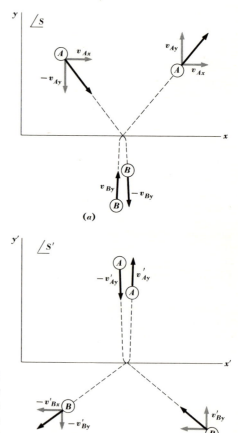

(a)

(b)

Fig. 2-1 (a) Collision of two bodies A and B as observed in S; body B has no x component of velocity in S. (b) The same collision viewed in a frame S' moving with speed $u = v_{Ax}$ relative to S. In this frame body A has no x' component of velocity.

reverse sign during the collision, the *total* y momentum in S' also reverses sign. That is, in S' the y component of momentum is *not* conserved!

This result contradicts the basic postulate of relativity that the laws of physics, and in particular the law of conservation of momentum, should be equally valid in *all* inertial frames of reference. Thus the *definition* of momentum itself must be in need of modification. As we shall now show, the problem is resolved by defining the momentum of a particle not as $\mathbf{p} = m\mathbf{v}$ but as

$$\mathbf{p} = \frac{m\mathbf{v}}{\sqrt{1 - v^2/c^2}} \tag{2-2}$$

In developing Eq. (2-2), we first note that the generalized momentum expression must still be proportional to m to preserve its additive properties, and that it must contain $\mathbf{v}$ as a factor in order for $\mathbf{p}$ and $\mathbf{v}$ to have the same direction. Thus it must have the general form

$$\mathbf{p} = \gamma m\mathbf{v} \tag{2-3}$$

where γ is a quantity depending only on the speed of the particle. Because this must reduce to the newtonian expression $\mathbf{p} = m\mathbf{v}$ in the limit of small velocity, we must also require $\gamma = 1$ when $v = 0$. The problem is to find the specific functional dependence of γ on v.

Returning to the collision discussed above, we consider as a special case a "grazing" collision where all the y components of velocity are very small. We make no restriction on the magnitudes of the x components. Since we have dropped the classical definition of momentum, we may no longer assume at the outset that $v_{Ay} = v_{By}$. Instead, we require that the y component of momentum be conserved in both S and S'. For momentum conservation in S, with Eq. (2-3)

$$m\gamma v_{Ay} = mv_{By} \tag{2-4}$$

We have set $\gamma = 1$ for body B because by assumption its speed is very small. Similarly momentum conservation in S' requires that

$$mv'_{Ay} = m\gamma v'_{By} \tag{2-5}$$

where $\gamma = 1$ for body A. Equations (2-4) and (2-5) express conservation of y momentum in S and S', respectively.

We can also use the velocity-transformation equations to express Eq. (2-5) in terms of components in S. Using Eqs. (2-1) and recalling that $v_{Ax} = u$, we obtain

$$\frac{mv_{Ay}}{\sqrt{1 - u^2/c^2}} = m\gamma v_{By}\sqrt{1 - \frac{u^2}{c^2}} \tag{2-6}$$

This must be consistent with Eq. (2-4) if momentum is to be conserved in both S and S'. One way to test this consistency is to solve Eqs. (2-4) and (2-6) for v_{Ax} and equate the results, as follows:

$$\frac{v_{By}}{\gamma} = \gamma v_{By}\left(1 - \frac{u^2}{c^2}\right)$$

This result could also be obtained by dividing Eq. (2-4) by Eq. (2-6) and rearranging. Solving for γ, we obtain

$$\gamma = \frac{1}{\sqrt{1 - u^2/c^2}} \qquad (2\text{-}7)$$

Now by assumption the y components of velocity are very small, so u is very nearly equal to the speed of body A in S and that of B in S'. Thus we may replace u by v, obtaining finally

$$\mathbf{p} = \frac{m\mathbf{v}}{\sqrt{1 - v^2/c^2}} \qquad (2\text{-}8)$$

as predicted.

The approximations in the above development should not distract one's attention from the generality of the result. For a general collision between two bodies of unequal mass with no restrictions on the velocities, one can use the generalized definition of momentum and the velocity-transformation equations to show that if momentum is conserved in S, it is also conserved in S'. Verifying this statement in detail is somewhat involved and is not essential for our purposes.

The new definition of momentum requires a revision of the concept of center of mass. It is customary to define the velocity of the center of mass as the velocity of a frame of reference in which the total *momentum* of the system is zero. This defines only the velocity, not the position, of the center of mass, but in most applications this is sufficient.

Example

A particle of mass m is at rest at the origin O of a system S, and a second particle with the same mass moves along the positive x axis with velocity v. Find the velocity of the center of mass.

Solution

We want to find a frame S' moving with velocity u relative to S such that in S' the total momentum is zero. The velocities in S', according to Eq. (1-19), are

$$v'_1 = \frac{v - u}{1 - vu/c^2} \qquad v'_2 = -u$$

For the total momentum in S' to be zero, these must be equal in magnitude:

$$\frac{v - u}{1 - vu/c^2} = u$$

This is a quadratic equation for u; one root is larger than c; the other is

$$u = \frac{1 - (1 - v^2/c^2)^{1/2}}{v/c^2} \tag{2-9}$$

We can check whether this reduces to the nonrelativistic result $u = v/2$ in the limit when $v \ll c$. We expand the radical using the binomial theorem, retaining only the first two terms:

$$\left(1 - \frac{v^2}{c^2}\right)^{1/2} = 1 - \frac{v^2}{2c^2} + \cdots$$

Equation (2-9) becomes

$$u = \frac{v^2/2c^2}{v/c^2} = \frac{v}{2}$$

as expected.

2-2 FORCE AND MOTION

Equation (2-8) can be interpreted in two ways. The point of view presented above is that it is a generalization of the definition of momentum; m is constant for a given particle and represents the inertial properties of the particle exhibited in low-speed (newtonian) collisions. An alternate viewpoint is that although momentum is still mass times velocity, the mass to be used is not just m but a "relativistic mass" given by

$$m_{\text{rel}} = \frac{m}{\sqrt{1 - v^2/c^2}} \tag{2-10}$$

The choice between these viewpoints is largely a matter of taste; one cannot say that either is right and the other wrong, since they say the same thing in different ways. It turns out that the first is more useful in finding the correct generalization of $\mathbf{F} = m\mathbf{a}$, our next problem. In either case, m is usually called the *rest mass* to distinguish it from the velocity-dependent relativistic mass used in some literature. The concept of "relativistic mass increase" is unnecessary and can be misleading (see Probs. 2-3 and 2-13), and it is not used in this book. In the following discussion m is *always* a constant, *not* a velocity-dependent quantity.

One may make two reasonable guesses how Newton's second law should be generalized to bring it into harmony with the principle of relativity. One of these is to retain the form $\Sigma\mathbf{F} = m\mathbf{a}$, using for m the relativistic mass given by Eq. (2-10). The other is to return to Newton's original form, $\Sigma\mathbf{F} = d\mathbf{p}/dt$ with $\mathbf{p}$ given by Eq. (2-8). The two are *not* equivalent; in the first case we have

$$\Sigma\mathbf{F} = \frac{m}{\sqrt{1 - v^2/c^2}}\frac{d\mathbf{v}}{dt}$$

while in the second

$$\Sigma\mathbf{F} = \frac{d}{dt}\frac{m\mathbf{v}}{\sqrt{1 - v^2/c^2}}$$

Which form if either agrees with the behavior of the physical world can be decided only by experiment.

This question has been investigated experimentally in a wide variety of situations, especially with high-speed electrically charged particles in electric (**E**) and magnetic (**B**) fields. It is found that the correct equation of motion is

$$q(\mathbf{E} + \mathbf{v} \times \mathbf{B}) = \frac{d}{dt}\frac{m\mathbf{v}}{\sqrt{1 - v^2/c^2}} \tag{2-11}$$

which agrees with the second of the two possibilities. The left side of Eq. (2-11) is called the *Lorentz force* expression. It is assumed that **E** and **B** are measured in the same frame of reference as **v** and that m and q are constants which characterize the inertial and electrical properties of the particle. Neither m nor q depends on the speed v of the particle; they are *invariant* under transformations from one inertial frame to another.

Observations with other types of forces are more difficult, but all such observations are consistent with the assumption that the generalized law of motion is

$$\Sigma\mathbf{F} = \frac{d\mathbf{p}}{dt} = \frac{d}{dt}\frac{m\mathbf{v}}{\sqrt{1 - v^2/c^2}} \tag{2-12}$$

In the above discussion, the term *force* has been used somewhat loosely and without a careful analysis of the role of the observer in its definition. One may ask whether if two observers in motion relative to each other measure a force, they obtain the same or different results. With electromagnetic forces, this question is avoided by using one coordinate system consistently in applying Eq. (2-11), measuring **E**, **B**, and **v** always with respect to the same inertial frame of reference. The transformation properties of **E** and **B** are discussed in Sec. 2-5.

Example

A charged particle with mass m and charge q is traveling at a speed $v = 0.8c$. Find the magnitude of electric field E required to give the particle an acceleration a along the original direction of motion. If this same field were applied to a particle at rest, what acceleration would it produce?

Solution

From Eq. (2-11),

$$qE = m\frac{d}{dt}\left(\frac{v}{\sqrt{1 - v^2/c^2}}\right)$$

$$= m\left[\frac{1}{\sqrt{1 - v^2/c^2}} + \frac{v^2}{(1 - v^2/c^2)^{3/2}}\right]\frac{dv}{dt}$$

Simplifying and writing $dv/dt = a$, we obtain

$$qE = \frac{m}{(1 - v^2/c^2)^{3/2}}a \qquad \text{or} \qquad a = \frac{qE(1 - v^2/c^2)^{3/2}}{m}$$

If the particle had been initially at rest, the factor $(1 - v^2/c^2)^{3/2} = {}^{27}\!/_{125}$ would not appear, and the acceleration with a given E would be larger by ${}^{125}\!/_{27} \cong 4.6$.

2-3 WORK AND ENERGY

The modifications of the laws of motion discussed in the previous section imply corresponding modification of the relationship between work and energy. Just as Newton's second law in its original form is used to derive the work-energy relation

$$\int_{x_1}^{x_2} F\,dx = \tfrac{1}{2}mv_2^2 - \tfrac{1}{2}mv_1^2$$

we use the generalized equation of motion, Eq. (2-12), to derive a relativistic generalization of this relationship. We retain the definition of work:

$$W = \int_{x_1}^{x_2} F\,dx \qquad\qquad (2\text{-}13)$$

We use Eq. (2-12) to convert this integral into a form containing only the *speed* of the particle, and then we perform the integration. The result is an expression containing the initial and final speeds, from which we can deduce an appropriate generalization of the definition of kinetic energy.

For simplicity, we consider only motion along a straight line. The force may vary during the motion but acts always along the x axis. Let the particle have velocity v_1 at point x_1 and time t_1 and velocity v_2 at x_2 and t_2. The momentum may be regarded as a function of x, v, or t, since these are all functionally related. Using the chain rule and $v = dx/dt$, we successively transform the integration variable in Eq. (2-13) as follows:

$$W = \int_{x_1}^{x_2} F\,dx = \int_{x_1}^{x_2} \frac{dp}{dt}\,dx = \int_{x_1}^{x_2} \left(\frac{dp}{dv}\frac{dv}{dt}\right)dx$$

$$= \int_{x_1}^{x_2} \frac{dp}{dv}\left(\frac{dv}{dx}\frac{dx}{dt}\right)dx = \int_{x_1}^{x_2} \frac{dp}{dv}\,v\,\frac{dv}{dx}\,dx = \int_{v_1}^{v_2} \frac{dp}{dv}\,v\,dv \tag{2-14}$$

Since p is given as a function of v by Eq. (2-8), we have

$$W = \int_{v_1}^{v_2} v\,\frac{d}{dv}\left(\frac{mv}{\sqrt{1 - v^2/c^2}}\right)dv \tag{2-15}$$

All that remains is to evaluate the integral, best done by first integrating by parts. The details are left as a problem (Prob. 2-7); the final result is

$$W = \frac{mc^2}{\sqrt{1 - v_2^2/c^2}} - \frac{mc^2}{\sqrt{1 - v_1^2/c^2}} \tag{2-16}$$

Equation (2-16) shows that the effect of the work is to produce a change in the quantity

$$E = \frac{mc^2}{\sqrt{1 - v^2/c^2}} \tag{2-17}$$

This cannot be the kinetic energy, however, because when $v = 0$, its value is not zero but mc^2. To obtain the analog of the classical kinetic energy, we must subtract mc^2, defining the kinetic energy E_k as

$$E_k = \frac{mc^2}{\sqrt{1 - v^2/c^2}} - mc^2 \tag{2-18}$$

This must reduce to $\frac{1}{2}mv^2$ when $v \ll c$. We can show that it does by expanding the binomial in Eq. (2-18), using the binomial theorem:

$$\left(1 - \frac{v^2}{c^2}\right)^{-1/2} = 1 + \frac{1}{2}\frac{v^2}{c^2} + \frac{3}{8}\frac{v^4}{c^4} + \frac{5}{16}\frac{v^6}{c^6} + \cdots$$

Combining this with Eq. (2-18) gives

$$E_k = mc^2\left(1 + \frac{1}{2}\frac{v^2}{c^2} + \frac{3}{8}\frac{v^4}{c^4} + \cdots\right) - mc^2$$

$$= \tfrac{1}{2}mv^2 + \frac{3}{8}m\frac{v^4}{c^2} + \cdots$$

The three dots stand for omitted terms. When $v \ll c$, all terms containing v/c or higher powers of this ratio can be neglected, and we have, approximately, $E_k = \tfrac{1}{2}mv^2$.

The validity of Eq. (2-18) has been confirmed directly by experiments making use of high-energy particle accelerators, as described in Sec. 1-2. This relation is illustrated graphically in Fig. 2-2, which also shows, for comparison, the nonrelativistic expression $\tfrac{1}{2}mv^2$.

The forms of Eqs. (2-17) and (2-18) suggest that in addition to having energy associated with motion, a particle of mass m has an energy mc^2 even when it is not moving. This energy may be thought of as associated with the mass, rather than with the motion. On the basis of this interpretation, Eq. (2-17) represents the *total* energy of a particle, including both kinetic energy and the energy mc^2 associated with its mass, which we call *rest energy*. This speculation is of course not a *proof* that rest energy is a physically meaningful concept, but it suggests a path for further inquiry. There is in fact very direct experimental evidence that mc^2 does represent an energy associated with mass; a few examples are discussed in Sec. 2-4.

Additional insight into the relation of mass and energy can be obtained by deriving an equation relating the total energy (including rest energy) of a particle and its momentum. To do this, we combine Eqs. (2-8) and (2-17) to eliminate v and obtain an expression relating E and p. This is most easily accomplished by the following manipulation: We divide Eq. (2-17) by mc^2

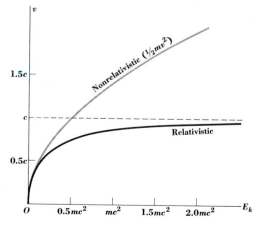

Fig. 2-2 Relation between the speed of a particle and its kinetic energy. The speed never exceeds c, no matter how great the kinetic energy. At speeds small compared to c, the kinetic energy is approximately $\tfrac{1}{2}mv^2$, but at larger speeds this expression deviates more and more from the relativistically correct equation.

and square the resulting equation; we divide Eq. (2-8) by mc and square the result:

$$\left(\frac{E}{mc^2}\right)^2 = \frac{1}{1 - v^2/c^2} \qquad \left(\frac{p}{mc}\right)^2 = \frac{v^2/c^2}{1 - v^2/c^2} \tag{2-19}$$

We then subtract the second of these expressions from the first and rearrange, obtaining

$$E^2 = (mc^2)^2 + (pc)^2 \tag{2-20}$$

This result shows again that the energy of a particle depends on its mass and momentum. In the nonrelativistic limit when $v \ll c$ and therefore $p \ll mc$, we expect this to reduce to $E = mc^2 + p^2/2m$; i.e., the rest energy plus the newtonian kinetic energy expressed in terms of the momentum. To show that this is indeed the case, we rewrite Eq. (2-20):

$$E = mc^2 \sqrt{1 + \left(\frac{p}{mc}\right)^2}$$

We now expand the radical using the binomial theorem, keeping only the first two terms. Completion of this calculation is left as a problem (Prob. 2-11).

The opposite extreme is a particle with a speed so close to c that p is much *larger* than mc. In this case, called the *extreme relativistic range*, the second term in Eq. (2-20) becomes so large that the first term may be neglected, and the energy-momentum relation becomes approximately $E = pc$. For an extreme relativistic particle the total energy is thus much larger than the rest energy.

Equation (2-20) also suggests the possibility of *massless* particles. Consider a particle with $m = 0$ and $v = c$; Eqs. (2-8) and (2-17) become indeterminate with these values, but such a particle is not *prohibited* by any of the above discussion. For a massless particle the energy-momentum relation is simply

$$E = pc \tag{2-21}$$

Such particles do indeed exist; the most familiar example is the *photon*, or quantum of electromagnetic radiation. Photons will be discussed in detail in later chapters, but we see already that one of their essential properties, the energy-momentum relation, follows directly from simple relativistic considerations.

Finally, we note that if the mass of a particle (zero or otherwise) is to be independent of its state of motion, it must be the same in all coordinate systems. The particle's velocity of course may be different in different systems, and so its energy and momentum also depend on the frame of reference, but if the mass is to be constant, Eq. (2-20) requires that the quantity $E^2 - p^2c^2$ must be the same in *all* frames of reference, i.e., must be *invariant* under coordinate transformations. This result may also be obtained directly by using the velocity transformation equations obtained in Sec. 1-6 to derive relations between the values of E and p in one system and their values in a second system. This derivation is suggested in Probs. 2-21 and 2-22. Similarly, it can be shown that for a system of particles having energies E_i and momenta $\mathbf{p}_i$ (where the index i labels the particles) the quantity

$$\mu^2 = (\Sigma E_i)^2 - (\mathbf{\Sigma p}_i)^2 c^2 \tag{2-22}$$

has the same value in all inertial frames. We omit formal proof of this statement; it is very useful in working out energy relations for high-energy collisions of fundamental particles. We return to this problem in our final chapter, Sec. 16-4.

2-4   MASS AND ENERGY

The mass-energy relation suggested in Sec. 2-3 has been confirmed by a wide variety of phenomena investigated during the past 50 years. The common characteristic is an interaction in which the total mass of the system is different in the final state and in the initial state; i.e., in which mass is not conserved. In every such case there is found to be a corresponding energy change which is consistent with associating an energy mc^2 with mass m.

The most familiar example is *nuclear fission;* a heavy nucleus at rest breaks into two parts which come away with considerable kinetic energy. The total mass of the fragments is *less* than that of the original nucleus, and the increase in kinetic energy is exactly accounted for by associating an energy mc^2 with the loss of mass m. The reverse phenomenon occurs when two light nuclei combine to form a single nucleus of mass slightly less than the total mass of the two initial nuclei; this is called *nuclear fusion,* and again the mass loss is exactly accounted for by excess energy in the final state. Fission and fusion reactions are discussed in more detail in Chap. 15.

More spectacular examples of the interchangeability of mass and energy occur in fundamental particle interactions, in which particles are created and destroyed. When an electron and a positron, each of mass m, collide, they both disappear, and electromagnetic radiation with total energy equal to $2mc^2$ is produced. The reverse process, *pair production,* occurs in high-energy particle collisions; as an example, a high-energy proton from an accelerator collides with a heavy nucleus; an electron and a positron are *created,* and the total energy of the proton decreases by at least $2mc^2$. The purest example of mass-energy conversion occurs in the decay of unstable particles. The π^0

meson, also called *neutral pion,* is an unstable particle about 264 times as massive as the electron, produced during high-energy collisions between nuclear particles; it lives only about 10^{-16} s, on the average, before decaying into electromagnetic radiation (gamma rays) with total energy exactly equal to mc^2, where m is the pion's mass. These and other fundamental-particle interactions are discussed in detail in Chap. 16.

Thus even without examining the details of the processes, we see that the equivalence of mass and energy are of central importance in understanding phenomena in nuclear physics and fundamental-particle phenomena. Although historically the principles of conservation of mass and of energy developed independently, they are very directly related. They now emerge as two aspects of a more general and inclusive principle, the *principle of conservation of mass and energy.*

2-5   ELECTROMAGNETIC FIELDS

In discussing the relativistic generalization of Newton's second law in Sec. 2-2, in connection with the Lorentz force law, we remarked on the importance of measuring the fields in the same frame of reference as the velocity of the particle; when this is done, Eq. (2-11) is found experimentally to be a correct description of the motion of charged particles.

But what happens when we measure **E** and **B** in another coordinate system, in motion relative to the first? An example will illustrate the problem that arises. Suppose a particle moves with constant velocity **v** in S, in which uniform electric and magnetic fields exist which are of just the right magnitude and direction so that in this frame of reference $q(\mathbf{E} + \mathbf{v} \times \mathbf{B}) = \mathbf{0}$. Now we look at the situation from a frame of reference S' which moves relative to S with a velocity **v** (so that the particle is at rest in S'). In this frame of reference $\mathbf{v} \times \mathbf{B} = \mathbf{0}$. But the particle has no acceleration in S'; hence there must be no force. Therefore **E** must be zero, although it was *not* zero in S.

This example shows that electric and magnetic fields look different to observers in different coordinate systems. Furthermore, it turns out that the components of *each* field **E'** and **B'** as measured in S' depend on *both* fields **E** and **B** as measured in S. This is the reason we must speak of *electromagnetic* fields rather than *electric* and *magnetic* fields; when one makes a Lorentz transformation from one frame to another, the two fields become mixed.

Equations relating the components of the two fields in two different frames of reference can be derived from the relativistic velocity transformation and the requirement that Eq. (2-11) must have the same form in both systems. We cannot discuss the details of this derivation here, but the results are quoted below. In addition, by using the Lorentz transformation, one can derive all the properties of the interactions between electric current or moving charges, usually expressed in terms of magnetic fields, from purely *electrostatic* considerations. This is an extremely important result and a beautiful example of the unifying effect relativity has had on the various parts of electromagnetic theory and its relation to other areas of physics.

In stating the transformation equations for the electric and magnetic fields, we represent each field in terms of a component *parallel* to the direction of relative motion of S and S' (in our usage the x axis) and a component *perpendicular* to this direction. These components measured in S are denoted by $\mathbf{E}_{\parallel}$, $\mathbf{E}_{\perp}$, $\mathbf{B}_{\parallel}$, and $\mathbf{B}_{\perp}$, and the corresponding components measured in S' are denoted by $\mathbf{E}'_{\parallel}$, $\mathbf{E}'_{\perp}$, $\mathbf{B}'_{\parallel}$, $\mathbf{B}'_{\perp}$. If $\mathbf{u}$ is the velocity of S' relative to S, then the transformation equations are

$$\mathbf{E}'_{\parallel} = \mathbf{E}_{\parallel}$$

$$\mathbf{E}'_{\perp} = \frac{\mathbf{E}_{\perp} + \mathbf{u} \times \mathbf{B}_{\perp}}{\sqrt{1 - u^2/c^2}}$$

$$\mathbf{B}'_{\parallel} = \mathbf{B}_{\parallel} \qquad\qquad (2\text{-}23)$$

$$\mathbf{B}'_{\perp} = \frac{\mathbf{B}_{\perp} - \mathbf{u} \times \mathbf{E}_{\perp}/c^2}{\sqrt{1 - u^2/c^2}}$$

We see that the components parallel to the direction of relative motion are the same in both systems, but the components perpendicular to this direction involve both fields in each system.

2-6 RELATIVITY AND NEWTONIAN MECHANICS

It may now appear that we have succeeded in demolishing the very foundations of newtonian mechanics. In one sense this is true; the absolute meanings of length and time in Newton's mechanics are inconsistent with the principle of relativity, and nearly all the other concepts have to be modified in one way or another. Yet all the relativistic formulations become equivalent to the newtonian ones when the velocities are sufficiently small. In such cases, time dilation, contraction of length, nonabsoluteness of simultaneity, and the various modifications of the dynamical principles are not observed. Thus the theory of relativity should be regarded not as a *refutation* of classical mechanics but a *generalization* of it. Every one of the principles of newtonian mechanics is contained in the relativistic theory as a special case, valid when the velocities are sufficiently small.

The relationship between newtonian mechanics and relativistic mechanics is an example of a general guiding principle of great importance in all scientific thought, the *correspondence principle*. According to this principle, when a new theory is in partial disagreement with an older, established theory, it must give the same results as the old theory in any areas in which the old theory has been found experimentally to be correct. Thus the correspondence principle insists that relativistic mechanics predict the same results as newtonian mechanics in situations where the latter has been found valid; as we have seen in several instances, relativistic mechanics does in fact satisfy this requirement.

Conversely, however, there are many physical situations for which newtonian mechanics is clearly inadequate. These include the interaction of electrically charged particles and electromagnetic fields at speeds approaching that of light and particularly the direct conversion of mass into energy, a phenomenon which newtonian mechanics is powerless to explain. But there still remains a large area, including practically all the behavior of macroscopic bodies and familiar mechanical systems, for which newtonian mechanics is perfectly adequate.

One further question may be raised in connection with the status of the theory of relativity: In stating the basic postulate of relativity, we insisted that all *inertial* frames of reference be equivalent. Why did we restrict this requirement to *inertial* frames? Why not *all possible* frames? This question provides the seed of Einstein's *general theory of relativity* (so called to distinguish it from the *special theory of relativity*, which we have been discussing up to now) and his theory of gravitation, developed in 1915. We cannot discuss these theories in any detail here, but an example will indicate their direction.

Consider the following situation: A man is standing in an elevator; the elevator cables have all broken, and the safety devices have all failed at once, so that the elevator is falling freely with an acceleration relative to the earth of $g = 9.80$ m/s^2 downward. The man observes that he is weightless, but he can interpret this observation in two ways: He may think that the elevator is in fact falling freely, and he with it, or he may think that somehow the force of gravity has been turned off, so that he is no longer attracted to the earth. If he confines his experiments to those which can be made within his own frame of reference, he cannot tell whether he is in an accelerated (noninertial) frame of reference or whether the force of gravity has been turned off.

A more realistic example concerns an astronaut in a space station in a circular orbit around the earth. Objects in the orbiting station appear weightless because both objects and station are constantly accelerated toward the earth under the action of its gravitational attraction. But there is no way to distinguish, by means of experiments performed in the station, between this situation and one in which the station is moving with constant velocity in a region of zero gravitational field. Just as with the falling elevator, there is no way to distinguish between a gravitational field and an accelerated reference system.

The heart of the *general* theory of relativity is the hypothesis that an accelerated reference system and a gravitational field are really two aspects of the same thing; if one cannot distinguish between them experimentally, it makes no sense to distinguish between them at all. This is called the *principle of equivalence*. Einstein postulated further that *any* gravitational field may be represented as equivalent to some modification of the coordinate system. It turns out that if the gravitational field is not uniform, we cannot simply use an accelerated frame of reference, but more drastic steps must be taken; in general, one must use a non-euclidean geometry. Thus if one accepts the principle of equivalence, one is led to the assumption that the space of the physical universe is in general non-euclidean.

The correspondence principle insists that if this new theory is correct, it must reduce to the older theory (in this case, the special theory of relativity) in areas in which the latter has been found valid. Conversely, however, there are several effects predicted by the general theory which are *not* included in the special theory. Most familiar of these is the interaction of electromagnetic radiation with a gravitational field. Roughly speaking, a ray of light from a distant star appears to bend as it passes near a massive object such as the sun, as though attracted toward it. Similarly, radiation traveling vertically downward in the earth's gravitational field experiences a very small increase in frequency which may be compared to the gain in kinetic energy of a falling body. Both these effects are extremely small and have required very careful and painstaking work for their observation.

Some details of the general theory of relativity and related theories of gravitation are still controversial in nature, but it is clear that these theories are of central importance in the study of the structure and evolution of stars and related astrophysical problems. One concept of great current interest is that of a *black hole*, a star which has collapsed to the point where its density is so great (the order of 10^{15} g/cm^3) that gravitational interactions prevent *any* radiation or matter from escaping from it. Proposed first as an unlikely mathematical curiosity, black holes are now believed by many astrophysicists actually to exist as the final state in the evolution of sufficiently massive stars.

Problems

2-1 Comparing the relativistic definition of momentum with the newtonian expression, by what fraction is the latter in error if

   a $v = 0.1c$

   b $v = 0.9c$

2-2 How much work must be done to accelerate a particle of mass m from rest to a speed of $0.1c$? To $0.9c$? Express your results as multiples of the rest energy.

2-3 A student proposed to compute the kinetic energy of a particle relativistically by using the expression $\frac{1}{2}mv^2$ with the "relativistic" mass of the particle. Is this correct? Explain.

2-4 Protons emerge from a certain synchrocyclotron with kinetic energy of about $0.5mc^2$. What is the speed of these particles? Compare your result with that obtained from the nonrelativistic relation between mass and kinetic energy.

2-5 What is the speed of a particle whose kinetic energy is equal to its rest energy? What percentage error is made if the nonrelativistic kinetic-energy expression is used?

2-6 A proton emerges from a particle accelerator with a speed of $0.75c$ and collides with another proton initially at rest.
 a What is the kinetic energy of the proton?
 b Find the velocity of a moving coordinate system such that in this system the total momentum of the two protons is zero.

2-7 Carry out the integral in Eq. (2-15) to obtain Eq. (2-16).

2-8 Find the speed of an "extreme relativistic" particle for which the total energy is $10mc^2$.

2-9 Show that the momentum p and kinetic energy T (*not* total energy) of a particle of rest mass m are related by the equation

$$p^2c^2 = T^2 + 2mc^2T$$

2-10 Construct a right triangle in which the length of one leg is mc^2 and the angle ϕ adjacent to this leg is given by $\sin \phi = v/c$.
 a Show that the hypotenuse length is the total energy and that the side opposite angle ϕ is c times the relativistic momentum.
 b Find a graphical procedure for obtaining the *kinetic* energy.

2-11 Show that the relativistic energy-momentum relation, Eq. (2-20), reduces to $E = mc^2 + p^2/2m$ in the nonrelativistic limit. Use the suggestions following Eq. (2-20).

2-12 Show that Eq. (2-12) can be rewritten as

$$\mathbf{F} = \frac{m\mathbf{a}}{\sqrt{1 - v^2/c^2}} + \frac{m(\mathbf{v} \cdot \mathbf{a})\mathbf{v}}{(1 - v^2/c^2)^{3/2}}$$

2-13 Write Eq. (2-12) in component form to show that for a particle with instantaneous velocity v along the x axis the components of acceleration are given by

$$F_x = \frac{ma_x}{(1 - v^2/c^2)^{3/2}} \qquad F_y = \frac{ma_y}{(1 - v^2/c^2)^{1/2}}$$

In the early days of relativity theory the coefficients of a_x and a_y were sometimes called the *longitudinal* and *transverse* masses, respectively, reflecting the fact that the relation of **F** to **a** is different for components parallel to **v** and perpendicular to **v**.

2-14 Show that a charged particle of mass m and charge q moving perpendicular to a uniform magnetic field B at relativistic speed v moves in a circle of radius R given by

$$R = \frac{mv}{qB\sqrt{1 - v^2/c^2}}$$

The results of Prob. 2-13 may be helpful.

2-15 In a hypothetical nuclear-fusion reactor two deuterium nuclei combine, or fuse, to form one helium nucleus. The mass of a deuterium nucleus, expressed in atomic mass units (u), is 2.0147; that of a helium nucleus is 4.0039 (1 u = 1.66×10^{-24} g).

   a   How much energy is released when 1 g of deuterium undergoes fusion? (Neglect the masses of the electrons, which do not participate in the nuclear reaction.)

   b   The annual consumption of electric energy in the United States is on the order of 10^{16} Wh. How much deuterium must react to produce this much energy?

2-16 According to newtonian mechanics, when a charged particle moves in a magnetic field, it moves with constant speed. Is this result correct in relativistic mechanics? Explain.

2-17 Consider the motion of a charged particle in a magnetic field in the situation of Prob. 2-14.

   a   Show that the nonrelativistic formulation predicts that the angular velocity of the particle is independent of its speed and hence of its energy.

   b   Using relativistic mechanics and the result of Prob. 2-14, derive a relationship between the angular velocity and the total energy of the particle.

   c   In a certain synchrocyclotron the angular velocity of very slow protons is about 30×10^6 r/s. What is the angular velocity when the particles have been accelerated in a kinetic energy equal to $0.5mc^2$?

2-18 A particle with mass m and initial speed v collides with a second particle of mass m, initially at rest, as observed in a frame S. The collision is completely *inelastic*; the two particles move off as one mass M after the collision.

   a   Show that v is related to the speed u of the center-of-momentum frame of reference S' in which the total momentum is zero by

$$v = \frac{2u}{1 + u^2/c^2}$$

   b   Find the final velocity of the composite particle M in S.

c   Using conservation of momentum in S, show that M is not equal to $2m$ but is given by

$$M = \frac{2m}{\sqrt{1 - u^2/c^2}}$$

In working out this result, the calculation is simplified somewhat by first establishing the relation

$$\frac{1}{\sqrt{1 - v^2/c^2}} = \frac{1 + u^2/c^2}{1 - u^2/c^2}$$

d   Find the kinetic energy in S' before and after the collision, and show that the difference is accounted for by the increased rest mass.

2-19   An electron in a uniform electric field E in the x direction starts from rest at the origin at time $t = 0$.

a   Show that its speed v after time t is given by

$$v = \frac{qEt/m}{\sqrt{1 + (qEt/mc)^2}}$$

b   Show that its position x after t is given by

$$x = \frac{mc}{qE}\left[\sqrt{1 + \left(\frac{qEt}{mc}\right)^2} - 1\right]$$

c   Show that after a very long time v approaches c and x approaches ct.

2-20   A positron with initial speed v collides with an electron initially at rest. Both particles are annihilated, and two photons of electromagnetic radiation are produced. Find the direction and energy of each photon if the photon energies are equal. Why is it not possible for only one photon to be produced?

2-21   A particle moving along the x axis has momentum p and total energy E as measured in a frame S. Show that in a frame S' moving with speed u relative to S, the momentum p' and energy E' are given by

$$p' = \frac{p - uE/c^2}{\sqrt{1 - u^2/c^2}} \qquad E' = \frac{E - up}{\sqrt{1 - u^2/c^2}}$$

Hence the transformation for the pair of quantities $(p, E/c^2)$ is the same as for (x, t).

2-22   Using the results of Prob. 2-21, show that the quantity $E^2 - p^2c^2$ has the same value in all frames of reference, i.e., is *invariant* under the Lorentz transformation.

2-23   Using Eqs. (2-23), show that the quantities $(E^2 - c^2B^2)$ and $\mathbf{E} \cdot \mathbf{B}$ have the same value in frame S' as in S; i.e., that they are *invariant* under the Lorentz transformation.

2-24 In a frame of reference S there is a uniform electric field $\mathbf{E}$ in the y direction and a uniform magnetic field $\mathbf{B}$ in the z direction. Using Eqs. (2-23), show that in a frame S' moving in the x direction with velocity u, one of these fields may always be made to vanish, by appropriate choice of u. Show that if $E < cB$, E' can be made to vanish, while if $E > cB$, B' can be made to vanish. What happens when $E = cB$?

2-25 A photon (the quantum of electromagnetic radiation) has energy E related to its frequency f by $E = hf$, where h is a universal constant called Planck's constant, as discussed in Chap. 8. Suppose we associate with a photon of energy E an equivalent mass $m = E/c^2$ and a corresponding gravitational potential energy in the earth's gravitational field of mgy, where y is the height above some reference level. When the photon "falls" through a height y, it gains energy and hence frequency. Show that the change in frequency is given approximately by

$$\frac{\Delta f}{f} = \frac{gy}{c^2}$$

2-26 An atom of mass m initially at rest absorbs a photon of energy E. Some of this energy becomes internal energy of the atom, while some of it is associated with center-of-mass motion as the atom recoils to conserve momentum. Call this recoil energy E_r, and show that if the kinetic energy of the atom can be treated nonrelativistically, then E_r is given by

$$E_r = \frac{E^2}{2mc^2}$$

Hence show that if the photon energy is much smaller than the atom's rest energy, the recoil energy is much smaller than the photon energy. In atomic transitions involving photons of visible or ultraviolet light or x-rays, recoil effects are usually negligible.

Wave Phenomena | 3

The wave concept lies at the heart of much of contemporary physics, including electrodynamics, optics, and quantum theory. Several general principles and concepts of wave phenomena are reviewed, and mathematical language for describing waves is introduced, with particular reference to mechanical waves on a stretched string. The dynamical basis of waves on a string is discussed, and then sinusoidal waves are introduced as an important example of periodic waves. Finally, we discuss the principle of superposition and its applications to the analysis of reflections, standing waves, and normal modes.

3-1 PROPERTIES OF WAVES

The study of wave propagation forms an important and interesting chapter in physical science, cutting across the boundaries that have traditionally divided physics into domains such as mechanics, electromagnetism, optics, and atomic physics. The concepts of waves and of wave propagation have played a central and overwhelmingly important role throughout the development of physical theory and have had the happy effect of bringing unity to the most diverse branches of physical science. Thus it is entirely appropriate that this book, which is devoted to the physics of the twentieth century, should be concerned in its early chapters with wave phenomena.

The next four chapters are concerned chiefly with optics, especially with phenomena requiring the use of wave concepts for their understanding. Although originally the term *optics* was used only for phenomena involving visible light, it is now used in a more general sense to include electromagnetic wave phenomena covering a wide range of frequencies and wavelengths, of which visible light forms a small but important part. Thus the study of optics is really the study of *electromagnetic waves.* In developing the topic, we first introduce in the present chapter some general wave concepts in the more familiar realm of *mechanical* waves; we then review the important principles of electrodynamics from which an understanding of electromagnetic waves emerges.

A wave is a disturbance from an equilibrium state that moves or *propagates* with time from one region of space to another. Examples of wave motion are numerous, both in everyday experience and in the various physical sciences. The classical example is that of waves on the surface of a pond. Dropping a stone into the water produces a disturbance which spreads out horizontally in all directions along the surface. An even more commonplace example is sound; a source of sound produces a fluctuation in pressure in the surrounding atmosphere, and this disturbance is propagated to distant points.

In both these examples the wave motion consists of successive displacements of various portions of a mechanical medium (water or air), but it is important to understand that the matter constituting the medium is not itself transported to distant points. In the case of water waves, the individual water molecules have an oscillating motion with respect to their equilibrium position (a smooth water surface). Similarly, travel of sound from a violin to a listener in a concert hall is a propagation of air pressure variations, not an actual transport of air molecules.

Some waves occur *without* a mechanical medium. One of the most important of these is an electromagnetic wave, in which the disturbance from equilibrium is the presence of time-varying electric and magnetic fields in a certain region of space, inducing corresponding electromagnetic disturbances at distant points. Although the physical nature of electromagnetic waves is quite different from that of mechanical waves, they share a number of common features and may be described with the same general language. Light, radio waves, x-rays, and γ rays are all examples of electromagnetic waves.

Further removed from ordinary experience is the wavelike nature of fundamental particles. In some respects a fundamental particle, such as an electron, behaves like a disturbance from an equilibrium (vacuum) state which propagates from one region of space to another as the particle moves. The concept of the wave nature of particles is one of the cornerstones of present-day quantum mechanics, and it will be discussed in detail in Chaps. 8 to 10.

A characteristic of all waves is the ability to transport *energy* from one region of space to another. Transmission of energy by an electromagnetic wave, such as sunlight or the radiation in a microwave oven, is familiar, and the destructive power of ocean surf is a convincing demonstration of the

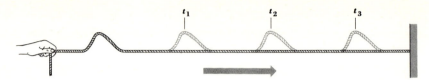

Fig. 3-1 Wave pulse on a stretched string, produced by giving one end a transverse "flipping" motion. The pulse is shown at several successive times; it moves with a definite speed and without change of shape.

energy carried by waves. Waves can also transport momentum and angular momentum. Energy transmission in both mechanical and electromagnetic waves will be discussed in detail in later sections.

As frequently happens in the formulation of physical principles, the most familiar phenomena are not always the simplest ones to analyze in detail. It is often instructive and useful to select a particularly simple situation to exhibit basic ideas, uncluttered by undue mathematical complexity. We select as our prototype of wave motion the propagation of mechanical waves on a stretched string or rope. We tie one end of a long string to a stationary support and then, keeping the tension constant, impart a motion to the other end, as shown in Fig. 3-1.

Observation of the resulting motion reveals several striking features. First the disturbance, which we may call a *wave pulse,* maintains its *shape* as it travels along the string. Second, experiment shows that the pulse moves with a definite speed, independent of its shape or size. Third, the displacements of individual points on the string are found to be perpendicular, or *transverse,* to the equilibrium position of the string and to the direction of propagation of the wave; any such wave is called a *transverse wave.*

A thorough understanding of these features must include their basis in the general principles of mechanics, namely, Newton's laws of motion. For this we need first a convenient language for *describing* wave phenomena. The situation is analogous to that in particle mechanics, where a *kinematic* description of particle motion in terms of displacement, velocity, and acceleration must precede the more general *dynamical* questions of the relation of motion to the forces that produce it. In the next section we consider such a descriptive language for a stretched string; several aspects will also be directly useful later in analyzing the relation of electromagnetic waves to the basic principles of electrodynamics, Maxwell's equations.

3-2 MATHEMATICAL DESCRIPTION OF WAVES

To describe wave motion on a stretched string, we introduce a coordinate system with its x axis along the equilibrium position of the string, as in Fig.

3-2. We neglect any sag due to gravity. Any point on the string is identified by its distance x from the origin, and the instantaneous displacement of this point from equilibrium is denoted by y. Because the displacement changes with time, and because at any time t the displacement is different for different points (different values of x), y is a function of both x and t, a fact represented symbolically by the expression

$$y = f(x,t) \tag{3-1}$$

This is called the *wave function* for the wave. When this function is known, we know everything there is to know about the motion. We can find the *position* of any point at any time by substituting appropriate values of x and t. We can find the transverse *velocity* v of any point, which is simply the rate of change of y with t,

$$v = \frac{\partial y}{\partial t} \tag{3-2}$$

and the instantaneous *slope* m at any point on the string,

$$m = \frac{\partial y}{\partial x} \tag{3-3}$$

We note that *partial derivatives* are used in the above expressions; in Eq. (3-2) we need the time rate of change of y with t, at a constant x, and in Eq. (3-3) we want the rate of change of y with x at a constant t, in accordance with the usual meaning of the partial derivative notation. How would we find the *acceleration* of a point? The *curvature* at a point?

Suppose we know that at time $t = 0$ the shape of the entire string is given by some function $y = f(x)$ and that the wave propagates in the $+x$ direction with constant speed u, without change of shape. It is then easy to find the general wave function $f(x,t)$. One approach is shown in Fig. 3-3; we view the traveling wave from a moving coordinate system S' with axes x' and y' which move along with the wave with speed u; the wave appears stationary in S'. If the origin O' of S' coincides with the other origin O at $t = 0$, then the wave is described for all time in S' by $y' = f(x')$. But from the figure we can see that

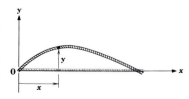

Fig. 3-2 Coordinate system for a mathematical description of transverse waves on a string. The x axis is the equilibrium position of the string; the displacement of a point whose equilibrium position is x is denoted as y. The equilibrium position of the string is shown as a shaded line.

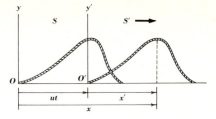

Fig. 3-3 A wave pulse moving with speed
u in a frame of reference appears
stationary in a frame of reference S'
moving relative to S with speed u. The
coordinates are related by $x' = x - ut$.

$$x' = x - ut$$
$$y' = y \qquad (3\text{-}4)$$

provided u is small enough so we do not need the relativistic coordinate
transformation. Thus in the original system S the wave is described by

$$y(x,t) = f(x - ut) \qquad (3\text{-}5)$$

that is, the function that described the shape at $t = 0$, with x replaced
everywhere by $(x - ut)$.

Here is an alternative view of Eq. (3-5). In time t the entire waveshape
moves to the right a distance ut, so the displacement y of point x at time
t is just the same as the displacement of a point a distance ut to the *left*
of x at time $t = 0$. That is, the displacement of point x at time t is equal
to the displacement of point $x - ut$ at time $t = 0$. This in turn is given
by $f(x - ut)$, a function with the same form as $f(x)$ but with x replaced
everywhere by $x - ut$. Thus if the waveshape at time $t = 0$ is $f(x)$ and if
the wave propagates to the right with constant speed u, the waveshape at
any later time t is given by $f(x - ut)$.

Example

Suppose a transverse wave pulse on a string is described at time $t = 0$ by
the equation

$$y = \frac{1}{1 + x^2}$$

where x and y are both measured in meters. The crest of the pulse is at
$x = 0$. If the wave speed is 2 m/s and the wave moves in the $+x$ direction,
write expressions for the shape of the wave at $t = 1$ s, $t = 2$ s, and for any
general value t.

Solution

In general, as just pointed out, the shape of the string at any time t is given
by

$$y = \frac{1}{1 + (x - ut)^2}$$

In the first case, $ut = (2 \text{ m/s})(1 \text{ s}) = 2 \text{ m}$, and the expression at time $t = 1 \text{ s}$ is

$$y = \frac{1}{1 + (x - 2)^2}$$

The crest is at $x = 2$ m. Similarly, at time $t = 2$ s the wave function is

$$y = \frac{1}{1 + (x - 4)^2}$$

with crest at $x = 4$ m. The waveshape has moved 2 and 4 m, respectively, from its position at time $t = 0$. The configurations of the string at these three times are shown in Fig. 3-4.

The preceding discussion has shown that any wave function $y = f(x,t)$ which describes a wave propagating in the $+x$ direction with wave speed u, must contain the variables x and t only in the particular combination $x - ut$. The discussion may be repeated for a wave traveling in the $-x$ direction to show that for such a wave the variables must appear only in the combination $x + ut$. An equivalent and sometimes more useful statement is that, for waves traveling in the $\pm x$ direction, the variables must appear in the combination $ax \mp bt$. This combination may be written as $a(x \mp bt/a)$, in which form it is clear that the wave speed u is given by $u = b/a$, that is, coefficient of t divided by the coefficient of x. This observation will be useful in a later discussion of the propagation of wave pulses.

The forms $y = f(x - ut)$ and $y = f(x + ut)$ for wave functions suggest another important observation. Since the wave function contains the two variables x and t, we can calculate its partial derivative with respect to either of these. These calculations are facilitated by introducing a single symbol to represent the combination $x \pm ut$. For a wave propagating in the $+x$ direction, let $z = x - ut$. Then application of the chain rule for derivatives leads to the following relations:

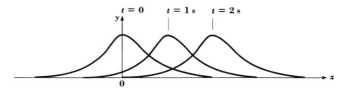

$t = 0$ $t = 1$ s $t = 2$ s

Fig. 3-4 Motion of a transverse wave pulse. The pulse is shown at three successive times.

$$\frac{\partial y}{\partial x} = \frac{dy}{dz}\frac{\partial z}{\partial x} = \frac{dy}{dz} \quad (1)$$

$$\frac{\partial y}{\partial t} = \frac{dy}{dz}\frac{\partial z}{\partial t} = \frac{dy}{dz}(-u)$$

From these we conclude that the two derivatives must be related by the equation

$$\frac{\partial y}{\partial x} = -\frac{1}{u}\frac{\partial y}{\partial t} \qquad \text{for } y = f(x - ut)$$

A similar calculation for a wave propagating in the $-x$ direction yields the relation

$$\frac{\partial y}{\partial x} = +\frac{1}{u}\frac{\partial y}{\partial t} \qquad \text{for } y = f(x + ut)$$

Repeated application of the same procedure yields a relation between the *second* derivatives; this relation is the same for waves propagating in either direction:

$$\frac{\partial^2 y}{\partial x^2} = \frac{1}{u^2}\frac{\partial^2 y}{\partial t^2} \tag{3-6}$$

This differential equation, which must be satisfied by any wave function representing a wave traveling in *either* the $+x$ or $-x$ direction, is called the *wave equation* for the system. It does not tell us directly what motion occurs in any particular situation, but its *solutions* represent all the possible motions. Thus a study of the functions which satisfy Eq. (3-6) is in effect a study of the possible wave motions on a stretched string.

To summarize: Any function $y = f(x,t)$ that describes a wave propagating in either direction on a string, with definite speed and unvarying waveshape, must satisfy Eq. (3-6). Correspondingly, such waves are physically possible if and only if this equation is consistent with the general laws of dynamics. Thus the next logical step is an attempt to derive the wave equation, which we have already deduced from *kinematic* considerations, from the principles of *dynamics*. In the course of this derivation it will become clear what properties the mechanical system must have in order to permit wave propagation.

The logical sequence just described will recur several times in our discussion of wave phenomena. In introducing the concept of electromagnetic waves in Sec. 4-3, we shall see that the functions describing the variation of electric and magnetic fields with position and time must satisfy a wave equation with exactly the same form as Eq. (3-6) if they are to be consistent with the appropriate general principles—in this case, Maxwell's equations.

3-3 DYNAMICS OF WAVES ON A STRING

We shall now derive the wave equation for the string from Newton's laws of motion. The string is not a point mass but rather a distribution of mass along a line, so we begin by applying the laws of motion to a very small section of string. Figure 3-5 shows a small element of string whose length in the equilibrium position is Δx. In the figure this element is displaced from the equilibrium position (represented by the x axis) and stretched, so that its actual length is somewhat greater than Δx. Assuming the string is uniform, we denote its mass per unit length in the equilibrium position by μ; this quantity is called the *linear mass density*. Thus the mass of this element is $m = \mu\,\Delta x$.

If gravity is neglected, the forces on this element of string are those shown in Fig. 3-5. The force applied to each end is in a direction tangent to the string at the corresponding point; these forces may be resolved into their x and y components. Under the assumption that the displacements are always transverse, there is no component of acceleration, hence of force, along the x axis. Thus it always must be true that $F_{1x} = F_{2x}$, where these symbols refer to the *magnitudes* of the corresponding components, regardless of sign. Since F_x does not change with the displacement of the string, each of these must be equal to the tension F in the string when it is not displaced from equilibrium. That is,

$$F_{1x} = F_{2x} = F \tag{3-7}$$

The transverse acceleration of the element of string is produced by the transverse component of force, $F_{2y} - F_{1y}$. To obtain the magnitudes of these forces, we note that the ratio F_{1y}/F_{1x} is equal to the *slope* of the string at the point x, and F_{2y}/F_{2x} to the slope at $x + \Delta x$. Thus we obtain the relations

$$\frac{F_{1y}}{F_{1x}} = \left(\frac{\partial y}{\partial x}\right)_x \qquad \frac{F_{2y}}{F_{2x}} = \left(\frac{\partial y}{\partial x}\right)_{x+\Delta x} \tag{3-8}$$

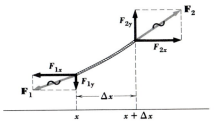

Fig. 3-5 Free-body diagram for an element of string whose length in its equilibrium position is Δx. The force at each end of the string is tangent to the string at the point of application; each force is represented in terms of its x and y components.

where the notation indicates that the derivatives are evaluated at the points x and $x + \Delta x$, respectively. Combining Eqs. (3-7) and (3-8),

$$F_{2y} - F_{1y} = F\left[\left(\frac{\partial y}{\partial x}\right)_{x+\Delta x} - \left(\frac{\partial y}{\partial x}\right)_x\right] \tag{3-9}$$

The net transverse force given by Eq. (3-9) is now to be equated to the product of the mass of the section and its acceleration:

$$F_{2y} - F_{1y} = \mu\,\Delta x\,\frac{\partial^2 y}{\partial t^2} \tag{3-10}$$

The question may arise as to whether the acceleration $\partial^2 y/\partial t^2$ should be evaluated at the point x or the point $x + \Delta x$. Since the next step is to let $\Delta x \to 0$, this is not really an important question.

Combining Eqs. (3-9) and (3-10) and dividing by $F\,\Delta x$,

$$\frac{(\partial y/\partial x)_{x+\Delta x} - (\partial y/\partial x)_x}{\Delta x} = \frac{\mu}{F}\frac{\partial^2 y}{\partial t^2} \tag{3-11}$$

We see that in the limit as $\Delta x \to 0$ the left side of this equation becomes simply the derivative with respect to x of $\partial y/\partial x$ which is $\partial^2 y/\partial x^2$; in this limit we therefore have

$$\frac{\partial^2 y}{\partial x^2} = \frac{\mu}{F}\frac{\partial^2 y}{\partial t^2} \tag{3-12}$$

Any wave function $y = f(x,t)$ that describes a physically possible wave on the string must agree with Eq. (3-12).

This equation has precisely the same form as Eq. (3-6), derived from more general considerations. Thus waves of the type under discussion *are* compatible with Newton's laws. Furthermore, comparing Eqs. (3-12) and (3-6) gives an additional important result; the fact that these two equations must be identical shows that the wave speed u is directly related to the mechanical properties of the system. That is, it must be true that $1/u^2 = \mu/F$, or

$$u = \sqrt{\frac{F}{\mu}} \tag{3-13}$$

Increasing the tension in the string increases the wave speed, but increasing the linear mass density decreases the speed, as might be expected intuitively. Thus deriving the wave equation for the system shows not only that wave propagation is physically possible but also how the wave speed is related to the properties of the system. An analogous calculation will be made in Sec. 4-3 for electromagnetic waves.

3-4 SINUSOIDAL WAVES

The discussion of wave motion on a string has been introduced with the idea of a wave pulse, localized at any given time in a certain region on the string, in which successive particles in the string undergo temporary displacements from equilibrium and then return. Some of the most important and interesting kinds of wave motion, however, are those in which each particle undergoes a repetitive, or *periodic*, motion. Suppose that the end of the string in Fig. 3-1 is given not just a single flip but a series of flips at regular time intervals. The number of repetitions per unit time is called the *frequency*, denoted by f, and the time for one repetition is called the period, denoted by T. Clearly, $T = 1/f$.

Frequencies are usually measured in hertz; one hertz $= 1\ \text{Hz} = 1$ cycle/second. The units kHz $(= 10^3\ \text{Hz})$ and MHz $(= 10^6\ \text{Hz})$ are also in common use.

Since the motion of the end of the string is periodic, the wave pattern on the string at any instant is also repetitive. During one period T of the motion, the wave travels along the string a distance uT. Let us denote this distance by $\lambda = uT$. At the end of the time interval T, the end of the string begins to repeat the motion of the first interval. By the end of the second period, the wave has traveled a total distance 2λ, and the wave pattern on the string consists of two separate patterns, each of length λ, identical in shape.

The distance λ is called the *wavelength*; it is the distance between any pair of corresponding points on two successive repetitions of the waveform. The important relationship

$$\lambda = uT = \frac{u}{f} \tag{3-14}$$

is valid for *any* periodic wave motion.

An important example of periodic wave motion occurs when the end of the string is given a *sinusoidal* (i.e., simple harmonic[1]) motion, in many respects the simplest periodic motion of a point. Let the end of the string be at $x = 0$, and let this point be given a transverse displacement $A \cos 2\pi ft$, a simple harmonic motion with amplitude A and frequency f. Then, at the point $x = 0$, the wave function is

$$y(0,t) = A \cos 2\pi ft \tag{3-15}$$

The resulting wave motion is shown in Fig. 3-6.

---

[1]Any reader who is not familiar with simple harmonic motion would do well to review this important concept in an elementary mechanics text, such as H. D. Young, "Fundamentals of Mechanics and Heat," 2d ed., secs. 10-1 and 10-2, McGraw-Hill Book Company, New York, 1974.

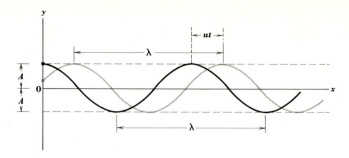

Fig. 3-6 A sinusoidal wave produced by giving the end of the string at $x = 0$ a sinusoidally varying displacement described by Eq. (3-15). The shape of the string at time $t = 0$, shown as a solid line, is described by the function $y(x,0) = A \cos 2\pi f \, (0 - x/u)$; the shape at a later time t, shown as a shaded line, is given by the general wave function of Eq. (3-16). In the time t the wave moves a distance ut to the right. The amplitude A and wavelength λ are also shown.

To find the complete wave function, we recall from Sec. 3-2 that the function for a wave propagating in the $+x$ direction must contain x and t only in the combination $x - ut$, which is equivalent to stating that the coefficient of t in the wave function must be $-u$ times the coefficient of x. Here the coefficient of t is $2\pi f$, and so the coefficient of x must be $-2\pi f/u$; the general function is

$$y(x,t) = A \cos\left(2\pi f t - \frac{2\pi f x}{u}\right)$$

$$= A \cos 2\pi f\left(t - \frac{x}{u}\right) \tag{3-16}$$

As a check, we may substitute Eq. (3-16) into Eq. (3-6), which must be satisfied by any possible wave function. It is in fact satisfied; the calculation is left as a problem.

The significance of the wave described by Eq. (3-16) may be appreciated more fully by noting first that every particle in the string undergoes simple harmonic motion; for a fixed value of x, corresponding to a particular point on the string, the displacement is a sinusoidal function of time. The motions of various points differ in *phase;* they are out of step with respect to each other, but nevertheless each point moves with simple harmonic motion. Second, at any instant the *shape* of the string is described by a sinusoidal function of x. That is, for any fixed value t, y is a sinusoidal function of x.

An alternative form of Eq. (3-16), obtained with the help of Eq. (3-14), is

$$y(x,t) = A \cos 2\pi\left(\frac{t}{T} - \frac{x}{\lambda}\right) \tag{3-17}$$

In this form, the wave function shows directly that, when t changes by an amount T, the argument of the sine function changes by 2π, corresponding to a complete cycle of motion of any point. Similarly, when x changes by λ, the argument again changes by 2π, corresponding to a complete repetition of the waveform.

This discussion may be adapted to the case of a wave propagating in the $-x$ direction. Such a wave cannot be produced by shaking the end of the string at $x = 0$, since there is no string to the left of this point. But we may easily imagine a wave motion somewhere in the middle of the string, arising from sinusoidal motion of a point to the right of the region we are observing. Since any wave propagating in the $-x$ direction must contain x and t only in the combination $x + ut$, a possible wave function for a sinusoidal wave of amplitude A, frequency f, and speed u is

$$y(x,t) = A \cos 2\pi f\left(t + \frac{x}{u}\right) = A \cos 2\pi \left(\frac{t}{T} + \frac{x}{\lambda}\right) \qquad (3\text{-}18)$$

To save writing factors of 2π, we introduce two new parameters; these are the *angular frequency* ω and the *wave number* k, defined as

$$\omega = 2\pi f \qquad k = \frac{2\pi}{\lambda} \qquad \omega = uk \qquad (3\text{-}19)$$

In terms of k and ω, Eq. (3-17) becomes

$$y(x,t) = A \cos (\omega t - kx) = A \cos (kx - \omega t) \qquad (3\text{-}20)$$

The second form of Eq. (3-20) is obtained from the identity $\cos(-a) = \cos a$.

One further generalization is useful. A simple harmonic motion described by the equation

$$y = A \cos (\omega t + \phi)$$

has the same general character as one described by

$$y = A \cos \omega t$$

The two motions have the same frequency, period, and amplitude; they differ only in that they are out of step with respect to each other. When ϕ, called the *phase angle*, is equal to π (180°), the two motions are precise opposites of each other; otherwise they are out of step by some fraction of a cycle. A quarter cycle is $\phi = \pi/2$, and so on. From the foregoing discussion, it should be clear that if the free end of a string is given a motion $y(0,t) = A \cos (\omega t + \phi)$ the resulting wave is described by the wave function

$$y(x,t) = A \cos (\omega t - kx + \phi) \qquad (3\text{-}21)$$

This wave differs from that described by Eq. (3-20) only in that at every point along the string, at any instant, the two waves are "out of step" by

$\phi/2\pi$ periods, with the second wave leading if ϕ is positive. The concept of *phase* is of vital importance for the understanding of many wave phenomena such as interference and diffraction, to be discussed in later chapters; in Sec. 5-2 we examine some mathematical techniques for combining waves having arbitrary phase differences.

3-5 ENERGY IN WAVE MOTION

We remarked in Sec. 3-1 that a wave can transport energy from one region of space to another. We are now ready to discuss the energy of a wave on a stretched string.

Since the string has mass in motion, it must have *kinetic energy*. An element of string whose equilibrium length is Δx has mass $\mu\,\Delta x$ and transverse speed $\partial y/\partial t$, so its kinetic energy E is

$$E = \frac{1}{2}\mu\left(\frac{\partial y}{\partial t}\right)^2 \Delta x \tag{3-22}$$

The kinetic energy *per unit length,* or energy *density,* is $\frac{1}{2}\mu(\partial y/\partial t)^2$.

The string also has *potential energy* because it is stretched, just as a stretched spring has potential energy. When an element with equilibrium length Δx is displaced and given a slope $\partial y/\partial x$, its new length Δs is given by

$$\Delta s = [(\Delta x)^2 + (\Delta y)^2]^{1/2} = \Delta x\left[1 + \left(\frac{\partial y}{\partial x}\right)^2\right]^{1/2} \tag{3-23}$$

The amount of stretching of this element is the difference $\Delta s - \Delta x$, and the associated potential energy is simply the work required for this stretching. The force doing the work is the tension F in the string, so the work is

$$W = F(\Delta s - \Delta x)$$

When $\partial y/\partial x$ is small, we may expand the expression in brackets in Eq. (3-23) using the binomial theorem, retaining only the first nonvanishing term:

$$\Delta s = \Delta x\left[1 + \frac{1}{2}\left(\frac{\partial y}{\partial x}\right)^2 + \cdots\right]$$

$$\Delta s - \Delta x = \frac{1}{2}\left(\frac{\partial y}{\partial x}\right)^2 \Delta x$$

$$W = \frac{1}{2}F\left(\frac{\partial y}{\partial x}\right)^2 \Delta x \tag{3-24}$$

Thus the potential energy *per unit length* is $\frac{1}{2}F(\partial y/\partial x)^2$.

The assumption that $\partial y/\partial x$ is always small compared to unity may cause some concern, but this assumption is actually implicit in our entire discussion; it can be shown that when the slope is *not* small, the displacements are not entirely transverse, and the problem becomes much more complex. Thus the assumption of small slope (and small displacements) is implicit in the assumption of transversality; this becomes part of our idealized *model* for this system, just as the assumption of small displacements of a simple pendulum is used to facilitate analysis of its motion.

The *total* energy per unit length, including both kinetic and potential energies, is

$$\frac{1}{2}\mu\left(\frac{\partial y}{\partial t}\right)^2 + \frac{1}{2}F\left(\frac{\partial y}{\partial x}\right)^2 \tag{3-25}$$

To find the total mechanical energy of a section of the string between points x_1 and x_2 at any instant, we integrate Eq. (3-25) between these limits, using derivatives of the wave function describing the particular wave under consideration.

A related problem is the mechanism by which energy is transferred along the string from one region to another. Consider a point P on the string as in Fig. 3-7a: energy is given to the part to the right of P when *work* is done on this part by the string to the left of P. The force on the right side of the string at P is shown in Fig. 3-7b. The horizontal component does no work because the displacement is always transverse; the vertical (transverse) component is

$$F_y = -F\frac{\partial y}{\partial x} \tag{3-26}$$

The rate at which this force does work on the right side is simply the product of F_y and the vertical *velocity*. The power P, or rate at which work is done, on the right side, is

$$P = F_y\dot{v} = -F\frac{\partial y}{\partial x}\frac{\partial y}{\partial t} \tag{3-27}$$

Fig. 3-7 (*a*) Energy is transported past a point P on the string; work is done on the string to the right of P as a result of the transverse force at P and its displacement. (*b*) Free-body diagram showing the force exerted on the string at P. Only the component F_y does work, since there is no displacement in the direction of F.

Example

Find the rate of energy transfer for the wave described by Eq. (3-20).

Solution

$$\frac{\partial y}{\partial x} = -Ak \sin (kx - \omega t)$$

$$\frac{\partial y}{\partial t} = A\omega \sin (kx - \omega t)$$

$$P = A^2 \omega k F \sin^2 (kx - \omega t)$$

$$= A^2 \omega^2 \frac{F}{u} \sin^2 (kx - \omega t) \tag{3-28}$$

For this wave P is always positive; energy is always transferred from left to right, never the reverse. At any given point P varies from zero to a maximum of $A^2 \omega^2 F/u$. The *average* rate of transfer of energy is this expression multiplied by the average value of $\sin^2 (kx - \omega t)$, which is $\frac{1}{2}$. Hence the rate of transfer of energy is proportional to the *square* of the frequency; it also depends on the mechanical properties of the system. The calculation can be repeated for a wave propagating in the $-x$ direction. The result is the same except that the sign is changed, showing that energy is transferred in the *negative* x direction as expected.

3-6   LONGITUDINAL WAVES

Several aspects of wave motion in a mechanical system have been discussed in the context of *transverse* waves on a stretched string. Another important kind of wave motion occurs in an elastic solid or fluid when the displacements are *parallel* to the direction of propagation of the wave. The result is called a *longitudinal* wave.

When one end of a long steel rod is given a sudden displacement, as might be achieved by striking it with a hammer, the immediate effect is a compression of the material in the region of the end. The compression induces stresses on the neighboring regions; the result is a *compression* wave which travels along the length of the rod. Figure 3-8 shows an example of such a wave. In this figure, the very heavily shaded regions have greater than average density. The actual particles of material, of course, do not travel down the length of the rod; what travels is the pattern of compression and associated stress.

Figure 3-8 might also be a longitudinal wave in a pipe filled with gas;

Fig. 3-8 Longitudinal wave pulse in an elastic rod, produced by displacing one end of the rod and then restoring it to its original position. The wave pulse is shown at several successive times; the shading represents the change in density in various regions of the rod. The instantaneous displacements of various points from equilibrium are shown by small arrows above the rod. The relationship between the density and the displacements should be studied carefully.

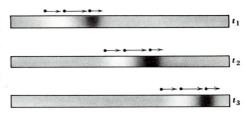

again the varied shading represents the density fluctuations accompanying the wave motion. In either case, the wave can be described by a *wave function* $y(x,t)$ giving the displacement y of each point from its equilibrium position as a function of time. The displacements y are now *parallel* to the direction of wave propagation, rather than perpendicular as with the stretched string.

We shall not analyze these kinds of waves in detail,[1] but shall quote a few results. By applying $F = ma$ to a section of material, one can derive a wave equation governing the wave functions for physically possible waves. The mass of an element is proportional to the *density* of the material, and the forces on the ends of the element are related to the changes in pressure accompanying the displacements. These in turn are related to the elastic properties of the material. For the solid rod the relevant elastic constant is *Young's modulus*, the ratio of change in pressure to the fractional change of length. For the gas the appropriate quantity is the *bulk modulus*, the ratio of change in pressure to fractional volume change. In either case, we expect the wave equation to contain a density ρ and an elastic constant E.

The wave equation for these systems turns out to be

$$\frac{\partial^2 y}{\partial x^2} = \frac{\rho}{E} \frac{\partial^2 y}{\partial t^2} \qquad (3\text{-}29)$$

Comparison with Eq. (3-6) shows that the wave speed is given by

$$u = \sqrt{\frac{E}{\rho}} \qquad (3\text{-}30)$$

Example

Find the speed of longitudinal waves in a steel rod.

---

[1] Longitudinal waves are analyzed in greater detail in the companion volume by H. D. Young, ibid., sec. 22-6.

Solution

The appropriate elastic modulus is Young's modulus, $E_Y = 20 \times 10^{10}$ N/m². The density is $\rho = 7 \times 10^3$ kg/m³, and the wave speed is

$$u = \sqrt{\frac{20 \times 10^{10}\ \text{N/m}^2}{7 \times 10^3\ \text{kg/m}}} = 5.3 \times 10^3\ \text{m/s}$$

some 15 times as great as the speed of sound in air at ordinary temperatures.

Equation (3-30) may also be applied to sound waves in a gas, which are always longitudinal. For an ideal gas the density ρ is given in terms of the pressure P, the molecular mass M, the gas constant R, and the absolute temperature T by

$$\rho = \frac{PM}{RT} \tag{3-31}$$

The relevant elastic constant in this case is the bulk modulus E_B. For an ideal gas at constant temperature the bulk modulus is simply P, but for sound waves in air a more realistic assumption is that the compression and rarefaction occur *adiabatically*, that is, without heat transfer from one region to another. In that case the relevant constant is the *adiabatic bulk modulus*, given by γP, where γ is the ratio of the specific heats at constant pressure and at constant value, $\gamma = C_P/C_V$. Under these conditions, the speed of sound in a gas is

$$u = \sqrt{\frac{\gamma RT}{M}} \tag{3-32}$$

Example

Find the speed of sound in air at $T = 300$ K (the temperature of a warm room).

Solution

Air is a mixture of diatomic gases, for which $\gamma = \frac{7}{5}$. The average molecular mass is $M = 29$ g/mol $= 29 \times 10^{-3}$ kg/mol. We find

$$u = \sqrt{\frac{\frac{7}{5}(8.314\ \text{J/mol K})(300\ \text{K})}{29 \times 10^{-3}\ \text{kg/mol}}} = 347\ \text{m/s}$$

which agrees well with the experimental value of 348 m/s.

In solid materials, both longitudinal and transverse waves are possible. In a *longitudinal* wave the stresses are purely compressive or tensile, without any shear stress, and the resulting deformations are expansions and compressions along the direction of wave propagation without shear deformation. A *transverse* wave is characterized by purely shear stresses and deformations, with no volume change. Since these two kinds of waves depend on different elastic properties, it is not surprising that they propagate with different speeds in the same material. The longitudinal wave, called a *pressure wave* or *p* wave, always has greater speed than the transverse wave, called a *shear wave* or *s* wave.

Measurement of speeds of these two kinds of waves in the earth has provided seismologists with valuable information concerning the structure of the earth. An area of particular interest is the recent discovery that slipping along fault zones, leading to earthquakes, is preceded by changes in the ratio of *s* to *p* wave speed; in the future this phenomenon may make it possible to predict the occurrence and magnitude of earthquakes.

3-7   SUPERPOSITION OF WAVES

In the wave phenomena discussed thus far, the wave motion originates in one region of the medium and propagates in one direction. But it may happen that two wave motions originate in different regions and propagate toward each other, such as the two wave pulses shown at the top of Fig. 3-9. While

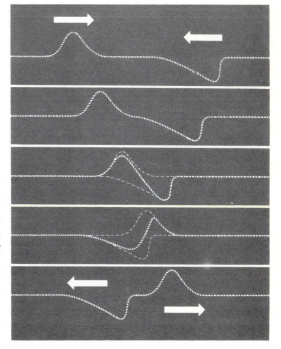

Fig. 3-9 Two pulses with different shapes, moving toward each other, are produced in two separate sections of a string. The position of the string is shown at several successive times. The positions of the individual pulses, during the time of overlap, are shown as broken lines. The actual displacement, shown as a solid line, is the sum of displacements corresponding to the separate pulses. After the two pulses pass, they proceed with their original shapes.

the two pulses are separated, no problem arises, but what happens when they reach the same region of the string and overlap?

Figure 3-9 shows a series of sketches made from a multiple-flash photograph of a string in which two pulses move toward each other and pass. Observation shows that, after they pass, each pulse has the same shape as originally. Furthermore, during the time of overlap the *total* displacement of each point on the string is just the *sum* of the displacements corresponding to the separate pulses. That is, *each pulse moves exactly as though the other were not present,* and the total displacement of any point at a given time is obtained by adding the corresponding displacements of the individual pulses.

Similar experiments can be carried out for other wave situations; again it is found that two different waves can exist in the same region of space at the same time, and the total disturbance at each point is the sum of those of the separate waves. This important result is the *principle of superposition;* a great many wave phenomena of physical importance are direct consequences of this principle. Although introduced here with reference to mechanical waves, it has important applications to other types of waves as well. The fact that two beams of light may cross and continue unchanged is an example of the principle of superposition for electromagnetic waves.

This principle may also be given a mathematical statement. If the wave functions $y_1(x,t)$ and $y_2(x,t)$ represent two different possible wave motions, another possible wave motion is given by their sum $Y(x,t) = y_1(x,t) + y_2(x,t)$. That is, if $y_1(x,t)$ is one solution of the wave equation and $y_2(x,t)$ another, their sum is also a solution. This result, in fact, follows directly from the *form* of the wave equation, specifically from the fact that it is a *linear* equation, containing derivatives of y only to the first power, so that a sum of any two solutions is also a solution. Thus the superposition principle, although introduced as an empirical observation, is really directly related to the form of the wave equation.

It is instructive to examine the superposition of *sinusoidal* waves on a string. Figure 3-10 illustrates two different possibilities. In Fig. 3-10*a*, the two waves, shown at one instant, are nearly in phase, and the maximum displacement is nearly equal to the sum of the amplitudes of the two waves. In Fig. 3-10*b* they are nearly 180° out of phase, and the maximum displacement is much *smaller* than the amplitude of either wave. Thus when sinusoidal waves are superposed, the resultant amplitude depends on the relative *phase* of the individual waves as well as their amplitudes.

An important example of superposition occurs when a wave on a string approaches a point which is held rigidly so that it cannot move. In Fig. 3-11 a wave pulse originates somewhere to the right of the picture and travels to the left toward the end of the string, which is tied to a wall. As the pulse arrives at the wall, the motion appears somewhat complicated, but the final

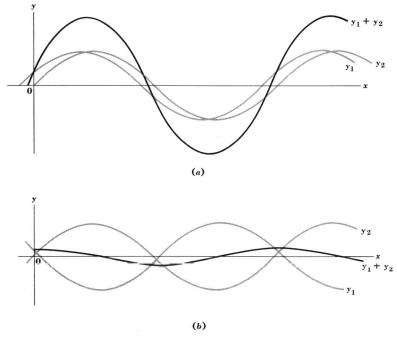

Fig. 3-10 Superposition of two sinusoidal waves with equal frequency and amplitude. (*a*) When the two waves are nearly in phase, the amplitude of the resultant wave is nearly equal to the sum of the separate amplitudes. (*b*) When the two waves are nearly 180° out of phase, the amplitude of the resultant wave is smaller than that of either separate wave.

result is an inverted pulse moving away from the wall, having the same shape as the original. What has happened is that the wave has been *reflected* at the fixed end. The phenomenon of *reflection* of waves is probably more familiar in other contexts. The reflection of a sound wave by a rigid surface produces echoes; reflection of an electromagnetic wave produces the image in a mirror. Figure 3-11 is a simple example of reflection of a mechanical wave on a string.

The mechanism of reflection can be understood by considering the forces at the end point. As the pulse arrives at the end of the string, it exerts an upward force on the fixed point, but the wall to which the string is attached supplies an equal and opposite force so that the point does not move. This *reaction* force generates a wave pulse having the same shape as that which arrived but inverted and progressing in the opposite direction. The reflected pulse must be such that the displacements corresponding to the incoming and reflected pulses always add to zero at the fixed point. This can be true at all times only if the two pulses have the same shape.

A reflection also occurs if the end of the string is mounted as in Fig.

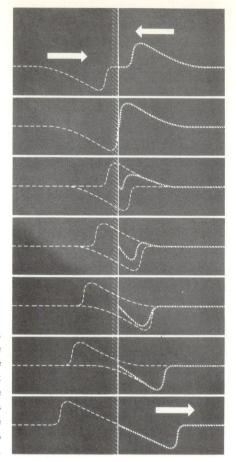

Fig. 3-11 As a wave pulse arrives at a fixed point on the string, the reaction force at the point generates a reflected pulse having the same shape as the original but inverted and moving in the opposite direction. The initial and reflected pulses are shown separately as broken lines; the actual displacement of the string, which is the sum of these, is shown as a solid line.

3-12. The ring maintains the tension of the string but exerts no vertical force because it slides without friction. The absence of vertical force means that the end of the string moves farther than it would if more string were attached. Roughly speaking, the inertia of this section of the string causes it to "overshoot" compared to the motion of the original wave pulse; this generates another wave traveling in the opposite direction. Again the wave pulse has the same shape as the incident pulse, but this time it is *not* inverted. In

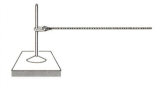

Fig. 3-12 Mechanism for anchoring the end of a string so that the tension is maintained without a transverse force at the end. When a wave pulse arrives at this point, the reflected pulse generated has the same shape as the incoming pulse and progresses in the opposite direction without inversion.

general, a wave pulse is reflected with inversion at a fixed end of a string and without inversion at a free end.

Reflection can readily be described in terms of wave functions for the various waves. Suppose $y = f(t + x/u)$ represents a wave function for a pulse traveling to the left, toward the fixed end of the string at $x = 0$. The function $-f(t - x/u)$ represents a wave traveling in the opposite direction, inverted (because of the negative sign in front) and having the same shape (because the function is the same). The total displacement at any point at any instant is given by

$$f\left(t + \frac{x}{u}\right) - f\left(t - \frac{x}{u}\right) \tag{3-33}$$

At the point $x = 0$ this reduces to $f(t) - f(t) = 0$, as must be the case if this end of the string is stationary. Similarly, the total disturbance corresponding to reflection of a wave from a *free* end at $x = 0$ where there is no inversion, can be expressed in the form $f(t + x/u) + f(t - x/u)$.

3-8   STANDING WAVES AND NORMAL MODES

The motion which results from reflection of sinusoidal waves is of particular interest. Suppose a sinusoidal wave moving in the $-x$ direction and described by the wave function $y_1(x,t) = A \cos (kx + \omega t)$ is reflected by a stationary end at $x = 0$. As discussed above, the periodically varying reaction forces at the end generate a second wave propagating in the $+x$ direction, with wave function $y_2(x,t) = -A \cos (kx - \omega t)$, a wave with the same amplitude, frequency, wavelength, and propagation speed but inverted and traveling in the opposite direction.

According to the principle of superposition, the total displacement $y(x,t)$ at any point is given by the sum $y = y_1 + y_2$. That is,

$$y(x,t) = A \cos (kx + \omega t) - A \cos (kx - \omega t) \tag{3-34}$$

We note immediately that the displacement at $x = 0$ is

$$y(0,t) = A \cos (0 + \omega t) - A \cos (0 - \omega t) = 0$$

satisfying the requirement that this point must not move.

Equation (3-34) can be simplified with the help of the trigonometric identity $\cos (a \pm b) = \cos a \cos b \mp \sin a \sin b$. Expanding each cosine function and combining the results, we obtain

$$y(x,t) = -2A \sin kx \sin \omega t \tag{3-35}$$

Equation (3-35) deserves careful study. First, the variables x and t *do not* appear in the combination $x \pm ut$ characteristic of waves propagating in a single direction. Second, each point undergoes simple harmonic motion, as shown by the factor $\sin \omega t$, but all points move *in phase*. Third, the amplitude of the motion of a point depends on its position, because of the factor $\sin kx$. Points for which $\sin kx = 0$ (that is, $kx = 0$ or an integer multiple of π) do not move at all, and those for which $|\sin kx| = 1$ (that is, $kx = \pi/2, 3\pi/2, \ldots$) have amplitude $2A$, which is twice the maximum displacement corresponding to each of the individual waves. In short, Eq. (3-35) does not represent a progressive wave but rather one with a stationary pattern which becomes larger and smaller with time. Such a wave is called a *standing wave*. The stationary points are called *nodes*, and the points of maximum amplitude are called *antinodes*.

Recalling from Eq. (3-19) that $k = 2\pi/\lambda$, we can find the distance between successive nodes. The first occurs at $x = 0$, the second at $x = \pi/k = \lambda/2$. Thus successive nodes are separated by a distance of half a wavelength. Similarly, successive *antinodes* are separated by $\lambda/2$. The standing wave represented by Eq. (3-35) is shown in Fig. 3-13. The positions of the nodes are given by

$$x = n\frac{\lambda}{2} \qquad n = 0, 1, 2, 3, \ldots \tag{3-36}$$

and the positions of the antinodes by

$$x = \left(n + \frac{1}{2}\right)\frac{\lambda}{2} \qquad n = 0, 1, 2, 3, \ldots \tag{3-37}$$

The above example refers to a mechanical situation. However, there is a completely analogous phenomenon for electromagnetic waves, in which a standing wave is formed by reflection of a wave from the surface of a conductor. This will be discussed in detail in Sec. 4-5.

A similar analysis can be made for reflection at a *free* end of a string. In this case, the reflection takes place without inversion, and it can be shown that if the incoming wave function is the same y_1 discussed above, the wave function for the resulting standing wave is

$$y(x,t) = 2A \cos \omega t \cos kx \tag{3-38}$$

Fig. 3-13 Standing wave resulting from the reflection of a sinusoidal wave at a fixed point. The position of the string is shown at several times. The amplitude of the pattern becomes larger and smaller with time, but it does not move along the length of the string; hence the term *standing wave*. The nodes and antinodes are shown.

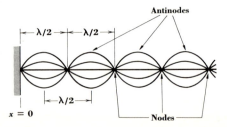

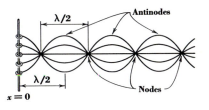

Fig. 3-14 Standing waves produced by reflection of a sinusoidal wave at a free end. In this case, the end is an antinode rather than a node because the wave is reflected without inversion. Positions of nodes and antinodes have the same relative spacing as in Fig. 3-13.

which represents the standing wave shown in Fig. 3-14; in this case the end of the string is an antinode rather than a node. At a free end there is no transverse force, so according to Eq. (3-26) the *slope* at this point must always be zero. This can be verified from Eq. (3-38) and also from Fig. 3-14. Derivation of Eq. (3-38) is left as a problem.

Proceeding further, we now ask what kind of wave motion is possible on a stretched string if *both* ends are held fixed and the string is given some initial motion. In this case, reflections occur at *both* ends, and these *may* produce standing waves. Clearly, however, a sinusoidal standing wave can exist only if *both* ends correspond to nodes of the standing wave, and this happens only when the total length of string, say L, is an integral number of half wavelengths. That is, when both ends are stationary, a sinusoidal standing wave can exist only when

$$L = n\frac{\lambda}{2} \qquad n = 1, 2, 3, \ldots \tag{3-39}$$

The corresponding frequencies of possible standing waves can be found by using the relation $u = \lambda f$ in Eq. (3-39); the result is

$$f = n\frac{u}{2L} \qquad n = 1, 2, 3, \ldots \tag{3-40}$$

This interesting result shows that when both ends of a string of length L are held fixed, a sinusoidal standing wave can exist only when the frequency is a whole-number multiple of the quantity $u/2L$. The frequencies given by Eq. (3-40) therefore constitute a set of characteristic frequencies with which the string can vibrate. Motion with any one of these natural frequencies is called a *normal mode* of vibration of the system, and the corresponding frequency is a normal-mode frequency. Standing waves corresponding to several normal modes are shown in Fig. 3-15.

According to the principle of superposition, such a system can vibrate in several normal modes simultaneously. Which normal modes occur in a particular motion depends on the initial conditions. The most familiar examples are the sounds produced by stringed instruments when the strings are initially displaced from equilibrium by plucking, bowing, or striking with hammers. After a string is set into motion, its motion can always be described

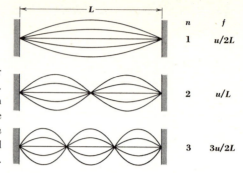

Fig. 3-15 Normal modes of vibration for a string of length L fixed at both ends. The frequency and the value of n in Eq. (3-39) for each normal mode are shown. It is seen that for each mode, n is equal to the number of antinodes and is less by 1 than the number of nodes.

as a superposition of normal modes. Hence any musical tone produced by a repetitive motion can always be described as a superposition of sinusoidal motions with various frequencies which are integral multiples of some lowest, or *fundamental*, frequency which determines the *pitch* of the tone. The various frequencies are called *harmonics* of the fundamental frequency; musicians call them *overtones*.

Sinusoidal standing waves are produced in many other situations. Organ pipes, whistles, and all other wind instruments, including the human voice, make use of standing waves in some kind of enclosure. In longitudinal sound waves in a pipe, such as an organ pipe or whistle, reflections at a closed end form a displacement *node* and a pressure *antinode*; an end open to the atmosphere is a pressure *node* but a displacement *antinode*. This situation is analogous to that of the string, for which a displacement node corresponds to a point of maximum slope of the string and hence of maximum transverse *force* (i.e., a force *antinode*), while a free end is a force node (no transverse force) and a displacement antinode, as shown in Fig. 3-14.

An organ pipe open at both ends has pressure nodes at both ends; the normal-mode frequencies are the same as for the corresponding string situation and are given by Eq. (3-40). When one end is open and the other closed, there is a node at one end and an antinode at the other, and the frequencies of the normal modes are determined by the condition that the length of the pipe must be an odd number of quarter wavelengths:

$$L = \frac{(2n - 1)\lambda}{4} = \frac{(2n - 1)u}{4f} \qquad n = 1, 2, 3, \ldots$$

$$f = \frac{(2n - 1)u}{4L}$$

Several problems at the end of this chapter deal with standing waves in organ pipes.

3-9 EXTENSIONS AND GENERALIZATIONS

The theory of mechanical waves can be extended in several directions, and we consider a few of them here. The first concerns the subject of *partial reflections*. Reflections in a stretched string have been discussed for two particular cases: an end is either *stationary* or *free* in the transverse direction. A third possibility is that the string may be tied to another string having different physical properties. The tension is the same in both strings, but the linear mass densities are different, so the wave speed is not the same in the two strings.

In Fig. 3-16, suppose a wave pulse originates to the left of the figure, on the light string. Experiment shows that the progress of the pulse is as illustrated. As the pulse reaches the boundary between the strings, a *reflected* pulse is formed with amplitude *smaller* than that of the incoming pulse; in addition, a pulse is *transmitted* to the heavier string. The wave speed is smaller in the heavier string, so the transmitted pulse is foreshortened. What has occurred is a *partial reflection* in which the incoming wave is partly transmitted and partly reflected. In this case the reflected wave is inverted; this is reasonable, since in the limit when the heavy string becomes infinitely heavy, the result must reduce to that in which the end of the light string is held stationary.

Similarly, when a wave originates on the heavy part of the string, it is partly transmitted without inversion and partly reflected without inversion from the boundary between the strings. In the limit when the second string is much lighter than the first, the situation approaches that in which the heavy string has a completely free end.

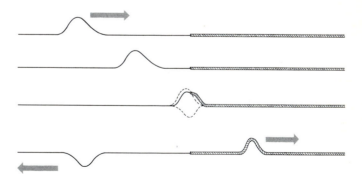

Fig. 3-16 Partial reflection of a wave pulse at a boundary point between two strings having different linear mass densities. In this case, the initial pulse is on the light string, and the reflected pulse traveling back on the light string is inverted with respect to the original pulse. The pulse transmitted to the heavy string is not inverted. The figures show that the wave speed is larger in the light string than in the heavy one, in agreement with Eq. (3-13).

It is instructive to compute the amplitude relations for the various waves. Let the boundary point between the two strings be at $x = 0$, and let the wave speeds be u_1 and u_2 for $x < 0$ and $x > 0$, respectively. Considering a sinusoidal incident wave, we write for the incoming wave in the region $x < 0$

$$y_i = A \sin \omega \left(t - \frac{x}{u_1} \right) \tag{3-41}$$

Then the transmitted wave (in the region $x > 0$) is

$$y_t = B \sin \omega \left(t - \frac{x}{u_2} \right) \tag{3-42}$$

and the reflected wave (in the region $x < 0$) is

$$y_r = C \sin \omega \left(t + \frac{x}{u_1} \right) \tag{3-43}$$

where the amplitudes B and C are to be related to the given amplitude A of the incoming wave.

To determine B and C, we first note that the wave function for the *total* displacement in the $x < 0$ region is $y_i + y_r$. At $x = 0$ the value of this function must agree with the value of y_t at $x = 0$; otherwise the two sections would not join at this point. This requirement yields the relation

$$A \sin \omega t + C \sin \omega t = B \sin \omega t \tag{3-44}$$

which is satisfied for all time only if

$$A + C = B \tag{3-45}$$

Furthermore, the *slopes* must also be equal on the two sides of $x = 0$; otherwise this point (which has no mass) would have an unbalanced force and hence an infinitely large acceleration. This condition yields a second amplitude relation, derivation of which is left as an exercise. The result is

$$\frac{A}{u_1} - \frac{C}{u_1} = \frac{B}{u_2} \tag{3-46}$$

Simultaneous solution of Eqs. (3-45) and (3-46), also left as an exercise, yields

$$\frac{B}{A} = \frac{2u_2}{u_1 + u_2} \qquad \frac{C}{A} = \frac{u_2 - u_1}{u_1 + u_2} \tag{3-47}$$

These amplitude ratios are called the *transmission coefficient* and *reflection coefficient*, respectively, terms used in describing many kinds of wave phenomena, especially in optics. We note that when $u_1 = u_2$, $B = A$ and $C = 0$, as we should expect.

Another phenomenon common to optics and transverse mechanical waves is *polarization*. It has been assumed throughout our discussion of waves on a string that the string always lies in the xy plane. But one could also consider displacements in the z direction, so that the string lies in the xz plane, or a more general displacement having components in both the y and z directions.

If all displacements lie in a single plane, the wave is said to be *plane-polarized*; all the waves discussed thus far have been plane-polarized in the xy plane. Similarly, a wave with displacements in the z direction is said to be polarized in the xz plane. More generally, consider a wave described by the functions

$$\begin{aligned} y(x,t) &= A \cos (kx - \omega t) \\ z(x,t) &= A \cos (kx - \omega t) \end{aligned}$$
(3-48)

At each instant a point on the string has equal displacements in the y and z directions; a little thought shows that the resultant wave has amplitude $A \sqrt{2}$ and is plane-polarized in a plane making $45°$ angles with the xy and xz planes.

Other wave motions can be obtained by combining two plane-polarized waves with a phase difference; then each particle, instead of moving back and forth in a straight line, describes a *circular* or *elliptical* path. For example, suppose a wave is formed from two plane-polarized waves with equal frequency and amplitude but differing in phase by $90°$, as shown in Fig. 3-17. The corresponding wave functions might be

$$\begin{aligned} y(x,t) &= A \cos (kx - \omega t) \\ z(x,t) &= A \sin (kx - \omega t) \end{aligned}$$
(3-49)

In particular, the motion of the point at $x = 0$ is given by

$$\begin{aligned} y &= A \cos \omega t \\ z &= -A \sin \omega t \end{aligned}$$
(3-50)

The distance r of this point from the x axis is

$$r = \sqrt{y^2 + z^2} = A \sqrt{\cos^2 \omega t + \sin^2 \omega t} = A$$
(3-51)

That is, the point moves in a circle of radius A, with angular velocity equal to ω. The reader should convince himself that the sense of the motion is *clockwise* as viewed looking back along the x axis (opposite to the direction of propagation). Such a wave is said to be *right-circularly polarized*; a wave with the opposite sense of rotation is left-circularly polarized. The motion in either case has the appearance of a rotating helix.

Polarization is a phenomenon common to all transverse waves. The most important examples of polarization occur in electromagnetic radiation, which

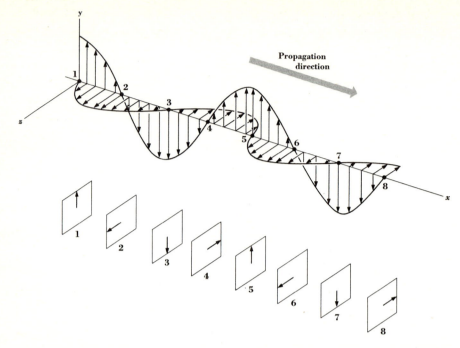

Fig. 3-17 Superposition of two plane waves with equal amplitudes and wavelengths, plane-polarized in perpendicular planes and 90° out of phase. The displacements of the separate waves are shown at one instant; the bottom diagrams show the resultant displacement at several numbered points. Each individual point moves in a circle with radius equal to the amplitude of each wave, with angular velocity ω.

is a transverse wave in the sense that the electric and magnetic fields representing the disturbance from equilibrium are perpendicular to the direction of propagation of the wave. Although the polarization of electromagnetic waves is of considerably more practical importance than that of mechanical waves, the basic ideas are shared by both. For *longitudinal* waves, on the other hand, there is no such thing as polarization.

Two additional phenomena in wave motion which deserve mention are *attenuation* and *dispersion*. Attenuation is associated with a loss of energy as the wave propagates. Our analysis of waves on a stretched string has not included any mechanism for energy dissipation, but there may be additional forces associated with air resistance and internal friction. If so, the governing differential equation contains additional terms to account for these forces; the result is that as a wave pulse or a sinusoidal wave propagates, its amplitude continuously decreases as its energy is dissipated. Similar effects occur with electromagnetic waves when the material through which the waves propagate is a conductor; currents induced in the material by the electric and magnetic fields of the wave dissipate its energy.

Dispersion results from the fact that the propagation speed of a sinusoidal wave may depend on its frequency. Like attenuation, dispersion is a phenomenon not predicted by the simple model we have used for mechanical waves, but it can be included as a refinement in the model. When dispersion is present, a wave pulse no longer propagates with a definite shape, and the usual result is that a pulse becomes more spread out as it travels. Dispersion of electromagnetic waves in matter is responsible for the fact that the index of refraction of glass depends on wavelength, and hence for the ability of a prism to spread out or *disperse* white light into its component spectrum colors. Dispersion of electromagnetic waves will be discussed in Chap. 6.

3-10   DOPPLER EFFECT

We conclude this chapter with a brief discussion of a phenomenon which, in this day of high-speed travel, is familiar to every child. When an automobile approaches, blowing its horn, the pitch seems to drop suddenly as the car passes the observer. Similarly, if the horn is stationary but the *observer* moves past, the pitch seems to drop as he passes. The frequency of a wave measured by an observer who is moving relative to the source is different from the frequency observed at the position of the source; when source and observer are approaching each other, the apparent frequency is increased, and when receding, decreased. This phenomenon, called the *Doppler effect*, occurs with all kinds of wave motion. Mechanical waves involve a material medium, while electromagnetic waves do not, and the nature of the effect is somewhat different in the two cases.

We consider first the case of sound waves when the observer is at rest in the medium, such as air or water, but the source is traveling toward it with speed v. Let the frequency of the source be f, with corresponding period $T = 1/f$, and let the wave speed be u. We assume u and v to be much smaller than the speed of light, so relativistic considerations do not enter. In a time interval T, during which one cycle of the wave is emitted, the wave progresses a distance uT; but in this same interval the source moves in the same direction a distance vT, as shown in Fig. 3-18. Then the wavelength, which is the

Fig. 3-18 Doppler effect with a moving source. The wave pulses represent successive maxima of a periodic wave. During a time interval T between the emission of two successive pulses, each pulse moves a distance uT and the source a distance vT. The distance between successive pulses, which is the wavelength, is given by $(u - v)T$.

distance between successive maxima in the wave, is not uT, as it would be with a stationary source, but rather $(u - v)T$. The corresponding frequency, which we denote by f', is given by

$$f' = \frac{u}{(u - v)T} = \frac{u}{u - v} f = \frac{f}{1 - v/u} \tag{3-52}$$

which represents an apparent *increase* in frequency, as already noted. Correspondingly, when the source is *receding* from the observer, the frequency is smaller by an amount obtained by changing the sign of the term v/u in Eq. (3-52).

When the source is stationary relative to the medium but the observer is moving, the situation is somewhat different. This case is most easily analyzed as follows: Suppose the observer is moving away from the source with speed v; then the wave speed *relative to the observer* is not u but rather $u - v$. The frequency f' with which successive maxima of the wave pass this observer is therefore given not by u/λ but rather by

$$f' = \frac{u - v}{\lambda} \tag{3-53}$$

where $\lambda = u/f$. Putting these equations together, we find for the apparent frequency

$$f' = \left(1 - \frac{v}{u}\right)f \tag{3-54}$$

When the observer is moving away from the source, f' is less than f; if, instead, he is moving toward the source, it is necessary only to change the sign of the term containing v to find the apparent *increase* in frequency.

The two results contained in Eqs. (3-52) and (3-54) may be combined to obtain a formula for the case where both source and observer are moving relative to the medium. This calculation is left as a problem.

The use of nonrelativistic kinematic considerations is justified by the fact that ordinarily the speed of sound and the speeds of both source and observer relative to the medium are very much smaller than the speed of light. When we consider the Doppler effect for light, relativistic kinematics *must* be used and the results are different. For light there is no material medium as there is for sound; light propagates in vacuum with a speed that is independent of the motion of either source or observer.

The Doppler frequency shift for light can be derived by an argument quite similar to that used for sound with a moving source. Suppose a light source moves toward an observer with speed v. Let T' be the period of the wave as measured by this observer. During this time, the wave moves a distance cT' and the source moves a distance vT', and so the wavelength λ' measured by the stationary observer is

$$\lambda' = (c - v)T' \tag{3-55}$$

Correspondingly, the frequency he observes is

$$f' = \frac{c}{\lambda'} = \frac{c}{(c-v)T'} \tag{3-56}$$

The period T' is related to the period T measured in the frame of reference of the source, but it is *not* identical, since in relativistic kinematics the time interval between two events depends on the frame of reference of the observer. Now T is a *proper-time* interval in the reference frame of the source, since it is measured between two events at the same space point in that frame. Thus T' is of *longer* duration than T, according to the usual formula for dilation of time,

$$T' = \frac{T}{\sqrt{1 - v^2/c^2}} \tag{3-57}$$

Furthermore, $T = 1/f$, where f is the frequency measured in the frame of reference of the source. Combining these results with Eq. (3-56), we obtain

$$f' = \frac{c}{c - v}\sqrt{1 - \frac{v^2}{c^2}}f = \sqrt{\frac{c + v}{c - v}}f \tag{3-58}$$

The corresponding expression for the apparent frequency when the observer is *receding* from the source is

$$f' = \sqrt{\frac{c - v}{c + v}}f \tag{3-59}$$

We note that there is no distinction between motion of source and motion of observer; only *relative* motion is significant.

The Doppler effect for light has important applications in astronomy. Spectroscopic analysis of light from distant nebulae reveals the presence of spectra which are characteristic of certain elements, except that all the frequencies are shifted by a constant factor. The interpretation is that the nebula is moving relative to the observer, and the shift in frequency is due to the Doppler effect. In practically all cases the Doppler shift is toward lower frequencies, indicating that it is *receding* from our solar system. Even more remarkable, the velocity predicted by this red shift, as it is called, is approximately proportional to the distance from us. Observations of this kind have provided practically all the evidence for the "exploding-universe" cosmological theories, which picture the universe as having originated in a great explosion several billion years ago in a relatively small region of space.

Problems

3-1 Suppose it is desired to produce on a string a wave pulse having the form shown
in Fig. 3-19.

    a If the wave speed is 50 m/s, describe in detail the motion which should
be given to the end of the string to produce this pulse.

    b How is the answer to (*a*) changed if the wave speed is 10 m/s?

0.1 m

Fig. 3-19   ←—2.0 m—→

3-2 Show that the function $f(x,t) = x^2 + 4axt - 4a^2t^2$ satisfies Eq. (3-6) if one
assumes a certain relationship between the constant a and the wave speed c.
What is this relationship?

3-3 A wave pulse on a stretched string is described by the equation

$$y(x,t) = \frac{0.10}{4 + (2x - 10t)^2}$$

where x and y are measured in meters and t in seconds.

    a Sketch the pulse at time $t = 0$ and at time $t = 0.1$ s.

    b What is the wave speed? In what direction does the pulse move?

    c Write an equation describing a similar pulse moving in the opposite direction.

3-4 A wave pulse on a stretched string is described by the equation

$$y(x,t) = 0.1e^{-(0.5x - 50t)^2}$$

where x and y are measured in meters and t in seconds.

    a What is the maximum displacement of a point on the string as the pulse
passes?

    b Sketch the shape of the pulse at time $t = 0$ and $t = 0.01$ s.

    c From the sketches, find the wave speed.

    d Find the wave speed directly from the functional form of the equation.

3-5 A certain wave motion on a string is represented by the function
$y = A \sin k(x - ut)$, where A, k, and u are constants.

    a Derive an expression for the transverse velocity of a point on the string
as a function of its equilibrium position x and time t.

    b Derive an expression for the slope of the string at point x and time t.

3-6 Verify that the wave function of Prob. 3-5 satisfies Eq. (3-6) by computing
the required derivatives and substituting.

3-7 One end of a stretched string is moved transversely with a uniform speed of
1.0 m/s until it is displaced 0.1 m; it is then returned to the original position
with the same uniform speed. The resulting wave pulse is found to travel with
a speed of 5.0 m/s.

    a Sketch the shape of the string at $t = 0, 0.1, 0.2, 0.3,$ and 0.4 s.

    b What is the length of the wave pulse on the string?

    c Draw a graph showing transverse velocity as a function of position on the string for $t = 0.4$ s.

3-8 Prove that, for any transverse wave on a string, the slope at any point x is equal to the ratio of the instantaneous transverse speed of the point to the wave speed.

3-9 A rope 40 m long has a total mass of 2.0 kg. If it is stretched horizontally to a tension of 500 N, what is the speed of transverse waves on the rope?

3-10 A rope 10 m long is hung from the ceiling. The mass of the rope is 0.5 kg, and an object with a mass of 0.5 kg is tied to the bottom end.

    a How does wave speed vary with position on the rope?

    b If a wave pulse with a length of 0.1 m is produced at the bottom end, what is its length when it reaches the top end?

3-11 Write a wave function for a sinusoidal wave propagating in the $+x$ direction with an amplitude of 0.1 m, wavelength of 2.0 m, and frequency of 5 Hz if the point $x = 0$ has zero displacement at time $t = 0$. What is the wave speed?

3-12 Solve Prob. 3-11 if the point $x = 0$ has its maximum positive displacement at time $t = 0$.

3-13 In transverse wave motion on a string, any section of string which instantaneously forms a straight line, i.e., has zero curvature, must be moving at that instant with constant speed. Explain physically why this is so.

3-14 It is impossible in practice to produce a waveform on a string which has "corners," i.e., points at which the slope of the string changes discontinuously. Explain physically why this is so.

3-15 The wave described in Prob. 3-11 is produced by giving a sinusoidal motion to the end of the rope at $x = 0$. Derive an expression for the force which must be applied to this point as a function of time. The expression may also contain the linear mass density and tension.

3-16 The equation of a sinusoidal wave on a string is

$$y = 0.05 \sin 2\pi(0.1x + 2.0t)$$

where the distances are measured in meters and t in seconds. Draw a diagram showing the position of the string at $t = 0$ and at $t = \frac{1}{8}$ s. From this diagram, find the wavelength, speed, and amplitude of the wave.

3-17 For the wave function of Prob. 3-16, find the wave speed, wavelength, period, frequency, wave number, and angular frequency directly from the wave function.

3-18 For the wave function of Prob. 3-16, find the maximum transverse speed of a point on the string and the maximum slope of the string.

3-19 One end of a stretched rope is given a periodic transverse motion with a frequency of 10 Hz. The rope is 50 m long, has a total mass of 0.5 kg, and is stretched with a tension of 400 N.

   a   Find the wavelength of the resulting waves.

   b   If the tension is doubled, how must the frequency be changed in order to maintain the same wavelength?

3-20 Compute the total energy of the wave pulse of Prob. 3-1 if $F = 500$ N and $\mu = 0.2$ kg/m.

3-21 Show that for a sinusoidal wave on a string, the average kinetic energy per unit length is equal to the average potential energy per unit length.

3-22 Show that the average power transmitted by a sinusoidal wave of amplitude A and angular frequency ω is given by $P = A^2\omega^2(\mu F)^{1/2}$. The quantity $(\mu F)^{1/2}$ is called the *characteristic impedance* of the string.

3-23 In Prob. 3-1, find the rate of transfer of energy past a given point during the time the pulse is passing the point. Also compute the time required for the entire pulse to pass this point, and show that the product of these two quantities is equal to the total energy obtained in Prob. 3-20. Use the values of F and μ given in Prob. 3-20.

3-24 For a sinusoidal wave on a string, show that the instantaneous rate of energy transfer past a given point is greatest when the point has zero displacement and least when it has maximum displacement.

3-25 Suppose a sinusoidal wave on a string, having amplitude A and traveling in the $-x$ direction, is partially reflected at the point $x = 0$, so that the reflected wave is in phase with the incident wave at $x = 0$ but its amplitude is kA, where k is a number between 0 and 1, sometimes called the reflection coefficient.

   a   Show that each point on the string undergoes simple harmonic motion with an amplitude that depends on x.

   b   Find the ratio of maximum to minimum amplitude, known as the standing-wave ratio.

3-26 Verify that when a sinusoidal wave on a string is reflected from a free end, the resulting standing wave is described by Eq. (3-38).

3-27 Find the frequencies of standing waves with wave speed u which can occur on a string of length L if one end is fixed but the other is anchored as in Fig. 3-12. In particular, show that the possible frequencies are odd-integer multiples $(1, 3, 5, \ldots)$ of a lowest, or fundamental, frequency. Sketch the standing-wave patterns of the three lowest frequency modes.

3-28 Find the normal-mode frequencies of an organ pipe of length L which is open (has antinodes) at both ends. What length of pipe is needed if the fundamental frequency is to be 16 Hz? (This is approximately the frequency of the note one octave below the lowest C on a piano; it is the lowest note found on most large organs.)

3-29 Answer the questions of Prob. 3-28 if the pipe is open at one end but closed at the other, as is often the case with large wood pipes.

3-30 If a pipe organ is tuned at a temperature of 20°C, by what fraction does the pitch change if the air is supplied to the pipes from a blower in the basement, where the temperature is 10°C? Is this a perceptible change?

3-31 If a guitar string is tuned to a certain note, how much must the tension be changed if the pitch is to be raised one octave, which corresponds to doubling the frequency?

3-32 Complete the calculation of the transmission and reflection coefficients, Eq. (3-47), for a sinusoidal wave at a boundary between two strings having different linear mass densities, as discussed in Sec. 3-9.

3-33 A sinusoidal wave on a string, traveling in the $-x$ direction, given by $y = A \cos (kx + \omega t)$, approaches the end at $x = 0$. This end is anchored to a device that exerts a transverse force F_y given by $F_y = -bv$, where b is a constant and v is the transverse velocity at $x = 0$.

    a   Show that at $x = 0$ the wave function must satisfy the condition

$$F\frac{\partial y}{\partial x} = b\frac{\partial y}{\partial t}$$

    b   Representing the reflected wave by $y = B \cos (kx - \omega t)$, use the condition of (*a*) to show that

$$B = \frac{F - ub}{F + ub} A$$

    c   Show that when b is small the reflected wave is not inverted, when b is large it is inverted, and when $b = (\mu F)^{1/2}$ there is *no* reflected wave. The last situation is analogous to terminating an electrical transmission line in an impedance equal to the characteristic impedance of the line, to eliminate reflections (cf. Prob. 3-22).

3-34 A wave on a string is formed by superposing the two plane-polarized waves $y(x,t) = A \sin (kx - \omega t)$ and $z(x,t) = B \cos (kx - \omega t)$. Show that each point moves in an elliptical path with half-axis lengths A and B. In what sense (clockwise or counterclockwise) is the path described, looking back along the x axis?

3-35 A train approaches a station platform at 10 m/s. Its whistle has a frequency of 100 Hz, as measured by the engineer. What frequency will be measured by an observer on the platform:

    a   When the train is approaching
    b   After the train has passed

3-36 A passenger in a train moving at 10 m/s measures the frequency of the whistle of a stationary train, which appears to its engineer to have a frequency of 100 Hz. What does the moving passenger measure:

a When his train is approaching the stationary train

b When the trains are separating

3-37 Show that in the limit when v/u is much smaller than unity, the expressions for the Doppler frequency shift for a moving source and for a moving observer [Eqs. (3-52), (3-54), and (3-58)] all become identical for both light and sound. [Hint: Expressions of the form $(1 + a)^n$ can be expanded using the binomial theorem; when a is very small, $(1 + a)^n \cong 1 + na$ and $(1 + a)^{-n} \cong 1 - na$.]

3-38 A certain spectrum line in the light from a distant nebula is known to correspond to the hydrogen Balmer line at 434 nm, but, because of the Doppler shift, appears to have a wavelength of 589 nm. Find the speed of the nebula with respect to the earth. Is it approaching or receding?

3-39 Radar systems utilizing the Doppler effect are used to measure velocities of moving objects, such as automobiles exceeding the speed limit. Derive an expression for the frequency shift for radiation reflected from a target moving at speed v relative to the source, and returned to the source position.

3-40 A spaceship approaching the earth at a speed of $0.2c$ emits a green light with a wavelength of 500 nm. What wavelength is observed on earth? What color?

3-41 Derive an expression for the Doppler frequency shift for sound when both source and observer are moving relative to the medium. Show that, when both move with the same velocity, no Doppler shift is observed.

3-42 A sound wave produced by a stationary source with frequency f is reflected from a surface which is moving away from the source with constant speed v; the reflected wave then returns to the position of the source. What is the frequency of the reflected wave, measured by an observer at this position?

PERSPECTIVE | I

In the first three chapters we have encountered two of the central themes of twentieth-century physics, the special theory of relativity and the wave concept. Einstein's principle of the invariance of the laws of physics, suggested by the observed constancy of the speed of light, postulates the equivalence of all inertial frames of reference. We have developed the modifications in newtonian mechanics required to bring them into harmony with this principle.

Our revised kinematic concepts include a generalization of the concepts of space and time, including the relative nature of simultaneity and of length and time measurements in various frames of reference. From the generalized space-time coordinate relations, given by the Lorentz transformation, comes a generalized velocity transformation. This, together with the requirement that conservation of momentum must hold equally in all coordinate systems, leads to generalizations of the concepts of momentum and energy and to the concept of the energy equivalent of rest mass. Throughout this development, the new generalized formulations reduce to the familiar newtonian relations when all speeds are small compared to the speed of light.

From relativistic mechanics we proceeded to a study of the most important characteristics of wave phenomena. The appropriate concepts were introduced in the familiar context of mechanical waves, but we indicated their relevance in many other areas of physics and their importance as a unifying thread running through all of physics.

Wave phenomena play a particularly important role in optics; we turn next to this topic, which has proved to be the most significant gateway from nineteenth-century physics to the quantum-mechanical principles of twentieth-century physics. Those branches of optics concerned with wave phenomena are a natural outgrowth of electrodynamics, and provide a beautiful example of the power of Maxwell's electromagnetic field equations. We shall show first that Maxwell's equations predict the existence of waves of electromagnetic nature. A variety of evidence shows that light is an electromagnetic wave and that it is a small part of a very broad spectrum of electromagnetic radiation with frequencies ranging from less than 1 Hz to at least 10^{25} Hz.

The wave model of light and other electromagnetic radiation provides the basis for understanding of several optical phenomena such as polarization, interference, and diffraction, and we shall study in detail several examples of these phenomena. Next we shall examine the special cases in which the wave picture can be simplified further by representing light propagation in terms of rays, the basis of geometrical optics. The ray representation is the model usually used in the analysis of lenses, mirrors, and optical instruments. Geometrical optics is much more limited in scope than the more general wave theory, but within its scope it is much simpler and is indeed one of the simplest of physical theories.

Electromagnetic Waves | 4

Various conceptions of the nature of light and its present position as part of the spectrum of electromagnetic radiation are reviewed. It is shown that Maxwell's electromagnetic field equations predict the existence of electromagnetic waves, and certain simple types of waves are discussed in detail. These waves transport energy and momentum; they are reflected by conducting surfaces and refracted by an interface between two media, and they exhibit polarization. The laws of reflection and refraction of geometrical optics can be derived from Maxwell's equations.

4-1 NATURE OF LIGHT

It is now known with a high degree of certainty that light is an electromagnetic disturbance, but this certainty was preceded by a long period of controversy as to the nature of light. Scientists of the seventeenth and eighteenth centuries were familiar with two general mechanisms by which disturbances were propagated through space: motion of *particles* and *wave* motion. The first involves transport of matter from one place to another; the other does not. It seemed natural to ask the question "Is light a particle or a wave?"

We now realize that this is an improper question; there is no reason to think that light should fall completely into one or the other of these categories. As we shall see, light partakes of *both* wave and particle properties. More precisely, the *model* used to describe optical phenomena partakes of both wave and particle properties; the function of any physical theory is to provide a model in terms of which phenomena may be described and understood. To ask "What is light?" suggests that it is some other familiar phenomenon in disguise, such as a high-frequency sound wave or small particles of green cheese in transit; in fact it has a fundamental identity of its own.

83

The *speed* of propagation of light has been measured by a variety of means. The earliest measurements, made by Roemer in 1676, made use of observations of the motion of the moons of Jupiter, and apparent variations in the periods of their orbits resulting from the finite speed of propagation of light from Jupiter to earth. The first completely *terrestrial* measurement was made by Fizeau in 1849. The speed of light is now one of the most precisely determined of all fundamental physical constants. Its value in vacuum, denoted by c, is

$$c = 2.997925 \times 10^8 \text{ m/s}$$

with a probable uncertainty of 0.000001×10^8 m/s. The approximate value $c = 3.00 \times 10^8$ m/s is in error by less than 0.1 percent.

During the seventeenth and eighteenth centuries a number of models were introduced to describe optical phenomena. *Geometrical* optics had its origins in the early seventeenth century. In this model, propagation of light is described in terms of *rays*, which travel in straight lines in a homogeneous medium and are bent by *reflection* at a shiny surface or *refraction* at an interface between two transparent media. All optical phenomena involving lenses and mirrors can be described with considerable precision with the ray model and two simple postulates regarding reflection and refraction. In this sense, geometrical optics is one of the *simplest* of all physical theories.

As early as 1650, however, *diffraction* effects were observed, in which light appears *not* to propagate in straight lines, but to bend around obstacles. About this time Huygens and others suggested that light is a *wave* phenomenon, and it was shown that the laws of reflection and refraction can be understood on a wave basis. This hypothesis was not generally accepted at this time, partly because of the prestige and influence of Newton, who did not accept the wave theory. Finally in 1802 Thomas Young, using what we now call the principle of superposition, showed that a variety of interference and diffraction effects can be understood on a wave model. His most famous experiment, the two-slit interference phenomenon, will be discussed in detail in Chap. 5. With this and other measurements he showed that the *wavelengths* of light waves are very small, ranging from 7×10^{-7} m at the red end of the visible spectrum to 4×10^{-7} m at the violet end. There is no doubt that the wave model does provide a description of one important aspect of the behavior of light.

James Clerk Maxwell, the great pioneer in electromagnetic theory, predicted in 1862 the existence of *electromagnetic waves,* consisting of fluctuating electric and magnetic fields which propagate through space. His predicted *speed* with which such waves should travel was identical with the measured value of the speed of light. This immediately suggested not only that light is a wave but that in particular it is an *electromagnetic* wave. In the words of Maxwell himself, the predicted speed of electromagnetic waves

. . . agrees so exactly with the velocity of light calculated from the optical experiments of M. Fizeau, that we can scarcely avoid the inference that light consists in the transverse undulations of the same medium which is the cause of electric and magnetic phenomena.

In 1887 Heinrich Hertz, for whom the unit of frequency, the hertz, is named, was able to *produce* electromagnetic waves with frequencies of the order of 10^6 to 10^8 Hz, using circuitry which today would be called an oscillator. The frequency was determined by computing the resonant frequency of an LC circuit, and the wavelength could be measured by various means, such as establishing standing waves with a reflector. In one experiment, in which the frequency of the oscillator was about $f = 3 \times 10^7$ Hz, Hertz measured the wavelength as $\lambda = 9.7$ m. The corresponding speed of propagation of the waves, given by $u = \lambda f$, is

$$u = \lambda f = (9.7 \text{ m}) (3 \times 10^7 \text{ s}^{-1}) = 2.9 \times 10^8 \text{ m/s}$$

which agrees well both with Maxwell's prediction and with the observed speed of light.

Hertz also showed that electromagnetic waves could be *reflected* by plane polished metallic surfaces and *focused* by concave metallic reflectors, and that their directions could be altered by passage through dielectrics, such as wood, paraffin, and glass, in the manner of *refraction* of light. In short, the behavior of electromagnetic waves was so similar to light as to leave little doubt that light is, in fact, electromagnetic in nature. In the words of Hertz:

The described experiments appear, at least to me, in a high degree suited to remove doubt in the identity of light, heat radiation, and electrodynamic wave motion.

Following Hertz, many other scientists investigated electromagnetic wave phenomena. In 1895, Marconi demonstrated the feasibility of wireless telegraphy, using "Hertzian waves," thus opening the door for radio and television communication. It is now known that electromagnetic waves exist over an enormous range of frequencies and wavelengths, Fig. 4-1 shows this range and the common names associated with waves in various frequency ranges.

4-2 MAXWELL'S EQUATIONS

In this section it will be shown that the existence of electromagnetic waves can be predicted from Maxwell's electromagnetic field equations. It is assumed that the reader has already acquired some familiarity with these equations in integral form, but we begin by reviewing briefly the equations and their experimental basis. We use mks units throughout. The fundamental fields are

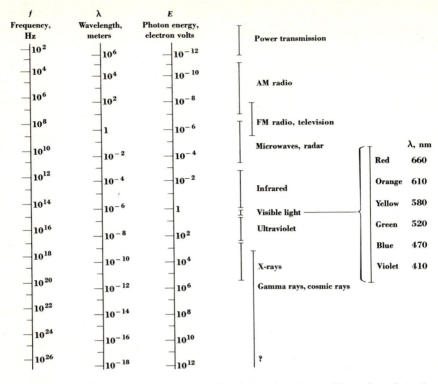

Fig. 4-1 The electromagnetic spectrum. All scales are logarithmic. The scale ends in the vicinity of the highest-energy secondary cosmic rays that have been observed up to the present time. [Wavelengths in the visible spectrum are sometimes expressed in angstroms $(1 \text{ Å} = 10^{-10} \text{ m})$, but the standard unit of measure is the nanometer $(1 \text{ nm} = 10^{-9} \text{ m})$.]

the electric field **E** and the magnetic induction field **B**. In vacuum (when no material medium is present) these are related to the electric charge density ρ and electric current density **j** by four equations, as follows:

$$\text{(I)} \qquad \int \mathbf{E} \cdot d\mathbf{s} = \frac{1}{\varepsilon_0} \int \rho \, dV \qquad\qquad (4\text{-}1)$$

The integral on the left is taken over a closed surface (surface element $d\mathbf{s}$), and the integral on the right over the volume bounded by that surface. This relation between the electric field **E** and its source (the charge density ρ) is Gauss' law of electrostatics, stating that the total flux of **E** out of a closed surface is proportional to the total electric charge in the enclosed volume. This in turn is derived from Coulomb's law, expressing the force of interaction between electric charges. When **E** is represented graphically by lines of force, Eq. (4-1) shows that the lines of **E** begin and end on charges.

$$\text{(II)} \qquad \int \mathbf{B} \cdot d\mathbf{s} = 0 \qquad\qquad (4\text{-}2)$$

The integral is again taken over a closed surface; this relation states that the total *magnetic* flux through a closed surface is always zero. There is no "magnetic charge" analogous to electric charge, and the lines of **B** never start or stop at a point.

$$\text{(III)} \qquad \oint \mathbf{E} \cdot d\boldsymbol{l} = -\int \frac{\partial \mathbf{B}}{\partial t} \cdot d\mathbf{s} \qquad\qquad (4\text{-}3)$$

The line integral on the left (line element $d\boldsymbol{l}$) is taken over a closed path, and the surface integral on the right over the open surface bounded by this path, with the convention that the direction of $d\boldsymbol{l} \times d\mathbf{s}$ is always *away from* the surface. This is Faraday's law of induction, showing that the induced electromotive force $\int \mathbf{E} \cdot d\boldsymbol{l}$ in a loop is equal to the time rate of change of magnetic flux $\int \mathbf{B} \cdot d\mathbf{s}$ through the loop. Since the *electrostatic* field due to a stationary charge configuration is always *conservative*, $\int \mathbf{E} \cdot d\boldsymbol{l}$ is always *zero* for such a field; hence Eq. (4-3) shows that the **E** field induced by a changing **B** field is *nonconservative* and of a sort that cannot be caused by any static charge distribution.

$$\text{(IV)} \qquad \oint \mathbf{B} \cdot d\boldsymbol{l} = \mu_0 \int \left(\mathbf{j} + \varepsilon_0 \frac{\partial \mathbf{E}}{\partial t} \right) \cdot d\mathbf{s} \qquad\qquad (4\text{-}4)$$

Again the line integral is taken over a closed path and the surface integral over the surface bounded by the path, with the same direction convention as for Eq. (4-3). This is a generalization of Ampère's law, relating the magnetic field **B** to its source, the current density **j**. Without the last term it is Ampère's law of magnetostatics, stating that the line integral of **B** around a closed path equals the total current ($\int \mathbf{j} \cdot d\mathbf{s}$) linked by that path. The last term, an essential generalization added by Maxwell, shows that a changing electric field also acts as a source of magnetic field. The term $\varepsilon_0 \partial \mathbf{E}/\partial t$ is called the *displacement current density* to emphasize its parallel with the ordinary current density **j** as a source of **B**.

The quantities ε_0 and μ_0 are constants characteristic of the MKS unit system. They are called the *permittivity* and *permeability* of vacuum, respectively. Their numerical values are

$$\varepsilon_0 = 8.854 \times 10^{-12} \text{ C}^2/\text{N} \cdot \text{m}^2 \qquad\qquad (4\text{-}5a)$$

$$\mu_0 = 4\pi \times 10^{-7} \text{ Wb/A} \cdot \text{m} \qquad\qquad (4\text{-}5b)$$

These values are directly related to the speed of light, as we shall see later in this chapter. The above value of μ_0 is *exact*, by definition, and ε_0 is defined in terms of the speed of light c as

$$\frac{1}{4\pi\varepsilon_0} = 10^{-7}c^2$$

The approximate value $1/4\pi\varepsilon_0 = 9 \times 10^9 \text{ N} \cdot \text{m}^2/\text{C}^2$ is often useful in calculations.

For electric and magnetic fields in matter, the equations have to be modified to include the phenomena of *polarization* and *magnetization.* Both free charge and polarization charge act as sources of **E**, and magnetization provides an additional source of **B**; the first and fourth equations, which relate the fields to their sources, have to be modified accordingly. The second and third equations retain their validity without modification.

We shall consider here only materials in which the polarization is proportional to **E** and the magnetization to **B**. For such materials we can simply replace ε_0 and μ_0 by ε and μ, which are properties of the material, called its *permittivity* and *permeability*, respectively. These are often expressed as

$$\varepsilon = K_E \varepsilon_0 \tag{4-6a}$$

$$\mu = K_M \mu_0 \tag{4-6b}$$

where the dimensionless constants K_E and K_M are called the *dielectric constant* and the *relative permeability* of the material. Finally, to include the possibility that the regions of integration may include more than one material, we include ε and μ *inside* the appropriate integrals. In regions where no free charges or currents are present, the Maxwell equations then become

$$\int \varepsilon \mathbf{E} \cdot d\mathbf{s} = 0 \tag{4-7a}$$

$$\int \mathbf{B} \cdot d\mathbf{s} = 0 \tag{4-7b}$$

$$\oint \mathbf{E} \cdot d\mathbf{l} = -\int \frac{\partial \mathbf{B}}{\partial t} \cdot d\mathbf{s} \tag{4-7c}$$

$$\oint \frac{1}{\mu} \mathbf{B} \cdot d\mathbf{l} = \int \varepsilon \frac{\partial \mathbf{E}}{\partial t} \cdot d\mathbf{s} \tag{4-7d}$$

These equations are sometimes expressed using the auxiliary fields **D** and **H**, called the *electric displacement* and *magnetic intensity*, respectively, and defined by the relations

$$\mathbf{D} = \varepsilon \mathbf{E} \tag{4-8a}$$

$$\mathbf{H} = \frac{\mathbf{B}}{\mu} \tag{4-8b}$$

Equations (4-7) can be used to derive relations governing the fields on two sides of a boundary surface between two dielectric materials or a dielectric and a conductor. These will be needed in our discussion of reflection and refraction of electromagnetic waves, and we state them here without proof.[1] The conditions are stated in terms of the components of the fields parallel to and perpendicular to the boundary surface.

First, at the surface of an ideal conductor (having zero resistivity),

$$E_{\parallel} = 0 \tag{4-9}$$

That is, just outside a conductor there can be no component of **E** parallel to the surface. Second, at a boundary surface between two dielectric materials (identified as 1 and 2 in the subscripts below) the following conditions must be satisfied:

$$\varepsilon_1 E_{\perp 1} = \varepsilon_2 E_{\perp 2} \tag{4-10a}$$

$$B_{\perp 1} = B_{\perp 2} \tag{4-10b}$$

$$E_{\parallel 1} = E_{\parallel 2} \tag{4-10c}$$

$$\frac{B_{\parallel 1}}{\mu_1} = \frac{B_{\parallel 2}}{\mu_2} \tag{4-10d}$$

That is, the perpendicular component of **B** and the parallel component of **E** must not change discontinuously at the boundary, and similarly the quantities $\varepsilon E_{\perp}$ and $B_{\parallel}/\mu$ must be continuous across the boundary.

We conclude this very brief review with the remark that only when the **E** and **B** fields are produced by static charge distributions and steady currents and are time-independent may the two fields be treated independently. In general, when either field varies with time, the two fields are interrelated and must be treated together. This is an important aspect of Eqs. (4-7c) and (4-7d).

4-3 PLANE ELECTROMAGNETIC WAVES

We now proceed to show that electromagnetic waves are permitted by Maxwell's equations. The procedure will be to make a simple assumption about a possible wave behavior of the **E** and **B** fields and then to show that the assumed field configurations are compatible with Maxwell's equations if the wave function for each field satisfies the wave equation. For simplicity, the discussion will be confined to a very simple wave.

The field configuration to be discussed has the following properties: The wave propagates in the $+x$ direction; the **E** field has a component only in the y direction, and the **B** field only in the z direction. These components

---

[1] The relations are derived in most introductory texts on electricity and magnetism; see, for example, the companion volume by A. F. Kip, "Fundamentals of Electricity and Magnetism," 2d ed., secs. 3-10, 5-10, and 10-6, McGraw-Hill Book Company, New York, 1969.

are denoted as E_y and B_z; each depends on x and t but *not* on y or z. That is, at any instant of time, each field is uniform over any plane perpendicular to the x axis. An example of a wave having these properties is shown schematically in Fig. 4-2.

To show that such a wave is compatible with Maxwell's equations, we first note that the first two equations, Eqs. (4-7a) and (4-7b), are satisfied automatically. At any instant the lines of **E** are parallel straight lines, parallel to the y axis. For any closed surface, precisely as many lines enter the enclosed volume on one side as leave it on the opposite side, and the *total* flux of **E** is always zero. The same argument also applies to **B**, and so Eqs. (4-7a) and (4-7b) are satisfied.

In applying Eq. (4-7c) it is useful to consider a surface lying parallel to the xy plane. By assumption, **B** is perpendicular to such a surface, and **E** is parallel to it. In particular, we consider the rectangular surface element shown in Fig. 4-3a, with dimensions Δx and Δy. We shall write approximate expressions for the integrals and then take the limit as Δx and Δy approach zero. Considering the integral $\int \mathbf{E} \cdot d\mathbf{l}$, the top and bottom sections of the boundary make no contribution, since for these the line element $d\mathbf{l}$ is perpendicular to **E**. Also, since E_y is independent of y, the two contributions from the other two sides are $-(E_y)_x \Delta y$ and $(E_y)_{x+\Delta x} \Delta y$, where the notation indicates the value of x at which E_y is evaluated. Thus

$$\oint \mathbf{E} \cdot d\mathbf{l} = [(E_y)_{x+\Delta x} - (E_y)_x] \Delta y \tag{4-11}$$

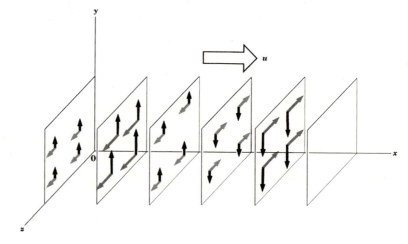

Fig. 4-2 Schematic representation of a plane electromagnetic wave. The electric field **E** at various points is shown by a solid vector; the magnetic field **B**, by a shaded vector. At each point, **E** and **B** are perpendicular to each other and to the direction of propagation. At any instant, each field is uniform over any plane perpendicular to the direction of propagation.

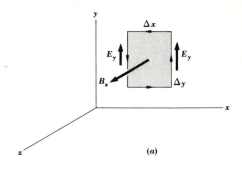

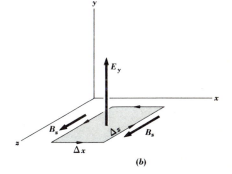

Fig. 4-3 (*a*) Time variation of B_z is associated with space variation of E_y. (*b*) Space variation of B_z is associated with time variation of E_y. The directions of the line integrals are shown.

Since the magnetic field is perpendicular to the surface element $\Delta x\,\Delta y$, the right-hand side of Eq. (4-7*c*) for this surface is simply

$$-\int \frac{\partial \mathbf{B}}{\partial t} \cdot d\mathbf{s} = -\frac{\partial B_z}{\partial t} \Delta x\,\Delta y \tag{4-12}$$

We now equate Eqs. (4-11) and (4-12), as indicated by Eq. (4-7*c*), and divide by $\Delta x\,\Delta y$:

$$\frac{(E_y)_{x+\Delta x} - (E_y)_x}{\Delta x} = -\frac{\partial B_z}{\partial t} \tag{4-13}$$

In the limit when $\Delta x \to 0$, the left-hand side becomes simply the partial derivative of E_y with respect to x, and we obtain

$$\frac{\partial E_y}{\partial x} = -\frac{\partial B_z}{\partial t} \tag{4-14}$$

This equation gives the electric field (expressed in terms of its x derivative) resulting from the time-varying magnetic field B_z.

A similar relationship emerges from Eq. (4-7*d*), which we apply to the surface shown in Fig. 4-3*b*. The calculation proceeds just as before:

$$\oint \frac{1}{\mu} \mathbf{B} \cdot d\mathbf{l} = -\frac{1}{\mu}[(B_z)_{x+\Delta x} - (B_z)_x]\,\Delta z$$

$$\int \varepsilon \frac{\partial \mathbf{E}}{\partial t} \cdot d\mathbf{s} = \varepsilon \frac{\partial E_y}{\partial t}\,\Delta x\,\Delta z$$

and finally, using Eq. (4-7d), dividing by $\Delta x\,\Delta z$, and taking the limit as $\Delta x \to 0$,

$$\frac{\partial B_z}{\partial x} = -\mu\varepsilon \frac{\partial E_y}{\partial t} \tag{4-15}$$

Equations (4-14) and (4-15) are two simultaneous differential equations which relate the derivative of one field with respect to x to the time derivative of the other. The component B_z can be eliminated from these two equations by taking the derivative of Eq. (4-14) with respect to x and the derivative of Eq. (4-15) with respect to t and combining the results. We obtain

$$\frac{\partial^2 E_y}{\partial x^2} = \mu\varepsilon \frac{\partial^2 E_y}{\partial t^2} \tag{4-16}$$

By a similar procedure, E_y can be eliminated; the resulting equation is

$$\frac{\partial^2 B_z}{\partial x^2} = \mu\varepsilon \frac{\partial^2 B_z}{\partial t^2} \tag{4-17}$$

Both these equations have the general form of the *wave equation*

$$\frac{\partial^2 f}{\partial x^2} = \frac{1}{u^2} \frac{\partial^2 f}{\partial t^2} \tag{4-18}$$

That is, the electric and magnetic fields we have postulated *do* satisfy Maxwell's equations, provided each varies with x and t in accordance with the wave equation. We see immediately that the speed u of the wave is given by

$$\mu\varepsilon = \frac{1}{u^2} \qquad \text{or} \qquad u = \frac{1}{\sqrt{\mu\varepsilon}} \tag{4-19}$$

We can now draw on our experience with solutions of the wave equation for the vibrating string to find possible wave functions for E_y and B_z. The simplest *periodic* solutions are sinusoidal. For example, a possible wave function for E_y is

$$E_y = E_0 \cos(kx - \omega t) \tag{4-20}$$

where E_0 is the amplitude of the wave, corresponding to the maximum value of E_y. The wave number k and angular frequency ω are related, as for any periodic wave, by $\omega = uk$, with u given by Eq. (4-19). The corresponding wave function for B_z can be found from Eq. (4-14). We find

$$\frac{\partial E_y}{\partial x} = -\frac{\partial B_z}{\partial t} = -kE_0 \sin (kx - \omega t)$$

$$B_z = \frac{k}{\omega} E_0 \cos (kx - \omega t) = \frac{E_0}{u} \cos (kx - \omega t) \qquad (4\text{-}21)$$

The above discussion has been somewhat formal, and it is well to pause here to consider its meaning. We have shown that Maxwell's electromagnetic field equations permit the existence of solutions representing electromagnetic *waves*, which in vacuum or a homogeneous medium propagate with a definite speed. In particular, we have found a solution corresponding to electric and magnetic fields which are perpendicular to the direction of propagation and to each other and which at any instant are uniform over a plane perpendicular to the direction of propagation. Because of this characteristic, such waves are called *plane* waves. Because both **E** and **B** are perpendicular to the direction of propagation, they are also *transverse* waves. In the case of sinusoidal waves, both **E** and **B** are, at any point in space, periodic functions of time, and at any point their time variations are *in phase*. At any instant,

$$B_z = \frac{E_y}{u} \qquad (4\text{-}22)$$

and this relationship is independent of the frequency or wave number of the wave.

In vacuum, the wave speed given by Eq. (4-19) is $(\mu_0\varepsilon_0)^{-1/2}$. This value will be denoted from now on by c. We find

$$c = \frac{1}{\sqrt{(4\pi \times 10^{-7})(8.854 \times 10^{-12})}} \text{ m/s} = 2.998 \times 10^8 \text{ m/s} \qquad (4\text{-}23)$$

which, as already pointed out, agrees with the observed value of the speed of light in vacuum. Since the days of Maxwell and Hertz, many other experimenters have measured the speeds of electromagnetic waves in vacuum over a wide range of frequency, and the results are all in agreement with Eq. (4-23).

The differential equations developed above are *linear* equations; thus electromagnetic waves obey the *principle of superposition* discussed in Chap. 3. For example, we could superpose a wave described by Eqs. (4-20) and (4-21) with another having the same amplitude and frequency but propagating in the $-x$ direction. The resultant electric and magnetic fields, obtained by adding the corresponding fields for the separate waves, represent a *standing wave*, completely analogous to those discussed in connection with the vibrating string. In following sections many important applications of the principle of superposition will appear.

4-4   ENERGY IN ELECTROMAGNETIC WAVES

It has been mentioned that electromagnetic waves carry energy and momentum, and we can now undertake a quantitative discussion of this matter. Energy is always associated with the presence of an electric or magnetic field in space or in a material. The energy in a charged capacitor can be regarded as residing in the electric field, with an energy density (energy per unit volume) of $\frac{1}{2}\varepsilon E^2$. Similarly, the energy of a solenoid carrying a current is consistent with an energy density in the *magnetic* field of $B^2/2\mu$.

When both **E** and **B** fields are present, the *total* energy density w is given by

$$w = \frac{1}{2}\left(\varepsilon E^2 + \frac{B^2}{\mu}\right) = \frac{1}{2}(\varepsilon E^2 + \mu H^2) \qquad (4\text{-}24)$$

In the second form **B** is expressed in terms of the magnetic intensity $\mathbf{H} = \mathbf{B}/\mu$ defined by Eq. (4-8b), anticipating later developments.

We now examine the implications of this expression for the plane waves introduced in Sec. 4-3. We consider a volume consisting of a small cube of dimensions Δx, Δy, and Δz, as shown in Fig. 4-4. The total electromagnetic field energy U in this volume is approximately

$$U = \frac{1}{2}\left(\varepsilon E_y{}^2 + \frac{B_z{}^2}{\mu}\right) \Delta x\, \Delta y\, \Delta z \qquad (4\text{-}25)$$

This energy may change as a result of energy transported in or out of the volume by the electromagnetic field.

The time rate of change of U is

$$\frac{dU}{dt} = \left(\varepsilon E_y \frac{\partial E_y}{\partial t} + \frac{B_z}{\mu}\frac{\partial B_z}{\partial t}\right)\Delta x\, \Delta y\, \Delta z \qquad (4\text{-}26)$$

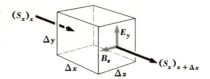

Fig. 4-4 Energy flow in an elemental cube. The energy-flow vector **S** shows that energy enters the left face of the cube at a rate $(E_y B_z/\mu)_x$ and leaves the right face at a rate $(E_y B_z/\mu)_{x+\Delta x}$, per unit surface area. The difference of these quantities is the net rate of change of energy in the cube, dU/dt.

With the help of Eqs. (4-14) and (4-15), this can be written

$$\frac{dU}{dt} = \left[\varepsilon E_y \left(-\frac{1}{\varepsilon \mu} \frac{\partial B_z}{\partial x} \right) + \frac{B_z}{\mu} \left(-\frac{\partial E_y}{\partial x} \right) \right] \Delta x \, \Delta y \, \Delta z$$

$$= -\left[\frac{\partial}{\partial x} \left(E_y \frac{B_z}{\mu} \right) \Delta x \right] \Delta y \, \Delta z \tag{4-27}$$

Since Δx is small, the quantity in brackets in the last equation represents approximately the change in quantity $E_y B_z / \mu$ from x to $x + \Delta x$. That is,

$$\frac{dU}{dt} = -\left[\left(\frac{E_y B_z}{\mu} \right)_{x+\Delta x} - \left(\frac{E_y B_z}{\mu} \right)_x \right] \Delta y \, \Delta z \tag{4-28}$$

This expression shows that the net rate of change of energy within the volume element depends on the *difference* of the values of the quantity $E_y B_z / \mu$ on the left and right faces and on the area $\Delta y \, \Delta z$ of these faces. This suggests that $E_y B_z / \mu$ represents a *time rate of energy flow per unit surface area;* $(E_y B_z / \mu)_x \, \Delta y \, \Delta z$ is the energy flow *into* the cube at the left face and $(E_y B_z / \mu)_{x+\Delta x} \, \Delta y \, \Delta z$ the energy flow *out* at the right face. The direction of energy transport is clearly the same as the direction of propagation of the wave, and so it is natural to regard $E_y B_z / \mu$ as the x component of a vector quantity which represents both the magnitude and direction of the energy flow per unit time, per unit surface area. Denoting this vector quantity by **S**, we have

$$S_x = \frac{E_y B_z}{\mu} \tag{4-29}$$

In this situation, the y and z components of **S** are zero.[1]

The vector quantity **S** is called the *Poynting vector.* Its units are energy per unit time, per unit area; the MKS units of **S** are watts per square meter. Equation (4-29) is consistent with the more general definition

$$\mathbf{S} = \mathbf{E} \times \frac{\mathbf{B}}{\mu} = \mathbf{E} \times \mathbf{H} \tag{4-30}$$

A more complete derivation, using Maxwell's equations and a theorem of vector calculus, yields the general result

$$\frac{d}{dt} \int (\tfrac{1}{2}\varepsilon E^2 + \tfrac{1}{2}\mu H^2) \, dV = -\int (\mathbf{E} \times \mathbf{H}) \cdot d\mathbf{s} \tag{4-31}$$

---

[1] In the following discussion, care must be taken to distinguish between capital **S**, representing the Poynting vector, and small **s**, representing the area element in surface integrals.

In this expression, the integral on the left side represents the total electro-magnetic field energy in the volume V, and that on the right the total rate of energy flow out of the closed surface bounding this volume. Thus Eq. (4-31) states that the time rate of change of total energy in the volume is equal to the negative of the surface integral of $\mathbf{S}$; this result justifies the inter-pretation of $\mathbf{S}$ as a rate of energy flow per unit area.

For the plane wave described by Eqs. (4-20) and (4-21) the Poynting vector is given by

$$S_x = \frac{E_0^2}{\mu u} \cos^2 (kx - \omega t)$$

$$= \sqrt{\frac{\varepsilon}{\mu}} E_0^2 \cos^2 (kx - \omega t) \tag{4-32}$$

Thus S_x is proportional to $\cos^2 (kx - \omega t)$; the average value of this function over one cycle is $\frac{1}{2}$, so the *average* rate of energy flow is

$$S_{av} = \frac{1}{2} \sqrt{\frac{\varepsilon}{\mu}} E_0^2 \tag{4-33}$$

The energy flow is proportional to the square of the electric-field amplitude. In optics, S_{av} is called the *intensity* of the radiation, and is often denoted by I.

Maxwell also demonstrated that electromagnetic waves transport *momentum*. When radiation carrying energy U is absorbed by a perfectly ab-sorbing surface, the quantity of momentum p transferred to the surface is $p = U/c$. This result implies that associated with the energy flow given by the Poynting vector there is also a *momentum flow*, given by $\mathbf{E} \times \mathbf{H}/c$. This result agrees with the prediction of the special theory of relativity (Sec. 2-3) that the energy-momentum relation for a particle with zero rest mass moving with speed c is $U = pc$. Remarkably, Maxwell's predictions preceded the development of the theory of relativity by over 30 years.

When an electromagnetic wave is absorbed or reflected by a surface, the associated momentum change causes a *pressure* on the surface. If the wave is absorbed, the momentum transferred to a surface element A per unit time is $(S/c)A$, and this rate of change of momentum must equal the force on the surface. The pressure P is the force per unit area, so a totally absorbed wave exerts a pressure

$$P = \frac{S}{c} \tag{4-34}$$

With a totally *reflected* wave the momentum change is twice as great, and in that case the pressure is $P = 2S/c$.

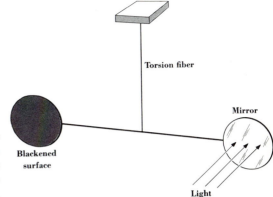

Fig. 4-5 Torsion balance used to measure radiation pressure. The amount of twist in the horizontal beam is proportional to the force that the radiation exerts on the mirror or blackened surface.

This pressure has been measured directly by means of an apparatus shown schematically in Fig. 4-5. A mirror or a blackened disk is suspended by a fine fiber, forming a torsion balance similar in principle to that used by Cavendish to investigate gravitational forces. The radiation pressure is measured by observing the angle through which the horizontal beam twists. The experiment is somewhat difficult to perform with precision; the pressure is very small (about 5×10^{-6} N/m² for direct sunlight), and the experiment must be performed in a high vacuum to eliminate spurious effects resulting from convection currents in the surrounding air. Results of this experiment, performed first in 1903 by Nichols and Hull, confirm the above predictions.

4-5   REFLECTION AND REFRACTION

Thus far, the discussion of electromagnetic waves has been confined to the propagation of waves in a homogeneous nonconducting medium. We now consider what happens when such a wave strikes a metallic conductor or an interface between two media having different electric and magnetic properties.

First, we suppose that a plane wave propagating in the $-x$ direction strikes a large perfectly conducting metallic plane coincident with the yz coordinate plane, as shown in Fig. 4-6a. Just outside the conductor (i.e., at $x = 0$) E must always be zero, as required by Eq. (4-9); there can be no field in the interior of an ideal conductor because of the mobile charges which cancel any applied field, and $E_\parallel$ is continuous across the boundary surface. The $\mathbf{E}$ field of the incident wave is *not* always zero at $x = 0$, so the currents induced in the conductor by this field must generate a reflected wave such that the *total* $\mathbf{E}$ resulting from the superposition of the incident and reflected waves is always zero everywhere in the plane $x = 0$.

This situation is completely analogous to that of reflection of waves at a fixed point on a vibrating string, discussed in Sec. 3-7. In that case the

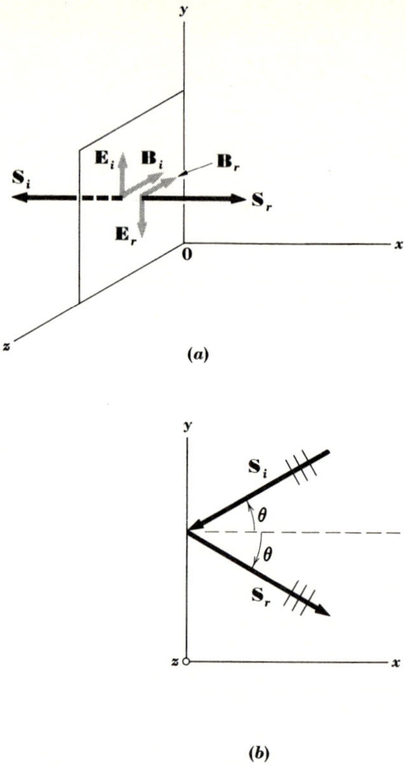

Fig. 4-6 (*a*) A plane wave strikes a metallic reflecting surface in the *Oyz* plane. The **E** and **B** fields and the Poynting vector for each wave are shown for a point near the surface. The total electric field **E** is zero near the surface, while **B** is not; the net rate of energy flow to the surface is zero if it is a perfect reflector (a metal with zero resistivity). (*b*) When the incoming wave direction is not perpendicular to the surface, the incident and reflected wave directions (shown by the directions of the **S** vectors) make equal angles with a perpendicular to the surface, and all three lines lie in a single plane.

displacement at the fixed point was always zero, just as the conductor requires that the electric field be zero in a certain plane. The fixed point exerts forces on the string such as to generate a reflected wave, and the currents induced in the conductor generate a reflected electromagnetic wave. In order to provide complete cancellation at $x = 0$, the electric field of the reflected wave at $x = 0$ must have the same amplitude as that of the incident wave but must be 180° out of phase with it. Thus if the electric field E_i of the incident wave is given by

$$E_i = E_0 \cos (kx + \omega t)$$

then that of the reflected wave E_r is given by

$$E_r = -E_0 \cos (kx - \omega t)$$

and the total electric field is

$$E = E_i + E_r = E_0 [\cos (kx + \omega t) - \cos (kx - \omega t)]$$
$$= -2E_0 \sin kx \sin \omega t \qquad (4\text{-}35)$$

Just as for the vibrating string, the result is a *standing wave*.

The corresponding expressions for the magnetic fields are

$$B_i = -\frac{E_0}{u} \cos (kx + \omega t)$$

$$B_r = -\frac{E_0}{u} \cos (kx - \omega t) \tag{4-36}$$

$$B = \frac{2E_0}{u} \cos kx \cos \omega t$$

The negative sign in the first equation arises because, for a wave in the $-x$ direction, $\mathbf{B}$ must be in the $-z$ direction when $\mathbf{E}$ is in the $+y$ direction. We note that $\mathbf{B}$ *does not* vanish at the surface of the conductor; there is no reason it should.

A similar but somewhat more complicated analysis shows that when the conducting plane is not perpendicular to the direction of propagation of the wave but is inclined at an angle, as shown in Fig. 4-6b, the reflected wave is not parallel to the incident wave but rather makes an angle with the plane equal to that of the incident wave, and in the opposite sense, as shown in the figure. Thus from the electromagnetic nature of light one can *derive* the familiar optical law that in reflection the angle of incidence equals the angle of reflection.

Next we consider the simplest possible example of *refraction* of an electromagnetic wave. Suppose that all space is divided by the yz plane into two regions, which are filled with different dielectric materials, with the material in the $x < 0$ half characterized by constants ε_1 and μ_1 and that in the $x > 0$ half by ε_2 and μ_2. When a plane electromagnetic wave propagating in the $+x$ direction strikes the boundary surface, some of the incident energy is reflected and the remainder is transmitted (refracted) in the second medium. A similar phenomenon occurs when one looks into a store window and sees both transmitted light from inside and reflected light from the street. The mechanical analog is a string with two sections of differing mass density, discussed in Sec. 3-9.

The frequency ω is the same in both media, but the wave number k is not, since the wave speed, given always by $u = (\mu\varepsilon)^{-1/2}$, is different. We denote the values for $x < 0$ by u_1 and k_1, and for $x > 0$ by u_2 and k_2. Figure 4-7a shows electric and magnetic fields corresponding to the incident, reflected, and transmitted waves; the Poynting vector for each is also shown to indicate the direction of propagation.

We let the subscript i denote the incident wave, r the reflected wave, and t the transmitted wave. Denoting the respective amplitudes by E_{0i}, E_{0r}, and E_{0t}, we may write for the *total* electric field E_1 in the region $x < 0$

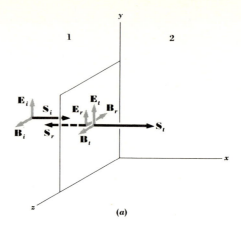

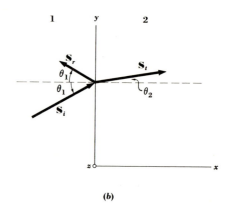

Fig. 4-7 (*a*) Reflection and refraction of a plane wave at an interface between two media. The **E** and **B** fields and the Poynting vector **S** are shown for the incident, reflected, and transmitted waves near the interface at one instant. (*b*) When the incident wave is not perpendicular to the surface, the incident and reflected wave directions make equal angles to a perpendicular to the surface, and the angles of incident and refracted waves are related by Eq. (4-48). All three **S** vectors lie in a single plane perpendicular to the interface.

$$E_1 = E_i + E_r = E_{0i} \cos (k_1 x - \omega t) + E_{0r} \cos (k_1 x + \omega t) \tag{4-37}$$

and for that (E_t) in the region $x > 0$

$$E_t = E_{0t} \cos (k_2 x - \omega t) \tag{4-38}$$

Equation (4-14) may be used as before to find the corresponding expressions for **B**, which are

$$B_1 = B_i + B_r = \frac{E_{0i}}{u_1} \cos (k_1 x - \omega t) - \frac{E_{0r}}{u_1} \cos (k_1 x + \omega t) \tag{4-39}$$

$$B_t = \frac{E_{0t}}{u_2} \cos (k_2 x - \omega t) \tag{4-40}$$

If the amplitude E_{0i} of the incident wave is known, the amplitudes E_{0t} and E_{0r} of the transmitted and reflected waves can be obtained by use of the fact that the fields on the two sides of the boundary surface must satisfy Eqs.

(4-10). In the present case all fields are parallel to the surface, and the relevant conditions are Eqs. (4-10c) and (4-10d).

According to Eq. (4-10c), when the value $x = 0$ is substituted into Eqs. (4-37) and (4-38), they must agree for all values of t. Carrying out this calculation and dividing out the common factor $\cos \omega t$, we obtain the relation

$$E_{0i} + E_{0r} = E_{0t} \tag{4-41}$$

A similar calculation using Eq. (4-10d) with Eqs. (4-39) and (4-40) leads to the relation

$$\frac{E_{0i}}{u_1 \mu_1} - \frac{E_{0r}}{u_1 \mu_1} = \frac{E_{0t}}{u_2 \mu_2} \tag{4-42}$$

These two simultaneous equations for E_{0r} and E_{0t} in terms of E_{0i}, which is supposedly known, may be solved simultaneously to obtain explicit expressions for E_{0r} and E_{0t}. This solution is left as an exercise; the results are

$$
\begin{aligned}
\frac{E_{0r}}{E_{0i}} &= \frac{u_2 \mu_2 - u_1 \mu_1}{u_2 \mu_2 + u_1 \mu_1} & \frac{E_{0t}}{E_{0i}} &= \frac{2 u_2 \mu_2}{u_1 \mu_1 + u_2 \mu_2} \\
&= \frac{\sqrt{\varepsilon_1/\mu_1} - \sqrt{\varepsilon_2/\mu_2}}{\sqrt{\varepsilon_1/\mu_1} + \sqrt{\varepsilon_2/\mu_2}} & &= \frac{2\sqrt{\varepsilon_1/\mu_1}}{\sqrt{\varepsilon_1/\mu_1} + \sqrt{\varepsilon_2/\mu_2}}
\end{aligned}
\tag{4-43}
$$

The second form of each expression is obtained by eliminating the wave speeds u_1 and u_2 using the relations $u_1 = (\varepsilon_1 \mu_1)^{-1/2}$ and $u_2 = (\varepsilon_2 \mu_2)^{-1/2}$ and multiplying numerator and denominator by $(\varepsilon_1 \varepsilon_2/\mu_1 \mu_2)^{1/2}$. We note that when the *same* material is on both sides of the interface ($\varepsilon_1 = \varepsilon_2$ and $\mu_1 = \mu_2$), the above results become $E_{0t} = E_{0i}$ and $E_{0r} = 0$, that is, total transmission and no reflection as we should expect.

In some cases of practical importance (e.g., transparent optical media such as glass) the permeability of the medium does not differ appreciably from that of vacuum, and we may assume with negligible error that $\mu_1 = \mu_2 = \mu_0$. In this case Eqs. (4-43) simplify to

$$
\frac{E_{0r}}{E_{0i}} = \frac{\varepsilon_1^{1/2} - \varepsilon_2^{1/2}}{\varepsilon_1^{1/2} + \varepsilon_2^{1/2}} \qquad \frac{E_{0t}}{E_{0i}} = \frac{2\varepsilon_1^{1/2}}{\varepsilon_1^{1/2} + \varepsilon_2^{1/2}}
\tag{4-44}
$$

These and other similar relations may also be expressed in terms of the index of refraction n of each material, defined as the ratio of the speed of light c in vacuum to its speed u in the material:

$$n = \frac{c}{u} = \sqrt{\frac{\varepsilon \mu}{\varepsilon_0 \mu_0}} = \sqrt{K_E K_M} \tag{4-45}$$

When the approximation $\mu = \mu_0$ is valid, we have simply

$$n = \sqrt{\frac{\varepsilon}{\varepsilon_0}} = \sqrt{K_E} \qquad (4\text{-}46)$$

and Eqs. (4-44) become

$$E_{0r} = \frac{n_1 - n_2}{n_1 + n_2} E_{0i} \qquad E_{0t} = \frac{2n_1}{n_1 + n_2} E_{0i} \qquad (4\text{-}47)$$

The first of Eqs. (4-47) shows that when $n_1 > n_2$, as with glass and air, the reflected wave near the boundary has the same phase as the incident wave, but when $n_2 > n_1$, the amplitudes E_{0r} and E_{0i} have opposite signs, indicating that the reflected wave has its **E** field *inverted* with respect to the incident wave. This result will be useful in understanding some interference phenomena to be discussed in Chap. 5.

This analysis can be carried out for the general case where the direction of the incident wave is not perpendicular to the interface. The calculation is more complicated, because each field has at least two components. It turns out that the *reflected* wave always makes an angle with the interface equal to that of the incident wave just as in reflection from a metallic surface. This is illustrated in Fig. 4-7b. The angle θ_2 of the *refracted* wave shown in Fig. 4-7b is always related to that of the incident wave θ_1 by

$$n_1 \sin \theta_1 = n_2 \sin \theta_2 \qquad (4\text{-}48)$$

which is the familiar *Snell's law* of geometrical optics. Thus it is possible to *derive* from electromagnetic theory all the familiar laws of geometrical optics. These were originally discovered as empirical laws long before their theoretical basis was well understood.

4-6 PLANE POLARIZATION

The electromagnetic waves discussed thus far in this chapter are *transverse;* the **E** and **B** fields are always perpendicular to the direction of propagation of the wave, which we have described by means of the Poynting vector **S**. Transverseness is in fact a general property of *all* electromagnetic waves, in regions of space whose distance from the source of radiation is large compared to the *dimensions* of the source.

Waves do not always have a single direction of propagation, but the concept of transverseness can be generalized. For example, an oscillating electric dipole is a source of electromagnetic radiation; at distances large compared to the size of the dipole, the radiation propagates radially outward in all directions, as shown in Fig. 4-8. There is no single direction of propagation, but at each point the directions of **E** and **B** are perpendicular to the

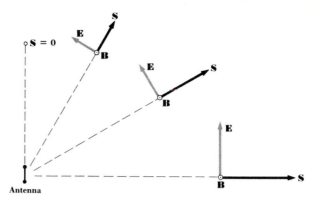

Fig. 4-8 Radiation from a simple electric dipole antenna. For all points in the plane, **E** is in the plane of the figure and **B** is perpendicular, out of the plane. The intensity is maximum in a direction perpendicular to the direction of the antenna, and zero along the line of the antenna.

radial direction and to each other. Thus at each point in space this wave is transverse.

It was mentioned in Sec. 3-9 that all transverse waves exhibit *polarization;* in a plane-polarized wave on a string, the displacements of points on the string lie in a plane containing the direction of propagation. Similarly, a plane-polarized electromagnetic wave is one in which in a given region of space **E** and **S** always lie in a plane, called the *plane of polarization.* The electromagnetic waves discussed thus far are plane-polarized, and for the wave introduced in Sec. 4-3 the plane of polarization is the *xy* plane. Figure 4-9 shows this wave and also a wave plane-polarized in the *xz* plane.

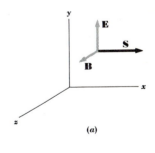

Fig. 4-9 E and **B** fields at one instant for two waves in the *x* direction. In (*a*) the wave is polarized in the *xy* plane; in (*b*) in the *xz* plane.

One *could* define the plane of polarization to be the plane of the **B** field; the reason the **E** field is chosen instead is that in many (though not all) instances of interaction of radiation with matter, such as darkening of a photographic film or the response of a photocell, it is the **E** field that causes the dominant part of the interaction. This can be understood qualitatively by considering the *force* a wave exerts on an electron moving with speed v in an atom of material. If the **E** amplitude is E_0, the **B** amplitude is E_0/c, as shown by Eq. (4-22). If the electron charge is e, the **E** field force $e\mathbf{E}$ has maximum magnitude eE_0, while the **B** field force $e\mathbf{v} \times \mathbf{B}$ has maximum magnitude eE_0v/c. Thus when v is small compared to c, the magnetic-field force is small compared to the electric-field force.

For visible light (as well as many other wavelength ranges) it is possible to make a *polarizing filter,* having the property that it is transparent to light plane-polarized in a certain plane but not to light plane-polarized perpendicular to this plane. Polarizing sunglasses and polarizing filters used for cameras are examples of such filters. The direction of the **E** field of the wave *transmitted* by a polarizing filter is called the *polarizing axis.*

When a wave is incident on a polarizing filter whose polarizing axis is at an angle ϕ to the **E** of the incident wave, as shown in Fig. 4-10, it is found that the wave is *partially* transmitted, and that the transmitted wave is plane-polarized in the direction of the polarizing axis. This phenomenon can be understood by reference to Fig. 4-10, in which the **E** of the incident wave is represented as the sum of a component $\mathbf{E}_\parallel$ parallel to the polarizing axis and a component $\mathbf{E}_\perp$ perpendicular to it. The parallel component is transmitted; the perpendicular component is not. We note that the validity of this component representation of the incident wave rests on the principle of superposition for electromagnetic waves, discussed earlier.

Ordinarily the property of the wave most easily measured is not the amplitude E_0 but the intensity I, defined by Eq. (4-33), which measures the energy carried by the wave. In the above example the amplitude of the

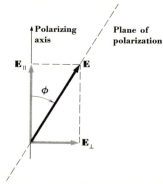

Fig. 4-10 The electric field of plane-polarized radiation is resolved into components parallel and perpendicular to the axis of a polarizing filter. Only the component parallel to the axis is transmitted.

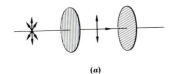

(a)

Fig. 4-11 (*a*) When radiation with a random mixture of polarizations is incident on a polarizing filter, only those components polarized parallel to the polarizing axis of the filter are transmitted. When a second polarizing filter with its axis perpendicular to the first is added, no light is transmitted. (*b*) A slotted sheet serves as a polarizing filter for unpolarized waves on a stretched string. Only components parallel to the slot are transmitted.

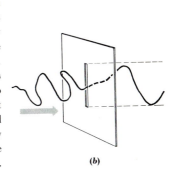

(b)

transmitted wave is smaller than that of the incident wave by a factor $\cos \phi$, so the *intensity* is reduced by a factor $\cos^2 \phi$. Thus if I_0 is the incident intensity, the transmitted intensity I is given by

$$I = I_0 \cos^2 \phi \tag{4-49}$$

Light from most ordinary sources is *not* plane-polarized. It is emitted not by a single atom but by a large number of atoms which ordinarily have no particular orientation. The light emitted by such a source is a random succession of all possible polarizations and is said to be *unpolarized*. When unpolarized light is incident on a polarizing filter, only the components parallel to the polarizing axis are transmitted, as shown in Fig. 4-11, which also shows a polarizing filter for *mechanical* waves on a string. For unpolarized light ϕ in Eq. (4-49) varies randomly from zero to π, and the *average* value of $\cos^2 \phi$ is $\frac{1}{2}$. Thus when unpolarized light of intensity I_0 is incident on a polarizing filter, the transmitted light is plane-polarized and has intensity $I_0/2$.

There are several other ways of producing polarized light from unpolarized light. When light is reflected obliquely at a dielectric interface, the relation of transmitted to reflected intensities is different for different states of polarization. It can be shown that when the angle of incidence is such that the transmitted and reflected waves are *perpendicular*, as shown in Fig. 4-12, the reflected wave is plane-polarized in a direction perpendicular to the plane containing the incident-, reflected-, and refracted-wave directions. That is, the component of incident radiation lying *in* this plane is completely *transmitted* to the second medium. This interesting result is called *Brewster's law*; it can be derived from electromagnetic theory in the same way as Eqs. (4-43), which apply to the particular case of *normal* incidence.

Fig. 4-12 When the reflected and refracted waves are perpendicular, the reflected wave is plane-polarized with its **E** field perpendicular to the plane of incidence. The component of the incident wave having its **E** field in this plane is completely transmitted. The angle θ_1 for which this occurs is called Brewster's angle.

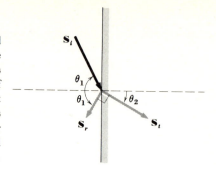

The critical angle of incidence is called *Brewster's angle*. Even when the angle of incidence is different from Brewster's angle, the reflected wave resulting from an unpolarized incident wave is *partially* polarized perpendicular to the plane of incidence, i.e., parallel to the reflecting surface. Thus polarizing sunglasses with vertical polarizing axes can reduce greatly the reflected glare from asphalt or wet road surfaces.

Some sources emit plane-polarized radiation. A radio-transmitter antenna often consists in principle of a straight wire into which is fed radio-frequency current from the transmitter. Such an antenna functions essentially as an oscillating dipole; at points far away from the antenna compared with its size and wavelength, the radiation is plane-polarized in a plane containing the wire and the line from it to the observer, as shown in Fig. 4-8. Light from an individual atom *may* be plane-polarized, but another possibility is *circularly* polarized light, to be discussed in Sec. 4-7.

A number of crystals exhibit the interesting property that their index of refraction is different for different states of polarization of light. The most familiar example is calcite (crystalline calcium carbonate). It is possible to arrange a series of such crystals in such a way that one component is refracted out of the crystal in one direction and the other in a different direction, so that waves with different states of polarization are separated in space. Such a device then functions as a polarizing filter. Any material that exhibits different indices of refraction for different polarizations is said to be *birefringent*.

A related phenomenon is *dichroism,* the selective *absorption* of light with certain polarization directions. The commercial material Polaroid is made from a polyvinyl alcohol whose long-chain molecules have been given a preferred orientation by stretching. The development of inexpensive polarizing filters has opened the door to numerous practical applications of polarized light. Polarizing sunglasses have been mentioned; another interesting example is *photoelasticity,* discussed in Sec. 4-7.

4-7   CIRCULAR POLARIZATION

Additional aspects of polarization are exhibited by an analysis of *superposition* of plane-polarized waves with different planes of polarization; the discussion parallels that of Sec. 3-9 for mechanical waves. Suppose two plane waves propagating in the $+x$ direction with equal amplitude E_0, one polarized in the xy plane, the other in the xz plane, are superposed. As we shall see, the behavior of the resultant wave depends critically on the relative *phase* of the two waves.

If the two waves are *in phase,* the two **E** fields at a given point reach their maximum magnitudes E_0 at the same time, are zero at the same time, and so on. Thus at any instant E_y and E_z at a point are equal, the resultant **E** makes a 45° angle with the y and z axes, and the resultant wave is *plane-polarized* at 45° to the y and z axes, with amplitude $\sqrt{2}\, E_0$.

Now, suppose the two waves are exactly half a cycle out of phase; then E_y is maximum positive when E_z is maximum negative, and so on. In this case the resultant **E** always lies in a plane at 45° to the $+y$ and $-z$ axes, *perpendicular* to that of the first case.

Next we consider a phase difference of 90° ($\pi/2$). Suppose the components of **E** are

$$E_y = E_0 \cos (kx - \omega t)$$

$$E_z = E_0 \cos \left(kx - \omega t - \frac{\pi}{2}\right) = E_0 \sin (kx - \omega t)$$

(4-50)

This pair of functions corresponds to Fig. 4-13 at time $t = 0$. Unlike the plane-polarized case, the total **E** field is never zero. Instead, it has constant magnitude, as shown by the fact that $(E_y^2 + E_z^2)^{1/2}$ is constant, and a direction that *rotates* uniformly about the direction of propagation with angular velocity equal to ω. This radiation is said to be *circularly polarized.* By convention, it is called *right-circularly* polarized when, as in this example, the **E** field at a fixed point in space rotates *clockwise,* as viewed looking backward toward the source, and *left-circularly* if *counterclockwise,* as would be the case if the phase difference had the opposite sign.

If the phase difference is other than $\pi/2$, or if the two amplitudes are unequal, it can be shown that the electric-field vector at a given point traces out not a circle but an ellipse, and such light is said to be *elliptically polarized.*

Circularly polarized light may be made readily from plane-polarized light by means of a birefringent crystal of such thickness that two perpendicularly polarized waves which are *in phase* when they enter the crystal are *out of phase* by 90° when they leave. Such a crystal is called a *quarter-wave plate.*

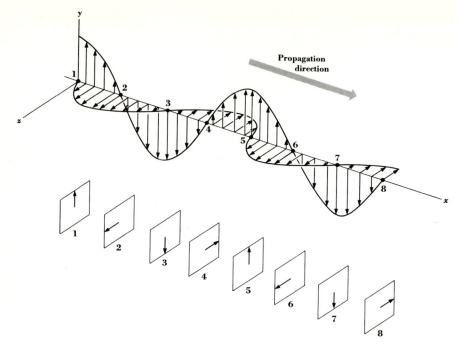

Fig. 4-13 Superposition of two plane waves with equal amplitudes and wavelengths, plane-polarized in perpendicular planes and 90° out of phase. The **E** fields are shown at one instant; the bottom diagrams show the resultant **E** field at several points. At any point, **E** is never zero; it has constant magnitude but rotates with the angular velocity of the wave. In the case shown, the resultant wave is right-circularly polarized.

Its action is most easily understood by observing that if the index of refraction of the material is different for the two planes of polarization, the wavelength is also different. Let us call the two wavelengths λ_1 and λ_2, and suppose that $n_2 > n_1$, so that $\lambda_1 > \lambda_2$. Then the object is to choose the thickness d of the plate so that it contains a certain number N of the longer wavelength but $N + \frac{1}{4}$ of the shorter, in order to introduce a phase difference of one-fourth cycle or of $\pi/2$. Thus the condition to be met is

$$d = N\lambda_1 = (N + \tfrac{1}{4})\lambda_2 \tag{4-51}$$

Furthermore, the wavelengths are simply related to the indices of refraction n_1 and n_2 in the two directions and to the wavelength λ_0 in vacuum by

$$\lambda_0 = n_1\lambda_1 = n_2\lambda_2 \tag{4-52}$$

Combining Eqs. (4-51) and (4-52) yields the result

$$d = \frac{\lambda_0}{4(n_2 - n_1)} \tag{4-53}$$

for the thickness of the plate. Details of this derivation are left as an exercise. Finally, the requirement of equal components in the two perpendicular directions corresponding to n_1 and n_2 is achieved simply by using a plane-polarized beam at $45°$ to these directions. In a similar manner, a quarter-wave plate can be used to convert circularly polarized light into plane-polarized, and a *half-wave* plate converts right- to left-circularly polarized light, and left to right. What effect does a half-wave plate have on plane-polarized light?

Some materials under stress become birefringent to a degree depending on the amount of stress. This phenomenon is the basis of *photoelasticity*, an important tool in experimental stress analysis. When two polarizing filters have their polarization axes "crossed," i.e., at right angles, no light is transmitted through the combination. But when a birefringent material is placed between them, the light emerging from the material is in general *elliptically polarized.* In regions where the stress causes a phase shift of π, 3π, 5π, and

Fig. 4-14 Photoelastic stress pattern formed with transparent model of part of a steel beam, seen in cross section. Closely spaced fringes at the curved surfaces show stress concentrations under bending stress. (*Photograph courtesy of Prof. W. F. Stokey, Carnegie-Mellon University.*)

so on, the light becomes polarized in the perpendicular plane and can pass through the second filter. The effect is a series of light and dark fringes, corresponding to regions of increasing phase shift and hence increasing stress. Figure 4-14 shows an example of such a pattern.

Many organic compounds in solutions, the most familiar examples being the sugars dextrose and levulose, have the effect of *rotating* the plane of polarization of a plane-polarized wave. This effect provides a useful analytical tool in distinguishing between two compounds which are so-called *mirror isomers,* that is, compounds whose molecular structures are mirror images of each other. The same effect can be used to measure concentrations of solutions of such compounds; the *optical activity,* or angle of rotation per unit path length, depends on concentration.

Problems

4-1 What is the wavelength of the radiation from (*a*) an AM radio station with a frequency of 1000 kHz; (*b*) an FM radio station with a frequency of 100 MHz?

4-2 What is the frequency of orange light with a wavelength of 600 nm?

4-3 A capacitor consisting of two parallel, coaxial disks is connected to a sinusoidal voltage source of frequency ω, and the resulting electric field between the disks varies with time according to $E = E_0 \cos \omega t$. Using Eq. (4-7*d*) for a circular path in a plane parallel to the disks and coaxial with them, find the induced magnetic field as a function of the distance from the axis.

4-4 Compare the magnitudes of conduction and displacement current for a vacuum tube operating at 100 MHz. For example, the vacuum tube might have two electrodes each 1 cm^2 in area, separated by the order of 1 cm, with a maximum potential difference of the order of 100 V and a maximum current of 10 mA. Compute the electric field between the electrodes, and from this find the displacement-current density. At what frequency would the two become comparable?

4-5 Consider the flow of alternating current in a bar of copper (resistivity $1.7 \times 10^{-8} \, \Omega \cdot$ m). At what frequency are the conduction-current density and the displacement-current density equal in magnitude? What is their relative phase?

4-6 For the plane electromagnetic wave discussed in Sec. 4-3, prove that the magnetic field B_z must satisfy Eq. (4-17).

4-7 The maximum electric field in the vicinity of a certain radio transmitter is 10^{-3} V/m.

    a What is the maximum magnetic field?

    b How does this compare in magnitude with the earth's magnetic field ($B = 0.5 \times 10^{-4}$ Wb/m²)?

4-8 An electromagnetic wave propagates in a ferrite material with the properties $K_E = 10$, $K_M = 1000$.

    a What is the speed of propagation?

    b What is the wavelength of a wave having a frequency of 100 MHz?

4-9 For the standing wave represented by Eqs. (4-35) and (4-36), show that the **E** and **B** fields are 90° out of phase and that the positions of nodes for **E** correspond to antinodes for **B**, and conversely.

4-10 Find the Poynting vector 1 m away from a 100-W light bulb, if it radiates uniformly in all directions. From this, calculate the radiation pressure at this distance on:

    a A perfectly absorbing black surface

    b A perfectly reflecting polished surface

4-11 For a 50,000-W radio transmitting station, find the maximum electric and magnetic fields at a distance of 100 km from the antenna, if it radiates equally in all directions.

4-12 *a* Compute the radiation pressure corresponding to total reflection of direct sunlight with an intensity of 1500 W/m².

    b If sunlight strikes a converging lens, such as an ordinary magnifying glass of diameter 10 cm and is concentrated to a spot 1 mm in diameter, find the radiation pressure on a mirror due to this spot if the light is totally reflected.

4-13 Find the *momentum density* (momentum per unit volume) in a beam of sunlight.

4-14 A radio station radiates 50,000 W uniformly in all directions. If an electric-field strength of 100 V/m is required to make a neon sign glow, how far away from the transmitter will it light neon signs?

4-15 For an electromagnetic wave, prove that the average energy associated with the **E** field is equal to that for the **B** field.

4-16 The intensity of sunlight on the surface of the earth is about 1500 W/m². Find the electric- and magnetic-field amplitudes for a sinusoidal wave of this intensity.

4-17 A certain microwave antenna uses a parabolic reflector to beam its radiation essentially in a single direction. If the radiated power is 1000 W, find the reaction force on the structure which supports the reflector. Is this likely to be an important consideration in the design of the structure?

4-18 Is the Poynting vector **S** corresponding to the superposition of two waves equal to the sum $\mathbf{S_1} + \mathbf{S_2}$ of the Poynting vectors of the individual waves? Explain.

4-19 The nineteenth-century inventor Nikola Tesla proposed to transmit large quantities of electric power via electromagnetic waves. What field strengths would be required if an amount of power comparable to that in modern transmission lines (of the order of 200 kV and 1000 A) is to be transmitted in a beam with a cross-section area of 100 m²?

4-20 Calculate the Poynting vector for the standing wave described by Eqs. (4-35) and (4-36), resulting from total reflection at normal incidence on the surface of an ideal conductor. Show that this represents a periodic flow from the antinodes of **E** to those of **B** and back, and that its average value is zero.

4-21 How is the momentum density related to the Poynting vector for an electromagnetic wave traveling in a material medium (not vacuum)?

4-22 Derive an expression for the radiation pressure resulting from partial reflection of an electromagnetic wave at normal incidence on an interface between two materials, as in Fig. 4-7a.

4-23 Find the index of refraction for a glass whose dielectric constant is 2.5.

4-24 A beam of light strikes the surface of a puddle of water, at normal incidence.
   a Find the amplitudes of reflected and transmitted waves, in terms of the amplitude of the incident wave.
   b What fraction of the energy is transmitted? What fraction is reflected?

4-25 For partial reflection at a dielectric interface, use Eqs. (4-43) to obtain expressions for the intensities of the transmitted and reflected waves in terms of the incident intensity, and show directly that energy is conserved in this process.

4-26 Write expressions for the components of **E** for a left-circularly polarized wave propagating in the $-x$ direction.

4-27 Unpolarized light is incident on a polarizing filter, and the emerging radiation strikes another polarizing filter with its polarizing axis at $45°$ to that of the first.
   a Describe the state of polarization of the light after the first filter, and after the second.
   b Find the electric-field amplitude and the intensity, after the first filter and after the second, in terms of the incident intensity.

4-28 Unpolarized light strikes a series of two polarizing filters whose polarizing axes make an angle θ with each other. Plot the emerging field amplitude and intensity as functions of θ. On the intensity graph, show the incident-light intensity.

4-29 A radio wave with a mixture of polarizations strikes a grid of parallel conducting wires. Describe the polarization of the radiation passing through the grid.

4-30 Three polarizing filters are stacked, with the axes of the second and third at 45 and $90°$, respectively, with that of the first.
   a If unpolarized light of intensity I_0 is incident on the stack, find the intensity and state of polarization after each filter.
   b If the second filter is removed, how does the situation change?

4-31 Complete the derivation of Eq. (4-53) indicated in the text, for the thickness of a quarter-wave plate.

4-32 It is desired to make a quarter-wave plate from quartz, whose indices of refraction in two perpendicular directions are about 1.54 and 1.55. The plate is to be used with orange light with a wavelength of 600 nm.
   a What should be the thickness of the plate?
   b How should the plate be used to convert plane-polarized light into right-circularly polarized? Left-circularly polarized?

4-33 How can a right-circularly polarized beam of light be converted into plane-polarized in a specified plane? Into left-circularly polarized?

4-34 Can sound waves be polarized? Explain.

4-35 Write equations for the magnetic fields of the component waves in Fig. 4-13. From these, show directly that the resultant magnetic field at any point has constant magnitude but a direction that rotates uniformly about the direction of propagation.

4-36 Prove that Brewster's angle (cf. Sec. 4-6) is given by $\tan^{-1}(n_2/n_1)$.

4-37 An electromagnetic wave in vacuum is described by the following **E** components:

$$E_y = E_1 \cos(kx - \omega t)$$
$$E_z = E_2 \sin(kx - \omega t)$$

   a Show that this wave is elliptically polarized, i.e., that the **E** vector traces out an ellipse. In what sense is the ellipse described (right or left)?
   b Show that this wave can be represented as the superposition of a plane-polarized wave and a circularly polarized wave. Find the amplitude of each; is the circularly polarized wave right- or left-circular?

Physical Optics I | 5

This chapter deals with phenomena associated with the superposition of waves. We begin with a discussion of spherical waves and their relationship to the plane waves discussed in Chap. 4. Mathematical methods are developed for adding several sinusoidal functions, and these are used to analyze effects associated with superposition of spherical waves from several coherent sources. Such effects are called *interference* phenomena; examples using both visible light and radio waves are analyzed. Then we discuss interference effects associated with thin films. Finally, we mention the various classes of interference phenomena and their relation to the *diffraction* effects to be discussed in Chap. 6.

5-1 SPHERICAL WAVES

The discussion of electromagnetic waves in Chap. 4 centered around plane waves. A plane wave propagates in one fixed direction, and the electric and magnetic fields at any instant are uniform over any plane perpendicular to this direction. At any point in space the fields are periodic functions of time, and in any plane perpendicular to the direction of propagation the electric field reaches its maximum intensity at all points simultaneously, is zero everywhere in the plane simultaneously, and so forth. Thus the wavefronts, planes perpendicular to the direction of propagation, are *planes of constant phase*.

Plane waves are unfortunately not so common in the real world as in the idealized world of Chap. 4. More familiar to our experience are waves that originate in a small source and radiate outward from it. A light bulb, a speaker in a sound system, a radio-transmitter antenna, all radiate waves in various directions. We now examine briefly a simple example of a wave having this multidirectional feature.

We take as a source an oscillating dipole, having a dipole moment p which varies sinusoidally with time, $p = p_0 \cos \omega t$. We place it at the origin of a coordinate system, aligned with the z axis. The electric field of the dipole also varies sinusoidally at each point in space; thus there is a displacement current and a time-varying *magnetic* field, and an electromagnetic wave is produced. Although a detailed calculation of the radiation pattern is beyond our scope, we can describe the pattern, observe its principal features, and quote the results of more detailed analysis.

Figure 5-1 is a cross section of the field pattern at one instant of time.

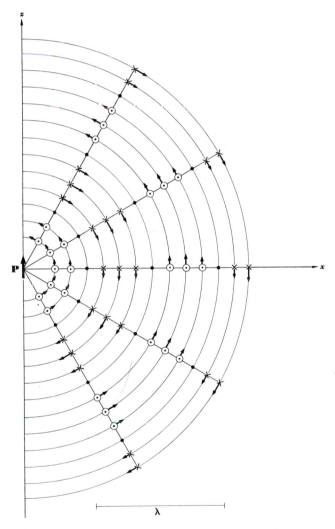

Fig. 5-1 Cross section in the xz plane of dipole radiation, showing electric-field vectors at one instant of time. At the points with circles the **B** field comes out of the plane of the figure; at the points with crosses, it is into the plane.

The curves are cross sections of spheres, the surfaces of constant phase. The wave propagates *radially* outward in all directions; at each point the **E** and **B** fields are perpendicular to the radial direction, so the wave is *transverse*. At every point **E** lies in the plane containing the point and the dipole source, and **B** is perpendicular to this plane. As time progresses, this entire pattern progresses outward, as the spheres of constant phase expand at a uniform rate equal to the wave speed.

To describe the pattern quantitatively, we introduce the spherical coordinate system shown in Fig. 5-2. We note that at each point **E** is in the direction of increasing θ and **B** in the direction of increasing ϕ. During half the cycle, of course, the directions are opposite to those shown. The Poynting vector **S** has the direction of **E** $\times$ **B** and is always radially outward.

Detailed calculation shows that at points far from the dipole compared to its size the fields are given by

$$E = \frac{p_0\omega^2}{4\pi\varepsilon u^2}\frac{\sin\theta}{r}\cos(kr - \omega t) \tag{5-1a}$$

$$B = \frac{p_0\omega^2}{4\pi\varepsilon u^3}\frac{\sin\theta}{r}\cos(kr - \omega t) \tag{5-1b}$$

These expressions deserve careful study. Each contains the factor $\cos(kr - \omega t)$, characteristic of a wave propagating radially outward in all directions from the source, with speed $u = \omega/k$. The factor $1/r$ indicates that the electric and magnetic fields become less intense as the distance from the source increases; this is to be expected, since the wave spreads out in space. Furthermore, the field intensities also depend on the *direction* relative to the orientation of the dipole, according to the factor $\sin\theta$; both fields are strongest in directions perpendicular to the dipole axis (i.e., in the *xy* plane) and are zero along the *z* axis. Neither field depends on ϕ; this is to be expected because of the axial symmetry of the source. The maximum value of B is $1/u$ times the maximum value of E. That is, the ratio of E to B is the same as for plane waves. The time variations of the two fields at any point in space

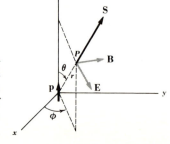

Fig. 5-2 Directions of **E**, **B**, and **S** at a point P with spherical coordinates r, θ, and ϕ. At each point **E** is in the direction of increasing θ, **B** in the direction of increasing ϕ, and **S** in the direction of increasing r.

are *in phase*, just as for plane waves. At any instant of time the loci of points in space at which the **E** or **B** field reaches its maximum magnitude, that is, the surfaces of *constant phase*, are spheres; hence the term *spherical waves*.

The energy transported by this spherical wave is given, as for all electromagnetic waves, by the Poynting vector $\mathbf{S} = \mathbf{E} \times \mathbf{B}/\mu$. We note that **E** and **B** are everywhere perpendicular; using the relation $u = (\varepsilon\mu)^{-1/2}$, we obtain,

$$S = \frac{p_0{}^2\omega^4}{16\pi^2\varepsilon u^3}\,\frac{\sin^2\theta}{r^2}\cos^2(kr - \omega t) \tag{5-2}$$

This equation reveals additional features of spherical waves. The rate of energy flow is proportional to $1/r^2$, the familiar "inverse-square" law for intensity of illumination and various other wave phenomena. The rate of radiation of energy is proportional to the *square* of the maximum dipole moment p_0 and to the *fourth power* of the angular frequency. The average value of $\cos^2(kr - \omega t)$ is $\frac{1}{2}$; thus the average value of S is

$$S_{\mathrm{av}} = \frac{p_0{}^2\omega^4}{32\pi^2\varepsilon u^3}\,\frac{\sin^2\theta}{r^2} \tag{5-3}$$

Recalling that this is average power *per unit area*, we can perform a surface integral over a sphere of radius r to find the average *total* power P_{av} radiated. This calculation is left as a problem; the result is

$$P_{\mathrm{av}} = \frac{p_0{}^2\omega^4}{12\pi\varepsilon u^3} \tag{5-4}$$

The wave just described is by no means the *only* kind of spherical wave. Another one, different but equally simple, results from the use of an oscillating *magnetic* dipole such as a small circular loop or coil of wire carrying a sinusoidal current. The result is a radiation field in which the directions of **E** and **B** are interchanged but with the same dependence on the field magnitudes on r and θ as for the electric dipole. More complicated arrangements of oscillating charge or current, such as quadrupoles or higher multipoles, produce more complicated radiation fields. In all cases, the wave at distances sufficiently far from the source is a spherical wave.

As observed previously, plane waves are easier to handle mathematically than spherical waves. Thus it is worthwhile to observe that at points far away from the source, a small segment of a spherical wave may be considered as approximately a plane wave, as shown in Fig. 5-3. The surfaces of constant phase, small spherical segments, become approximately plane. In the language of *geometrical* optics, the propagation of light is described not by means of waves and constant-phase surfaces but by means of *rays*. For a spherical wave,

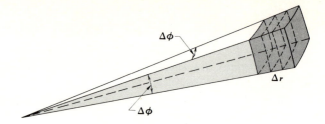

Fig. 5-3 In a small region far removed from the source, a small segment of a spherical wave is very nearly a plane wave.

the ray picture consists of many straight lines radiating out from the central source. For plane waves, the rays are simply straight parallel lines in the direction of propagation. In each case, the lines used to represent the light in the ray picture are perpendicular to the constant-phase surfaces, or wavefronts, which represent the real physical basis of light. Thus the wave and ray descriptions are more closely related than it might seem at first glance.

5-2 VECTORS AND COMPLEX EXPONENTIAL FUNCTIONS

The principal content of this chapter is the analysis of the behavior of several superposed waves. A problem encountered frequently is the addition at a certain point in space of several sinusoidal $\mathbf{E}$ fields having the same direction and frequency but different phases; it is useful to develop mathematical techniques for handling such problems easily.

We first note that a sinusoidal function such as $E_1 = E_0 \cos \omega t$ can always be represented by a *rotating vector* as in Fig. 5-4. The coordinate

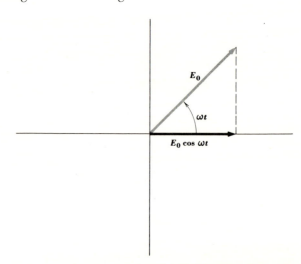

Fig. 5-4 Rotating vector used to represent the quantity $E_0 \cos \omega t$. This vector rotates counterclockwise with constant angular velocity ω.

axes represent not real space but a fictitious two-dimensional space introduced as a computational aid. A vector of length E_0 rotates with constant angular velocity ω, and its *horizontal* component at any instant is $E_0 \cos \omega t = E_1$. Similarly a function with the same amplitude but different phase, say $E_2 = E_0 \cos (\omega t + \phi)$ is represented by a rotating vector with the same length and angular velocity as the first, but rotated counterclockwise by an angle ϕ relative to the first. The horizontal component of this vector is E_2.

The sum $E_1 + E_2$ is the sum of the horizontal components of the two vectors, and this is equal to the horizontal component of their *vector sum.* This procedure is shown in Fig. 5-5, which shows each vector and the vector sum at two different times. The triangle representing the vector sum rotates; the function $E_1 + E_2$ varies sinusoidally with amplitude E equal to the magnitude of this vector sum. To find E, it is sufficient to draw the vector diagram at one instant of time (say $t = 0$) and from it determine the magnitude of the vector sum. This depends on the relative orientation of the vectors, which is determined by the *phases* of the individual functions.

In the present problem we need only to apply the law of cosines to the vector diagram of Fig. 5-5 to obtain the amplitude E of the resultant function:

$$\begin{aligned} E^2 &= E_0{}^2 + E_0{}^2 - 2E_0{}^2 \cos (\pi - \phi) \\ &= 2E_0{}^2(1 + \cos \phi) \end{aligned} \tag{5-5}$$

These calculations are often facilitated by making use of the close relationship between sine and cosine functions and exponential functions with imaginary arguments. We recall that i represents the imaginary unit, having

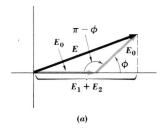

(a)

Fig. 5-5 Vector diagram showing vector addition of the two vectors whose projections on the horizontal axis are E_1 and E_2. The vectors are shown at two different times; the triangle representing the vector sum rotates, and the projection of the vector sum on the horizontal is the instantaneous value of $E_1 + E_2$. The amplitude of this sinusoidally varying total is the magnitude of the vector sum.

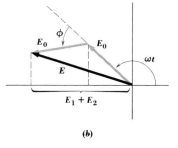

(b)

the property $i^2 = -1$. The equations relating the trigonometric and exponential functions, called *Euler relations*, are as follows:

$$e^{i\alpha} = \cos\alpha + i\sin\alpha$$
$$e^{-i\alpha} = \cos\alpha - i\sin\alpha$$

(5-6)

These equations are derived in most texts on elementary calculus. From them one can obtain algebraically the inverse relations

$$\sin\alpha = \frac{e^{i\alpha} - e^{-i\alpha}}{2i}$$

$$\cos\alpha = \frac{e^{i\alpha} + e^{-i\alpha}}{2}$$

(5-7)

Any number containing imaginary as well as real parts is called a *complex number*. The number z is said to be a complex number if it can be expressed as $z = x + iy$, where x and y are real quantities. Every complex number can be written as the sum of a real and an imaginary quantity. The following notations are frequently used:

Real part of $z = \text{Re}(z) = x$
Imaginary part of $z = \text{Im}(z) = y$

Thus the real and imaginary parts of the complex quantity $e^{i\alpha}$ are, respectively,

$\text{Re}(e^{i\alpha}) = \cos\alpha$
$\text{Im}(e^{i\alpha}) = \sin\alpha$

Complex numbers may be represented graphically on a plane, using a rectangular coordinate system with horizontal axis corresponding to the *real* part of the complex number and vertical axis to the *imaginary* part. These may also be called the *real* and *imaginary* axes, respectively. Any complex number is then represented as a point in this plane or as a *vector* joining the origin and the point, as shown in Fig. 5-6. The *length* of this vector (the distance from the origin to the point) is given by $(x^2 + y^2)^{1/2}$. This quantity is called the *absolute value* of the complex quantity z and is usually denoted by $|z|$. That is, if $z = x + iy$, then $|z| = (x^2 + y^2)^{1/2}$.

One additional notation is that of the *complex conjugate* of z, denoted by z^*, defined as a quantity with the same real part as z but an imaginary part with the opposite sign. That is, if $z = x + iy$, then by definition $z^* = x - iy$. More generally, the complex conjugate of any complex quantity can be obtained by replacing i everywhere by $-i$, provided all algebraic symbols represent real quantities. In terms of the complex conjugate, the absolute value of z may be written

$$|z| = (x^2 + y^2)^{1/2} = (zz^*)^{1/2}$$

(5-8)

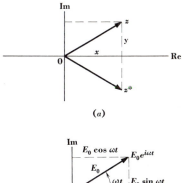

Fig. 5-6 Complex plane. (*a*) Geometrical representation of a complex number *z* and of its real and imaginary parts. The complex conjugate z^* is also shown. (*b*) Geometrical representation of the complex number $E_0 e^{i\omega t}$, showing its real and imaginary parts, $E_0 \cos \omega t$ and $E_0 \sin \omega t$, respectively, and its magnitude $|E_0 e^{i\omega t}| = E_0$. As the vector representing this complex number rotates counterclockwise with constant speed, its projection on the real axis varies sinusoidally, with "simple harmonic motion."

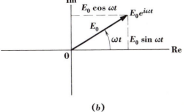

The usefulness of complex numbers in the vector representation introduced above should now be apparent. Every vector in the plane can be represented by a complex number. Corresponding to the function $E_0 \cos \omega t$ and its associated rotating vector is the complex number whose real and imaginary components are, respectively, $E_0 \cos \omega t$ and $E_0 \sin \omega t$. In view of Eq. (5-6), this is just $E_0 e^{i\omega t}$. That is, the function $E_1 = E_0 \cos \omega t$ is the real part of $E_0 e^{i\omega t}$:

$$E_1 = \mathrm{Re}\,(E_0 e^{i\omega t})$$

We note that the *absolute value* of $E_0 e^{i\omega t}$ is the amplitude of E_1, since

$$|E_0 e^{i\omega t}| = (E_0{}^2 \cos^2 \omega t + E_0{}^2 \sin^2 \omega t)^{1/2} = E_0 \qquad (5\text{-}9)$$

To add the two functions $E_1 = E_0 \cos \omega t$ and $E_2 = E_0 \cos (\omega t + \phi)$, we simply write

$$
\begin{aligned}
E_1 + E_2 &= \mathrm{Re}\,(E_0 e^{i\omega t}) + \mathrm{Re}\,(E_0 e^{i(\omega t + \phi)}) \\
&= \mathrm{Re}\,(E_0 e^{i\omega t})(1 + e^{i\phi})
\end{aligned}
\qquad (5\text{-}10)
$$

where $E_0 e^{i\omega t}(1 + e^{i\phi})$ is the complex-number representation of the rotating vector in Fig. 5-5 representing the vector sum. Thus the amplitude E of the function $E_1 + E_2$ is the absolute value of this complex expression:

$$E^2 = |E_0 e^{i\omega t}(1 + e^{i\phi})|^2 \qquad (5\text{-}11)$$

To evaluate this, we use Eq. (5-8):

$$
\begin{aligned}
E^2 &= [E_0 e^{i\omega t}(1 + e^{i\phi})][E_0 e^{-i\omega t}(1 + e^{-i\phi})] \\
&= E_0(2 + e^{i\phi} + e^{-i\phi}) \\
&= 2E_0{}^2(1 + \cos \phi)
\end{aligned}
\qquad (5\text{-}12)
$$

in agreement with Eq. (5-5). The factor $e^{i\omega t}$ disappears when we compute the absolute value because the magnitude of the vector sum in Fig. 5-5 does not depend on time. This also shows that we could have omitted the factor $e^{i\omega t}$ from the beginning, corresponding to calculating the vector sum at the particular time $t = 0$, when $e^{i\omega t} = 1$.

Equations (5-5) and (5-12) show that when two sinusoidal functions of equal amplitude are added, the sum is also a sinusoidal function. If they are in phase ($\phi = 0$), the amplitude of the resultant is $2E_0$; if they are a half cycle out of phase ($\phi = \pi$), the amplitude is zero. Intermediate phases give amplitudes between zero and $2E_0$. In Sec. 5-3 we apply these calculations to *interference* phenomena.

5-3   INTERFERENCE FROM TWO COHERENT SOURCES

To introduce the basic concepts of interference, we consider the following prototype problem. Two identical radio transmitting antennas are fed from the same oscillator; they emit sinusoidal waves which are identical in frequency, amplitude, phase, and state of polarization. They are separated by a distance d which is the same order of magnitude as the wavelength λ of the emitted radiation. What are the characteristics of the resulting superposed radiation pattern?

For simplicity, we consider only the region far from the antennas. The two waves may then be assumed to have the same intensity and direction of propagation, although their phases differ. The situation is shown in Fig. 5-7. At point O, equidistant from the two antennas, the maxima of the two waves arrive simultaneously, resulting in values of **E** and **B** twice as great as from each separate wave, and an intensity *four* times as great.

Point P in the figure is one-half wavelength closer to one antenna than the other. Because the two waves do not travel equal distances to P, they do not arrive at point P in phase but rather one-half cycle out of phase. When one wave has its maximum electric field in one direction, the other has its maximum in the opposite direction; the result is that the *vector sum* of the two electric fields at this point is zero *at every instant*, and therefore the intensity of the total radiation field at this point is zero.

Thus the superposition of the two radiation fields produces a field which is *more* intense at some points and *less* intense at others than that corresponding to either wave separately. In terms of the angle θ in Fig. 5-7, the path difference between the two waves is $d \sin \theta$. When this is zero or any integer number of wavelengths, waves from the two antennas arrive exactly in phase; when it is any half-integer number of wavelengths, they arrive out of phase by $180°$. These two conditions are called complete *constructive interference* and complete *destructive interference* or *cancellation*, respectively.

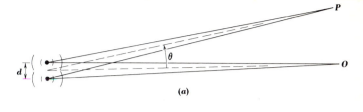

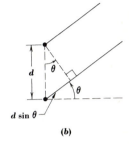

Fig. 5-7 (*a*) Two identical radio antennas separated by a distance *d*. The antennas could be, for example, dipoles perpendicular to the plane of the figure, in which case the waves at points in the plane are plane-polarized perpendicular to it. (*b*) Detail showing the path difference for the two waves, in terms of the angle *θ*. The distance to *P* is so great that the lines from the two antennas may be considered parallel.

The condition for a direction of maximum intensity is

$$d \sin \theta = n\lambda \qquad n = 0, 1, 2, \ldots \tag{5-13}$$

and that for zero intensity is

$$d \sin \theta = (n + \tfrac{1}{2})\lambda \qquad n = 0, 1, 2, \ldots \tag{5-14}$$

Wavelengths for radio transmission typically range from 1000 m for the longest wave transmission to a few centimeters for radar and for television relay equipment. Thus this is a macroscopic effect which can readily be observed with fairly modest equipment. Precisely the same phenomenon can be observed with sound waves by replacing the transmitter antennas by two loudspeakers driven from the same amplifier. An analogous phenomenon with water waves is shown in Fig. 5-8, an interference pattern produced by the superposition of water waves from two point sources. Each source produces sinusoidal waves with circular wavefronts spreading out from the source. The total disturbance at any point on the surface of the water is equal to the sum of the two disturbances corresponding to the individual waves. The two disturbances reinforce each other along certain lines, but they cancel along other lines.

Returning to the radiation pattern of the two antennas, we may obtain the intensity in any direction *θ* by adding the **E** fields at point *P* to obtain

Fig. 5-8 Photograph of an interference pattern in water waves formed by the superposition of waves from two sources oscillating in phase with the same frequency. (*Photo courtesy of Educational Services Incorporated.*)

the total field. Because point P is very distant from the sources, both **E** fields lie along the same line and have equal amplitudes, and the problem is one of adding two sinusoidal functions with equal amplitude and frequency but with a phase difference ϕ which depends on θ. This problem was solved by two different methods in Sec. 5-2; if the amplitude of each field is E_0 and the phase difference ϕ, the amplitude E of the resultant field is

$$
\begin{aligned}
E^2 &= E_0{}^2 + E_0{}^2 - 2E_0{}^2 \cos (\pi - \phi) \\
&= 2E_0{}^2(1 + \cos \phi)
\end{aligned}
\tag{5-15}
$$

The *intensity*, according to Eq. (4-33), is given by

$$
I = \frac{1}{2} \sqrt{\frac{\varepsilon}{\mu}} E^2 = \sqrt{\frac{\varepsilon}{\mu}} E_0{}^2(1 + \cos \phi)
\tag{5-16}
$$

The intensity I_0 from a single antenna would be

$$
I_0 = \frac{1}{2} \sqrt{\frac{\varepsilon}{\mu}} E_0{}^2
\tag{5-17}
$$

In terms of this quantity, we have

$$
I = 2I_0(1 + \cos \phi)
\tag{5-18}
$$

Finally, we determine the phase difference ϕ in terms of the path difference $d \sin \theta$. When the path difference is one-half wavelength, the phase difference is π, and for a whole wavelength it is 2π. In general ϕ is 2π times the *number of wavelengths* contained in the path difference; thus

$$
\phi = 2\pi \frac{d \sin \theta}{\lambda} = kd \sin \theta
\tag{5-19}
$$

where k is the usual wave number, $k = 2\pi/\lambda$. A *path* difference δ always introduces a *phase* difference ϕ given by

$$\phi = k\delta = 2\pi\delta/\lambda \tag{5-20}$$

Finally, from Eqs. (5-18) and (5-19), the intensity distribution is given by

$$
\begin{aligned}
I &= 2I_0[1 + \cos{(kd \sin \theta)}] \\
&= 4I_0 \cos^2{(\tfrac{1}{2}kd \sin \theta)}
\end{aligned}
\tag{5-21}
$$

Example

A certain radio station, operating at a frequency of $1500\ \text{kHz} = 1.5 \times 10^6\ \text{Hz}$, has two identical vertical dipole antennas spaced 400 m apart. What is the intensity distribution in the resulting radiation pattern?

Solution

First, the wavelength is $\lambda = c/f = 200$ m. The directions of the intensity *maxima* are those for which the path difference is zero or an integer number of wavelengths, as given by Eq. (5-13). Inserting the appropriate numerical values yields the following:

$$\sin \theta = \frac{n\lambda}{d} = \frac{n}{2} \qquad \theta = 0,\ 30°,\ 90°$$

In this example, values of n greater than 2 give values of $\sin \theta$ greater than unity and thus have no meaning; there is *no* direction for which the path difference is three or more wavelengths. Similarly, the directions having zero intensity (complete destructive interference) are given by Eq. (5-14):

$$\sin \theta = \frac{(n + \tfrac{1}{2})\lambda}{d} = \frac{n + \tfrac{1}{2}}{2} \qquad \theta = 14.5°$$

In this case values of n greater than 1 have no meaning, for the reason just mentioned.

The complete intensity-distribution pattern is given by Eq. (5-21); we have $k = 2\pi/(200\ \text{m})$, $kd = 4\pi$, and

$$I = 2I_0[1 + \cos{(4\pi \sin \theta)}]$$

This pattern is most conveniently represented graphically by a polar plot as in Fig. 5-9.

It should be noted that, if the distance between antennas is less than one-half wavelength, there is *no* direction for which the intensity is zero. Even so, the variation of intensity with direction is given correctly by Eq. (5-21).

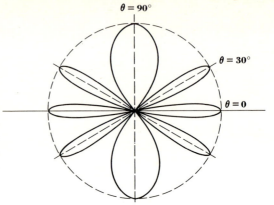

$\theta = 90°$

$\theta = 30°$

$\theta = 0$

Fig. 5-9 Polar plot of the intensity distribution in the interference pattern for two antennas in phase, for the particular case $d = 2\lambda$. For any angle θ, the distance of the curve from the origin represents the intensity in the corresponding direction. The line joining the antennas is vertical.

The crucial consideration in interference phenomena is the relative *phase* of waves arriving at a given point from various sources. This in turn depends on the existence of a definite phase relationship between the sources and on the difference in path length from source to observation point. In calculating the intensity pattern in an interference situation one must always add the amplitudes first, then calculate the intensity from the resultant amplitude; it would *not* be correct to calculate the intensity of each wave and then add intensities. That is, if the fields for two waves are E_1 and E_2, the intensity pattern is determined by $|E_1 + E_2|^2$, not by $(|E_1|^2 + |E_2|^2)$, which in general is a quite different quantity.

Interference with radio waves can occur with a single source, if the wave reaches the observer by two different paths. An example of practical importance is the case when radio waves reach a receiver by "straight line" transmission and also by refraction in the ionosphere, with a different path length. If the waves arrive with nearly equal amplitudes, there can be either almost complete constructive or destructive interference, depending on the relative phase. Since the ionosphere constantly changes in constitution, the path length of the refracted wave constantly changes. This accounts in part for the fading or rapid "buffeting" sound which sometimes occurs when one is trying to receive weak, distant AM radio transmission. Similarly, the fluttering of a television picture when an airplane flies over is due to interference between the wave received directly from the transmitter and that reflected from the metallic surfaces of the plane.

Do similar interference effects occur with sources of visible light? Offhand, the answer might seem to be negative. One does not have to look far to find a lamp with two bulbs in it, but interference effects are not observed. However, consider the situation of Fig. 5-10. We form two very narrow slits or apertures, perhaps by coating a sheet of glass with an opaque material and then scratching two very fine lines in it. We illuminate one side of this plate with monochromatic (single-frequency) light, to avoid complications from a mixture of wavelengths, and we look at the intensity of radiation at various points on a screen placed on the opposite side of the plate, as shown in Fig. 5-10. The pattern has precisely the same characteristics as that corresponding to interference of two radio waves, discussed above. The difference is one of *scale*. The conditions for maximum and minimum intensity are still Eqs. (5-13) and (5-14), but the wavelengths are very much smaller than for radio waves and are of the order of 4 to 7×10^{-7} m.

This experiment was performed by Thomas Young in 1802, and he presented it as evidence of the wave nature of light. He was able to make determinations of wavelengths of light which, considering the crudeness of his apparatus, were remarkably precise.

Why are interference effects not observed with two ordinary light bulbs? The two sources are not monochromatic, it is true; furthermore, the distance between them is ordinarily very much larger than a wavelength of light. But there is a much more fundamental reason, namely the lack of a definite *phase relationship* between the two sources. In the basic mechanism of emission of light, atoms are given excess energy by thermal agitation, collisions of other atoms, or excitation in electric fields, and they subsequently radiate this energy away as electromagnetic radiation. Each atom radiates for a time (typically of the order of 10^{-8} s) and then ceases when it has lost all the energy it can. Meanwhile, other atoms have begun to radiate. The phases of these emitted radiations are *random;* if there are two such sources, there can be no definite phase relationship between the two radiations.

It is as though the two radio antennas discussed earlier were driven by different transmitters, each turned on and off at random to prevent a definite phase relationship. In this case no interference pattern would be observed, the phase relationship at a given point would vary randomly with time, and so therefore would the intensity. By using a single transmitter we avoid this difficulty; similarly, when the two slits in Thomas Young's experiment are

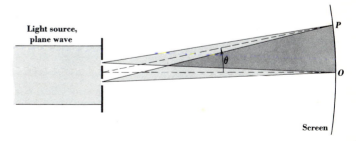

Fig. 5-10 Interference pattern formed by two narrow slits illuminated from the left by a monochromatic plane wave. The interference pattern is formed on the screen at the right.

illuminated by the same source, radiation from them is in a definite phase relationship at each instant of time. Two sources having a definite phase relationship are said to be *coherent*, and those that do not are *incoherent*. Clearly, coherent sources are an essential ingredient for the observation of interference phenomena. The most significant feature of light emitted by a *laser* is that the microscopic mechanism of emission in effect *synchronizes* the emission of many atoms, so that the emitted light maintains its definite phase relationship for time intervals much longer than that corresponding to the emission of a single atom. The operation of lasers is discussed in Sec. 12-7.

5-4 INTERFERENCE FROM SEVERAL SOURCES

The analysis of Sec. 5-3 can easily be extended to situations involving more than two sources. Figure 5-11*a* shows an array of four radio transmitting antennas, equally spaced along a straight line. Also shown in this figure are vector diagrams corresponding to the addition of amplitudes for various directions as shown. Just as with two antennas, the phase difference ϕ between signals from adjacent antennas is given by Eq. (5-19).

Figure 5-11*b* represents the general behavior of an interference pattern from several coherent sources equally spaced along a straight line. We can

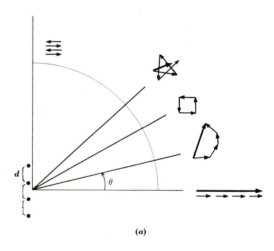

(a)

Fig. 5-11 (*a*) Interference from four antennas in a row, for the case $d = \lambda/2$. Vector diagrams show the addition of amplitudes from individual waves at several points. (*b*) Graph showing intensity as a function of phase angle for the case of four sources.

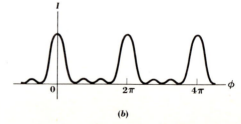

(b)

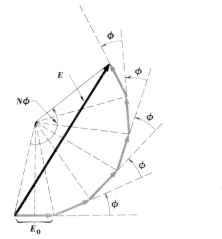

Fig. 5-12 Graphical addition of amplitudes for N sources of equal strength with a phase difference ϕ between adjacent sources. The case $N = 6$ is shown.

work out an expression for the intensity in the interference pattern, as a function of the angle θ, just as in the case of two sources. This is so easy that instead of doing it for four sources, we shall do it for the general case of N sources of equal amplitude spaced equally along a straight line. Since there is a constant phase difference ϕ between waves arriving at P from adjacent sources, the vector diagram consists of a series of N vectors with equal magnitude E_0 and equal angle ϕ between directions of adjacent vectors. The vector diagram for the addition of amplitudes is shown in Fig. 5-12, which shows the constant phase difference ϕ between adjacent sources. As shown in the figure, the ends of the vectors lie on a circle whose radius R is given by

$$\tfrac{1}{2}E_0 = R \sin \frac{\phi}{2} \tag{5-22}$$

The resultant amplitude E is the length of the chord subtended at the center of the circle by the angle $N\phi$, as shown. The length of a chord which subtends an angle $N\phi$ on a circle of radius R is given by $2R \sin (N\phi/2)$. Combining this with Eq. (5-22), we find for the resultant amplitude

$$E = 2R \sin \frac{N\phi}{2} = E_0 \frac{\sin (N\phi/2)}{\sin (\phi/2)} \tag{5-23}$$

The intensity is

$$I = \frac{1}{2}\sqrt{\frac{\varepsilon}{\mu}} E^2 = \frac{1}{2}\sqrt{\frac{\varepsilon}{\mu}} E_0{}^2 \frac{\sin^2 (N\phi/2)}{\sin^2 (\phi/2)}$$

$$= I_0 \frac{\sin^2 (N\phi/2)}{\sin^2 (\phi/2)} \tag{5-24}$$

where again I_0 is the intensity from a single source as in Eq. (5-17).

The functional dependence of I on ϕ, which in turn depends on the angle θ in Fig. 5-11, consists of a rapid fluctuation given by the factor $\sin^2 (\phi/2)$ modulated by the more slowly varying function $1/\sin^2 (\phi/2)$. Each factor, together with the product of the two functions, is plotted in Fig. 5-13. The expression is indeterminate at $\phi = 0, 2\pi, 4\pi, \ldots$; it may be evaluated at $x = 0$ by recalling that for very small angles $\sin x \cong x$, so that we have approximately, for small ϕ,

$$\frac{\sin^2 (N\phi/2)}{\sin^2 (\phi/2)} \cong \frac{(N\phi/2)^2}{(\phi/2)^2} = N^2$$

Thus at $\phi = 0, 2\pi, 4\pi, \ldots$,

$$I = \frac{1}{2} \sqrt{\frac{\epsilon}{\mu}} N^2 E_0^2 = N^2 I_0 \tag{5-25}$$

This corresponds physically to the case where signals from all N sources arrive at P in phase, and the total amplitude is just NE_0.

To complete the intensity-distribution calculation, the phase difference ϕ must be expressed in terms of the angle θ giving the direction from the array of sources to the observer. When the sources are all in phase, this is

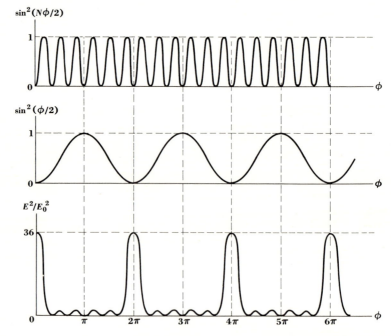

Fig. 5-13 Interference pattern for six sources. The individual factors of Eq. (5-24) are plotted, with their quotient, which represents the intensity. The principal maxima are separated by several much smaller subsidiary maxima.

determined entirely by the path difference and is given by Eq. (5-19), just as in the two-source case. If there are phase differences between sources, they must be added to the phase angle resulting from the path difference. For example, if adjacent sources differ in phase by 45°, then $\phi = kd \sin \theta + \pi/4$.

The interference pattern is seen to consist of sharp, large maxima, separated by several much smaller subsidiary peaks. The larger the value of N, the sharper and more intense are the peaks, in contrast to the two-slit diffraction pattern, where the maxima are broad. Practical use is made of this behavior in the design of directional radio antennas, when it is desirable to beam most of the power from a radio transmitter along a single line, as is the case in many communication situations.

Equation (5-24) can also be derived by using the complex exponential-function representation. The rotating vectors are represented by the quantities

$$E_0{}^{i\omega t}, \; E_0 e^{i(\omega t+\phi)}, \; E_0 e^{i(\omega t+2\phi)}, \; \ldots, \; E_0 e^{i[\omega t+(N-1)\phi]}$$

and their vector sum by

$$E = E_0 e^{i\omega t}(1 + e^{i\phi} + e^{2i\phi} + \cdots + e^{i(N-1)\phi}) \tag{5-26}$$

As explained above, the magnitude of this vector sum is constant, and we are at liberty to calculate it at any instant of time. We choose $t = 0$; then $e^{i\omega t} = 1$. The expression in parentheses is a geometric series, and can be represented more simply by use of the formula for the sum of a geometric series:

$$1 + a + a^2 + \cdots + a^{N-1} = \frac{a^N - 1}{a - 1} \tag{5-27}$$

which can be verified by division. Dropping the factor $e^{i\omega t}$ and using this formula, we obtain

$$E = E_0 \frac{e^{iN\phi} - 1}{e^{i\phi} - 1} \tag{5-28}$$

which can be rearranged in the following form:

$$E = E_0 \frac{e^{iN\phi/2}}{e^{i\phi/2}} \frac{e^{iN\phi/2} - e^{-iN\phi/2}}{e^{i\phi/2} - e^{-i\phi/2}}$$

$$= E_0 e^{i(N-1)\phi/2} \frac{\sin (N\phi/2)}{\sin (\phi/2)} \tag{5-29}$$

The intensity I is given by

$$I = \frac{1}{2} \sqrt{\frac{\epsilon}{\mu}} |E|^2 = \frac{1}{2} \sqrt{\frac{\epsilon}{\mu}} EE^*$$

and so, finally,

$$I = \frac{1}{2} \sqrt{\frac{\varepsilon}{\mu}} E_0{}^2 \frac{\sin^2 (N\phi/2)}{\sin^2 (\phi/2)} = I_0 \frac{\sin^2 (N\phi/2)}{\sin^2 (\phi/2)} \qquad (5\text{-}30)$$

which agrees with Eq. (5-24).

The corresponding phenomena with visible light are of considerable practical importance. One can construct an apparatus similar to that used in the two-slit experiment described above but having *many* slits. For interference effects to be readily observable, the spacing between sources should be of the same order of magnitude as the wavelength, which for visible light is less than 0.001 mm. A common procedure is to scratch a series of very fine grooves with a diamond point on a highly polished plane glass surface or a polished metal mirror used as a reflector. Grids have been made with up to about 1000 lines/mm. Such grids are called *diffraction gratings;* those made from a transparent material and used in transmission are called *transmission gratings,* and those used as reflectors are called *reflection gratings.*

As noted above, the maxima in the interference pattern become sharper with increasing numbers of slits; when N is very large, they become extremely sharp, and essentially all light of a given wavelength comes out at angles θ which satisfy the condition that the path difference for light from adjacent slits is an integer number of wavelengths; that is,

$$d \sin \theta = n\lambda \qquad n = 0, 1, 2, 3, \ldots \qquad (5\text{-}31)$$

In practice a narrow parallel beam is formed by a slit oriented parallel to the lines of the diffraction grating; if a screen is placed behind the grating, a series of images of this slit appear at angles which satisfy Eq. (5-31) with various values of n. The central undeviated maximum corresponds to $n = 0$.

If the incident light consists of a mixture of wavelengths, images for different wavelengths appear at different angles, the short wavelengths being bent less than the longer ones. Continuous-spectrum white light is dispersed into a continuous spectrum; but unlike a prism, which produces a single spectrum, the grating forms a *series* of spectra on each side of the central maximum, one for each value of n. The $n = 1$ spectrum is called the first-order spectrum, the $n = 2$ the second order, and so on. If the grating spacing is known, wavelengths can be measured directly by measuring the angle θ.

Diffraction gratings have found wide application in spectroscopy. By proper choice of the line spacing in the grating, one can adjust the amount of spread or *dispersion* between maxima for different wavelengths. This is a considerable advantage over the prism spectrometer, in which one is at the mercy of the dispersive properties of the glass used; thus diffraction gratings are very widely used for precise spectroscopic measurements.

5-5   THIN FILMS

An interesting example of interference is seen when light is reflected from two nearly parallel surfaces. An example is shown in Fig. 5-14. Two perfectly flat glass plates are in contact along one edge but are separated by a certain distance on the opposite edge, so as to form a wedge-shaped air space. Monochromatic light is incident from above. Reflections occur at all four surfaces; we consider in particular the interference between reflections from the two surfaces adjacent to the air wedge. In traveling from the source to the observer's eye, the wave reflected from the bottom surface has to travel somewhat farther than that from the top surface. The path difference varies with the distance from the line of contact between the plates, and so we expect an interference pattern. Near the line of contact, the path difference is nearly zero, and we expect a region of maximum *constructive* interference. Another region of constructive interference should occur when the path difference is one wavelength λ, corresponding to an air space of $\lambda/2$; the second bright fringe should occur at a distance d from the line of contact, given approximately by

$$\alpha = \frac{\lambda/2}{d} \qquad \text{or} \qquad d = \frac{\lambda}{2\alpha} \tag{5-32}$$

More generally, there should be a succession of bright and dark fringes, with adjacent bright fringes separated by the amount d given by Eq. (5-32).

   This experiment is easy enough to perform; results are as predicted, with one important exception. Near the line of contact, where we expect a bright fringe, a *dark* fringe is observed. The succession of alternate bright and dark fringes appears as predicted, but the positions are exactly reversed, showing that one of the reflected waves had suffered an additional phase shift of one-half cycle. This can be understood on the basis of the analysis of Sec. 4-5, where transmission and reflection coefficients were calculated for a plane

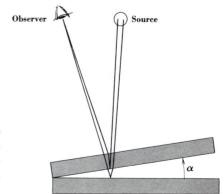

Fig. 5-14 Reflection of light from the two surfaces shown. Depending on the difference in path length, constructive or destructive interference occurs. The angle α is greatly exaggerated for clarity.

wave striking an interface between two dielectric media. We found that when the second medium has a larger index of refraction than the first, the reflected wave is *inverted* with respect to the incident wave; that is, the reflection introduces a phase change of π. When the index in the first medium is *greater* than that in the second, *no* phase change occurs. In the present situation, the wave reflected internally from the top surface suffers no phase change, but that reflected from the bottom surface is inverted. This additional phase change accounts for the position of the fringes in the experiment just described and provides an interesting confirmation of the predictions of Sec. 4-5.

These *interference fringes,* as they are called, have many practical applications. One of the simplest is testing the flatness of a glass plate by putting it in contact with another plate known to be flat and observing the pattern of interference fringes resulting from the irregularities of the surface. These fringes are generally not along straight lines, as in the idealized situation described above, but are *contour lines* representing the irregularities of the surface. Two examples are shown in Fig. 5-15. By making use of these interference fringes, it is possible to make surfaces that are flat within a fraction of a wavelength, much more precisely than would be possible using ordinary mechanical measuring devices.

A similar phenomenon is responsible for the brightly colored rings observed when a thin film of oil floats on water. Here the radiation is not ordinarily monochromatic, and constructive interference occurs at different positions for different colors of light; hence the interference pattern appears as fringes of various colors rather than simply as light and dark fringes.

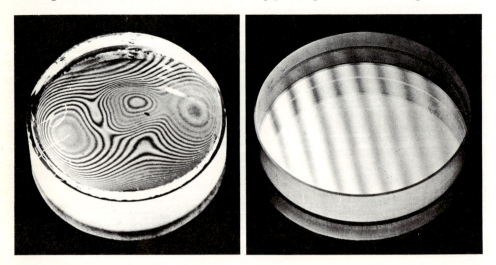

Fig. 5-15 Interference fringes produced by interference between reflections at two air-glass interfaces. The ring-shaped fringes were first observed by Newton and are called Newton's rings.

Another important practical application of the interference between reflections from two adjacent surfaces is antireflection coating of lenses. A lens is coated with a thin film of material whose thickness is chosen to achieve maximum destructive interference of the reflected waves, with corresponding maximum transmitted intensity through the lens. Some of the details of design of such nonreflecting coatings are included in the problems for this chapter.

5-6 INTERFERENCE AND DIFFRACTION

The terms *interference* and *diffraction* are both used, to a certain extent interchangeably, to describe phenomena resulting from superposition of waves

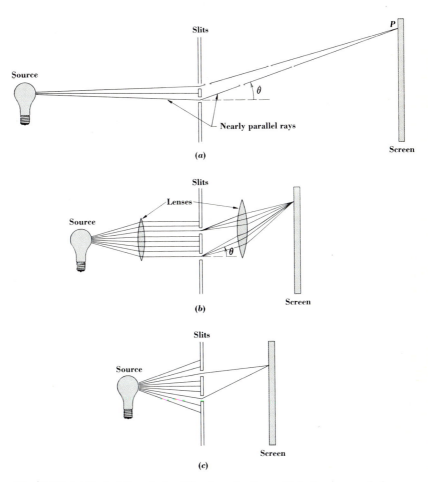

Fig. 5-16 (*a*) Typical Fraunhofer diffraction situation, with both source and observer very far from the diffracting object. (*b*) Lens arrangement used to observe Fraunhofer diffraction with finite source and observer distances. (*c*) Typical Fresnel diffraction situation, with both source and observer at finite distances from the diffracting object.

with phase differences. Ordinarily *interference* refers to the superposition of a small number of coherent sources, such as two slits, reflection from two surfaces, or two radio-transmitter antennas. *Diffraction* usually refers to superposition of a large number of waves, as in a diffraction grating. Additional examples of diffraction, including x-ray diffraction in crystals, diffraction from apertures and edges, and holography, will be discussed in Chap. 6. It is important to understand that despite the variety of terminology used, all interference and diffraction phenomena are governed by the same basic principles.

In the discussion of interference of light emerging from slits, it was assumed that all slits radiate *in phase;* this is true only when the primary source of light is far enough away so that the waves striking the slits may be considered plane waves, or when a lens system is used to convert spherical waves from a source at a finite distance into plane waves. Correspondingly, it was assumed that the position of the observer is essentially an infinite distance away. For historical reasons, interference phenomena in which both source and observer are infinitely far from the slit array are called *Fraunhofer diffraction.* An example is shown in Fig. 5-16a. By using lenses to convert spherical waves into plane waves, it is possible to observe Fraunhofer diffraction with finite distances. An example of a possible experimental arrangement is shown in Fig. 5-16b.

Phenomena in which either source or observer, or both, are at finite distances from the slits or other obstacle, are called *Fresnel diffraction;* an example is shown in Fig. 5-16c. In this case both source-to-slit and slit-to-screen distances have to be considered in computing phase differences, and this makes Fresnel diffraction patterns more difficult to compute in detail than Fraunhofer. Nevertheless, the same basic principles are involved in both.

Problems

5-1 Derive Eq. (5-2) for the Poynting vector for a spherical wave from the expressions for **E** and **B** for the wave, Eqs. (5-1).

5-2 Derive Eq. (5-4) for the total energy radiated from an oscillating dipole, from the expression for S_{av}, Eq. (5-3). Use as an area element for the integration a ring concentric with the z axis, whose inner and outer edges subtend angles θ and $\theta + d\theta$, respectively, at the origin. Show that the area of such a ring is $2\pi r^2 \sin \theta \, d\theta$, and that S_{av} is constant over the ring. The surface integral is then a single integral on θ.

5-3 Two identical oscillating dipoles are located at the origin of a coordinate system, at right angles to each other, one along the y axis, one along the z axis. The two oscillators are in phase. Find the total radiation field for points along each of the three coordinate axes. Describe the state of polarization of the radiation in each case.

5-4 Repeat Prob. 5-3 for the case where the two oscillators are 90° out of phase. Also show that the total radiation field is the same as that produced by a permanent dipole p_0 which *rotates* in the yz plane with angular velocity ω.

5-5 A dipole is made from two small metallic spheres separated by a distance of 1 m. A sinusoidal potential difference is applied to produce an oscillating dipole, and the maximum charge on each sphere is 10^{-8} C. If the frequency is 10^6 Hz, find the total power radiated from the dipole.

5-6 An electric-dipole antenna for a radio station operating at 1000 kHz produces a maximum electric field of 10^{-3} V/m at a distance of 10 km. If the dipole is vertical, find the maximum dipole moment of the antenna.

5-7 When the functions $E_1 = E_0 \cos \omega t$ and $E_2 = E_0 \cos (\omega t + \phi)$ are added, plot a graph showing the amplitude of the resulting sinusoidal function, as a function of the phase angle ϕ. What is the amplitude when $\phi = 0$? $\pi/4$? $\pi/2$? $3\pi/4$? π?

5-8 Find the amplitude and phase of the sinusoidal function which results from adding $A \cos \omega t$ and $2A \cos (\omega t + \pi/2)$.

5-9 For any two complex numbers A and B, prove that $\text{Re}(A + B) = \text{Re}(A) + \text{Re}(B)$.

5-10 For any complex number A, prove that $\text{Re}(A) = \frac{1}{2}(A + A^*)$ and $\text{Im}(A) = (A - A^*)/2i$.

5-11 Show that the complex number $-\frac{1}{2} + i\sqrt{3}/2$ is a cube root of unity.

5-12 Show that the sixth roots of unity are represented by points in the complex plane which lie on a circle of unit radius and are spaced 60° apart around the circle. Using this information, write each of the roots in the standard form $x + iy$.

5-13 Using Euler's relations, prove that $(\cos x + i \sin x)^n = \cos nx + i \sin nx$, which is called De Moivre's theorem.

5-14 Starting with Eqs. (5-7), prove the identity $\sin^2 x + \cos^2 x = 1$.

5-15 Evaluate $e^{i\pi/2}$, $e^{i\pi}$, $e^{3i\pi/2}$, and $e^{2\pi i}$.

5-16 Show that for any complex number z, $|z|^2 = zz^*$.

5-17 Two identical radio antennas separated by one-half wavelength operate 180° out of phase.
   a Draw vector diagrams to determine the resultant intensity, for intervals of 30° around the antennas.
   b Derive an expression for the intensity as a function of angle, in terms of the intensity that would be produced by a single antenna.

5-18   Two identical radio antennas separated by one-half wavelength are operated with a phase difference of ϕ. Derive an expression for the intensity of the resultant radiation pattern, as a function of angle, in terms of the intensity of a single antenna.

5-19   Two radio antennas are driven from the same source, in phase, but are oriented so that for points on a horizontal plane the radiation of one is polarized in this plane but that of the other is polarized in a vertical plane. Find the intensity of the resultant radiation as a function of angle, for points in the horizontal plane.

5-20   In a two-slit interference experiment with light of wavelength 500 nm, what must be the spacing of the slits if the distance from the central maximum to the first adjacent maximum, on a screen 10 m away, is 1 cm?

5-21   If the apparatus of Prob. 5-20 is immersed in water, what should the slit spacing be?

5-22   Two identical radio antennas spaced one-quarter wavelength apart are fed from the same source but are $90°$ out of phase because of phase-shifting networks. Find the resultant intensity as a function of angle.

5-23   Four identical radio antennas in a line, spaced one-half wavelength apart, are all driven in phase. Calculate the resulting intensity pattern, and draw vector diagrams showing addition of amplitudes at several points.

5-24   A diffraction grating is to be constructed to give the first maximum at $30°$ for the sodium line at 589.0 nm.
   a   What should be the line spacing of the grating?
   b   What is the angular separation of the lines in the sodium doublet (589.0 and 589.6 nm)?

5-25   A certain diffraction grating has 5000 lines/cm. For a certain spectrum line a maximum is observed at $30°$ to the normal. What are the possible wavelengths of the line?

5-26   Suppose the range of the visible spectrum is defined as 400 to 700 nm. Design a diffraction grating which spreads (disperses) the first diffraction maxima over $30°$ for this range.

5-27   An antenna array consists of N identical antennas in a straight line one-quarter wavelength apart. The phase difference between successive antennas in the row is $90°$. Calculate the resulting intensity distribution, and show that for large N this scheme directs nearly all the energy in a single direction.

5-28   Lenses are often coated with magnesium fluoride ($n = 1.38$) to reduce reflections. How thick should the layer be if reflections from the coating surface interfere destructively with those from the coating-glass interface for a wavelength in the center of the visible spectrum (say yellow light at 550 nm)? Assume that, for the glass, $n = 1.50$.

5-29. Suppose the coating material in Prob. 5-28 has an index of refraction of 1.70. What should be the thickness of the film?

5-30 Lenses coated with magnesium fluoride as described in Prob. 5-28 appear bluish. Why?

5-31 Suppose that the plates of Fig. 5-14 are 10 cm wide and are separated at one edge by 0.1 mm. The plates are made of glass with $n = 1.50$, and the space between them is filled with an oil having $n = 1.33$. Taking $\lambda = 500$ nm, compute the spacing between interference fringes. Is the fringe at the line of contact light or dark?

5-32 Repeat Prob. 5-31 for the case when the space between the plates is filled with carbon disulfide, for which $n = 1.62$.

5-33 A plano-convex lens rests with its convex surface on a plane glass surface. The radius of curvature is 30 cm, and the setup is illuminated from above with light of wavelength 600 nm.
   a   Is the point of contact a bright or dark area in the interference pattern?
   b   Derive expressions for the radius of the nth bright ring of the pattern, and for the nth dark ring.

5-34 Show that the intensity pattern for N sources, Eq. (5-24), reduces to that for two sources, Eq. (5-18), when $N = 2$.

Physical Optics II | 6

In this chapter we continue the discussion of phenomena associated with superposition of waves, concentrating primarily on those usually called *diffraction* phenomena. In x-ray diffraction a crystal serves as a three-dimensional diffraction grating for radiation of appropriate wavelength. We consider patterns formed when a parallel beam (plane wave) emerges from an aperture or encounters an obstruction. Closely related considerations lead to a qualitative understanding of holography, the recording and reproduction of three-dimensional images. Finally, we consider some aspects of the interaction of radiation with matter, particularly the variation of wave speed with frequency, and some interference phenomena with waves having different frequencies.

6-1 CRYSTAL DIFFRACTION

This section is concerned with diffraction of x-rays by a crystal lattice; we begin with a discussion that may seem unrelated, but the connection will emerge shortly. In Chap. 5 the discussion of interference patterns from coherent sources was limited to sources equally spaced along a *line*. Sources may also be distributed over a plane or throughout a region of space; calculation of the resulting interference pattern may be more complex, but the principles are exactly the same as for the linear array.

An example is shown in Fig. 6-1. Each source in the square array emits radiation with the same amplitude and phase. We observe the resultant interference pattern in the direction θ as shown. Constructive interference occurs between successive antennas in a horizontal row if the condition

$$d \cos \theta = m\lambda \qquad m = 1, 2, 3, \ldots \tag{6-1}$$

is satisfied, and constructive interference between successive elements in a vertical column occurs if

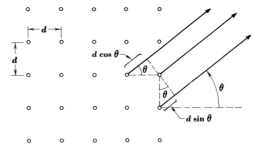

Fig. 6-1 A two-dimensional array of antennas. For radiation from all antennas to arrive at a distant point in phase, two conditions must be satisfied simultaneously; they are Eqs. (6-1) and (6-2).

$$d \sin \theta = n\lambda \qquad n = 1, 2, 3, \ldots \tag{6-2}$$

For all the waves from the antennas to arrive at the point of the observer with identical phases, these two relations must be satisfied simultaneously. Depending on the relative magnitude of d and λ, there may be several pairs of integers for which this relationship is satisfied, or perhaps none at all. As a particular example, suppose that $d = \lambda \sqrt{2}$; then both conditions are satisfied with $m = 1$ and $n = 1$ when $\theta = 45°$, and we expect a strong maximum in the interference pattern in this direction.

Additional interesting features appear if, instead of being primary sources of radiation, the elements in the square array in Fig. 6-1 are *scatterers* of incident radiation. Suppose, for example, they are small metal spheres and that a plane electromagnetic wave of wavelength comparable to d is directed at the array. The electric field at the position of each sphere induces an oscillating electric dipole, so each sphere emits a spherical wave. The total interference pattern is then the superposition of the incident plane wave and the scattered spherical waves, one for each sphere. Since the scatterers are at various distances from the primary source of the plane wave, the oscillating dipoles are not all in phase. To compute the interference pattern, we need to consider not just the differences in path lengths between the various scatterers and the observation point but the *total* path difference from the primary source to each scatterer, thence to the observation point.

Let us consider a plane wave incident upon a square array, as shown in Fig. 6-2. The path length from source to observer is the same for all scatterers in a single row if the lines to the source and observer are at equal angles, as shown in the figure. Under some conditions scattered radiation from adjacent rows may *also* be in phase. As shown, the path difference for two scatterers in the same column but adjacent rows is $2d \sin \theta$. For constructive interference to occur, this must be an integer number of wavelengths. For radiation from the *entire array* to arrive at the observer in phase, we must have

$$2d \sin \theta = n\lambda \qquad n = 1, 2, 3, \ldots \tag{6-3}$$

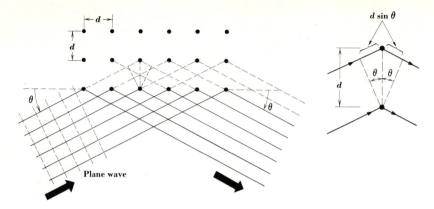

Fig. 6-2 Scattering of radiation from a square array. Interference from successive scatterers in a row is constructive when the angles of incidence and reflection are equal. When Eq. (6-3) is satisfied, interference from adjacent rows is also constructive.

When this condition is satisfied, a strong maximum in the interference pattern is observed. If the condition is not satisfied, no strong maximum is observed, since there is then *no* position of the observer for which all the radiation will arrive in phase from all scatterers. Equation (6-3) is called the *Bragg condition*, in honor of Sir William Bragg, one of the pioneers in x-ray diffraction analysis.

It is convenient to describe this interference effect in terms of *reflections* of the wave from the horizontal rows in Fig. 6-2. When strong interference maxima do occur, they are always at angles such that the angles of incidence and reflection are equal, and the additional condition of Eq. (6-3) must also be satisfied. In principle one could enclose the array in a black box and determine the spacing of the radiators by observing the interference pattern, provided the wavelength of the radiation is known.

The entire discussion can be extended to a three-dimensional array. Again the concept of reflection planes is useful; if the array has regular structure, it is possible to construct several different sets of parallel planes passing through all radiators. All radiators in a given plane interfere constructively if the angles of incidence and reflection with respect to this plane are equal, and the condition for constructive interference between adjacent planes spaced a distance d apart is again Eq. (6-3). Because there are several different sets of parallel planes, there are various sets of angles corresponding to directions of maximum intensity. Figure 6-3 illustrates several sets of planes for a cubic array of radiators.

We are now ready to relate this discussion to x-ray phenomena. X-rays were discovered in 1895 by Roentgen; circumstances of their production, to be discussed in Chap. 8, immediately suggested that they were electromagnetic waves. All attempts at dealing with them by the usual optical

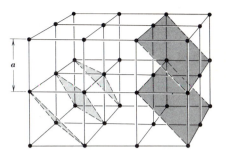

Fig. 6-3 Simple cubic crystal lattice, showing two different families of crystal planes. The spacing of the planes on the left is $a/\sqrt{3}$; that of the planes on the right is $a/\sqrt{2}$. There are also three sets of planes parallel to the cube faces, with spacing a.

methods were unsuccessful, however, and it became clear that their wavelength must be much *shorter* than that of visible light. In 1912 Laue suggested that, if x-ray wavelengths were of the same order of magnitude as the atomic spacing in crystals, a crystal could be used as a three-dimensional diffraction grating for the analysis of x-rays.

Laue's suggestion proved to be an extremely fruitful one. Directing a narrow beam of x-rays at a large single crystal whose orientation can be varied, and recording on photographic film the positions of the various maxima in the interference pattern, one can analyze the structure of crystals in considerable detail. An example of an x-ray diffraction pattern is shown in Fig. 6-4.

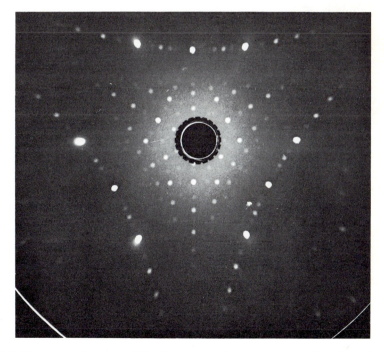

Fig. 6-4 Photograph of an x-ray diffraction pattern; the spots represent directions of strong maxima in the interference pattern.

In the ensuing years, x-ray diffraction from crystals has been by far the most important experimental tool in the investigation of crystal structure of solids. It has been possible to measure atomic spacings in crystals quite precisely and to determine the details of crystal structure even in complex crystals. More recently, x-ray diffraction experiments have played a considerable role in investigations of the structure of liquids and even of organic molecules. Yet the basic principles involved in x-ray diffraction, those of superposition and interference, are the same ones responsible for a wide variety of other interference and diffraction phenomena.

6-2 DIFFRACTION FROM APERTURES AND EDGES

In this section we consider *diffraction* effects which occur when a plane wave strikes a barrier with an aperture or an edge. A typical situation is shown in Fig. 6-5; a plane electromagnetic wave is incident upon a sheet of material which is opaque to radiation except in one region where a hole has been cut. We place a screen at a considerable distance from the aperture and observe the radiation pattern on this screen. What do we see?

The *ray* model of light would provide a simple, clear-cut answer to this question. If light travels in straight lines, the screen should be dark except for a uniformly illuminated spot the same size and shape as the aperture. Similarly, if instead of an opaque screen with an aperture we used a small opaque *obstacle*, the result should be a shadow on the screen with definite edges, the same size and shape as the obstacle. When observations are made, however, the edges are always somewhat fuzzy; if the experiment is done with monochromatic light, *fringes* appear at the edge of the shadow, reminiscent of interference fringes. Such phenomena cannot be explained on the basis of a ray picture of light.

Even more strange, when a circular obstacle is used, a *bright spot* appears at the center of the shadow. The existence of this spot was predicted in the year 1818 by the French mathematician Poisson, on the basis of a wave theory of light. Poisson himself was *not* a believer in the wave theory; he published this calculation, the result of which seemed absurd, as a final death blow

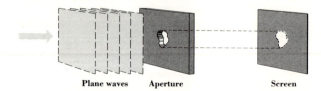

Plane waves   Aperture   Screen

Fig. 6-5 Plane monochromatic waves are incident on a barrier with an aperture, in the same plane as that of the waves. The intensity pattern on the screen is observed.

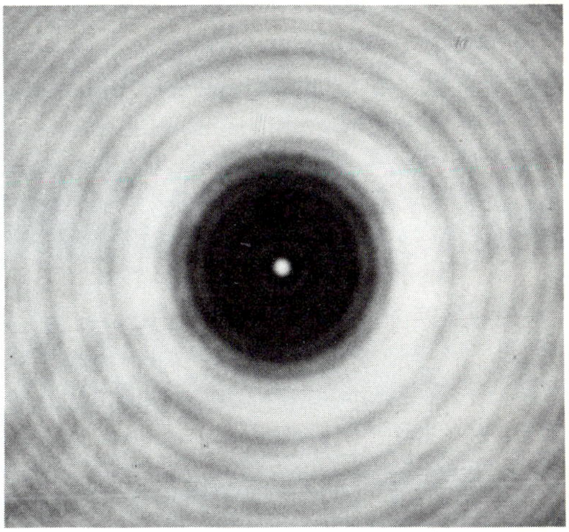

Fig. 6-6 Shadow of a $\frac{1}{8}$-in-diameter ball bearing, showing the Poisson bright spot. The ball was glued to a microscope slide and illuminated by a He-Ne laser beam. (*From Hecht and Zajak, "Optics," Addison-Wesley Publishing Company. Used by permission.*)

to the wave theory. Almost immediately, however, the existence of the bright spot was verified experimentally by Arago. It had in fact been observed as early as 1723 by Maraldi, but his work had attracted no attention at the time. Figure 6-6 shows an example of the Poisson spot.

Phenomena that involve departures from straight-line ray behavior of radiation are called *diffraction* phenomena. Calculations of diffraction patterns are often quite complicated, but there are a few cases which can be handled quite simply; we discuss the basic ideas here. For light, diffraction patterns are calculated from the following principle: *In diffraction of a plane wave by an aperture in an opaque sheet, the radiation field for all points beyond the sheet is the same as would be produced by a uniform distribution of sources over the area of the aperture.* We confine our attention to the case in which the opaque sheet is parallel to the planes of the incident wave, in which case we assert further that *all the sources in this distribution are in phase.*

This principle is called *Huygens' principle* in honor of Christian Huygens, a contemporary of Newton, who discovered it in the course of an investigation of the properties of water waves, long before the wave nature of light was understood. In effect we have already used Huygens' principle in the analysis of a diffraction grating, which is an opaque screen containing a series of parallel slits equally spaced, illuminated by a plane wave. We treated each slit as a new source of radiation and calculated the resulting interference pattern. For an aperture of more general shape, we must consider not just a discrete set of sources but a continuous distribution over the plane of the aperture.

The procedure prescribed by Huygens' principle may not seem to make any physical sense at all, since it is clear that there are no real sources of radiation in the aperture. Nevertheless, the assumption of a uniform distribution of sources across the aperture leads to correct predictions of diffraction patterns. We first discuss an example of the use of this procedure and then present an argument to justify the use of the fictitious source distribution.

Let us use the above prescription to calculate the diffraction pattern produced by an aperture in the form of a long, thin slit. In Fig. 6-7 the short dimension of the slit is vertical and its long dimension perpendicular to the page. The radiation pattern is the same as would be produced by a continuous distribution of *sources* over the area of the slit. Assuming that the length of the slit is much larger than its width, we may regard this as essentially a two-dimensional problem. We divide the slit into a series of elemental strips perpendicular to the figure. A typical strip is shown in the figure; its width is ds. We can think of this strip as generating cylindrical wavefronts, that is, waves whose surfaces of constant phase are coaxial cylinders, with their axis along the strip.

To calculate the total intensity in the direction θ toward the distant point P, we sum the contributions of these strips to the total field at P, taking into account the phase differences resulting from the differences in path length. The path difference for the two paths shown is $s \sin \theta$, and the corresponding phase difference, according to Eq. (5-20), is

$$\phi = ks \sin \theta \tag{6-4}$$

The phase changes continuously with s across the slit. Correspondingly, the *total* phase difference Φ between the bottom and the top of the slit is:

$$\Phi = ka \sin \theta \tag{6-5}$$

The intensity may be found by means of a vector diagram very similar to that used for the interference pattern for N slits in Fig. 5-12. Instead of the N slits, there is a *continuous* distribution of sources across the slit;

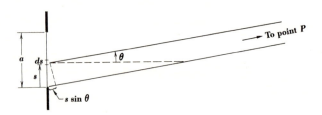

Fig. 6-7 Calculation of the diffraction pattern for a slit of width a. The path difference between light from the bottom edge and that from a strip a distance s from the bottom edge is $s \sin \theta$. From this the phase difference of the two radiations can be found. The total intensity at any angle θ is found by adding the contributions of the source strips (integrating on s), taking account of the varying phase.

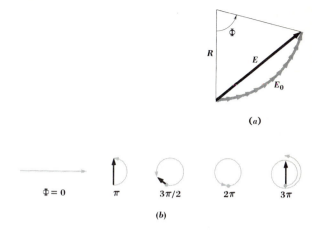

(a)

$\Phi = 0$ π $3\pi/2$ 2π 3π

(b)

Fig. 6-8 (a) Vector diagram for addition of amplitudes for a single slit. The length of the curve is the same for all angles; the angle subtended is the total phase difference between the top and bottom edges of the slit. The chord represents the resultant amplitude. (b) Vector diagrams for several points in the diffraction pattern.

correspondingly, the construction to find the total amplitude is not a vector sum of N vectors with equal magnitudes but rather an infinite sum of infinitesimal vectors, forming a smooth curve of constant radius of curvature R, as shown in Fig. 6-8a. The *length* of this curve E_0, representing the sum of the *magnitudes* of the vectors, is constant, and the *chord length* E represents the *amplitude* of the resultant radiation. The angle Φ subtended at the center of the circle is the total phase difference between top and bottom of the slit, given by Eq. (6-5).

Just as in Fig. 5-12, the chord length E is given by $\frac{1}{2}E = R \sin (\Phi/2)$; the constant arc length E_0 is $E_0 = R\Phi$. Eliminating R and solving for E, we find

$$E = E_0 \frac{\sin (\Phi/2)}{\Phi/2} \tag{6-6}$$

where Φ is given by Eq. (6-5) and E_0 is the value of E when $\theta = 0$ and $\Phi = 0$. The intensity is

$$I = I_0 \frac{\sin^2 (\Phi/2)}{(\Phi/2)^2} = I_0 \frac{\sin^2 (\frac{1}{2}ka \sin \theta)}{(\frac{1}{2}ka \sin \theta)^2} \tag{6-7}$$

where I_0 is the intensity at $\theta = 0$. Vector diagrams corresponding to several points in the diffraction pattern are shown in Fig. 6-8b.

This result may also be obtained by use of the complex-number representation. The electric field dE resulting from a strip of width ds at the bottom of the slit ($s = 0$) is

$$dE = E_0 \operatorname{Re} [e^{i\omega t}] \frac{ds}{a} \qquad (6\text{-}8)$$

where the factor $1/a$ is included for dimensional consistency and so that in the final result E_0 will represent the amplitude in the direction $\theta = 0$. Similarly, the contribution dE from a strip of width ds a distance s from the bottom is

$$dE = E_0 \operatorname{Re} [e^{i(\omega t + \phi)}] \frac{ds}{a} \qquad (6\text{-}9)$$

where the phase angle ϕ is given as before by Eq. (6-4).

To find the total field at P, we integrate Eq. (6-9) over the width of the slit, using for ϕ the expression given by Eq. (6-4). Since the factor $e^{i\omega t}$ drops out in taking the absolute value, we omit it from here on. The amplitude at P is then given by

$$E = E_0 \left| \frac{1}{a} \int_0^a e^{iks\sin\theta}\, ds \right| = E_0 \left| \frac{e^{ika\sin\theta} - 1}{ika\sin\theta} \right|$$

$$= E_0 \left| e^{(1/2)ika\sin\theta} \frac{\sin\left(\tfrac{1}{2}ka\sin\theta\right)}{\tfrac{1}{2}ka\sin\theta} \right| \qquad (6\text{-}10)$$

The intensity distribution is

$$I = I_0 \frac{\sin^2\left(\tfrac{1}{2}ka\sin\theta\right)}{\left(\tfrac{1}{2}ka\sin\theta\right)^2} \qquad (6\text{-}11)$$

in agreement with Eq. (6-7).

Figure 6-9 shows a graph of this function and under it a photograph of a diffraction pattern, which agrees well with the theoretical prediction. Thus in this case, Huygens' principle leads to a result which agrees with experimental observations.

We now sketch an argument to show *why* the fictitious source distribution across apertures leads to correct results in diffraction-pattern calculations. If the opaque sheet has *no* aperture, it blocks the radiation completely. But how does it accomplish this? A plane wave incident on the left side of the sheet induces oscillating dipoles in the sheet; these produce an additional radiation field which, when superposed on the incident field, results in a *total* field with zero intensity at all points to the right of the sheet. If the incident wave is a plane wave, the sources of this secondary wave, which cancel the incident wave at points to the right of the sheet, must be a uniform distribution of sources over the sheet.

When we *remove* a certain area of the sheet, we remove the secondary sources in that area. Let a typical secondary source be S_i, and let its radiation

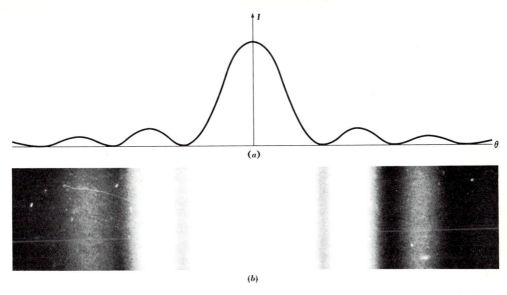

Fig. 6-9 (*a*) Intensity distribution for the diffraction pattern formed from a single slit on a distant screen. (*b*) Photograph made by placing photographic film in the plane of the screen.

field be $\mathbf{E}_i$. We could produce the same effect as removing these sources if, instead, we allowed them to remain but *added* to each one a corresponding source S_i', which produces a radiation field precisely the negative of that of S_i, that is, $-\mathbf{E}_i$. But the latter arrangement also corresponds to the superposition of the waves associated with an opaque sheet with no aperture (i.e., *no* radiation to the right of the screen) and the radiation from the sources S_i'. Thus on the right side the total radiation field is just that of the uniform distribution of sources S_i' over the area of the aperture; this fact justifies calculating the radiation pattern on this basis.

Some important points are left out of this argument. One is that we have not considered any peculiarities associated with induced sources at the *edges* of the aperture. To the extent that we have neglected these, our results are independent of the material of which the opaque sheet is made. But in cases where edge effects cannot be neglected, the properties of the material *are* relevant, and the calculations become considerably more complicated. In general, it is usually legitimate to neglect edge effects whenever the dimensions of the aperture are much larger than the wavelength of the radiation. This is usually the case with visible light, but it is practically never the case with radio waves of microwave frequencies, in which case more detailed calculations must be made.

The above analysis may be applied to a more complete treatment of the interference pattern from two slits, discussed in Sec. 5-3. In the initial discussion of this problem we neglected the widths of the slits and considered only the phase differences resulting from the distance d between slits. We may now compute the diffraction pattern from two slits of *finite* width a separated by a distance d between centers. The pattern, as might be guessed, is a superposition of the two-slit pattern for zero-width sources, Eq. (5-21), and the single-slit diffraction pattern obtained above, Eq. (6-7) or (6-11). That is, the intensity pattern is found to be

$$I = I_0 \cos^2\left(\frac{\Psi}{2}\right) \frac{\sin^2(\Phi/2)}{(\Phi/2)^2} \tag{6-11a}$$

where $\Psi = kd \sin \theta$ and $\Phi = ka \sin \theta$. This result is obtained the same way as Eq. (6-11) except that the integral in Eq. (6-10) goes from 0 to a and form d to $d + a$. Derivation of Eq. (6-11a) is left as an exercise. Because for a given value of θ, Ψ is larger than Φ by a factor of d/a, Ψ varies more rapidly with θ than does Φ, and the first factor in Eq. (6-11a) goes through zero several times for each zero of the second factor. Thus the pattern consists of relatively closely spaced peaks characteristic of the two-slit pattern, with the amplitudes of the peaks varying slowly as in the single-slit diffraction pattern.

Huygens' principle may also be used to obtain the diffraction pattern from a circular aperture, a problem of practical interest in connection with the resolving power of optical instruments. The integral cannot be evaluated in terms of elementary functions, and numerical approximations are necessary. The pattern consists of a central bright spot surrounded by concentric bright rings. The angular size θ of the dark ring separating the bright spot from the first bright ring is found to be given by

$$\sin \theta = 1.22 \frac{\lambda}{a} \tag{6-11b}$$

where a is the diameter of the circle. For example, when light of wavelength 500 nm is incident on an aperture 1 mm in diameter, the angular size of the first dark ring is

$$\theta = \sin^{-1} \frac{(1.22)(500 \times 10^{-9} \text{ m})}{10^{-3} \text{ m}} = 6.1 \times 10^{-4}$$

On a screen 10 m away from the aperture, the radius of this ring is $(6.1 \times 10^{-4})(10 \text{ m}) = 6.1$ mm. This radius measures the approximate size of the central bright spot, and we see that this is considerably larger than the aperture itself.

Diffraction patterns can be calculated for other shapes of apertures and for single edges. The calculations are usually complex and are made numeri-

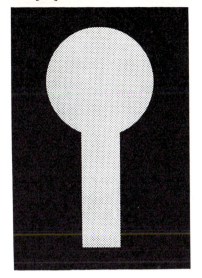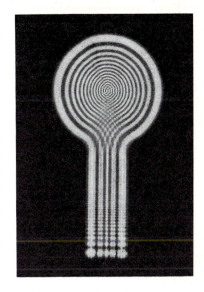

Fig. 6-10 Diffraction pattern formed by an irregularly shaped aperture.

cally with the aid of a high-speed computer. An interesting example of diffraction from an aperture is shown in Fig. 6-10. Photographs such as this are usually made not by placing the photographic film a very great distance from the aperture but by using a converging lens as shown in Fig. 5-16*b*.

6-3 HOLOGRAPHY

Holography is a technique for storing and reproducing a three-dimensional image[1] of a three-dimensional object. Ordinary photography, by comparison, always records two-dimensional images. The lens in a camera forms an image of the object being photographed. If the object is plane and the lens free from aberration, the image is also plane and can be recorded by placing a photographic film in the image plane. But in general the image is three-dimensional; portions of the image which happen to lie in the film plane are recorded without distortion, but those which are in front of or behind this plane simply appear out of focus. The three-dimensional character of the image is not recorded on film; what is recorded is distinctly two-dimensional, as is the image formed on a screen by a slide projector.

Holography, however, does produce true three-dimensional images with all the attributes such images should have. Such an image can be viewed from different directions to reveal different sides of the image, and from

---

[1]The concepts of real and virtual *images* are discussed in Secs. 7-1 and 7-2, and a reader unfamiliar with these concepts would do well to read those sections before proceeding.

different distances to reveal changing perspective. In fact, to anyone who has not seen a hologram image, and to many who have, the whole phenomenon seems quite impossible.

Holography was invented *in principle* by Gabor in 1947; because it involves interference effects over substantial regions of space, an extremely monochromatic light source is required, and such a source was not readily available until the invention of the laser in 1960. Laser operation will be discussed in Sec. 12-7; for the present we simply remark that lasers *do* produce very nearly monochromatic light and can be used for holography. Gabor received the Nobel Prize for physics in 1971.

We first describe a simple setup to produce a hologram and reproduce its images; then we give a brief discussion of how and why the images are formed. The basic setup to make a hologram is shown in Fig. 6-11a. The beam from a laser, spread out by means of suitable lenses, is split, part of it striking a photographic film directly, the other part illuminating the object to be holographed. *Scattered* light from the object also strikes the film; since the light is monochromatic and coherent, the direct light and scattered light have a definite *phase* relation at each point on the film, and an *interference pattern* is formed and recorded.

The images are formed by simply projecting laser light through the developed film, as in Fig. 6-11b. A *virtual* image is formed in the same position relative to the film as that of the original object, and a *real* image is formed on the opposite side in the mirror-image position. The virtual image may be viewed directly, or a converging lens may be used to form a real image on a screen of this virtual image. The real image formed is not easily viewed directly, but again it may be projected on a screen or a second image formed with a converging lens.

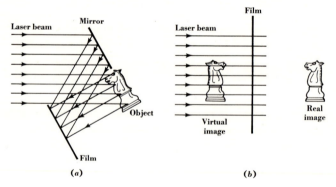

Fig. 6-11 (a) A hologram is formed on the film by interference between direct light reflected from the mirror and light scattered by the object being holographed. (b) Three-dimensional images are formed when light from a laser is sent through the hologram obtained in (a).

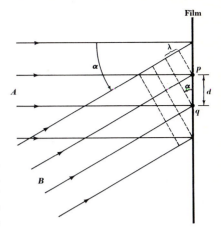

Fig. 6-12 The interference pattern formed by two plane waves is recorded on a photographic film. Adjacent intensity maxima are separated by a distance $d = \lambda/\sin \alpha$.

As a first step in understanding how hologram images are formed, we consider the interference pattern formed by two coherent parallel beams A and B incident on a photographic film, as shown in Fig. 6-12. One beam is normal to the film, the other is at an angle α to the normal. The broken lines represent wavefronts of B, spaced one wavelength apart. If the two waves are in phase at point p, they are also in phase at point q, and constructive interference (maximum intensity) occurs at both points. Midway between is a point where the phase difference is π and the intensity is minimum. The intensity of the resultant wave is in fact a *sinusoidal* function of position along the film; successive maxima are separated by a distance d given by

$$d \sin \alpha = \lambda \tag{6-12}$$

In the developed film, the blackest regions are those of maximum intensity in the interference pattern; the most nearly transparent are those of minimum intensity. Now we make a positive print on transparent film, which reverses light and dark. This step is not essential, but it helps clarify the basic ideas.

The resulting record of the interference pattern is a series of stripes of maximum transmittance corresponding to the interference *maxima*, separated by equal distances $d = \lambda/\sin \alpha$, as given by Eq. (6-12). We now project the same laser beam used before through this pattern on the film. We can guess the result by noting the similarity of this arrangement to a diffraction grating, discussed in Sec. 5-4. We found there that when a parallel beam is incident normally on a grating with spacing d between adjacent slits, the result is a series of maxima in the resulting interference pattern, at angles θ to the normal given by

$$d \sin \theta = n\lambda \qquad n = 0, \pm 1, \pm 2, \pm 3, \ldots \tag{6-13}$$

In our situation the transmission of the grating does not change abruptly from zero to maximum and back as we go across the lines; instead it changes *sinusoidally*. It is not obvious what effect this should have on the interference pattern. We state without proof the result that only the $n = 0$ and $n = \pm 1$ maxima predicted by Eq. (6-13) actually appear; all higher-order maxima are absent.

Proof of this statement is beyond our scope, but we can draw an analogy for the reader with a little knowledge of Fourier series. Any periodic wave can be represented as a sum of *sinusoidal* waves whose frequencies are integer multiples of the frequency of the wave. A "square wave" contains the fundamental frequency together with all possible harmonics or multiples of the fundamental, while a sine wave contains only the fundamental-frequency component. To make a long story short, the diffraction pattern represents a Fourier analysis of the grating, which is, after all, a periodic function of position. The intensities of the various "orders" (values of n) correspond to the amplitudes of the various sine functions in the series. The "square wave" grating has all orders, corresponding to all possible harmonics, whereas the "sine wave" grating has only the first order, corresponding to the fundamental frequency.

Thus the diffraction pattern from our sinusoidal grating, formed initially by the interference of two parallel beams, one normal to the grating and one at angle α, is a pair of parallel beams, both at angle α, one on either side of the normal, as shown in Fig. 6-13.

Now we consider the interference of two coherent waves, one a *plane* wave at normal incidence as before, the other a *spherical* wave emitted from a point source, as in Fig. 6-14. Again, we expose and develop the film and project laser light through the resulting transparency. What does the interference pattern look like?

Consider a small region near point a in Fig. 6-14. The corresponding small segment of the spherical wave is nearly a plane wave, as discussed in Sec. 5-1, and the contribution from this portion of the grating can be predicted from our previous result. It is simply a pair of segments of waves in the

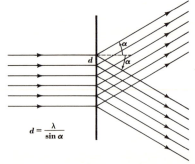

Fig. 6-13 When a laser beam passes through the film obtained from the interference pattern in Fig. 6-12, the result is two plane waves at angles α equal to the angle of the original beam.

$$d = \frac{\lambda}{\sin \alpha}$$

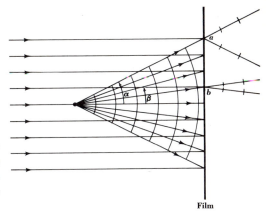

Fig. 6-14 Interference of a plane wave and a spherical wave. Each small segment of the spherical wave can be treated as a plane wave, and the ray picture can be used to represent the resulting pattern.

Film

direction shown, which we have represented in the figure as rays. The same argument can be made for other points in the transparency, such as point *b*.

Taken together, these sets of rays show the formation of two images, as shown in Fig. 6-15. One is a *real* image, where the rays actually do converge, at a point to the right of the film the same distance as the original source point was to the left. The other is a virtual image, corresponding to the diverging rays whose directions are the same *as though* they had originated at a point in the same location as the original source point. Thus, at least for single points, the images are indeed formed as advertised.

Now suppose the original object consists not just of one point source but of many. Since each interference pattern results from adding amplitudes of the component waves, the principle of linear superposition holds, both for the formation of the pattern on the film and for formation of the final image. That is, the final image for many point sources is just the sum of the images

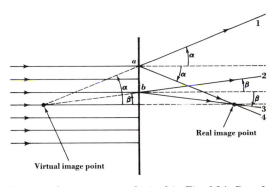

Real image point

Virtual image point

Fig. 6-15 Formation of images from interference pattern obtained in Fig. 6-14. Rays 1 and 2 diverge *as if* they had originated at the virtual image point; rays 3 and 4 actually do diverge from the real image point.

of the individual sources. This completes our demonstration of the assertion that the arrangement described at the beginning actually does form three-dimensional images.

6-4 DISPERSION AND SCATTERING

Dispersion is the dependence of wave speed on frequency. The index of refraction n of a material was defined in Sec. 4-5 as the ratio of the speed of light c in vacuum to its value u in the material, $n = c/u$. Thus

$$n = \sqrt{\frac{\mu\varepsilon}{\mu_0\varepsilon_0}} \tag{6-14}$$

In terms of the dielectric constant K_E and the relative permeability K_M, introduced in Eqs. (4-6),

$$n = \sqrt{K_E K_M} \tag{6-15}$$

Furthermore, as mentioned in Sec. 4-5, K_M for most materials (with the notable exception of the ferromagnetic materials) differs from unity by at most a few parts in 10^4, and often by less than one part in 10^6. With the approximation $K_M = 1$,

$$n = \sqrt{K_E} \tag{6-16}$$

It is necessary, however, to use a certain amount of discretion in applying this result, as the following example will show. Water is composed of highly polar molecules and in a static electric field has an unusually large relative dielectric constant, approximately $K_E = 80$. Equation (6-16) gives a predicted value of the index of refraction of about 9. The *measured* index of refraction for water, for visible light, is about $n = 1.33$. What went wrong?

To understand the nature of the difficulty, we have to look at the *microscopic* basis of K_E for water. There are two mechanisms; the first is the slight displacement of electrons relative to their associated nuclei, under the action of an **E** field, leading to an *induced* dipole moment; the second is that each water molecule has a significant *permanent* dipole moment even in the absence of a field. An applied **E** field then tends to rotate the molecules to orient their dipoles parallel to the field; this tendency is opposed by thermal motion, which tends to randomize the orientations.

In a static field the second mechanism is dominant, and the large static value of K_E is associated with orientation of permanent moments. At optical frequencies there is not time for the molecules to rotate appreciably, the first mechanism is dominant, and K_E decreases to about 1.8.

In general both K_E and K_M vary with frequency; hence the index of refraction of a material, given by Eq. (6-15), is also frequency-dependent.

The variation of index of refraction with wavelength (and therefore with frequency) is a well-known phenomenon. Newton discovered in 1666 that the refraction of a beam of light by a glass prism is different for different colors, although the relation between color and wavelength was not firmly established until 140 years later. This variation in refractive power, called *dispersion*, is the mechanism by which white light is broken up into a rainbow; the effect is used in prism spectrometers. For most glasses at optical frequencies, the index of refraction *increases* with increasing frequency; in refraction the shorter wavelengths (the violet end of the spectrum) are bent more sharply than the longer ones (the red end of the spectrum). Variation of index of refraction with wavelength for two glasses is shown in Fig. 6-16.

The dependence of index of refraction on frequency can be understood on the basis of the microscopic structure of matter. We consider here only the simplest possible model. Electrons are assumed to be distributed through the material, with an average density of N electrons per unit volume. Each has charge e and mass m, and is bound to its equilibrium position by a force proportional to the displacement from that position. Thus the particles can vibrate with simple harmonic motion about their equilibrium positions. The actual behavior of electrons in atoms is not this simple, but this model still affords some insight into the mechanism of dielectric polarization.

In the presence of a sinusoidal **E** field the electrons vibrate with the frequency of the field. As a result, each has a time-varying dipole moment

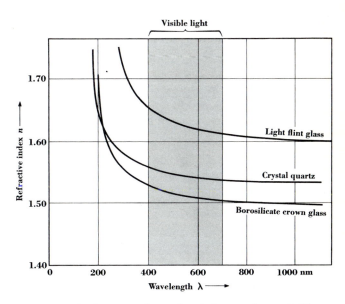

Fig. 6-16 Variation of index of refraction with wavelength for two glasses of different composition and for crystalline quartz.

resulting from its displacement with respect to the positive charge of the atom. Our program is to calculate this displacement as a function of time, from which we can calculate the *polarization* of the material, which is the dipole-moment density, as a function of time. The electric displacement **D** is given by $\mathbf{D} = \varepsilon_0\mathbf{E} + \mathbf{P} = \varepsilon\mathbf{E}$. As the calculation will show, **P** is proportional to **E**, so we can determine ε.

In the presence of a sinusoidal field $E = E_0 \cos \omega t$, an electron experiences a force $F = eE_0 \cos \omega t$ in addition to the elastic force $(-kx)$ tending to restore it to its equilibrium position. Newton's second law gives

$$-kx + eE_0 \cos \omega t = m \frac{d^2x}{dt^2} \tag{6-17}$$

As pointed out above, the resulting forced oscillation of the electron is sinusoidal with the frequency ω of the radiation:

$$x = A \cos \omega t \tag{6-18}$$

where the amplitude A is to be determined. Substituting Eq. (6-18) and its second derivative into Eq. (6-17), we find that this is a solution of the differential equation only if A obeys the condition $-kA + eE_0 = -m\omega^2 A$, or

$$A = \frac{eE_0}{k - m\omega^2} = \frac{eE_0/m}{\omega_0{}^2 - \omega^2} \tag{6-19}$$

where ω_0 is the natural frequency of the oscillator, defined by $\omega_0 = (k/m)^{1/2}$. Combining Eqs. (6-18) and (6-19) yields

$$x = \frac{e/m}{\omega_0{}^2 - \omega^2} E_0 \cos \omega t = \frac{e/m}{\omega_0{}^2 - \omega^2} E \tag{6-20}$$

The displacement x from equilibrium of each electron is proportional to E. When ω is *less* than the natural frequency ω_0, the displacement is *in phase* with the field; when larger, x and E have opposite signs and are 180° out of phase.

Each electron contributes a dipole moment xe, and so the polarization or density of dipole moments is $P = xeN$; thus

$$P = \frac{eNE/m}{\omega_0{}^2 - \omega^2} \tag{6-21}$$

The electric displacement is

$$\mathbf{D} = \varepsilon_0\mathbf{E} + \mathbf{P} = \left(\varepsilon_0 + \frac{e^2N/m}{\omega_0{}^2 - \omega^2}\right)\mathbf{E} \tag{6-22}$$

from which

$$\varepsilon = \varepsilon_0 + \frac{e^2 N/m}{\omega_0^2 - \omega^2} \qquad K_E = 1 + \frac{e^2 N/\varepsilon_0 m}{\omega_0^2 - \omega^2} \qquad (6\text{-}23)$$

Thus a frequency-dependent dielectric constant results from even this simple model. Equation (6-23) also shows that, when ω is close to ω_0, K_E becomes very *large*, corresponding to a very *small* velocity of propagation. In that case energy is strongly *absorbed* from the incident radiation. Our model contains no mechanism for energy absorption, but one can easily be included by adding to the equation of motion [Eq. (6-17)] a velocity-dependent damping force as in a damped harmonic oscillator. The analysis will not be given in detail; Fig. 6-17 shows the variation of permittivity and energy absorption with frequency for this model.

The phenomena illustrated by Fig. 6-17 are observed in many common materials. Ordinary glass has a dielectric constant which is very nearly independent of frequency at low frequencies; in the region of visible light n and K_E increase with frequency, and the material becomes opaque in the ultraviolet region. The quantitative details of the preceding discussion should not be taken too seriously, but it does give some *qualitative* insight into the microscopic mechanisms of dispersion and absorption.

A rather similar analysis leads to understanding of the *scattering* of light by air molecules, dust and smoke particles, crystal imperfections, and the like, leading to visual phenomena such as haze, blue sky, red sunsets, and so on. The **E** field of an incident wave induces oscillating dipoles, and these scatter the incident radiation by emitting spherical waves as described in Sec. 5-1. For an elastically bound electron as described above, the maximum dipole moment p_0 is given by

$$p_0 = \frac{e^2 E/m}{\omega_0^2 - \omega^2} \qquad (6\text{-}24)$$

This may be combined with Eq. (5-4) to find the average *rate* at which energy is scattered from an incident wave. The frequency dependence of this rate means that some colors of light are scattered more than others. Which are scattered most?

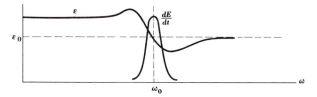

Fig. 6-17 Permittivity and rate of energy absorption as functions of frequency.

6-5 INTERFERENCE WITH DIFFERENT FREQUENCIES

We conclude this chapter with an introduction to interference phenomena with waves of different frequency and wavelength. To begin, we consider two waves whose **E** fields at a certain point in space have the same direction and the same amplitude E_0 but different frequencies ω_1 and ω_2. The total field at this point is then

$$E = E_0 \cos \omega_1 t + E_0 \cos \omega_2 t \tag{6-25}$$

This expression is more illuminating when written in terms of the average frequency $\omega_0 = (\omega_1 + \omega_2)/2$ and the amount $\Delta\omega$ by which each differs from the average. That is, we write

$$\begin{aligned} \omega_1 &= \omega_0 - \Delta\omega \\ \omega_2 &= \omega_0 + \Delta\omega \end{aligned} \tag{6-26}$$

In terms of these, Eq. (6-25) becomes

$$E = E_0 \left[\cos (\omega_0 - \Delta\omega)t + \cos (\omega_0 + \Delta\omega)t\right] \tag{6-27}$$

Using the cosine sum and difference formulas and simplifying, we obtain

$$E = (2E_0 \cos \Delta\omega t) \cos \omega_0 t \tag{6-28}$$

This function represents a field oscillating with frequency ω_0, with a time-dependent amplitude (in parentheses) which varies with a smaller frequency $\Delta\omega$.

For sound waves, this phenomenon is the familiar one of *beats*. When two tuning forks with frequencies 440 and 442 Hz are sounded together the ear perceives a sound with a frequency of 441 Hz with an intensity which varies from zero to maximum and back with a frequency of 2 Hz. This is *twice* the frequency ($\Delta\omega = 1$ Hz) with which the amplitude factor varies, since the ear perceives the *magnitude* of the amplitude, not its sign.

Equation (6-28) can also be understood on the basis of the rotating-vector representation of Sec. 5-2. The two vectors representing the individual functions rotate at different angular velocities. If they start out in phase, corresponding to constructive interference, the one with the larger ω eventually gets a half revolution ahead of the other, and destructive interference occurs. After another equal time period they are back in phase again. The frequency with which one vector gains a complete revolution over the other is determined by the *difference* $\Delta\omega$ in their angular velocities.

Next, we consider the *space* variation of the waves. For variety we use the complex-number representation. If both waves are plane waves propagating in the $+x$ direction, the superposed-wave function is

$$E = E_0 \operatorname{Re} \left[e^{i(k_1 x - \omega_1 t)} + e^{i(k_2 x - \omega_2 t)}\right] \tag{6-29}$$

where each wave number k is related to the corresponding frequency ω by $\omega = uk$, as usual. At the particular time $t = 0$, this is

$$E = E_0 \, \text{Re} \, [e^{ik_1x} + e^{ik_2x}] \tag{6-30}$$

We introduce the quantities k_0 and Δk:

$$\begin{aligned} k_1 &= k_0 - \Delta k \\ k_2 &= k_0 + \Delta k \end{aligned} \tag{6-31}$$

In terms of k_0 and Δk, Eq. (6-30) becomes

$$\begin{aligned} E &= E_0 \, \text{Re} \, [e^{i(k_0 + \Delta k)x} + e^{i(k_0 - \Delta k)x}] \\ &= [2E_0 \cos (\Delta k)x] \cos k_0 x \end{aligned} \tag{6-32}$$

This equation is plotted in Fig. 6-18, which also shows the individual wave functions at the time $t = 0$.

This picture can also be obtained directly by a graphical superposition of the two waves. They are in phase at $x = 0$, and the maximum amplitude there is $2E_0$. Moving along the x axis, the two waves grow farther and farther out of phase because of their slightly different wavelengths, until a point is reached where a maximum in one direction for one wave corresponds to a maximum in the opposite direction for the other, and then cancellation occurs. The resulting wave has the appearance of a sinusoidal wave whose amplitude changes slowly as a function of x, over a distance long compared with the individual wavelength. The factor in Eq. (6-32) that represents the varying amplitude is

$$2E_0 \cos \Delta kx \tag{6-33}$$

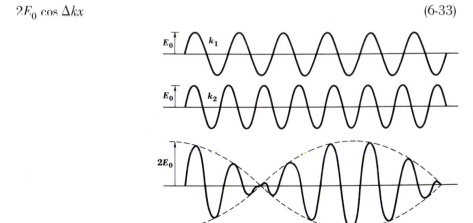

Fig. 6-18 Superposition of sinusoidal waves with different wave numbers ($k_1 < k_2$) results in a wave whose amplitude varies from zero to $2E_0$. The locally sinusoidal nature is described by $k_0 = \frac{1}{2}(k_1 + k_2)$, while the envelope curve has a slower variation with x given by the smaller wave number $\Delta k = \frac{1}{2}(k_2 - k_1)$.

This factor is called the *envelope* of the wave; it is the boundary line along which the maxima of the function lie.

If both waves have the same speed u, the entire pattern, including the envelope curve, also moves with that speed. But the speed of electromagnetic waves in matter depends on frequency, and this leads to some important new features. Let us again superpose two sinusoidal waves with frequencies ω_1 and ω_2 and wave numbers k_1 and k_2, and ω_1 and k_1 slightly larger than ω_2 and k_2, respectively. The wave speeds u_1 and u_2 are given by $\omega_1 = u_1 k_1$ and $\omega_2 = u_2 k_2$. Suppose also that the wave speed is an *increasing* function of frequency, so that $u_1 > u_2$. We now observe the two waves by running alongside them with the same speed u_2 as the *slower* of the two waves. Figure 6-19 shows the individual waves and their superposition at two different times. In the first case, the envelope of the interference pattern has a maximum at the position of the observer. In the second case, the observer and the second wave have traveled the same distance, and so the second wave still looks the same, but the first has *gained* a little, as shown in the figure. The region where the two waves interfere constructively has moved considerably farther than the first wave; thus the speed of the *envelope* is considerably *greater* than that of *either* of the waves. Conversely, if the first wave travels more *slowly* than the second wave, the envelope travels more *slowly* than either of the two waves.

A precise relationship between the individual wave speeds and the speed of the envelope can be derived. In terms of the quantities ω_0, $\Delta\omega$, k_0, and Δk defined by Eqs. (6-26) and (6-31), the superposed wave is

$$
\begin{aligned}
E &= E_0 \operatorname{Re} \left[e^{i(k_1 x - \omega_1 t)} + e^{i(k_2 x - \omega_2 t)} \right] \\
&= E_0 \operatorname{Re} \left[e^{i[(k_0 + \Delta k)x - (\omega_0 + \Delta\omega)t]} + e^{i[(k_0 - \Delta k)x - (\omega_0 - \Delta\omega)t]} \right] \\
&= E_0 \operatorname{Re} \left[e^{i(k_0 x - \omega_0 t)} \left(e^{i(\Delta k x - \Delta\omega t)} + e^{-i(\Delta k x - \Delta\omega t)} \right) \right] \\
&= \left[2E_0 \cos(\Delta k x - \Delta\omega t) \right] \cos(k_0 x - \omega_0 t)
\end{aligned}
\tag{6-34}
$$

In the last line, the quantity in brackets represents the envelope of the superposed wave, and the second term represents a sinusoidal wave with the average frequency ω_0 and wave number k_0. We recall from Sec. 3-2 that a wave function for a wave traveling in the $+x$ direction always contains x and t in the combination $ax - bt$, where a and b are constants, and that the wave speed is given by b/a. Examining the last form of Eq. (6-34), we see that the factor containing k_0 and ω_0 corresponds to a speed $u_0 = \omega_0/k_0$, but the speed of the *envelope* of the wave is something quite different. Denoting that speed by v, we find

$$
v = \frac{\Delta\omega}{\Delta k}
\tag{6-35}
$$

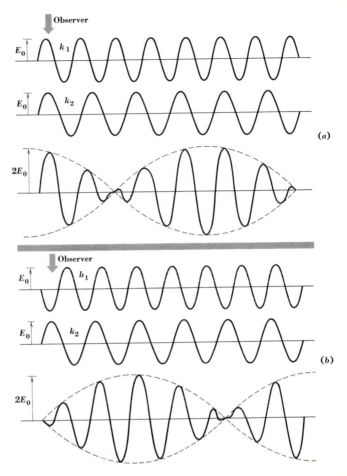

Fig. 6-19 (*a*) Interference pattern seen by an observer moving with the second wave. At this instant he is at a maximum in the envelope. (*b*) Slightly later, the second wave has not moved relative to the observer, but the first has moved ahead slightly. The envelope of the interference pattern has now moved so that the observer is at a minimum rather than a maximum. The velocity of the envelope is greater than that of either of the waves.

If the speed u were the same for all frequencies, the ratio ω/k would be constant, and $\Delta\omega/\Delta k$ would be equal to ω/k. But in general this is *not* the case, and *the speed of the envelope is different from that of either individual wave.* The speed of propagation of the *envelope* of an interference pattern is called the *group velocity.* Group *speed* would be more precise, but that term is not commonly used. Equation (6-35) holds more generally in dispersive wave propagation.

Superposing two waves with different wave numbers has the interesting effect of *bunching* the wave, that is, of concentrating the wave in certain

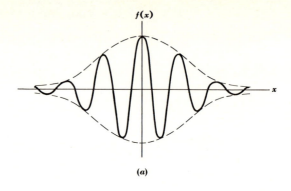

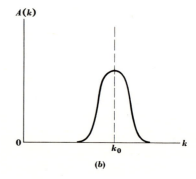

Fig. 6-20 (*a*) Wave pulse formed by the superposition of a continuous spectrum of sinusoidal waves with wave numbers centered around k_0. (*b*) The corresponding function $A(k)$. It can be shown that successive zeros of the wave pulse (corresponding to half wavelengths of a sinusoidal wave) are spaced a distance π/k_0 apart.

regions of space. Although the superposed wave, like each of the individual waves, extends throughout space and is not localized, the superposed wave has a considerably more "lumpy" nature than the individual waves. This suggests that adding more waves of still different frequencies and wave numbers might produce a *wave pulse* with a finite extension in space such as, for example, the wave shown in Fig. 6-20, which resembles a half cycle of the superposition of two sinusoidal waves. A more general superposition of several sinusoidal waves can be represented, at one instant of time, as

$$E = \sum_n A_n e^{ik_n x} \tag{6-36}$$

or even

$$E = \int A(k) e^{ikx} \, dk \tag{6-37}$$

in which a continuous distribution of values of k is used, and the function

$A(k)$ represents the amplitude of the component wave having wave number k. Representation of functions as superpositions of sinusoidal functions is called *Fourier analysis*. The expression in Eq. (6-36) is called a Fourier series, and Eq. (6-37) a Fourier integral. Fourier analysis is very useful in many different areas of physics.

By an appropriate choice of the function $A(k)$ it is possible to construct a localized *wave pulse*, also called a *wave packet*. If the speed u of the individual sinusoidal waves is independent of frequency (and therefore of k), the pulse also moves with this speed, and its shape is constant. But if the wave speed is a function of frequency, then the pulse speed is the *group velocity* introduced above, which is, in general, different from the wave speed. It can be shown that, if the pulse is constructed from waves whose wave numbers are all in the vicinity of a central wave number k_0, the group velocity is given by

$$v = \frac{d\omega}{dk} \tag{6-38}$$

where the derivative is evaluated at $k = k_0$. This agrees with Eq. (6-35), which was derived for the special case of the superposition of only two sinusoidal waves. Equation (6-38) is derived in Appendix C.

Wave packets are of great importance in quantum mechanics. In some experiments, elementary particles behave as though they were waves instead of particles. The concept of a wave packet provides the means of reconciling the apparently incompatible wave and particle aspects of the behavior of matter. We shall return to this important subject in Chap. 9.

Problems

6-1 A simple cubic crystal lattice has a lattice spacing of 0.2 nm. At what angles will constructive interference from planes parallel to a cube face occur, if x-rays with a wavelength of 0.1 nm are used?

6-2 In Prob. 6-1, at what angles will constructive interference be observed for each of the sets of planes shown in Fig. 6-3?

6-3 In a laboratory demonstration, a model of a crystal lattice is made by arranging small steel balls (1-cm diameter) in a cubic lattice with 10 cm spacing, embedding them in 10-cm-thick styrofoam slabs and stacking the slabs. If such an arrangement is then irradiated by 3-cm microwaves, find the angles at which the beam must strike the crystal face for Bragg reflection from planes parallel to the cube faces.

6-4 Small steel balls (1-cm diameter) are arranged in a square array in a plane, with 10-cm spacing. A microwave beam of wavelength 3 cm strikes the plane at normal incidence. In what direction will strong maxima in the resulting diffraction pattern be observed?

6-5 Ordinary rock salt (sodium chloride) has a cubic crystal lattice similar to Fig. 6-3, with the sodium and chlorine ions in alternate lattice sites. The lattice spacing a is 0.282 nm.
    a   Using the fact that the molecular mass of NaCl is 58.5 g/mol, compute the *density* of NaCl.
    b   For what wavelength x-rays is a Bragg reflection observed at $\theta = 10°$ in Fig. 6-2?

6-6 Potassium chloride (KCl) has the same crystal structure as NaCl, described in Prob. 6-5. Its molecular mass is 74.6 g/mol and its density is 3.13 g/cm^3.
    a   Compute the lattice spacing.
    b   At what angles is the Bragg condition satisfied for x-rays of wavelength 0.12 nm?

6-7 In a single-slit diffraction experiment, the slit is 0.1 mm wide and is illuminated by monochromatic light with a wavelength of 500 nm. The diffraction pattern is observed on a screen 10 m away. What is the spacing between successive minima in the pattern?

6-8 Derive a formula for the angular spacing of dark fringes in the diffraction pattern for a single slit, by observing that when the width of the slit is divided into halves, there are certain angles for which corresponding regions in the two halves are exactly 180° out of phase so that complete destructive interference occurs.

6-9 Consider the limit of the intensity distribution for diffraction from a single slit [Eq. (6-7)] when the width of the slit is much larger than a wavelength. Describe the resulting pattern.

6-10 Suppose the pattern shown in Fig. 6-9 was formed using a slit of a certain width d, a screen 2.0 m away from the slit, and light of wavelength 500 nm. Find the slit width.

6-11 A single slit is illuminated by light of wavelength 500 nm. A diffraction pattern is formed on a screen 50 cm away from the slit, and the distance between the first and third minima in the pattern is found to be 2.0 mm. What is the width of the slit?

6-12 A parallel beam of green mercury light of wavelength 546 nm passes through a slit of width 0.2 mm to a screen 4.0 m away.
    a   What is the width of the central maximum in the diffraction pattern, i.e., the distance between the two minima on either side of the central maximum?
    b   What is the width of the first maximum on either side of the central maximum?

6-13 A two-slit diffraction setup is made with two slits 0.05 mm wide, spaced 0.2 mm between centers.

    a   How many maxima in the two-slit interference pattern appear between the first minima of the fringe envelope (the single-slit diffraction pattern) on either side of the central maximum?

    b   If the wavelength is 500 nm, what is the angular separation between the second and third fringes in the interference pattern?

    c   What is the ratio of the intensity of the second fringe to the side of the center to that of the central fringe?

6-14 In a certain two-slit diffraction experiment, two slits 0.02 mm wide are spaced 0.2 mm between centers.

    a   How many fringes appear between the first minima of the single-slit "envelope" on either side of the central maximum?

    b   If the angle between the central maximum and the second fringe to either side of the central maximum is 0.17°, what is the wavelength?

6-15 A parallel beam of light of wavelength 500 nm is incident on a circular aperture 0.10 mm in diameter, forming a diffraction pattern on a screen 5.0 m away.

    a   What is the radius of the first dark ring in the pattern?

    b   If the wavelength is changed to 600 nm, what is the radius of the first dark ring?

6-16 A loudspeaker for a sound system is made in the form of a plane disk 20 cm in diameter. The radiation from this disk when it vibrates back and forth along its axis may be treated like that from a circular aperture. The speed of sound is about 360 m/s. Find the angular size of the central maximum in the resulting diffraction pattern if the frequency is:

    a   18 kHz

    b   3600 Hz

    c   180 Hz

This problem illustrates the tendency of loudspeakers to focus high-frequency sounds in a narrow beam.

6-17 Suppose a hologram is made with light of wavelength 600 nm (orange) and then viewed with light of wavelength 500 nm (green). How will the images differ from those that would be formed with the orange light?

6-18 How does image formation by a hologram compare with stereoscopic photography, in which two cameras take pictures from two slightly different positions? What are the most significant differences?

6-19 What would be the appearance of the image formed when a hologram is viewed with white light?

6-20 Do a hologram negative and the corresponding positive print (with black and white reversed) make the same image? (Note that changing the phase of the reference beam by 180° would reverse black and white on the hologram.)

6-21 The relative dielectric constant K_E of water is strongly temperature-dependent, decreasing from 88 at $0°C$ to 55 at $100°C$. How can this behavior be understood?

6-22 Is the phenomenon described in Prob. 6-21 consistent with the fact that the index of refraction of water for visible light (600 mm) varies only from about 1.33 to 1.32 over the same temperature range? Explain.

6-23 Make a calculation of the dielectric constant of a material, similar to that leading to Eq. (6-23), but starting with the assumption that the electrons are completely free instead of elastically bound. This resembles the state of affairs in the ionosphere. Show that the displacements are exactly $180°$ out of phase with the electric field, and so the relative dielectric constant is less than unity.

6-24 By combining Eq. (6-24) for the induced dipole moment of an elastically bound electron with the formulation of Sec. 5-1 concerning energy radiated by an oscillating dipole, find the total rate of energy scattering by an elastically bound electron in the presence of an electromagnetic wave of amplitude E_0 and frequency ω. What is the limit of this expression as the binding force becomes very small (a nearly free electron)? Express your results also in terms of the incident intensity I_0.

6-25 Why is the sky blue?

6-26 Why does the sky appear red in a sunset?

6-27 Calculate the energy density and the Poynting vector for a superposition of two sinusoidal electromagnetic waves, as discussed in Sec. 6-5, for the case where the wave speeds are slightly different. Show that the speed of energy transport is given by the group velocity, not the wave velocity of either wave.

Geometrical Optics | 7

Geometrical optics is an approximate method of calculating optical phenomena; it is based on a description of light as *rays* which travel in straight lines in a homogeneous medium. We discuss first the relationship of the ray and wave pictures. Reflection and refraction of spherical waves at plane surfaces are discussed, first using the wave description and then in terms of rays, and it is shown that the laws of reflection and refraction for rays can be derived from wave considerations. In this connection, the concept of *images* is introduced. Next, reflection and refraction of a spherical wave at a spherical surface are considered, and an approximate analysis of a thin lens is given. Finally, we discuss briefly some applications of lenses and mirrors in optical instruments.

7-1 WAVES AND RAYS

Although light is fundamentally a wave phenomenon, some important aspects of its propagation can be described in terms of lines called *rays* in the direction of propagation and perpendicular to the wavefronts. For a plane wave the rays are parallel lines in the direction of propagation; for spherical waves they radiate outward from the source. Figure 7-1 shows the relation between rays and wavefronts for these two kinds of waves. Description of light in terms of rays is the central concept in *geometrical optics,* and when diffraction and interference effects can be neglected, geometrical optics provides a very simple and convenient model for calculating the behavior of optical systems such as mirrors and lenses.

The principles of geometrical optics were discovered empirically before their relation to the wave picture was understood. They are as follows:

1 In a homogeneous medium each ray is a straight line.

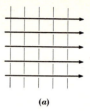

(a)

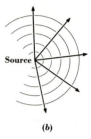

Source

(b)

Fig. 7-1 Relation of wave and ray descriptions. Solid lines are rays; broken lines are wavefronts (surfaces of constant phase). The two sets of lines are perpendicular at their intersections. (a) Plane wave; (b) spherical wave.

2 When a ray is *reflected* by a reflecting surface, the incident ray, the reflected ray, and the normal to the surface all lie in a single plane, and the incident and reflected rays make equal angles with the normal.

3 When a ray is *refracted* at an interface between two optical media with indices of refraction n_1 and n_2, the incident and transmitted rays and the normal to the surface all lie in a single plane, and the angles θ_1 and θ_2 which the incident and transmitted ray, respectively, make with the normal are related by

$$n_1 \sin \theta_1 = n_2 \sin \theta_2 \tag{7-1}$$

This relation is called *Snell's law* after Willebrord Snell (1591–1626), although there is some doubt whether he actually discovered it. Values of index of refraction for a few materials are given in Table 7-1.

Table 7-1 Index of Refraction of Various Materials (for $\lambda = 589$ nm)

Carbon disulfide (CS_2)	1.63
Diamond	2.42
Glass, crown	1.52
Glass, flint	1.65
Glass, heaviest flint	1.89
Ice	1.31
Quartz, fused	1.46
Rock salt (NaCl)	1.54
Water	1.33

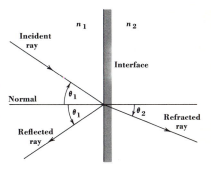

Fig. 7-2 Partial reflection and partial transmission of a ray at an interface between two optical media. The incident, reflected, and transmitted rays and the normal to the interface all lie in the plane of the figure.

At an interface between two media, a ray is in general partly reflected and partly transmitted; the above geometrical relations are illustrated in Fig. 7-2.

The above principles of geometrical optics, originally empirical in nature, can be derived from a general wave picture using Huygens' principle, discussed in Sec. 6-2 in connection with diffraction calculations. To derive Snell's law, for example, we consider the construction in Fig. 7-3; a wave is incident on an interface between two media, and the position of a wavefront is shown at three times. Secondary wavelets emitted from points a and b on the front ab reach points a' and b', respectively, at the same time. The secondary wavelet emitted from b', at the interface, has reached point b'' by the time the wavelet from a' has reached point a'' at the interface, and the line $a''b''$ defines the direction of the wavefront in the second medium.

Now the distances d_1 and d_2 in the figure are not equal because the wave speeds are different in the two media. By definition (Sec. 4-5), the index of refraction n in each medium is the ratio of the speed c in vacuum to the speed u in the medium; thus we have

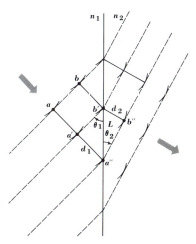

Fig. 7-3 Construction for deriving Snell's law from Huygens' principle. The broken lines represent wavefronts in the two media, and the arcs suggest the secondary wavelets proceeding from each front. For the case shown, n_2 is greater than n_1.

$$\frac{d_1}{d_2} = \frac{n_2}{n_1}$$

(7-2)

The distances d_1 and d_2 are also related by the geometry of the figure, which shows that

$$d_1 = L \sin \theta_1 \qquad \text{and} \qquad d_2 = L \sin \theta_2$$

or

$$\frac{d_1}{d_2} = \frac{\sin \theta_1}{\sin \theta_2}$$

(7-3)

Combining Eqs. (7-2) and (7-3) and rearranging, we obtain

$$n_1 \sin \theta_1 = n_2 \sin \theta_2$$

in agreement with Eq. (7-1). The law of reflection can be derived from Huygens' principle by a similar construction.

The laws of reflection and refraction can also be derived from electromagnetic theory, as indicated in Sec. 4-5; the *intensities* of the transmitted and reflected rays, and their variation with angle, can also be predicted. This analysis is much more complex than that based on Huygens' principle, but it is of fundamental importance because it supports the electromagnetic nature of light and also because the intensity relations cannot be obtained with the simpler theories.

We next consider the reflection and refraction of a *spherical* wave at a plane surface. Consider a small sector of a spherical wavefront, striking a small area of the reflecting surface. A sufficiently small sector of a spherical surface can be considered as approximately plane; the reflection from this small area is therefore expected to behave in the same way as the reflection of a plane wave, which results in another plane wave reflected with equal angles to the surface. Thus the part of the wave reflected from this element of surface is part of a spherical wave having the property that perpendiculars to the new spherical wavefronts (represented by the rays in Fig. 7-4a) emerge as though they had all originated at a point Q to the right of the reflecting surface, as shown.

In terms of the ray picture, a ray originates at point P, is reflected, and reaches the observer's eye so that the angles of incidence and reflection are equal. The observer in Fig. 7-4a judges the position of the source by the directions of the rays (or wavefronts) reaching his eyes; to this observer it appears that the source is at point Q. Thus the mirror is said to produce an *image* of the source P at the point Q. A plane mirror *always* produces an image, behind the mirror a distance equal to the source distance, such that the line joining P and Q is perpendicular to the plane of the mirror.

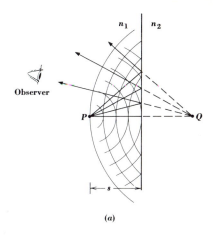

(a)

Fig. 7-4 (a) Spherical wave partially reflected by the interface between two media. The reflected wave is as though it had originated at point Q, independent of the relative magnitudes of n_1 and n_2. (b) Spherical wave partially transmitted through the interface. The refracted wave near the horizontal axis is approximately a spherical wave with its center at the point Q, whose position is given by Eq. (7-4). For the case shown, $n_2 > n_1$; note that the wavelength is smaller in the second medium.

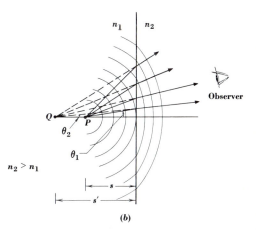

(b)

A similar analysis can be carried out for *refraction* of spherical waves by a plane surface between two media having different indices of refraction. Just as above, we consider a small area of the interface and regard the spherical wave striking that small area as practically a plane wave. The reflected wave obeys the law of reflection, and the direction of the refracted wave is determined by Snell's law. Thus, the small segments of spherical wave can be expected to proceed as shown in Fig. 7-4b, in which the ray representation of the segments is shown.

The result is a *reflected* spherical wave in the first medium, and a *transmitted* wave in the second medium. Just as in the previous case of reflection, the reflected wave proceeds backward in the first medium as though it had originated at a point Q in the second medium, as in Fig. 7-4a. The transmitted wave is somewhat more complicated. For a transmitted ray near the axis of Fig. 7-4b, the backward projection of the corresponding ray crosses the axis at a distance s' given by

$$s \tan \theta_1 = s' \tan \theta_2 \tag{7-4}$$

If the rays are nearly parallel to the axis, the angles θ_1 and θ_2 are small, so that, approximately,

$$\tan \theta_1 \cong \sin \theta_1 \qquad \text{and} \qquad \tan \theta_2 \cong \sin \theta_2 \tag{7-5}$$

Making this approximation in Eq. (7-4) and combining the result with Eq. (7-1), we find

$$\frac{s'}{s} = \frac{n_2}{n_1} \tag{7-6}$$

The *central part* of the transmitted spherical wave, that is, the part proceeding nearly perpendicular to the refracting surface, has the same shape as though it had been emitted by a source at Q as shown; it is said that there is an *image* of the real source at this point. It is important to note that this result is correct *only* for that part of the wave whose propagation is approximately perpendicular to the interface. Taken as a whole, the refracted wave is *not* precisely a spherical wave but has a more complicated form. Thus Eq. (7-6) is an approximation, valid for the condition known as "normal incidence," that is, when the rays are all nearly normal (perpendicular) to the interface. This approximation is also called the *paraxial approximation*, and the rays nearly parallel to the normal are called *paraxial rays*.

The image associated with the refracted wave in the above discussion is responsible for the fact that, when one looks down at a body of water from the air above, objects under water always seem to be *closer* than they really are. In this case, n_2 is the index of refraction of air, approximately unity, while n_1 is the index of refraction of water, about 1.33. Thus the image position s' is closer to the surface than the actual position s. At highly oblique viewing angles the object always appears distorted and blurred, corresponding to the failure of the paraxial approximation; this effect is noticeable when looking obliquely into an aquarium.

The three principles of geometrical optics stated at the beginning of this section form the basis for a complete ray treatment of light. They describe all phenomena in geometrical optics and are sufficient to solve any problem. In this sense, geometrical optics is one of the *simplest* of all physical theories. Detailed calculations of optical phenomena can easily become extremely complicated, however. Even in the simple case of refraction of a spherical wave by a plane surface between two media, we found it necessary to make an approximation in order to obtain a simple result. Similar approximations have to be made in the next section, where we deal with the reflection and refraction of spherical waves by spherical surfaces in lenses. In the remainder of this chapter we shall concentrate on the simplest possible calculations, making approximations where necessary to avoid complications inherent in more precise treatments.

7-2 REFLECTION AT A SPHERICAL SURFACE

We consider next the reflection of a spherical wave by a spherical surface. We can distinguish two general cases. In the first, the source is much *closer* to the mirror than its center of curvature C, as in Fig. 7-5a. In this case, the reflected wave should have characteristics similar to the case of a spherical wave reflected from a *plane* surface and thus should proceed away from the mirror as though it had originated at an image point Q, as shown in the figure. But, if the distance from the source to mirror is *large* compared with the radius of curvature of the mirror, a spherical wavefront strikes the edges of the mirror before striking its center; consideration of the resulting phase relationship shows that the curvature of the reflected wave should have the opposite sense; that is, it should *converge* toward an image point Q, as shown in Fig. 7-5b. This also happens when the source P is located *at* the center

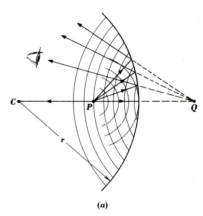

(a)

Fig. 7-5 Reflection of a spherical wave from a spherical mirror of radius r. (a) When the source P is much closer than the center of curvature C, the reflected wave proceeds as though it had originated at Q, which is the image of P. (b) When the source P is much farther away than the center of curvature, the reflected wave converges toward a real image point Q.

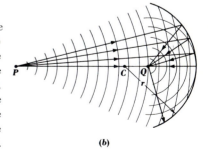

(b)

of curvature, for then spherical waves reach all parts of the spherical mirror simultaneously and are reflected back exactly in phase, so that the reflected spherical wave has precisely the same center of curvature as the original spherical wave. In this case, the image point and the source coincide.

Now we analyze this reflection in detail, using the ray picture together with appropriate approximations. The basis for the calculations is Fig. 7-6. The line through the center O of the mirror, perpendicular to a tangent plane at that point, is called the *optic axis*. A ray originates at point P, a distance p from O, making a small angle α with the optic axis. It is reflected through the point Q, a distance q from O. The radius of curvature of the mirror is r; C is its center of curvature, and, following the law of reflection, the incident and reflected rays make equal angles with the radius line from the center to the mirror surface. In terms of the angles in Fig. 7-6, the distance y in the figure may be variously expressed as

$$y = p \tan \alpha = r \sin (\alpha + \beta) = q \tan (\alpha + 2\beta) \tag{7-7}$$

If the angles α and β are sufficiently small, the angle, its sine, and its tangent are all very nearly equal. Thus Eqs. (7-7) become approximately

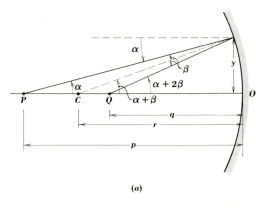

(a)

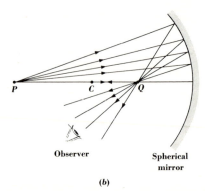

Fig. 7-6 (a) Ray diagram used to derive the object and image distance relation for a spherical mirror. For rays nearly parallel to the axis, all rays originating at P are reflected through Q, resulting in a real image at Q. (b) Several rays originating at P, reflected through Q.

(b)

$$p\alpha = r(\alpha + \beta) = q(\alpha + 2\beta) \tag{7-8}$$

We may divide these equations by β and eliminate the ratio α/β to obtain

$$\frac{1}{p} + \frac{1}{q} = \frac{2}{r} \tag{7-9}$$

The most important feature of this equation is that it does *not* contain the angles α and β. This shows that a ray originating from point P is reflected through point Q, no matter at what angle it leaves P, provided that the angle is *small*.

Figure 7-6b shows several rays originating at P and reflected through Q. The rays then diverge again from Q, so that to an observer to the left of this point it seems that Q is the source of the rays. Thus Q is an *image* of the source at P. In contrast to some of the images previously considered, the rays actually *do* diverge from this point. For this reason, Q is said to be a *real* image. Conversely, images consisting of rays that only *appear* to diverge from a certain point are usually called *virtual* images.

When the source distance becomes very great, $p \to \infty$, the incoming waves are very nearly plane waves. In this case, Eq. (7-9) gives for the image distance $q = r/2$. Thus, an incoming plane wave is reflected through a point at a distance $r/2$ away from the mirror. Conversely, a source at this point is reflected as a parallel beam, that is, a plane wave. This point, labeled F in diagrams, is called the *focus* of the mirror; its distance from the mirror is the *focal length*, usually denoted by f. Thus, for a spherical mirror, $f = r/2$ and

$$\frac{1}{p} + \frac{1}{q} = \frac{1}{f} \tag{7-10}$$

We emphasize again that, because of the approximations made in deriving this equation, only those rays striking the mirror near its center can be expected to be reflected *precisely* through the focus. The deviations occurring for rays far from the optic axis or making large angles with it are called *spherical aberrations*. It is possible to design a mirror that precisely focuses a parallel beam (plane wave); such a mirror is *paraboloidal* in shape. Reflecting astronomical telescopes are always used to view very distant objects, where the light rays are very nearly parallel, and mirrors for such telescopes are usually paraboloidal rather than spherical.

When the source distance p is *less* than the focal length f, Eq. (7-10) gives a *negative* value for the image distance q. This corresponds to a reflected wave which is a diverging spherical wave, appearing to originate from a virtual source to the right of the mirror, as in Fig. 7-5a. Thus a negative value of q means a virtual image to the right of the mirror, rather than a real image to the left. A similar consideration can be applied to the case where the incoming wave is produced by another mirror or lens and is a *converging* spherical wave, as shown in Fig. 7-7, rather than a wave that appears to originate from a point. In this case it is useful to introduce the concept of a *virtual object,* defined as the point at which the incoming rays *would* converge if they were not first reflected by the mirror. Point P in Fig. 7-7 is such a virtual object, and the corresponding object distance p is negative. Finally, the mirror may be *convex* rather than concave. A parallel beam is then reflected as though it had originated from a point a distance $f = r/2$ to the right of the mirror. This case is consistent with Eq. (7-10) provided we regard f and r as *negative* quantities.

The discussion of formation of images by a spherical mirror can easily be extended to the more general case when the source, or *object,* is not a single point but is extended in space. For each point P of the object there is a corresponding image point Q, lying on the line through P and the center of curvature C. The distance q of each image point from the center O of the mirror is again related to the distance p of the corresponding object point by Eq. (7-10). An immediate corollary is that, for an object whose points all lie in a *plane* perpendicular to the optic axis, the distance p is (in the paraxial approximation) the same for all points, and so all the image points are also equidistant from O. That is, in this approximation, *the image of a plane object is also plane.*

Understanding of the formation of images of extended objects is facilitated by a construction called a *principal-ray diagram.* We select a point on the object, such as point P in Fig. 7-8. There are four rays which can always be located easily:

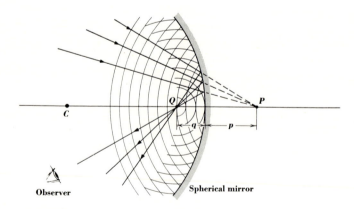

Fig. 7-7 A converging incident spherical wave can be represented as a virtual source at
P, toward which the wave would converge if the mirror were not present. The
corresponding object distance p is negative.

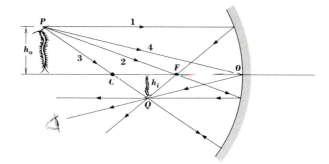

Fig. 7-8 Principal-ray diagram, showing the formation of a real image by a spherical mirror. Numbers on the four principal rays correspond to those in the text.

1 A ray that leaves P parallel to the optic axis is reflected through the focus F.

2 Conversely, a ray from P that passes through the focus F is reflected back parallel to the optic axis.

3 A ray that passes through the center of curvature C strikes the mirror perpendicularly and is reflected back along itself.

4 A ray striking the center O of the mirror is reflected so as to make equal angles with the optic axis.

These four rays are shown in Fig. 7-8. They converge at a point Q, which is therefore a real image of point P. This figure could be used for an alternative derivation of Eq. (7-10); it also provides a useful relation between the *sizes* of object and image. By considering the similar triangles formed by P, Q, O, and the optic axis, we see that the sizes of object and image, which we may call h_o and h_i, respectively, are directly proportional to the distances from the mirror:

$$\frac{h_i}{h_o} = -\frac{q}{p} \tag{7-11}$$

The negative sign shows that when p and q are positive, the image is *inverted* relative to the object. This equation is useful in computing magnifying powers of optical instruments, to be discussed in Sec. 7-5.

As a numerical example, if in Fig. 7-8 $f = 20$ cm, $p = 60$ cm, and $h_o = 4$ cm, then

$$\frac{1}{60 \text{ cm}} + \frac{1}{q} = \frac{1}{20 \text{ cm}} \qquad q = 30 \text{ cm}$$

$$\frac{h_i}{4 \text{ cm}} = -\frac{30 \text{ cm}}{60 \text{ cm}} \qquad h_i = -2 \text{ cm}$$

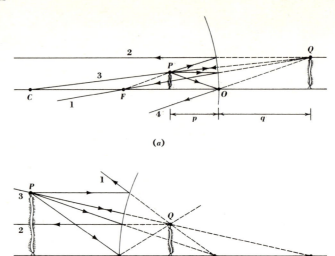

(a)

(b)

Fig. 7-9 Principal-ray diagrams for image formation by mirrors. (a) Concave mirror with object closer to mirror than focus. (b) Convex mirror.

Figure 7-9 shows two more examples of principal-ray diagrams. In Fig. 7-9a, the object distance p is less than f, and the image is virtual. In Fig. 7-9b, $p > f$ but the mirror is convex and again the image is virtual. In both these cases the principal rays must be extended backward (broken lines) to the point from which they appear to originate. In Fig. 7-9a, if $f = 20$ cm, $p = 10$ cm, and $h_o = 4$ cm, then

$$\frac{1}{10\text{ cm}} + \frac{1}{q} = \frac{1}{20\text{ cm}} \qquad q = -20\text{ cm}$$

$$\frac{h_i}{4\text{ cm}} = -\frac{-20\text{ cm}}{10\text{ cm}} \qquad h_i = 8\text{ cm}$$

In Fig. 7-9b, if $f = -20$ cm, $p = 20$ cm, and $h_o = 4$ cm, then

$$\frac{1}{20\text{ cm}} + \frac{1}{q} = \frac{1}{-20\text{ cm}} \qquad q = -10\text{ cm}$$

$$\frac{h_i}{4\text{ cm}} = -\frac{-10\text{ cm}}{20\text{ cm}} \qquad h_i = 2\text{ cm}$$

7-3   REFRACTION AT A SPHERICAL SURFACE

Next, as a step toward analysis of the behavior of lenses, we consider the *refraction* of a spherical wave by a spherical surface between two optical

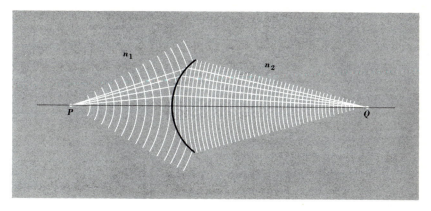

Fig. 7-10 A spherical wave from P in the first medium is refracted at the spherical interface, resulting in an approximately spherical wave converging toward the real image point Q in the second medium. Corresponding rays are shown. In this example, $n_2 > n_1$.

media. The wave is partly reflected and partly refracted (transmitted); the reflected wave is governed by the considerations given in Sec. 7-2, and so in this section we concentrate on the *refracted* wave. In Fig. 7-10 a spherical wave originating at point P is refracted at a spherical interface with radius of curvature r between two media with indices of refraction n_1 and n_2. The resulting wave is, at least in the paraxial approximation, a converging spherical wave corresponding to rays which converge at the point Q in the second medium. Thus Q is a *real image* of the source, or object, at P.

Just as with the spherical mirror, we can derive a relationship between object and image distances. The appropriate ray diagram is shown in Fig. 7-11. The various angles are related by the requirement that the sum of interior angles in a triangle must be $180°$. Applying this to each of the triangles that share the side passing through C, we obtain the relations

$$\alpha + \gamma + (180° - \theta_1) = 180° \qquad \text{or} \qquad \theta_1 = \alpha + \gamma$$
$$\theta_2 + \beta + (180° - \gamma) = 180° \qquad \text{or} \qquad \gamma = \theta_2 + \beta \tag{7-12}$$

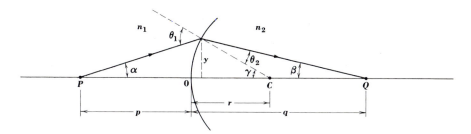

Fig. 7-11 Ray diagram for the derivation of the equation relating object and image distances for refraction by a spherical surface. All angles are actually very small but are exaggerated here for clarity. For the case shown, $n_2 > n_1$.

Next, the distance y can be expressed in a variety of ways, as follows:

$$y = p \tan \alpha = q \tan \beta = r \sin \gamma \qquad (7\text{-}13)$$

which, for small angles, gives

$$\alpha p = \beta q = \gamma r \qquad (7\text{-}14)$$

Finally, Snell's law in the small-angle approximation is

$$n_1 \theta_1 = n_2 \theta_2 \qquad (7\text{-}15)$$

Now it is possible to combine the five simultaneous equations for the angles, Eqs. (7-12), (7-14), and (7-15), to eliminate all the angles, just as with the spherical mirror. The reader can supply the details of this calculation; the result is

$$\frac{n_1}{p} + \frac{n_2}{q} = \frac{n_2 - n_1}{r} \qquad (7\text{-}16)$$

the general form of which is pleasingly similar to Eq. (7-9) for the spherical mirror.

Just as with the spherical mirror, it is possible for the image distance q to turn out negative. In such a case, the refracted wave does not converge to the right of the interface but *diverges* in such a way as to appear to have originated at a point to the left of the surface a distance $-q$. Correspondingly, when the incident wave is a converging spherical wave that *would* converge at a certain distance to the *right* of the interface if the interface were not there, the object distance p is negative. Lastly, the curvature of the surface may be opposite to that shown. When the center of curvature is to the left, r is a negative quantity. These sign conventions are summarized as follows:

1 p is positive when the object point is to the left, negative otherwise.

2 q is positive when the image point is to the right, negative otherwise.

3 r is positive if the center of curvature is to the right, negative otherwise.

We might now proceed to discuss the action of a spherical surface on plane waves and define a focus and a focal length, just as in the case of the spherical mirror. In practical situations, however, spherical surfaces are usually used in pairs, in the form of *lenses*, and so we proceed immediately to a discussion of the situation where there are two adjacent spherical surfaces.

7-4 THIN LENSES

We now consider an optical system consisting of a thin piece of material of index of refraction n_2, with spherical surfaces of radii r_1 and r_2, respectively, embedded in a medium of index of refraction n_1. Such a system is called a *lens*. When the lens is in vacuum, $n_1 = 1$; for air at ordinary temperature and pressure, $n = 1.00028$, and the approximation $n_1 = 1$ is usually used. It is, however, useful to include in the analysis the possibility that the lens may be immersed in some other fluid, for which n_1 is different from unity.

The analysis proceeds as follows: If the second surface were not present, the first would form an image of any object placed to the left of it. The second surface may interfere with the actual formation of this image, but it does not alter the fact that rays emerge from the first surface in directions characteristic of a particular image position. If they are converging, the image position is to the right of the first surface; if diverging, to the left. Thus it is perfectly legitimate to regard this image as an *object* for the second surface, even though it may not actually be formed when the second surface is present. The image still exists in the sense that the directions of the rays emerging from the first surface are characteristic of a certain image position. Let p_1 and q_1 represent the object and image positions for the first surface, and p_2 and q_2 those for the second surface, with the usual sign conventions. Applying Eq. (7-16) to each of the two surfaces, we find

$$\frac{n_1}{p_1} + \frac{n_2}{q_1} = \frac{n_2 - n_1}{r_1} \tag{7-17a}$$

$$\frac{n_2}{p_2} + \frac{n_1}{q_2} = \frac{n_1 - n_2}{r_2} \tag{7-17b}$$

In the second equation the roles of n_1 and n_2 are reversed, since for the second surface the medium characterized by n_1 is on the right rather than on the left.

Next, we note that the *image* formed by the first surface is the *object* for the second. Furthermore, if the first image distance q_1 is positive, the corresponding object distance for the second surface is negative, and conversely; thus if the thickness of the lens is negligible, we have $q_1 = -p_2$. Using this relationship together with Eqs. (7-17), we can eliminate q_1 and p_2 to obtain a single equation relating the original object distance p_1 and the final image distance q_2. The result is

$$\frac{1}{p_1} + \frac{1}{q_2} = \left(\frac{n_2}{n_1} - 1\right)\left(\frac{1}{r_1} - \frac{1}{r_2}\right) \tag{7-18}$$

Having obtained this equation, we may now describe the lens as a single unit; we drop the subscripts on p and q and simply state that the first object position p and the final image position q are related by

$$\frac{1}{p} + \frac{1}{q} = \left(\frac{n_2}{n_1} - 1\right)\left(\frac{1}{r_1} - \frac{1}{r_2}\right) \tag{7-19}$$

The same sign conventions apply to this equation as for the single-surface equation (7-16).

When the source or object is very far away, the incident waves are practically plane waves. The point at which such plane waves are focused is called the *focus,* and the corresponding value of q is called the *focal length* of the lens, denoted by f, just as for the spherical mirror. That is, an incident plane wave, corresponding to rays parallel to the axis, is brought to focus at a distance f from the lens, where

$$\frac{1}{f} = \left(\frac{n_2}{n_1} - 1\right)\left(\frac{1}{r_1} - \frac{1}{r_2}\right) \tag{7-20}$$

Equation (7-20), called the *lensmaker's equation,* shows that, within the approximations we have made, the lens is *symmetric;* if it is reversed, side to side, the focal length and all the other characteristics remain unchanged. This can be verified by noting that turning it over corresponds to interchanging r_1 and r_2 and changing the signs on both. Once the focal length f is known, the lens equation can be written somewhat more simply:

$$\frac{1}{p} + \frac{1}{q} = \frac{1}{f} \tag{7-21}$$

For an ordinary lens in air, $n_2 > n_1$; in that case examination of Eq. (7-20) shows that f is positive whenever the lens is thicker at the center than the edge. This is true, for example, when $r_1 > 0$ and $r_2 < 0$ (double-convex lens) or when both r_1 and r_2 are positive and $r_2 > r_1$ (concavo-convex lens). But some lenses are thicker at the edge than the middle, as is the case if $r_1 < 0$ and $r_2 > 0$ (double-concave lens) or if r_1 and r_2 are positive but $r_2 < r_1$. In all such cases f is a *negative* quantity. In this case a beam of parallel rays is not brought to a real focus but rather *diverges* from the lens as though it had originated from a virtual focus a distance f to the left of the lens; such a lens is called a *diverging lens.*

Similarly, it is possible for q to be negative, indicating a virtual image to the left of the lens, or for p to be negative, corresponding to a virtual *object* describing rays which converge as they approach the first surface, as though they would meet a distance p to the right of the lens. Finally, the lens may have a *plane* surface, in which case we set the corresponding radius equal to infinity and the term drops out of the lensmaker's equation.

Understanding of the formation of an image by a lens is facilitated by constructing a principal-ray diagram of the same sort used for the spherical mirror. The principal rays which are most easily drawn are:

1 A ray parallel to the optic axis, which is refracted through the focus

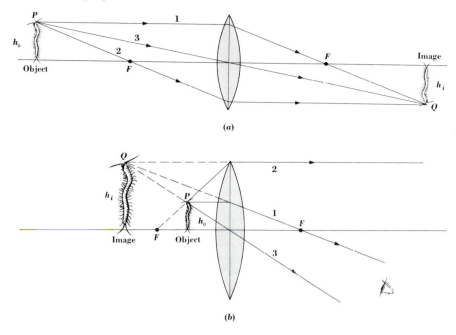

Fig. 7-12 Principal-ray diagrams showing image formation by a convex lens. (*a*) When the object distance is greater than the focal length, a real, inverted image is formed. (*b*) When the object distance is less than the focal length, a virtual, erect image is formed; its position is obtained by projecting the principal rays backward. The rays appear to come from point *Q*.

2 A ray passing through the focus, refracted parallel to the optic axis

3 A ray which passes straight through the center of the lens and which is not deviated at all

Figure 7-12 shows two principal-ray diagrams. In Fig. 7-12*a* the object is farther from the lens than the focal length, and a real image results. In Fig. 7-12*b* the object is closer than the focal length, resulting in a virtual image. In this case it is necessary to project the rays backward to find the intersection point corresponding to the position of the virtual image. Figure 7-13 shows a principal-ray diagram for a diverging lens. We note that such a lens always forms a virtual image if the object is real, and that the image is always smaller and closer to the lens than the object.

In all the above cases, as the principal-ray diagrams show, the object and image heights h_o and h_i, respectively, are related to the object and image distances by

$$\frac{h_i}{h_o} = -\frac{q}{p}$$

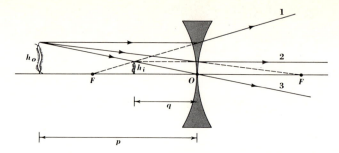

Fig. 7-13 Formation of virtual image of real object by diverging lens. Ray 1 starts parallel to the axis and emerges as though it had come from the first focus F; ray 2 starts as though it were going through the second focus F and emerges parallel to the axis. The first two rays must be extended backward to obtain the apparent point of origin, the position of the virtual image.

just as for spherical mirrors. For example, if in Fig. 7-13 $f = -20$ cm, $p = 30$ cm, and $h_o = 5$ cm,

$$\frac{1}{30 \text{ cm}} + \frac{1}{q} = \frac{1}{-20 \text{ cm}} \qquad q = -12 \text{ cm}$$

$$\frac{h_i}{5 \text{ cm}} = -\frac{-12 \text{ cm}}{30 \text{ cm}} \qquad h_i = 2 \text{ cm}$$

We emphasize again that this entire discussion of lenses is an approximate one. We have assumed throughout that all rays are very nearly parallel to the optic axis. For rays sufficiently far from the optic axis, various deviations, called *aberrations*, begin to appear. In the design of precise optical equipment, such as camera lenses, it is always necessary to use several lenses in combination, to cancel partially the effects of these aberrations.

Another important factor in many optical devices is *dispersion;* in general the index of refraction of the material varies with wavelength, so that the focal length of the lens is a function of wavelength. This results in *chromatic aberration,* which in precise optical equipment is corrected in part by using combinations of lenses having different indices of refraction and dispersion.

The design of such optical systems is an extremely complex operation, frequently involving a considerable amount of trial-and-error calculation. The development of high-speed digital computers in recent years has made possible the design of lens systems which otherwise would be hopelessly complicated to calculate. These include zoom lenses with variable focal length, extremely wide-angle lenses, and many other special-purpose lenses. Even in the most complicated cases, however, the same basic principles are involved as in the simple examples discussed here.

7-5 OPTICAL INSTRUMENTS

We conclude this chapter on geometrical optics with a very brief discussion of several simple applications of lenses and mirrors in optical instruments. One of the simplest is the use of a lens in a *camera*, as shown in Fig. 7-14*a*. The function of the lens is simply to create at the position of the film a real image of the object being photographed, as shown. The simplified discussion of this chapter would indicate that this can be accomplished with a single lens; actually camera lenses usually contain several elements, in order to reduce various aberrations.

A similar problem is that of a slide or motion-picture projector. Here the function is just opposite that of a camera lens: The lens creates an enlarged real image on a screen of a transparent film or slide, as shown in Fig. 7-14*b*. These two applications of lenses have several features in common. In both cases the ratio of object to image size is the same as the ratio of object and image distance from the lens; the image is *real* and is *inverted* with respect to the object. These features and the same general principles are also characteristic of the operation of the human eye, in which the lens produces a real inverted image on the retina.

A slightly more subtle application of a single lens is that of a simple magnifying glass. The closer an object is to the eye, the more detail can be seen, but most persons cannot focus their eyes comfortably on an object closer than about 25 cm. The function of a magnifying glass is to form an enlarged

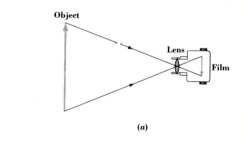

(a)

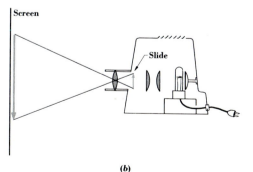

Fig. 7-14 (*a*) A camera lens forms a real inverted image, reduced in size, at the position of the film. (*b*) Projector forms a real, inverted, enlarged image of a slide or other transparent object, on a projection screen. The lenses between bulb and slide serve to concentrate light from the bulb on the slide; they are called condenser lenses.

(b)

image at a distance sufficiently far away from the eyes to be comfortable for viewing. Unlike the case of the camera or slide projector, the image need not be real. Figure 7-15, which is drawn approximately to scale, shows how a magnifying glass with $f = 5$ cm forms an enlarged, erect virtual image of an object located closer to the lens than the focus.

It is customary to define the *magnification* of an optical system as the ratio of the *angular size* (ratio of size to distance from the eye) of the image using the instrument to that without the instrument, under the most favorable conditions. For the magnifying glass, "most favorable conditions" means as close as possible with comfort, namely, 25 cm away from the eye. Thus in the example of Fig. 7-15 the magnification is about 4, often written as $4\times$. In practice, lens aberrations usually limit the magnification of simple magnifying glasses to about $3\times$.

For greater magnification it is often desirable to use two or more lenses in combination. We consider here only the two simplest examples, the compound microscope and the astronomical telescope. Figure 7-16 shows the general construction of a compound microscope. The lens closest to the object, called the *objective lens*, forms a real, enlarged, inverted image of the object in the barrel of the microscope. The second lens, called the *eyepiece lens*, uses this image as its object and forms a final virtual, enlarged, erect image, which can be located at a distance from the eye convenient for comfortable viewing. Compound microscopes constructed according to this general scheme

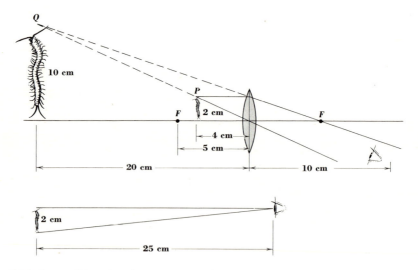

Fig. 7-15 A magnifying glass forms an enlarged, erect virtual image. The angular size of this image in the situation shown is approximately 10 cm/30 cm or $\frac{1}{3}$. The angular size of the object at the closest distance for comfortable viewing is 2 cm/25 cm or $\frac{2}{25}$. The magnification in this situation is $\frac{1}{3} / \frac{2}{25}$, or about 4.

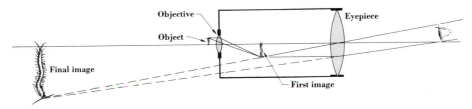

Fig. 7-16 A compound microscope. The objective lens, whose focal length is usually only a few millimeters, forms a real image in the microscope barrel. This image forms the object from which the eyepiece forms the final virtual image. Sizes of object and images, as well as the diameter of the barrel, have been exaggerated for clarity.

but using more complex lens groupings can be made with a magnification of several hundred.

The operation of the refracting astronomical telescope, shown in Fig. 7-17, is very similar to that of the compound microscope, except for differences in magnitudes of the various focal lengths. Like the compound microscope, it makes use of an objective lens, forming a real image in the barrel of the telescope, and an eyepiece lens which forms an enlarged virtual image of the first image. The final image, as in the case of the compound microscope, is inverted with respect to the object. This is the principle of operation of most ordinary binoculars, which also use a pair of *prisms* for each eye, in which internal reflections invert the image (up and down and right to left) back to the same orientation as the object. Binoculars typically have a magnification of 5 to 20, although telescopes with much greater magnifying powers can be made using this principle.

Finally, we consider briefly the principle of the reflecting telescope. Its operation is similar to that of the telescope just described, except that the

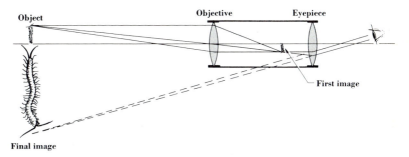

Fig. 7-17 A refracting astronomical telescope. The objective lens forms a real image in the telescope barrel, and the eyepiece forms a final virtual image. Object and image sizes are exaggerated. In telescopic sights and transits, the cross hairs may be located at the position of the first image; they then appear to be superimposed on the actual object. The final image is usually located far away, for most comfortable viewing.

objective lens is replaced by a concave mirror. When the telescope is to be used only with very distant objects, this scheme has several advantages. One is that a mirror is intrinsically free from chromatic aberration. Another is that by making the mirror paraboloidal instead of spherical, the spherical aberrations mentioned in Sec. 7-2 can be completely eliminated in the first image. A third is that it is usually easier and cheaper to make large mirrors than lenses of comparable size. The general shape of a reflecting telescope is shown in Fig. 7-18.

Throughout this chapter we have neglected effects associated with *diffraction*. Since the apertures involved in optical instruments for visible light are usually very large compared with the wavelengths of light, it might seem that diffraction effects are completely negligible. Nevertheless, in very precise work, such as photographic work requiring very high resolution, diffraction effects usually determine the ultimate limit of sharpness of the image produced by a lens. The image of a point object is not really a point,

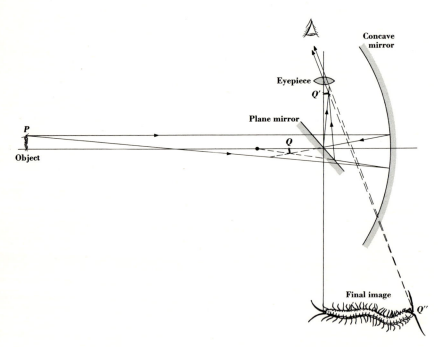

Fig. 7-18 A reflecting telescope. The image formed by the mirror is brought away from the optic axis by a small plane mirror placed at 45° to the optic axis. Q shows the image the concave mirror would form if the plane mirror were not present; Q' is the (real) image formed of this image by the plane mirror. Alternatively, the plane mirror may be placed normal to the optic axis and the first image brought out to the right through a hole in the mirror. The eyepiece forms a final virtual image as shown. Not all the rays in this diagram are principal rays.

even with perfectly accurate lens surfaces, but is a *diffraction pattern* characteristic of the emergence of light from a circular aperture, as discussed in Sec. 6-2. The angular size of the central maximum in this pattern is given by

$$\sin \theta = 1.22 \frac{\lambda}{a} \qquad (7\text{-}22)$$

where a is the diameter of the lens or mirror from which the light emerges to form the image. In the idealization of *geometrical* optics the angular size of the diffraction pattern would be zero; larger and larger values of θ correspond to greater and greater departures from this idealization and to increasing fuzziness of the image. Thus diffraction effects are more troublesome with small apertures than large; this is part of the motivation for constructing reflecting telescopes with extremely large reflectors, such as the 200-in-diameter reflector of the Hale telescope at Mount Palomar. (Increased *intensity* of the final image is also an important consideration.)

A useful rule of thumb called *Rayleigh's criterion* is that images of two point objects can barely be distinguished ("resolved") as separate points if their diffraction patterns overlap so that the central maximum of one coincides with the first minimum of the other. This occurs when the angular separation of the points is the angle θ given by Eq. (7-22). Thus the ultimate limit on the resolution of a camera or telescope lens is set by this criterion. In ordinary lenses the accuracy of the optical surfaces is usually the determining factor for the resolution, but in lenses and mirrors of the highest precision the quality of the image is limited by diffraction effects.

Example
If the resolution of a telescope is limited by diffraction at its 5-cm-diameter objective lens, what is the minimum distance between two objects that can be resolved at a distance of 2 km?

Solution
We take $\lambda = 500$ nm, characteristic of the center of the visible spectrum. According to Rayleigh's criterion, the minimum angular separation of the objects is given by

$$\sin \theta = 1.22 \frac{500 \times 10^{-9} \text{ m}}{5 \times 10^{-2} \text{ m}} = 1.2 \times 10^{-5}$$

The angular separation at 2 km of two objects a distance d apart is

$$\theta = \frac{d}{2 \times 10^3 \text{ m}}$$

We set this equal to the above angle, noting that no appreciable error is introduced by taking $\sin \theta = \theta$. We find

$$d = 2.4 \times 10^{-2} \text{ m} = 2.4 \text{ cm}$$

Problems

7-1 A fish in a pool appears to a fisherman to be 5 ft below the surface. What is its real depth below the surface?

7-2 An observer 1 m away from a glass slab 1 m thick, having $n = 1.5$, looks at an object 1 m away from the opposite side of the slab, 3 m away from him.
   a How far away does the object appear to be?
   b At what distance would a camera have to be focused to photograph the object in this situation?

7-3 Consider a "corner" constructed from three mutually perpendicular plane mirrors, such as an inside corner of a cube. Show that a ray of light directed into this corner always emerges after reflection in a direction parallel to its original direction. This principle is used in the design of reflectors for highway safety and other uses.

7-4 It is often said that the image formed by a plane mirror reverses right and left but not top and bottom. Is this true? Explain.

7-5 What minimum height must a wall mirror have, and how should it be located on a vertical wall, so that a person 6 ft tall whose eyes are 6 in below the top of his head can see himself from shoes to top of head?

7-6 Show that a mirror with parabolic cross section exactly focuses a parallel beam to a point.

7-7 Show that reflections from the inside of a prolate ellipsoid of revolution have the property that light from a source at one focus of the ellipsoid is focused at the other focus. A similar effect with sound accounts in part for the unusual acoustic properties of some buildings with rounded ceilings, such as the Mormon Tabernacle in Salt Lake City.

7-8 For a concave spherical mirror of radius r, plot a graph showing the image distance q as a function of object distance p. Indicate the radius and focal length on the p scale.

7-9 A concave spherical mirror has a radius $r = 10$ cm. Find the location, size, and orientation of the image of an object 1 cm high, and draw a principal-ray diagram showing formation of the image, for the cases:

    a $p = 10$ cm

    b $p = 4$ cm

7-10 Consider a convex spherical mirror with $r = -10$ cm.

    a   Under what conditions does the mirror form a real image of a real object?

    b   Describe the position, size, and orientation of the image formed of an object 1 cm high 10 cm from the mirror. Draw a principal-ray diagram.

7-11 For a spherical interface of radius r between two optical media, with the same orientation as Fig. 7-10, draw graphs showing image position q as a function of object position p when:

    a $n_2 > n_1$

    b $n_2 < n_1$

7-12 A spherical interface of radius $r = 5$ cm separates two media whose indices of refraction are $n_1 = 1$ and $n_2 = 1.5$. The surface is concave to the right. Find the image size, position, and orientation for an object 1 cm high placed:

    a   20 cm to the left of the surface

    b   5 cm to the left

7-13 Repeat Prob. 7-12 for the case where the surface is concave to the left.

7-14 A parallel beam (plane wave) strikes a transparent sphere of radius R and index of refraction n. At what point is the beam focused?

7-15 A long solid glass cylinder of index of refraction 1.5 is 10 cm in diameter, and one end is a hemispherical surface with radius 5 cm. A small object is placed on the axis; find the position, size, orientation, and nature of the image if the object is:

    a   20 cm from the hemispherical end

    b   5 cm from the hemispherical end

7-16 The glass cylinder of Prob. 7-15 is immersed in water ($n = 1.33$). Find the image positions under the same conditions as in that problem.

7-17 A small object is located in the center of a transparent glass marble of radius 1.0 cm and index of refraction 1.5. Where does the object appear to be, and how does its apparent size compare with its actual size?

7-18 Show from Eq. (7-20) that any thin lens which is thicker at the center than at the edges has a positive focal length, and conversely.

7-19 Discuss quantitatively the effect of a *cylindrical* interface between two media on a parallel beam incident on the interface.

7-20 For a thin lens with spherical surfaces, plot the image position q and the image size as functions of the object distance p, for an object of a given size, for the case $f > 0$.

7-21 Repeat Prob. 7-20 for the case $f < 0$.

7-22 A thin lens of refractive index 1.50 is double-convex, with radii 10 cm and

30 cm. If an object 2 cm high is placed 40 cm to the left of the lens, find the location, size, and orientation of the image. Draw a principal-ray diagram.

7-23 A double-concave lens has radii of 3 cm and 6 cm and refractive index 1.60.
    a   Find the focal length of this lens.
    b   An object 1 cm high is placed 10 cm to the left of this lens. Find the location, size, orientation, and nature of the image. Draw a principal-ray diagram.

7-24 The equation relating object and image distances for a thin lens, Eq. (7-21), can be expressed in terms of the distances of object and image from the focal points, rather than from the lens. Denoting these distances by *s* and *s'*, respectively, prove that

$$ss' = f^2$$

This form of the thin-lens equation was developed by Newton.

7-25 Two thin lenses whose focal lengths are f_1 and f_2 are placed in contact. Prove that the effect of this combination is the same as that of a single thin lens of focal length *f* given by

$$\frac{1}{f} = \frac{1}{f_1} + \frac{1}{f_2}$$

7-26 A double-convex lens whose surfaces both have radii of curvature of 10 cm is silvered on one side. The index of refraction is $n = 1.5$. Show that this lens acts as a mirror of focal length *f*, and find *f*:
    a   When the light approaches from the silvered side
    b   When the light approaches from the unsilvered side

7-27 For a converging lens, show that, in the case of real images, $p + q \geq 4f$.

7-28 A compound microscope is made using an objective lens with focal length 0.5 cm. The first image is 20 cm from the objective, the second 25 cm from the eye.
    a   What is the magnification of this microscope?
    b   If the unaided eye can barely distinguish two points 0.01 cm apart at a distance of 25 cm, what is the minimum separation that can be distinguished using this microscope?

7-29 A compound microscope is to be built using an objective with $f = 0.2$ cm. The distance between objective and eyepiece is 20 cm. If the first image is formed 15 cm from the objective, and the final image is at infinity,
    a   What focal-length eyepiece should be used?
    b   Where is the first image formed by the objective?
    c   What is the angular magnification?

7-30 The size of film used for a single picture in a 35-mm camera is about 24 by 36 mm, or roughly 1 by 1½ in. What focal-length lens should be used to take a picture of:
    a   A mountaineer 10 ft away?
    b   A deer 50 ft away?

7-31 A slide projector designed for 35-mm slides (about 1 by $1\frac{1}{2}$ in) projects a picture on a screen 40 by 60 in, 10 ft away.
   a   What is the focal length of the lens?
   b   What is the distance from slide to lens?

7-32 A compound microscope has objective and eyepiece lenses of focal lengths 0.5 and 5.0 cm, respectively. The first image is formed 10 cm from the objective lens. Find the magnification:
   a   If the final image is 25 cm from the eyepiece
   b   If the final image is at infinity

7-33 A telescope is to be made from two lenses, having focal lengths of 5 and 1 cm.
   a   What should be the distance between lenses if the initial object and the final virtual image are both very far away?
   b   What is the magnification under these circumstances?

7-34 The eyepiece of a certain telescope has a focal length of 10 cm, and the distance between objective and eyepiece is 2.1 m. What is the angular magnification?

7-35 A reflecting telescope uses a mirror with radius of curvature 0.50 m and an eyepiece with focal length 1.0 cm. Both the object and the final image are at infinity.
   a   What is the position of the image formed by the mirror?
   b   What is the angular magnification?

7-36 The first image of a reflecting telescope is formed 5 m from the mirror, and the image is observed with a compound microscope having $200\times$ magnification.
   a   What is the radius of curvature of the mirror?
   b   What is the overall magnification?

7-37 A lens commonly found in 35-mm cameras has a focal length of 50 mm and a diameter of 25 mm, corresponding to a maximum aperture of $f/2$. The resolution of a lens is commonly expressed as the maximum number of lines per millimeter *in the image* that can be resolved. If the resolution of this lens is diffraction-limited, approximately what is the resolution in lines per millimeter? (Good-quality 35-mm camera lenses typically have a resolution of the order of 100 lines/mm, determined by surface precision rather than diffraction.)

7-38 Assuming the resolution of the 200-in Hale telescope is diffraction-limited, find its angular resolution. What is the minimum separation at which two objects on the moon (6×10^{10} m away) could be resolved? For simplicity the diameter of the mirror may be taken as 5 m.

7-39 Camera lenses usually contain an aperture of variable diameter to control exposure. Consider a lens of focal length 50 mm and diameter 25 mm, with a resolution (as defined in Prob. 7-37) of 200 lines/mm. How much can this lens be "stopped down" (i.e., aperture decreased) before diffraction effects begin to limit the image quality? Determine the minimum aperture diameter that should be used if diffraction effects are to be avoided.

PERSPECTIVE II

In the preceding four chapters we have been concerned primarily with classical optics, that is, with optical phenomena that can be understood on the basis of a ray or wave model. We began by developing the idea of electromagnetic waves, using the same basic concepts and language developed in Chap. 3 for mechanical waves. The existence of electromagnetic waves was predicted by Maxwell's electromagnetic field equations, which form the foundation of classical electrodynamics. A variety of experimental evidence demonstrates conclusively that light is an electromagnetic wave and that it is a small part of a very broad spectrum of electromagnetic waves with frequencies ranging from less than 1 Hz to at least 10^{25} Hz.

The wave model of light and other electromagnetic radiation proves to be satisfactory for the understanding of a variety of phenomena associated with propagation of light, including interference and diffraction, polarization, and related physical phenomena. Furthermore, in certain special cases the wave picture of light can be simplified even more by representing the propagation of wavefronts by rays. The ray representation forms the basis of geometrical optics, the model usually used in the analysis of optical instruments such as lenses, mirrors, and combinations of these. The scope of geometrical optics is much more limited than that of the more general wave theory, but within its range it is much simpler.

In summary, the wave and ray models of classical optics provide a description of a wide variety of optical phenomena associated with the propagation of light and other electromagnetic radiation, and within this context the theory is fairly complete. Yet there are many other phenomena, especially those associated with emission and absorption of radiation, in which the wave picture is far from complete. The latter class of phenomena forms the subject matter for the next three chapters.

197

First, although we have regarded the propagation of an electromagnetic wave as a continuous process, a variety of evidence shows that the energy associated with this radiation is emitted and absorbed only in discrete units, sometimes called quanta. The wave model gives no hint as to why these quanta should exist or how they are emitted or absorbed.

Second, the existence of characteristic spectra of elements, in which each element emits radiation only of a number of discrete frequencies, different for each element, shows that the emission of radiation by atoms of an element must be related to the internal structure of the atoms. But again, wave optics, based as it is on classical electrodynamics, provides no clue to the understanding of this relationship.

As we shall see in the next three chapters, the understanding of phenomena associated with the emission and absorption of radiation and of its interaction with matter requires sweeping changes in our concepts of the nature both of radiation and of matter itself. First, there is the apparent inconsistency of the discreteness of the energy of radiation with the continuous nature of wave propagation. Then there is the problem of describing and understanding the internal structure of atoms. As we shall see, an atom is basically a mechanical system; yet when classical newtonian mechanics is applied to the system, even in the simplest cases, the results cannot account for the existence of characteristic spectra and so cannot be a completely correct description of the internal structure of atoms.

The key to the understanding of these problems is quantum mechanics, which involves fundamental changes in our conception of how a mechanical system is to be described. In particular, it is necessary to abandon the idea of describing a particle as a localized point in space, moving at each instant with a definite velocity. Instead, particles must be regarded as spread-out entities which are not completely localized in space. As these entities move with time, the spread-out nature partakes of some of the characteristics of a wave. Thus under some circumstances particles exhibit wave properties, and in fact these wave properties can be demonstrated very directly in some experiments.

Thus while the preceding four chapters have concentrated on the successes of classical optics, the next three chapters will concentrate on its failures. But from these failures emerges a more sophisticated physical theory which does provide at least a partial basis for the understanding of emission and absorption of radiation and its relation to the internal structure of atoms. In recognition of the discrete, or quantum, nature of the energy associated with radiation and with changes of internal states of atoms, this new theory is called quantum mechanics.

Particle Nature of Radiation 8

Many optical phenomena can be understood on the basis of the *wave* nature of light and other electromagnetic radiation. Many other phenomena, however, exhibit a different aspect of the nature of light and suggest that it should be regarded not as a wave but as a stream of *particles*. Several phenomena which exhibit the particle nature of light are discussed and interpreted in terms of the fundamental assumptions of the quantum theory. Finally, it is shown that the wave and particle aspects of radiation are not necessarily inconsistent and that they can be regarded as two aspects of a single phenomenon.

8-1 EMISSION AND ABSORPTION

In order to comprehend the enormous significance of the discoveries outlined in this chapter, we first consider briefly the state of knowledge of optics and the structure of matter around 1890. The wave theory of light accounted completely for the phenomena then known involving the *propagation* of light, such as geometrical optics, interference, diffraction, and polarization. Insofar as these phenomena were concerned, the wave theory was *complete*.

Furthermore, the development of electromagnetic theory, crowned by the brilliant achievements of James Clerk Maxwell, predicted the existence of *electromagnetic waves* whose speed in vacuum should be the same as the observed value of the speed of light. These developments, together with the experimental work of Heinrich Hertz, who in 1887 demonstrated experimentally the existence of electromagnetic radiation, provided conclusive evidence that light is indeed an electromagnetic wave.

With respect to the structure of matter, the existence of *atoms* was firmly established by an abundance of chemical phenomena, the kinetic theory of gases, and other evidence. The work of Faraday and others on electrolysis showed that there exist elementary units of electric charge; by 1890 it was fairly clear that atoms consist of positive and negative charges and that part of the negative charge can be removed under some conditions. Finally, in 1897, the experimental work of J. J. Thomson with what were then called "cathode rays" demonstrated the existence of electrons and provided a measurement of their charge-to-mass ratio. Thus it became clear that atoms are not indivisible, as had once been thought, but have internal structure. The details of this structure, however, were completely unknown and had to wait until the pioneering experiments of Rutherford and his colleagues in 1911.

Phenomena associated with the *emission* and *absorption* of light by matter were not nearly so well understood as its *propagation*. There was some *qualitative* understanding; it was clear that electromagnetic radiation is produced by oscillating charges or currents, just as Hertz had produced electromagnetic radiation by means of oscillations in a resonant circuit. To account for the wavelengths of light determined from interference and diffraction experiments, the frequency must be of the order of 10^{15} Hz, compared with frequencies of the order of 10^8 Hz in the experiments of Hertz. It was suspected that vibrations of optical frequency must be associated with motion of individual charges within atoms. In fact, as early as 1862, Faraday had placed a light source between the poles of a strong magnet and looked for changes in wavelength in the spectrum emitted. His apparatus was not sensitive enough to detect changes, but in 1896 Zeeman, using improved spectrometers, found that measurable shifts *do* occur. This lent further support to the model of vibrations of electric charge within atoms as the fundamental sources of light.

Aside from this qualitative picture, there was very little understanding of the process of emission of light. It was known as early as 1752 that when substances in the gaseous state are excited by heating or by an electric discharge, they ordinarily emit light that contains only certain wavelengths, rather than a continuous spectrum. Because spectrometers often employ a slit to define a narrow beam, which is then dispersed by a prism or diffraction grating, the various wavelengths appeared as *lines* of various colors; hence such spectra came to be known as "line spectra." By 1823 it had been shown that each element has a characteristic line spectrum and that elements can be identified by their spectra.

The phenomenon of *absorption spectra* was also observed early in the nineteenth century. When light passes through an element in the gaseous state, some wavelengths are *absorbed* much more strongly than others, and it was found that the wavelengths absorbed were the same as some of those *emitted* by the same element when thermally or electrically excited.

No real progress was made in finding regularities or patterns in the observed spectra of elements until the work of Balmer, who in 1885 found an empirical rule governing the wavelengths of the visible spectrum emitted by hydrogen, the simplest atom. Even then, this rule had no fundamental basis. This groping for schemes to correlate or systematize spectra reminds one of the long struggle of Kepler, culminating in his three empirical rules governing the motion of the planets, and of the struggles of chemists trying to find order among the chemical elements, culminating in the periodic table of Mendeleev. Such groping is a vital part of the advancement of scientific knowledge.

There were corresponding mysteries regarding the light emitted by *solid* matter. It was known in the nineteenth century that when solid bodies are heated very hot ("red hot" or "white hot"), they emit light in a *continuous* spectrum, that is, a continuous distribution of wavelengths, rather than a line spectrum. It was observed that the frequency of the most intense radiation is directly proportional to the absolute temperature of the radiating body and that the *total* energy radiated per unit time is proportional to the fourth power of the absolute temperature. Some partially successful attempts were made to provide a theoretical basis for the observations, but full understanding had to wait until the first years of the twentieth century, when one of the key pieces of the puzzle was found by Max Planck.

There were several other phenomena that were difficult to understand on the basis of the classical theory of light. One was the *photoelectric effect,* discovered by Hertz in 1887 and investigated in detail by Hallwachs and Lenard, in which electrons are liberated from the surface of a material when it absorbs electromagnetic radiation. Another was the production of x-rays in cathode-ray tubes, discovered by Röntgen in 1895.

Thus by the turn of the century it was clear that, while the electro-magnetic theory of light was adequate for understanding the *propagation* of light, it was completely inadequate for *emission* and *absorption* of light. We can sense the excitement that must have pervaded scientific circles in those times. Only radical new ideas could bring understanding into these diverse areas, and in 1900 the time was ripe for such ideas. The revolution in physical theory which took place in the 25 years following the turn of the century was one of the most significant in the entire history of scientific thought. This period witnessed the birth and flowering of the quantum theory and of the theory of relativity, both of which lie at the very heart of contemporary physical science.

The development of new ideas does not always take place in a systematic and orderly way but sometimes seems to present the appearance of a partly assembled jigsaw puzzle. The reader may feel disappointment at the lack of a coherent, orderly scheme of development. The fact is, however, that physical theories, especially those representing as dramatic a departure from established thought as we are discussing here, virtually *never* develop in an orderly manner. There is always guesswork, much of which turns out to be wrong; blind alleys are followed, and unsuccessful hypotheses are discarded in favor of more promising ones. By examining the search for understanding at the beginning of the twentieth century, we gain a heightened appreciation of the conceptual basis of the new theories and of their significance.

8-2 PHOTOELECTRIC EFFECT

The first hint of the photoelectric effect was discovered in 1887 by Hertz, quite by accident, in the course of his investigation of electromagnetic radiation. As a detector of radiation, Hertz used a rudimentary antenna made of a piece of wire with a small polished metal sphere on each end, bent into a circle to form a narrow gap between the spheres. Electromagnetic waves induced a potential difference across the gap, as shown by sparks jumping across it. Hertz observed that sparks jumped more readily when the gap was illuminated by light from another spark gap in the apparatus *producing* the waves. This suggested that light facilitated the escape of charges from the spheres.

This idea in itself was not revolutionary. It was already known that mobile charges in conducting materials are prevented from escaping from the material by potential-energy barriers at the surface and that by various means the charged particles can gain enough energy to surmount this barrier and escape. In *thermionic emission,* first observed in 1883 by Edison, the energy is supplied by heating the material to a very high temperature, liberating electrons by a process analogous to boiling a liquid. Figure 8-1 shows a scheme for observing the flow of electrons from a heated filament

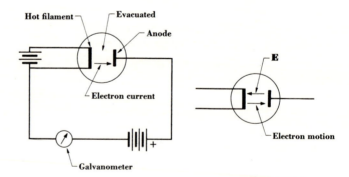

Fig. 8-1 An apparatus for observing thermionic emission. The filament is heated by an electric current. The anode is kept at a positive potential with respect to the filament; the resulting electric field pushes the negatively charged electrons toward the anode, and the resulting current is detected by the galvanometer.

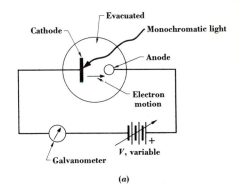

(a)

Fig. 8-2 (a) An apparatus for observing photoelectric emission of electrons. The cathode is illuminated by monochromatic light, and the resulting current is measured with a galvanometer, as a function of the potential difference V. The intensity of illumination can also be varied. (b) Graphs of current I as a function of voltage V for various intensities of incident light. Saturation current is directly proportional to light intensity, but the stopping potential V_0 is independent of intensity.

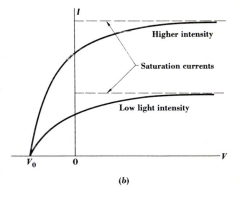

(b)

to another electrode inside an evacuated tube as a result of thermionic emission from the filament. Electrons may also be liberated from a surface by bombardment by other charged particles or by imposing very strong electric fields at the surface to pull the particles away.

Although the basic idea of photoelectric emission of electrons was not startling, the *details* of the phenomenon observed by Hallwachs and Lenard were quite unexpected. An apparatus used to investigate the photoelectric effect is shown schematically in Fig. 8-2a. Two electrodes are sealed in an evacuated glass bulb and connected to a source of variable potential difference V. Monochromatic light, perhaps provided by a continuous-spectrum source with a prism spectrometer, illuminates the cathode, liberating electrons, some of which travel to the anode and around the external circuit. The resulting current may be measured with a galvanometer, as shown. As the potential difference V is varied, the current is found to vary in the manner shown in Fig. 8-2b. This curve shows that at sufficiently high potential difference, *all* the electrons liberated from the cathode are collected by the anode, and then the current is not increased by a further increase in potential difference. This maximum current is called the *saturation current*.

For smaller values of V not all the electrons are collected, but even for small *negative* values of V (opposite polarity to that shown in Fig. 8-2a), some current still flows, despite the fact that the force on the electrons is then toward the cathode rather than toward the collecting anode. This indicates that the electrons leave the cathode with a certain kinetic energy, and some have enough energy to reach the anode despite the repulsive force. When the potential difference V reaches a certain critical value, labeled V_0 in the figure, the current drops to zero, showing that no electrons leave the photocathode with kinetic energies greater than eV_0. This critical value of V is called the *stopping potential.*

Now let us change the *intensity* of the light, keeping its wavelength the same. More energy is then available to liberate electrons, and the saturation current should increase; this is, in fact, observed. Correspondingly, however, it might be thought that the electrons should leave the surface with more energy, and so *larger* negative value of V_0 should be necessary to reduce the current to zero. Instead, it is found that the value of V_0 is *independent* of the intensity of the radiation. This suggests that the maximum kinetic energy with which electrons leave the cathode depends only on the *wavelength* of the radiation and *not* on its intensity. Specifically, it was found that V_0 is directly proportional to the *frequency* of the radiation. That is, the maximum kinetic energy of emitted electrons is a *linear* function of frequency. This relationship is illustrated in Fig. 8-3.

In 1905 Einstein showed that this relationship could be understood on the basis of a revolutionary new hypothesis regarding the nature of light. Einstein hypothesized that the energy transported by electromagnetic radiation is composed of individual and indivisible bundles of energy, each having a quantity of energy proportional to the *frequency* of the corresponding radiation. If radiation of a given frequency is made more intense, *more* bundles of energy are transmitted, but the amount in each bundle remains unchanged. In photoelectric emission, each electron absorbs only one such bundle. These bundles of energy were originally called *quanta* and are now more commonly known as *photons.* Expressing this hypothesis mathematically, we may say that the energy E of one photon of light of frequency f is

$$E = hf \qquad (8\text{-}1)$$

where h is a proportionality constant.

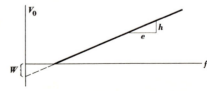

Fig. 8-3 Graph showing stopping potential V_0 as a function of frequency f of incident radiation. The intercept determines the work function W, and the slope determines the ratio h/e.

The idea that the energy associated with electromagnetic radiation is packaged in units of magnitude proportional to the frequency (usually called the *quantum hypothesis*) was not entirely original with Einstein. It had been proposed 5 years earlier by Planck as part of an attempt to understand the continuous spectrum emitted by very hot solid bodies. Planck, however, regarded it as a calculational technique without any fundamental physical significance, while Einstein regarded it as a fundamental property of light. Revolutionary though this new concept was, it was in a sense a natural development, inasmuch as it introduced an *atomistic* aspect to the theory of electromagnetic radiation, which may be compared to the atomistic aspect of the structure of matter introduced by Dalton a hundred years earlier.

Returning to the experimental situation, we now consider the energy relationships in detail. For an electron to leave the surface of a conductor, it must surmount a potential-energy barrier. The amount of energy necessary for an electron to be removed from the surface is called the *work function* for the material and is denoted by W. Thus when an electron absorbs a photon of energy $E = hf$, its kinetic energy just outside the surface is $hf - W$. Recalling that electrical potential is potential energy per unit charge, we see that, when the anode is at a *negative* potential V with respect to the cathode, an electron with charge e which travels from cathode to anode undergoes an *increase* in potential energy of eV, with a corresponding *decrease* in kinetic energy. If this potential difference is greater than the kinetic energy with which electrons leave the cathode, they can never reach the anode. Thus the critical potential difference V_0 to just stop the flow of current from cathode to anode is given by

$$eV_0 = hf - W \qquad (8\text{-}2)$$

By measuring this critical potential for various frequencies, one can draw a graph of V_0 versus f, as in Fig. 8-3; from this graph both h and W can be determined, if e is known. The constant h is called *Planck's constant*; its value is found to be

$$h = 6.626 \times 10^{-34} \text{ J} \cdot \text{s} \qquad (8\text{-}3)$$

Work functions for common conductors typically are on the order of 10^{-19} J.

In energy relationships for electrons, it is often convenient to measure energies not in joules but in a unit called the *electronvolt*, abbreviated eV. By definition, 1 electronvolt is the amount of energy acquired or lost by an electron (or any charged particle with charge equal to that of the electron) in moving through an electrical potential difference of 1 volt. Electrical potential is potential energy per unit charge, and 1 volt is equal to 1 joule/coulomb (1 V = 1 J/C); thus the two units of energy are related simply by the fact that $1 \text{ eV} = (1 \text{ electron charge})(1 \text{ V})$. The charge of the electron has been found to be $1.602 \times 10^{-19} \text{ C}$; therefore

$$1 \text{ eV} = 1.602 \times 10^{-19} \text{ J} \qquad (8\text{-}4)$$

The electronvolt is a unit of *energy*, not of potential. Expressed in these units, work functions typically range from 0.5 to 5 eV. Similarly, the energy of a photon of visible light, for example, with a wavelength of $500 \text{ nm} = 5 \times 10^{-7} \text{ m}$, is

$$E = hf = \frac{hc}{\lambda} = \frac{(6.62 \times 10^{-34} \text{ J} \cdot \text{s})(3.00 \times 10^8 \text{ m/s})}{5 \times 10^{-7} \text{ m}}$$

$$= 3.98 \times 10^{-19} \text{ J} = 2.48 \text{ eV}$$

In problems such as this it is often useful to express h in units of $\text{eV} \cdot \text{s}$ rather than $\text{J} \cdot \text{s}$; in these units its value is

$$h = 4.136 \times 10^{-15} \text{ eV} \cdot \text{s}$$

Other common units derived from the electronvolt are

$$1 \text{ keV} = 10^3 \text{ eV}$$

$$1 \text{ MeV} = 10^6 \text{ eV}$$

$$1 \text{ GeV} = 10^9 \text{ eV}$$

The rest energy of the electron is

$$mc^2 = (9.11 \times 10^{-31} \text{ kg})(3.00 \times 10^8 \text{ m/s})^2 = 8.18 \times 10^{-14} \text{ J}$$

Expressed in electronvolts, this is

$$mc^2 = \frac{8.18 \times 10^{-14} \text{ J}}{1.60 \times 10^{-19} \text{ J/eV}} = 5.11 \times 10^5 \text{ eV} = 0.511 \text{ MeV}$$

In this section we have seen that quantitative observations of the photoelectric effect led to the concept of an atomistic or *quantum* aspect of the nature of electromagnetic radiation. Revolutionary though this hypothesis was in its day, it provided insight into a phenomenon which could not be understood on the basis of classical electromagnetic theory.

8-3 X-RAY PRODUCTION AND SCATTERING

Several phenomena involving x-rays give additional support to the quantum hypothesis for electromagnetic radiation. X-rays were first produced in 1895 by W. K. Röntgen, using an apparatus similar in principle to that shown schematically in Fig. 8-4. Electrons released from the heated cathode by

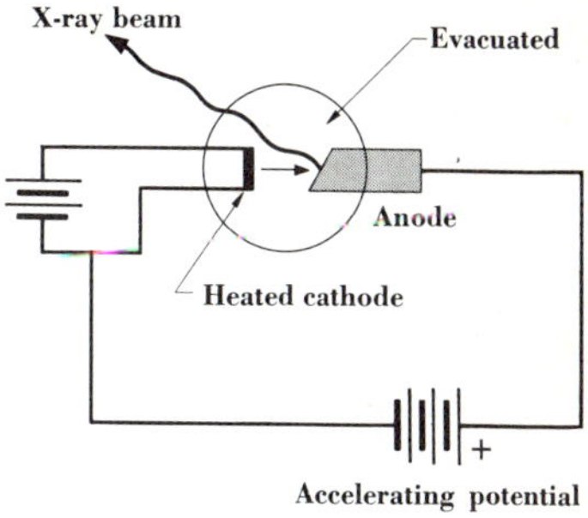

Fig. 8-4 Apparatus used to produce x-rays. Electrons are emitted thermionically from the heated cathode and are accelerated toward the anode; when they strike it, x-rays are produced.

thermionic emission are accelerated toward the anode by a large potential difference, as shown. At sufficiently high potentials (several thousand volts) a very penetrating radiation is emitted from the surface of the anode. It was suspected early that this radiation was electromagnetic in nature, and further experiments confirmed this suspicion. In 1913 W. H. Bragg discovered x-ray diffraction by crystals, discussed in Sec. 6-1. This technique permitted precise measurements of *wavelengths* of x-rays and thus became the basis for a study of *x-ray spectra*.

In subsequent investigations, several important observations emerged. Ordinarily, a continuous spectrum of frequencies of x-rays is emitted, but the *maximum* frequency was observed to be proportional to the accelerating voltage between the electrodes and independent of electrode material. These observations can be understood on the basis of the quantum hypothesis. In its travel from cathode to anode, an electron acquires a kinetic energy equal to eV, where V is the potential difference between the electrodes. On striking the anode, it loses this kinetic energy, and a corresponding amount of energy is emitted as electromagnetic radiation. If one photon is produced in each collision, then

$$eV = hf = \frac{hc}{\lambda} \tag{8-5}$$

For example, an accelerating voltage of 10,000 V should lead to a photon energy of 10,000 eV and an x-ray wavelength of

$$\lambda = \frac{hc}{eV} = \frac{(6.62 \times 10^{-34} \text{ J} \cdot \text{s})(3.00 \times 10^8 \text{ m/s})}{(1.60 \times 10^{-19} \text{ C})(10^4 \text{ V})}$$

$$= 1.24 \times 10^{-10} \text{ m} = 0.124 \text{ nm}$$

Such calculations agree with measured values of λ obtained by diffraction experiments and therefore lend strong support to the quantum aspect of electromagnetic radiation.

Even more complete confirmation of the particle nature of x-rays is provided by the phenomenon of *Compton scattering*. In the course of experimental investigations of x-ray scattering from matter, the American physicist A. H. Compton discovered in 1923 that some of the scattered radiation had *longer* wavelength and correspondingly smaller frequency than the incident radiation. This phenomenon cannot be understood on the basis of *classical* electromagnetic theory, in which the scattered radiation results from electron vibration induced by the incident radiation and therefore must have the *same* frequency as the incident radiation. Conversely, the *quantum* theory provides a beautifully clear and simple understanding of the basic features of Compton scattering. The scattering is described as a collision between two *particles,* the incident photon and an electron initially at rest. After the collision, the electron has energy and momentum, and the outgoing photon has less energy and smaller frequency than the incident one. Such a process is shown diagrammatically in Fig. 8-5.

Compton scattering is so important and useful as an illustration of the properties of photons that it is worth discussing in considerable detail. The wavelength of the scattered radiation is found to depend on the *scattering angle,* θ in Fig. 8-5. Using the familiar principles of conservation of energy and momentum, we can derive a relationship between the two wavelengths and the scattering angle θ. The analysis of this collision proceeds in exactly the same manner as the analysis of a collision between two billiard balls. Since the system is isolated, the total momentum must be the same before and after the collision. Furthermore, we assume that the collision is completely *elastic,* so that energy is also conserved.

Because the energies involved may be comparable to the electron's rest energy, we use for the electron the relativistic energy-momentum relation:

$$E^2 = P^2c^2 + m^2c^4 \qquad (8\text{-}6)$$

where E is the total electron energy, including the rest energy mc^2, and P the magnitude of momentum. Since photons always travel with the speed of light c, their rest mass must be zero, and the energy-momentum relationship for a *photon* is simply

$$E = pc \qquad (8\text{-}7)$$

This relationship is also confirmed by measurements of radiation pressure as discussed in Sec. 4-4.

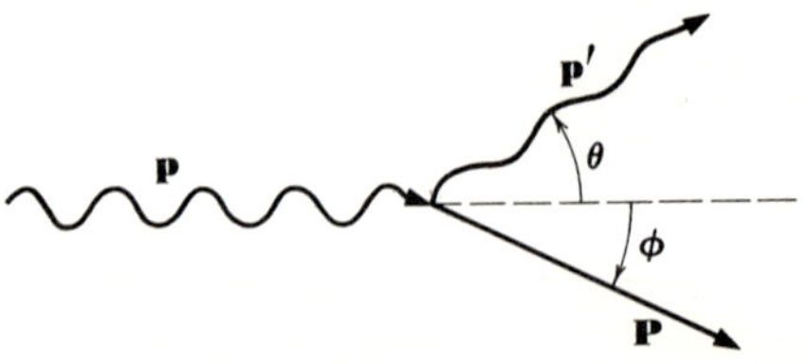

Fig. 8-5 Diagram showing particle interpretation of Compton scattering. Wavy lines represent photons; the solid line, the electron, which is initially at rest. The particles are labeled according to their momenta.

Let **p** be the momentum of the photon before scattering and **p'** its momentum after scattering. We resolve each into its components parallel and perpendicular to the direction of the incident photon. Conservation of these two components of total momentum leads to the equations

$$p = p' \cos \theta + P \cos \phi$$
$$0 = p' \sin \theta - P \sin \phi$$

(8-8)

Since we are seeking a relationship which involves the direction θ of the scattered photon, it is useful first to eliminate the angle ϕ, which represents the direction of the final electron momentum. To do this, we solve Eqs. (8-8) for $P \cos \phi$ and $P \sin \phi$, respectively, square, and add, using the identity $\sin^2 \phi + \cos^2 \phi = 1$. The result is

$$P^2 = p^2 + p'^2 - 2pp' \cos \theta$$

(8-9)

To obtain an expression involving only the *photon* momenta p and p', we eliminate the electron momentum P using energy relations. Energy conservation during the collision requires that

$$pc = p'c + T$$

(8-10)

where T is the electron kinetic energy after the collision, related to its *total* energy E by

$$E = T + mc^2$$

(8-11)

In terms of T, Eq. (8-6) becomes

$$(T + mc^2)^2 = P^2c^2 + m^2c^4$$

(8-12)

We substitute the expression for T from Eq. (8-10) into Eq. (8-12) and simplify, obtaining

$$P^2 = (p - p')^2 + 2mc(p - p')$$

(8-13)

Finally, we combine Eqs. (8-9) and (8-13) to eliminate P and again simplify, obtaining

$$mc(p - p') = pp'(1 - \cos \theta)$$

or

$$mc \left(\frac{1}{p'} - \frac{1}{p} \right) = 1 - \cos \theta$$

(8-14)

This expresses the relationship between the momenta p and p' of the incident and scattered photons and the scattering angle θ.

Finally, Eq. (8-14) can be written in terms of the *wavelengths* of the photons. Combining the basic relation $E = hf$ for the energy of a photon with the energy-momentum relation $E = pc$, we have $p = hf/c$. Since for any wave $c = \lambda f$, the momentum and wavelength of a photon are related simply by

$$p = \frac{h}{\lambda} \qquad\qquad (8\text{-}15)$$

Using this relation in Eq. (8-14), we obtain

$$\lambda' - \lambda = \frac{h}{mc}(1 - \cos\theta) \qquad\qquad (8\text{-}16)$$

In view of the somewhat involved derivation, this is a remarkably simple result, showing that the wavelength λ' of the scattered photon is *longer* than that (λ) of the incident photon, the difference depending on the scattering angle. Experiments with x-ray scattering, in which the wavelengths are measured directly by x-ray diffraction techniques, agree with Eq. (8-16) within the limits of precision of the experiment.

The above analysis has assumed that the electron that scatters the photon is *free*. In actual fact, some of the electrons in any atom are rather tightly bound to the nucleus. When such electrons scatter x-rays, the recoil is not that of the electron alone, but of the entire atom. In such cases, Eq. (8-16) still gives the correct shift in wavelength, provided one uses for m not the mass of an electron alone but the mass of the entire atom, which is several thousand times larger. These wavelength shifts are so small as to be unnoticed in usual x-ray scattering experiments but are, in fact, the predominant events in most cases.

Thus we have seen that the phenomenon of Compton scattering provides additional strong support for the particle picture of electromagnetic radiation and also helps justify the description and analysis of electron-photon collisions in mechanical terms.

8-4   LINE SPECTRA

The existence of line spectra gives further support to the particle picture of light and also provides valuable insight into an important aspect of atomic structure. In fact, atomic spectroscopy has been by far the most important experimental tool in investigating atomic structure in detail.

The existence of line spectra has been known for over 200 years, and in Sec. 8-1 we commented briefly on the characteristic emission and absorption spectra of elements. But as late as 1880, although line spectra were a familiar phenomenon, their basic nature was not understood. An enormous amount of effort went into searching for some pattern or orderly relationship among various lines in a spectrum, but no real progress was made until 1885, when a Swiss schoolteacher, Johann Balmer, succeeded, after a long period of trial and error, in finding an empirical formula relating various lines in the spectrum of hydrogen, the simplest atom.

Balmer's formula is most transparent when written in the following form:

$$\frac{1}{\lambda} = R\left(\frac{1}{2^2} - \frac{1}{n^2}\right) \qquad n = 3, 4, 5, \ldots \tag{8-17}$$

The constant R is called the *Rydberg constant* after J. R. Rydberg, who, following Balmer, made considerable progress in the search for various spectral series. The currently accepted value of R is

$$R = 0.0109677 \text{ nm}^{-1}$$

As Table 8-1 shows, the predictions of Balmer's formula agree extremely well with observed wavelengths of lines in the hydrogen spectrum. Balmer also speculated on the possible existence of other series of spectrum lines corresponding to replacing the 2^2 in his formula by other numbers such as 1^2, 3^2, 4^2, and so forth, leading to possible spectral series given by

$$\frac{1}{\lambda} = R\left(\frac{1}{1^2} - \frac{1}{n^2}\right) \qquad \frac{1}{\lambda} = R\left(\frac{1}{3^2} - \frac{1}{n^2}\right) \qquad \text{etc.} \tag{8-18}$$

Calculation of numerical values shows that the first of these should lie in the far-ultraviolet region of the spectrum, 91.2 to 121.4 nm, while the others should be in the infrared region, $\lambda > 820.4$ nm. In the course of subsequent investigation, all these predicted spectral series were found to exist, and their wavelengths agreed extremely well with the predictions of Eqs. (8-18).

In the 25 years following Balmer's original paper, various physicists made some additional progress in systematizing the spectra of various elements. Ritz discovered that the spectrum of an element can always be represented by means of a set of characteristic numbers called *terms* such that the *wave*

Table 8-1 Data on Hydrogen Spectrum

	Wavelength, nm	
n	Balmer's formula	Ångström's measurements
3	656.208	656.210
4	486.08	486.074
5	434.00	434.01
6	410.13	410.12

number of each observed spectrum line is given by the *difference* of two terms. This scheme was called the *combination principle*. These terms and the corresponding spectrum lines were found to fall naturally into groups or series, suggesting the existence of some simple underlying principle, but there was as yet no inkling of what this principle could be.

Balmer's formula and the Ritz combination principle suffered from the same deficiency as Kepler's laws of planetary motion; they were *empirical* descriptions of phenomena without any fundamental basis. They provided no understanding of the *mechanism* of emission and absorption of light or of the basis of the observed regularities in spectra. A more complete understanding of the fundamental basis of spectra had to wait until the next generation. Two key pieces of the puzzle were missing; one was the idea of the quantization of electromagnetic wave energy, as described by the *photon* theory, and the other was a new and revolutionary picture of the structure of the atom.

The key idea was finally found in 1913 by Niels Bohr with an insight which, from a historical vantage point 60 years later, seems almost obvious; yet in its time it represented a bold and brilliant stroke. Bohr reasoned that if the atoms of a particular element can emit photons of only certain particular energies (corresponding to the spectrum of that element) then *the atoms themselves* must be able to possess only certain particular quantities of energy. That is, corresponding to the discrete spectrum of an element there must be a discrete series of possible energies that the atom can possess.

This bold hypothesis immediately shed new light on Balmer's formula. For the series of wavelengths given by Eq. (8-17) the corresponding photon energies are

$$E = \frac{hc}{\lambda} = hcR\left(\frac{1}{2^2} - \frac{1}{n^2}\right) \tag{8-19}$$

Thus if the hydrogen atom can exist only in states characterized by the series of possible energy levels

$$E_n = -\frac{hcR}{n^2} \qquad n = 1, 2, 3, \ldots \tag{8-20}$$

then all the spectral series of hydrogen predicted by the Balmer formula can be understood as originating from transitions between pairs of these allowed energy levels. Correspondingly, the *terms* in the Ritz combination principle are reinterpreted as representing corresponding *energy levels*.

Thus one can start with the observed spectrum of an element, reconstruct the energy-level scheme, and identify individual spectrum lines with particular transitions between energy levels. It is convenient to represent energy-level schemes graphically as in Fig. 8-6, which shows energy-level diagrams for

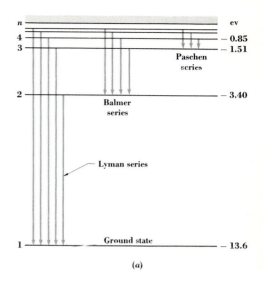

(a)

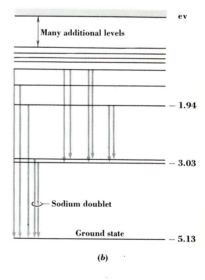

Fig. 8-6 Energy-level diagrams. (a) Hydrogen. The series of transitions ending at the ground state ($n = 1$) give the Lyman series, in the ultraviolet. Those ending at $n = 2$ give the Balmer series, in the visible region, and at $n = 3$ the Paschen series in the infrared. (b) Sodium. Some energy levels are closely spaced doublets, and transitions involving these lead to doublet spectrum lines. The transitions leading to the (589.0, 589.6 nm) doublet are shown.

(b)

two elements. In such a diagram, transitions accompanying emission or absorption of particular photons are indicated by arrows.

The above discussion has centered around emission spectra, but atomic energy levels are equally satisfactory in accounting for *absorption* spectra. An atom can gain energy by absorbing a photon of appropriate energy; the photon disappears and the atom is left in a higher energy state. Atoms can also acquire energy through collisions; in the spectra emitted in flames and other very hot gases, some of the energy of random thermal motion of atoms is converted through collisions into *internal* energy of individual atoms,

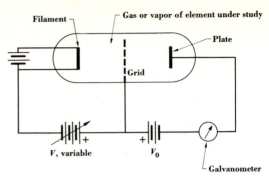

Fig. 8-7 Apparatus for the Franck-Hertz experiment. Electrons emitted thermionically from the heated filament are accelerated toward the grid by the potential difference V. They have enough energy to proceed on to the plate despite the smaller retarding potential V_0, unless they collide inelastically with atoms on the way. Measuring the potential differences V for which inelastic collisions set in gives a direct measurement of the excitation potentials, or energy levels.

leaving the atoms in energy states higher than the lowest or *ground state.* Such an atom is said to be in an *excited state,* and the subsequent photon emission and return to the ground state or a lower state is sometimes called *decay.*

A detailed study of conduction of electricity through gases provides additional and persuasive evidence for the existence of atomic energy levels. Such a study was made by J. Franck and G. Hertz starting in 1914. Using an apparatus shown schematically in Fig. 8-7, Franck and Hertz bombarded vapors of various elements with electrons emitted thermionically from the filament and accelerated toward the grid by the potential difference V. A smaller retarding potential V_0 slows the electrons somewhat as they approach the plate, and the current of electrons that reach the plate is measured by the galvanometer in this circuit.

As the accelerating potential V is increased, more and more electrons arrive at the plate and the current increases. But when a certain critical potential is reached, the plate current *drops* suddenly, as shown in Fig. 8-8. This can be understood in terms of atomic energy levels. For small values of V, an electron collides elastically with atoms; since the electron is so much less massive, it loses practically no energy in such collisions and arrives at the grid with energy very nearly equal to eV. Then it can proceed to the plate, losing energy eV_0 in the process. But when the electron kinetic energy becomes as large as the energy difference between the two lowest levels in the atoms, an electron can collide *inelastically* with an atom, giving up some

Fig. 8-8 Galvanometer current as a function of accelerating voltage V in the Franck-Hertz experiment. The breaks in the curve indicate the onset of inelastic collisions, with corresponding energy loss eV, and thus give a direct measurement of energy levels, in electronvolts.

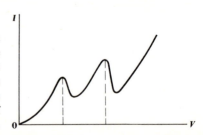

of its energy and leaving the atom in an excited state. When this happens, it may reach the grid with insufficient energy to proceed on to the plate, and the plate current is reduced. For example, with mercury vapor Franck and Hertz found that one of the breaks in the plate-current graph came at $V = 4.9$ V (electron energy of 4.9 eV). This suggests that atoms are being excited by collisions with electrons to an energy level 4.9 eV above the ground state. As V is increased further, the plate current again increases and then eventually drops sharply again, corresponding to excitation of a higher energy level. Thus a series of energy levels called *excitation potentials* is observed.

To check this interpretation, Franck and Hertz observed the *spectra* emitted by the vapors during this process. In the previous example, an atom excited to an energy level of 4.9 eV above the ground state should emit a 4.9-eV photon when it returns to the ground state. This transition corresponds to a wavelength of 253.6 nm. This spectrum line was, in fact, observed, but only when V was greater than 4.9 V. For smaller potentials, it disappeared. Similarly, by increasing V further, spectrum lines of other wavelengths could be excited. These experiments gave very direct and convincing confirmation of the existence of atomic energy levels and their relationship to line spectra.

8-5 BOHR MODEL OF HYDROGEN ATOM

The foregoing discussion cannot be considered a complete theory of atomic spectra because it has provided no basis for *predicting* atomic energy levels. At the same time Bohr proposed his theory relating atomic spectra to energy levels, he also attempted to make an actual calculation of energy levels for the simplest atom, hydrogen, on the basis of a simple model which has come to be known as the *Bohr model*. Although this model has serious conceptual defects, it is important historically, for it was the first attempt to predict atomic energy levels that achieved any measure of success.

The Bohr theory comprises a *dynamic* model of the atom in which the electron is pictured as moving in a circular orbit around the nucleus (a single proton), just as the planets move around the sun in nearly circular orbits. Both particles are treated as points. The electron is assumed to be subject to the classical laws of mechanics and electromagnetism, but an additional assumption is needed to introduce a restriction as to the possible orbits in which the electron can move. Since the electron is so much less massive than the proton, we assume that the latter is stationary; the electron is attracted to it with a force given by Coulomb's law. Each particle has a charge of magnitude e, and the attractive force has magnitude

$$F = \frac{1}{4\pi\varepsilon_0} \frac{e^2}{r^2} \qquad (8\text{-}21)$$

where r is the radius of the orbit. This is the force responsible for the centripetal acceleration of the electron toward the center of its circle, given by v^2/r, where v is the electron's orbital speed. According to Newton's second law, this force equals the mass times the acceleration, and so we have

$$\frac{e^2}{4\pi\varepsilon_0 r^2} = \frac{mv^2}{r} \tag{8-22}$$

This equation shows that the kinetic energy T of the electron is inversely proportional to the radius of its orbit:

$$T = \tfrac{1}{2}\,mv^2 = \frac{e^2}{8\pi\varepsilon_0 r} \tag{8-23}$$

The potential energy also depends on r. Taking the potential energy as 0 at $r = \infty$, it is easily shown, by integrating Eq. (8-21), that the potential energy $V(r)$ at any value of r is

$$V(r) = -\frac{e^2}{4\pi\varepsilon_0 r} \tag{8-24}$$

The *total* energy E of the electron is given by

$$E = T + V = -\frac{e^2}{8\pi\varepsilon_0 r} \tag{8-25}$$

The assumption which Bohr introduced in order to decide what particular values of r should be permitted has been justified by more recent developments in quantum mechanics, but in Bohr's day it was a brilliant and remarkable guess. Bohr hypothesized that the *angular momentum* of the electron must be an integer multiple of the quantity $h/2\pi$, where h is the same Planck's constant which relates the energy and frequency of a photon. It may be remarked in passing that this is not a completely unreasonable guess, since h does have the same units as angular momentum, and since the condition that governs the possible orbit radii must be related somehow to the existence of photons. The quantity $h/2\pi$ is now usually abbreviated $\hbar$, read "h-bar."

The electron angular momentum is given by $\mathbf{r} \times \mathbf{p} = \mathbf{r} \times m\mathbf{v}$. In a circular orbit $\mathbf{r}$ and $\mathbf{v}$ are always perpendicular, so the magnitude of this quantity is simply mvr. Bohr's hypothesis therefore becomes

$$mvr = \frac{nh}{2\pi} = n\hbar \qquad n = 1, 2, 3, \ldots \tag{8-26}$$

Combining this with Eq. (8-22) to eliminate v, and solving the resulting equation for r, we find that the permitted radii, which we may call r_n, are

$$r_n = \frac{4\pi\varepsilon_0 n^2 \hbar^2}{me^2} \qquad n = 1, 2, 3, \ldots \tag{8-27}$$

Finally, inserting this expression into Eq. (8-25), we find that the allowed energies E_n are

$$E_n = -\left(\frac{e^2}{4\pi\varepsilon_0}\right)^2 \frac{m}{2n^2\hbar^2} \qquad n = 1, 2, 3, \ldots \tag{8-28}$$

The form of this equation is identical to that deduced from the Balmer formula, Eq. (8-20); in both cases the energy levels are given by a certain constant divided by the square of an integer. Furthermore, Eq. (8-28) permits a theoretical prediction of the Rydberg constant. If Eqs. (8-20) and (8-28) are to agree, it must be true that

$$hcR = \left(\frac{e^2}{4\pi\varepsilon_0}\right)^2 \frac{m}{2\hbar^2} \tag{8-29}$$

Thus this is the really crucial test of the Bohr theory. It turns out, in fact, that the value of R obtained from Eq. (8-29), using the measured values of m, e, c, and h, *does* agree with the value of R obtained directly from spectroscopic data and thus provides direct and rather astonishing confirmation of the Bohr theory.

This model also yields a prediction of the *dimensions* of the hydrogen atom. As Eq. (8-27) shows, the orbit radius increases with energy; for the lowest level, or *ground state*, corresponding to $n = 1$, the radius is given by $r_1 = 4\pi\varepsilon_0\hbar^2/me^2$, which has the numerical value 0.529×10^{-10} m. This value agrees at least qualitatively with other estimates of the size of the hydrogen atom, such as those obtained from the density of solid hydrogen and from the deviations from ideal-gas behavior of gaseous hydrogen resulting from finite molecular size.

The Bohr theory was a remarkable combination of classical principles and of new postulates completely inconsistent with classical theory. Ordinarily it would be expected that an electron traveling in a circular orbit would radiate energy continuously, just as an oscillating dipole radiates, but this is not observed. Even worse, the *frequencies* of the emitted radiation are not the same as the frequencies of orbital motions predicted by the Bohr theory. The Bohr model achieved stability by simply *postulating* that radiation does not occur as long as an electron moves in one of its permitted orbits. But this stability was bought at the expense of throwing away the only classical picture available at that time of the *mechanism* by which energy is radiated. That is, the Bohr theory provided no description of what happens during a transition from one stable orbit to another.

This hybrid character of the Bohr theory was felt by many physicists to be unsatisfactory, and it suffered from other equally serious deficiencies. It was not clear how it should be applied to atoms containing more than one electron, and all attempts to predict energy levels of more complicated atoms failed. Furthermore, later evidence accumulated from a variety of experiments with electrons showed that in many respects the classical picture of the electron as a charged particle with a definite position in space had to be modified drastically. The present-day concept of the electron, which will be discussed in considerable detail in later chapters, is of an *extended* entity which ordinarily is *not* localized at a particular point in space. Thus by present-day standards the Bohr theory was completely wrong conceptually. Still, it was an important milestone, inasmuch as it was the first successful attempt at predicting atomic energy levels, thus paving the way for more detailed understanding of the structure of atoms and the behavior of elementary particles.

8-6 CONTINUOUS SPECTRA

The discussion of the preceding section centered on the understanding of *line spectra* produced by elements in the gaseous state, when interactions between atoms are negligible. Similar and closely related problems arise in connection with the *continuous spectra* emitted by very hot materials in the solid and liquid states. By 1900 it was well known that the spectrum of radiation emitted by matter in condensed states (liquid or solid) is *continuous,* rather than a line spectrum, and that its details are nearly independent of the material emitting the radiation. Studies were made of the distribution of emitted energy among the various wavelengths and of the dependence of this distribution on the temperature of the radiating body. The results of such studies are conveniently represented graphically, as shown in Fig. 8-9. The area under the curve between any two values of λ represents rate of emission of energy in radiation having wavelengths in this interval.

The empirical facts known in 1900 were these: First, the *total* rate of radiation of energy, represented by the total area under the curve, is proportional to T^4, where T is the absolute temperature; this relation is called the

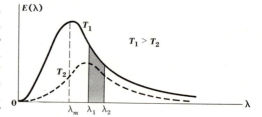

Fig. 8-9 Energy distribution in continuous-spectrum radiation. The area under the curve between any two wavelengths, such as the shaded area shown, represents the rate of energy radiation by waves with wavelengths in the corresponding interval. The total area under the curve represents the total rate of radiation of energy. The broken line shows the distribution for a lower temperature; the maximum is shifted in the direction of longer wavelengths, and the total area is decreased.

Stefan-Boltzmann law. The rate of radiation from an area A of an ideal radiating surface at temperature T is given by

$$P = A\sigma T^4 \tag{8-30}$$

where σ is a numerical constant given by $\sigma = 5.67 \times 10^{-8}$ W/m$^2 \cdot$ K^4.

Second, the wavelength λ_m at which the *maximum* rate of energy emission occurs (corresponding to the maximum of the curve in Fig. 8-9) is inversely proportional to absolute temperature:

$$\lambda_m T = \text{const} = 2.90 \times 10^{-3} \text{ m} \cdot \text{K} \tag{8-31}$$

As the temperature of a body rises, its radiated energy is concentrated in shorter and shorter wavelengths; a glowing body which appears yellow is hotter than one which appears red. This observation is called the *Wien displacement law.* Third, the *shape* of the energy-distribution curve does not change with temperature. A curve for one temperature can be made to fit any other temperature by simply changing the scales on the graph.

In the closing years of the nineteenth century, many attempts were made to understand this behavior. Light was known to be electromagnetic radiation, and it seemed natural to assume that it was produced by vibrations of elementary charges within a material. Attempts were made to *derive* the energy distribution shown in Fig. 8-9, treating the electrons as harmonic oscillators with average energies determined by the equipartition theorem of kinetic theory, discussed in Sec. 13-5. According to the equipartition theorem, each oscillator should have an *average* kinetic energy of $3kT/2$, where k is Boltzmann's constant. None of these attempts was completely successful, but in 1900 Max Planck succeeded in deriving a formula which agreed with observed energy distributions in continuous spectra by adding to the classical equipartition theorem the hypothesis that a harmonic oscillator with frequency f can gain or lose energy only in units hf, where h is Planck's constant.

Planck himself, along with many other physicists of the time, tended to regard this *quantum hypothesis* more as a calculational trick than as a new fundamental principle. As we have already seen, however, evidence for the existence of "particles" of light accumulated to an impressive collection in the years following 1900, so that by 1920 there was no longer any doubt of the validity of this concept. In a sense, the existence of microscopic energy levels may be said to have originated with Planck rather than with Bohr, since this concept is contained implicitly in his picture of the energy relationships of microscopic harmonic oscillators.

The details of Planck's derivation are somewhat involved and need not concern us here; the formula for the energy distribution which he derived with the aid of the quantum hypothesis is as follows:

$$F(\lambda) = \frac{2\pi hc^2}{\lambda^5} \frac{1}{e^{hc/\lambda kT} - 1} \tag{8-32}$$

This function represents the rate of energy radiation per unit surface area of an ideal radiating substance. It agrees with experimental observations of the energy distribution in continuous spectra. It also contains the Wien displacement law and the Stefan-Boltzmann law as consequences. For the first of these, we take the derivative of Eq. (8-32) with respect to λ and set it equal to zero to find the wavelength λ_m of maximum energy radiation. The details of this calculation are left as a problem; the result is

$$\lambda_m = \frac{hc}{4.965kT} \tag{8-33}$$

where the number 4.965 is a numerical constant, the root of the equation

$$5 - x = 5e^{-x} \tag{8-34}$$

obtained when the derivative of Eq. (8-32) is set equal to zero.

The form of Eq. (8-33) is to be expected. Photons are emitted from a body by microscopic oscillating charges, which typically have energies of the order of a few times kT, as shown by the equipartition theorem. A photon of energy kT has a wavelength $\lambda = hc/kT$; a photon whose wavelength is given by Eq. (8-33) has energy of $4.965kT$.

The Stefan-Boltzmann law is obtained by integrating Eq. (8-32) over λ to find the *total* rate of radiation of energy per unit area. This calculation is also left as a problem; the result is

$$\int_0^\infty F(\lambda)\,d\lambda = \frac{2\pi^5 k^4}{15c^2 h^3} T^4 = \sigma T^4 \tag{8-35}$$

This shows that the total rate of energy radiation is proportional to T^4, in agreement with experimental observations, and it also relates σ to other fundamental constants.

8-7   WAVE-PARTICLE DUALITY

We have now examined a variety of phenomena involving light and other electromagnetic radiation. One group of phenomena, comprising what is usually called classical optics, points to the *wave* nature of light, in accordance with the predictions of classical electromagnetic theory. Another class of phenomena, observed in more recent years, points with equal force to the *particle* nature of light. These two aspects of the behavior of electromagnetic radiation seem at first glance to be in direct conflict; nevertheless, the accepted viewpoint today is that they are *not* incompatible. The situation may be

OPTICAL SPECTRA

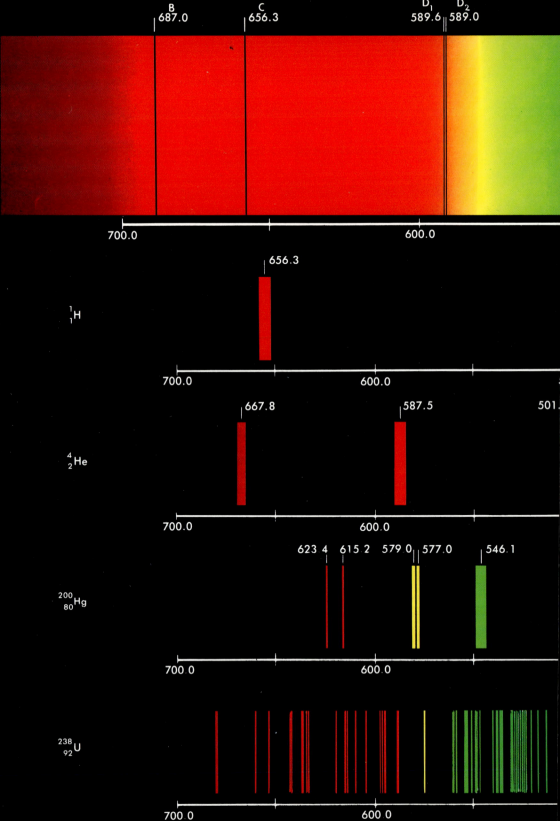

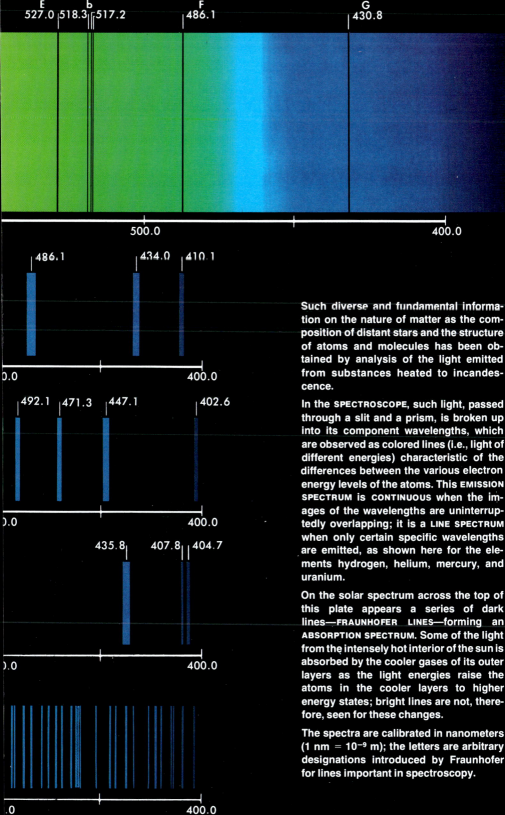

E	b	F	G
527.0	518.3 517.2	486.1	430.8

500.0   400.0

486.1   434.0   410.1

0.0   400.0

492.1 471.3 447.1   402.6

0.0   400.0

435.8   407.8 404.7

0.0   400.0

0.0   400.0

Such diverse and fundamental information on the nature of matter as the composition of distant stars and the structure
of atoms and molecules has been obtained by analysis of the light emitted
from substances heated to incandes-
cence.

In the SPECTROSCOPE, such light, passed
through a slit and a prism, is broken up
into its component wavelengths, which
are observed as colored lines (i.e., light of
different energies) characteristic of the
differences between the various electron
energy levels of the atoms. This EMISSION
SPECTRUM is CONTINUOUS when the images of the wavelengths are uninterrup-
tedly overlapping; it is a LINE SPECTRUM
when only certain specific wavelengths
are emitted, as shown here for the elements hydrogen, helium, mercury, and
uranium.

On the solar spectrum across the top of
this plate appears a series of dark
lines—FRAUNHOFER LINES—forming an
ABSORPTION SPECTRUM. Some of the light
from the intensely hot interior of the sun is
absorbed by the cooler gases of its outer
layers as the light energies raise the
atoms in the cooler layers to higher
energy states; bright lines are not, therefore, seen for these changes.

The spectra are calibrated in nanometers
(1 nm = 10^{-9} m); the letters are arbitrary
designations introduced by Fraunhofer
for lines important in spectroscopy.

compared to the fable about the blind men trying to describe an elephant after touching various parts of its anatomy. The blind men can explore various aspects of the elephant's structure, but it is difficult for any of them to get a correct overall picture. So it is with light. We have to accept the fact that light has both particle and wave properties and that different experiments reveal different aspects of its nature.

We have seen in Sec. 6-5 a hint that wave and particle descriptions of light are not necessarily incompatible. Superposing two waves with slightly different wavelengths results in a wave having a lumpy character not possessed by either separate wave. By superposing a large number of waves having frequencies close to a given central frequency, it is possible to construct a *wave pulse* such as that shown in Fig. 8-10. This wave has regular spacing between successive maxima, equal to the wavelength of the central waves out of which it was constructed, but at any instant of time it is localized in a finite region of space. Such a wave packet clearly partakes of both wave and particle characteristics.

One should not claim that Fig. 8-10 is an illustration of a photon, for various reasons. In the first place, the fact that various wavelengths were used to construct this wave packet indicates a corresponding spread of *energies*, and this clearly is incompatible with the concept of a photon as having a definite energy. Furthermore, such a simplified picture gives no indication of why the energy should be restricted to the value $E = hf$, as observed experimentally. Nevertheless, this picture is useful as an illustration of a phenomenon having both wave and particle aspects.

As an example of the difficulties that arise from attempts to picture a photon too specifically as a particle localized in space or as a wave spread out over a large region, one may consider the quantum interpretation of the two-slit interference experiment discussed in Sec. 5-3. The intensity-distribution pattern corresponds to the numbers of *photons* emerging in various directions; the intensity at any point is directly proportional to the number of photons per unit area, per unit time, in the vicinity of that point.

In the two-slit situation it is tempting to suppose that each individual photon must pass through either one or the other of the slits. But if this is the case, it should be possible to produce a two-slit interference pattern

Fig. 8-10 A wave pulse, or wave packet, which has a more or less definite wavelength but is localized in a finite region of space. Such a wave packet can be constructed as a linear superposition of sinusoidal waves with wavelengths close to that corresponding to successive maxima of the pulse.

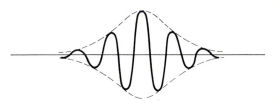

on a photographic film by opening one slit for a certain time interval, then closing it and opening the other slit for the same time. Experiment shows, however, that this procedure does *not* result in a two-slit interference pattern but rather in two superposed single-slit diffraction patterns, quite different from the two-slit pattern. In the wave picture it is easy to see why this procedure fails, since it is essential for the radiation from the two slits to be *coherent* to produce the characteristic two-slit pattern.

The only way to reconcile this apparent paradox is to assume that *every* photon goes partly through *both* slits; only then can the radiation from the two slits be coherent. We must recognize that there is nothing conceptually wrong with this point of view. The photon is not a single point in space, and there is no reason it should have to pass through one slit or the other.

The interference pattern mentioned above can be recorded with a device which detects individual photons. The most common such device is called a *photomultiplier,* and its details need not concern us. To observe the interference pattern, we place the photomultiplier at various positions for equal time intervals and count photons at various positions, as shown in Fig. 8-11. *On the average,* the photon distribution obtained agrees with the intensity of the two-slit pattern. But if the intensity is reduced to the point where there are only a few photons per second, there is no way of predicting precisely where any individual photon will go.

The interference pattern now emerges as a *statistical distribution* of photons, describing how many photons go in each direction, or alternatively

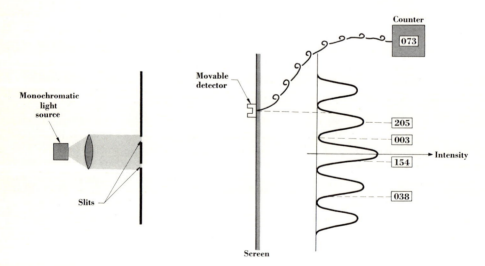

Fig. 8-11 Two-slit interference pattern observed with photomultipliers. The curve shows the intensity distribution predicted by the wave picture, and the photon distribution is shown schematically by the numbers of photons counted at various positions.

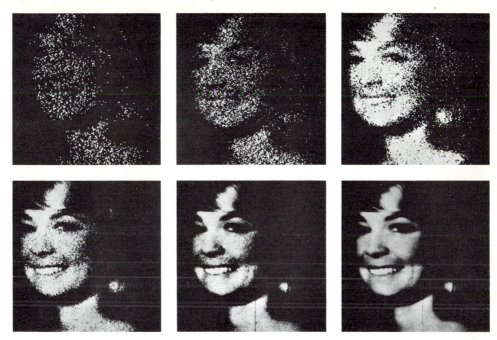

Fig. 8-12 Images formed by small numbers of photons, recorded by using electronic image amplification. Each spot in the upper pictures corresponds to a single photon; with increasing intensity the pattern becomes smoother and the quantum nature of the process is no longer visible. (*From Hecht and Zajak, "Optics." Copyright 1974, Addison-Wesley Publishing Company. Used by permission. Pictures by RCA Laboratories.*)

the *probability* for an individual photon to go in each direction, but *not* where any individual photon will go. Thus the photon picture reveals an intrinsically statistical aspect of the description of interference phenomena. The idea of describing radiation in statistical language is an important concept, and as we shall see in the following chapters, this concept reappears in the quantum-mechanical description of particles.

Figure 8-12, made by using electronic image amplification techniques, also illustrates the statistical nature of light. In the upper pictures each white dot represents an individual photon. When the *total* number of photons is small, the pattern appears almost random; with increasing numbers the pattern emerges and the quantum nature of the process is no longer apparent.

A comprehensive theory of light encompassing both its wave and particle aspects, has been developed only in the past 25 years, in the branch of physics called *quantum electrodynamics.* The concept of energy levels of an atomic system is extended to electromagnetic fields; just as an atom exists only in certain definite energy states, so the electromagnetic field has certain well-defined energy states, corresponding to the presence of various numbers of photons of various energies. Present-day quantum electrodynamics is capable of making extremely precise predictions of energy levels of atoms and of other phenomena involving interaction of matter with electromagnetic radiation. For this subject to come to full flower required 50 years after the conceptual birth of quantum mechanics with Planck's original quantum hypothesis of 1900.

Problems

8-1 Roughly how many photons does a 100-W light bulb emit per second? At what distance is the photon flux equal to 100 per square centimeter of surface, per second?

8-2 A certain radio station broadcasts at a frequency of 1000 kHz with an average power output of 5000 W.
   a What is the energy of a photon in electronvolts?
   b How many photons does the station emit per second?
   c Why are no quantum effects observed in radio transmission at frequencies such as this?

8-3 A γ-ray photon emitted in a certain nuclear reaction has an energy of 1 MeV. Find its wavelength and frequency. How does the wavelength compare with typical nuclear sizes (the order of 10^{-15} m)?

8-4 What minimum accelerating voltage is needed in an x-ray tube in order to produce x-rays with a wavelength of 0.1 nm?

8-5 A radioactive isotope of cobalt, ^{60}Co, emits a γ ray with a wavelength of about 0.932×10^{-12} m. The nucleus contains 27 protons and 33 neutrons.
   a Find the photon energy, in electronvolts.
   b If the nucleus is at rest before emission, what is its recoil speed afterward?
   c Is it necessary to use the relativistic expression for momentum to find this speed?

8-6 Suppose that the cobalt atom of Prob. 8-5 is in a metallic crystal containing 0.01 mol of cobalt (about 6.02×10^{21} atoms) and that the crystal recoils as a whole, rather than only the single nucleus. Find the recoil velocity. (This recoil of the whole crystal rather than a single nucleus is called the Mössbauer effect, in honor of its discoverer, who first observed it in 1958.)

8-7 In a photoelectric-effect experiment, it is observed that for light with wavelength 400 nm a stopping potential $V_0 = 2$ V is needed, and for light with wavelength 600 nm, a stopping potential of 1 V. From these data, calculate the work function for the material, and Planck's constant.

8-8 What energy (in electronvolts) must a photon have so that its wavelength is of the order of magnitude of nuclear diameters (10^{-15} m)?

8-9 Why is the Compton effect not observed for visible light?

8-10 For what wavelength photon does Compton scattering produce a 1 percent increase in wavelength, at a photon scattering angle of 45°? In what region of the electromagnetic spectrum does such a photon lie?

8-11 For what wavelength photon does Compton scattering result in a photon whose energy is one-half that of the original photon, at a photon scattering angle of 45°? In what region of the electromagnetic spectrum does such a photon lie?

8-12 Compton scattering has been observed from *protons* (in targets containing hydrogen) as well as from electrons. For what order of magnitude of photon energy (in electronvolts) would this effect be observable? For example, for what photon energy would the energy loss be of the order of 1 percent?

8-13 Why are the energy levels of the hydrogen atom less than zero?

8-14 A certain atom has the following energy-level scheme: -8, -5, -2, -1, -0.5 eV. Calculate the wavelengths corresponding to all possible transitions between these levels. Which ones lie in the visible spectrum? The ultraviolet? The infrared?

8-15 A certain atom emits spectrum lines at 300, 400, and 1200 nm. Assuming that three energy levels are involved in the corresponding transitions, calculate the spacing of these levels, in electronvolts.

8-16 An electron with mass m collides inelastically with an atom of mass M, initially at rest, and excites it to an energy E above the ground state. By applying the principles of conservation of energy and momentum, show that the initial energy of the electron must be at least $(1 + m/M)E$.

8-17 What minimum electron energy (in electronvolts) is necessary for an electron to excite a hydrogen atom from $n = 1$ to $n = 2$? Is the effect illustrated by Prob. 8-16 significant in this case?

8-18 A proton collides with a hydrogen atom and excites it from $n = 1$ to $n = 2$. What minimum energy must the proton have if the hydrogen atom is initially at rest? Compare your result with that of Prob. 8-17.

8-19 A hydrogen atom makes a transition from $n = 3$ to $n = 1$, with emission of a photon. If it is initially at rest, what is its recoil velocity after emission?

8-20 In a hydrogen glow discharge tube, the atoms are in motion with various velocities, according to the kinetic theory of gases. As a result of the corresponding Doppler frequency shifts, spectrum lines appear not as perfectly sharp lines but as somewhat spread-out distributions of wavelengths. Make a rough estimate of the spread of wavelengths corresponding to Doppler broadening for the $n = 3$ to $n = 2$ transition in hydrogen, for a temperature $T = 1000$ K.

8-21 For the ground state of the hydrogen atom, as described by the Bohr model, find the radius of the orbit, the speed of the electron, its angular velocity, and angular momentum, in the usual mechanical units.

8-22 How do the various mechanical quantities mentioned in Prob. 8-21 depend on the quantum number n?

8-23 A helium atom with one of its two electrons removed (a "singly ionized atom," denoted as He^+) resembles a hydrogen atom in its electron configuration. How are the energy levels and the orbit radii related to the corresponding quantities for the hydrogen atom?

8-24 A *positron* is a particle having the same mass as an electron but opposite charge. A positron and an electron can form a bound state in much the same manner as an electron and proton form a hydrogen atom. This "atom" is called *positronium*. Make an analysis like that of the Bohr model to find the energy levels and orbit radii of the positronium atom. Hint: Neither particle is at rest, but if the distance between them is d, then each particle travels in a circle of radius $d/2$, with its center midway between the particles.

8-25 Derive Eq. (8-33) using the root of Eq. (8-34) given in the text.

8-26 Integrate Eq. (8-32) to obtain the Stefan-Boltzmann law, Eq. (8-35). In the integral, make the change of variable $x = hc/\lambda kT$ and use the following fact:

$$\int_0^\infty \frac{x^3 \, dx}{e^x - 1} = \frac{\pi^4}{15}$$

which can be derived by mathematical trickery.

8-27 What is the total rate of radiation per unit area from:
  a A frying pan at $300°C$
  b A tungsten lamp filament at $3000°C$
if each behaves as an ideal radiator in accordance with Eq. (8-30)?

8-28 Calculate the numerical value of the Stefan-Boltzmann constant σ from Eq. (8-35) and compare the result with the empirical value given following Eq. (8-30).

8-29 A 100-W light bulb operates at a temperature of 3000 K. Assuming it loses energy only by radiation, what must be the total surface area of the filament? Is your result reasonable, considering actual light bulbs?

8-30 A body glows red when heated to 1200 K. Use the Wien displacement law to find λ_m at this temperature. Note that the maximum intensity is in the far infrared even though some visible light is emitted.

8-31 The temperature in the gaseous outer layers of the sun is about 6000 K. At what wavelength is the maximum radiated intensity? In what range of the electromagnetic spectrum does this wavelength lie?

8-32 Show that for sufficiently long wavelengths the Planck radiation law, Eq. (8-32), becomes approximately

$$F(\lambda) = \frac{2\pi ckT}{\lambda^4}$$

Hint: In this limit the exponent is small; for small x, e^x may be expanded in a power series and only the first two terms retained. Thus for small x, $e^x - 1 = x$. The above result is significant because it does not contain h and is identical with a result derived by Rayleigh without Planck's quantum hypothesis. When $\lambda = 10hc/kT$ $(hc/\lambda kT = 0.1)$, this approximate function is in error by about 5 percent.

Wave Nature of Particles | 9

Corresponding to the wave-particle duality for electromagnetic radiation, the fundamental *particles*, such as electrons, exhibit *wave* properties in some situations. This dual nature of material particles was first predicted theoretically and then observed experimentally soon afterward. The discovery of the wave properties of particles necessitates sweeping changes in the fundamental concepts of the description of particles. In general, it is not possible to specify the position of a particle precisely, nor its velocity. Instead, the particle is described as a *wave function* which is not localized in space and which moves with time. The wave function describing a particle is found to be a solution of a certain equation analogous to the wave equation for classical waves.

9-1 DE BROGLIE WAVES

In the year 1924 a young French graduate student, Louis de Broglie, put forth a revolutionary hypothesis which was to shake the very foundations of mechanics and open the door to solution of many of the baffling problems concerning the structure of the atom and its interaction with electromagnetic radiation.

Reduced to its bare skeleton, de Broglie's hypothesis was approximately as follows: Nature loves symmetry and simplicity in physical phenomena. The two great classes of entities which are basic to the structure of matter are electromagnetic radiation and material particles. The first of these, electromagnetic radiation, has been demonstrated conclusively to have a dual wave-particle nature. Therefore, it is reasonable to suppose that *particles* also have a dual nature and that in some circumstances they may behave like waves rather than particles.

De Broglie drew an analogy with the various branches of optics. *Geo-*

metrical optics, with its description of light in terms of rays, is an approximation of the more general *wave* analysis of optics, an approximation which is valid whenever interference and diffraction phenomena can be neglected. Perhaps the particle description of electrons and other particles and the description of their motion in terms of line trajectories are approximations which are valid under certain circumstances, but perhaps there are other conditions under which a more general description is necessary, embodying a *wave* description of electrons and other particles.

If an electron behaves like a wave, what determines its wavelength and frequency? The two fundamental dynamic qualities in the motion of a particle are its energy and its momentum, and these presumably should determine the wavelength and frequency. Pursuing the analogy with electromagnetic radiation, de Broglie proposed that the wavelength and frequency should be determined by the momentum and energy, respectively, in exactly the same way as for photons, namely,

$$\lambda = \frac{h}{p} \qquad f = \frac{E}{h} \tag{9-1}$$

which may be compared with Eqs. (8-1) and (8-15). It was not clear at first whether the energy E should be the total energy of the particle, which would include potential energy and, in the case of relativistic dynamics, the rest energy, or whether it should be just *kinetic* energy. For the moment we consider only nonrelativistic motion of free particles, and E is the kinetic energy.

The wave hypothesis has an interesting consequence in connection with the Bohr theory of the hydrogen atom. We recall that Bohr introduced the somewhat artificial assumption that the angular momentum of the electron must be an integer multiple of $h/2\pi$, expressed by Eq. (8-26) as

$$mvr = \frac{nh}{2\pi} \qquad n = 1, 2, 3, \ldots \tag{9-2}$$

Now mv is just the momentum of the electron, $mv = p$, and according to de Broglie this is related to its wavelength by Eq. (9-1). Therefore $(h/\lambda)r = nh/2\pi$, and

$$2\pi r = n\lambda \qquad n = 1, 2, 3, \ldots \tag{9-3}$$

That is, the orbit circumference $2\pi r$ must be an integral number of wavelengths. This result seems somehow reasonable and suggests some sort of *standing wave* associated with a circular orbit. This is, to be sure, a rather vague and not very satisfactory picture, but the relationship is too remarkable to be a coincidence and must, instead, be an indication that de Broglie's hypothesis *does* have something to do with the description of electrons in atoms.

To appreciate the magnitude of de Broglie's work, we must recall that at the time there was no direct experimental evidence that particles have wave characteristics. It is one thing to suggest a new hypothesis to explain experimental observations; it is quite another to propose such a radical departure from established concepts on theoretical grounds alone. But it was clear that a radical idea was needed; the dual nature of electromagnetic radiation had forced just such a revolutionary proposal in that area, and the relatively complete lack of success in understanding atomic structure and spectra indicated that a similar revolution was needed in the mechanics of particles. Thus, in a sense, the time was ripe for de Broglie's hypothesis, and so it was that in the following years he and other physicists developed it into a detailed theory, even before there was any direct experimental verification of the wave properties of particles.

9-2 DIFFRACTION OF PARTICLES

Three years after de Broglie first advanced his theory about the wave nature of particles, direct experimental confirmation of his hypothesis was obtained. During 1926 and 1927 Davisson and Germer, working at the Bell Telephone Laboratories, were studying the scattering of electrons from the surface of a solid. Electrons emitted from a heated filament were accelerated by electrodes, and the resulting beam of electrons was directed at a block of nickel. The numbers of electrons scattered in various directions were then measured. The experimental setup is shown schematically in Fig. 9-1.

In the midst of the experiments, an accident occurred which permitted air to enter the vacuum chamber enclosing the apparatus. This resulted in the formation of a film of oxide on the target surface. To reduce this oxide, the target was baked in a high-temperature oven; unknown to Davisson and Germer, this had the effect of *annealing* the sample, which had originally been a polycrystalline specimen, so that after the heat treatment it became a large single crystal. After the accident the experimental results were quite different. At certain particular angles there were sharp maxima and minima in the intensity of scattered electrons, in contrast to the smooth variation with angle which had been observed before the accident. Furthermore, the angular positions of these maxima and minima depended on electron energy. Typical results from these experiments are shown in the polar graphs of Fig. 9-2. The similarity of these results to corresponding results from x-ray diffraction experiments, especially in the light of the de Broglie hypothesis, suggested to Davisson and Germer that the electrons were being *diffracted*. If so, this experiment would provide a direct test of the de Broglie hypothesis.

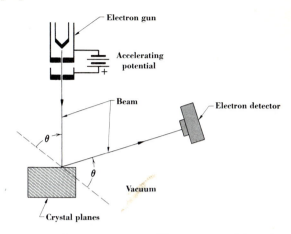

Fig. 9-1 Apparatus for the Davisson-Germer experiment. Electrons emitted from the heated filament are accelerated by the electrodes in the electron gun and directed at the crystal, and the electrons in the scattered beam are observed by a suitable detector. The relative orientation of the electron gun, crystal, and detector can be varied. The entire apparatus is enclosed in an evacuated chamber.

In one particular measurement, using an electron energy of 54 eV, an intensity maximum was observed when both the incident beam and the detector for the scattered beam made an angle of 65° with a particular family of crystal planes (cf. Sec. 6-1) whose spacing had been measured by x-ray diffraction techniques and found to be 0.91×10^{-10} m. (We note that $\theta = 65°$ corresponds to a *scattering* angle ϕ of 50°; since $\phi = \pi - 2\theta$.) As shown in Sec. 6-1, the Bragg condition for constructive interference of waves scattered at an angle θ from planes spaced a distance d apart is

$$2d \sin \theta = n\lambda \qquad n = 1, 2, 3, \ldots \tag{9-4}$$

Thus the electron scattering in this particular experiment is characteristic of

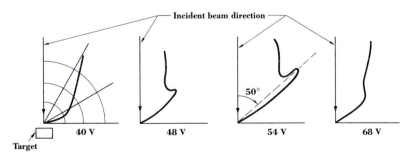

Fig. 9-2 Polar plots of the intensity of a scattered electron beam as a function of angle between incident and scattered beams, showing an intensity maximum in a particular direction for certain electron energies.

a wave whose wavelength is given (with $n = 1$) by

$$\lambda = 2(0.91 \times 10^{-10} \text{ m}) \sin 65° = 1.65 \times 10^{-10} \text{ m}$$

This value is to be compared with the wavelength obtained from the de Broglie hypothesis. The momentum of the particle can be expressed in terms of its energy, which in turn is equal to eV, where V is the potential difference through which the electron was accelerated. That is,

$$E = \frac{p^2}{2m} = eV \qquad (9\text{-}5)$$

Solving this equation for p and inserting the result in the de Broglie relation, Eqs. (9-1), we find

$$\lambda = \frac{h}{p} = \frac{h}{\sqrt{2meV}} \qquad (9\text{-}6)$$

Inserting the appropriate numerical values,

$$\lambda = \frac{6.62 \times 10^{-34} \text{ J} \cdot \text{s}}{\sqrt{2(9.11 \times 10^{-31} \text{ kg})(1.60 \times 10^{-19} \text{ C})(54 \text{ V})}}$$

$$= 1.67 \times 10^{-10} \text{ m}$$

in remarkable agreement with the direct determination from the electron diffraction data.

The following year a similar experiment was performed by the British physicist G. P. Thomson, using a thin film of metal consisting of many microscopic crystals with random orientation. A similar technique had been developed some years earlier by Debye and Scherrer to observe x-ray diffraction with powdered specimens. Again the results were in agreement with the de Broglie hypothesis. It is of interest to note that G. P. Thomson was the son of J. J. Thomson, who 30 years earlier had performed the definitive experiment to establish the *particle* nature of electrons.

Further investigation of the wave properties of particles was carried out by many physicists throughout the world. In Germany, Estermann and Stern diffracted doubly ionized helium atoms (α particles) from a lithium fluoride crystal, establishing that they too had wavelike properties. More recently, *neutron* diffraction experiments have been performed. Thus the wave properties of particles have become well established.

To the extent that an electron or other elementary particle behaves as a wave, it should be possible to describe it with a *wave function*. Waves on a vibrating string are described by a function which represents the displacement of each point in terms of its equilibrium position and time, and in the description of an electromagnetic wave, each field component is represented as a function of the space coordinates and time.

The nature of this wave function for a particle needs to be clarified. For the vibrating string, the function represents a displacement, and for electromagnetic waves it is an electric or magnetic field at a point. But what is it for a "particle wave"? There is some doubt about whether this is a proper question. Just as the concept of electric field is an abstraction introduced to describe the interaction between electric charges, the concept of a wave function associated with a particle is an abstraction introduced to describe the motion of the particle. It would not be appropriate to ask what an electric field is made of, and one may question whether it is proper to ask similar questions about the wave function for a particle. Perhaps we should just accept the fact that using a wave function provides a description of phenomena, and let it go at that.

Nevertheless, the wave function can be discussed in somewhat more definite terms. To the extent that a particle behaves as a wave, it can no longer be regarded as localized at a single point, as in the classical conception of a particle. Thus the question whether the particle lies in a specified region of space at a particular instant of time cannot, in general, have a definite yes-or-no answer. As we shall see later, the wave function provides an answer to such questions in terms of the *probability* of finding the particle in a given region, in an experiment which measures position. Thus we are led naturally to a *statistical* description of the particle's position, quite analogous to the statistical interpretation of interference patterns discussed in Sec. 8-7 in connection with the photon concept. This interpretation helps to round out the symmetry between the description of radiation and that of particles, in the spirit of de Broglie's original hypothesis; it will be discussed in greater detail in Sec. 10-1.

A somewhat easier question to resolve is the apparent inconsistency of the wave and particle points of view. It has already been mentioned in Secs. 6-5 and 8-7 that by superposition of sinusoidal waves with various wavelengths it is possible to construct a wave pulse, or wave packet, which has a more or less definite wavelength and yet is localized in a finite region of space. Such a wave will show interference or diffraction effects only in experiments whose scale is of the same order of magnitude as the wavelength; in any experiment of grosser scale it will appear as a particle, not a wave. For example, electrons accelerated in a television picture tube have to pass through apertures in the accelerating electrodes, and in principle diffraction effects should be observed. But the electron wavelength is exceedingly small compared with the size of the aperture, and the resulting diffraction pattern on the fluorescent screen of the picture tube is so small as to be unobservable.

9-3 WAVE PACKETS

The key to understanding the relationship between the wave and particle properties of electrons and other particles is found in the consideration of wave packets. We now consider in detail how sinusoidal waves can be superposed to form a wave packet which has a characteristic wavelength and yet is localized in a finite region of space. In order to illustrate principles in as simple a context as possible, the present discussion will be limited to waves in one space dimension. The wave function for a particle will be denoted by Ψ.

It is convenient to characterize sinusoidal waves by means of the *wave number* k and the angular frequency ω, related to the wavelength λ and frequency f, respectively, just as in Sec. 3-4:

$$k = \frac{2\pi}{\lambda} \qquad \omega = 2\pi f \tag{9-7}$$

As in Sec. 3-4, the wave speed u is related to k and ω by

$$\omega = uk \tag{9-8}$$

Sinusoidal waves corresponding to wave number k and frequency ω have the following functional forms:

$$\sin (kx \pm \omega t)$$
$$\cos (kx \pm \omega t) \tag{9-9}$$
$$e^{i(kx \pm \omega t)}$$

For mechanical or electromagnetic waves we must use the *real parts* of complex exponential functions, since mechanical displacements and electric and magnetic fields are always real quantities. At this stage in our discussion the wave function for particles is of completely unknown nature, so there is no a priori reason for ruling out complex functions. We shall find, in fact, that the complex exponential is often the most convenient function with which to work.

The above functions are not localized in space but rather extend over all possible values of the coordinate x. But, as pointed out earlier, it is possible to superpose several waves of this form having different values of k and ω so as to obtain a composite wave which *is* localized in space. The simplest example is a wave obtained by superposing two sinusoidal waves with slightly different wave numbers, say k_1 and k_2, with equal amplitudes A. This case was discussed in detail in Sec. 6-5, and it would do no harm for the reader to review that discussion. The result, we recall, is an interference pattern resembling a series of pulses. Even superposition of only two waves has the effect of "bunching" the resultant wave in some regions of space. Furthermore,

as mentioned in Sec. 6-5, there is nothing to prevent our constructing a wave
function $\Psi(x,t)$ which is more general superposition of waves such as

$$\Psi(x,t) = \sum_n A_n e^{i(k_n x - \omega_n t)} \tag{9-10}$$

in an effort to construct a wave which is more localized. If we add waves
with a *continuous* distribution of ω and k, the sum becomes an integral:

$$\Psi(x,t) = \int A(k) e^{i(kx - \omega t)} \, dk \tag{9-11}$$

The function $A(k)$ gives the amplitude of each component wave and is thus
a function of k.

It turns out that by using an appropriate function $A(k)$ we can construct
a wave pulse with *any* desired shape. The process of representing an arbitrary
function as a superposition of sinusoidal functions is called *Fourier analysis*,
and the representations themselves are called Fourier series or Fourier integrals.

Of particular interest are wave pulses constructed with sinusoidal waves
having wave numbers in the vicinity of some central wave number k_0. For
example, suppose the amplitude function has the form shown in Fig. 9-3.
An example of a function $A(k)$ having this general shape is

$$A(k) = Ce^{-a^2(k-k_0)^2} \tag{9-12}$$

In Eq. (9-12), C represents the maximum value of the function, and a
characterizes the *width* of the curve; when a is large, it is sharply peaked,
dropping away rapidly from its maximum at the central wave number k_0,
but when a is small the curve is broader and flatter. Thus a characterizes
the range or spread of values of k used.

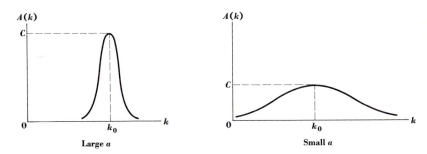

Fig. 9-3 Graphs of Eq. (9-12). The central wave number is k_0, and the maximum height
C. Curves for two different values of a are shown; the width of the curve is inversely
proportional to a.

The analytical expression for the resulting wave function $\Psi(x,t)$ is obtained by substituting Eq. (9-12) into Eq. (9-11) and performing the integration. That is,

$$\Psi(x,t) = \int_{-\infty}^{\infty} Ce^{-a^2(k-k_0)^2} e^{i(kx-\omega t)}\, dk \tag{9-13}$$

To see the general shape of the wave function Ψ, it is sufficient to consider only one instant of time; at time $t = 0$, the wave function is

$$\Psi(x,0) = \int_{-\infty}^{\infty} Ce^{-a^2(k-k_0)^2} e^{ikx}\, dk \tag{9-14}$$

The evaluation of this integral is straightforward but somewhat involved. The details are given in Appendix D; the result is

$$\Psi(x,0) = \frac{C\sqrt{\pi}}{a} e^{-x^2/4a^2} e^{ik_0 x} \tag{9-15}$$

The real and imaginary parts of this complex function are, respectively,

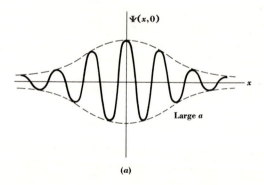

(a)

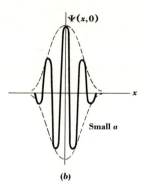

(b)

Fig. 9-4 Graphs of Eq. (9-15a) for one value of k_0 but two different values of a. The width of the curve is directly proportional to a.

$$\text{Re} \left[\Psi(x,0) \right] = \frac{C\sqrt{\pi}}{a} e^{-x^2/4a^2} \cos k_0 x \qquad (9\text{-}15a)$$

$$\text{Im} \left[\Psi(x,0) \right] = \frac{C\sqrt{\pi}}{a} e^{-x^2/4a^2} \sin k_0 x \qquad (9\text{-}15b)$$

Each of these represents a sinusoidal wave, $\cos k_0 x$ or $\sin k_0 x$, multiplied by the envelope function $e^{-x^2/4a^2}$. The real part of this function, Eq. (9-15a), is plotted in Fig. 9-4.

Thus by superposing an infinite number of sinusoidal waves with wave numbers in the vicinity of k_0, we have obtained a localized wave pulse having successive maxima and minima characteristic of a wave number k_0, but with a decreasing amplitude so that the wave pulse is localized in space. The constant a again characterizes the width of the envelope function $e^{-x^2/4a^2}$, but its role is just the inverse of that in Eq. (9-12). When a is small, the exponent $-x^2/4a^2$ quickly becomes large and negative when x becomes different from zero, and the curve drops sharply from its maximum. When a is large, the envelope is less peaked. Thus a sharply peaked function $A(k)$ corresponds to a rather flat function $\Psi(x,0)$, while if $A(k)$ is broad (corresponding to a wide range of component wave numbers), $\Psi(x,0)$ is sharply peaked. This reciprocal relationship has an important significance which will be explored in the next section.

The preceding discussion is designed to persuade the reader that perhaps an electron can be a particle and a wave at the same time. Wave properties are visible in the structure of the packet, yet the *envelope* of the wave packet is localized in space.

We now come to a crucial question. How does the particle move? That is, how does the envelope of the wave packet move? It is clear that we must identify the classical velocity of the particle with the motion of the wave packet envelope, and we must now investigate how to calculate this motion. If we were dealing with electromagnetic radiation in vacuum, there would be no difficulty. All the individual waves would propagate with speed c, independent of the wave number k, and any superposition of such waves would also move with speed c; as a result the entire picture in Fig. 9-4 would move with the speed of light.

When the speeds are different for the various component waves, the situation changes, as shown in Sec. 6-5 for the superposition of two sinusoidal waves with different wave numbers and speeds. In that case, as Eq. (6-34) shows, the sinusoidal wave itself moves with speed $u = \omega_0/k_0$, the speed corresponding to the *average* wave number and frequency, but the *envelope* of the wave moves with a speed called the *group velocity*, given by

$$v = \frac{\Delta\omega}{\Delta k} \tag{9-16}$$

which, if ω is not directly proportional to k, is not at all the same thing. In the limit when Δk is very small, the group velocity approaches the value

$$v = \frac{d\omega}{dk} \tag{9-17}$$

A similar calculation may be performed for the wave packet described by Eq. (9-13). The details of the calculation are somewhat more complicated than in the simple case considered in Sec. 6-5, but the end result is precisely the same; the peak of the envelope is found to move with a speed given by Eq. (9-17). In fact, it is possible to prove this relationship quite generally for any wave packet constructed of sinusoidal waves with wave numbers in the vicinity of a central value k_0. A proof of the general validity of this relation is given in Appendix C.

Now let us see how all this applies to waves describing particles. The de Broglie hypothesis states that the energy and momentum of a particle are related to the frequency and wavelength, respectively, by Eqs. (9-1). Expressing these in terms of k and ω, with Eqs. (9-7), and introducing the notation $\hbar = h/2\pi$, we find

$$
\begin{aligned}
p &= \frac{h}{\lambda} = \frac{h}{2\pi}\frac{2\pi}{\lambda} = \hbar k \\
E &= hf = \frac{h}{2\pi}2\pi f = \hbar\omega
\end{aligned}
\tag{9-18}
$$

The energy E and momentum p are also related by the familiar expression from classical mechanics, $E = p^2/2m$. Therefore,

$$\hbar\omega = \frac{\hbar^2 k^2}{2m} \tag{9-19}$$

from which we immediately obtain

$$u = \frac{\omega}{k} = \frac{\hbar k}{2m} = \frac{p}{2m} \tag{9-20}$$

showing that the *wave speed* u of a matter wave is directly proportional to its wave number, unlike the situation for light, for which c is independent of k.

Equation (9-20) may seem a little alarming, inasmuch as this is exactly *one-half* the classical velocity $v = p/m$ of a particle. But we remember that the significant velocity in the description of a particle in terms of waves is the *group* velocity, given by Eq. (9-17). Applying this to Eq. (9-19), we find for the group velocity of matter waves

$$v = \frac{d\omega}{dk} = \frac{\hbar k}{m} = \frac{p}{m} \tag{9-21}$$

which agrees with the definition of momentum $p = mv$ familiar from classical mechanics.

In the wave description of particles, the classical concept of velocity has meaning only when redefined in terms of the motion of the envelope of a wave packet. Still, this is a natural extension of classical kinematics, and it is helpful in understanding how a single entity can exhibit wave properties in certain experiments and particle properties in others.

There is, however, a serious difficulty in this description, at least from the point of view of classical mechanics. In constructing wave packets we superpose waves having a spread of values of k. Since $p = \hbar k$, this implies that the particle does not have a definite momentum but rather has a spread of values of p, corresponding to the different values of k. From the point of view of classical mechanics, dealing as it does with point masses having definite positions and velocities at each instant, this is clearly nonsense. But as we shall see in the following sections, the wave description of matter forces us to accept the possibility that, just as a particle described by a wave packet does not have a precisely defined *position*, it also need not have a definite *momentum*.

If this idea seems strange and even contrary to common sense, it is because of the prejudices created by newtonian mechanics. Common sense tells us that a body must move with a definite velocity at any instant, and must therefore at that instant have a definite momentum. But common sense is based on everyday observations, and these do not include looking directly at the motions of electrons and atoms. Thus we must be prepared to question our "common sense" when dealing with situations and phenomena far-removed from everyday experience, in areas where intuition may be misleading. In the next section we shall explore in more detail the concepts of *uncertainty* of momentum and position of a particle and the relationship between them.

9-4 UNCERTAINTY PRINCIPLE

A localized wave packet can be obtained only by using a spread of wave numbers. A wave corresponding to a single wave number k is a sine wave with no beginning or end, spreading throughout space. In mechanical language, a particle described by such a wave may have a definite momentum

$p = \hbar k$ only if its position is completely *indefinite*. Conversely, a wave packet with a finite extension requires a spread of values of k, which means in turn a spread of values of momentum, such as the superposition given by Eq. (9-11). In particular, the amplitude function of Eq. (9-12) leads to the wave packet of Eq. (9-15). Let us examine these equations in more detail, with particular attention to the role of the constant a.

As observed in Sec. 9-3, when a is large, the function $A(k)$ is sharply peaked, as in Fig. 9-5a; when a is small, the graph of $A(k)$ is relatively flat, without a sharp maximum, as in Fig. 9-5b. The shape of the envelope of the resulting wave packet, given by Eq. (9-15), depends on a in a similar manner, but here a appears in the *denominator* of the fractional exponent, rather than the *numerator*, so that the dependence is just opposite to the situation for the function $A(k)$. Thus a large a gives a broad, flat envelope for Ψ, as in Fig. 9-5c, while a small a gives a sharply peaked envelope, as in Fig. 9-5d.

The indeterminacy in position or momentum of a particle depends on the width of the functions $\Psi(x,0)$ or $A(k)$, respectively. A particle with relatively *little* uncertainty in its momentum has correspondingly *great* uncertainty in position, as in Fig. 9-5a and c, and a particle with great uncertainty in momentum can have relatively small uncertainty in position, as in Fig. 9-5b and d. This whole situation is in sharp contrast to that of classical mechanics, in which it is possible in principle to determine both the position

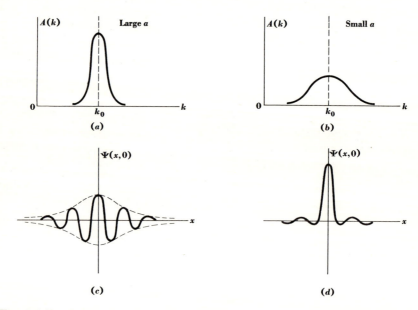

(a)

(b)

(c)

(d)

Fig. 9-5 Two different functions $A(k)$ and the corresponding functions $\Psi(x,t)$, at time $t = 0$. The width of $\Psi(x,0)$ is inversely proportional to that of $A(k)$.

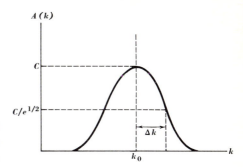

Fig. 9-6 The half-width Δk is the interval over which the curve drops from its maximum value at k_0 to $e^{-1/2}$ of this maximum.

and momentum of a particle precisely. Here we can define the position precisely only if the momentum is uncertain to a high degree, and conversely. Thus we are forced to abandon the classical notion of specifying position and velocity with arbitrarily great precision and, instead, to be content with a somewhat less precise description including *uncertainties* in both position and momentum, which appear in a complementary way.

The relationship between the uncertainty in position and that in momentum can be put in a more quantitative form by first defining more precisely what we mean by the widths of the function $A(k)$ and $\Psi(x,0)$. We arbitrarily define the *half-width* of $A(k)$ as the interval in k over which the function drops from maximum to $e^{-1/2}$ times maximum, or about 0.61 of its maximum value, as shown in Fig. 9-6. Reference to Eq. (9-12) shows that the exponent is zero when $k = k_0$ and equals $-\frac{1}{2}$ when $-a^2(k - k_0)^2 = -\frac{1}{2}$ or

$$k = k_0 \pm \frac{1}{\sqrt{2}a} \tag{9-22}$$

Thus the half-width of $A(k)$, which we may call Δk, is given by

$$\Delta k = \frac{1}{\sqrt{2}\,a} \tag{9-23}$$

Similarly, Eq. (9-15) shows that the envelope of $\Psi(x,0)$ drops from its maximum (at $x = 0$) to $e^{-1/2}$ times maximum when $-x^2/4a^2 = -\frac{1}{2}$, or

$$x = \sqrt{2}\,a \tag{9-24}$$

Thus the half-width Δx of $\Psi(x,0)$ is

$$\Delta x = \sqrt{2}\,a \tag{9-25}$$

Our definition of half-width is of course arbitrary; it does *not* represent a *maximum* departure of k or x from the average value, but it does provide a reasonable characterization of the shapes of the curves. The half-width also corresponds to the quantity known in statistics as the *standard deviation* of the function, which can be used to define the half-width of a function of arbitrary shape.

Each of the uncertainties Δk and Δx depends on a, but their *product* is independent of a:

$$\Delta x \, \Delta k = 1 \tag{9-26}$$

The fact that Δx is inversely proportional to Δk is no surprise; Fig. 9-5 and the accompanying discussion strongly suggest such a relationship. Equation (9-26) can also be expressed in terms of *dynamical* quantities, using $p = \hbar k$. The result is

$$\Delta x \, \Delta p = \hbar \tag{9-27}$$

Although we have developed this equation only with reference to one specific wave packet, it can be generalized for an arbitrary wave packet. The derivation will not be discussed in detail here, but the result is as follows: No matter what amplitude function $A(k)$ is used in the construction of the wave packet, it is always true that

$$\Delta x \, \Delta p \geq \hbar \tag{9-28}$$

The physical content of Eq. (9-28) is as follows: If the position of a particle is known to within an uncertainty Δx, its momentum must necessarily be uncertain by an amount Δp which is at *least* as great as $\hbar/\Delta x$, and conversely. This statement is one form of a famous principle first enunciated by Werner Heisenberg in 1927 and is known as *Heisenberg's uncertainty principle*. Although the original derivation used reasoning somewhat different from the above, this principle is a natural outgrowth of the description of particles in terms of waves.

Additional insight into this important principle can be gained by considering it from a purely particle point of view. In studying the motion of a classical particle, such as a rifle bullet, we have no difficulty in determining the position and velocity with great precision. (For example, we can use high-speed stroboscopic photography.) But as Heisenberg pointed out, this is possible only because, on the scale of observation used in such measurements, the uncertainty required by Eq. (9-28) is so minute that it is much smaller than the experimental errors. On an *atomic* scale things are quite different. Suppose we try to determine the position of an electron with a precision of 10^{-10} m, the order of the size of an atom, by scattering light from it. In order to have sufficient resolving power, the light must have a very small wavelength and correspondingly large energy and momentum per photon. If we are to "see" the electron, at least one photon must bounce off it and enter the microscope or other detector. But the scattering of this photon occurs in an unpredictable direction, and there is a corresponding unpredictable recoil momentum of the electron. The more closely we look, the shorter wavelength and therefore higher-energy photons we must use, and the uncertainty in the electron's momentum becomes correspondingly larger. This argument can be made more quantitative, and the result is in agreement with Eq. (9-28).

Arguments such as this can be misleading, however, inasmuch as they imply that the particle *has* a definite position and that we cannot determine it precisely only because of the inadequacy of our measuring instruments. But the difficulty is more fundamental than this. The electron or other particle is *not* a point with a definite position and momentum, but rather a wave packet, and it is not correct to say that it *has* precisely a certain position or momentum. Thus we are forced to revise our fundamental model for describing what we are accustomed to call *particles*. Although we continue to use the term *particle*, it must now be understood in this more general sense.

Any attempt to observe the position or motion of a "particle" must involve an interaction with the particle which inevitably changes the shape of its wave function. A particle detector can "find" a particle in a certain region of space only if the wave function is initially large in that region, and it turns out that the square of the absolute value of Ψ, that is, $|\Psi|^2$, provides a measure of the *probability* of an interaction with the detector which leads to a temporary localization of the particle and the registering of a count in the detector. Thus we arrive at interpretation of the wave function in terms of *probability* of interaction in a certain region, sometimes described as the probability of *finding* the particle in a certain region.

A particle with uncertain momentum also has uncertain *energy*, and there is an uncertainty principle relating the uncertainty ΔE in energy of a given state of motion to the *time* interval Δt during which the motion is observed. This relation is

$$\Delta E \, \Delta t \geq \hbar \tag{9-29}$$

We can give an illustration of this principle (not to be confused with a real derivation) in the context of the wave packet discussed above. The energy is given by $E = p^2/2m = \hbar^2 k^2/2m$. If there is a small uncertainty Δk in k, the corresponding uncertainty ΔE in E is given approximately by $(dE/dk) \, \Delta k$, with the derivative evaluated at k_0:

$$\Delta E = \hbar^2 k_0 \frac{\Delta k}{m} \tag{9-30}$$

The appropriate time interval Δt is the time taken for the pulse to pass a given observer; this is characterized by the half-width Δx divided by the group velocity $v = \hbar k_0/m$ as in Eq. (9-21):

$$\Delta t = \frac{m\,\Delta x}{\hbar k_0} \qquad\qquad (9\text{-}31)$$

Combining Eqs. (9-30) and (9-31), we obtain

$$\Delta E\,\Delta t = \Delta k\,\Delta x \hbar \qquad\qquad (9\text{-}32)$$

But $\Delta k\,\Delta x = 1$, as shown by Eq. (9-26); so

$$\Delta E\,\Delta t = \hbar \qquad\qquad (9\text{-}33)$$

The energy-time uncertainty relation, which has much more general validity than the above example may suggest, has many applications. When an atom in an excited state emits a photon and decays to the ground state, the process is not instantaneous; during the transition the wave function of the system is a superposition of functions for the two states, hence does not correspond to definite energy. If the atom remains in its excited state for a long time, the energy uncertainty is *small,* but if the transition occurs quickly, there is a *larger* energy uncertainty. We shall return to this principle several times in later chapters in connection with the operation of lasers, width of spectrum lines, fundamental-particle interactions, and other topics.

We have been led in this chapter to a fundamental revision of the concept of the *state* of a system. In classical mechanics, the state of motion of a point particle is described by its position and velocity at any instant of time, and a complete description of motion consists in specifying the position at all times. In *wave mechanics,* this is not possible; a complete description of the state of a particle at one instant of time consists in specifying its *wave function,* and a complete description of its *motion* consists in specifying the wave function for every instant of time. In some respects this is a less precise description than that of classical mechanics, but the nature of things is that this is as complete a description as it is possible to give. In classical mechanics the goal of a problem is frequently to find the position and velocity of a particle as functions of time; in the new *quantum mechanics* the goal is frequently to find the *wave function* describing a particle as it varies with time. The final section of this chapter and most of Chap. 10 will deal with this general problem.

9-5   SCHRÖDINGER EQUATION

In the examples of wave phenomena discussed in Chaps. 3 and 4, we derived from basic principles a differential equation governing the possible wave functions for the system. For transverse waves on a stretched string, the wave function $y(x,t)$ must satisfy the wave equation

$$\frac{\partial^2 y}{\partial x^2} = \frac{\mu}{F} \frac{\partial^2 y}{\partial t^2} \tag{9-34}$$

which is derived from Newton's laws of motion. For the one-dimensional *electromagnetic* waves considered in Chap. 4, the equation obtained from Maxwell's equations is

$$\frac{\partial^2 F}{\partial x^2} = \mu \varepsilon \frac{\partial^2 F}{\partial t^2} \tag{9-35}$$

where F denotes a component of **E** or **B**.

Although we have discussed wave functions for *particles* in considerable detail, we have no corresponding *wave equation* governing such functions. Worse than that, we have no general principle corresponding to Newton's laws or Maxwell's equations from which to *derive* such an equation. Nevertheless, it seems reasonable that a wave equation should exist. The publication of de Broglie's wave hypothesis in 1924 stimulated a great deal of discussion at various centers of research in theoretical physics. At the University of Zurich, the eminent physical chemist Peter Debye suggested to a young German physicist named Erwin Schrödinger that he make a careful study of de Broglie's theory and present it for discussion in a seminar at Zurich. In the course of this study, Schrödinger developed the wave equation which bears his name and which we shall now discuss. Our development will not precisely parallel Schrödinger's original work, but the principles are identical.

It is tempting to try an equation having the classical wave-equation form, as in Eqs. (9-34) and (9-35), with second derivatives with respect to both the space coordinates and time. But the solutions of these equations represent waves propagating with a speed which is independent of wavelength (provided the coefficients are constant), whereas Eq. (9-20) shows that the wave speed for a particle wave *does* depend on wavelength. However, the *form* of the relation of ω and k suggests a possible form of the wave equation. The simplest periodic wave is a *sinusoidal* wave, which in complex exponential form is

$$\Psi(x,t) = Ae^{i(kx-\omega t)} \tag{9-36}$$

For such a function, taking the derivative with respect to x yields the same result as multiplying by ik, while taking the derivative with respect to time is equivalent to multiplying by the factor $-i\omega$.

Now the energy-momentum relationship $E = p^2/2m$ leads, as Eq. (9-19) shows, to the wave-number–frequency relation $\hbar\omega = \hbar^2 k^2/2m$. Thus for the above sinusoidal wave,

$$\hbar\omega e^{i(kx-\omega t)} = \frac{\hbar^2 k^2}{2m} e^{i(kx-\omega t)} \tag{9-37}$$

This suggests that perhaps the differential equation which we seek contains a *first* derivative with respect to time and a *second* derivative with respect to the space coordinate, corresponding to the appearance of ω and k^2, respectively, in Eq. (9-37), which may be rearranged as follows:

$$- \frac{\hbar^2}{2m} (ik)^2 e^{i(kx-\omega t)} = i\hbar(-i\omega)e^{i(kx-\omega t)} \qquad (9\text{-}38)$$

As just pointed out, this is equivalent to

$$- \frac{\hbar^2}{2m} \frac{\partial^2}{\partial x^2} e^{i(kx-\omega t)} = i\hbar \frac{\partial}{\partial t} e^{i(kx-\omega t)} \qquad (9\text{-}39)$$

In other words, when the wave function $\Psi(x,t)$ is *sinusoidal,* it must satisfy the differential equation

$$- \frac{\hbar^2}{2m} \frac{\partial^2 \Psi}{\partial x^2} = i\hbar \frac{\partial \Psi}{\partial t} \qquad (9\text{-}40)$$

We have already discussed at length the fact that a wave of arbitrary shape can be represented as a superposition of sinusoidal waves. If each sinusoidal wave is a solution of Eq. (9-40), any *sum* of such solutions is also a solution. That is, because Eq. (9-40) is *linear,* its solutions obey the *superposition principle.* Thus it is reasonable to surmise that Eq. (9-40) must be satisfied by every wave function that represents a physically possible state of the particle. All this is, of course, conjecture, and the conjecture must stand or fall by the test of experiment. It is clear that this equation passes one experimental test: it is consistent with the observed relationship between energy, momentum, and wavelength for particle waves. In following chapters we shall see much more detailed evidence for the correctness of this equation. The appearance of the imaginary unit i in Eq. (9-40) is significant; it shows that in general the solutions of this equation can be expected to contain complex quantities, and it corroborates the suspicion expressed at the beginning of Sec. 9-3 that wave functions for particles need not be *real* quantities but may sometimes be complex.

Equation (9-40) is the *Schrödinger wave equation.* In the form presented here, it applies only to a *free* particle. That is, its solutions describe a particle that is the quantum-mechanical analog of a classical particle moving in a straight line with constant velocity, with no interactions. Thus this equation plays a role in quantum mechanics analogous to that of Newton's first law in classical mechanics. Most of the problems to which quantum mechanics must address itself involve *interactions* among particles. The electron in the hydrogen atom, for instance, moves under the action of the electrical attraction toward the nucleus. Our next task will be to understand how interactions can be introduced into the wave equation, to enable us to determine the possible wave functions for a particle interacting with a force field. This area is the principal subject for the next chapter.

Problems

9-1 A certain electron microscope uses a beam of 20-keV electrons. If the smallest detail that can be "seen" is equal in size to the electron wavelength, find this size, and compare it with resolution of typical optical microscopes.

9-2 Find the wavelengths of:
    a   1-MeV protons
    b   1-MeV electrons
    c   1-MeV photons
    Which of these would be suitable as a probe to investigate the shapes of nuclei, for which a typical radius is 2×10^{-15} m?

9-3 A "thermal neutron" is a neutron that has come to thermal equilibrium with its surroundings and therefore has, according to the equipartition principle, an average energy $\frac{3}{2}kT$, where k is Boltzmann's constant and T is the absolute temperature. For $T = 300$ K,
    a   What is the energy of such a particle, in electronvolts?
    b   What is the wavelength of such a particle?

9-4 Scattering of high-energy electrons is used as a means of investigating the structure of nuclei. For this purpose the electrons must have a wavelength smaller than nuclear diameters (of the order of 10^{-15} m). What energy (in electronvolts) must an electron have for its wavelength to be 10^{-16} m? Note that this energy is in the "extreme relativistic" range; i.e., the energy is much larger than mc^2, and so the energy and momentum are related approximately by $E = pc$.

9-5 Find the wavelength of a bullet with a mass of 5 g traveling at 300 m/s. Do you think diffraction effects have anything to do with marksmanship?

9-6 Find the energy (in electronvolts) corresponding to a wavelength of 0.1 nm for:
    a   A photon
    b   An electron
    c   A neutron

9-7 Plot graphs showing wavelength as a function of energy, up to about 10^4 eV, for:
    a   Photons
    b   Electrons

9-8 In the Davisson and Germer experiment, for the particular numerical data given, what electron energy would be needed to observe the second-order diffraction maximum at the same angle as the first-order maximum described?

9-9 What order of magnitude energy of α particles would be appropriate for crystal diffraction experiments?

9-10 Find the wave velocity and the group velocity for a wave packet described by the wave function

$$\Psi(x,t) = \frac{1}{4 + (2x - 4t)^2} \sin\left(\tfrac{1}{2}x - 2t\right)$$

9-11 For particles moving at relativistic speeds, $E = p^2c^2 + m^2c^4$, and the corresponding relation for ω and k for the associated waves is $\omega^2 = c^2(k^2 + \mu^2)$, where $\mu = mc/\hbar$. Show that the wave velocity $u = \omega/k$ is always greater than c but that the group velocity $v = d\omega/dk$ is always less than c, and that $uv = c^2$ always.

9-12 A wave packet is constructed using the function

$$A(k) = Ae^{-b|k-k_0|} \qquad \text{where } |k - k_0| = k - k_0 \qquad \text{if } k > k_0$$
$$|k - k_0| = k_0 - k \qquad \text{if } k < k_0$$

Find the corresponding function $\Psi(x,0)$ at time $t = 0$ and the envelope of the function. To evaluate the integral, divide the interval of integration into two regions, $k < k_0$ and $k > k_0$. Make estimates of the "widths" of $A(k)$ and $\Psi(x,0)$ and show that $\Delta x\, \Delta k \cong 1$.

9-13 A wave packet is constructed using for $A(k)$ a function which has the value A (a constant) when $k_0 - a < k < k_0 + a$ and is zero for values of k outside this interval. Find the corresponding function $\Psi(x,0)$ and the envelope of the function. Estimate the widths of $A(k)$ and $\Psi(x,0)$, and show that $\Delta x\, \Delta k \cong 1$.

9-14 For the wave pulse given by Eq. (9-14) at time $t = 0$, find the general wave function $\Psi(x,t)$ for any x and t, if the wave speed is $c = \omega/k$ and is independent of k. By examining the resulting wave function, show that in this case the wave and group velocities are equal.

9-15 Show that the wave function obtained in Prob. 9-14 is a solution of the wave equation

$$\frac{\partial^2 \Psi}{\partial x^2} = \frac{1}{c^2}\frac{\partial^2 \Psi}{\partial t^2}$$

9-16 Find the uncertainty in momentum for an electron with energy of 10 eV and an uncertainty of position of 10^{-10} m, quantities characteristic of electrons in atoms. Compare this momentum uncertainty with the momentum of an electron in a hydrogen atom in the $n = 1$ state.

9-17 An electron in a television picture tube emerges from a hole of 1.0-mm diameter with an energy of 10^4 eV. Calculate the uncertainty in the transverse component of momentum, and from this find the uncertainty of the point where the electron strikes the screen, 0.25 m away. Is this uncertainty likely to have significant effects on the quality of the picture?

9-18 For a particle which has an uncertainty in position equal to its de Broglie wavelength, find the corresponding uncertainty in velocity, and compare with the magnitude of the velocity.

9-19 The minuteness of detail that can be seen with a microscope is limited by the wavelength of the radiation used. To "see" the internal structure of an atom, one would have to use "light" with a wavelength of the order of 0.01 nm. If an electron is "seen" by using this method, find the uncertainty of momentum of the electron:

a By using the uncertainty principle directly
b By considering the momentum transfer to the electron in a head-on collision with a photon of the specified wavelength

9-20 Repeat Prob. 9-19, using an electron instead of a photon.

9-21 A particle is confined in a region of space of dimensions the order of 10^{-15} m, comparable to the dimensions of nuclei. Find the minimum uncertainty in momentum, and from that the minimum uncertainty in energy, if the particle is a proton, and if it is an electron. Compare this energy to the interaction energy of a proton and an electron 10^{-15} m apart. In the early days of nuclear physics this calculation was used as an argument that there cannot be electrons in the nucleus.

9-22 A hydrogen atom is excited by electron bombardment to the $n = 2$ state, about 10 eV above the ground state ($n = 1$). After remaining in this state for 10^{-8} s, it radiates a photon and returns to the ground state. Compute the uncertainty in energy of the excited state, and express as a fraction of the photon energy.

9-23 In the meson theory of nuclear forces a proton or neutron emits an unstable particle called a π meson or *pion*, of mass equal to about 270 times the electron mass. This process violates classical energy conservation, but the uncertainty principle permits such a state to exist for a time limited by Eq. (9-29). Using for ΔE the rest energy mc^2 of the pion, find a typical lifetime for such a state, which is called a "virtual state." How far can the pion travel in this time, if its speed is comparable to c? The pion is eventually absorbed by another proton or neutron, and the distance computed above is an estimate of the maximum *range* of the nuclear force.

9-24 Show that any function in the form

$$\Psi(x,t) = Ae^{i(kx-\omega t)}$$

is a solution of Eq. (9-40), provided ω is given by $\hbar\omega = \hbar^2 k^2/2m$.

9-25 Show that if $\Psi_1(x,t)$ and $\Psi_2(x,t)$ are solutions of Eq. (9-40), then the sum

$\Psi_1 + \Psi_2$ is also a solution. This important result shows that "matter waves" obey the principle of superposition, so useful in calculations of optical phenomena.

9-26 Show that Eq. (9-40) has solutions in the form

$$\Psi(x,t) = e^{at} f(x)$$

Find the function $f(x)$. Do you think such solutions are likely to be physically meaningful? Explain.

Quantum Mechanics | 10

In quantum mechanics, the state of a system is described in terms of a *wave function* for the system. A state may have a mixture of values of momentum, or energy, or other dynamical quantities. For any given system, Schrödinger's equation, together with subsidiary restrictions, determines the possible wave functions that can describe this system and, at the same time, determines the possible energy states. We examine solutions of Schrödinger's equation for two specific systems, a particle in a box and the harmonic oscillator. Finally, we discuss the fact that in some cases other dynamical quantities such as angular momentum are "quantized," and we discuss briefly the general operator formalism by which allowed values of these quantized quantities can be determined. This chapter provides the foundation for the discussion of atomic structure in the following chapters.

10-1 STATE OF A SYSTEM

To introduce general principles in as simple a context as possible, we consider in this chapter only one-dimensional systems. The quantum-mechanical description of such a system uses a wave function $\Psi(x,t)$ which is a function of one space coordinate and time. We regard $\Psi(x,t)$ as a *complete* description of the state of the system; that is, this wave function contains all the information that it is possible to know about the system. We have already remarked that in some respects this is somewhat less specific than the classical description of particle motion, in which it is possible to specify the position and velocity at every instant of time. Nevertheless, the nature of the physical world is such that this more detailed description is not always possible; this is a fact of life which must be accepted.

The *spatial* dependence of the function $\Psi(x,t)$ shows how the particle is distributed in space. This function may be positive or negative, real or complex; the quantity $\Psi^*\Psi = |\Psi|^2$ at a given point in space represents the extent to which the particle is localized in the vicinity of that point. This dependence on the *square of the absolute value* of the wave function is analogous to the situation in optics, where the *intensity* of a wave, which determines the rate of energy transmission, is proportional to the square of the electric-field amplitude.

In an experiment designed to ascertain whether or not a particle is in an interval of space Δx, the *probability* that the particle will be found in this interval is given by

$$\Psi^*\Psi \, \Delta x \tag{10-1}$$

This statement requires further explanation. First any such experiment involves an interaction with the particle, so that after the experiment, if the particle has been found in the interval, the final wave function describing the system is concentrated for the moment in the interval Δx, although the particle may not have had such a definite location *before* the experiment. In the interaction between the system and the measuring apparatus, the wave function describing the system is most likely to be transformed into one concentrated in the interval Δx if the quantity $\Psi^*\Psi$ was initially large in that interval. It is in this sense that Eq. (10-1) represents the probability that the particle will be found in this interval.

The wave function can also be used to obtain information about the *momentum* of the particle in a certain state. As we have seen, a wave function with a mixture of different values of momentum can be represented as

$$\Psi(x,t) = \int_{-\infty}^{\infty} A(k)e^{i(kx-\omega t)} \, dk \tag{10-2}$$

The function $A(k)$ represents the extent to which the particle's wave number is "localized" in the vicinity of k, corresponding to momentum $p = \hbar k$, and $A^*(k)A(k) \, \Delta k$ represents the probability that a measurement of the momentum of the particle will yield a result between $\hbar k$ and $\hbar(k + \Delta k)$. Again, this is not to say that the particle actually *has* this momentum initially; before the experiment it may have a mixture of values of momentum, and it is given a definite momentum in the course of the experiment only because the interaction with the measuring apparatus changes the wave function.

Equation (10-2) shows how the wave function $\Psi(x,t)$ is represented in terms of the momentum distribution $A(k)$; conversely if $\Psi(x,t)$ is known, $A(k)$ can be found. In the language of Fourier analysis, each of these is the Fourier transform of the other. The inverse relation to Eq. (10-2), which we state here without proof, is

$$A(k) = \frac{1}{2\pi} \int_{-\infty}^{\infty} \Psi(x,0)e^{-ikx} \, dx \tag{10-3}$$

Later in this chapter we shall see how other kinds of information can be extracted from the wave function, such as information concerning the angular momentum of the particle.

One of the important goals of quantum mechanics is to predict *energy levels*. The discussion of Chap. 9 showed that, at least for a free particle, a state with energy E has a dependence on the time variable given by the factor $e^{-i\omega t}$, where $E = \hbar\omega$. This relation turns out to be correct even for interacting systems, so in searching for states of definite energy we often begin with the assumption that the wave function has the general form

$$\Psi(x,t) = \psi(x)e^{-i\omega t} \qquad \omega = E/\hbar \tag{10-4}$$

In addition, experience shows that when the particle is in a *bound state*, such as an electron in an atom, it does not spread over all space but is at least partly *localized;* hence in these cases we require that the spatial factor $\psi(x)$ in the wave function must go to zero far away from the center to which the particle is bound. A final restriction on $\Psi(x,t)$ is that it must be a *continuous* function. This requirement is difficult to establish a priori, and is best justified by the fact that it leads to correct energy predictions. There are of course corresponding continuity requirements for solutions of the classical wave equation.

We now summarize the problems that lie ahead. We need to develop a wave equation that includes *interactions* of the particle with a force field. This will be the quantum-mechanical analog of Newton's second law, $F = ma$, whereas the Schrödinger equation for a *free* particle is the analog of Newton's *first* law. Having developed this equation, we then try to find functions that are solutions and therefore represent possible states of the system. In the process, we hope to be able to predict the energy levels of the possible states. Finally, we shall use the wave functions so obtained to develop whatever additional information is needed concerning particular states of the system.

10-2 PARTICLE IN A BOX

As often happens with physical theories, the most interesting problems are not always the easiest ones. Often, in a first encounter with new principles, it is profitable to consider very *simple* applications as illustrations of the principles. The following problem illustrates some ideas not found in the discussion of wave functions for a free particle. We consider a particle which moves along the x axis and is restricted to the interval $0 \leq x \leq L$ by rigid walls at $x = 0$ and $x = L$, as shown in Fig. 10-1. This situation could be

Fig. 10-1 Particle in a one-dimensional box of width L. The particle is confined to the region $0 < x < L$; the wave function must become zero at $x = 0$ and $x = L$. An alternative statement of the problem is a particle in a force field such that the potential energy is zero for $0 < x < L$ but is infinite outside these limits. Such a potential-energy function is called a potential well.

a model for a bead sliding along a perfectly smooth straight wire with rigid barriers at $x = 0$ and $x = L$. What are the wave functions for the possible states of this system, and what are their characteristics?

We begin by searching for states having a definite energy E. As remarked above, any such state is represented by a wave function Ψ whose time dependence is sinusoidal with frequency ω, related to the energy by $E = \hbar\omega$. Such a function may therefore be expressed as

$$\Psi(x,t) = e^{-i\omega t}\psi(x) \tag{10-5}$$

where the function $\psi(x)$ does not contain the variable t. Substituting Eq. (10-5) into the Schrödinger equation (9-40), we obtain

$$-\frac{\hbar^2}{2m}\frac{\partial^2\psi}{\partial x^2}e^{-i\omega t} = i\hbar\psi\frac{\partial}{\partial t}e^{-i\omega t}$$

$$= \hbar\omega\psi e^{-i\omega t} = E\psi e^{-i\omega t} \tag{10-6}$$

That is, $\Psi(x,t)$ is a solution of the Schrödinger equation if and only if $\psi(x)$ satisfies the equation

$$-\frac{\hbar^2}{2m}\frac{\partial^2\psi}{\partial x^2} = E\psi \tag{10-7}$$

which is usually called the *time-independent Schrödinger equation*. In the following discussion the capital letter Ψ is always used for the complete wave function containing both x and t, and the lowercase letter ψ for the corresponding time-independent function.

Equation (10-7) may be rewritten

$$\frac{\partial^2\psi}{\partial x^2} = -\frac{2mE}{\hbar^2}\psi \tag{10-8}$$

from which it is evident that the possible solutions have the form

$$\psi(x) = A \begin{Bmatrix} \sin \\ \cos \end{Bmatrix} \sqrt{\frac{2mE}{\hbar^2}} \, x \qquad (10\text{-}9)$$

where A is a constant. Furthermore, these are solutions of the equation for *every* value of E, and so this does not yet tell us anything about what values of E are permitted.

Now we must use the *continuity condition* introduced in Sec. 10-1. Since the particle is confined to the region $0 \le x \le L$, the wave function $\psi(x)$ must be zero outside this interval, and if it is to be continuous at $x = 0$ and $x = L$, it must be zero at these points. Thus we require $\psi(0) = 0$ and $\psi(L) = 0$. The first condition eliminates the cosine functions in Eq. (10-9) from consideration, since they are *not* zero at $x = 0$. The sine functions *do* satisfy this condition, but they must also be zero at $x = L$; that is, we must have

$$\sin \frac{\sqrt{2mE}}{\hbar} L = 0 \qquad (10\text{-}10)$$

which is true only when

$$\frac{\sqrt{2mE}}{\hbar} L = n\pi \qquad n = 1, 2, 3, \ldots \qquad (10\text{-}11)$$

Thus the Schrödinger equation and the continuity condition are both satisfied only for values of E that are consistent with Eq. (10-11); hence the possible energy levels for the system have been determined! Solving this equation for E, we find that the possible energies E_n are given by

$$E_n = \frac{1}{2m} \left(\frac{\pi\hbar}{L}\right)^2 n^2 \qquad n = 1, 2, 3, \ldots \qquad (10\text{-}12)$$

and the corresponding wave functions, which we may call $\psi_n(x)$, are

$$\psi_n(x) = A \sin \frac{n\pi}{L} x \qquad (10\text{-}13)$$

Writing the wave function in this form makes it easy to see that the boundary condition at $x = L$ is satisfied. We also note that there is *no* state with $E = 0$, for then $\psi(x)$ is zero *everywhere*, corresponding to no particle anywhere! Hence the lowest-energy state, or *ground state*, has $E = (\pi\hbar/L)^2/2m$.

Several wave functions in the series are shown in Fig. 10-2. In each case the number of *nodes* (points where $\psi = 0$) is $n + 1$ and the number of *antinodes* is n. The lowest-energy states have the smoothest wave functions, and as the energy increases, the functions become increasingly peaked. This

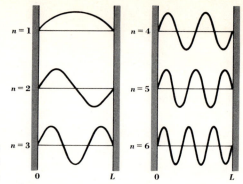

Fig. 10-2 Wave functions for particle in a box. The energy of each state is proportional to n^2.

figure also illustrates the analogy of this problem to that of the normal modes of a stretched string of length L, discussed in Sec. 3-8.

We discussed in Sec. 10-1 the interpretation of the quantity $\Psi^*\Psi\,dx$ as the probability of finding the particle in the interval dx. Referring to Eq. (10-4), we see that

$$\Psi^*(x,t)\Psi(x,t) = \psi^*(x)e^{i\omega t}\psi(x)e^{-i\omega t}$$
$$= \psi^*(x)\psi(x) \tag{10-14}$$

which shows that *for any state having definite energy the probability distribution is independent of time.*

It is customary to define probabilities so that the *total* probability for all possible events is unity. This corresponds to saying that the probability of finding the particle *somewhere* in the region $0 \le x \le L$ is unity. Thus it is convenient to choose the constant A in Eq. (10-13) so that

$$\int_0^L \psi^*(x)\psi(x)\,dx = 1 \tag{10-15}$$

In this case $\psi(x)$ happens to be *real*, $\psi^*(x)$ and $\psi(x)$ are equal, and inserting Eq. (10-13) in Eq. (10-15) gives

$$\int_0^L A^2 \sin^2 \frac{n\pi}{L} x\,dx = 1 \tag{10-16}$$

Evaluation of this integral is left for the reader; the result is that Eq. (10-16) is satisfied by choosing $A = (2/L)^{1/2}$.

A wave function that satisfies Eq. (10-15) is said to be *normalized*. It is usually convenient to deal with normalized wave functions whenever possible, and we shall do so in all future discussions. Thus, the normalized wave functions for this problem are

$$\psi_n(x) = \sqrt{\frac{2}{L}} \sin \frac{n\pi}{L} x \qquad n = 1, 2, 3, \ldots \tag{10-17}$$

To summarize the above procedure: We first obtained an infinite set of solutions for the differential equation governing wave functions for this problem. From this infinite set, we selected a series of functions satisfying not only the differential equation but also the *boundary* conditions resulting from the continuity condition. While the differential equation itself is satisfied for *any* value of E in the solutions, only for a certain discrete set of values of E is it possible to satisfy *both* the differential equation and the boundary conditions. This situation is typical of those found in solutions of Schrödinger's equation. In Sec. 10-5 we shall consider a similar problem in which the boundary condition is slightly more subtle. The problem discussed there is the harmonic oscillator, in which there is a *potential energy* $\frac{1}{2}kx^2$; the boundary condition is that the wave function should *approach* zero at distances very far away from the center of force, rather than that it should *equal* zero at some finite distance. Before discussing this problem, however, we need to develop methods for finding the differential equation corresponding to any given force field. This is the subject of the next section.

10-3 SCHRÖDINGER EQUATION WITH INTERACTIONS

The preceding sections have been devoted to the wave equation for a free particle, the quantum-mechanical analog of a classical particle moving with constant velocity under the action of no force. Now we shall generalize this equation to include *interaction* of the particle with its surroundings by means of a force field. The resulting equation corresponds to Newton's *second* law in classical mechanics, just as the free-particle wave equation corresponds to Newton's *first* law.

The experimental evidence on which this new equation is based is of a rather indirect nature, consisting mostly of data on energy levels of atoms, together with the observation that free particles behave like waves. From such data it is not possible to *derive* the general dynamical law without making a bold guess at some point, just as 300 years ago it required the genius of Newton to make the leap from a mass of empirical data on planetary and terrestrial motion to a compact set of dynamical laws. Equipped with the hindsight provided by the 50-year history of quantum mechanics, we can try to make this new dynamical law look *reasonable*, but it would be misleading to pretend that it can be rigorously *derived*.

As previously, we concentrate for the moment on one-dimensional problems with coordinate x. In addition, we consider only an interaction described by a *conservative* force field,[1] that is, a force $F(x)$ which is a function

---

[1]See H. D. Young, "Fundamentals of Mechanics and Heat," 2d ed., sec. 9-7, McGraw-Hill Book Company, New York, 1974.

only of position and can be represented in terms of a potential-energy function $V(x)$, where $F(x) = -dV/dx$. A familiar example from classical mechanics is the spring force in a harmonic oscillator, $F = -kx$, with corresponding potential energy $V = \frac{1}{2}kx^2$. The restriction to conservative force fields is justified at least in part by the fact that many of the important interactions between particles, including electrical and gravitational interactions, *are* represented by conservative force fields.

In general, a particle does not have a definite position, and so neither will it have a definite potential energy V at any instant. But the particle's momentum and thus its kinetic energy are also uncertain, and so a state with definite *total* energy may be possible, despite the fact that kinetic or potential energy separately may not have a definite value. Thus the classical concept of potential energy can be taken over into quantum-mechanical problems without difficulty.

Because a particle has both kinetic and potential energies, it is not obvious which of these, if either, should be used to determine the *frequency* of the wave function. In making the choice, we are guided by the analogous situation in classical wave propagation; when a wave in one medium enters another medium in which the wave speed is different, its *wavelength* changes but its *frequency* is the same in both media. It is reasonable to expect a similar state of affairs with "matter waves." At each point x the wave function is some periodic function of time, and in analogy with the classical wave situation we expect the *frequency* of this time dependence to be the same at various points even though the potential energy is, in general, different. For this to be true, the frequency must be determined by the *total* energy of the system. This observation provides an important clue to the development of the generalized wave equation.

In developing the free-particle wave equation in Sec. 9-5 we wrote the energy-momentum relation $p^2/2m = E$ as a wave-number–frequency relation $\hbar^2 k^2/2m = \hbar\omega$. Then associating ik with the operation $\partial/\partial x$ and $-i\omega$ with the operation $\partial/\partial t$ led to the wave equation

$$-\frac{\hbar^2}{2m}\frac{\partial^2\Psi}{\partial x^2} = i\hbar\frac{\partial\Psi}{\partial t} \tag{10-18}$$

We now retrace this path; for a conservative system the sum of kinetic and potential energies is the constant total energy E.

$$\frac{p^2}{2m} + V(x) = E \tag{10-19}$$

The corresponding wave-number–frequency relation, associating frequency with *total* energy as discussed above, is

$$\frac{\hbar^2 k^2}{2m} + V = \hbar\omega \tag{10-20}$$

Making the same associations $ik \leftrightarrow \partial/\partial x$ and $-i\omega \leftrightarrow \partial/\partial t$ as before, we obtain the equation

$$-\frac{\hbar^2}{2m}\frac{\partial^2\Psi(x,t)}{\partial x^2} + V(x)\Psi(x,t) = i\hbar\frac{\partial\Psi(x,t)}{\partial t} \tag{10-21}$$

which differs from the free-particle Schrödinger equation, Eq. (9-40), in having the additional term containing the potential energy.

Equation (10-21) is thus a more general form of the *Schrödinger equation*. With one further generalization, to be discussed in Sec. 10-6, it provides the key to the application of the concepts of quantum mechanics to a wide variety of systems. Solutions for this equation contain, in principle, detailed information about the structure of atoms, including electron configurations, energy levels, and so on. To be sure, applications of this equation often pose formidable *mathematical* difficulties, but as far as *principles* are concerned, we are now well on our way to an understanding of atomic structure.

We now return briefly to the continuity condition introduced in Sec. 10-1. If Eq. (10-21) is to be satisfied at every value of x at every instant of time, the derivatives $\partial^2\Psi/\partial x^2$ and $\partial\Psi/\partial t$ must *exist* for all x and t; a necessary condition for the existence of these derivatives is for Ψ to be a *continuous* function of x and t, and for $\partial\Psi/\partial x$ also to be a continuous function. The only exception to this requirement occurs when $V(x)$ has an infinite discontinuity; at such a point it is sufficient for Ψ itself to be continuous.

Any wave function corresponding to a state having a definite total energy E has a definite frequency $\omega = E/\hbar$; the time dependence of such a wave function is contained in a factor

$$e^{-i\omega t} = e^{-iEt/\hbar} \tag{10-22}$$

just as for a free particle. Thus any wave function $\Psi(x,t)$ representing a state with a definite, constant total energy E can be written in the form

$$\Psi(x,t) = e^{-iEt/\hbar}\psi(x) \tag{10-23}$$

Inserting this in Eq. (10-21), we find that $\psi(x)$ must satisfy the differential equation

$$-\frac{\hbar^2}{2m}\frac{d^2\psi(x)}{dx^2} + V(x)\psi(x) = E\psi(x) \tag{10-24}$$

in which the factor $e^{-iEt/\hbar}$ has been divided out. This is the *time-independent Schrödinger equation*. It is less general than Eq. (10-21) because it is valid only for states that have definite total energy. Nevertheless, one of the important problems in atomic structure is to predict energy levels, and so this is a very useful equation.

10-4 SOLUTIONS OF SCHRÖDINGER EQUATION

Many of the most important problems of quantum mechanics are concerned directly with finding and interpreting the solutions of Eq. (10-24) or a similar equation for problems in three dimensions. Solving such equations often involves considerable mathematical complexity, and we shall consider only a few particularly simple examples. First, however, it is instructive to make a *qualitative* study of properties of solutions for certain simple potential-energy functions. In this preliminary discussion the relation between classical and quantum-mechanical descriptions of motion will be emphasized.

First we show that in any region where the potential energy V is *constant*, the solution of Eq. (10-24) is a *sinusoidal* function. The equation can be rewritten as

$$\frac{d^2\psi}{dx^2} + \frac{2m(E - V)}{\hbar^2}\psi = 0 \tag{10-25}$$

where the coefficient of ψ is constant. The solutions of this equation are

$$\psi(x) = A \begin{Bmatrix} \sin \\ \cos \end{Bmatrix} kx \tag{10-26}$$

where k is the wave number, related to the wavelength λ as usual by $k = 2\pi/\lambda$, and A is a constant amplitude factor. Substitution of Eq. (10-26) into Eq. (10-25) shows that the wave number is given by

$$k^2 = \frac{2m(E - V)}{\hbar^2} \tag{10-27}$$

and the corresponding wavelength is

$$\lambda = \frac{h}{\sqrt{2m(E - V)}} \tag{10-28}$$

This result agrees with the de Broglie relation $\lambda = h/p$, with the momentum p determined from the energy relation $p^2/2m + V = E$.

Using this result, we can predict some general features of wave functions corresponding to a "step-function" potential energy such as that shown in Fig. 10-3. In each of the two regions the potential energy is constant; the constant total energy E is also shown. According to Eq. (10-28), the wave function for $x > 0$, where $V = V_0$, should have a *longer* wavelength than

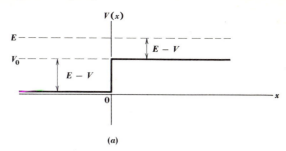

(a)

Fig. 10-3 (a) A two-level potential-energy function. The broken line labeled E represents the constant total energy, and the distance between this and the potential-energy line represents the kinetic energy. (b) A possible wave function. The left side is a region of larger kinetic energy and correspondingly shorter wavelength and smaller amplitude than the right side; the two functions must join smoothly at $x = 0$.

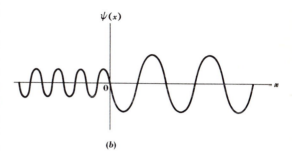

(b)

in the region $x < 0$, where $V = 0$. Furthermore, since the particle's *speed* is greater in the region where $V = 0$ than in the region where it is V_0, it spends a relatively smaller time on the left side than the right; hence we expect the *amplitude* of the wave function to be smaller on the left than the right. The general behavior of the wave function is shown in Fig. 10-3b. We also note that different amplitudes for the two sides are necessary in order for the two functions to join smoothly at $x = 0$, as required by the *continuity condition* that the function and its first derivative must be continuous at $x = 0$.

When the total energy E is *less than* V_0. as in Fig. 10-4a, a new consideration enters. In classical mechanics, in a region where the potential energy is greater than the total energy, the kinetic energy is *negative;* this is impossible, and so classically a particle can never enter such a region. But Eq. (10-25) still has solutions in this region; the coefficient of ψ is now negative, so that the solutions are not sinusoidal but rather *real exponential* functions. The reader can verify that the solutions are

$$\psi(x) = Ae^{\pm\gamma x} \qquad \gamma^2 = \frac{2m(V_0 - E)}{\hbar^2} \tag{10-29}$$

In the present problem, the function with the positive exponent is not permitted because it grows large without bound in the classically forbidden region $x > 0$. Thus the wave function for $x > 0$ must be a decreasing exponential function. According to the continuity condition, this must join smoothly onto the sinusoidal solution for $x < 0$, so that the solutions have the general form shown in Fig. 10-4b. There is some penetration of the wave function into the region of negative kinetic energy, a phenomenon which has no analog in classical mechanics.

An interesting situation occurs when two regions of positive kinetic energy are separated by a potential-energy *barrier* of height greater than the total energy, as shown in Fig. 10-5a. In the central region the wave function is *exponential*, and in the side regions sinusoidal; at each boundary the function and its first derivative are continuous. Such a function, representing a state of definite total energy, is not localized in space. However, just as for free particles, a wave packet can be constructed by superposing several wave functions with slightly different energies and a corresponding spread of wavelengths. As we have seen, these functions are not precisely zero in the classically forbidden region. Thus if such a wave packet approaches such a potential barrier, there is a finite probability that it will appear at a later time on the opposite side of the barrier! This behavior, which has no analog in classical mechanics, has been described as "tunneling through a potential hill" which could not be surmounted classically. Although this phenomenon makes no sense in the context of classical mechanics, it is a very real quantum-mechanical phenomenon. It is by this mechanism that α particles escape from radioactive nuclei despite the potential-energy barriers that bind the particles to their nuclei. In the electronic circuit device called the *tunnel*

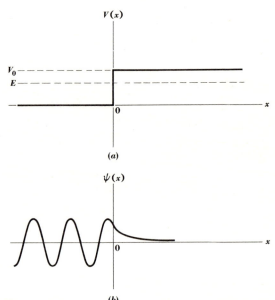

(a)

Fig. 10-4 A possible wave function for the two-level potential-energy function of Fig. 10-3a for the case $E < V_0$. The function is sinusoidal in the region of positive kinetic energy and exponential in the region of negative potential energy; the two functions must join smoothly at $x = 0$.

(b)

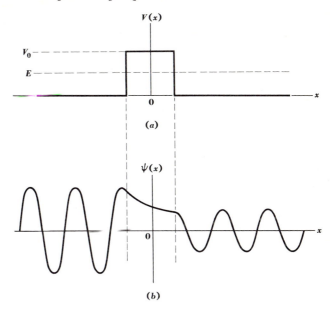

Fig. 10-5 (a) A potential-energy barrier. A particle whose energy E is less than the height V_0 of the barrier can move from one side to the other even though they are separated by a region of negative kinetic energy. (b) A possible wave function. This function is sinusoidal on each side and exponential in the middle. The functions must join smoothly at each boundary.

diode, electrons traverse a region of negative kinetic energy in traveling across a boundary layer from one region of a germanium crystal to another.

For the "step" and "barrier" potential-energy functions the particle is not *bound* in the sense of being localized in a certain region. Correspondingly, there are no restrictions on the energy of the particle; the continuity conditions can be satisfied for *any* value of E. Conversely, in the particle-in-a-box problem of Sec. 10-2, the particle *is* localized or "bound," and the appropriate boundary conditions can be satisfied only with certain particular total energies. To illustrate this situation further, we consider the potential-energy "well" shown in Fig. 10-6a, for total energy E less than V_0.

Just as before, the solution of the Schrödinger equation is sinusoidal in the regions where $E > V$, that is, when $-L \le x \le L$, and exponential in the other two regions, and the function and its first derivative must be continuous at the points $x = \pm L$. If we choose E arbitrarily, it may be necessary to use growing exponentials to satisfy these continuity conditions, as in Fig. 10-6b. Such a wave function grows very large at large positive or negative x and it thus cannot represent a bound state. When this happens, E is not one of the permitted energies of the system. Only when the chosen E yields *decreasing* exponentials on both sides, as in Fig. 10-6c, is it a

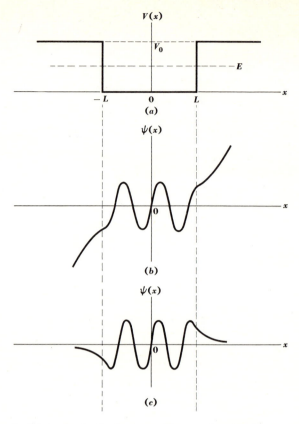

Fig. 10-6 (a) A potential well of finite depth. (b) An impossible wave function. For the energy chosen, boundary conditions require growing exponentials in the end regions, which have no physical meaning. Hence this energy is not a permitted energy level for the system. (c) A possible wave function. The function is sinusoidal in the central region and a decaying exponential on each end. The functions must join smoothly at the boundaries.

permissible energy value. Hence the boundary conditions at $x = \pm L$ limit the possible energies to a discrete set of levels, each with its own wave function.

This general discussion can be extended to problems in which the potential-energy function $V(x)$ is a continuously varying function rather than a series of steps. In the vicinity of a point at which $E > V$, the function behaves like a small segment of a sinusoidal function with a wavelength characteristic of the kinetic energy at that point, according to Eq. (10-28). For some functions the potential energy may vary sufficiently rapidly compared with a wavelength so that the resulting wave function bears little resemblance to a sinusoidal function. Still, the concept of a "locally sinusoidal" wave often is a useful one; this viewpoint is helpful in understanding the properties of the wave functions for the quantum-mechanical harmonic oscillator to be discussed in the next section.

10-5 HARMONIC OSCILLATOR

We now consider a quantum-mechanical analysis of the harmonic oscillator, which consists in classical mechanics of a point mass m attracted to a center of force at the origin ($x = 0$) with a force given by $F = -kx$, where x is the displacement from the origin and k is the force constant. The potential energy of the particle at point x is $V(x) = \frac{1}{2}kx^2$. Newton's second law leads to the differential equation

$$\frac{d^2x}{dt^2} + \frac{k}{m}x = 0 \tag{10-30}$$

whose solutions are

$$x = A\cos(\omega t + \phi) \qquad \omega = \sqrt{\frac{k}{m}} \tag{10-31}$$

where A and ϕ are constants, and ω is the angular frequency, determined by the mass and force constant as shown. In the discussion which follows, we continue to use ω as an abbreviation for the quantity $(k/m)^{1/2}$.

Just as in classical mechanics, the harmonic oscillator in quantum mechanics is of considerable importance, not only because situations involving harmonic motion occur frequently, but also because there are a great many situations, such as molecular vibrations, in which the harmonic oscillator provides a simplified *model* of a more complicated system. Planck, in his original work on radiation, represented the *sources* of radiation as harmonic oscillators with various frequencies. Energy is emitted by these oscillators in bundles of size $hf = \hbar\omega$, so it would not be surprising if the quantum-mechanical harmonic oscillator turned out to have energy levels with spacing $\hbar\omega$ between adjacent levels.

The wave functions representing states of definite total energy must be solutions of the time-independent Schrödinger equation, which for the present problem takes the form

$$-\frac{\hbar^2}{2m}\frac{d^2\psi}{dx^2} + \frac{1}{2}kx^2\psi = E\psi \tag{10-32}$$

This equation becomes considerably easier to handle if we make two changes of variable. To accomplish this, we multiply the entire equation by the factor

$$\frac{2}{\hbar\omega} = \frac{2}{\hbar}\sqrt{\frac{m}{k}} \tag{10-33}$$

obtaining the following result:

$$-\frac{\hbar}{\sqrt{mk}}\frac{d^2\psi}{dx^2} + \frac{\sqrt{mk}}{\hbar}x^2\psi = \frac{2E}{\hbar\omega}\psi \tag{10-34}$$

The form of this equation suggests the following substitutions:

$$y^2 = \frac{\sqrt{mk}}{\hbar}x^2 \qquad \alpha = \frac{2E}{\hbar\omega} \tag{10-35}$$

This step has the advantage that the new variables y and α are *dimensionless* quantities. Proof of this statement is left as a problem. The change from x to y corresponds to changing the scale of length measurement, and changing from E to α corresponds to measuring energy in different units.

In terms of the new variables, the wave equation becomes

$$\frac{d^2\psi}{dy^2} = (y^2 - \alpha)\psi \tag{10-36}$$

We note that the points $y^2 = \alpha$ have a special significance; reference to Eqs. (10-35) shows that at these points

$$\frac{\sqrt{mk}}{\hbar}x^2 = \frac{2E}{\hbar\omega}$$

Since $\omega = (k/m)^{1/2}$, this can be rewritten

$$\tfrac{1}{2}kx^2 = E$$

That is, at $y^2 = \alpha$ the *potential* energy $\tfrac{1}{2}kx^2$ is equal to the *total* energy; this therefore represents the classical limit of motion; the *amplitude* for the dimensionless variable y in a classical description of the motion is $\alpha^{1/2}$. The regions $y^2 > \alpha$ correspond to the classically forbidden regions of negative kinetic energy. If the function is to represent a particle localized in space, it must approach zero in these regions.

Thus the problem is to find solutions of Eq. (10-36) that approach zero as $y \to \pm\infty$. To understand why this condition is met only for certain values of α, we examine the behavior of the function in the region $y^2 > \alpha$. If the function and its slope are both *positive* in this region, $d^2\psi/dx^2$ is also positive; the slope continuously increases, and the function goes off toward infinity. The same thing happens if the function and its slope are both negative. Only when the function and its slope have *opposite* sign, and when the two have just the right relation, can the function curve asymptotically toward zero at large y. This behavior occurs only for a discrete set of values of α, and hence of E.

Thus, just as for the particle in a box, the admissible wave functions and corresponding energies are those which satisfy not only the wave equation but also the *boundary conditions*. For the particle in a box, the boundary condition was that the wave function should equal zero at the walls. In this case, we require instead that the wave function *approach* zero at large y. Solutions of the differential equation having this property exist only for certain specific values of α, and they are therefore the values corresponding to the possible states.

Obtaining the admissible solutions of Eq. (10-36) and the corresponding values of α requires some mathematical acrobatics which we shall omit. The results turn out to be rather simple in form; the functions all have the form $e^{-y^2/2}$ multiplied by a *polynomial* in y which contains either only even-power terms or only odd-power terms. These polynomials are known as Hermite polynomials, and the functions, each consisting of a polynomial multiplied by the exponential factor, are called Hermite functions. For reference, the first few Hermite functions and the corresponding values of α are listed in Table 10-1. These are customarily labeled according to the index n representing the maximum power of y that appears in the polynomial. The functions are labeled $\psi_n(y)$ and the corresponding values of α are $\alpha_n = 2n + 1$. The reader is invited to verify by substitution into Eq. (10-36) that these are indeed solutions of the equation; the exponential factor guarantees that they approach zero at large y, no matter what the degree of the polynomial.

As the table shows, it is customary to define the Hermite functions so that the coefficient of the highest power of y in the polynomial is equal to 2^n in each case. When defined in this way, the functions are not *normalized* in the sense of Sec. 10-2. To normalize them, each function $\psi_n(y)$ must be multiplied by a numerical factor which turns out to be $(\pi^{1/2}\, 2^n n!)^{-1/2}$, but this is a mathematical detail. Graphs of the first few Hermite functions are shown in Fig. 10-7. For each, the corresponding "classical limits" of motion

Table 10-1 Hermite Functions, Solutions of the Equation

$$\frac{d^2\psi}{dy^2} = (y^2 - \alpha)\psi$$

n	$\psi_n(y)$	$\alpha_n = 2n + 1$
0	$e^{-y^2/2}$	1
1	$2ye^{-y^2/2}$	3
2	$(4y^2 - 2)e^{-y^2/2}$	5
3	$(8y^3 - 12y)e^{-y^2/2}$	7
4	$(16y^4 - 48y^2 + 12)e^{-y^2/2}$	9
5	$(32y^5 - 160y^3 + 120y)e^{-y^2/2}$	11

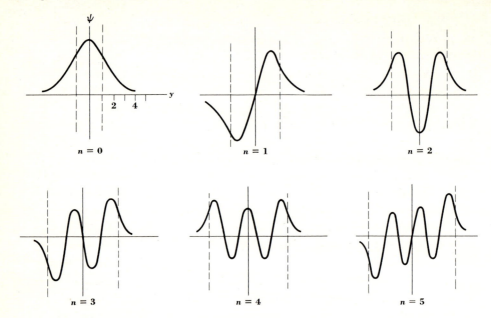

Fig. 10-7 The first six harmonic-oscillator wave functions. These are graphs of the Hermite functions in Table 10-1. The number of nodes in each function is equal to the quantum number n. The scale for y is the same for all functions, but the vertical scales are different. The classical limits of motion (amplitudes) are shown as broken lines; these correspond to inflection points on the curves, and are determined in each case by the condition $y^2 = \alpha = 2n + 1$.

(the amplitude of a classical system having the same energy) are shown as broken lines. At these points $y^2 = \alpha$ and $d^2\psi/dx^2 = 0$, so they are *points of inflection.*

The permissible values of α are given by the expression $\alpha_n = 2n + 1$. The second of Eqs. (10-35) shows that the corresponding energies are given by

$$E_n = (n + \tfrac{1}{2})\hbar\omega \qquad n = 0, 1, 2, 3, \ldots \tag{10-37}$$

As anticipated, the energy-level scheme consists of a series of equally spaced levels, separated by $\hbar\omega$. This result confirms Planck's hypothesis, which preceded the solution of the Schrödinger equation for the harmonic oscillator by 25 years! The number n is called a *quantum number;* just as for the hydrogen-atom energy levels predicted by the Bohr theory, it is an integer that labels the possible quantum-mechanical *states* and their corresponding energies.

Equation (10-37) shows another interesting feature. The ground-state energy, or lowest energy level ($n = 0$), is not zero but rather $E_0 = \tfrac{1}{2}\hbar\omega$. A harmonic oscillator cannot exist in a state with *zero* energy; the minimum energy is $\frac{1}{2}\hbar\omega$. This energy is unobservable, since in interactions of the oscillator with an external system only *changes* in energy are observed. The existence of this minimum energy corresponds to the fact that, in a quantum-mechanical sense, the particle can never exist in a state in which it has zero velocity and lies precisely at the origin. Such a state would violate the uncertainty principle, so it is not surprising that it is also forbidden by the Schrödinger equation.

It is instructive to compare the *probability* function $|\psi(y)|^2$ for each state with the corresponding probability for a *classical* harmonic oscillator having the same energy, by which we mean the probability of finding the classical oscillator at various positions if we make observations at randomly chosen times. This is obtained by noting that the probability for finding the particle in an interval dx near x is equal to the fraction of the total period during which it is in this interval. The time dt required to traverse this interval is given by

$$dt = \frac{dx}{v} \tag{10-38}$$

To find v in terms of x, we use the classical energy relation

$$\tfrac{1}{2}mv^2 + \tfrac{1}{2}kx^2 = \tfrac{1}{2}kA^2 = E \tag{10-39}$$

where A is the classical amplitude. Solving this for v and inserting in Eq. (10-38),

$$dt = \frac{dx}{\omega\sqrt{A^2 - x^2}} \tag{10-40}$$

Since the particle traverses the element dx twice during each cycle, the probability $P(x)\,dx$ of finding it in this interval is $2dt/T$, where T is the period, given by $T = 2\pi/\omega$. Combining these relations, we find

$$P(x)\,dx = \frac{dx}{\pi\sqrt{A^2 - x^2}} \tag{10-41}$$

This holds, of course, only for $|x| \leq A$. When $|x| > A$, $P(x) = 0$ in the classical case.

In terms of the dimensionless variable y, the probability function P becomes

$$P(y) = \frac{1}{\pi\sqrt{\alpha - y^2}} \tag{10-42}$$

Figure 10-8 shows the classical and quantum-mechanical probability functions for several values of n. The classical probability functions are largest

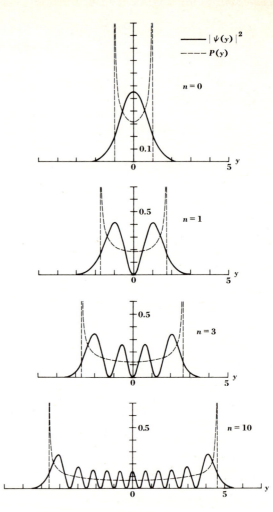

Fig. 10-8 Quantum-mechanical probability functions $|\psi(y)|^2$ for the harmonic oscillator. The corresponding classical probabilities P for the same energies are shown as broken lines, along with the classical amplitudes.

at the end points, where the classical particle is moving most slowly and hence spends most of its time. For $n = 0$ there is very little resemblance between $|\psi|^2$ and the classical probability, but with increasing n the quantum-mechanical description takes on some of the general shape of the classical one. It can also be seen that the wavelength of the wave function is longer in the end regions of small kinetic energy and momentum than in the central region of larger momentum.

As already mentioned, the solutions of the Schrödinger equation for the harmonic oscillator provide justification of the Planck quantum hypothesis. This development is also useful in other contexts. The classical harmonic oscillator is an idealized model for more complicated vibrating systems which can be *approximated* by this model, and so it is in the quantum-mechanical case. Molecular vibrations provide an important example. The potential energy

Fig. 10-9 A potential-energy curve describing the attractive force for atoms in a diatomic molecule. The potential energy has been chosen to be zero at the equilibrium separation r_0 and as a result has the value V_0 at large separations. The approximation given by Eq. (10-43) is equivalent to approximating a section of this curve near $r = r_0$ by a parabola, as shown by the broken curve.

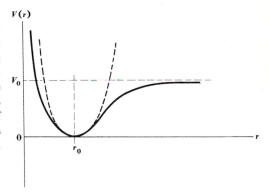

associated with the interaction of atoms in a diatomic molecule may behave in a manner similar to that shown in Fig. 10-9, where r is the spacing between atoms. The potential-energy function $V(r)$ has a minimum at the equilibrium distance r_0, and in the vicinity of this point it can be approximated in terms of the distance $x = r - r_0$ from the equilibrium position, as

$$V(x) = \frac{1}{2} \left(\frac{d^2 V}{dr^2} \right)_{r=r_0} x^2 \tag{10-43}$$

Thus the foregoing development can be applied directly to finding energy levels associated with vibrations of diatomic molecules. Even the vibrational motions of more complicated molecules can be represented as combinations of simple harmonic motions, and there is a corresponding simplicity of energy levels for such vibrations. We shall return to this subject in Chap. 12 in connection with molecular spectra.

10-6 SCHRÖDINGER EQUATION IN THREE DIMENSIONS

For simplicity in presenting basic concepts, the discussion of the Schrödinger equation has thus far been restricted to one-dimensional systems. The entire formulation can readily be extended to three dimensions, and this extension is in fact necessary for an analysis of even the simplest atoms. The wave function is then a function of three space coordinates and time; in rectangular coordinates it may be written as $\Psi(x, y, z, t)$. The probability interpretation of the wave function is generalized so that $\Psi^* \Psi \, dV$ represents the probability of finding the particle in a volume element dV.

As in Sec. 10-3, we are guided by the correspondence between terms in the classical energy relation and terms in the Schrödinger equation. The momentum of the particle is now a vector quantity and may be represented in terms of its rectangular components p_x, p_y, p_z in a specified coordinate system. The magnitude p of the momentum is given by $p^2 = p_x^2 + p_y^2 + p_z^2$. The potential energy is a function of the three space coordinates and is written as $V(x,y,z)$. The energy relation in three dimensions is

$$\frac{p_x^2 + p_y^2 + p_z^2}{2m} + V(x,y,z) = E \tag{10-44}$$

Following the same reasoning as in Sec. 10-3, we conclude that the Schrödinger equation in three dimensions is

$$-\frac{\hbar^2}{2m}\left(\frac{\partial^2 \Psi}{\partial x^2} + \frac{\partial^2 \Psi}{\partial y^2} + \frac{\partial^2 \Psi}{\partial z^2}\right) + V(x,y,z)\Psi = i\hbar\frac{\partial \Psi}{\partial t} \tag{10-45}$$

For states of definite total energy we again represent the time-dependent wave function $\Psi(x,y,z,t)$ as in Eq. (10-23); the generalization to three dimensions is

$$\Psi(x,y,z,t) = e^{-iEt/\hbar}\psi(x,y,z) \tag{10-46}$$

where $\psi(x,y,z)$ must satisfy the three-dimensional time-independent Schrödinger equation

$$-\frac{\hbar^2}{2m}\left(\frac{\partial^2 \psi}{\partial x^2} + \frac{\partial^2 \psi}{\partial y^2} + \frac{\partial^2 \psi}{\partial z^2}\right) + V\psi = E\psi \tag{10-47}$$

For a free particle, $V(x,y,z) = 0$ everywhere, and there are sinusoidal solutions of Eq. (10-47) analogous to the functions $\psi = Ae^{ikx}$, with $p = \hbar k$, for the one-dimensional problem. We introduce a wave vector $\mathbf{k}$, with components k_x, k_y, k_z, the three-dimensional generalization of the wave number k in one dimension: the momentum of the particle is given by $\mathbf{p} = \hbar\mathbf{k}$. The position vector $\mathbf{r}$ is represented by its components x, y, z; the reader can verify that the functions

$$\psi = Ae^{i\mathbf{k}\cdot\mathbf{r}} \tag{10-48}$$

are solutions of the three-dimensional Schrödinger equation (10-47) with $V = 0$, and that they represent states of definite energy and momentum, with completely undefined position. These functions have the additional feature that they can be written as products of three functions, each of which contains only one of the three coordinates, as follows:

$$Ae^{i\mathbf{k}\cdot\mathbf{r}} = Ae^{i(k_x x + k_y y + k_z z)} = Ae^{ik_x x}e^{ik_y y}e^{ik_z z} \tag{10-49}$$

This decomposition of a wave function into functions of one variable is a logical extension of the separation of the factor containing t, exhibited by Eq. (10-46), and is a very useful procedure in many problems.

There is nothing particularly sacred about rectangular coordinates; for some problems other coordinate systems are more convenient. An example is the hydrogen atom, to be discussed in Chap. 11. In this problem, the electron is attracted to a fixed center of force (the nucleus) by the Coulomb force, with corresponding potential energy

$$V = -\frac{e^2}{4\pi\varepsilon_0}\frac{1}{r} = -\frac{e^2}{4\pi\varepsilon_0}\frac{1}{\sqrt{x^2 + y^2 + z^2}} \tag{10-50}$$

This potential-energy function is represented more simply in spherical coordinates than rectangular because it depends on only one of the three spherical coordinates r, θ, ϕ. The derivatives with respect to x, y, and z can be expressed in terms of derivatives with respect to r, θ, and ϕ. The resulting expressions are more complicated, but the simplification of the potential-energy function more than compensates, making the problem much more tractable in spherical coordinates than in rectangular.

10-7 OPERATORS AND EIGENVALUES

The energy levels for a quantum-mechanical system are determined by the solutions of the time-independent Schrödinger equation for the system. The solutions of this equation, therefore, represent in every case states with definite total energies. This problem can be restated in an illuminating form. We define an *operator H* as follows:

$$H = -\frac{\hbar^2}{2m}\frac{d^2}{dx^2} + V(x) \tag{10-51}$$

The significance of this operator is that the indicated operations, multiplication or differentiation, are to be performed on any function that follows the operator in an algebraic expression. That is,

$$H\psi(x) = \left[-\frac{\hbar^2}{2m}\frac{d^2}{dx^2} + V(x)\right]\psi(x) = -\frac{\hbar^2}{2m}\frac{d^2\psi}{dx^2} + V(x)\psi \tag{10-52}$$

With this notation, Schrödinger's equation becomes simply

$$H\psi(x) = E\psi(x) \tag{10-53}$$

That is, the states of definite total energy have the property that when the operator H is applied to any one of them the result is *the same function, multiplied by a constant equal to the total energy*. For other functions, which are *not* solutions of this equation, there is no reason for $H\psi(x)$ to be a multiple of the original function $\psi(x)$, but for functions that satisfy the equation, it *is*. Mathematicians describe this situation by saying that $\psi(x)$ is an *eigen-*

function of the operator H. The corresponding constant E for each function is called the *eigenvalue. Every wave function that represents a state of definite total energy is an eigenfunction of the energy operator, and the corresponding eigenvalue is equal to the total energy.*

This observation gives a clue to how to find states with a definite value of some other dynamical quantity such as momentum or angular momentum rather than definite total energy. Perhaps there is an *operator* corresponding to each dynamical quantity, so that a state having a definite value of that quantity is represented by an eigenfunction of the corresponding operator. To test this hypothesis, we consider states having definite total momentum. We have already seen in Chap. 9 that such states, at least for a free particle, are sinusoidal waves. For momentum $p = \hbar k$, the time-dependent wave function is

$$\Psi(x,t) = Ae^{i(kx-\omega t)} = Ae^{i(px/\hbar-\omega t)} \tag{10-54}$$

This wave function has the property that

$$\frac{\hbar}{i}\frac{\partial \Psi}{\partial x} = p\Psi \tag{10-55}$$

Therefore, it is reasonable to conclude that the operator corresponding to momentum is

$$p \rightarrow \frac{\hbar}{i}\frac{\partial}{\partial x} \tag{10-56}$$

Checking this with Eq. (10-51), we see that the two are consistent, since if we start with the classical expression for total energy, $E = p^2/2m + V$, and make the substitution suggested by Eq. (10-56), the result is precisely the energy operator of Eq. (10-51).

We can now state the principles of quantum mechanics in a considerably more general form than previously. *For every observable physical quantity there is a corresponding operator. The states of the system corresponding to definite values of that physical quantity are represented by eigenfunctions of the operator, and the corresponding eigenvalues are the possible values of the physical quantity.* Thus if A is an operator corresponding to a physical quantity and a is one of the permissible values of that quantity, the states of the system having a definite value of that physical quantity are represented by wave functions that are solutions of the equation

$$A\Psi = a\Psi \tag{10-57}$$

where A may be a differential operator, or a function of the space coordinates, or both, and a is a constant.

This more general formalism paves the way for the quantization of other physical quantities. An important example is angular momentum. We have seen that angular momentum played a central role in early studies of the hydrogen atom; Bohr's quantum hypothesis is essentially the assumption that the angular momentum of the electron in the hydrogen atom must be an integer multiple of $\hbar$. Furthermore, there is now a variety of more direct experimental evidence, to be discussed in Chap. 11, that angular momentum and its components are *quantized*. In any experiment that measures angular momentum or a component in a specified direction, the result is never a continuous distribution of values but rather a discrete set.

The above discussion of operators shows, at least in principle, how to find the permitted values of angular momentum for any system. We first develop an angular-momentum *operator*. The classical definition of angular momentum is

$$\mathbf{L} = \mathbf{r} \times \mathbf{p} \qquad \text{or} \qquad \begin{array}{l} L_x = yp_z - zp_y \\ L_y = zp_x - xp_z \\ L_z = xp_y - yp_x \end{array} \tag{10-58}$$

The corresponding operators for the components of angular momentum are

$$L_x \rightarrow \frac{\hbar}{i}\left(y\frac{\partial}{\partial z} - z\frac{\partial}{\partial y}\right) \tag{10-59a}$$

$$L_y \rightarrow \frac{\hbar}{i}\left(z\frac{\partial}{\partial x} - x\frac{\partial}{\partial z}\right) \tag{10-59b}$$

$$L_z \rightarrow \frac{\hbar}{i}\left(x\frac{\partial}{\partial y} - y\frac{\partial}{\partial x}\right) \tag{10-59c}$$

Correspondingly one can develop an operator for the square of the total angular momentum, $L^2 = L_x^2 + L_y^2 + L_z^2$.

For many systems of physical interest, including electrons in atoms, it can be shown that the permitted values of angular momentum are given by

$$L^2 = l(l+1)\hbar^2 \qquad l = 0, 1, 2, 3, \ldots \tag{10-60}$$

and the possible values for the *component* of angular momentum in the direction corresponding to any particular measurement are integral multiples of $\hbar$. Thus if we design an apparatus which measures the component of momentum along the z axis, the possible values are

$$L_z = m\hbar \tag{10-61}$$

where m is an integer which can take any value between $-l$ and $+l$. It is interesting to note that while the magnitude of the total angular momentum is

$$L = \sqrt{l(l+1)}\,\hbar \tag{10-62}$$

its *component* in any direction cannot be quite as large as this. This corresponds to a basic uncertainty in angular momentum associated with the uncertainties of position and momentum already discussed. That is, the *direction* of the angular-momentum vector is never completely well defined. It is often useful to classify states of atomic systems according to angular momentum and its components. Such classifications will be discussed in Chaps. 11 and 12.

We have now developed several important general principles which can be applied to a variety of problems associated with the microscopic structure of matter. In the following chapters we shall see that these principles, along with a few additional ones, provide the key to understanding the structure of atoms, molecules, and solids. These areas are the principal subjects of the next four chapters.

Problems

10-1 A certain particle has a normalized wave function

$$\psi(x) = \frac{1}{\pi^{1/4}}e^{-x^2/2}$$

Estimate roughly the probability that, in an experiment to determine its position, the particle will be found between $x = 1$ and $x = 2$. This estimate can be made by plotting the appropriate function on graph paper and counting squares to find the relevant areas.

10-2 For the wave packet of Prob. 9-13, find the probability that, in an experiment which measures momentum, the particle's momentum will be found to lie between $\hbar(k_0 - a/2)$ and $\hbar(k_0 + a/2)$.

10-3 For a particle in a box, discussed in Sec. 10-2, find the probability that in the lowest energy state the particle is in the interval $L/4$ to $3L/4$.

10-4 For a particle in a one-dimensional box, find the energy of the lowest energy state, and from this find the momentum of the particle. The *direction* of the momentum is indefinite. Show that the corresponding uncertainty in momentum and the uncertainty of position given by the size of the box are consistent with the uncertainty principle.

10-5 Find the lowest energy for a neutron in a box with a width of 5×10^{-15} m, the order of magnitude of the nuclear diameter for heavy elements. Express your result in electronvolts.

10-6 Carry out the normalization integral [Eq. (10-15)] for the particle-in-a-box wave functions to show that the functions given in Eq. (10-17) are normalized.

10-7 Find the probability functions $|\psi(x)|^2$ for the particle-in-a-box wave functions in Eq. (10-17), and sketch the functions for the lowest three energy levels.

10-8 Show that in regions of positive (classical) kinetic energy, ψ and $d^2\psi/dx^2$ always have opposite signs, while in classically forbidden regions of negative kinetic energy they always have the same sign.

10-9 Show that the classical kinetic energy of a particle in one dimension corresponds to the quantity $-(\hbar^2/2m)d^2\psi/dx^2$ in the Schrödinger equation.

10-10 For the wave functions in Eq. (10-17), show that for any two functions $\psi_n(x)$ and $\psi_{n'}(x)$

$$\int_0^L \psi_n(x)\psi_{n'}(x)\,dx = 0$$

unless $n = n'$. This is called the *orthogonality* property of the functions.

10-11 Show that for a particle in a two-dimensional box the Schrödinger equation for states with definite energy is

$$-\frac{\hbar^2}{2m}\left(\frac{\partial^2\psi}{\partial x^2} + \frac{\partial^2\psi}{\partial y^2}\right) = E\psi$$

10-12 Show that the solutions of the two-dimensional Schrödinger equation for a particle in a box (Prob. 10-11) have the form

$$\psi = A\begin{Bmatrix}\sin\\\cos\end{Bmatrix}mx\begin{Bmatrix}\sin\\\cos\end{Bmatrix}ny$$

Find the energy levels for a box of length a and width b by using the same boundary conditions as for the one-dimensional box. Also find the normalized wave functions.

10-13 Show that the variables y and α defined by Eqs. (10-35) are dimensionless.

10-14 Show by direct substitution that the first three functions in Table 10-1 are solutions of Eq. (10-36).

10-15 Estimate the width of the harmonic-oscillator wave function for the $n = 0$ state, in terms of k, m, and $\hbar$, and compare this with the amplitude of a classical (non-quantum-mechanical) harmonic oscillator having the same energy.

10-16 Find the constant factors needed to normalize the harmonic-oscillator wave functions for $n = 0$ and $n = 1$. The following integral will be useful:

$$\int_{-\infty}^{\infty} e^{-x^2}\,dx = \sqrt{\pi}$$

This is derived by mathematical trickery. The normalization integrals for all values of n can be reduced to this integral by successive integrations by parts.

10-17 Integrate Eq. (10-41) to show that the total probability for finding the particle in the range $-A \leq x \leq A$ is unity.

10-18 Suppose an oxygen atom experiences a force proportional to its displacement from an equilibrium position, with force constant 50 N/m.

a Find the classical frequency of vibration.

b Find the spacing between adjacent energy levels.

c Find the frequency of the three lowest-energy photons that can be emitted or absorbed during transitions among these levels.

d Find the wavelengths of the photons in (c). In what region of the electromagnetic spectrum do they lie?

10-19 Show that the harmonic-oscillator wave functions $\psi_n(y)$ can all be written in the form

$$\psi_n(y) = e^{-y^2/2} H_n(y)$$

where $H_n(y)$ is a polynomial of the nth degree in y. By substituting this expression into Eq. (10-36), show that $H_n(y)$ must satisfy the differential equation

$$H_n''(y) - 2y H_n'(y) + (\alpha_n - 1) H_n(y) = 0 \qquad \text{with } \alpha_n = 2n + 1$$

Taking the polynomials $H_n(y)$ from the functions in Table 10-1, show by direct substitution that they satisfy this equation for $n = 2$ and $n = 4$. These are called Hermite polynomials.

10-20 For the $n = 1$ harmonic-oscillator wave function, find the probability that, in an experiment which measures position, the particle will be found within a distance $\frac{1}{2}\hbar^{1/2}(mk)^{-1/4}$ of the origin.

10-21 Show that, in transitions between energy states of a harmonic oscillator, the frequency of the emitted or absorbed radiation is always an integer multiple of the classical oscillator frequency $(k/m)^{1/2}$.

10-22 For a harmonic oscillator whose mass is that of a hydrogen atom and whose spring constant is typical of interatomic forces in molecules (say $k = 50$ N/m), how does the spacing of adjacent energy levels compare with typical energies associated with thermal motion at ordinary temperatures (kT at 300 K, where k is Boltzmann's constant)?

10-23 Verify that Eq. (10-48) is a solution of the three-dimensional Schrödinger equation (10-47) with $V = 0$.

10-24 Show that in one-dimensional problems any function which is an eigenfunction of the momentum operator is also an eigenfunction of the kinetic-energy operator. Is the converse also true?

10-25 For a particle in a plane, suppose polar coordinates (r,θ) are used instead of cartesian coordinates (x,y). Use the coordinate transformations $x = r\cos\theta$, $y = r\sin\theta$ together with the chain rule for differentiation to transform the angular-momentum operator L_z to polar coordinates, and show that it is given by

$$L_z \to \frac{\hbar}{i} \frac{\partial}{\partial\theta}$$

PERSPECTIVE III

The three preceding chapters have introduced some of the most important concepts of quantum mechanics. Various phenomena associated with the emission and absorption of radiation exhibit a discrete or quantum aspect of electromagnetic radiation which cannot be understood on the basis of classical electrodynamics. Correspondingly, there are phenomena associated with the behavior of particles which cannot be understood adequately on the basis of newtonian mechanics but rather suggest a wave aspect of particle behavior.

More generally, both particles (in the old sense) and radiation exhibit both wave and particle aspects. As we have seen, these two kinds of behavior are not mutually exclusive but rather are complementary; an entity which shows wave characteristics in one kind of experiment may exhibit particle characteristics in another, and both can be understood as aspects of a more general description. Thus the wave concept has the happy effect of bringing unity into the description of both particles and radiation; it is on this basis that we have claimed that wave concepts are central and essential to contemporary theories of matter and radiation and their interaction.

In developing a language for describing this dual wave-particle nature of matter, we have found that in quantum mechanics the state of a particle or of a system of particles is described not by the position and velocity of a point but rather by a wave function which depends on spatial coordinates and time. Some systems, especially those associated with "bound states" of particles, can exist only in states with certain discrete energy levels. When such a system interacts with an electromagnetic field, the emission or absorption of radiation is understood on the basis of a transition from one energy state to another, with emission or absorption of a photon of electromagnetic energy of corresponding magnitude. Thus this analysis provides the key for

279

an understanding of the characteristic spectra of elements, in terms of the structure of their atoms.

Our next task is to pursue further the analysis of atomic structure and its relation to the spectra and other properties of atoms. The logical place to begin is with the simplest atom, hydrogen. It is found that the solutions of the Schrödinger equation for the hydrogen atom predict correctly the energy levels of hydrogen already established from spectrum analysis and also describe the electron configurations in the various quantum states.

We then proceed to the analysis of more complicated atoms containing several electrons. When more than one electron is present, the analysis immediately becomes much more complicated because of the interactions between electrons, but it is found that with the help of certain approximations we can still make considerable progress in the analysis of the structure of more complicated atoms. Central to this analysis is a "zoning ordinance" called the exclusion principle, which forbids two electrons in an atom from occupying the same quantum state. This principle is responsible for the periodically recurring properties of elements exhibited by the periodic table of the elements.

The same principles used to understand the structure of individual atoms can be extended to an analysis of systems containing several interacting atoms. In particular, the various kinds of molecular binding and the structure of complex molecules can be understood on the basis of the electron configurations of the constituent atoms. Thus quantum mechanics provides the fundamental basis for the phenomenon of valence. With systems containing several atoms, there are additional effects associated with relative motion of the nuclei, called molecular vibrations. The energy levels associated with these vibrations and with rotational motion of molecules lead to additional interesting features in the spectra of molecules.

Next, we consider systems containing such a large number of atoms, molecules, or other subsystems that it is impractical to describe the state of each subsystem in detail. In such cases, it is helpful to employ a statistical description of the state of the system, in which one abandons hope of describing the state of every subsystem and instead describes the statistical distribution of states of individual atoms or molecules. The classical version of this description is the kinetic theory of gases, which relates the macroscopic behavior of a gas to a statistical description of its microscopic constituents. By extending this analysis to quantum-mechanical systems, we are able to formulate a statistical description of the states of electrons in a solid, the quantum states of molecules in a gas, and similar problems. The methods of statistical mechanics provide very useful and powerful tools for the analysis of complex systems containing many interacting subsystems.

The Hydrogen Atom | 11

The concepts of quantum mechanics are applied to an analysis of the simplest atom, hydrogen. The Schrödinger equation is applied to the hydrogen atom, and it is shown that solution of this equation with the appropriate boundary conditions leads naturally to the energy levels of the atom and its possible angular-momentum states. Transitions from one quantum state to another during emission or absorption of radiation are discussed. The changes in energy levels resulting from the application of magnetic field are discussed, and it is shown that this behavior and other details of the hydrogen spectrum point to the existence of an intrinsic angular momentum and magnetic moment of the electron, conveniently pictured as "spin."

11-1 THE NUCLEAR MODEL

To place our discussion of the hydrogen atom in context, we review briefly the nuclear model of the atom. By the beginning of the twentieth century it was well established that the constituent parts of atoms carry electric charges and that the negative charges, electrons, can be removed from atoms. In 1897 the English physicist J. J. Thomson measured the charge-to-mass ratio (e/m) for electrons by observing their trajectories in electric and magnetic fields, and thereby established that the electron mass accounts for only a small fraction of the total mass of the atom, about $\frac{1}{2000}$ for the hydrogen atom.

There were several independent indications of the magnitude of atomic dimensions. These included the van der Waals correction to the ideal-gas equation (associated with finite molecular sizes), observations on density of matter in the solid state, and a variety of experiments on diffusion and mean free paths of molecules in the gaseous state. All these indicated atomic diameters of the order of 10^{-10} m.

There were a number of proposals regarding the *internal structure* of atoms. In a model proposed by J. J. Thomson, the positive charge was pictured as being spread out over the entire volume of the atom, with the negative electrons embedded in it like raisins in a pudding. This model had certain advantages; by ascribing elastic properties to the positive charge, one could imagine the electrons as being elastically bound and therefore able to *vibrate* about their equilibrium positions, providing a mechanism for absorption and emission of electromagnetic waves. There was, however, no basis on which to account for the existence of particular spectrum lines, such as the Balmer series.

Starting in 1909, Ernest Rutherford and his collaborators at the University of Manchester (England) obtained experimental evidence showing conclusively that the Thomson model was in need of drastic revision. Rutherford's experiments consisted in observing the deflections in the trajectories of α particles (emitted by radioactive elements such as uranium) as they passed through thin films of metal. It was known that α particles have positive charges and a mass about 8000 times that of the electron. Because of this mass difference, the atomic electrons should have relatively little effect on the motion of an α particle, just as a truck can drive through a hailstorm without having its motion altered appreciably. Any significant deflection of the particles would have to be produced by interaction with the more massive *positively* charged constituents of the atoms. Thus the extent of the deflections provided information regarding the *distribution* of the positive charge.

Suppose the positive charge is distributed uniformly through a sphere of radius R. Gauss' law shows that for points outside the sphere the field has the same $1/r^2$ behavior as though all the charge were concentrated at the center, and for points inside the sphere the field is directly proportional to r, as shown in Fig. 11-1. The maximum field occurs at the surface ($r = R$) of the charge distribution, and the magnitude of this maximum value is proportional to $1/R^2$.

Rutherford's calculations[1] showed that if the positive charge extends over a sphere of radius $R = 10^{-10}$ m, the maximum electric field is sufficient to deflect an α particle only a few degrees at most. Instead, he found that some particles were scattered through rather large angles, and a few almost exactly backward. Thus the forces must be much *larger* than predicted by the Thomson model, and the positive charge must be concentrated in a much smaller region. Quantitative observations showed that the positive charge of the atom is concentrated in a region no larger than 10^{-14} m in radius, 10,000 times smaller than the overall size of the atom itself.

---

[1] For a more detailed discussion of the dynamics of Rutherford scattering, see H. D. Young, "Fundamentals of Mechanics and Heat," 2d ed., sec. 12-3, McGraw-Hill Book Company, New York, 1974.

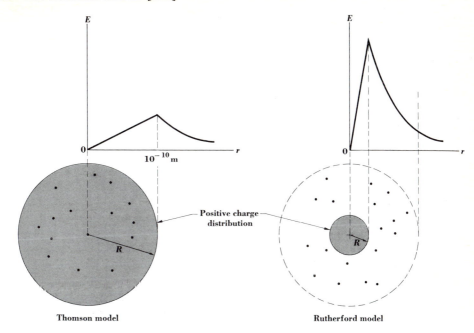

Fig. 11-1 Electric field produced by a uniform distribution of charge throughout a sphere of radius R. The maximum value of E occurs at the surface of the sphere and is greater for small R than for larger R.

Although the Rutherford nuclear model shed important new light on the internal structure of atoms, it left many questions unanswered, including the *stability* of an atom. If the electrons are stationary, what holds them in place? If they move in orbits, why do they not emit electromagnetic radiation continuously, losing energy and spiraling into the nucleus? Also unexplained were the phenomena of line spectra. Why does an atom emit only certain frequencies of radiation rather than a continuous spectrum?

The Bohr theory of the hydrogen atom, introduced just 4 years after Rutherford's discoveries, gave a prediction of the spectrum of the hydrogen atom and a partial explanation of its stability. As pointed out in Chap. 8, however, this model had problems. Its *conceptual* defects included the artificial nature of the assumption necessary to achieve discrete energy levels and the mixing of classical and quantum-mechanical concepts in a seemingly inconsistent way. Among the *practical* disadvantages was the fact that the Bohr theory failed completely for atoms more complicated than hydrogen. Thus, although the Bohr theory achieved a certain measure of success in understanding the properties of the hydrogen atom, it was by no means a complete theory.

With the introduction of the wave concept of electrons by de Broglie in 1925 and its subsequent development into a detailed theory by Schrödinger,

Heisenberg, and others, an important new tool for the analysis of atomic structure became available. In the next section we shall see how the Schrödinger equation can be applied to an analysis of the structure of hydrogen. The discreteness of energy levels appears in a natural way, rather than having to be inserted artificially as in the Bohr theory. Furthermore, the Schrödinger equation also gives new insight into a number of other phenomena associated with the hydrogen atom and into the structure of more complicated atoms.

11-2 SPHERICALLY SYMMETRIC WAVE FUNCTIONS

We are now ready to apply the Schrödinger equation to the hydrogen-atom problem. We remark at the outset that although the problem can be solved exactly, the complete solution involves a fair amount of mathematical acrobatics. To discuss it in full detail would require introducing a number of mathematical techniques with which the reader may not be familiar. Rather than do this, we shall concentrate on certain simple aspects of the analysis, quote some results of the more complete treatment, and then discuss what it all means.

In our model the nucleus is represented as a stationary point charge $+e$ at the origin of our coordinate system, and the electron of mass m and charge $-e$ is represented by a wave function surrounding the nucleus. The classical force associated with the interaction is

$$F = \frac{1}{4\pi\varepsilon_0} \frac{e^2}{r^2} \tag{11-1}$$

where r is the distance between the particles, given in cartesian coordinates by $(x^2 + y^2 + z^2)^{1/2}$. The corresponding potential energy, defined to be zero at infinite separation, is

$$V = -\frac{1}{4\pi\varepsilon_0} \frac{e^2}{r} = -\frac{1}{4\pi\varepsilon_0} \frac{e^2}{\sqrt{x^2 + y^2 + z^2}} \tag{11-2}$$

Because one of the primary goals is to predict energy levels, we consider first the time-independent Schrödinger equation, discussed in Sec. 10-6, Eq. (10-47). With the potential energy given by Eq. (11-2), the equation is

$$-\frac{\hbar^2}{2m}\left(\frac{\partial^2\psi}{\partial x^2} + \frac{\partial^2\psi}{\partial y^2} + \frac{\partial^2\psi}{\partial z^2}\right) - \frac{1}{4\pi\varepsilon_0}\frac{e^2}{\sqrt{x^2 + y^2 + z^2}}\psi = E\psi \tag{11-3}$$

The object is to find solutions of this equation representing bound states, and the corresponding energy levels. We first note that since the potential is *spherically symmetric*, i.e., dependent only on the distance from the origin, not the direction, at least *some* of the solutions should also have this symmetry. As it turns out, there are additional solutions that are *not* spherically symmetric, but let us begin by looking for those that *are*.

Spherical symmetry means that ψ depends on x, y, z, only through the single variable r, so we should be able to express Eq. (11-3) entirely in terms of r. This involves only repeated application of the chain rule for differentiation. For example,

$$\frac{\partial \psi}{\partial x} = \frac{d\psi}{dr} \frac{\partial r}{\partial x} \tag{11-4}$$

Now $\partial r/\partial x$ is easy to evaluate:

$$\frac{\partial r}{\partial x} = \frac{\partial}{\partial x}(x^2 + y^2 + z^2)^{1/2} = \frac{x}{(x^2 + y^2 + z^2)^{1/2}} = \frac{x}{r} \tag{11-5}$$

so

$$\frac{\partial \psi}{\partial x} = \frac{x}{r} \frac{d\psi}{dr} \tag{11-6}$$

Similarly we may find $\partial^2\psi/\partial x^2$ by differentiating Eq. (11-6), which is a product of three factors:

$$\frac{\partial}{\partial x}\left(\frac{x}{r}\frac{d\psi}{dr}\right) = \frac{1}{r}\frac{d\psi}{dr} - \frac{x^2}{r^3}\frac{d\psi}{dr} + \frac{x}{r}\left(\frac{d^2\psi}{dr^2}\frac{x}{r}\right)$$
$$= \frac{1}{r}\frac{d\psi}{dr} - \frac{x^2}{r^3}\frac{d\psi}{dr} + \frac{x^2}{r^2}\frac{d^2\psi}{dr^2} \tag{11-7}$$

This kind of manipulation becomes tedious very quickly, but we are almost finished. The derivatives $\partial^2\psi/\partial y^2$ and $\partial^2\psi/\partial z^2$ have exactly the same form as Eq. (11-7) except that x is replaced everywhere by y and z, respectively. Thus we can write down immediately the expression for the *sum* of the three second derivatives:

$$\frac{\partial^2\psi}{\partial x^2} + \frac{\partial^2\psi}{\partial y^2} + \frac{\partial^2\psi}{\partial z^2} = \frac{3}{r}\frac{d\psi}{dr} - \frac{x^2 + y^2 + z^2}{r^3}\frac{d\psi}{dr}$$
$$+ \frac{x^2 + y^2 + z^2}{r^2}\frac{d^2\psi}{dr^2} = \frac{d^2\psi}{dr^2} + \frac{2}{r}\frac{d\psi}{dr} \tag{11-8}$$

Finally, the Schrödinger equation for spherically symmetric functions is

$$-\frac{\hbar^2}{2m}\left(\frac{d^2\psi}{dr^2} + \frac{2}{r}\frac{d\psi}{dr}\right) - \frac{e^2}{4\pi\varepsilon_0}\frac{1}{r}\psi = E\psi \tag{11-9}$$

In considering possible solutions of this equation, we note that two terms contain the factor $1/r$; in one it is multiplied by $d\psi/dr$, and in the other by ψ itself. The *sum* of these two terms can be made to equal zero for all values of r by choosing for ψ an exponential function of r. Furthermore, with an appropriate choice of E the term containing $d^2\psi/dr^2$ can be made to equal the term $E\psi$ for all values of r. Thus there must be a solution with the general form

$$\psi(r) = Ce^{-r/a} \tag{11-10}$$

where C and a are constants.

For dimensional consistency, a must have units of length. The negative exponent reflects the fact that ψ must approach zero at large r if it is to represent a *bound state* in which the electron is localized in the vicinity of the nucleus.

Substituting Eq. (11-10) into Eq. (11-9), rearranging, and dividing out the common factor $Ce^{-r/a}$, we find

$$\left[-\frac{\hbar^2}{2m}\left(\frac{1}{a^2} - \frac{2}{ar}\right) - \frac{e^2}{4\pi\varepsilon_0}\frac{1}{r} \right] Ce^{-r/a} = ECe^{-r/a}$$

and

$$-\frac{\hbar^2}{2ma^2} + \left(\frac{\hbar^2}{ma} - \frac{e^2}{4\pi\varepsilon_0}\right)\frac{1}{r} = E \tag{11-11}$$

This equation is satisfied for all values of r if, and only if, the coefficient of $1/r$ is zero and the two constant terms are equal. These requirements determine the values of a and E. We find

$$\frac{\hbar^2}{ma} - \frac{e^2}{4\pi\varepsilon_0} = 0 \qquad \rightarrow \qquad a = \frac{4\pi\varepsilon_0\hbar^2}{me^2} \tag{11-12}$$

and

$$E = -\frac{\hbar^2}{2ma^2} = -\left(\frac{e^2}{4\pi\varepsilon_0}\right)^2 \frac{m}{2\hbar^2} \tag{11-13}$$

With these values of E and a, Eq. (11-10) is a solution of the Schrödinger equation. The constant E is the energy of the state, and a characterizes the extension in space of the wave function; at a distance $r = a$ from the origin the function has dropped to $1/e$ of its value at $r = 0$.

These results are exactly equal to the orbit radius and energy of the $n = 1$ state in the Bohr model, as given by Eqs. (8-27) and (8-28). Therefore this wave function must represent the *ground state* of the hydrogen atom. By replacing *one* of the factors of a in Eq. (11-13) by the expression of Eq.

(11-12), we obtain

$$E = -\frac{1}{2}\frac{e^2}{4\pi\varepsilon_0 a} \tag{11-14}$$

which shows directly that the energy is equal to the total energy of an electron in a Bohr orbit of radius a, as given by Eq. (8-25).

Equation (11-10) is a solution of the Schrödinger equation for *any* value of C. Thus we are free to choose a value of C to *normalize* the wave function, as discussed in Sec. 10-2. The probability of finding the particle in the volume element dV is $\psi^*\psi\,dV$, provided ψ is normalized so that $\int\psi^*\psi\,dV = 1$. For the spherically symmetric situation it is natural to choose for dV a spherical shell with inner and outer radii r and $r + dr$, respectively. The surface area of the shell is $4\pi r^2$ and its thickness is dr, so $dV = 4\pi r^2\,dr$. Thus the normalization condition becomes

$$\int_0^\infty (Ce^{-r/a})^2 4\pi r^2\,dr = 1 \tag{11-15}$$

The integral can be evaluated by two successive integrations by parts or by one reference to a table of integrals. The result is

$$\pi C^2 a^3 = 1 \qquad \text{or} \qquad C = \frac{1}{\sqrt{\pi a^3}} \tag{11-16}$$

The normalized ground-state wave function for the hydrogen atom is

$$\psi(r) = \frac{1}{\sqrt{\pi a^3}}e^{-r/a} \tag{11-17}$$

with a given by Eq. (11-12). Thus the Schrödinger equation yields a wave function representing a state with the same energy as the ground state in the Bohr model, which has already been shown to agree with experimental observations; furthermore the "size" of the wave function is of the same order of magnitude as the Bohr radius.

The angular-momentum properties of this state are worth noting. We recall from Sec. 10-7 that a state with a definite value of a component of angular momentum is an *eigenfunction* of the corresponding operator. Suppose we apply the operator L_x given by Eq. (10-59a) to the ground-state wave function of Eq. (11-17). This involves computing the quantities

$$y\frac{\partial}{\partial z}e^{-r/a} \qquad \text{and} \qquad z\frac{\partial}{\partial y}e^{-r/a}$$

It is not difficult to show that these are *equal*; the details are left as a problem. The result is that for this particular wave function, $L_x\psi = 0$. That is, ψ is an eigenfunction of L_x, and the eigenvalue is zero. Thus this state has a definite value of L_x, and it is zero! In exactly the same way one can show that L_y and L_z are zero, so the total angular momentum of the state is zero. More generally, it can be shown that *every* spherically symmetric state must have zero total angular momentum. Proof of this statement is left as a problem.

This result differs from the Bohr model, in which the angular momentum in the ground state is $\hbar$. Indeed, it may seem contrary to common sense that the electron can exist in a stable state with no dynamical quantity corresponding to rotational motion. Yet the function *is* a proper solution of the Schrödinger equation, and this result, which has no classical analog, is correct. Further consideration shows that the state *cannot* have a nonzero component of momentum in any direction; this would imply a directional nature of the wave function, and we have already seen that the function has *no* directional nature since it is spherically symmetric. From this point of view, therefore, the fact that $L_z = 0$ is to be expected.

Equation (11-17) is the first of a set of spherically symmetric solutions. Another is

$$\psi(r) = C\left(1 - \frac{r}{2a}\right)e^{-r/2a} \tag{11-18}$$

This function corresponds to the energy of the $n = 2$ level in the Bohr model, and the "size" of the wave function corresponds to the radius of the $n = 2$ orbit. Verification of these statements is left as a problem. More generally, it can be shown that corresponding to each value of n in the Bohr model there is a spherically symmetric wave function consisting of a polynomial of degree $n - 1$ in r, multiplied by $e^{-r/na}$, and representing a state with the same energy E_n as the corresponding state in the Bohr model. Thus the spherically symmetric solutions of the Schrödinger equation reproduce the energy-level scheme of the hydrogen atom, and in addition provide a description of the electron distribution for each state.

11-3   GENERAL WAVE FUNCTIONS

Not all the solutions of Eq. (11-3) are spherically symmetric. As soon as the restriction of spherical symmetry is dropped, however, the calculations become considerably more complex. The usual procedure is first to express Eq. (11-3) in spherical coordinates, shown in Fig. 11-2. From this figure the following relations can be obtained:

$$\begin{aligned} x &= r \sin\theta \cos\phi \\ y &= r \sin\theta \sin\phi \\ z &= r \cos\theta \end{aligned} \tag{11-19}$$

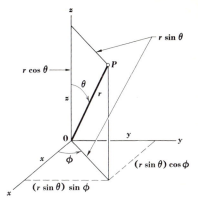

Fig. 11-2 Diagram showing the spherical coordinates (r,θ,ϕ) of a point P and their relation to the rectangular (cartesian) coordinates (x,y,z).

The derivatives with respect to x, y, and z can be transformed into derivatives with respect to the spherical coordinates, by making use of the chain rule. The result is

$$-\frac{\hbar^2}{2m}\left[\frac{1}{r^2}\frac{\partial}{\partial r}\left(r^2\frac{\partial\psi}{\partial r}\right) + \frac{1}{r^2\sin\theta}\frac{\partial}{\partial\theta}\left(\sin\theta\frac{\partial\psi}{\partial\theta}\right) + \frac{1}{r^2\sin^2\theta}\frac{\partial^2\psi}{\partial\phi^2}\right]$$
$$-\frac{e^2}{4\pi\varepsilon_0}\frac{1}{r}\psi = E\psi$$

(11-20)

in which ψ is now a function of the spherical coordinates r, θ, and ϕ. We note that if ψ depends only on r, all the derivatives with respect to θ and ϕ are zero and it reduces to Eq. (11-9).

The key to finding general solutions of Eq. (11-20) is a technique known as *separation of variables*, which consists in representing the function $\psi(r,\theta,\phi)$ as a product of three functions, each containing only one of the three coordinates. Denoting these functions by $R(r)$, $\Theta(\theta)$, and $\Phi(\phi)$, respectively, we write

$$\psi(r,\theta,\phi) = R(r)\Theta(\theta)\Phi(\phi)$$

(11-21)

When this expression is substituted into Eq. (11-20), it is found to be a solution only if each individual function satisfies a certain ordinary differential equation.

We now abandon derivation and quote the following results, asking the reader to take them on faith until he attains, perhaps in a later course, the necessary fluency in partial differential equations to derive them. For both the Bohr model and the spherically symmetric functions, the solutions were labeled by a single integer index or *quantum number n*. For the general wave functions we need a set of three integer quantum numbers (n,l,m_l). The energy is still determined entirely by n, which is called the *principal quantum number:*

$$E_n = -\left(\frac{e^2}{4\pi\varepsilon_0}\right)^2 \frac{m}{2n^2\hbar^2} \qquad n = 1, 2, 3, \ldots \tag{11-22}$$

The second quantum number (l) can be zero or any positive integer up to $n - 1$, and the third (m_l) can be zero or any positive or negative integer up to $\pm l$. Thus the following sets of quantum numbers are possible: $(3, 1, 1)$, $(4, 3, -2)$, $(1, 0, 0)$. But these are *not* possible: $(2, 2, 2)$, $(2, 1, 2)$, $(2, 3, -4)$.

The third quantum number m_l is usually written in the literature simply as m. This is slightly hazardous, inasmuch as m is also used universally to denote the electron mass. From now on we conform to convention and call it m, at the same time cautioning the reader to beware of possible ambiguities.

With reference to the individual functions in Eq. (11-21), it is found that $R(r)$ depends on n and l, $\Theta(\theta)$ depends on l and m, and $\Phi(\phi)$ depends only on m. Thus the product wave function can be written

$$\psi_{nlm}(r,\theta,\phi) = R_{nl}(r)\Theta_{lm}(\theta)\Phi_m(\phi) \tag{11-23}$$

The first few functions $R_{nl}(r)$ and $\Theta_{lm}(\theta)$ are shown in Tables 11-1 and 11-2. The Φ functions are given by

$$\Phi(\phi) = e^{im\phi} \tag{11-24}$$

The functions $R_{nl}(r)$ are expressed in Table 11-1 in terms of the dimensionless variable $\rho = r/a$, where a is the first Bohr radius, defined by Eq. (11-12). Each function contains a factor $e^{-\rho/n}$ multiplied by a polynomial of degree $n - 1$ in ρ; the coefficients in the polynomials are different for

Table 11-1   Radial Functions $R_{nl}(r)$ for Hydrogen Atom; $\rho = r/a$

$$R_{10}(r) = 2a^{-3/2}e^{-\rho}$$

$$R_{20}(r) = \frac{1}{\sqrt{2}a^{3/2}}\left(1 - \frac{\rho}{2}\right)e^{-\rho/2}$$

$$R_{21}(r) = \frac{1}{2\sqrt{6}a^{3/2}}\rho e^{-\rho/2}$$

$$R_{30}(r) = \frac{2}{3\sqrt{3}a^{3/2}}\left(1 - \frac{2\rho}{3} + \frac{2\rho^2}{27}\right)e^{-\rho/3}$$

$$R_{31}(r) = \frac{8}{27\sqrt{6}a^{3/2}}\rho\left(1 - \frac{\rho}{6}\right)e^{-\rho/3}$$

$$R_{32}(r) = \frac{4}{81\sqrt{30}a^{3/2}}\rho^2 e^{-\rho/3}$$

Table 11-2 Angular Functions $\Theta_{lm}(\theta)$ for Hydrogen Atom*

$$\Theta_{00} = \frac{1}{\sqrt{2}} \qquad \Theta_{10} = \tfrac{1}{2}\sqrt{6}\cos\theta$$

$$\Theta_{11} = \tfrac{1}{2}\sqrt{3}\sin\theta$$

$$\Theta_{20} = \tfrac{1}{4}\sqrt{10}(3\cos^2\theta - 1)$$

$$\Theta_{21} = \sqrt{15}\sin\theta\cos\theta$$

$$\Theta_{22} = \tfrac{1}{4}\sqrt{15}\sin^2\theta$$

*For any Θ_{lm}, $\Theta_{l-m} = \Theta_{lm}$. This relation may be used for negative values of m.

different values of l and the same n. Similarly, in Table 11-2, each function is a polynomial of degree l in $\sin\theta$ and $\cos\theta$.

We have now exhibited a complete set of solutions of the Schrödinger equation for the hydrogen atom, each identified by a set of three quantum numbers n, l, m. The energy levels, determined by the principal quantum number n, are given by Eq. (11-22), which agrees exactly with the energy levels deduced from the spectrum of hydrogen. Of course, if the energy levels had come out differently, it would have been clear immediately that the Schrödinger equation cannot provide the correct description of the behavior of atoms, and it would have been forgotten or modified. But in 1925 the discovery that the solutions *do* predict the hydrogen energy levels correctly was a discovery of the first magnitude and provided very direct support for the basic correctness of the new concepts.

The "size" of a wave function, that is, the dimensions of the region in which it differs appreciably from zero, is determined by the radial function $R(r)$. Table 11-1 shows that the size depends primarily on a factor of the form $e^{-\rho}$, $e^{-\rho/2}$, or in general $e^{-\rho/n}$. Thus the radius outside which the wave function is negligibly small *increases* with n. To examine this matter in more detail, we make use of the fact that the probability of finding the electron in the radius interval dr is given by $|\psi|^2 4\pi r^2\,dr$, which is proportional to $r^2|R(r)|^2$. This quantity is plotted for several radial functions in Fig. 11-3. Furthermore, it is possible to show that for the functions having the maximum l for a given n (that is, $l = n - 1$), $r^2|R(r)|^2$ attains its *maximum* value at

$$r_{\max} = n^2 a = n^2 \frac{4\pi\varepsilon_0\hbar^2}{me^2} \tag{11-25}$$

where a is as usual the radius of the first Bohr orbit, $a = 0.529 \times 10^{-10}$ m. This is just equal to the Bohr-orbit radius for state n, as given by Eq. (8-27).

It is useful to visualize electron wave functions as clouds whose density is proportional to $|\psi|^2$ at various points. This picture should not be taken

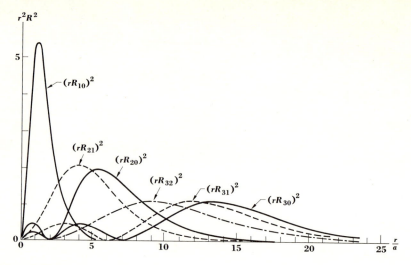

Fig. 11-3 Graphs of the quantity $r^2|R(r)|^2$ for several radial functions. Each graph represents the probability of finding the particle at various radii, for the corresponding state.

too seriously; the size of the atom itself is smaller by 10^4 than wavelengths of visible light, and scattering a light photon would seriously distort the wave function, so there is no hope of actually *seeing* a hydrogen wave function. Nevertheless, visualizing electron wave functions as clouds is useful in clarifying basic ideas. Pictorial representations of a few functions are shown in Fig. 11-4. This figure also shows an abbreviated scheme for labeling states, introduced by spectroscopists but now used quite generally, in which a state is labeled by a number equal to the principal quantum number n, followed by a lowercase letter which corresponds to the angular-momentum number l according to the following scheme:

l	Spectroscopic notation
0	*s*
1	*p*
2	*d*
3	*f*
4	*g*
5	*h*

Thus a state with $n = 2$ and $l = 1$ is called a $2p$ state, and so on. In this notation the value of m is not specified.

In general, for a given n there are several values of l and m, corresponding to different states, which give the same total energy. Two or more distinct states having the same energy are said to be *degenerate*. This is not to imply that the quantum numbers l and m are of no significance in describing the state. These quantum numbers are related to the angular distribution of the wave function about the nucleus, and it will be shown in the next section that they are directly related to the *angular momentum* and its z component.

In the above discussion we have considered only time-independent wave functions. Just as for the harmonic oscillator, discussed in Sec. 10-5, the complete time-dependent wave function Ψ is obtained by multiplying ψ by the factor $e^{-iEt/\hbar}$, which expresses the time dependence of a wave function with a definite total energy E. Thus we may write

$$\Psi_{nlm}(r,\theta,\phi,t) = \psi_{nlm}(r,\theta,\phi)e^{-iE_nt/\hbar} \tag{11-26}$$

with E_n given by Eq. (11-22). Correspondingly, the complex conjugate of the time-dependent wave function is given by

$$\Psi^*_{nlm}(r,\theta,\phi,t) = \psi^*_{nlm}(r,\theta,\phi)e^{+iE_nt/\hbar} \tag{11-27}$$

The quantity $|\Psi|^2 = \Psi\Psi^*$, which represents the probability density, is independent of time at each point in space. As pointed out in Sec. 10-4, this is a property of *all* wave functions for states of definite total energy. On the other hand, the wave function Ψ itself varies with time according to the factor $e^{-iE_nt/\hbar}$. That is, the real and imaginary components of the wave function both vary sinusoidally with time with an angular frequency ω given by

$$\omega = \frac{E_n}{\hbar}$$

In summary, we have now seen how the solutions of the Schrödinger equation for the hydrogen atom can be used to predict the energy levels of the atom, as well as the electron distribution. The analysis is considerably more complex mathematically than in the Bohr theory, but the Schrödinger equation has the tremendous advantage that the energy levels and the permitted wave functions arise naturally from physically reasonable boundary conditions which the wave functions must satisfy, rather than having to be introduced artificially by ad hoc assumptions as in the Bohr theory.

11-4 ANGULAR MOMENTUM

We now examine the angular-momentum characteristics of the wave functions developed in the preceding section. In the Bohr theory, the quantization of angular momentum was introduced as an explicit postulate, and the assumption that the angular momentum of the electron is an integral multiple of $\hbar$ led to the correct energy levels of the hydrogen atom. Thus it is of interest

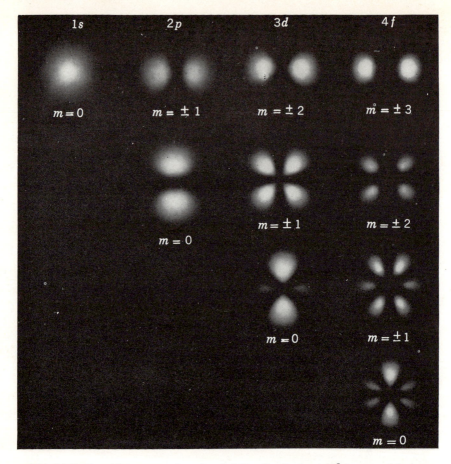

Fig. 11-4 Pictorial representation of probability distribution $|\psi|^2$ for several hydrogen wave functions. Each figure is a cross section in a plane containing the polar axis (z axis), which is vertical and in the plane of the paper. The scale varies from figure to figure.

to examine the wave functions just developed to ascertain whether they too have definite angular momentum, and if so what correspondence exists between this angular momentum and that associated with the Bohr theory.

According to the discussion of Sec. 10-7, a state has a definite value of a component of angular momentum in a given direction only if its wave function is an *eigenfunction* of the corresponding angular-momentum operator. The operators for the components of angular momentum in cartesian coordinates are given by Eqs. (10-59). For a state to have a definite value of L_z, it must be true that

$$\frac{\hbar}{i}\left(x\frac{\partial}{\partial y} - y\frac{\partial}{\partial x}\right)\psi = (\text{const})\psi \tag{11-28}$$

and the constant is the value of L_z for the state.

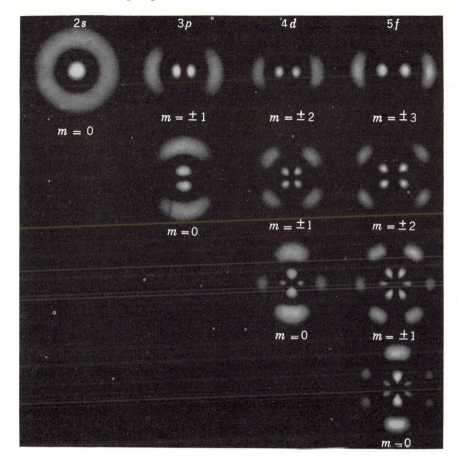

Since the hydrogen wave functions have been represented in terms of spherical coordinates, it is most convenient to transform the angular-momentum operators to these coordinates, using Eqs. (11-19). The L_z operator in spherical coordinates is simply

$$L_z \rightarrow \frac{\hbar}{i} \frac{\partial}{\partial \phi} \qquad (11\text{-}29)$$

This result is obtained most easily by starting at the end and working backward, using the chain rule for differentiation. The details are left as a problem.

We now apply the operator for L_z to a hydrogen-atom wave function. The factor in each function that depends on ϕ is given by Eq. (11-24) and so we have

$$\frac{\hbar}{i}\frac{\partial}{\partial\phi}\psi_{nlm} = \frac{\hbar}{i}R_{nl}\Theta_{lm}\frac{\partial}{\partial\phi}e^{im\phi}$$

$$= \frac{\hbar}{i}(im)R_{nl}\Theta_{lm}\Phi_m \qquad (11\text{-}30)$$

$$= m\hbar\psi_{nlm}$$

This result shows that applying the operator for L_z to the wave function ψ_{nlm} yields the same function, multiplied by $m\hbar$. That is, this function is an *eigenfunction* of the L_z operator, with eigenvalue $m\hbar$. Thus ψ_{nlm} represents a state with a definite value of L_z equal to $m\hbar$; the quantum number m determines the value of L_z, just as n determines the energy of the state.

Similarly, an operator can be derived for the square of the total angular momentum, $L^2 = L_x^2 + L_y^2 + L_z^2$. This operator is somewhat more complicated than that for L_z, and the details of its derivation need not be discussed here. The result is

$$L^2 \rightarrow -\hbar^2\left[\frac{1}{\sin\theta}\frac{\partial}{\partial\theta}\left(\sin\theta\frac{\partial}{\partial\theta}\right) + \frac{1}{\sin^2\theta}\frac{\partial^2}{\partial\phi^2}\right] \qquad (11\text{-}31)$$

When the operator for L^2 is applied to ψ_{nlm}, the result is the quantity $l(l + 1)\hbar^2\psi_{nlm}$. That is, ψ_{nlm} is an eigenfunction of the L^2 operator, with eigenvalue $l(l + 1)\hbar^2$, and ψ_{nlm} represents a state with a definite value of L^2, given by

$$L^2 = l(l + 1)\hbar^2 \qquad (11\text{-}32)$$

It is now clear that each quantum number has a definite physical significance. The *principal quantum number* n determines the energy of the state. The angular momentum is determined by l, called the *orbital quantum number* or the *angular-momentum quantum number*. The *component* of angular momentum in the z direction is determined by m, called the *magnetic quantum number* for reasons which will become clear in Sec. 11-7.

The maximum value of L_z for any value of l is $l\hbar$. It might be thought that this corresponds to the case where the angular momentum is aligned with the z axis, and that L^2 should equal $l^2\hbar^2$. Instead it is $l(l + 1)\hbar^2$; the *magnitude* of the total angular momentum is somewhat larger than its maximum component in any given direction. In classical mechanics this would make no sense; quantum-mechanically it means the *direction* of the angular-momentum vector is not well defined. In fact, a state with a definite value of L_z *cannot* have definite values of L_x and L_y. This fundamental uncertainty in the direction of the angular-momentum vector is analogous to the uncertainty in position and momentum discussed in Sec. 9-4.

It may seem strange that the hydrogen-atom wave functions have a definite value of one particular component of angular momentum. Does this imply that not all directions in space are equivalent? On the contrary; the fact that we have obtained states with definite L_z is a result of the particular coordinate system used. It is possible to construct states having, instead, a definite value of L_x or of L_y, but because of the fundamental uncertainty, it is *not* possible to construct states that have definite values of two or more components of **L,** except in the special case $l = 0$.

It is also possible to construct a mixture of states in which *no* component of angular momentum has a definite value. An example is a function in the form

$$a\Psi_{nlm_1} + b\Psi_{nlm_2}$$

where a and b are constants. The two functions correspond to the same energy and angular momentum, but there are two different values of L_z. Therefore this state has definite E and L^2 but *not* L_z. Correspondingly, adding wave functions with different values of l or n produces a state in which L^2 or E does not have a definite value. The fact that several possible wave functions can be combined to obtain a new possible state of the system is an example of the *superposition principle* which we have already seen in action in various other contexts. Applied to the hydrogen atom, the superposition principle says that if any two wave functions Ψ_1 and Ψ_2 are individually possible states of the system, then any linear combination

$$\Psi = a_1\Psi_1 + a_2\Psi_2 \tag{11-33}$$

is also a possible state of the system. That is, such a state is a solution of the time-dependent Schrödinger equation. It is *not* in general a solution of the time-independent Schrödinger equation, unless all states in the mixture have the same energy. The superposition principle is useful in the analysis of *transitions* of a system from one state to another, to be discussed in Sec. 11-6.

11-5 HYDROGENLIKE ATOMS

The above analysis of the hydrogen atom can be applied with only a little additional effort to a number of similar systems. First, the assumption that the nucleus is infinitely massive and stationary is not an essential restriction. If the nucleus has finite mass, both it and the electron move. The corresponding two-body problem in classical mechanics can be reduced to an equivalent one-body problem with a fixed center of force by introducing the *reduced mass* of the system.[1] If the individual masses are m_1 and m_2, the reduced mass μ is defined as

$$\mu = \frac{m_1 m_2}{m_1 + m_2} \tag{11-34}$$

With the coordinate r interpreted as the position of the electron *relative to the nucleus*, the entire analysis goes through just as before, with the electron mass m replaced by the reduced mass. Since the proton mass is about $1836m$, the reduced mass of the hydrogen atom is

$$\mu_{\text{H}} = \frac{m(1836m)}{m + 1836m} = 0.99946m$$

Reference to Eqs. (11-12) and (11-13) shows that the energy levels are proportional to m and are slightly reduced compared to their values with an infinitely massive nucleus, while the radii are slightly increased. Similarly, for the *deuterium* atom, whose nucleus contains a proton and a neutron and is twice as massive as that of ordinary hydrogen, the reduced mass is $0.99973m$. This may look like an insignificant difference, less than three parts in 10,000, but sensitive spectroscopic equipment can easily detect this *isotope shift*, the difference between the spectrum lines of ordinary hydrogen and those of deuterium.

Another example is a bound state of an ordinary electron and a positron, or positive electron. This system, called a *positronium atom*, has no nucleus in the usual sense, but it has energy levels and wave functions closely related to those of the hydrogen atom. We leave it to the reader to show that the reduced mass of this system is $m/2$, and to work out the relation of the energies and wave functions to those of hydrogen.

Another class of systems to which the hydrogen analysis can be applied is an atom which ordinarily has several electrons but from which all but one have been removed. An atom with Z protons in the nucleus ordinarily has Z electrons, where Z is the *atomic number*. For helium, $Z = 2$, for lithium $Z = 3$, and so on. The principal difference between such a stripped-down atom and the hydrogen atom, aside from the small reduced-mass correction, is that the nuclear charge is Ze rather than just e. The potential energy contains the factor Ze^2 instead of e^2. The energy levels are given by

$$E_n = -\left(\frac{Ze^2}{4\pi\varepsilon_0}\right)^2 \frac{\mu}{2n^2\hbar^2} \tag{11-35}$$

and the first Bohr radius is

[1] See, for example, Young, ibid, sec. 10-5.

$$a = \frac{4\pi\varepsilon_0\hbar^2}{Zme^2} \tag{11-36}$$

Thus the energies are *larger* by a factor Z^2, and the wave functions *smaller* by a factor of Z, than for hydrogen. Spectrum lines corresponding to transitions between these levels of singly ionized helium can be seen in the light from a helium glow discharge lamp.

11-6 TRANSITIONS

Thus far we have discussed states of the hydrogen atom with definite energy. But in experimental observations what is always observed is *not* the energy of a particular state but the *change* in energy when a system makes a transition from one state to another. The wavelengths and frequencies of spectrum lines are determined not by the positions of the energy levels but by the *differences* between various energy levels. Thus it is of interest to examine the mechanisms by which transitions from one energy state to another take place.

First, an atom in a state with definite E, L^2, and L_z cannot make a transition to another state having different values of these dynamical quantities unless it *interacts* with its surroundings. Since the atom consists of charged particles, this interaction is *electromagnetic* in nature. In emission or absorption of radiation, the electron in the hydrogen atom is acted upon by the electric and magnetic fields of an electromagnetic wave. An atom can also change its energy state in a collision with another charged particle, such as an ion in a gas, in which case the interaction is the Coulomb force between the two charges.

Corresponding to the interaction of the atom with its surroundings, there is an interaction *energy*, represented by an additional term in the Schrödinger equation; in general, this term depends explicitly on time, since the interaction is time-dependent. As a result, the state of the atom is *not* ordinarily a state with definite energy but rather a time-dependent mixture of states with various energies. That is, the state of the atom is described by a function of the form

$$\Psi = \sum_i a_i \Psi_i \tag{11-37}$$

where Ψ_i is a state with energy E_i, and the coefficients a_i are functions of time. Suppose an atom in a state

$$\Psi_1 = \psi_1 e^{-iE_1 t/\hbar} \tag{11-38}$$

with energy E_1 makes a transition to another state

$$\Psi_2 = \psi_2 e^{-iE_2 t/\hbar} \tag{11-39}$$

with energy E_2 by emitting an electromagnetic photon of energy $E_1 - E_2$ and frequency

$$\omega = \frac{E_1 - E_2}{\hbar} \tag{11-40}$$

Then during the transition the state of the atom is represented by a function of the form

$$\Psi = a_1(t)\Psi_1 + a_2(t)\Psi_2 \tag{11-41}$$

in which we have explicitly shown that the coefficients a_1 and a_2 are functions of time. If the system starts in one state and ends in the other, the variation of the coefficients a_1 and a_2 might be as shown in Fig. 11-5.

It is of interest to examine the probability density $|\Psi|^2 = \Psi^*\Psi$ for such a mixture of two states of different energies. Combining Eqs. (11-38), (11-39), and (11-41), we find

$$\begin{aligned} \Psi^*\Psi &= (a_1^*\psi_1^* e^{iE_1 t/\hbar} + a_2^*\psi_2^* e^{iE_2 t/\hbar})(a_1\psi_1 e^{-iE_1 t/\hbar} + a_2\psi_2 e^{-iE_2 t/\hbar}) \\ &= |a_1\psi_1|^2 + |a_2\psi_2|^2 + a_1^* a_2 \psi_1^* \psi_2 e^{i(E_1 - E_2)t/\hbar} \\ &\qquad\qquad + a_1 a_2^* \psi_1 \psi_2^* e^{-i(E_1 - E_2)t/\hbar} \end{aligned} \tag{11-42}$$

This is a significant result; the quantity $|\Psi|^2$ at a given point in space is *not* independent of time, as it is with states of definite energy. If the variation of the coefficients a_1 and a_2 is very *slow* compared with that of the wave functions themselves, then the first two terms in this expression also vary slowly. But the last two terms vary sinusoidally with a frequency given by

$$\omega = \frac{E_1 - E_2}{\hbar} \tag{11-43}$$

which is the same as the frequency of the emitted radiation! The superposition of the two wave functions with different energies thus causes an oscillation

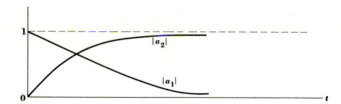

Fig. 11-5 Possible time variation of coefficients a_1 and a_2 in a superposition of two wave functions, corresponding to a transition from state Ψ_1 to state Ψ_2. Graphs show the absolute values of a_1 and a_2, which may be complex. Normalization requires that $|a_1|^2 + |a_2|^2 = 1$.

in the charge distribution in the atom with just the right frequency to produce electromagnetic radiation of the observed frequency.

In atomic transitions the time during which the transition occurs is typically of the order of 10^{-8} s, while the frequency of the emitted radiation, on the other hand, is typically of the order of 10^{15} Hz. Thus usually a very *large* number of cycles occur during the emission of a photon. By considering the mechanism of the interaction of the atom and electromagnetic field in detail, it is possible actually to *calculate* the amount of time involved in a transition. This time, in turn, is closely related to the *intensity* of the resulting spectrum line; the most intense spectral lines are those corresponding to transitions with the greatest transition rates. The prediction of intensities of spectral lines is one of the successes of quantum mechanics in an area where the Bohr theory was completely powerless.

We have mentioned the oscillating charge density in an atom, resulting from the superposition of the two wave functions with different energies. The angular distribution of the resulting radiation depends on the spatial distribution of this oscillating charge. The transitions most likely to occur are those in which the charge distribution resembles an oscillating electric *dipole*. Much *less* likely are transitions for which the two superposed functions resemble a quadrupole, octupole, etc. The dipole-like charge distribution occurs when the two states have values of l that differ by unity and values of m that differ by zero or unity. Other transitions are not impossible, but they are much less likely.

Thus we obtain the following *selection rules* for transitions from one state to another:

$$\Delta l = \pm 1$$
$$\Delta m = 0, \pm 1$$

(11-44)

Transitions that violate these rules are said to be *forbidden*, not because they cannot occur but because they are so much *less likely* than the others that they are not usually observed in optical spectra.

11-7   THE ZEEMAN EFFECT

The Zeeman effect is the phenomenon of *splitting* of lines in atomic spectra when the atoms are placed in a magnetic field. Although this effect was first observed experimentally by the Dutch physicist Pieter Zeeman, the idea was not original with him. As early as 1862, Michael Faraday had speculated that, if vibrating electric charges in matter are responsible for the emission of line spectra, then imposing a magnetic field might change the frequencies of the vibrations and of the emitted light. The resolution of Faraday's spectroscope was not sufficient to detect any effect, but when Zeeman performed similar experiments at the University of Leyden in 1896, using improved

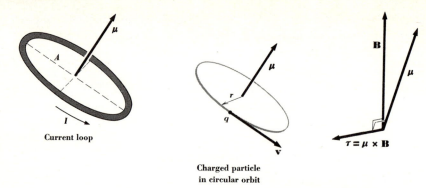

Current loop

Charged particle
in circular orbit

Fig. 11-6 A current loop or a charged particle in a circular orbit possesses a magnetic moment $\boldsymbol{\mu}$. In the presence of a magnetic field **B** the loop experiences a torque $\boldsymbol{\tau} = \boldsymbol{\mu} \times \mathbf{B}$ tending to orient the magnetic moment parallel to **B**. The potential energy $V = -\boldsymbol{\mu} \cdot \mathbf{B}$ of this interaction is minimum when $\boldsymbol{\mu}$ and **B** are parallel, maximum when they are antiparallel, and zero when they are perpendicular.

spectroscopic equipment, he discovered that in the presence of a magnetic field individual spectrum lines are *split* into a number of closely spaced lines. Furthermore, following a suggestion by H. A. Lorentz, Zeeman discovered that the component lines have different but definite states of *polarization*.

To understand the effect of a magnetic field on energy levels of the hydrogen atom, it is useful to regress briefly to the language of the Bohr model. In that model, the electron moving in its circular orbit can be thought of as equivalent to a circular current loop. In classical electromagnetism[1] a plane conducting loop of area A carrying a current I has a magnetic moment $\boldsymbol{\mu}$ whose magnitude is $\mu = IA$ and whose direction is determined by the right-hand rule, as shown in Fig. 11-6. In the presence of a magnetic field this magnetic moment experiences a torque $\boldsymbol{\tau}$ given by

$$\boldsymbol{\tau} = \boldsymbol{\mu} \times \mathbf{B} \tag{11-45}$$

which tends to orient the dipole in the direction of the field. Corresponding to this interaction is a potential energy given by

$$V = -\boldsymbol{\mu} \cdot \mathbf{B} = -\mu B \cos \theta \tag{11-46}$$

where θ is the angle between the directions of **B** and $\boldsymbol{\mu}$.

We may evaluate $\mu = IA$ in terms of the electron motion. When the electron, with mass m and charge e, moves in a circular orbit of radius r with speed v, the circumference of the orbit is $2\pi r$, and the electron makes $v/2\pi r$ revolutions per second. The equivalent current (the amount of charge passing a given point per unit time) is

---

[1]See A. F. Kip, "Fundamentals of Electricity and Magnetism," 2d ed., secs. 8.3 and 8.8, McGraw-Hill Book Company, New York, 1969.

$$I = \frac{ev}{2\pi r} \tag{11-47}$$

The area A of the current loop is πr^2, and the magnetic moment associated with the electron's motion is

$$\mu = \frac{ev}{2\pi r}\pi r^2 = \frac{evr}{2} \tag{11-48}$$

When this expression is multiplied and divided by m, the factor mvr appears in the numerator. This is the magnitude of the angular momentum L of a particle with momentum mv moving in a circle of radius r. Thus

$$\mu = \frac{e(mvr)}{2m} = \frac{e}{2m}L \tag{11-49}$$

Thus the magnitude of the magnetic moment is directly proportional to that of the angular momentum L, with the proportionality factor $e/2m$. This factor is called the *gyromagnetic ratio*. For a positive charge the vectors $\boldsymbol{\mu}$ and $\mathbf{L}$ have the same direction. The electron charge is negative, and the correct *vector* relationship for electrons is

$$\boldsymbol{\mu} = -\frac{e}{2m}\mathbf{L} \tag{11-50}$$

The above discussion has been based on the Bohr model, which has already been shown to be inadequate. The existence of a magnetic moment is less easy to visualize in the wave-mechanical description, but experiment shows that Eq. (11-50) holds there also. The most direct experimental evidence is in fact the Zeeman effect, as we shall see.

In computing the interaction energy of the magnetic moment $\boldsymbol{\mu}$ in the magnetic field $\mathbf{B}$, it is convenient to choose the coordinate axes so that $\mathbf{B}$ lies along the direction of the $+z$ axis. In that case, combining Eqs. (11-46) and (11-50), we obtain

$$V = \frac{e}{2m}\mathbf{L}\cdot\mathbf{B} = \frac{e}{2m}L_z B \tag{11-51}$$

If there were no restrictions on possible values of L_z, it could take any value from $-L$ to $+L$, and Eq. (11-51) could have any value from $-eLB/2m$ to $+eLB/2m$. An energy level with the value E in the absence of a field might have any value between $E - eLB/2m$ and $E + eLB/2m$ in the field. Correspondingly, any spectrum line resulting from a transition to or from this level would become smeared out by the corresponding amount.

In actual fact, L_z is *quantized,* and this smearing-out is not observed experimentally. Instead, individual spectrum lines are *split* into several distinct lines which are displaced various amounts from the zero-field positions, as shown in Fig. 11-7; this indicates corresponding splitting in energy levels. The possible values of L_z, as discussed in Sec. 11-4, are given by $m_l\hbar$, where m_l is the magnetic quantum number for the state, an integer between $-l$ and l. We now see the reason for the name "magnetic quantum number."

Using the above expression for L_z together with Eq. (11-51), we find that a level with magnetic quantum number m_l is shifted by an amount ΔE given by

$$\Delta E = m_l \frac{e\hbar}{2m} B \tag{11-52}$$

In the presence of a magnetic field, then, the energy scheme of the hydrogen atom takes the form shown in Fig. 11-8. Levels with the same n and l but different m_l, which are *degenerate* in the absence of a **B** field, become *nondegenerate* in the presence of **B**.

It is of interest to examine the numerical magnitude of the splitting of energy levels. A magnetic field of 1 Wb/m² (1 T or 10^4 G) is easily produced in modern laboratories. For such a field, the value of the coefficient of m_l in Eq. (11-52) is

$$\frac{e\hbar B}{2m} = \frac{(1.60 \times 10^{-19}\,\text{C})(1.054 \times 10^{-34}\,\text{J}\cdot\text{s})(1\,\text{Wb/m}^2)}{2(9.11 \times 10^{-31}\,\text{kg})}$$

$$= 9.27 \times 10^{-24}\,\text{J} = 5.79 \times 10^{-5}\,\text{eV}$$

For comparison, the energy of the $n = 3$ to $n = 2$ transition corresponding to the longest-wavelength line in the Balmer series, as Fig. 11-8 shows, is $3.40 - 1.51$ eV, or about 1.9 eV. The *fractional* change in transition energy is about 3×10^{-5}; the wavelength of the line in question is 656.2 nm, and

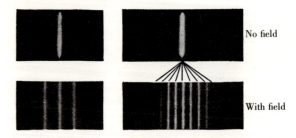

No field

With field

Fig. 11-7 Photographs of spectrum lines, illustrating the Zeeman effect. When the source of radiation is placed in a magnetic field, some individual lines split into sets of lines, as shown, as a result of the interaction of the magnetic moments of the atoms with the magnetic field. The fact that discrete lines appear rather than a continuous smear demonstrates the quantization of the component of magnetic moment, and thus of angular momentum, in the direction of the magnetic field.

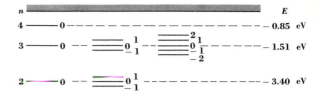

Fig. 11-8 Energy-level diagram showing the splitting of energy levels resulting from the interaction of the magnetic moment of the electron's orbital motion with an external magnetic field. Values of m_l are shown adjacent to the various levels; relative magnitudes of splittings are exaggerated for clarity. Some of the $n = 4$ levels are not shown; the reader should try to draw them in.

so the corresponding shift in wavelength should be of the order of

$$\Delta\lambda = (656.2 \text{ nm})(3 \times 10^{-5}) \cong 0.02 \text{ nm}$$

a shift which is well within the resolution of present-day grating spectrometers.

Referring again to Fig. 11-8, we can now predict into *how many* component lines each spectrum line should be split. As an example, we consider again the $n = 3$ to $n = 2$ transition. As Eq. (11-52) shows, the $n = 3$, $l = 2$ level (3d in spectroscopic notation) is split into five equally spaced levels corresponding to the five values of m_l. Correspondingly, the $n = 2$, $l = 1$ (2p) level is split into three levels. Let the splitting of *adjacent* levels be ΔE and the level spacing in the absence of a magnetic field E_0. If there were no selection rules, there would be 15 distinct transitions, ranging in energy from $E_0 - 3\,\Delta E$ for the $m_l = -2 \rightarrow \vert 1$ transition to $E_0 + 3\,\Delta E$ for the $m_l = +2 \rightarrow -1$ transition, and differing by intervals of ΔE. The selection rule $m_l = 0, \pm 1$ eliminates several of these; the nine transitions consistent with this rule are shown in Fig. 11-9. As the figure shows, these all have energy E_0 or $E_0 \pm \Delta E$, and the Zeeman effect splits this particular line into *three* lines.

The predictions of Lorentz regarding the *polarization* of the components of Zeeman-split lines are also borne out experimentally. It turns out that in any transition for which m_l does not change, the resulting line is *plane-*

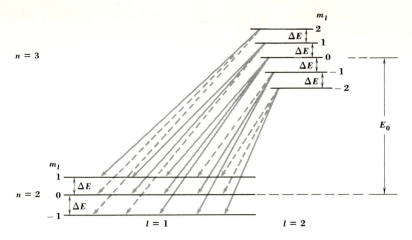

Fig. 11-9 Detail of part of the hydrogen energy-level diagram, showing Zeeman-effect splitting of the 3d and 2p levels. Transitions forbidden by the selection rule $\Delta m = 0, \pm 1$ are shown as broken lines.

polarized in the plane of **B**, while when m_l changes by one unit, the line is *circularly* polarized. These results can be understood qualitatively on the basis of the oscillating charge cloud which is present during the transition, as discussed in Sec. 11-6. When m_l does not change, this cloud resembles an electric dipole along the z axis, while when m_l changes by unity, it resembles two superposed dipoles along the x and y axes, 90° out of phase.

Thus the Zeeman effect provides direct confirmation of a number of predictions of quantum mechanics, as applied to the hydrogen atom. Not only does the Schrödinger equation provide a correct prediction of spectrum lines; it also provides a basis for computing *intensities* of lines, *shifts* resulting from the application of magnetic field, and states of *polarization* of the component lines in the Zeeman effect. The theory is not yet complete, however. Careful examination of the details of various spectra reveals some discrepancies in the Zeeman splittings, and some lines show splitting even in the absence of an external magnetic field. In some cases there are an *even* number of component lines, although the above discussion suggests that there should always be an *odd* number, since the number of values of m_l for a given level is always odd. These and numerous other features of atomic spectra point to the necessity for further refinements. One of the most important of these is the concept of *electron spin* with its associated magnetic moment and magnetic interaction energy.

11-8 ELECTRON SPIN

The principles of quantum mechanics discussed thus far account for many features of atomic spectra and related phenomena, but there are some observations that suggest the need for further generalization. Some spectra reveal a pair of closely spaced levels (a *doublet*) where the Schrödinger equation predicts only one. An example is the spectrum of sodium, with energy levels as shown in Fig. 8-6b. In the Zeeman effect, sometimes five or seven lines are found instead of the three predicted in Sec. 11-7, and when there *are* three, the spacing is sometimes greater than predicted. Several examples of this *anomalous Zeeman effect* are shown in Fig. 11-10.

Another important set of observations is provided by the experiments of Stern and Gerlach, beginning in 1921. Their object was to measure the magnetic moments of atoms by evaporating atoms from an oven, using apertures to form a *beam* of atoms, and then passing this beam (in an evacuated chamber) through a strongly inhomogeneous magnetic field, as shown in Fig. 11-11. In a *uniform* field a magnetic moment experiences a *torque* but no net force; in a *nonuniform* field there is a *force*, which has the effect of deflecting the beam vertically by an amount proportional to the component of the magnetic moment along the field. This permits a direct measurement of magnetic moments.

Stern and Gerlach anticipated a continuous vertical distribution, corresponding to the various possible values of this component; because of quantiza-

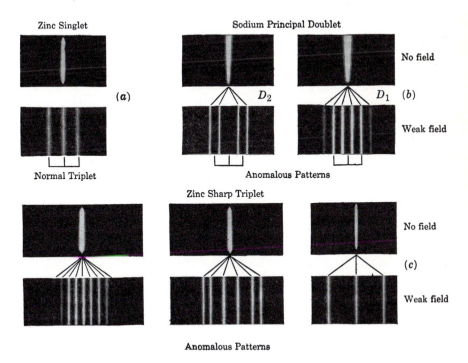

Fig. 11-10 Photographs showing the normal and anomalous Zeeman effects for several elements. The brackets under each photograph show the "normal" splitting predicted by neglecting the effect of electron spin.

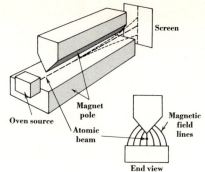

Fig. 11-11 Apparatus for Stern-Gerlach experiment. A beam of atoms from the oven moves through an inhomogeneous magnetic field, causing vertical deflections of the beam.

tion of angular momentum, they found instead a *discrete* set of deflections. For some atoms the beam was split into three, five, seven, or more components, corresponding to $l = 1, 2, 3$, or more, but in some cases the number of components was *even*, suggesting a *half-integer* angular momentum. For example, if $l = \frac{3}{2}$, we could have $m_l = \frac{3}{2}, \frac{1}{2}, -\frac{1}{2}$, or $-\frac{3}{2}$, and the beam would be split into four components. The problem is that the quantum mechanics discussed thus far does not permit half-integer angular-momentum quantum numbers!

To account for these various anomalies, Goudsmit and Uhlenbeck postulated in 1925 the existence of *electron spin*, in which the electron is assumed to have an *intrinsic* angular momentum and corresponding magnetic moment, in addition to the angular momentum and magnetic moment resulting from its *orbital* motion about the nucleus. In the Bohr model the electron is now pictured not as a point but rather as a small sphere which *spins* on its axis as it travels around the orbit, thereby making additional contributions to the angular momentum and magnetic moment. This picture may be compared with the angular momentum of the earth, one part associated with the *spin* of the earth on its axis and the other with its *orbital* motion around the sun. The terms *spin* and *orbital angular momentum*, in fact, originated in celestial mechanics.

In wave mechanics there is no simple way to picture the phenomenon of electron spin, but the concept can be incorporated into the Schrödinger equation by use of a wave function with two components, corresponding to two possible orientations of electron spin relative to a specified direction.

The anomalies mentioned above are all consistent with the assumption that the electron possesses an intrinsic magnetic moment which can have a component

$$\mu = \pm \frac{e\hbar}{2m} \tag{11-53}$$

in any specified direction, such as the direction of an external magnetic field.

Unlike the orbital magnetic moment, the spin magnetic moment cannot have *zero* component in the direction of the field; this fact suggests that the corresponding angular momentum must have a component $\pm\frac{1}{2}\hbar$ in the direction of a given reference axis. This component may then change by $\pm\hbar$ in a transition between states, just as with orbital angular momentum. Correspondingly, in the presence of a magnetic field B the intrinsic magnetic moment gives an additional interaction energy $\pm e\hbar B/2m$.

The first direct measurement of the gyromagnetic ratio of electron spin (ratio of spin magnetic moment to spin angular momentum) was suggested by Einstein and performed by De Haas, using an experimental arrangement shown schematically in Fig. 11-12. A cylinder of ferromagnetic material is suspended by a fine fiber inside a solenoid, which magnetizes the sample axially. When the direction of the magnetic field is reversed, the electron magnetic moments (and thus their spins) change direction as the direction of magnetization reverses. Since there is no external torque along the axis of rotation, the *total* angular momentum must be constant, and this can happen only if the sample as a whole begins to rotate. By measuring the angular velocity of rotation immediately after field reversal, one can calculate the total change in angular momentum of the electron spin. The total change in magnetic moment can also be measured from the magnetization of the sample, so the *ratio* of angular momentum to magnetic moment can be measured.

The results of this measurement are consistent with the assumption that the component of angular momentum in the direction of the field is $\pm\frac{1}{2}\hbar$ and that the gyromagnetic ratio for the intrinsic angular momentum is not $e/2m$, as for orbital angular momentum and magnetic moment, but rather

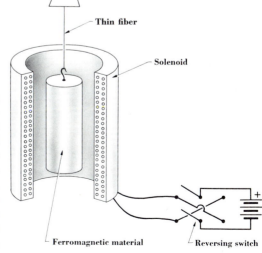

Fig. 11-12 Apparatus for measuring electron-spin angular momentum. A cylinder of ferromagnetic material is suspended by a fine fiber in a solenoid (shown in cross section), which magnetizes the material by orienting the electron magnetic moments parallel to the field. When the field is reversed, the spins flip over; since the *total* angular momentum cannot change, the specimen begins to rotate.

Thin fiber

Solenoid

Ferromagnetic material

Reversing switch

twice that value, e/m. This result is unique to quantum mechanics; within the framework of *classical* electrodynamics, there is no possible configuration of charge that leads to a gyromagnetic ratio different from $e/2m$.

The intrinsic magnetic moment of the electron also shifts energy levels even when *no* external field is applied. The reason is that, in the moving frame of reference of the electron, the positively charged nucleus appears to be in motion, and so the electron "sees" not just a static electric field but also a *magnetic* field, as shown by the relativistic field transformations, Eqs. (2-22). Relativistic electrodynamics must be used to calculate the resulting interaction energy. The apparent motion of the nucleus can be expressed in terms of the electron's *orbital* angular momentum **L**, and the interaction energy depends on the relative orientation of **L** and the electron spin. Denoting the spin angular momentum by **S**, we can express the interaction energy in terms of the quantity **L**•**S** and the electrical potential $V(r)$ corresponding to the electric field of the nucleus. Specifically, the interaction energy is given by

$$E = \frac{e}{2m^2c^2r}\frac{dV(r)}{dr}\mathbf{L}\cdot\mathbf{S} \qquad (11\text{-}54)$$

Because of its dependence on the spin and orbital angular momenta of the electron, this interaction is called *spin-orbit coupling*.

Energy shifts resulting from spin-orbit coupling are typically comparable to those of the strong-field Zeeman effect. As an example, we evaluate Eq. (11-54) for the $n = 2$ state of the Bohr atom. The electrical potential is $V(r) = e/4\pi\varepsilon_0 r$, and **L**•**S** is of the order of $\hbar^2$. Taking dV/dr and inserting $\hbar^2$ for **L**•**S**, we find that the spin-orbit energy is roughly

$$E \cong \frac{1}{2m^2c^2}\frac{e^2\hbar^2}{4\pi\varepsilon_0 r^3}$$

For the second Bohr orbit,

$$r = (2)^2\frac{4\pi\varepsilon_0\hbar^2}{me^2} = 2.12 \times 10^{-10}\text{ m}$$

Inserting this and the other numerical values, we find

$$E \cong 2 \times 10^{-24}\text{ J} \cong 10^{-5}\text{ eV}$$

This is comparable to our numerical example of Zeeman-effect splitting. Furthermore, the spin-orbit coupling energy increases rapidly with n, which governs the average value of r for the wave function. As an example, the splitting of the $3p$ level of the sodium atom leading to the famous yellow sodium doublet (589.0, 589.6 nm) in the $3p \longrightarrow 3s$ transition is the result of spin-orbit coupling.

The concept of electron spin may appear to be merely an ad hoc hypothesis, introduced to explain experimental facts but without any fundamental basis. This is indeed a deficiency of this formulation. In the *relativistic* wave equation for the electron, the *Dirac equation*, the spin and its associated interaction energy come out automatically rather than having to be added separately. Furthermore, the Schrödinger equation can be obtained from the Dirac equation as an approximation when the energies are sufficiently small compared with mc^2. Thus the concept of electron spin, although introduced here as an ad hoc explanation of certain spectral anomalies, can be justified thoroughly on *theoretical* grounds, through the methods of *relativistic quantum mechanics*.

The electron spin introduces a fourth quantum number to describe the state of the electron in the hydrogen atom. The component of spin angular momentum in the direction of a given axis (for example, the z axis) must be $\pm\frac{1}{2}\hbar$, corresponding to a quantum number s which takes the values $\pm\frac{1}{2}$. Thus the *four* quantum numbers n, l, m, and s constitute a complete description of the state. As we shall see in the next chapter, this description is especially useful in more complex atoms.

Problems

11-1 A 10-MeV α particle collides head on with an electron at rest. Assuming the particles can be treated classically, find the electron energy after the collision. What fraction of the initial α-particle energy is transferred to the electron?

11-2 An α particle of energy 1 MeV makes a head-on collision with a gold nucleus initially at rest. Find the distance of closest approach of the two particles.

11-3 The radius of the gold nucleus is about 7×10^{-15} m. In a Rutherford-scattering experiment, what minimum energy must the α particle have to measure this radius? That is, what energy is needed for it to approach within 7×10^{-15} m of the center of the nucleus? Express your result in electronvolts.

11-4 Verify by direct substitution that the wave function given by Eq. (11-18) is a solution of the spherically symmetric Schrödinger equation (11-9), and find the energy of the state described by this function.

11-5 Find the value of the constant C necessary to normalize the wave function given by Eq. (11-18). The calculation is simplified by making the change of variable $x = r/2a$ and by using a table of integrals.

11-6 For the hydrogen wave function ψ_{100}, what is the probability that the electron is in the region *outside* a sphere of radius equal to the first Bohr radius, given by Eq. (11-12)?

11-7 The Lyman series in the hydrogen spectrum consists of those lines resulting from transitions which end in the $n = 1$ state. Compute the wavelengths of the three longest-wavelength lines. In what region of the electromagnetic spectrum do they lie?

11-8 The Paschen series in the hydrogen spectrum consists of those lines resulting from transitions which end in the $n = 3$ state.
 a Compute the wavelengths of the three longest-wavelength lines. In what region of the electromagnetic spectrum do they lie?
 b What minimum energy would have to be given to an atom initially in the ground state for all of these lines to be observed?

11-9 The average translational kinetic energy of gas molecules at absolute temperature T is $3kT/2$, where k is Boltzmann's constant. At what temperature is this equal to the ionization energy of hydrogen?

11-10 The longest-wavelength line in the Balmer series results from the transition from $n = 3$ to $n = 2$. Find the difference in wavelength between the line emitted by normal hydrogen and that emitted by deuterium.

11-11 Hydrogen-atom transitions have recently been observed in the laboratory and in astrophysical observations which involve states with n values of the order of 100.
 a Compute the energy and Bohr radius for a hydrogen atom with $n = 100$.
 b Compute the energy, frequency, and wavelength of the photon emitted in a transition from $n = 100$ to $n = 99$. In what range of the electromagnetic spectrum does such a photon lie?

11-12 Consider the positronium atom discussed in Sec. 11-5.
 a Compute the ionization energy, in electronvolts.
 b What wavelength photon is needed to ionize a positronium atom?
 c What wavelength photon is emitted in the $n = 2$ to $n = 1$ transition in positronium?

11-13 The He$^+$ ion has one electron and a nuclear charge $+2e$.
 a What is the Bohr radius for the electron in its ground state?
 b What energy is needed to remove the electron, i.e., to *doubly* ionize the atom?
 c Considering spectral series for this ion, which series lie in the visible spectrum? The language of Sec. 8-4 is helpful.

11-14 The doubly ionized lithium atom Li^{++} has one electron and a nuclear charge $+3e$.
 a What is the energy of the remaining electron in its ground state?
 b Find the wavelength and frequency of the photon corresponding to the transition $n = 2$ to $n = 1$.
 c Estimate the size of the ground-state wave function.
 d In (b), determine the difference in wavelength of a photon emitted by the common isotope ^{7}Li and one emitted by the uncommon isotope ^{6}Li.

11-15 For the radial functions R_{21} and R_{32} in Table 11-1, show that the quantity $r^2|R(r)|^2$ has a maximum at $\rho = 2^2$ and $\rho = 3^2$, respectively. Compare these results with the predictions of Eq. (11-25).

11-16 For the radial functions given in Table 11-1, show that $R(0) = 0$, except when $l = 0$.

11-17 Show that the Φ functions given by Eq. (11-24) are not single-valued unless m is an integer. The points (r,θ,ϕ) and $(r,\theta,\phi + 2\pi)$ are the same point, so $\Phi(\phi)$ must equal $\Phi(\phi + 2\pi)$ if Φ is to be single-valued.

11-18 For the angular functions in Table 11-2, show that, for a given value of l, the function is most concentrated along the polar axis for $m = 0$ and that, for increasing values of m, it becomes more and more concentrated in the equatorial plane (the xy plane).

11-19 A student asserts that any wave function for the hydrogen atom can be multiplied by a factor $e^{i\alpha}$, where α is a real constant, without changing any of the physical properties of the corresponding state. Discuss this assertion.

11-20 Express the ground-state hydrogen wave function, Eq. (11-17), in terms of x, y, and z, and apply the angular-momentum operator L_z given by Eq. (10-59c) to show that for this state $L_z = 0$.

11-21 Show that *every* spherically symmetric wave function (that is, ψ a function only of r) is an eigenfunction of each component of angular momentum, with eigenvalue zero. This is the only exception to the general rule that no two components of $\mathbf{L}$ can have definite values.

11-22 Derive the spherical-coordinate form of the angular-momentum operator $L_z = (\hbar/i)\,\partial/\partial\phi$ from the cartesian form, Eq. (10-59c) and the coordinate transformations of Eqs. (11-19).

11-23 Show that the functions $\sin m\phi$ and $\cos m\phi$ are *not* eigenfunctions of the L_z operator, but each can be represented as a linear combination of eigenfunctions with eigenvalues $m\hbar$ and $-m\hbar$.

11-24 Consider the ion He$^+$, which has one electron. How are the wave functions for this ion related to those of the hydrogen atom?

11-25 A quantum-mechanical harmonic oscillator makes a transition from the state $n = 3$ to the state $n = 2$ by emitting an electromagnetic photon.
  a   Find the frequency of the time variation of each of the functions Ψ_2 and Ψ_3.
  b   Find the frequency of the time variation of the quantity $\Psi^*\Psi$ during the transition.
  c   Find the frequency of the emitted radiation.

11-26 The transition $n = 2$ to $n = 1$ in hydrogen occurs in a time of the order of 10^{-8} s. Compute the *period* of the corresponding radiation; how many cycles of radiation occur during the radiation?

11-27 Consider the $4p \longrightarrow 3d$ transitions in hydrogen, in the presence of a magnetic field of 2.0 Wb/m^2, and assume that the electron has zero spin.

    a Draw an energy-level diagram showing the Zeeman-effect splitting, and calculate the magnitude of the splitting.

    b Indicate the permitted transitions, and calculate the shifts in their energies compared with the zero-field values.

    c Calculate the wavelength shifts of the resulting spectrum lines.

11-28 In the Bohr model of the hydrogen atom, how does the spin-orbit coupling energy depend on the quantum number n?

11-29 Draw an energy-level diagram showing the Zeeman-effect splitting of the $3d$ and $2p$ levels in hydrogen, including electron spin. Analyze the splitting of the line resulting from $3d \longrightarrow 2p$ transitions.

11-30 From Eq. (11-54), estimate the spin-orbit interaction energy for the $2p$ state of the hydrogen atom, by evaluating the quantities $1/r$ and dV/dr at $r = 4a$, where a is the first Bohr radius, given by Eq. (11-12).

11-31 In the Bohr model, calculate the magnetic moment of the electron in the $n = 1$ state. From this, calculate the energy-level splitting in a magnetic field $B = 1.0$ Wb/m^2. Into how many levels is the original level split, and how are their positions related to that of the original level?

Atomic and 12
Molecular Structure

In this chapter the principles of quantum mechanics are applied to many-electron atoms and to molecules. An additional new principle, the *exclusion principle*, is needed to understand the structure of many-electron atoms, the chemical properties of elements, and the periodic table of elements. Next we discuss x-ray spectra, associated with transitions of inner electrons in many-electron atoms. The relation of electronic structure of atoms to valence is discussed next, together with some important properties of molecules, including molecular spectra associated with transitions between vibration and rotation states.

12-1 EXCLUSION PRINCIPLE

In introducing the fundamental principles of quantum mechanics, we have concentrated on one-electron systems, just as in classical mechanics one must first understand the dynamical laws for a single point mass, and then apply these laws to more complicated systems. To begin the corresponding extension of quantum mechanics, we consider first the helium atom, with two electrons and a nuclear charge of $+2e$, and its relation to the hydrogen atom. The definite-energy states of the hydrogen atom are described by time-independent wave functions of a single position vector $\mathbf{r}$ or a set of three coordinates such as (x,y,z); the states of a two-electron atom are represented by a wave function containing the coordinates of *both* particles, such as $\psi(x_1,y_1,z_1,x_2,y_2,z_2)$ or $\psi(\mathbf{r}_1,\mathbf{r}_2)$. Just as the quantity

$$\psi^*(\mathbf{r})\psi(\mathbf{r})\, dV \tag{12-1}$$

for a one-electron wave function represents the probability that the particle

315

will be found in a volume element dV in the vicinity of the point $\mathbf{r}$, the quantity

$$\psi^*(\mathbf{r}_1,\mathbf{r}_2)\psi(\mathbf{r}_1,\mathbf{r}_2)\,dV_1\,dV_2 \tag{12-2}$$

for a two-electron wave function represents the probability that the first particle will be found in a volume element dV_1 near point $\mathbf{r}_1$ and simultaneously the second particle will be found in a volume element dV_2 near $\mathbf{r}_2$. In general, the wave function is a function of as many position vectors or sets of three coordinates as there are particles in the system.

Correspondingly, the total-energy operator, introduced in Sec. 10-7, depends on the coordinates of both particles. There are terms for the kinetic energy of each particle, a potential energy associated with the interaction of each particle with the nucleus, and an additional term representing interaction of the two particles with each other. Thus the time-independent Schrödinger equation for two electrons in a helium atom, including all these energies, is

$$-\frac{\hbar^2}{2m}\left(\frac{\partial^2\psi}{\partial x_1{}^2} + \frac{\partial^2\psi}{\partial y_1{}^2} + \frac{\partial^2\psi}{\partial z_1{}^2} + \frac{\partial^2\psi}{\partial x_2{}^2} + \frac{\partial^2\psi}{\partial y_2{}^2} + \frac{\partial^2\psi}{\partial z_2{}^2}\right)$$

$$+ \frac{e^2}{4\pi\varepsilon_0}\left(-\frac{2}{r_1} - \frac{2}{r_2} + \frac{1}{|\mathbf{r}_1 - \mathbf{r}_2|}\right)\psi = E\psi \tag{12-3}$$

The term containing $|\mathbf{r}_1 - \mathbf{r}_2|$, representing the interaction between the two electrons, complicates the mathematical problem enough so that this equation cannot be solved exactly. The situation is comparable to the classical problem of the interaction of three bodies, such as the sun, the earth, and the moon. The differential equations resulting from applying Newton's laws and the law of gravitation are impossible to solve in the general case, except by numerical approximation. Similarly, one must resort to approximations with the helium atom and nearly all more complex systems.

To any reader who feels disappointment at having to make approximations at so early a stage, we remark that such is often the case in applying physical principles to new situations and, furthermore, that it can be an *advantage* rather than a *disadvantage*. Even when exact solutions exist, they are often so complex mathematically that their physical meaning is not readily grasped. One can often obtain approximate results that are reasonably good representations and are much *simpler*, facilitating a grasp of their physical meaning. Equally important, there are many cases in which even approximate quantum-mechanical discussions bring understanding to areas where classical mechanics is powerless, with or without approximations.

The simplest approximation for many-electron atoms is simply to disregard the interelectron interactions and include only the interaction of each electron with the nucleus. In this model, each electron moves as though the others were not present, and its wave functions are the same as those for the hydrogen atom, except that the nuclear charge is Ze, where Z is the atomic number, equal to the number of protons in the nucleus. In this approximation, the wave function for the two-electron system of the helium atom is a product of two one-electron hydrogenlike wave functions, and the total energy of the state is the sum of the energies of the two electrons.

Formally, let $\psi_1(x_1,y_1,z_1)$ be a solution of the equation

$$-\frac{\hbar}{2m}\left(\frac{\partial^2\psi_1}{\partial x_1{}^2} + \frac{\partial^2\psi_1}{\partial y_1{}^2} + \frac{\partial^2\psi_1}{\partial z_1{}^2}\right) - \frac{2e^2}{4\pi\varepsilon_0 r_1}\psi_1 = E_1\psi_1 \tag{12-4}$$

with energy E_1 and $\psi_2(x_2,y_2,z_2)$ a solution of the corresponding equation for the second particle, with energy E_2. Then it can be shown that the product function $\psi = \psi_1(\mathbf{r}_1)\psi_2(\mathbf{r}_2)$ is a solution of Eq. (12-3) with the term in $|\mathbf{r}_1 - \mathbf{r}_2|$ omitted and that the energy of the state is $E_1 + E_2$. Detailed proof of this statement is left as a problem. The state of each electron is described by a set of four quantum numbers, just as for the hydrogen atom, and the state of the composite system is described by a set of eight quantum numbers.

This approximation is quite drastic; especially when there are many electrons, the interactions of the electrons with each other are as important as the interaction of each with the nucleus. Fortunately, a considerably better approximation can be made without sacrificing the essential features of the simple one. Instead of ignoring the electron-electron interactions, we regard each electron as moving in an electric field which is the combined result of the nuclear charge and the charges of the other electrons and which, on an average, can be assumed to be spherically symmetric. Thus the wave function for each electron is a solution of a Schrödinger equation similar in form to that of the hydrogen atom but with the $1/r$ potential-energy term replaced by a different function $V(r)$. The state of each electron may then be described by a set of four quantum numbers, just as with the hydrogen atom, although since the potential-energy function is different, the relation of the energy levels to the quantum numbers is not the same as for the hydrogen atom.

The scheme just described is called the *central-field approximation;* it includes the interactions between the electrons in an approximate way, while keeping the simplicity of the description in terms of quantum numbers for one-electron states. Much of the discussion of complex atoms which follows is based on this model.

Every atom, no matter what its structure, has a "ground state," or state of lowest energy; for the hydrogen atom the $1s$ state ($n = 1$, $l = 0$) is the ground state. In the central-field model, how does the ground state of a many-electron atom look? Offhand, one might expect that in the ground state all the electrons would fall into the lowest-energy states, so that every electron would be in a 1s state. In that case, looking at atoms with increasing numbers of electrons, we should expect gradual changes in the chemical and physical properties of the elements corresponding to these atoms.

There are several different kinds of evidence that this is *not* what happens. First the chemical properties of elements change quite abruptly with atomic number. Consider, for example, the elements fluorine, neon, and sodium, with 9, 10, and 11 electrons, respectively. Fluorine tends strongly to form compounds in which it acquires an extra electron, sodium forms compounds in which it *loses* an electron, and neon forms no compounds at all. If the chemical behavior of elements is to be understood in terms of electronic structure, the picture of a ground state with all the electrons in the 1s states cannot be correct.

The key to understanding the structure of many-electron atoms was discovered in 1925 by a Swiss theoretical physicist, Wolfgang Pauli, in a principle now known as the *Pauli exclusion principle*. This principle can be stated very simply, and yet it is of the utmost importance in the understanding of many-electron systems. It is this: *In a system containing several electrons, no two electrons can be in states in which all four of their quantum numbers are the same.*

As an example, we consider the lithium atom, with three electrons. For the $n = 1$ states, there can be only $l = 0$ and $m = 0$, and the spin quantum number can be $+\frac{1}{2}$ or $-\frac{1}{2}$. Thus only two electrons can be accommodated in the $n = 1$ states. The third electron must be in a state farther from the nucleus, with $n = 2$ or higher. This accounts for the fact that this electron is loosely bound and is readily lost when lithium forms compounds. The $n = 1$ states are "full," and the third electron must be content with the $n = 2$ states.

The exclusion principle immediately offers hope of understanding the periodic table of the elements. We picture the electronic structure of complex atoms in terms of successive filling up of higher and higher energy levels, with the assumption that the chemical properties of elements are determined mostly by the loosely bound outer electrons. For example, an atom with one electron considerably farther away from the nucleus than the others should have a tendency to lose this electron and thus behave chemically as an element with a valence of $+1$. The periodic table will be discussed in detail in Sec. 12-2.

The Pauli exclusion principle can be stated in more general terms without reliance on the central-field approximation. The general form is somewhat abstract, and we can only indicate its general nature here. Very briefly, the principle states that in any permissible wave function for a many-electron system, the effect of interchanging all the coordinates of any pair of electrons (including the description of the spin state) is simply to change the *sign* of the function. In mathematical terms, the wave function must be *antisymmetric* with respect to interchange of all coordinates (space and spin) of any pair of electrons. It can be shown that this is equivalent in the central-field approximation to our original statement that two electrons cannot be in the same state, i.e., cannot have all four quantum numbers the same. The more general statement is useful in analysis of molecular bonds and in many more complex problems.

12-2 PERIODIC TABLE

The variation of the chemical and physical properties of the elements with atomic number forms a pattern exhibited by the periodic table of the elements, Table 12-1. One of the important features of the table is that all elements in a particular column or *group* have similar chemical and physical properties. We now consider the relation of these properties to the electron configurations of atoms. Most of this discussion will be based on the central-field model introduced in the previous section, in which each electron is represented as moving in a potential resulting from the nucleus and the average positions of all the other electrons; each electron is described by a set of four quantum numbers n, l, m, s. The number of electrons in the atom, called the atomic number, is denoted by Z. This is also equal to the number of protons in the nucleus, and each proton has charge $+e$. Thus, an atom with atomic number Z has total nuclear charge Ze.

In the Bohr theory the radius of the electron orbit is proportional to n^2, as shown by Eq. (8-27). Correspondingly, the sizes of the *wave functions* for the hydrogen atom increase proportionately to n^2. A similar dependence on n also occurs for complex atoms, and it is in fact enhanced, for the following reason. Electrons close to the nucleus move in the field of the full nuclear charge Ze, while for electrons moving in the outer periphery of the atom the positive nuclear charge is partly canceled by the negative charge of the inner electrons. An electron *much farther* from the nucleus (on the average) than the other $(Z - 1)$ electrons "sees" a *net* charge not of $+Ze$ but of $+Ze - (Z - 1)e$, or simply $+e$. At intermediate distances the net field of the nucleus and the inner electrons can be described approximately by an effective value of Z, denoted by Z_{eff}, intermediate between unity and Z. This concept is useful in the analysis of x-ray spectra, to be discussed in Sec. 12-3. At present, the main point is that the outer electrons experience a smaller electric field and hence are more loosely bound than would be the case if the inner electrons were not present. This partial cancellation of the nuclear field by inner electrons is called *shielding* or *screening*, and it is a very important concept in the understanding of the structure and properties of many-electron atoms.

Table 12-1 The Periodic Table of the Elements

The number above the symbol of each element is its atomic mass, and that below is its atomic number. The elements whose atomic masses are given in parentheses do not occur in nature, but have been prepared artificially in nuclear reactions. The atomic mass in such a case is the mass number of the most long-lived radioactive isotope of the element.

Period	Group I	Group II												Group III	Group IV	Group V	Group VI	Group VII	Group VIII
1	1.00 H 1																		4.00 He 2
2	6.94 Li 3	9.01 Be 4												10.81 B 5	12.01 C 6	14.01 N 7	16.00 O 8	19.00 F 9	20.18 Ne 10
3	22.99 Na 11	24.31 Mg 12												26.98 Al 13	28.09 Si 14	30.98 P 15	32.07 S 16	35.46 Cl 17	39.94 Ar 18
4	39.10 K 19	40.08 Ca 20	44.96 Sc 21	47.90 Ti 22	50.94 V 23	52.00 Cr 24	54.94 Mn 25	55.85 Fe 26	58.93 Co 27	58.71 Ni 28	63.54 Cu 29	65.37 Zn 30		69.72 Ga 31	72.59 Ge 32	74.92 As 33	78.96 Se 34	79.91 Br 35	83.8 Kr 36
5	85.47 Rb 37	87.66 Sr 38	88.91 Y 39	91.22 Zr 40	92.91 Nb 41	95.94 Mo 42	(99) Tc 43	101.1 Ru 44	102.91 Rh 45	106.4 Pd 46	107.87 Ag 47	112.40 Cd 48		114.82 In 49	118.69 Sn 50	121.75 Sb 51	127.60 Te 52	126.90 I 53	131.30 Xe 54
6	132.91 Cs 55	137.34 Ba 56	* 57–71	178.49 Hf 72	180.95 Ta 73	183.85 W 74	186.2 Re 75	190.2 Os 76	192.2 Ir 77	195.09 Pt 78	197.0 Au 79	200.59 Hg 80		204.37 Tl 81	207.19 Pb 82	208.98 Bi 83	(210) Po 84	(210) At 85	222 Rn 86
7	(223) Fr 87	226.05 Ra 88	† 89–103																

* Rare earths														
138.91 La 57	140.12 Ce 58	140.91 Pr 59	144.24 Nd 60	(145) Pm 61	150.35 Sm 62	152.0 Eu 63	157.25 Gd 64	158.92 Tb 65	162.50 Dy 66	164.92 Ho 67	167.26 Er 68	168.93 Tm 69	173.04 Yb 70	174.97 Lu 71

† Actinides														
227 Ac 89	232.04 Th 90	231 Pa 91	238.03 U 92	(237) Np 93	(242) Pu 94	(243) Am 95	(247) Cm 96	(249) Bk 97	(251) Cf 98	(254) Es 99	(253) Fm 100	(256) Md 101	(254) No 102	(257) Lw 103

Thus the average distance of an electron from the nucleus is strongly dependent on n, and it is customary to speak of *shells* of electrons for various values of n. The innermost shell of electrons consists of those in the $n = 1$ states, the next shell those in the $n = 2$ states, etc. These shells are sometimes identified by capital letters, starting with K, as follows:

$$n: \quad 1 \quad 2 \quad 3 \quad 4 \quad \ldots$$
$$\text{Shell:} \quad K \quad L \quad M \quad N \quad \ldots$$

Although in the hydrogen atom the *energy* of the state depends *only* on n, this is an accident resulting from the simple $1/r$ form of the potential-energy function. For the *screened* potential-energy functions resulting from the combined effect of the nucleus and the other electrons, the electron energies depend on *both* n and l. In most cases the smallest values of l for a given n have the lowest energy levels, since for a given n the electron is, on the average, somewhat closer to the nucleus for small values of l than for large values. Thus each shell is subdivided into *subshells* according to the value of l.

These subshells are often labeled with the spectroscopic notation introduced in Sec. 11-3. Table 12-2 summarizes the various notations in common use as well as the *number* of levels in each shell and subshell, including the possibility of two electrons with opposite spins for each set of values of n, l, and m. For each l there are $2l + 1$ values of m, and for each of these there are two values of the spin quantum number s. Thus the subshell identified by n and l has $2(2l + 1)$ states and can accommodate that number of electrons. Correspondingly, a shell with a given n can have values of l ranging from 0 to $n - 1$, so the *total* number of electrons that can be accommodated in shell n is

Table 12-2

Shell	n	l	m	Spectroscopic notation	Number of levels	
K	1	0	0	$1s$	2	
L	2	0	0	$2s$	2	8
	2	1	$0, \pm 1$	$2p$	6	
M	3	0	0	$3s$	2	18
	3	1	$0, \pm 1$	$3p$	6	
	3	2	$0, \pm 1, \pm 2$	$3d$	10	
N	4	0	0	$4s$	2	32
	4	1	$0, \pm 1$	$4p$	6	
	4	2	$0, \pm 1, \pm 2$	$4d$	10	
	4	3	$0, \pm 1, \pm 2, \pm 3$	$4f$	14	

$$\sum_{l=0}^{n-1} 2(2l + 1) = 4 \sum_{l=0}^{n-1} l + 2n$$
$$= 2(n - 1)n + 2n$$
$$= 2n^2 \qquad\qquad (12\text{-}5)$$

where we have used the fact that the sum of the first r integers is $r(r + 1)/2$.

We can now describe simply the electron configuration of any atom. For hydrogen, the ground state is simply $1s$. In the ground state of the helium atom, *both* electrons are in $1s$ levels, with opposite spins, a state denoted as $1s^2$. In the ground state of helium the K shell is completely filled, and there are no electrons in any other shells. The fact that the total angular momentum of the helium atom is zero is confirmed by the Stern-Gerlach experiment, described in Sec. 11-8. With helium, *no* splitting of the beam is observed.

Next in the list of elements is lithium, with three electrons. In the ground state two are in the K shell and one in the L shell; the ground state of lithium is denoted as $1s^2 2s$. The $2s$ electron is, on the average, considerably farther from the nucleus than the $1s$ electrons, and so the *net* charge influencing its motion is approximately e, as shown schematically in Fig. 12-1, rather than the nuclear charge $3e$. Thus we expect this electron to be rather loosely bound. The observed chemical behavior of lithium bears out this prediction;

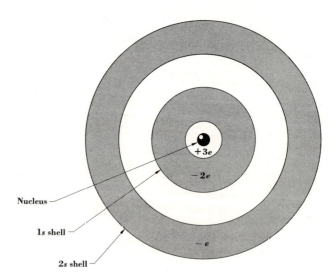

Fig. 12-1 Schematic representation of the shell structure of the lithium atom. The nucleus has a charge $+3e$; the two $1s$ electrons are, on the average, much closer to the nucleus than the $2s$ electron. Hence the $2s$ electron moves in a field approximately equal to that of a charge $+3e - 2e$, or simply e.

it forms ionic compounds in which each atom loses an electron, and thus in chemical language it is said to have a valence of $+1$. Salts of lithium in aqueous solution dissociate into positively charged lithium ions with the $2s$ electron removed, and negatively charged anions.

The *first ionization potential* of the lithium atom (the energy required to remove the outer electron) is 5.4 eV, compared to 13.6 eV for hydrogen and 24.5 eV for helium. If the screening due to the $1s$ electrons were completely effective, Z_{eff} would be 1 and the ionization potential would be the same as the energy required to remove an electron from a hydrogen atom initially in the $n = 2$ state, namely 3.4 eV. The fact that it is somewhat *larger* shows that there is some overlap of the $1s$ and $2s$ wave functions: the $2s$ electron spends some of its time *inside* the charge cloud of the $1s$ electrons. The *second ionization potential* (the energy required to remove a second electron) would be expected to be much larger, since the $1s$ electrons are much closer to the nucleus than the $2s$ electron and are not screened from the nuclear charge. The second ionization potential for lithium is in fact found to be 75.6 eV.

Proceeding down the list of elements, we note that beryllium, with four electrons, has the ground-state configuration $1s^2 2s^2$, with two electrons in the L shell, and thus behaves chemically with a valence of $+2$.

The ground-state electron configurations of the next several elements are shown in Table 12-3. At $Z = 10$ the L shell, with a capacity for eight electrons, is completely filled, and there are no electrons in the M shell. Thus we should expect this to be a particularly stable configuration, with no pronounced tendency either to gain or to lose electrons. The element is, in fact, neon, an inert gas with no known compounds. The preceding element, with $Z = 9$, lacks one electron for a filled shell and thus might be expected to have an affinity for electrons and a tendency to form electrovalent bonds in which it acquires an extra electron. This element is fluorine, and it is observed to have just these properties. The other element adjacent to neon, sodium, has filled K and L shells, and one electron in the M shell. Thus its electron configuration is similar to that of lithium, and, as expected, it tends to form compounds in which it has a valence of $+1$. Lithium and sodium are the first two of the alkali metals, and they both have the "filled-shell-plus-one-s-electron" configuration.

One can proceed similarly through the entire periodic table. With the M and N shells a slight complication arises because of the dependence of energy levels on l. The $3d$ and $4s$ levels overlap in energy, so that some electrons go into the N shell before the M shell is completely filled. Potassium, with $Z = 19$, is the first element exhibiting this effect; its outermost electron is $4s$ rather than $3d$. This effect gives rise to a series of metallic elements with fairly similar chemical properties, having one or two electrons in $4s$

Table 12-3 Ground-State Electron Configurations*

Element	Symbol	Atomic number (Z)	Electron configuration
Hydrogen	H	1	$1s$
Helium	He	2	$1s^2$
Lithium	Li	3	$1s^22s$
Beryllium	Be	4	$1s^22s^2$
Boron	B	5	$1s^22s^22p$
Carbon	C	6	$1s^22s^22p^2$
Nitrogen	N	7	$1s^22s^22p^3$
Oxygen	O	8	$1s^22s^22p^4$
Fluorine	F	9	$1s^22s^22p^5$
Neon	Ne	10	$1s^22s^22p^6$
Sodium	Na	11	$1s^22s^22p^63s$
Magnesium	Mg	12	$1s^22s^22p^63s^2$
Aluminum	Al	13	$1s^22s^22p^63s^23p$
Silicon	Si	14	$1s^22s^22p^63s^23p^2$
Phosphorus	P	15	$1s^22s^22p^63s^23p^3$
Sulfur	S	16	$1s^22s^22p^63s^23p^4$
Chlorine	Cl	17	$1s^22s^22p^63s^23p^5$
Argon	Ar	18	$1s^22s^22p^63s^23p^6$
Potassium	K	19	$1s^22s^22p^63s^23p^64s$
Calcium	Ca	20	$1s^22s^22p^63s^23p^64s^2$

*A complete table of ground-state configurations for all the elements is given in Appendix F.

levels and partially filled $3d$ subshells. These elements form the first *transition series* starting with scandium ($Z = 21$) and terminating with zinc ($Z = 30$), at which point the $3d$ subshell is completely filled.

The partially filled $3d$ subshell in the transition elements is responsible for the ferromagnetic behavior of the transition elements iron, cobalt, and nickel. Because the $3d$ subshell is only partially full, the exclusion principle permits several electrons in these levels to have parallel spins; thus each atom can have a substantial magnetic moment. In a filled shell, conversely, the magnetic moments must add up to zero because of the opposite spins of pairs of electrons.

A complete list of the probable electron configurations of the elements is given in Appendix F. From this it can be seen that the order of filling up of energy levels is

$$1s,\ 2s,\ 2p,\ 3s,\ 3p,\ 4s,\ 3d,\ 4p,\ 5s,\ 4d,\ 5p,\ 6s,\ 4f,\ 5d,\ 6p,\ 7s,\ 6d$$

Appendix F is worthy of careful study. It can be seen that all the inert gases (helium, neon, argon, krypton, xenon, and radon) have configurations consisting of completely filled shells or subshells. All the alkali metals (lithium, sodium, potassium, rubidium, cesium, francium) have "filled-shell-plus-one-electron" configurations, and all the halogens (fluorine, chlorine, bromine, iodine, astatine) have "filled-shell-minus-one" configurations.

Thus a qualitative understanding of the principal features of the periodic table of the elements emerges from this table of electron configurations. In all cases, two atoms having similar configurations of their outermost electrons are found to have similar chemical properties, corroborating the view that the chemical properties of an element are determined mostly by the behavior of its outer electrons. This also accounts for the very close similarity of behavior of the lanthanide or *rare-earth* series, including elements 57 through 71. These elements differ only in the number of electrons in $4f$ and $5d$ levels, not in the $6s$ electrons which determine the chemical properties. A similar phenomenon occurs with the actinide series, starting with element 91. The reader is encouraged to check the electron structure of other groups in the periodic table, to see the basis for the similarities of chemical behavior of the various elements in a group.

Some physicists like to say that all of chemistry is contained in the Schrödinger equation. This may be a slight exaggeration, but it is true that the Schrödinger equation provides the theoretical foundation and the basic principles needed to understand the chemical behavior of matter in terms of its microscopic structure.

As an introduction to the analysis of the origins of x-ray spectra in the following section, we now consider the configuration of the *innermost* electrons in a many-electron atom. First, in most complex atoms the energy required to remove one of the *outer* electrons, called the *ionization energy* or *ionization potential*, has the same order of magnitude as that for hydrogen, namely, about 1 to 20 eV. The reason, as already pointed out, is that the effect of the nuclear charge $+Ze$ is largely canceled or *shielded* by the negative charges of the inner electrons. Thus the total electric field at the position of an outer electron is not radically different from that in hydrogen.

For the *inner* electrons, the situation is quite different. According to Gauss' law of electrostatics, any spherically symmetric charge distribution which lies entirely *outside* a certain radius r produces no electric field at points *inside* that radius. Thus, for example, the electrons in the K shell are affected only slightly by those in the L, M, and outer shells, since the charge distributions corresponding to the latter shells are mostly outside the region of the K shell. Thus the K electrons experience the field of almost the entire nuclear charge Ze, and $Z_{eff} \cong Z$.

It is easy to see how the energy levels and sizes of wave functions are affected. The Coulomb interaction between two particles of charge e contains the factor e^2. The corresponding factor for an electron and a nucleus with

Z protons is Ze^2. Thus the energy level for a K electron, which in the case of hydrogen would be given by Eq. (11-22) with $n = 1$, is given instead by a similar formula but with e^4 replaced by Z^2e^4. That is, the energy should be *larger* by a factor of the order of Z^2 than for hydrogen. Correspondingly, the size of the $1s$ wave function, as characterized by the Bohr-orbit radius given by Eq. (11-25) with $n = 1$, becomes *smaller* by a factor of Z. Thus in a complex atom the inner electrons are closer to the nucleus, and much more tightly bound, than in the ground state of hydrogen.

Conversely, the *outer* electrons in a complex atom are fairly completely shielded from the nucleus, so that they interact with a net charge of the order of only e, rather than Ze. Thus the *energies* associated with transitions between levels of the outer electrons are of the same order of magnitude (1 to 20 eV) as for hydrogen, a fact that is borne out by the optical spectra of various elements. Similarly, the *sizes* of the outer electron wave functions are not drastically different from those of hydrogen in similar states, and so the *sizes* of complex atoms are not in general significantly different from those of the hydrogen atom. This prediction is borne out by measurements of the spacing of atoms in crystals, using x-ray diffraction techniques. Various studies have shown that lattice spacings are *not* strongly dependent on the atomic number of the material and, in fact, are of the same order of magnitude, typically 0.1 to 0.5 nm, for all elements, with few exceptions. Correspondingly, the *density* of an element in the solid state is determined primarily by the mass of its nucleus, with the "volume" of an atom varying in a manner of only secondary importance. Thus the elements that are most dense in the solid state are those near the end of the periodic table, and the least dense ones are generally toward the beginning.

12-3 X-RAY SPECTRA

In the discussion of x-ray production in Sec. 8-3, it was pointed out that the *maximum* energy of an x-ray photon produced in a collision between a high-energy electron and a stationary target is determined by the energy of the electron. This prediction is borne out by measurements of wavelengths by crystal diffraction techniques, as discussed in Sec. 6-1. Experiment also shows, however, that some x-ray photons produced in such collisions have energies considerably smaller than this maximum. In fact, one sometimes finds a *discrete* set of energies, analogous to *line spectra* in optical spectroscopy, which are independent of the energy of the original electron but depend on the target material. The origin of these lines can be understood in terms of the atomic structure of the target atoms.

Just as optical spectra result from transitions between two energy states of the *outer* electrons of an atom, discrete x-ray spectra, with photon energies typically 10^3 to 10^4 times as great as those of optical spectra, result from transitions between energy states of *inner* electrons. As a simple example, suppose we remove one of the K electrons completely from an atom, leaving a *vacancy* in the K shell. Then an electron in the L, M, or other shell can drop into the K shell, in a transition accompanied by the emission of a photon of energy equal to the difference of the two levels.

We can estimate the magnitudes of the inner-electron energy levels, using the *screening* or *shielding* considerations introduced in Sec. 12-2. For an atom with atomic number Z and nuclear charge Ze, each inner electron is shielded by considerably *less* than the other $Z - 1$ electrons. On an average, a K electron is shielded only by the other K electron, and therefore it should see a net charge of approximately $(Z - 1)e$, corresponding to $Z_{eff} = Z - 1$. Thus we expect the K energy level to be *larger* than for hydrogen by a factor $(Z - 1)^2$. The $1s$ energy for hydrogen is about -13.6 eV, and so for an element of atomic number Z it should be about $-(Z - 1)^2(13.6 \text{ eV})$. Correspondingly, the $2p$ subshell of the L shell is shielded by two K electrons, by two L electrons in the $2s$ subshell, and perhaps, on the average, by three of the six L electrons in the $2p$ subshell, for an average total of about seven. Thus we might guess that for a $2p$ electron in the L shell, $Z_{eff} = Z - 7$, giving an energy of $-(Z - 7)^2(3.4 \text{ eV})$, where 3.4 eV is the corresponding energy for hydrogen. A transition of an inner electron from such an L state to a previously vacant K level should be accompanied by the emission of a photon whose energy is the difference of these two energies. For example, if the atom is iron, with $Z = 26$, this energy difference should be

$$\Delta E = (26 - 1)^2(13.6 \text{ eV}) - (26 - 7)^2(3.4 \text{ eV})$$
$$= 7270 \text{ eV} = 1.16 \times 10^{-15} \text{ J} \tag{12-6}$$

and the corresponding wavelength should be

$$\lambda = \frac{hc}{E} = \frac{(6.62 \times 10^{-34} \text{ J} \cdot \text{s})(3.00 \times 10^8 \text{ m/s})}{1.16 \times 10^{-15} \text{ J}}$$
$$= 1.72 \times 10^{-10} \text{ m} = 0.172 \text{ nm} \tag{12-7}$$

As a matter of fact, a prominent x-ray line for iron is observed at a wavelength of 0.193 nm, which agrees reasonably well with Eq. (12-7), considering our relatively primitive approximations.

Any state of an atom in which an electron has been completely removed from an inner shell, leaving a vacancy, is called an *x-ray energy level*. Although these levels have been introduced with reference to the energies of individual electrons, they are actually energies of the entire atom viewed as a system. The K energy state is the state in which a K electron has been removed and is at rest; this state of the system has higher energy than the state in which the electron occupies the K level. In the above example, the K level for iron is *higher* than that of the ground state by

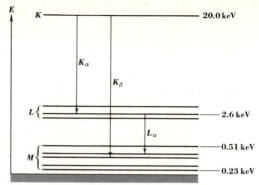

Fig. 12-2 X-ray energy diagram for molybdenum, not to scale. Zero energy corresponds to the ground state of the neutral atom. A few transitions are shown.

about $(26 - 1)^2 \times 13.6$ eV $= 8500$ eV. Similarly, the L level is about $(26 - 7)^2 \times 3.4$ eV $= 1230$ eV above the ground state. The x-ray energy levels for an atom can be shown in a diagram just as with optical spectra; an example is shown in Fig. 12-2. Most of the levels are multiple, due to dependence of energy on the angular-momentum quantum number and to spin-orbit coupling.

Transitions between these levels lead to a series of x-ray spectrum lines for each element. When the vacancy is originally in the K shell, an electron can drop in from the L shell, leaving a vacancy in the L shell which can be filled from the M shell, and so on. Or an electron can drop directly from the M shell to the K shell. In the usual notation, a transition in which the electron ends in the K shell is called a K line, and so on, and a Greek letter is added to designate the initial shell, as shown in Table 12-4.

The usual mechanism for *exciting* x-ray energy levels leading to the production of characteristic x-ray spectra is collision of high-energy electrons (or other charged particles) with the inner electrons of an atom. The electrostatic repulsion sometimes transfers enough energy to one of these electrons

Table 12-4   X-Ray Spectrum Notation

Transition	Notation
$L \rightarrow K$	$K\alpha$
$M \rightarrow K$	$K\beta$
$N \rightarrow K$	$K\gamma$
$O \rightarrow K$	$K\delta$
$M \rightarrow L$	$L\alpha$
$N \rightarrow L$	$L\beta$
$O \rightarrow L$	$L\gamma$
$\vdots$	$\vdots$

to remove it from the atom completely. Thus $K\alpha$ x-ray lines are observed only when the energy of the initial bombarding electron is sufficient to remove an electron from the K shell. This energy is determined by the accelerating voltage in the x-ray tube, so measurement of the voltage at which the K lines begin to appear provides a direct measurement of the energy required to remove a K electron, i.e., of the K energy level. This procedure is analogous to the use of the Franck-Hertz experiment (Sec. 8-4) for investigation of energy levels associated with optical spectra.

Just as with optical spectra, one can observe *absorption* spectra as well as *emission* spectra for x-ray transitions. Unlike optical spectra, the absorption wavelengths are not the same as those for emission. For example, the $K\alpha$ line results from the transition from a K level to an L level, in which the electron goes from L to K shell. The reverse transition cannot be observed ordinarily because there is no vacancy in the L shell in the target atom. Thus the incident radiation must have enough energy to remove an electron *completely*, not just boost it to the L shell. As a result, as the energy of the incident x-rays is gradually increased, sudden increases in absorption are observed, called *absorption edges*, corresponding to energies just sufficient to remove electrons from a certain shell. An example of dependence of x-ray absorption on energy is shown in Fig. 12-3.

Thus x-ray spectra can be understood in terms of the same basic concepts used for optical spectra and several other phenomena associated with atomic structure. In fact, the extension of these concepts to the understanding of x-ray spectra seems almost obvious. Still, it must be recalled that in the years when x-ray spectra were first investigated in detail, that is, in the decade from 1910 to 1920, the relation of atomic spectra to atomic energy levels was just beginning to be understood. Thus the analysis of x-ray spectra provided in those days additional strong support of the explanation of optical spectra in terms of atomic-energy-level transitions.

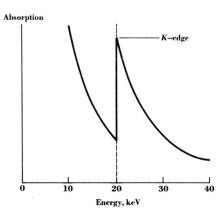

Fig. 12-3 X-ray absorption in molybdenum. A beam of x-rays is passed through a slab of molybdenum and the absorption measured, as a function of energy. A sharp increase in absorption occurs at the K absorption edge, corresponding to excitation of the K x-ray energy level.

12-4 IONIC BOND

The principles of quantum mechanics provide important insight into the phenomenon of *chemical binding,* that is, the association of two or more atoms in a stable structure called a *molecule.* The simplest chemical bond is the *ionic bond,* in which one or more electrons from one atom are transferred completely or nearly so to another atom. A common example is the molecule of sodium chloride, NaCl, in which the sodium atom gives its outermost electron completely to the chlorine atom and becomes positively charged.

As mentioned in Sec. 12-2, sodium and the other alkali metals have an electronic structure characterized by filled shells with one additional *s* electron. The filled shell, corresponding to a spherically symmetric charge distribution, shields the outermost electron almost completely from the nuclear charge, and it moves in a field corresponding to a charge *e* rather than the total nuclear charge *Ze*. Relatively little energy is needed to detach the *s* electron, and the alkali metals form positive ions readily. Atoms with more than one electron in the outermost shell form positive ions less readily than the alkali metals, that is, have higher ionization potentials, since the shielding of the nuclear charge is less complete than for the filled-shell configuration of the alkali metals. Thus across any period in the periodic table a more or less steady *increase* in ionization potential could be expected. This prediction is substantiated by the experimental values of ionization potentials in Table 12-5.

As the table shows, the last element in the second period, neon, has a large ionization potential, with a correspondingly small tendency to form

Table 12-5 Ionization Potentials (in Electronvolts)

				Group				
Period	I	II	III	IV	V	VI	VII	VIII
1	H 13.6							He 24.5
2	Li 5.4	Be 9.3	B 8.3	C 11.3	N 14.5	O 13.6	F 17.4	Ne 21.6
3	Na 5.1	Mg 7.6					Cl 13.0	Ar 15.7
4	K 4.3	Ca 6.3					Br 11.8	Kr 13.9
5	Rb 4.2	Sr 5.7					I 10.6	Xe 12.1
6	Cs 3.9	Ba 5.2						

Table 12-6	Electron Affinities
Fluorine	3.6 eV
Chlorine	3.8
Bromine	3.5
Iodine	3.2

positive ions. Furthermore, neon has a filled-shell configuration and therefore has little tendency to *acquire* additional electrons; thus it is chemically *inert*. But the element adjacent to neon, fluorine, has a "filled-shell-minus-one" structure. Because of this incomplete outer shell, the electrons, even in a neutral fluorine atom, do not completely shield the nuclear charge except at rather large distances. An additional electron can be added to the outermost ($2p$) shell, in a region where it is only partially shielded by the other $2p$ electrons and hence is *bound* by the nuclear attraction. Thus a neutral fluorine atom tends to acquire an additional electron to become a negative ion with a filled-shell electron configuration, and this ion has a *lower energy* than a neutral atom with an extra electron a great distance away. The energy that must be added to *remove* the extra electron is called the *electron affinity*. Electron affinities for the halogens are shown in Table 12-6.

Now we return to the sodium chloride molecule. To remove an electron from a sodium atom requires 5.1 eV. When this electron is attached to a chlorine atom, 3.8 eV is returned, for a net loss of 1.3 eV. But now there are two ions, one positive and one negative, a great distance apart. When they approach each other, there is an attractive electrostatic force and thus a negative potential energy which, if the ions are not too close together, is given approximately by $-e^2/4\pi\varepsilon_0 r$. At distances typical of atomic diameters, say 0.2 to 0.3 nm, this energy is of the order of -5 eV, more than enough to repay the 1.3-eV investment in creating the ions initially, and so the bound state is energetically favorable, by a balance of the order of 4 eV. Experiment shows that the energy necessary to dissociate a sodium chloride molecule into the separate atoms is 4.2 eV. This close agreement is partly fortuitous, inasmuch as we have ignored the distortion of the filled-shell electron configuration of each ion caused by the electric field of the other, but the calculation does illustrate why the ionic bond is energetically favorable.

In view of the electrostatic attraction between the two ions, we might well ask why the two atoms do not continue to approach each other until the electron structures overlap *completely*. In that case the electrons would no longer shield the nuclei so effectively, and so there would be a strong electrostatic repulsion of the nuclei. In addition, when the electron clouds of the two atoms begin to overlap, they must be considered not as independent systems but as parts of a single system, and the Pauli exclusion principle must be applied to the whole system. Roughly speaking, the exclusion principle is the quantum-mechanical analog of the classical statement that two objects cannot occupy the same space at the same time. When the overlap becomes significant, some of the electrons have to go into higher energy states in order to avoid violating the exclusion principle. At sufficiently close distances, the energy required to produce these configurations is greater than the corresponding decrease in potential energy, and this limits the minimum separation of the atoms.

The equilibrium spacing of the two nuclei in a sodium chloride molecule is about 0.24 nm. Thus the interaction is attractive up to a certain critical distance. At the critical distance, they are neither attracted nor repelled. Near the equilibrium position the interaction can be represented as a force proportional to the displacement from equilibrium; this can be described in terms of a fictitious *spring* with a force constant determined by the strength of the interionic force. Such a molecule can undergo a *vibrational* motion in which each atom undergoes approximately simple harmonic motion with respect to its equilibrium position. This fact is important in the analysis of molecular spectra, to be discussed in Sec. 12-6.

Some metallic elements can become doubly ionized by losing *two* electrons and form ionic bonds with two halogen or other atoms. This does *not* occur for sodium; the first ionization potential is 5 eV, but the second ionization potential (the energy necessary to remove a second electron from a singly ionized atom) is over 47 eV, and there is no case where the removal of the second electron is energetically favorable. But for magnesium, the element following sodium in the periodic table, the first ionization potential is 7.6 eV, the second only 15 eV, and the third about 80 eV. Thus magnesium forms ionic compounds, such as $MgCl_2$, in which it loses two electrons, one to each of two chlorine atoms, to become doubly ionized. An analysis of the energy balance of such a process can be made precisely in the same way as that made above for the sodium chloride molecule. All the other elements in group II, the *alkaline-earth metals*, have the same filled-shell-plus-two-electrons structure, and all behave chemically in a similar manner.

In all cases, the number of ionic bonds a given atom can form is determined by the successive ionization potentials, which in turn depend on the shell structure of the electrons. In chemical language, elements that tend to take the role of *positive* ions in ionic bonds are called metals. Elements having a strong tendency to become *negatively* ionized in ionic bonds are called *nonmetals;* the strongest nonmetals, as we have seen, are the halogens. An important feature of ionic bonds is the absence of *directional* character of the interatomic force. Each ion has a filled-shell electron configuration and is therefore spherically symmetric, and there is no reason for the interaction to be stronger in one direction than any other. This behavior is in sharp contrast to that of the *covalent bond*, discussed in the next section, which is often highly directional. This distinction is important in connection with the structure of crystalline solids, to be discussed in Sec. 14-1.

12-5   COVALENT BOND

The ionic bond provides insight into the structure of molecules involving strong metals and nonmetals, such as the alkali halides (compounds of an alkali metal with a halogen). But many chemical bonds have a more symmetric configuration; the simplest examples are diatomic gas molecules such as hydrogen, nitrogen, oxygen, and chlorine. Specific-heat measurements, infrared spectroscopy, and molecular-mass determination all show that the gaseous state of these elements consists of *diatomic* molecules. The corresponding bond, in which the two atoms of the molecule participate equally, is called a *covalent* or *homopolar* bond.

Just as in the analysis of atomic structure, the simplest example of the homopolar bond is that of hydrogen, which serves as a prototype problem. To understand why a bound state of two hydrogen atoms should be energetically favorable, we consider first a very crude pictorial model. Figure 12-4 shows two electric dipoles, which can be thought of as two separated hydrogen atoms. In Fig. 12-4a the two dipoles are far apart. In Fig. 12-4b they are brought together with opposite orientations. Because pairs of *unlike* charges are closer together than pairs of like charge, there is a net *attractive* force between the dipoles and correspondingly a negative potential energy. In Fig. 12-4c and d the repulsion between like charges is greater than the attraction of unlike charges, and so there is a net *repulsive* force. Thus in this simple model, the configuration in which the two electrons lie between the two nuclei and are shared by them is energetically more favorable than that of two separated atoms.

A slightly less crude picture can be built using the Bohr model. We imagine the two electrons in an orbit lying in a plane perpendicular to the

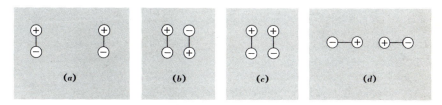

Fig. 12-4 Interaction of two electric dipoles. In (b) the net force between the dipoles is attractive; in (c) and (d) it is repulsive.

Fig. 12-5 Bohr model of the hydrogen molecule. The two protons are stationary, held in equilibrium by a balance of their mutual repulsion and the attraction of the electrons, which move in a circular orbit in the midplane between the protons. This state has lower total energy than one in which the two atoms are separated.

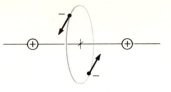

line joining the nuclei, as shown in Fig. 12-5. Calculation shows that the total energy of the system in the state shown is lower than that corresponding to the lowest energies of the two separated atoms. It is not surprising that this model does not yield correct *quantitative* results for the energy levels of the hydrogen molecule, but at least it makes the existence of a bound state *plausible*. The point of both these simple models is that the state in which the two electrons lie between the protons and are shared by them is energetically more favorable than the state in which each proton has its own electron and the two atoms are separated by a considerable distance. Figure 12-5 is readily translated into wave-mechanical language, in which we visualize the charge clouds corresponding to the electron wave functions as concentrated in the region *between* the nuclei, as in Fig. 12-6 (middle), or in the *outer* regions, as in Fig. 12-6 (bottom).

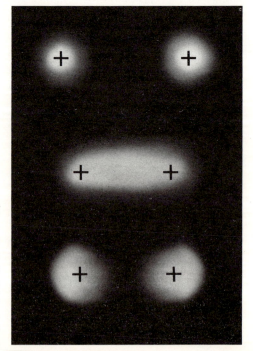

Fig. 12-6 Pictorial representation of electron clouds in the hydrogen molecule. Top: two separated atoms. Middle: charge cloud concentrated in the region between the nuclei, resulting in an attractive interaction. In this state the electron spins must be antiparallel. Bottom: charge cloud depleted in the region between the nuclei, resulting in a repulsive interaction. In this state the electron spins are parallel.

Thus we are led to the notion of a *shared-electron bond*, in which two atoms each contribute an electron to the region between them, with a resultant decrease in the total energy of the state. In the quantum-mechanical description of the hydrogen molecule the *wave function* describing the electrons is more concentrated in the region between the two nuclei, and less concentrated outside, than for individual atoms.

If the two electrons are to occupy more or less the same region of space between the two nuclei, they must have more or less the same wave function and therefore the same quantum-mechanical *state*. According to the exclusion principle, this is possible only when the two electrons have opposite spins. When the spins are parallel, the state that is energetically most favorable is forbidden by the exclusion principle, and the lowest *permitted* energy state is one in which the electrons are concentrated in the region *outside* the pair of nuclei. In this case, the nuclei are not shielded, they repel each other, and no molecular binding occurs.

Thus *antiparallel spins* are an essential characteristic of the covalent bond; no more than two electrons can participate in such a bond, since the exclusion principle would not permit this. On the other hand, an element can have several electrons in its outermost shell, and *each* of them can form an electron-pair or covalent bond with another atom. This occurs frequently in hydrocarbon molecules. An isolated carbon atom has two electrons in the K shell and four in the L shell. In the presence of other atoms, with their associated noncentral electrical forces, the state of each L electron becomes a mixture of angular-momentum states, and the wave functions correspondingly take on a directional, lopsided appearance. In the molecule of methane (CH_4), the simplest hydrocarbon, the nucleus of the carbon atom is at the center of a regular tetrahedron, with the nuclei of four hydrogen atoms at the four corners. In the vicinity of the line joining the center to each corner, the wave functions for the electrons have large amplitudes, corresponding to the presence of *pairs* of electrons with opposite spins. Because of the symmetry of the situation, the bond angles are all equal; this is the state having the lowest total energy consistent with the Pauli principle. The structure of the methane molecule is shown pictorially in Fig. 12-7. In more complex organic molecules, a carbon atom often forms four covalent bonds with other atoms. Each bond consists of a pair of electrons, one from each atom, and the two always have opposite spins.

In any molecule containing several covalent bonds, the relative directions of these bonds are always determined by energy considerations and by the Pauli principle. The angular-momentum states of the associated electrons play a significant role. As we have seen, electrons in s states have spherically symmetric wave functions, while those with $l \neq 0$ have directional characteristics. For a given n, three p functions can be formed that are somewhat

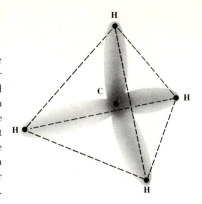

Fig. 12-7 Pictorial representation of the methane (CH$_4$) molecule, showing the four covalent bonds. The electron cloud between the central carbon atom and each of the four hydrogen nuclei represents the two electrons of a covalent (shared-electron) bond. The four bonds are arranged symmetrically, with the hydrogen nuclei at the corners of a regular tetrahedron.

elongated or football-shaped in three mutually perpendicular directions. Furthermore, in the presence of the multicentered field of several nuclei the wave functions become *mixtures* of angular-momentum states; an appropriate superposition of a *p* function with an *s* function yields a wave function with a "lobe" on one side only, and three different such functions can be constructed with lobes in three perpendicular directions. Such a mixture of angular-momentum states is called a *hybrid* wave function.

Thus in a state where an atom forms two covalent bonds with electrons having these hybrid *s-p* wave functions, one might expect the two bonds to be perpendicular. In the molecules H$_2$O and H$_2$S, the actual bond angles are 105° and 92°, respectively. Similarly, in the NH$_3$ molecule we should expect the three hydrogen bonds to have three mutually perpendicular directions; the actual bond angle is 109°. These deviations are a result of the mutual repulsion of the hydrogen nuclei for each other.

In all cases, the *directions* of the bonds are determined by the electron configurations of the individual atoms. This directionality is also a dominant factor in determining the crystal structure of solids. A crystal of a solid element is essentially a very large molecule held together by ionic or covalent bonds. When the bonding is covalent, the crystal structure is determined by the number and directions of the covalent bonds that are energetically most favorable. Sometimes one form is favored under some conditions of temperature and pressure, and another under other conditions; hence the existence of various crystalline forms of the same chemical substance.

Another characteristic feature of the covalent bond is *saturation*; a given atom can form only a certain maximum number of covalent bonds. Thus the hydrogen molecule always has *two* atoms, never three, and there is no compound CH$_5$ because carbon can form only four covalent bonds. The *nuclear* force, the interaction responsible for the stability of nuclei, also exhibits saturation; it will be discussed in Chap. 15.

12-6 MOLECULAR SPECTRA

Thus far in the discussion of atomic energy levels we have ignored the possibility of motion of the nucleus. For a single atom, we can make the approximation that the nucleus is so much more massive than the electrons that it can be considered as stationary, or we can assume that the *center of mass* is stationary, in which case the motion of the nucleus is included by using the reduced mass, introduced in Sec. 11-5. One could, of course, consider additional energy of motion of the center of mass, corresponding to a free particle moving in some kind of container. As shown in Sec. 10-2, the energy levels associated with this motion are so very closely spaced for a container of reasonable size that they can be regarded as a continuum rather than a discrete set.

In diatomic or polyatomic molecules, new features appear. Even when the center of mass is stationary, the individual nuclei can still move. The simplest example is *rotation* about an axis through the center of mass. The classical kinetic theory of gases and the experimentally determined specific heats of polyatomic gases (to be discussed in Secs. 13-1 and 13-5) show that molecules of these gases *do* have kinetic energy associated with rotational motion in addition to the energy of translational motion of the center of mass of each molecule.

In a quantum-mechanical description of rotation of a polyatomic molecule, we anticipate that the energy may be *quantized*. That is, there may be discrete energy levels, just as the electron rotating about the nucleus in the hydrogen atom has discrete energy levels. Also, in classical mechanics the *energy* and the *angular momentum* of rotational motion are closely related, since each can be expressed in terms of moments of inertia and angular velocity. In the systems examined thus far, angular momentum is quantized, and so we expect the rotational kinetic energy of a molecule also to have discrete levels.

In order to exhibit principles as simply as possible, the following discussion will be confined entirely to *diatomic* molecules. We consider first a model in which the molecule is represented as a rigid dumbbell, with two point masses m_1 and m_2 separated by a constant distance r, as shown in Fig. 12-8. This model is consistent with the fact that practically all the mass of an atom is concentrated in the nucleus, whose dimensions are smaller by a factor of the order of 10^5 than the separation between nuclei in a molecule or crystal. The angular position of such a dumbbell is described completely by two angular coordinates, and any rotational motion can be represented as a combination of rotations about two mutually perpendicular axes through the center of mass, perpendicular to the axis of the dumbbell.

From the definition of the center of mass, $m_1 r_1 = m_2 r_2$, and from the figure $r = r_1 + r_2$. Solving these two equations for r_1 and r_2, we find

Fig. 12-8 Model of a diatomic molecule, regarded as a rigid dumbbell consisting of two point masses m_1 and m_2 separated by a constant distance r. The rotational motion of the molecule can be described as a combination of rotations about two mutually perpendicular axes through the center of mass, as shown.

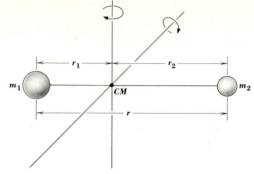

$$r_1 = \frac{m_2 r}{m_1 + m_2} \qquad r_2 = \frac{m_1 r}{m_1 + m_2} \tag{12-8}$$

The moment of inertia I about an axis through the center of mass, perpendicular to the dumbbell axis, is

$$I = m_1 r_1{}^2 + m_2 r_2{}^2 = \frac{m_1 m_2{}^2 r^2}{(m_1 + m_2)^2} + \frac{m_1{}^2 m_2 r^2}{(m_1 + m_2)^2}$$

$$= \frac{m_1 m_2}{m_1 + m_2} r^2 \tag{12-9}$$

In the last form we recognize the reduced mass μ of the system, defined as

$$\mu = \frac{m_1 m_2}{m_1 + m_2} \tag{12-10}$$

in terms of which the moment of inertia becomes simply

$$I = \mu r^2 \tag{12-11}$$

In a complete quantum-mechanical analysis of the rotational motion, the next step is to express the kinetic energy of the system in terms of the components of momentum of each particle and then to construct the corresponding energy operator H for use in the Schrödinger equation, as discussed in Sec. 10-7. Solutions of the time-independent Schrödinger equation then give the possible energy levels for rotational motion of the molecule.

Instead of giving this complete analysis, we shall take a shortcut which uses the classical relationship between rotational kinetic energy and angular momentum. In classical mechanics, the rotational kinetic energy of a rigid body rotating with angular velocity ω about a fixed axis is

$$E = \tfrac{1}{2} I \omega^2 \tag{12-12}$$

where I is the moment of inertia of the body about the axis of rotation.

Similarly, the angular momentum **L** has a magnitude L given by

$$L = I\omega \qquad (12\text{-}13)$$

Strictly speaking, this holds only when the axis of rotation is a *principal axis of inertia*. However, for any body having axial symmetry, as in the case of the diatomic molecule, *any* axis perpendicular to the molecular axis is a principal axis.

Combining Eqs. (12-12) and (12-13) to eliminate the kinematic quantity ω in favor of the two dynamical quantities E and L, we obtain

$$E = \frac{L^2}{2I} \qquad (12\text{-}14)$$

With angular momentum of electrons in atoms, the square of the magnitude of the total angular momentum is given by

$$L^2 = l(l + 1)\hbar^2 \qquad l = 0, 1, 2, \ldots \qquad (12\text{-}15)$$

In the present case the angular momentum is associated with the motion of *nuclei* rather than electrons, but since it is the same dynamical quantity, it is reasonable that Eq. (12-15) should also govern rotational angular momentum of a diatomic molecule. Hence, substituting the above expression for the permitted values of L^2, we find that the permissible energies associated with rotation of a diatomic molecule are

$$E_l = l(l + 1)\frac{\hbar^2}{2I} \qquad l = 0, 1, 2, \ldots \qquad (12\text{-}16)$$

Although this derivation is somewhat intuitive, a complete and rigorous calculation based on solution of the Schrödinger equation yields the same result. As we shall see, the rotational energy levels given by Eq. (12-16) also agree with experimental observations. This energy-level scheme is illustrated in Fig. 12-9.

As an indication of the magnitudes involved, we estimate the value of $\hbar^2/2I$ for a typical diatomic molecule, say oxygen. The atomic mass of oxygen is 16, which means that a mole of oxygen (6.02×10^{23} molecules) has a mass of 16 g. Thus the mass of one oxygen atom is approximately

$$m = \frac{16 \times 10^{-3}\,\text{kg}}{6.02 \times 10^{23}} = 2.7 \times 10^{-26}\,\text{kg} \qquad (12\text{-}17)$$

To obtain an estimate of the distance r between nuclei, we note that molecular binding of two atoms is the same phenomenon in principle as that of the binding atoms in a crystalline solid, in which x-ray diffraction experiments have shown that the spacing of atoms is typically of the order of 2×10^{-10} m.

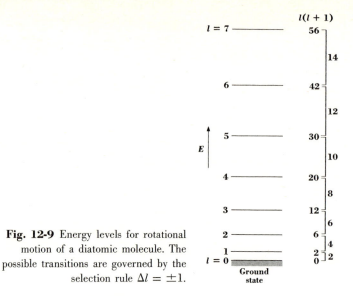

Fig. 12-9 Energy levels for rotational motion of a diatomic molecule. The possible transitions are governed by the selection rule $\Delta l = \pm 1$.

This approximate magnitude also agrees with estimates of the *size* of the oxygen molecule obtained from measurements of the mean free path of molecules in the gaseous state, observations of van der Waals corrections to the ideal-gas equation, and other data.

Using these numbers, we find for the moment of inertia of an oxygen molecule

$$I = \tfrac{1}{2}(2.7 \times 10^{-26} \text{ kg})(2 \times 10^{-10} \text{ m})^2 = 5.4 \times 10^{-46} \text{ kg} \cdot \text{m}^2 \qquad (12\text{-}18)$$

Finally, the constant $\hbar^2/2I$ has the numerical value

$$\frac{\hbar^2}{2I} = \frac{(1.06 \times 10^{-34} \text{ J} \cdot \text{s})^2}{2(5.4 \times 10^{-46} \text{ kg} \cdot \text{m}^2)} = 1.0 \times 10^{-23} \text{ J}$$

$$= 0.6 \times 10^{-4} \text{ eV} \qquad (12\text{-}19)$$

This energy may be compared with energies corresponding to optical spectra, which in the visible region are typically 2 to 3 eV. The spacing of these rotational energy levels is *smaller* by a factor of the order of 10^4, and transitions from one level to another correspond to photons in the far-infrared region of the electromagnetic spectrum. According to the classical equipartition theorem, the *average* rotational kinetic energy for a diatomic molecule with two rotational degrees of freedom is kT, which at ordinary temperatures, say $T = 300$ K, is

$$kT = (1.38 \times 10^{-23} \text{ J/K})(300 \text{ K}) = 4.14 \times 10^{-21} \text{ J}$$

$$= 0.0258 \text{ eV} \simeq \tfrac{1}{40} \text{ eV} \qquad (12\text{-}20)$$

Comparing this number with Eq. (12-16) and the numerical value given in Eq. (12-19), we see that a diatomic molecule with this much rotational energy is in a state with a quantum number of the order of $l = 20$. Thus, in a transition between two adjacent quantum states, the gain or loss of energy is relatively *small* compared with the average *total* energy at ordinary temperatures.

The infrared spectrum associated with transitions between rotational states may be obtained from the energy-level diagram shown in Fig. 12-9. Just as for atomic spectra, there are *selection rules* based on the transitions corresponding to electric-dipole radiation patterns, which are ordinarily the only transitions with significant probabilities. The selection rules, as before, are that the angular momentum must change by one unit, and its component in a given direction by one unit or zero That is,

$$\Delta l = \begin{cases} +1 & \text{absorption} \\ -1 & \text{emission} \end{cases}$$

$$\Delta m_l - 0, \pm 1$$

(12-21)

As Fig. 12-9 shows, the level spacing increases uniformly with l, and so the *frequencies* in the rotation spectrum of a diatomic molecule are all integral multiples of a fundamental frequency given by $\omega = \hbar/I$. Detailed proof of this statement is left as a problem.

Pure rotation spectra of diatomic molecules are observable only when all other kinds of energy transitions can be neglected; this occurs for some diatomic molecules at sufficiently low temperatures. At higher temperatures *vibrational* motion yields additional energy levels and corresponding complications in the molecular spectrum. Thus the next generalization in our model should be to picture the two nuclei as *elastically bound* so that a *vibrational* motion along the axis of the molecule is possible. In a classical description of this motion,[1] there is a certain equilibrium spacing of the two nuclei, and for small displacements from equilibrium the interatomic force is approximately proportional to the displacement. As a result, each nucleus undergoes *simple harmonic motion* with an angular frequency ω given by

$$\omega = \sqrt{\frac{k}{\mu}}$$

(12-22)

where μ is the reduced mass defined by Eq. (12-10) and k is the force constant for the interatomic force. The latter can be estimated from the macroscopic elastic properties of solids, by using a simple model of the structure of the solid.[2] Such calculations suggest that typical molecular force constants are

[1] H. D. Young, "Fundamentals of Mechanics and Heat," 2d ed. sec. 10-5, McGraw-Hill Book Company, New York, 1974.
[2] Ibid., sec. 9-4.

of the order of 50 N/m. Thus, in a classical calculation, the frequency of oscillation of the atoms in the diatomic oxygen molecule discussed above is

$$\omega = \sqrt{\frac{k}{\mu}} = \sqrt{\frac{50 \text{ N/m}}{1.4 \times 10^{-26} \text{ kg}}} = 6 \times 10^{13} \text{ s}^{-1} \qquad (12\text{-}23)$$

In classical mechanics the behavior of a two-body oscillator is equivalent in all respects to the motion of a harmonic oscillator whose mass is the reduced mass of the two-body system, and there is no reason not to expect the same to be true in the quantum-mechanical formulation. The harmonic oscillator has been discussed in detail in Sec. 10-5, using Schrödinger's equation. The energy levels are

$$E = (n + \tfrac{1}{2})\hbar\omega = (n + \tfrac{1}{2})\hbar\sqrt{\frac{k}{\mu}} \qquad n = 0, 1, 2, 3, \dots \qquad (12\text{-}24)$$

This expression represents a series of equally spaced levels, with adjacent levels separated by $\hbar\omega$. For the frequency given by Eq. (12-23).

$$\hbar\omega = (1.06 \times 10^{-34} \text{ J} \cdot \text{s})(6 \times 10^{13} \text{ s}^{-1}) = 6 \times 10^{-21} \text{ J}$$
$$= 0.014 \text{ eV}$$

Thus the energy associated with a transition between *vibrational* states of a diatomic molecule is typically of the order of 10^{-2} of optical-spectrum energies, and the corresponding radiation is in the near-infrared region of the spectrum.

For the oxygen molecule, the vibrational level spacing is of the order of 100 times as great as that of the rotational states and is also of the same order of magnitude as the quantity kT at ordinary temperatures, indicating that, according to the equipartition theorem, at room temperature most of the oxygen atoms are in the lowest few quantum states, with a fairly large number in the $n = 0$ state. This observation has important implications in the quantum theory of specific heats, to which we shall return in Sec. 13-5.

At sufficiently high temperatures, a molecule has both vibrational and rotational energy; the composite energy-level scheme is shown in Fig. 12-10, which shows several relatively widely spaced vibrational levels, each with a set of more closely spaced rotational levels. In transitions between these states, there are several transitions for given initial and final values of n, corresponding to different initial values of l. The result is a *series* of closely spaced spectrum lines. Originally, the resolution of infrared spectroscopic equipment was not sufficient to resolve these as separate lines, and they were called *band spectra*. It is now understood that each band corresponds to a definite pair of values of n with various values of l, according to the selection rules

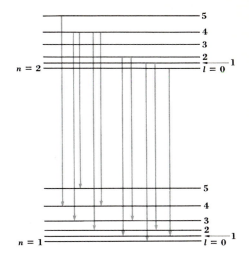

Fig. 12-10 Vibration-rotation energy-level scheme. For each vibrational level there is a series of more closely spaced rotational levels. Several transitions consistent with the selection rule $\Delta l = \pm 1$ are shown.

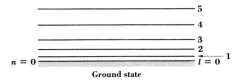

$$\Delta l = \pm 1$$
$$\Delta m_l = 0, \pm 1$$

(12-25)

For a molecule containing more than two atoms, additional interesting features appear. A triatomic molecule whose atoms do not lie along a single line has nonzero moments of inertia along all three principal axes, and thus there are three degrees of freedom associated with rotational motion. For such a triatomic molecule, such as water or CO_2, there are also several varieties of vibrational motion. Each of these is called a *normal mode*; and each normal mode has its characteristic frequency ω and set of energy levels with spacing $\hbar\omega$. The three normal modes for a linear triatomic molecule are shown in Fig. 12-11.

Analysis of the infrared spectrum resulting from transitions among various vibrational and rotational states provides a wealth of information concerning molecular structure, strength and rigidity of bonds, and other

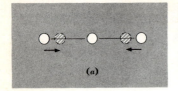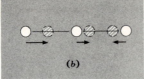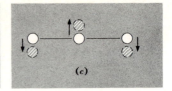

Fig. 12-11 Normal modes of vibrational motion for a linear triatomic molecule. Modes (a) and (b) correspond to stretching and compressing the bonds, and mode (c) to bending. Thus the energy levels of these modes, determined from infrared spectra, provide information about the strength and rigidity, respectively, of the bonds.

aspects of interatomic interactions. Infrared spectroscopy has been enormously important as a tool for the investigation of molecular structure. It is also very useful in quantitative analysis; for example, infrared absorption spectroscopy is widely used in instrumentation for air-pollution monitoring. Astrophysicists use absorption and emission spectra of molecules to obtain information about stellar atmospheres and the composition of interplanetary space.

12-7 LASERS AND MASERS

We conclude this chapter with a brief discussion of a somewhat specialized topic of great current interest. *Maser* is an acronym for Microwave Amplification by Stimulated Emission of Radiation; this device is basically an extremely low-noise, sharply tuned microwave amplifier. *Laser* is the same acronym with "light" in place of "microwave." Despite this name, the laser is *not* primarily a light amplifier but rather a *source* of extremely coherent monochromatic light which can also be extremely intense.

Both the laser and the maser depend for their operation on *stimulated emission*. To explore this concept, we consider two energy states, say E_1 and E_2 (with $E_2 > E_1$) of a quantum-mechanical system such as a molecule. We have discussed in some detail two aspects of the interaction of this system with electromagnetic radiation; one is the *absorption* of a photon of energy $\hbar\omega = E_2 - E_1$ during which the system makes a transition from E_1 to the higher state E_2, and the other is the spontaneous *emission* of a photon of energy $E_2 - E_1$ during which the system drops from state E_2 to state E_1. What we have not yet mentioned is the fact that emission can be triggered or *stimulated* by the presence of *another* photon of the same energy and polarization. That is, a photon is more likely to be emitted by a system in an excited state if there are already one or more photons of the same energy present.

This phenomenon is called *stimulated emission* to distinguish it from the *spontaneous* emission that occurs ordinarily. In stimulated emission, an incoming photon induces an atom or molecule in an excited state to make a downward transition, emitting another photon of the same energy, direction, phase, and polarization as the first; thus the two photons are *coherent*. This property is essential for laser and maser operation. Complete understanding of the relation of spontaneous to stimulated emission requires quantum electrodynamics, and here we must simply take stimulated emission as a fact of life. Those who like to ascribe personalities to particles say that a photon likes to go where his friends and relatives are, while the electron is governed by the exclusion principle and hence is a hermit!

Now suppose we somehow manage to raise a lot of molecules to the state E_2 at the same time. Never mind how we do it, for the moment. Suppose one molecule spontaneously emits a photon, which, as it passes through the region of the other molecules, stimulates them to emit; the result is an avalanche of "synchronized" photons, all with the same frequency, phase, polarization, and direction as the original one. If we can keep supplying molecules in the excited state E_2, the process can continue indefinitely, and the result is a stream of radiation that is very much more coherent and monochromatic than it would be if the molecules emitted independently. This is the basic process in a laser.

Getting the molecules into the excited state E_2 is not a trivial problem. At any temperature there is a statistical distribution of energies, the lower energies always being more common than the higher. If $E_2 - E_1$ is a few electronvolts, then at any reasonable temperature the number of molecules in state E_2 is a *very* small fraction of the total. We must somehow create a *population inversion*, in which E_2 is populated significantly more than it would be under conditions of thermal equilibrium. We note that it would not do simply to irradiate the molecules with strong light of energy $E_2 - E_1$. This would stimulate upward transitions to state E_2 but would also stimulate emission, so that on the average we would lose ground. To prepare molecules in state E_2, we must resort to subterfuge; as an example of how this is accomplished, we consider the helium-neon gas laser, a common and perhaps familiar device which is portable and inexpensive.

In the He-Ne laser, a mixture of helium and neon is sealed into a glass envelope provided with two electrodes; an applied voltage creates an electric field, which sets up a glow discharge. Some of the atoms are ionized, and the ions and electrons carry the discharge current. The electrons in turn can collide with gas atoms, exciting them to various energy states. The laser transition occurs between two excited states of neon, and energy is fed in to provide the necessary population inversion by a happy coincidence in the relation of the neon energy levels to those of helium.

A partial energy-level diagram for this system is shown in Fig. 12-12. Electron impact excites some of the He atoms to the $1s2s$ state (spectroscopic notation) shown and to higher states from which some atoms cascade down

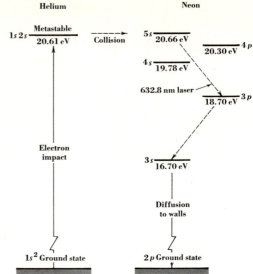

Fig. 12-12 Energy-level diagram for helium and neon, showing laser action. The excited states of neon are identified by the state of the one excited electron; the other nine electrons are in the ground state $1s^2 2s^2 2p^5$.

to this state. Ordinarily an atom in such an excited state would quickly emit a photon of energy 20.61 eV and decay back to the ground state. In this case, however, both the excited state and the ground state have zero angular momentum, and there is a selection rule forbidding "zero-zero" transitions. The rule results from the fact that a photon always carries away at least one unit of angular momentum. Such a state, in which radiative decay is forbidden by a selection rule, is called a *metastable state*.

The He atoms can lose energy by another mechanism, however. The $5s$ level of Ne has almost exactly the same energy as the $1s2s$ level of He, and an energy-exchange collision between an excited He atom with a little translational kinetic energy and an unexcited Ne atom can leave the He atom in the ground state and the Ne atom in the $5s$ excited state. This state is again metastable; the Ne atom cannot decay directly to the ground state because of selection rules, but it *can* decay to the $3p$ level shown, and in fact this is the transition involved in the laser action. Finally, from the $3p$ state the Ne atom makes another radiative transition to the metastable $3s$ state and from there decays to the $2p$ ground state, usually by collision with the walls of the container. We note that it is important that the $3p \rightarrow 3s$ transition occur rapidly; if there were an appreciable buildup of atoms in $3p$ states, the probability of *absorption* of laser radiation and reexcitation to the $5s$ state would be appreciable, and this would inhibit the laser action.

In practical He-Ne lasers the gas pressures are typically 1.0 mm of He and 0.1 mm of Ne. Two parallel mirrors are sealed into the envelope; light is reflected back and forth, forming a standing-wave pattern. One of the mirrors is only partly silvered, so part of the beam emerges from the envelope.

This is only one of many kinds of lasers. The *first* laser was a solid-state device using a cylinder of ruby (Al_2O_3 with a small percentage of Cr_2O_3) with polished parallel ends to serve as the reflectors. Laser action is provided by a metastable state of the chromium ion. There are many other varieties, some solid-state devices using rare-earth ions, others using various gases. The corresponding microwave devices (masers) use various molecular vibration or rotation energy levels.

Problems

12-1 Prove the statement following Eq. (12-4).

12-2 The ion He^+ has only one electron and therefore has hydrogenlike wave functions and energy levels.
    a   What is the relationship between the energy-level scheme for He^+ and that for H?
    b   In what regions of the spectrum do the Lyman, Balmer, and Paschen series (transitions terminating at $n = 1, 2, 3$, respectively) lie?

12-3 Show that in any "filled-shell" electron configuration the total z component of angular momentum is zero.

12-4 If for some reason atoms could contain only electrons with principal quantum numbers up to and including $n = 5$, how many elements would there be? Use the energy-level sequence given in Sec. 12-2.

12-5 Long before the details of atomic structure were understood, it was observed that the atomic numbers (Z) of the inert gases are given by the following scheme:

He: $Z = 2(1^2) = 2$
Ne: $Z = 2(1^2 + 2^2) = 10$
Ar: $Z = 2(1^2 + 2^2 + 2^2) = 18$
Kr: $Z = 2(1^2 + 2^2 + 2^2 + 3^2) = 36$
Xe: $Z = 2(1^2 + 2^2 + 2^2 + 3^2 + 3^2) = 54$
Rn: $Z = 2(1^2 + 2^2 + 2^2 + 3^2 + 3^2 + 4^2) = 86$

How can this sequence be understood in terms of the electron configurations of the atoms?

12-6 The ionization potentials of the transition metals (atomic numbers 21 to 30) are very nearly equal. How can this observation be understood on the basis of their electron configurations?

12-7 Considering the difference in ionization potentials of the various alkali metals, as shown in Table 12-5, which would you expect to be most active chemically, in terms of propensity to form compounds rather than exist as an element? Explain. Why are the ionization potentials different?

12-8 Considering the difference in electron affinity of the halogens, as shown in Table 12-6, which would you expect to be most active chemically, in terms of propensity to form compounds? Explain. Why are the electron affinities different?

12-9 Which of the "inert gases" is most likely to be capable of forming compounds? Explain.

12-10 Although the $2s$ and $2p$ states for hydrogen have exactly the same energy, the $2s$ state for the valence electron of lithium has lower energy than the $2p$ state. How can this difference be understood qualitatively on the basis of difference in wave-function shapes?

12-11 Calculate the ionization energy of a neutral sodium atom by assuming that the energy of the outer electron is the same as that of an electron with $n = 3$ in the hydrogen atom. Compare your result with the observed ionization energy, and explain the difference.

12-12 For a singly ionized beryllium atom, compute the approximate wavelength corresponding to the transition $4p \longrightarrow 3s$ of the remaining valence electron.

12-13 In a simple model of the lithium atom, the valence electron moves in the field of the nuclear charge $+3e$ and of the two $1s$ electrons, represented by a uniform charge density over a sphere of radius a.

    a Use Gauss' law to find the electric field and the potential as functions of r.

    b Show that at small r the potential is essentially that of a point charge $+3e$, but at large r it is that of a point charge $+e$. Hence show that the wave functions of the valence electron become more and more hydrogenlike for increasing values of the principal quantum number n.

12-14 A "screened potential" often used in atomic physics as an approximate representation of the field of the nucleus and the inner electrons is

$$V(r) = -\frac{Ze^2}{4\pi\varepsilon_0}\frac{e^{-r/a}}{r} \qquad a = \frac{4\pi\varepsilon_0\hbar^2}{me^2Z^{1/3}}$$

    a Find the charge density, as a function of r, corresponding to this potential.

    b Find the electric field as a function of r. Show that for $r \ll a$ it is the same as that of a point charge $+Ze$. At what value of r is the field the same as that of a point charge $+Ze/2$? Note that $a = a_0/Z^{1/3}$, where a_0 is the first Bohr radius.

12-15 Estimate the K and L x-ray energy levels for molybdenum, and compute the wavelength corresponding to the $K\alpha$ transition.

12-16 What minimum voltage is necessary in an x-ray tube to excite the K x-ray energy level in an aluminum target?

12-17 Calculate the position of the K absorption edge for nickel.

12-18 For an atom of atomic number Z, assume a K electron is screened from the nuclear charge only by the other K electron, so $Z_{eff} = Z - 1$.

a Show that in this approximation the K x-ray energy level is given by $A^2(Z-1)^2$, where A is a constant. Obtain an expression for A in terms of m, e, and $\hbar$.

b Using the same approximation, show that the $K\alpha$ x-ray line for element Z has a wavelength given approximately by $2\pi\hbar c/A^2(Z-1)^2$. This relationship was discovered empirically by Moseley in 1913.

12-19 The nuclei (protons) in the hydrogen molecule are subject to the exclusion principle; this has the consequence that when the spins are parallel (*ortho*-hydrogen), only *odd* values of the rotational quantum number l are permitted, while when the spins are antiparallel (*para* hydrogen), only *even* numbers are permitted. Draw separate energy-level diagrams for the two species, and describe which spectrum lines are missing which would be observed if each molecule could have any integer value of l.

12-20 Consider the molecule KBr. Using a consideration similar to that given in Sec. 12-4, calculate the maximum separation of the ions that still permits the existence of a stable molecule.

12-21 Consider the molecule $MgCl_2$. Using the ionization potentials and electron affinities given in Sec. 12-4, calculate the values of ion spacing for which this molecule should be stable.

12-22 Using the considerations of Sec. 12-4, analyze the energy balance for formation of the molecule HF, assuming that the bond is ionic. From the results, can you draw any conclusions about the probable actual nature of this bond?

12-23 An approximate wave function for the hydrogen molecule can be constructed from products of one-electron wave functions centered on the two nuclei, or from sums of such products. For example, if ψ_1 is a $1s$ wave function centered on nucleus 1, with ψ_2 a corresponding function centered on nucleus 2, then an approximate wave function is some combination of the products.

$$\psi_1(\mathbf{r}_1)\psi_2(\mathbf{r}_2) \qquad \text{and} \qquad \psi_1(\mathbf{r}_2)\psi_2(\mathbf{r}_1)$$

where $\mathbf{r}_1$ and $\mathbf{r}_2$ are the coordinates of the two electrons. If the two electrons have parallel spins, the wave function must be *antisymmetric* with respect to interchange of electron coordinates. Show that in this case the wave function is zero at a point halfway between the two nuclei.

12-24 Discuss the valence-bond structure of the ethylene molecule, C_2H_4.

12-25 Compute the energy levels in the Bohr model of the hydrogen molecule, shown in Fig. 12-5, using the condition that the total angular momentum must be an integer multiple of $\hbar$. For a stable molecule, the repulsion of the two protons must just cancel the attractive forces of the electrons, and the vector sum of all forces on each electron must be equal to mv^2/r for that electron. These conditions, together with the quantization of angular momentum, are sufficient to determine the spacing of the protons and the orbit radii, from which the energy levels can be obtained.

12-26 The rotation spectrum of HCl contains the following wavelengths:

$120.4 \, \mu m$
$96.4 \, \mu m$
$80.4 \, \mu m$
$69.0 \, \mu m$
$60.4 \, \mu m$

Find the distance between nuclei in the HCl molecule.

12-27 In the vibration-rotation spectrum of HCl, there appear two lines at $3.43 \, \mu m$ and $3.48 \, \mu m$, which correspond to the transitions $\Delta n = -1$, $\Delta l = \pm 1$.
a   For which wavelength is $\Delta l = +1$?
b   From these data, find the effective spring constant for the interatomic force in the HCl molecule. The data in Prob. 12-26 may be useful.

12-28 How is the vibration-rotation energy-level scheme of the oxygen molecule for the common isotope ^{16}O related to that for the rare isotope ^{18}O?

12-29 Show that the frequencies in a pure rotation spectrum are all integer multiples of the quantity $\hbar/I$. [Cf. statement following Eq. (12-21).]

12-30 When a molecule undergoes both vibrational and rotational motion, the moment of inertia of the molecule is not constant because of the varying distance between atoms. How should this fact affect the rotational energy levels?

12-31 Find the separation of the first two rotational energy levels for the H_2 molecule, and the corresponding wavelength. How does the wavelength for the corresponding transition in the deuterium molecule D_2 differ? The equilibrium spacing of atoms in each molecule is 7.5×10^{-11} m.

Statistical Mechanics | 13

In a physical system containing a very large number of particles, atoms, molecules, or other constituents, it is usually impossible, for practical reasons, to apply the basic physical laws directly to each particle. Instead, it is often advantageous to take a *statistical* approach in which one describes the distribution of particles in various states in a statistical manner; the existence of a very large number of parts of a system can often be used to advantage in this statistical description. We begin with a discussion of the classical kinetic-molecular model of an ideal gas. The basic ideas of a statistical description of a state of a many-particle system are then introduced, and the Maxwell-Boltzmann distribution function is derived. A simple application of this function to the calculation of specific heats of gases is discussed in detail. Finally we show that the quantum-mechanical notion of *indistinguishability* of identical particles necessitates changes in the development of the distribution function, and the appropriate modifications are developed.

13-1 KINETIC MODEL OF IDEAL GAS

The ideal-gas equation of state is a relation between the pressure, volume, temperature, and quantity of matter of a gas. At sufficiently high temperatures and low pressures, many different gases are found to obey this relation quite well. The usual forms of the equation are

$$PV = nRT \quad \text{and} \quad PV = \frac{m}{M}RT \tag{13-1}$$

where P is pressure, V volume, T *absolute* temperature, n number of moles, m the mass of gas, M the molecular mass, and R a universal constant. In the usual MKS units, P is measured in newtons per square meter, V in cubic meters, T in kelvins, m in kilograms, and M in kilograms per mole. With these units the gas constant R is found to have the value

$$R = 8.314 \text{ J/mol} \cdot \text{K} \tag{13-2}$$

We recall that *one mole* of any substance contains a number of molecules equal to *Avogadro's number* N_o, where

$$N_o = 6.022 \times 10^{23} \text{ molecules/mol} \tag{13-3}$$

The fact that a large number of gaseous substances can be described by the same simple equation of state suggests strongly the existence of a corresponding simplicity in the *structure* of gases, and in the latter part of the nineteenth century a microscopic model was developed to relate behavior of gases to their microscopic structure. The central idea is to apply the laws of mechanics to the motion of individual molecules and then to use the *average* behavior of these molecules to predict *macroscopic* properties such as temperature and pressure.

Here are the principal features of the kinetic-molecular model. We assume that a gas consists of a very large number of identical molecules which may be treated as particles. The total volume of the molecules themselves is assumed to be negligibly small compared to the volume in which they move; this assumption is based on the fact that a gas may change its volume over a wide range and ordinarily is much less dense than the same compound in the liquid or solid state. The molecules are constantly in motion, colliding with each other and with the walls of the container; as a result, the average *density* of molecules is the same everywhere, and the position and direction of motion of an individual molecule are completely random. The collisions are perfectly *elastic*, and occur in a time interval very short compared to the average time between collisions.

Our first objective is to *derive* the ideal-gas equation from this model. Before embarking on the calculations, we must be sure we understand the nature of the problem. The pressure a gas exerts on a wall of its container results from very large numbers of collisions; we do not observe the individual collisions, but rather the *average* force due to many collisions. Similarly, the *temperature* of a gas is related to the *average* energy of its molecules. *Temperature and pressure are inherently macroscopic concepts*, and they have no meaning for an individual molecule. Only by considering the *average* behavior of gas molecules can we hope to make a connection between a *microscopic* model and *macroscopic* properties.

When a molecule makes an elastic collision with a wall of its container, as shown in Fig. 13-1, its x component of momentum changes by an amount

$$\Delta p_x = p_{2x} - p_{1x} = -2mv_x \tag{13-4}$$

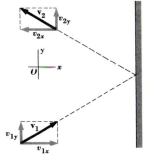

Fig. 13-1 Elastic collision of a molecule with a wall. If the force is perpendicular to the wall, the component of velocity perpendicular to the wall changes direction; the other components do not change.

where m is the mass of a molecule. If every molecule had the same v_x, and if we could find the *number* of collisions on a given area, per unit time, we could calculate the time rate of change of momentum by multiplying the momentum change for each collision, given by Eq. (13-4), by the number of collisions per unit of time. This would then be equal to the *force* which the area exerts on the colliding molecules; the force *on* this area would be just the negative of this.

The x components of velocity are *not* all equal in magnitude, but suppose for the moment that they are, half the molecules having v_x and the other half $-v_x$. How many molecules strike an area of wall A per unit time? In a time interval Δt, a particle moves in the x direction a distance $v_x \Delta t$. The particles which strike the wall during this interval are those which were at most a distance $v_x \Delta t$ from the wall at the beginning of the interval; at the beginning of Δt these particles had to be in a cylinder of base area A and height $v_x \Delta t$. The volume of this cylinder is simply $Av_x \Delta t$.

If the total number of particles is N and the total volume V, the number of particles *per unit volume* is N/V, and the number of particles in this cylinder is

$$Av_x \Delta t \frac{N}{V} \tag{13-5}$$

Because of the randomness of the direction of velocity, half these particles are moving *toward* the wall and the other half *away from* the wall; only those moving toward the wall will strike it during the interval Δt, so the number of collisions during Δt is just one-half of Eq. (13-5). The number of collisions *per unit time*, obtained by dividing by Δt, is

$$\tfrac{1}{2}Av_x \frac{N}{V}$$

The total rate of change of momentum is the number of collisions per unit time multiplied by the momentum change in each collision:

$$\frac{dp_x}{dt} = \tfrac{1}{2}Av_x\frac{N}{V}(-2mv_x) = -Amv_x{}^2\frac{N}{V} = F_x \tag{13-6}$$

This expression therefore represents the average total *force* which the wall exerts on all the molecules which strike it. The force exerted *on* the wall is the negative of this; the *pressure* is the force per unit area:

$$P = \frac{F_x}{A} = \frac{Nmv_x{}^2}{V} \tag{13-7}$$

The initial assumption that v_x has the same magnitude for all molecules is not correct, but we can separate the molecules into groups such that *in each group* every molecule has very nearly the same v_x. Then we calculate the pressure due to each *group*; the *total* pressure is the sum of all the pressures due to these groups. Since the pressure due to each group depends only on $v_x{}^2$ for that group, the total pressure is obtained simply by using the *average* value of $v_x{}^2$ for all the molecules. We denote this average by $(v_x{}^2)_{\text{av}}$. Thus the total pressure is

$$P = \frac{Nm(v_x{}^2)_{\text{av}}}{V} \tag{13-8}$$

We can relate the average value of $v_x{}^2$ to the average of the squares of the *speeds* of the molecules. We call this latter quantity the *mean-square speed* and denote it by $(v^2)_{\text{av}}$. The speed v of a molecule is related to the components of its velocity by $v^2 = v_x{}^2 + v_y{}^2 + v_z{}^2$. This is true for every molecule, so it must also be true for the averages. That is,

$$(v^2)_{\text{av}} = (v_x{}^2)_{\text{av}} + (v_y{}^2)_{\text{av}} + (v_z{}^2)_{\text{av}}$$

But all directions of motion are equally likely, so $(v_x{}^2)_{\text{av}} = (v_y{}^2)_{\text{av}} = (v_z{}^2)_{\text{av}}$. Thus,

$$(v^2)_{\text{av}} = 3(v_x{}^2)_{\text{av}}$$

Using this result in Eq. (13-8), we find

$$P = \tfrac{1}{3}\frac{Nm(v^2)_{\text{av}}}{V} \tag{13-9}$$

To make this resemble the ideal-gas equation more closely, we express the total number of molecules N in terms of the number of moles n and Avogadro's number N_0, $N = nN_0$, and multiply both sides by V. The result is

$$PV = n\tfrac{1}{3}N_0 m(v^2)_{\text{av}} \tag{13-10}$$

Comparing this with the empirical ideal-gas equation (13-1), we see that the two agree if the right-hand side of Eq. (13-10) is proportional to the absolute temperature, i.e., if

$$\tfrac{1}{3}N_0 m(v^2)_{av} = RT$$

This equation is more illuminating when rewritten:

$$\tfrac{1}{2}m(v^2)_{av} = \frac{3}{2}\frac{R}{N_0}T \tag{13-11}$$

Now $\tfrac{1}{2}m(v^2)_{av}$ is the average translational kinetic energy of a molecule. That is, our kinetic-theory pressure calculation agrees with the empirical ideal-gas law if and only if the translational kinetic energy is proportional to the absolute temperature. This, then, is the experimental justification for the assumption expressed in Eq. (13-11).

The constant R/N_0 appears so frequently in kinetic-theory calculations that it is usually abbreviated $R/N_0 = k$, and called *Boltzmann's constant.* Its value is

$$k = \frac{R}{N_0} = 1.381 \times 10^{-23}\ \text{J/K} \tag{13-12}$$

Boltzmann's constant may be regarded as a new kind of gas constant in which the quantity of gas referred to is one molecule rather than 1 mol. With this constant, the ideal-gas equation can be written

$$PV = NkT \tag{13-13}$$

where N is again the total number of molecules. In terms of k, the average translational kinetic energy of a molecule is simply

$$E_{av} = \tfrac{3}{2}kT \tag{13-14}$$

We also note that since m is the mass of a single molecule, and the molecular mass M is by definition the mass of a *mole* of molecules, the two are related by

$$M = N_0 m \tag{13-15}$$

That is, M and m bear the same relationship as R and k; in each case the first is a "per mole" quantity, the second "per molecule."

The square root of $(v^2)_{av}$ is called the *root-mean-square speed,* denoted as v_{rms}. If there are N molecules, and if the speed of a typical one is v_i, then by definition

$$v_{rms} = \sqrt{\frac{1}{N}\sum_{i=1}^{N} v_i{}^2} \tag{13-16}$$

In terms of v_{rms}, Eq. (13-11) can be rewritten

$$v_{rms} = \sqrt{\frac{3RT}{N_o m}} = \sqrt{\frac{3RT}{M}} = \sqrt{\frac{3kT}{m}} \qquad (13\text{-}17)$$

As an example we compute v_{rms} for nitrogen molecules at room temperature, $20°C = 293$ K. The molecular mass of nitrogen is 28 g/mol $= 28 \times 10^{-3}$ kg/mol. Thus, from Eq. (13-17),

$$v_{rms} = \sqrt{\frac{3(8.314 \text{ J/mol} \cdot \text{K})(293 \text{ K})}{28 \times 10^{-3} \text{ kg/mol}}} = 511 \text{ m/s}$$

This speed is about half again as great as the speed of sound u in air at this temperature, given by Eq. (3-32). We note that the general expression for u is identical to that for v_{rms} except that it contains γ where v_{rms} contains 3. In both cases, one can verify that the expressions have the correct units by recalling that $1 \text{ J} = 1 \text{ kg} \cdot \text{m/s}^2$.

13-2 STATISTICAL DESCRIPTIONS OF STATES

As we have seen, the pressure of an ideal gas depends only on the *average* of the squares of the molecular speeds. When a more detailed description of molecular motion is useful, we do not try to specify the velocity or energy of an individual molecule but instead describe how many molecules have speeds or energies in various intervals by means of a *distribution function*.

Figure 13-2 shows an apparatus to measure the distribution of molecular speeds in a gas. A substance is vaporized in an oven, and molecules of vapor are permitted to escape, through a hole in the oven wall, into an evacuated region. A series of slits is constructed to block all molecules except those in one direction, so as to form a well-defined *beam*; this beam is aimed at a series of rotating disks as shown. The entire apparatus is enclosed in a container which is evacuated so that the molecules may move freely without colliding with air molecules. When the disks are rotating, a molecule passing through the slit in the first disk will arrive at the second at just the right time to pass through its slit only if it has a certain speed. Other molecules

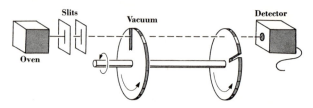

Fig. 13-2 Apparatus for producing a molecular beam and observing the distribution of molecular speeds in the beam.

with different speeds will strike the second disk. This apparatus may therefore be used as a speed selector which blocks all molecules except those in a narrow range of speeds. One may then measure *how many* molecules have speeds in various ranges.

The distribution of molecular speeds can be described by a function $f(v)$ having the property that $f(v)\, dv$ is the fraction of all the molecules having speeds in the interval dv. If there are N molecules, the total number dN having speeds in the interval dv is

$$dN = Nf(v)\, dv \tag{13-18}$$

Since every molecule must have some speed, the integral of Eq. (13-18) over all possible speeds must be equal to N. That is,

$$N = \int dN = \int_0^\infty Nf(v)\, dv \tag{13-19}$$

Thus $f(v)$ must satisfy the condition

$$\int_0^\infty f(v)\, dv = 1 \tag{13-20}$$

Any distribution function satisfying this requirement is said to be *normalized*. In the following discussion only normalized functions will be used.

The distribution function can also be interpreted in terms of *probability*. If a molecule is selected at random, the probability that its speed will fall in the interval dv is given by $f(v)\, dv$; the probability of finding an object with specified characteristics among a large group is proportional to the *number* of objects in the group having these characteristics.

If the distribution function $f(v)$ is known, various quantities of interest can be calculated. They include the *average* speed, denoted by v_{av}, given by

$$v_{av} = \int_0^\infty vf(v)\, dv \tag{13-21}$$

and the average of v^2, denoted as $(v^2)_{av}$ given by

$$(v^2)_{av} = \int_0^\infty v^2 f(v)\, dv \tag{13-22}$$

As we have seen, the latter quantity is significant because of its relation to the average *kinetic energy* of the molecules,

$$(\tfrac{1}{2}mv^2)_{av} = \tfrac{1}{2}m(v^2)_{av}$$

where m is the mass of a molecule.

The function which describes the distribution of molecular speeds in an ideal gas in thermodynamic equilibrium at absolute temperature T is the Maxwell-Boltzmann distribution; its expression is

$$f(v) = 4\pi \left(\frac{m}{2\pi kT}\right)^{3/2} v^2 e^{-mv^2/2kT} \qquad (13\text{-}23)$$

where k is the Boltzmann constant, as in Eq. (13-12). This expression is derived in detail in Sec. 13-4 after some preliminary developments.

From the statistical description of the speeds of the various molecules, given by the function $f(v)$, or from a corresponding function for the distribution of molecular *energies* or other dynamical quantities, various macroscopically observable properties of the system such as temperature, pressure, specific heat, and magnetization can be calculated. Thus, although such distributions do not give detailed information about individual molecules, they are nevertheless very useful.

There are analogous problems in quantum-mechanical systems. Suppose we have a large number of identical atoms or molecules, each of which has a series of energy levels. Under given conditions, how many molecules are in the lowest state (the ground state), how many are in the next state, and so on? As a specific example, suppose we want to know the temperature to which sodium vapor must be heated in order to obtain a certain intensity of emitted light resulting from radiative transitions from the first excited state (2.1 eV above the ground state) to the ground state. We can answer this question if we know what fraction of sodium atoms are in the first excited state (due to collisions from thermal motion) as a function of temperature of the vapor.

The next section addresses this general kind of question. Our procedure will be to derive, from very general considerations, a distribution function which gives the numbers of molecules that are in various energy states or, alternatively, the *probability* for each molecule to be in a given state. The distribution functions can then be used to compute the total *energy* of the system, its specific heat, and other physical quantities of interest.

13-3 MAXWELL-BOLTZMANN DISTRIBUTION

Let us consider a system consisting of a very large number N of identical components, each of which has a series of energy levels ε_i. For definiteness, we shall usually refer to these components as *molecules*, although they might also be atoms, electrons, or other entities.

The Maxwell-Boltzmann distribution law is as follows: In a system of N identical molecules in thermodynamic equilibrium, each having a set of possible states with energies ε_i, the number of molecules in a specified state with energy ε_i is proportional to the quantity

$$e^{-\varepsilon_i/kT}$$

where T is the absolute temperature and k is Boltzmann's constant. The remainder of this section is devoted to *deriving* this law from fundamental probability considerations. The derivation requires several steps, and the logic is not always simple, but the reader who is able to comprehend this development will have enhanced greatly his understanding of the origin and nature of the law. Otherwise, one can skip directly to the end of this section to admire the final results, which are used in later sections.

We assume that the molecules are nearly independent, so that at any instant each molecule has a definite energy, but there are nevertheless interactions of sufficient strength to permit energy interchange for the establishment of thermal equilibrium.

In general, each molecule may have a number of different possible states with the same energy. For example, if the molecule is a hydrogen atom, there are various angular-momentum states, identified by the quantum numbers l and m, for each value of the principal quantum number n, which determines the energy of the state. It was shown in Sec. 12-2 that the total number of states having the principal quantum number n is $2n^2$. The existence of several physically distinct states with the same energy is called *degeneracy*; the energy level is said to be *degenerate,* and the number of distinct states having a given energy ε_i is called the *degree of degeneracy*, denoted by g_i. Thus the degree of degeneracy of the hydrogen-atom energy levels is $g_i = 2i^2$, where we have used i rather than n for the principal quantum number to conform to later usage.

How shall we describe the possible states of the *entire system?* Two possibilities come to mind. We could specify the state of each of the N molecules, by making a chart showing which molecules are in each of the states having energy ε_1, which in the states ε_2, and so on. This description specifies a state of the system which we shall call a *microscopic* state or simply a *micro* state. We can count the *total number* of possible micro states. Since there are g_i different states associated with energy ε_i for an individual molecule, the total number of distinct states in which a given molecule can exist is

$$\sum_i g_i \tag{13-24}$$

Each molecule has its choice of any one of these states, and so the total number of ways the N molecules can be arranged among the various states is

$$\left(\sum_i g_i\right)^N = M \tag{13-25}$$

where M denotes the *total* number of micro states.

Usually the micro states themselves are not very useful. Since the molecules are identical, it is of no concern precisely *which* molecules are in which energy states. Instead, we want to know *how many* are in each energy state, without regard to *which* molecules they are. Thus a different and more directly useful kind of state description consists in specifying only the *total* number of molecules having each energy, n_1 molecules with energy ε_1, n_2 with ε_2, and in general n_i with ε_i. We shall call this description a *macroscopic* state of the system, or *macro* state; it consists of the set of numbers n_i. This name is appropriate, inasmuch as this description is most directly related to the macroscopic properties of the system. Our objective is to derive a *distribution* function $n = f(\varepsilon)$ which gives the number of molecules n_i in each energy level ε_i and thus describes the macro state for a system in thermodynamic equilibrium.

Since the macro state is a less detailed specification than the micro state, there are in general several micro states for each macro state. As a simple example, suppose there are four molecules numbered from 1 to 4, with two energy states. If these states are not degenerate, then $g_1 = 1$ and $g_2 = 1$, $N = 4$, and the total number of micro states is

$$M = (1 + 1)^4 = 16$$

These states are shown schematically in Table 13-1. The number of macro states, on the other hand, is only five. As the table shows, one macro state has six corresponding micro states, two have four micro states each, and the other two have one each.

The heart of the derivation of the Maxwell-Boltzmann distribution, as will be seen shortly, is the assumption that the *most probable* macro state, that is, the macro state in which the system is most likely to exist, is the one with the largest number of corresponding micro states. Thus it is useful to work out a general formula for the number of micro states corresponding to any given macro state. Suppose we want to put n_i molecules in the states with energy ε_i. Since the corresponding degeneracy is g_i, *each* of the n_i molecules can be put in any one of the g_i states with energy ε_i, and the *total* number of ways the states can be chosen for any particular set of n_i molecules is $(g_i)^{n_i}$. There is a corresponding number of choices for each energy level, and so for a macro state described by the set of numbers n_1, n_2, . . . the *total* number of choices is

Table 13-1 States of Four Particles with Two Energy Levels

Micro states		Macro states	
ε_1	ε_2		
Molecule numbers		n_1	n_2
1234	— }	4	0
123	4		
124	3		
134	2	3	1
234	1		
12	34		
13	24		
14	23		
23	14	2	2
24	13		
34	12		
1	234		
2	134		
3	124	1	3
4	123		
—	1234 }	0	4

$$g_1{}^{n_1}g_2{}^{n_2}g_3{}^{n_3}\cdots \tag{13-26}$$

where the product ranges over all the energy states.

This is by no means the end of the possible choices, however. There are still different combinations if we *permute* the various particles. Instead of taking the *first* n_1 molecules and putting them in the first states, we may select n_1 molecules from anywhere in the collection, and similarly for the other states. The number of distinct ways N molecules can be rearranged, which is called the *number of permutations of N molecules*, is simply $N!$ To see this, we observe that any of the N molecules may be placed first in the sequence; for each of these N choices we have $N - 1$ choices for the second in the sequence, for each of these $N - 2$ for the third, and so on, so that the total number of ways of arranging (permuting) N molecules is

$$N(N - 1)(N - 2) \cdots (3)(2)(1) = N! \tag{13-27}$$

where $N!$ is read "N factorial" and is simply an abbreviation for the left side of Eq. (13-27).

It might appear that the number of micro states corresponding to any macro state is the product of Eqs. (13-26) and (13-27). However, if we include *all* the possible permutations of N molecules, of which there are $N!$, we are *overcounting* the number of possibilities, for the following reason: A permutation in which the molecules are simply rearranged within a given energy state should not be counted, since we need to know only *which* molecules are in the n_i in energy level ε_i, not *in what sequence* they appear. Thus we should *divide* the total number of permutations $N!$ by a factor $n_i!$ for each energy level.

Putting all the pieces together, we find that the total number of micro states corresponding to a macro state specified by the numbers n_1, n_2, . . . is given by

$$\frac{N!}{n_1!n_2!n_3! \cdots} g_1{}^{n_1} g_2{}^{n_2} g_3{}^{n_3} \cdots \tag{13-28}$$

We now make a fundamental postulate concerning the relative likelihood of occurrence of the various states. The postulate is this: *In a state of thermal equilibrium with a certain total energy, all the various micro states with that energy are equally likely to occur.* This postulate seems reasonable, but perhaps somewhat arbitrary; its ultimate justification is that results derived from it agree with observations of the macroscopic properties of matter.

If the micro states are all equally probable, the macro states are *not* equally probable, since they correspond to different numbers of micro states. Thus the *probability* of occurrence of a given macro state is equal to the number of micro states corresponding to it, divided by the *total* number M of micro states. Denoting the probability of a certain macro state $(n_1, n_2, . . .)$ by $P(n_1, n_2, . . .)$, we have

$$P(n_1, n_2, . . .) = \frac{1}{M} \frac{N!}{n_1!n_2! \cdots} g_1{}^{n_1} g_2{}^{n_2} \cdots \tag{13-29}$$

Because ordinarily a large number of molecules are involved, some macro states are much more likely to occur than others. The *most probable* macro states are of greatest significance in characterizing the actual observed behavior of a system. It turns out, in fact, that a relatively small number of closely related macro states are so very much more probable than *all* the others that it can be said, to a very good approximation, that only *one* macro state has an appreciable probability of occurrence, and this macro state is therefore a suitable description of the state of the real physical system!

Thus the next task is to find the distribution of particles $(n_1, n_2, . . .)$ which *maximizes* the value of Eq. (13-29). Rather than maximize this quantity itself, it is more convenient to deal with its *logarithm*; since $\ln P$ is a monotonic increasing function of P, maximizing the logarithm is equivalent to maximizing the function itself. Using the familiar properties of logarithms, we find

$$\ln P = -\ln M + \ln N! - \sum_i \ln n_i! + \sum_i n_i \ln g_i \tag{13-30}$$

In varying the numbers $n_1, n_2, \ldots$ to maximize $\ln P$, the n_i cannot all be varied independently, for two reasons. First their sum must be equal to the constant total number N of molecules:

$$N = \sum_i{}' n_i \tag{13-31}$$

Second, the sum of the energies of all the molecules must equal the total energy of the system, which is also constant. Since there are n_i molecules in the states with energy ε_i, the total energy of these molecules is $n_i \varepsilon_i$, and the total energy E of the entire system is

$$E = \sum_i{}' n_i \varepsilon_i \tag{13-32}$$

Any set of numbers n_i appearing in Eq. (13-30) must be consistent with these two constraints.

Now, because N is very large, the n_i are also large, and so only an insignificant error is introduced if we regard them as *continuous* variables rather than as integers. This has the great advantage that in maximizing Eq. (13-30) we can take *derivatives* with respect to the n_i. Another useful approximation, also based on the assumption that the n_i are very large, is to represent $n!$ by a continuous function of n, as follows:

$$\ln n! \cong n \ln n - n \tag{13-33}$$

This formula, known as *Stirling's approximation*, is derived in Appendix G. As an example, for $n = 50$, we have

$$\ln 50! = 148.5$$
$$50 \ln 50 - 50 = 145.6$$

Even for this small value of n, the error in the approximation is only 2 percent. In practical problems, where the number of molecules typically ranges from 10^{10} to 10^{25}, the error is completely negligible. With the help of Eq. (13-33), Eq. (13-30) can be written

$$\ln P = -\ln M + \ln N! + \sum_i n_i \ln g_i - \sum_i (n_i \ln n_i - n_i) \tag{13-34}$$

We must now find the values of the n_i that maximize this function. The function attains an extreme (or at least stationary) value when all the quantities $\partial \ln P / \partial n_i$ are simultaneously zero. But, as already pointed out, the n_i cannot all be varied independently; they are subject to the constraints $\Sigma n_i = N$ and $\Sigma n_i \varepsilon_i = E$. We could use these two equations to eliminate two of the n's, take the derivatives with respect to the remaining ones, and solve the resulting set of simultaneous equations for the values of n_i that make the function a maximum. Instead, it is easier to preserve the symmetry of the expressions with respect to all the n's by making use of a trick developed by Lagrange, known as the *method of undetermined multipliers*. We shall not prove the validity of this method in detail, but it is plausible even without formal proof. The procedure is as follows: Instead of taking the derivatives of $\ln P$ as indicated, we consider the following function:

$$f(n_i) = \ln P - \alpha \left(\sum_i n_i - N \right) - \beta \left(\sum_i n_i \varepsilon_i - E \right) \tag{13-35}$$

where α and β are arbitrary constants. The two terms on the right are zero no matter what values α and β have, and so this function is equal to $\ln P$. Now we take the derivative of Eq. (13-35) with respect to each n_i and set it equal to zero. The resulting set of equations can then be solved for the n_i that maximize the function.

This procedure can be justified roughly as follows: For any set of n_i satisfying $\Sigma n_i = N$ and $\Sigma n_i \varepsilon_i = E$, Eq. (13-35) is identical with $\ln P$. But because of the constraints, not all the n_i can be varied independently; if all but two are specified, the last two are determined by the constraints. Suppose n_1 and n_2 are the two that are *not* independent. Then for each of the others, all of which can be varied independently, we are at liberty to require that $\partial f / \partial n_i = 0$. But by appropriate choices of α and β the derivatives with respect to n_1 and n_2 can *also* be made to vanish. Thus the solutions of the set of equations $\partial f / \partial n_i = 0$ are the set of n_i that maximizes $\ln P$, subject to the constraints.

Carrying out this program, we have

$$\frac{\partial f}{\partial n_i} = \frac{\partial}{\partial n_i} \ln P - \alpha - \beta \varepsilon_i = 0 \tag{13-36}$$

with $\ln P$ given by Eq. (13-34). Carrying out the derivative, recalling that N and M are constants, we find

$$\frac{\partial}{\partial n_i} \ln P = \ln g_i - \left(\ln n_i + n_i \frac{1}{n_i} - 1 \right)$$

$$= \ln g_i - \ln n_i \tag{13-37}$$

Combining this result with Eq. (13-36), we find

$$\frac{\partial f}{\partial n_i} = \ln g_i - \ln n_i - \alpha - \beta \varepsilon_i = 0 \tag{13-38}$$

Solving for n_i,

$$n_i = g_i e^{-\alpha} e^{-\beta \varepsilon_i} \tag{13-39}$$

This is the Maxwell-Boltzmann distribution.

The number n_i of molecules in states with energy ε_i is proportional to an exponential function of ε_i. The meaning of the parameters α and β is not yet clear. The constant α simply contributes a multiplicative factor $e^{-\alpha}$; since Eq. (13-39) must satisfy $\Sigma n_i = N$, we have

$$N = \sum_i n_i = e^{-\alpha} \sum_i g_i e^{-\beta \varepsilon_i} \tag{13-40}$$

Now N, g_i, and ε_i are presumably known properties of the system, so this determines α if the other parameter β is known. Thus α is associated with the *normalization* of the distribution function, and from now on we denote the normalization constant as $e^{-\alpha} = A$.

The significance of β is less obvious but more fundamental than that of α. Suppose we draw a histogram of Eq. (13-39) for the particular case of nondegenerate energies (all $g_i = 1$), as in Fig. 13-3. Because of the

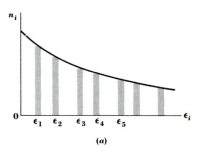

(a)

Fig. 13-3 Maxwell-Boltzmann distributions for different values of β. (a) When β is small, corresponding to high temperature, the populations of the levels decrease only slowly with increasing energy, showing that states with rather high energy have substantial populations. (b) When β is large, corresponding to low temperature, the population drops off rapidly with increasing energy, showing that most molecules are in the lowest energy states.

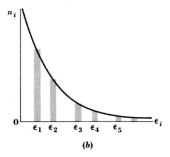

(b)

exponential function, n_i is a *decreasing* function of ε_i, and the *rate* at which the function drops off with increasing ε_i depends on β. When β is very *small*, it drops off relatively slowly; for large β it drops off with increasing ε_i, as shown in the figure. This suggests a relationship between β and the *temperature* of the system; at very low temperatures nearly all the molecules are in the lowest energy states, whereas for very high temperatures there should be a wide range of energy states that are nearly equally populated. Thus it appears that β is *inversely* proportional to the temperature of the system.

This interpretation of β is supported by other results which will be obtained later in this chapter. For example, from Eq. (13-39) it will be shown that the average kinetic energy associated with translational motion of molecules in an ideal gas is given by $\varepsilon_{av} = 1/2\beta$. But as we saw in Sec. 13-1, this average energy is equal to $\frac{3}{2}kT$. Thus at least in this case, β must be related to T by the equation

$$\beta = \frac{1}{kT} \tag{13-41}$$

Further support of this interpretation of β will appear later. Thus the Maxwell-Boltzmann distribution, Eq. (13-39), may be rewritten

$$n_i = Ag_ie^{-\varepsilon_i/kT} \tag{13-42}$$

although for some calculations it is more convenient to express the distribution function in terms of β rather than kT.

As a simple application of the Maxwell-Boltzmann distribution, we consider a fictitious gas of diatomic molecules which have only rotational kinetic energy, with energy levels as discussed in Sec. 12-6, given by

$$\varepsilon_l = \frac{l(l + 1)\hbar^2}{2I} \qquad l = 0, 1, 2, \ldots \tag{13-43}$$

At a given temperature, what is the ratio of the number of molecules in the $l = 1$ states to the number in the $l = 0$?

First it should be noted that, for any energy ε_l, the angular momentum is $[l(l + 1)]^{1/2} \hbar$, and its z component can have any of the $2l + 1$ values between $-l\hbar$ and $+l\hbar$. Thus the degeneracy of this state is $g_l = 2l + 1$. Specifically, $g_0 = 1$, $g_1 = 3$, $g_2 = 5$, and so on. The Maxwell-Boltzmann distribution, giving the number of molecules in each rotational energy state, then gives

$$n_l = A(2l + 1)e^{-l(l+1)\hbar^2/2IkT} \tag{13-44}$$

The constant A is not known, but since only the ratio n_1/n_0 is required, we find immediately

$$\frac{n_1}{n_0} = \frac{A(3)e^{-\hbar^2/Ikt}}{A(1)e^{-0}}$$

$$= 3e^{-\hbar^2/IkT} \tag{13-45}$$

For the oxygen molecule discussed in Sec. 12-6, $\hbar^2/I = 2 \times 10^{-23}$ J. At room temperature (say 300 K),

$$kT = (1.38 \times 10^{-23} \text{ J/K})(300 \text{ K}) = 4.14 \times 10^{-21} \text{ J}$$

$$\frac{\hbar^2}{IkT} = \frac{2 \times 10^{-23} \text{ J}}{4.14 \times 10^{-21} \text{ J}} \cong 0.005$$

$$\frac{n_1}{n_0} = \frac{A(3)e^{-0.005}}{A(1)} = 2.985$$

and we find $n_1/n_0 \cong 3$. But at $T = 1$ K, $\hbar^2/IkT = 1.4$ and $n_1/n_0 = 3e^{-1.4} = 0.75$. At sufficiently *low* temperatures, the exponent becomes very large and negative, $n_1/n_0 \ll 1$, and practically *no* molecules are in the $l = 1$ states. As T increases, n_1/n_0 increases; at *high* temperatures the exponent approaches zero, $n_1/n_0 \to 3$, and there are three times as many molecules in the $l = 1$ as in the $l = 0$ states. That is, in the low-temperature limit *all* the molecules are in the lowest energy state, while in the high-temperature limit the distribution is determined entirely by the degeneracy.

13-4 MOLECULAR SPEEDS

Equation (13-42) is the general form of the *Maxwell-Boltzmann distribution*. Although derived in terms of a *discrete* set of energy levels, it may also be applied to a system in which the energy levels form a *continuum*. Let us consider again the ideal gas, represented as a collection of N molecules in a container, where ε is the translational kinetic energy of a molecule. For any container of reasonable size the energy levels are so closely spaced that they may be regarded as a continuum. The Maxwell-Boltzmann distribution can be used to obtain the distribution of molecular speeds.

The energy levels are degenerate, since the energy of a state depends on the *magnitude* of momentum of the molecule ($\varepsilon = p^2/2m$) but not on its *direction*. To determine the degree of degeneracy, we introduce a fictitious three-dimensional space whose coordinates p_x, p_y, and p_z are the components of momentum of a molecule. Each point in this space represents a possible momentum and therefore a possible state of motion of a molecule. The magnitude of momentum $p = (p_x^2 + p_y^2 + p_z^2)^{1/2}$ is the distance from the origin to the point.

Any volume element in this *momentum space* represents a certain range of momentum, and the number of states in this range is proportional to the volume of the element. In calculating the degree of degeneracy, however, we are interested in the number of states in an *energy* interval, say ε to $\varepsilon + d\varepsilon$. All points corresponding to a given energy ε lie on a *sphere* in momentum space of radius $p = (2m\varepsilon)^{1/2}$. Likewise, points corresponding to the energy range ε to $\varepsilon + d\varepsilon$ lie within a spherical shell whose thickness dp is determined from the interval $d\varepsilon$ by taking the derivative of the energy-momentum relation:

$$\varepsilon = \frac{p^2}{2m} \qquad d\varepsilon = \frac{p\,dp}{m} \tag{13-46}$$

The *volume* of this spherical shell, assuming it is very thin, is approximately its surface area multiplied by its thickness; that is,

$$dV = 4\pi p^2\,dp$$

which may be written in terms of energy with the help of Eqs. (13-46):

$$dV = 4\pi m p \frac{p\,dp}{m} = 4\pi m (2m\varepsilon)^{1/2}\,d\varepsilon \tag{13-47}$$

Thus the number of states in the interval $d\varepsilon$ is proportional to $\varepsilon^{1/2}\,d\varepsilon$, and the degeneracy factor simply to $\varepsilon^{1/2}$.

The Maxwell-Boltzmann distribution function for an ideal gas therefore may be written

$$n(\varepsilon)\,d\varepsilon = A\varepsilon^{1/2}e^{-\beta\varepsilon}\,d\varepsilon \tag{13-48}$$

The quantity $n(\varepsilon)\,d\varepsilon$ is the number of particles with energies in the interval $d\varepsilon$, and A is a normalization constant, chosen to satisfy the equation

$$\int_0^\infty n(\varepsilon)\,d\varepsilon = A\int_0^\infty \varepsilon^{1/2}e^{-\beta\varepsilon}\,d\varepsilon = N \tag{13-49}$$

Evaluation of this integral requires some mathematical trickery, the details of which need not concern us. Its value, which can be found in integral tables, is

$$\int_0^\infty \varepsilon^{1/2}e^{-\beta\varepsilon}\,d\varepsilon = \frac{\sqrt{\pi}}{2\beta^{3/2}} \tag{13-50}$$

A similar integral which is useful is

$$\int_0^\infty \varepsilon^{3/2}e^{-\beta\varepsilon}\,d\varepsilon = \frac{3\sqrt{\pi}}{4\beta^{5/2}} \tag{13-51}$$

Using Eq. (13-50) to evaluate Eq. (13-49), we find

$$A = 2\pi N \left(\frac{\beta}{\pi}\right)^{3/2} \tag{13-52}$$

and the energy distribution for an ideal gas becomes

$$n(\varepsilon) = 2\pi N \left(\frac{\beta}{\pi}\right)^{3/2} \varepsilon^{1/2} e^{-\beta\varepsilon} \tag{13-53}$$

This function can be used to calculate the *average* kinetic energy ε_{av} of a gas molecule. There are $n(\varepsilon)\,d\varepsilon$ molecules with energies ε in the interval $d\varepsilon$, and the total energy of these molecules is $\varepsilon n(\varepsilon)\,d\varepsilon$; the total energy of *all* the molecules is the integral of this expression; to obtain the average, we divide by the total number of molecules:

$$\varepsilon_{av} = \frac{1}{N} \int_0^\infty \varepsilon n(\varepsilon)\,d\varepsilon = \frac{A}{N} \int_0^\infty \varepsilon^{3/2} e^{-\beta\varepsilon}\,d\varepsilon \tag{13-54}$$

Using Eq. (13-51), we find

$$\varepsilon_{av} = \frac{2\pi N(\beta/\pi)^{3/2}}{N} \frac{3\sqrt{\pi}}{4\beta^{5/2}} = \frac{3}{2\beta} \tag{13-55}$$

The kinetic-molecular model of an ideal gas (Sec. 13-1) shows that the average translational kinetic energy is $3kT/2$, and this agrees with Eq. (13-55) if we again set $\beta = 1/kT$.

The Maxwell-Boltzmann distribution for an ideal gas can also be expressed in terms of the distribution of *speeds* of gas molecules, using the relation $\varepsilon = \frac{1}{2}mv^2$. Deriving the expression in terms of v is left as a problem; the result is

$$n(v)\,dv = 4\pi N \left(\frac{m}{2\pi kT}\right)^{3/2} v^2 e^{-mv^2/2kT}\,dv \tag{13-56}$$

which agrees with Eq. (13-23). This function may be used with Eqs. (13-21) and (13-22) to find the average and root-mean-square speeds. These calculations are left as a problem; the results are

$$v_{av} = \sqrt{\frac{8kT}{\pi m}} \qquad v_{rms} = \sqrt{\frac{3kT}{m}} \tag{13-57}$$

The second of these agrees with Eq. (13-17), obtained from the kinetic-theory argument.

Equation (13-56) may be compared with experimental molecular-speed distributions from experiments such as the one described in Sec. 13-2. This is a much more detailed comparison of theory and experiment than the ideal-gas equation, and the excellent agreement gives strong support to the

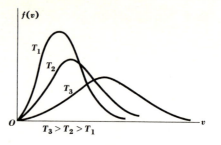

Fig. 13-4 Maxwell-Boltzmann distribution curves for various temperatures. As the temperature increases, the curve becomes flatter, and its maximum shifts to higher temperature.

assumption of equal probability of micro states, the equating of β with $1/kT$, and in fact our entire analysis.

Figure 13-4 shows how the distribution of molecular speeds in a gas changes with temperature. The general shape of the distribution curve remains the same, but the scales change. The figure shows the Maxwell-Boltzmann distribution for three different temperatures. As temperature increases, the curve becomes flattened and extends farther in the direction of large speeds, as we should expect.

13-5 SPECIFIC HEATS OF GASES

The kinetic-molecular theory of gases leads naturally to the assumption that the average translational kinetic energy is proportional to the absolute temperature. This result can be used to predict the *specific heat* of a gas, since heat is a transfer of microscopic mechanical energy.

According to Eq. (13-14), the average translational kinetic energy is $3kT/2$ per molecule, or $3N_0kT/2 = 3RT/2$ per mole. To increase the temperature of a mole of gas by an amount ΔT, we must add an amount of energy $3R\Delta T/2$, and therefore we predict that the molar specific heat C (also called the molar heat capacity) should be $C = 3R/2$, no matter what the nature of the gas!

Table 13-2 gives some experimental results, expressed in mechanical units and as multiples of R. For the inert gases the values agree quite well with the above prediction, but the *diatomic* gases have specific heats closer to $5R/2$ than to our prediction, and polyatomic gases have still larger values, indicating that the molecules have additional energy. One possibility is *rotational* kinetic energy. A diatomic molecule, considered as a rigid dumbbell, can rotate about either of two perpendicular axes perpendicular to its own axis, and we might guess that just as there is an average energy $\frac{1}{2}kT$ for each of the three components of *translational* motion, there is an additional $\frac{1}{2}kT$ for each of the two rotational components, for an average total energy of $5kT/2$ per molecule, or $5RT/2$ per mole. The corresponding molar specific heat is $5R/2$, which agrees quite well with the values in the table.

The idea that each distinct kind of motion should have associated with it, on the average, a kinetic energy of $\frac{1}{2}kT$ per molecule is called the *principle of equipartition of energy*. It is customary to call each distinct kind of motion a *degree of freedom*. A monatomic molecule has three degrees of freedom, corresponding to the three components of velocity. A diatomic molecule has five degrees of freedom, corresponding to three components of velocity and two of angular velocity. For a triatomic molecule, if the atoms are not all in a straight line, there are moments of inertia and rotational energies for all three mutually perpendicular axes. In such cases, there are six degrees of freedom, and we expect the molar specific heat to be $C = 3R$. We see in Table 13-2 that the observed specific heats of several triatomic gases are somewhat larger than this value.

Further refinements can be made; the molecules may not be completely rigid but may have internal *vibrational* motion as well as translation and rotation. A more refined model of a diatomic model would regard it not as a rigid dumbbell but as two point masses connected by a spring. Then there would be additional kinetic and potential energies associated with *vibrational* motion. This effect accounts for the specific heat of Cl_2 shown in Table 13-2.

Table 13-2 Specific Heats of Gases at $T = 300$ K and Constant Volume

Gas	Specific heat, cal/g·K	Molar specific heat, J/mol·K	× R
He	0.755	12.6	1.52
Ne	0.153	13.0	1.56
Ar	0.075	12.5	1.51
Kr	0.036	12.1	1.46
Xe	0.0228	12.6	1.51
H_2	2.4	20.1	2.42
O_2	0.155	20.9	2.51
N_2	0.176	20.6	2.48
NO	0.166	20.8	2.50
CO	0.179	21.0	2.52
HCl	0.137	21.0	2.52
Cl_2	0.0848	25.2	3.02
CO_2	0.153	28.7	3.45
SO_2	0.117	31.4	3.78
NO_2	0.152	28.9	3.47
H_2O	0.471	27.3	3.28
$(C_2H_5)_2O$	0.416	128.9	15.5

From the above discussion, the predicted specific heats are constant, independent of temperature. Although some gases are observed to have specific heats which are more or less independent of temperature over a wide range, others show a marked dependence on temperature. Figure 13-5 shows the specific heat of hydrogen as a function of temperature. At low temperatures the molar specific heat is about $\frac{3}{2}R$, characteristic of a *monatomic* gas, despite the fact that other evidence indicates that hydrogen is *diatomic* at these temperatures. At successively higher temperatures it increases to $\frac{5}{2}R$ and becomes relatively constant; then at still higher temperatures it increases to a final value of $\frac{7}{2}R$. This clearly suggests that at sufficiently low temperatures there is no energy associated with rotational or vibrational motion.

The reason is not far to seek. We have observed in connection with the discussion of molecular spectra in Sec. 12-6 that energies associated with both rotational and vibrational motion of a diatomic molecule are quantized. The vibrational energy levels, for example, are given by $E_n = (n + \frac{1}{2})\hbar\omega$. But now suppose that the temperature is so low that kT is much *smaller* than $\hbar\omega$. In this case most molecules should be in the $n = 0$ vibrational state, and there is little chance for a molecule to acquire enough energy from a collision to reach any higher energy state, since very few molecules *have* this much energy. Thus only a small fraction of molecules change their vibrational state at all when the temperature changes slightly, and as a result the vibrational motion contributes much *less* to the specific heat than would be expected on the basis of the equipartition theorem. Under these circumstances, the vibrational degree of freedom is said to be "frozen out." The same argument is valid for the rotational energy levels.

The temperature dependence of the specific heat of hydrogen suggests that at very low temperatures both the vibrational and rotational degrees of freedom are "frozen out." Molecular spectroscopy shows that the rotational energy levels are much more closely spaced than the vibrational, and so we expect that as the temperature increases, the rotational levels will begin to contribute to the specific heat before the vibrational levels. Thus at intermediate temperatures the specific heat becomes $\frac{5}{2}R$, corresponding to the contributions of the translational and rotational degrees of freedom but not

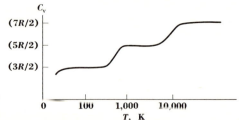

Fig. 13-5 Observed value of the molar specific heat (at constant volume) of hydrogen as a function of temperature.

of vibrational energy, which is still frozen out. At still higher temperatures the vibrational energy begins to contribute, and the specific heat attains a final value of $\frac{7}{2}R$. At still higher temperatures we might expect to obtain further contributions to the specific heat arising from the possibility of electron-energy-level excitation. As we have seen, the electron energy levels are spaced far apart compared with vibrational or rotational levels, and so any such contributions to the specific heat will occur only at extremely high temperatures. At such temperatures, enough of the hydrogen molecules are dissociated into single atoms to make the situation even more complicated.

To clarify and illustrate some of the above discussion and to show how more detailed calculations of specific heats can be made, we consider the vibrational specific heat of a diatomic gas. We assume that the temperature is such that the translational and rotational degrees of freedom contribute the classical $\frac{5}{2}R$ to the molar specific heat but the vibrational motion is just beginning to contribute. That is, we assume that most of the molecules are in the $n = 0$ vibrational state, and only a few in higher states.

We now apply the Maxwell-Boltzmann distribution derived in Sec. 13-3 to this problem. To make the notation consistent with that of Sec. 13-3, we use i for the vibrational quantum number. That is, the possible vibrational energies of a molecule are given by

$$\varepsilon_i = (i + \tfrac{1}{2})\hbar\omega = (i + \tfrac{1}{2})\varepsilon_0 \tag{13-58}$$

where ε_0 is an abbreviation for the quantity $\hbar\omega$. If there are N molecules, the number n_i in the energy state ε_i is given by Eq. (13-39). Since for each molecule there is only one vibrational state corresponding to the given quantum number i, the degeneracy factors g_i are all equal to unity and may be omitted. Thus the number of molecules in state i is given by

$$n_i = Ae^{-\beta(i+1/2)\varepsilon_0} \tag{13-59}$$

with $\beta = 1/kT$. The constant A is chosen to satisfy the condition

$$\sum_{i=0}^{\infty} n_i = A \sum_{i=0}^{\infty} e^{-\beta(i+1/2)\varepsilon_0} = N \tag{13-60}$$

To determine A, we note that this sum can be written

$$\sum_{i=0}^{\infty} e^{-\beta(i+1/2)\varepsilon_0} = e^{-\beta\varepsilon_0/2}(1 + e^{-\beta\varepsilon_0} + e^{-2\beta\varepsilon_0} + e^{-3\beta\varepsilon_0} + \cdots) \tag{13-61}$$

The sum in parentheses is simply the sum of terms of a geometric progression and may be evaluated by using the relation

$$1 + a + a^2 + a^3 + \cdots = \frac{1}{1 - a} \tag{13-62}$$

which is valid when $a < 1$. This formula can be verified directly by long division. Using it, we find

$$\sum_{i=0}^{\infty} e^{-\beta(i+1/2)\varepsilon_0} = \frac{e^{-\beta\varepsilon_0/2}}{1 - e^{-\beta\varepsilon_0}} = \frac{1}{e^{\beta\varepsilon_0/2} - e^{-\beta\varepsilon_0/2}}$$

$$= \frac{1}{2 \sinh \frac{1}{2}\beta\varepsilon_0} \tag{13-63}$$

Using this result in Eq. (13-60), we find

$$A = 2N \sinh \tfrac{1}{2}\beta\varepsilon_0 \tag{13-64}$$

and the complete distribution function is

$$n_i = 2N \sinh \tfrac{1}{2}\beta\varepsilon_0 e^{-\beta(i+1/2)\varepsilon_0} \tag{13-65}$$

At very low temperatures, when β is very large, the distribution falls off very *rapidly* with increasing i, and most molecules are in the $i = 0$ state. On the other hand, when $kT = 1/\beta$ is equal to ε_0, a sizable fraction of the molecules are in higher vibrational states, and we expect the vibrational energy to contribute considerably to the specific heat of the gas.

To calculate the vibrational contribution to the specific heat, we first find the total vibrational energy of the whole gas, given by

$$E = \sum_i n_i \varepsilon_i \tag{13-66}$$

with n_i and ε_i given by Eqs. (13-65) and (13-58), respectively. Dividing this quantity by N gives the average energy *per molecule*, and taking the derivative of that quantity with respect to T gives the rate of change of energy with temperature per molecule, which is the specific heat per molecule.

The sum in Eq. (13-66) can be evaluated by means of a trick based on the observation that

$$e^{-\beta\varepsilon_i}\varepsilon_i = -\frac{\partial}{\partial\beta}e^{-\beta\varepsilon_i} \tag{13-67}$$

Thus

$$\sum_i n_i \varepsilon_i = \sum_i A e^{-\beta\varepsilon_i}\varepsilon_i = -A\frac{\partial}{\partial\beta}\sum_i e^{-\beta\varepsilon_i}$$

$$= -A\frac{\partial}{\partial\beta}\sum_i e^{-\beta(i+1/2)\varepsilon_0} \tag{13-68}$$

This last sum has already been evaluated in Eq. (13-63), and we have

$$\sum_i n_i \varepsilon_i = -A \frac{\partial}{\partial \beta} \frac{1}{2 \sinh \frac{1}{2}\beta\varepsilon_0}$$

$$= -N \sinh \frac{1}{2}\beta\varepsilon_0 \frac{\partial}{\partial \beta} \frac{1}{\sinh \frac{1}{2}\beta\varepsilon_0} \tag{13-69}$$

Carrying out the differentiation and simplifying, we find

$$E = \sum_i n_i \varepsilon_i = \frac{N\varepsilon_0}{2} \operatorname{ctnh} \frac{1}{2}\beta\varepsilon_0 = \frac{N\varepsilon_0}{2} \operatorname{ctnh} \frac{\varepsilon_0}{2kT} \tag{13-70}$$

The average vibrational energy *per molecule* is

$$\varepsilon_{av} = \frac{\varepsilon_0}{2} \operatorname{ctnh} \frac{\varepsilon_0}{2kT} = \frac{\hbar\omega}{2} \operatorname{ctnh} \frac{\hbar\omega}{2kT} \tag{13-71}$$

It is instructive to examine this last expression in the limit of very high temperatures, when $\varepsilon_0/2kT \ll 1$. For very small x, sinh x is approximately equal to x, and cosh x to unity, as can be seen by expanding the exponentials used to define these functions in power series. Thus at small x the function ctnh x approaches $1/x$; in the high-temperature limit Eq. (13-71) becomes

$$\varepsilon_{av} = \frac{\varepsilon_0}{2} \frac{2kT}{\varepsilon_0} = kT \tag{13-72}$$

which is just the result predicted by the classical equipartition theorem! Conversely, at very low temperatures ctnh $(\varepsilon_0/2kT) \to 1$ and Eq. (13-71) approaches the value $\frac{1}{2}\varepsilon_0$, corresponding to every molecule being in the ground state $i = 0$.

The vibrational specific heat C per molecule is simply the derivative of Eq. (13-71) with respect to T. The details of this calculation are left as a problem; the result is

$$C = k \left[\frac{\varepsilon_0/2kT}{\sinh (\varepsilon_0/2kT)} \right]^2$$

$$= k \left[\frac{\frac{1}{2}\beta\varepsilon_0}{\sinh \frac{1}{2}\beta\varepsilon_0} \right]^2 \tag{13-73}$$

In the high-temperature limit ($\beta \to 0$) the vibrational specific heat approaches the classical value k per molecule (or R per mole), but at low temperatures it approaches zero, as expected.

Equations (13-71) and (13-73) are plotted as functions of T in Fig. 13-6. For comparison, the values of these quantities predicted by the equipartition

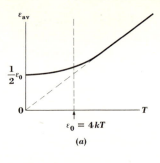

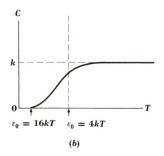

Fig. 13-6 (*a*) Average vibrational energy of a molecule as a function of temperature. For comparison, the prediction of the classical equipartition theorem is shown as a broken line. The temperature at which $\varepsilon_0 = 4kT$ is shown for reference. (*b*) Specific heat (per molecule) as a function of temperature. For comparison, the prediction of the classical equipartition theorem is shown as a broken line. The temperatures at which $\varepsilon_0 = 16kT$ and $4kT$ are shown. The value of this function for a given value of T is proportional to the slope of the ε_{av} versus T graph at the same T.

theorem are also shown. We see that the temperature dependence of the specific heat agrees qualitatively with the observed behavior of hydrogen at temperatures of several thousand degrees. A more quantitative comparison can be made by using the value of ε_0 obtained from the infrared spectrum of the hydrogen molecule. This value is found to be approximately 0.5 eV, which is equal to kT at a temperature of about 6000 K, characteristic of the temperature of the outer layers of the sun. This calculation thus shows in detail why at ordinary temperatures the vibrational motion of the hydrogen molecule makes no contribution to its specific heat.

In principle, this entire calculation can be repeated for the rotational energy levels. Because the degeneracy is different for different levels and because the energy states are expressed in terms of the square of a quantum number, the sums cannot be evaluated exactly and approximations must be made. Similar calculations may be carried out for polyatomic molecules having several different modes of vibration. The *total* specific heat, which ordinarily is the only quantity which can be measured directly, is always the sum of the translational, vibrational, and rotational contributions. In general these involve several different functions of temperature, and the various vibrational and rotational degrees of freedom begin to make significant contributions to the specific heat each at a different temperature. In all cases, it is possible to establish the relationship between molecular energy levels determined from molecular spectroscopy and the resulting temperature dependence of specific heats.

Similar considerations can be applied to calculating the specific heats of *solids*. For a solid, there is usually no energy corresponding to the rotational kinetic energy of a molecule but, instead, a large number of *vibrational* modes corresponding to various vibrations of the crystal lattice. For metals, there is an additional contribution to the specific heat resulting from closely spaced *electron* energy levels, and so electrons as well as nuclear motion contribute to the specific heat. For this reason, we postpone a detailed discussion of the quantum theory of specific heats of solids until Sec. 14-2. Meanwhile, we shall develop in the next section some statistical considerations which are fundamental to the understanding of the behavior of materials in the solid state.

13-6   QUANTUM STATISTICS

In this section we shall consider the modifications that must be made in the statistical description of states of a system when the components are not molecules but *electrons*. This development is essential in understanding the properties of solids, which, as will be shown in Chap. 14, are intimately connected with electron energy distribution in a solid. Thermal and electrical conductivity, magnetic properties, specific heats, and a number of other properties of solid materials are directly related to the electron energy states, and so it is essential to be able to describe quantitatively the distribution of electrons in these states.

The correct distribution function for electrons differs from the Maxwell-Boltzmann distribution in two important and closely related respects. First, electrons are governed by the *exclusion principle*; no quantum state may be occupied by more than one electron. In the Maxwell-Boltzmann case, conversely, the molecules are treated as independent entities, and there are no restrictions as to how many particles can occupy a given state.

Second, in the Maxwell-Boltzmann case we have assumed implicitly that the various molecules, although identical, can be *distinguished* from each other; that is, that in principle it is possible to *label* the molecules number 1, number 2, and so on. Thus a micro state in which molecule number 1 is in one energy state and number 2 in another is counted as distinct from the micro state in which they are reversed, even though the two molecules are identical. A quantum-mechanical description of a state containing several electrons does *not* distinguish among the particles in this way. The exclusion principle requires, to be sure, that the wave function be antisymmetric with respect to interchange of any two electrons, but quantum mechanics provides no basis on which to identify individual electrons in a given state, since *they are not in principle distinguishable*.

The distribution function that results from these two considerations differs in some important respects from the Maxwell-Boltzmann distribution. In honor of its discoverers, it is called the *Fermi-Dirac* distribution function. To develop this distribution, we retrace our path through the derivation of the Maxwell-Boltzmann distribution, making modifications where necessary. Again we consider a set of energy levels ε_i with degeneracies g_i. That is, level ε_i can accommodate g_i electrons without violating the exclusion principle. We assume equal probability of micro states, count the number of micro states corresponding to a given macro state, and find the most probable macro state. Because of the fundamental indistinguishability of electrons, however, the definition of a micro state and the procedure of counting micro states have to be revised carefully. We can no longer state that a certain specific particle is in a particular state with energy ε_i; the most detailed description that is possible *in principle* is to specify *how many* electrons (always zero or one) are in each of the g_i states of energy ε_i but not *which* electrons they are, since that question now has no meaning.

A micro state is now specified by specifying which of the g_i states corresponding to each energy ε_i are occupied by electrons; this is the most detailed possible description of the state of the system. A macro state is specified by the number n_i of electrons in each energy ε_i, without regard for *which* of the degenerate states with this energy are occupied. Thus the distinction between micro and macro states lies in the selection of the various levels with a given energy ε_i, and the number of micro states in a given macro state is determined by counting for each energy level the number of different ways n_i particles can be placed in the g_i states with energy ε_i.

If the electrons were distinguishable, this would be easy. The first particle could be placed in any one of the g_i states. For each of these choices there would be a choice of $g_i - 1$ for the second particle; for each of these, $g_i - 2$ for the third, and so on, to $g_i - (n_i - 1)$ for the last. The total number of possible ways of placing these n_i particles in the g_i states would be the product of all these factors, which is

$$g_i(g_i - 1)(g_i - 2) \cdots (g_i - n_i + 2)(g_i - n_i + 1) = \frac{g_i!}{(g_i - n_i)!} \quad (13\text{-}74)$$

But now, since the particles are, in principle, indistinguishable, permuting the n_i particles among the various states does not produce a physically different state of the system. We have *overcounted* the number of possibilities by a factor of the number of permutations of n_i particles, which is $n_i!$ and the number of P_i of physically different ways of putting n_i particles into g_i states of energy ε_i is not Eq. (13-74) but rather

$$P_i = \frac{g_i!}{(g_i - n_i)! n_i!} \quad (13\text{-}75)$$

For those familiar with combinatorial analysis, we point out that what we have done is to compute the number of *combinations* of g_i things taken n_i at a time, in this case, the number of different ways a group of n_i states can be selected from a larger group g_i.

Each macro state is characterized by a set of numbers $(n_1, n_2, \ldots)$, and the number of micro states corresponding to a given macro state is obtained by multiplying the factors P_i given by Eq. (13-75) for all the energies. That is, the number P of micro states corresponding to the macro state specified by the set of numbers n_i is

$$P = P_1 P_2 P_3 \cdots = \frac{g_1! g_2! \cdots}{(g_1 - n_1)!(g_2 - n_2)! \cdots n_1! n_2! \cdots} \tag{13-76}$$

We now assume again that all the micro states corresponding to a given total energy are equally likely. Again because of Eq. (13-76), the macro states are *not* all equally likely, and the most probable macro state, which is also the most probable state of the actual system, is found by maximizing Eq. (13-76). The resulting macro state is the best estimate we can make of the actual state of the system. Just as before, it turns out that a group of closely related macro states are so very much more likely than all the others that we are justified in asserting that these represent *the* state of the system.

Maximizing P is equivalent to maximizing $\ln P$, which is

$$\ln P = \sum_i \ln g_i! - \sum_i \ln (g_i - n_i)! - \sum_i n_i!$$

$$= \sum_i [g_i \ln g_i - g_i - (g_i - n_i) \ln (g_i - n_i) + (g_i - n_i)$$

$$- n_i \ln n_i + n_i] \tag{13-77}$$

where we have again used Stirling's approximation. To maximize this quantity, subject to the two subsidiary conditions $\Sigma n_i = N$ and $\Sigma n_i \varepsilon_i = E$, we again take the derivative with respect to each n_i of the quantity

$$\ln P - \alpha \left(\sum_i n_i - N \right) - \beta \left(\sum_i n_i \varepsilon_i - E \right) \tag{13-78}$$

and set each derivative equal to zero. Carrying out this operation,

$$\ln (g_i - n_i) - \ln n_i - \alpha - \beta \varepsilon_i = 0 \tag{13-79}$$

or

$$\ln \frac{g_i - n_i}{n_i} = \alpha + \beta \varepsilon_i \tag{13-80}$$

Rearranging this and solving for n_i,

$$n_i = \frac{g_i}{e^{\alpha + \beta \varepsilon_i} + 1} \tag{13-81}$$

which is the general form of the Fermi-Dirac distribution.

An argument similar to that used with the Maxwell-Boltzmann distribution can be used to show that the constant β is again related to the temperature of the system by $\beta = 1/kT$. The value of the constant α must again be chosen to satisfy the condition $\Sigma n_i = N$. It is customary to express α in terms of another constant ε_f, as follows:

$$\alpha = -\frac{\varepsilon_f}{kT} \tag{13-82}$$

Since α is a dimensionless quantity, ε_f has units of energy; it is called the *Fermi energy* for the distribution. With this notation, the Fermi-Dirac distribution function becomes

$$n_i = \frac{g_i}{e^{\beta(\varepsilon_i - \varepsilon_f)} + 1} \tag{13-83}$$

It is instructive to compare the general behavior of this function with that of the Maxwell-Boltzmann distribution. For simplicity, we consider only a system in which the energy levels are nondegenerate, so that all the g_i are unity. In this case, the n_i are always numbers between zero and unity, and each n_i represents the probability that the nondegenerate state ε_i is occupied, sometimes called the *occupation index* for the state. For very low temperature (large β), the exponent is a large *positive* quantity when ε_i is even slightly greater than ε_f; the denominator of the fraction is then very large, resulting in a value of n_i close to zero. When ε_i is slightly *less* than ε_f, the exponent is a large *negative* number, the exponential is near zero, and n_i is close to unity. The general shape of the function n_i is shown in Fig. 13-7. At successively higher temperatures, the function drops less rapidly from values near unity to values near zero, as ε_i passes the Fermi energy ε_f. Conversely, in the limit of extremely low temperatures, the function has nearly square corners.

Fig. 13-7 Fermi-Dirac distribution function. At very low temperatures, all states below ε_f are occupied, and all those above ε_f are unoccupied. At higher temperatures the break becomes less sharp as more of the states above ε_f become occupied.

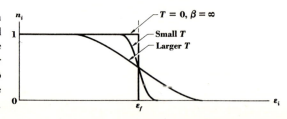

This behavior is in sharp contrast to that of the Maxwell-Boltzmann distribution and is a direct result of the exclusion principle. Without the exclusion principle, at very low temperatures nearly all the electrons would drop into the lowest energy states, but the exclusion principle prevents this. Instead, the lowest energy states are filled up successively, to whatever energy level is necessary to accommodate all the electrons, and from there on all energy states are empty. We also see that, at *any* temperature, ε_f represents the energy for which $n_i = \frac{1}{2}$.

It should be pointed out that ε_f is not a universal constant for any system but is a function of temperature. At very low temperatures, as we have seen, it is the highest energy state that is occupied; at extremely high temperatures, ε_f usually becomes large and negative. In this case, the exponent is always a fairly large positive number, and the exponential function in the denominator is much larger than unity. Thus in the high-temperature limit Eq. (13-83) becomes approximately

$$n_i = \frac{g_i}{e^{\beta(\varepsilon_i - \varepsilon_f)}} = e^{\beta \varepsilon_f} g_i e^{-\beta \varepsilon_i} \tag{13-84}$$

which is the Maxwell-Boltzmann distribution. In this case, we note further that all the n_i are numbers much smaller than unity. That is, in the high-temperature limit, electrons occupy energy levels sufficiently high so that the probability of occupation of even the lowest levels is considerably less than unity. In this limit the exclusion principle and the indistinguishability of particles become irrelevant and the function becomes identical with the Maxwell-Boltzmann form.

The discussion of this section has been confined entirely to a statistical description of indistinguishable particles which obey the exclusion principle. There are other particles which, although indistinguishable in a quantum-mechanical sense, do *not* obey the exclusion principle. It has been found, in fact, that all particles with a spin angular momentum that is a *half-integer* multiple of $\hbar$ obey the exclusion principle and hence are governed by the Fermi-Dirac distribution function. Conversely, all particles with spin angular momentum zero or an *integer* multiple of $\hbar$ are immune to the exclusion principle. The distribution function appropriate for these particles, which takes into account their indistinguishability, is called the *Bose-Einstein distribution function*. Rather surprisingly, it has exactly the same functional form as the Fermi-Dirac distribution except that the term $+1$ in the denominator becomes -1. Examples of particles obeying this distribution are photons and the various mesons. These particles are often collectively called *bosons*, with reference to this statistical behavior. Conversely, particles with half-integer intrinsic angular momentum, obeying the exclusion principle and the Fermi-Dirac distribution function, are called *fermions*. We shall return to this important distinction between classes of particles in Chap. 16.

Problems

13-1 Calculate the density of nitrogen at standard temperature and pressure.

13-2 Show that the density of an ideal gas is given by PM/RT, where M is the molecular mass.

13-3 What pressure would be necessary to compress air to a density equal to that of water, at a temperature of $0°C$, if it behaves as an ideal gas? Is it likely that its behavior under these conditions *is* described accurately by the ideal-gas equation? Explain.

13-4 For a mixture of gases, show that the total pressure is equal to the sum of the pressures which the separate gases would exert if each were in the container alone. These are called the *partial pressures* of the gases comprised in the mixture.

13-5 If the speeds of 10 molecules in a gas are 1, 1, 2, 2, 2, 3, 3, 4, 6, and 10 m/s, find the average and root-mean-square speeds.

13-6 Experiment shows that the dimensions of an oxygen molecule are of the order of 2×10^{-10} m. Make a rough estimate of the pressure at which the gas would exhibit noticeable deviations from ideal-gas behavior, as a result of the finite size of the molecules, at ordinary temperatures ($T = 300$ K).

13-7 For nitrogen at standard temperature and pressure, calculate the average number of molecules that collide with a 1-cm^2 area of the container wall in 1 s.

13-8 A machine is built which fires hard steel ball bearings at a steel plate. Each ball has a mass of 0.01 kg and is fired perpendicular to the plate with a speed of 50 m/s. If five balls are fired per second, and if the collisions are elastic, find the average force exerted on the plate.

13-9 A number of hard particles move between two parallel flat rigid walls a distance d apart. All collisions are perfectly elastic; all particles have speed v and always move perpendicular to the walls. There are N particles in all, each having mass m.
   a   What average force is exerted on each wall? What average pressure?
   b   If the kinetic energy of each particle is equal to $kT/2$, calculate the specific heat of the system.
   c   How does the pressure vary with temperature for this system?

13-10 Consider a gas consisting of N molecules confined in a cubical box with sides of length l whose edges are parallel to the x, y, and z axes. Suppose that one-third of the molecules move parallel to each coordinate axis and none in any other direction. Furthermore, suppose that as many are moving in the $+x$ direction at any instant as in the $-x$ direction, that collisions with the wall are perfectly elastic, and that all molecules have the same speed v.
   a   Calculate the pressure on any wall.
   b   If the kinetic energy of a molecule is $\frac{3}{2}kT$, derive a relationship between P, V, and T for this peculiar gas.

13-11 Find the root-mean-square speeds of:

    a   Oxygen molecules at $20°C$

    b   Helium atoms at $20°C$

    c   Helium atoms at 1 K

13-12 Smoke particles in the air typically have masses of the order of 10^{-17} to 10^{-15} kg. The motion of these particles resulting from collisions with air molecules, readily observed with a microscope, is called *brownian motion*. Find the root-mean-square speed of brownian motion for a particle of mass 10^{-16} kg in air at 300 K. Is the speed the same or different if the smoke particle is in hydrogen gas at the same temperature? Explain.

13-13 The best vacuum (lowest pressure) which can be attained in the laboratory is of the order of 10^{-10} mmHg, or about 10^{-13} atm. At this pressure and room temperature (about 300 K), how many molecules are present in a volume of 1 cm^3?

13-14 The sun contains a large quantity of hydrogen. The temperature at its surface is about 6000 K. What is the root-mean square speed of hydrogen molecules near the surface?

13-15 Find the approximate fraction of the molecules in a gas which have speeds between v_{rms} and $1.1v_{rms}$. Does this fraction depend on temperature? Explain.

13-16 A certain fictitious gas has the following distribution of molecular speeds: $f(v) = Av$ if v is between zero and v_m, and $f(v) = 0$ if v is larger than v_m, where A and v_m are constants.

    a   How must the constants A and v_m be related in order for Eq. (13-20) to be satisfied? Express A in terms of v_m.

    b   Calculate v_{av} and v_{rms} in terms of v_m. Also find the most probable speed v_0. Are these quantities related in the same way as in the Maxwell-Boltzmann distribution? Should they be?

    c   Is Eq. (13-17) correct for this distribution? Explain.

    d   What fraction of the molecules have speeds greater than $\frac{1}{2}v_m$?

13-17 Approximately what fraction of the molecules in an ideal gas have translational kinetic energy less than $0.1kT$? Hint: In the Maxwell-Boltzmann function, when mv^2 is much smaller than kT, the exponential factor is very close to unity and may be omitted.

13-18 Derive Eq. (13-56) for the Maxwell-Boltzmann distribution in terms of v, from Eq. (13-53).

13-19 The gas that leaks into a vacuum system almost always contains a larger fraction of hydrogen and helium than that found in the outside atmosphere. How can this observation be understood on the basis of kinetic energy?

13-20 Derive from Eq. (13-56) expressions for the *average* speed v_{av} and *root-mean-square* speed v_{rms} of molecules in an ideal gas.

13-21 For a gas obeying the Maxwell-Boltzmann distribution, find the *most probable* molecular speed, and show that a molecule having this speed has a kinetic energy equal to kT.

13-22 For a gas governed by the Maxwell-Boltzmann distribution, find the average translational kinetic energy of molecules by integrating Eq. (13-22), using the function given by Eq. (13-23). The following integral, will be useful:

$$\int_0^\infty v^4 e^{-v^2/b^2} \, dv = \frac{3\sqrt{\pi}}{8} b^5$$

Compare your result with the prediction of the equipartition theorem.

13-23 Are relativistic corrections to the masses of gas molecules significant at ordinary temperatures? At approximately what temperature do they become significant? Does this temperature depend on the molecular mass?

13-24 List all the possible micro states for six particles in two energy states. Also list all the macro states, and count the number of micro states for each macro state. If all micro states are equally likely, find the probability for each macro state.

13-25 For molecules obeying the Maxwell-Boltzmann distribution, show that the number n_1 of molecules in a nondegenerate energy state ε_1 is related to the number n_2 in another state ε_2 by

$$\frac{n_1}{n_2} = e^{-(\varepsilon_1 - \varepsilon_2)/kT}$$

13-26 Using the result of Prob. 13-25, calculate the approximate temperature at which 1 percent of a gas of hydrogen atoms are in the $n = 2$ state, assuming most are in the $n = 1$ state.

13-27 At what temperature does kT equal 1 eV?

13-28 A certain mixture of diatomic gases contains n_1 mol of a gas with molecular mass M_1 and n_2 mol of a gas with molecular mass M_2. Compute the molar specific heat and the specific heat per unit mass for the mixture.

13-29 Compute the specific heat (per unit mass) of hydrogen gas. How does this compare with the specific heats of familiar solid and liquid materials?

13-30 How can one understand qualitatively the large molar specific heat of diethyl ether, $(C_2H_5)_2O$, given in Table 13-2?

13-31 At standard temperature and pressure, sulfur dioxide, SO_2, has a molar specific heat of about 31.4 J/K. How can this value be understood on the basis of kinetic theory?

13-32 For the HCl molecule, a transition in vibrational energy level corresponding to $\Delta n - -1$ results in the emission of a photon with a wavelength of 3.5×10^{-6} m. From this information, calculate the approximate fraction of HCl molecules that are in the $n = 1$ state at $T = 300$ K.

13-33 Suppose that the two nuclei in an oxygen molecule are separated by 2×10^{-10} m.

    a   Compute the moment of inertia of the molecule about an axis through the midpoint of the line joining the two nuclei, and perpendicular to it.

    b   At $T = 300$ K, if an oxygen molecule has a rotational kinetic energy equal to kT, what is its quantum state; i.e., what is the value of the rotational quantum number l?

13-34 Estimate the temperature at which rotational kinetic energy begins to make a significant contribution to the specific heat of diatomic oxygen, assuming it is in the gaseous state at this temperature. Is this latter assumption realistic?

13-35 The rotational energy levels of a diatomic molecule are given by $E = E_0 l(l + 1)$, where E_0 is a constant characteristic of the molecule and $l = 0, 1, 2, \ldots$. In transitions between rotational levels in which a photon is absorbed, the selection rule $\Delta l = \pm 1$ is obeyed. If $E_0 = 0.01$ eV, estimate the relative intensities of the $2 \rightarrow 1$ and $1 \rightarrow 0$ spectrum lines for a gas at $T = 300$ K by calculating the relative populations of the various states.

13-36 For a gas of diatomic molecules, the rotational energy begins to contribute significantly to the specific heat at a certain temperature T. How does T depend on the molecular mass, assuming all diatomic molecules have more or less the same dimensions?

13-37 Derive Eq. (13-73) for vibrational specific heat from Eq. (13-71). Verify that in the limit as $T \rightarrow \infty$, it approaches k, and that as $T \rightarrow 0$, it approaches zero.

13-38 Write an expression for the *total* molar specific heat of a diatomic gas if all contributions except that of the vibrational energy are given by the equipartition theorem.

13-39 For a gas whose molecules have energy levels ε_i with degeneracies g_i we may define a function $Z(\beta)$ called the *partition function*:

$$Z(\beta) = \sum_i g_i e^{-\beta \varepsilon_i}$$

    a   Show that the normalization constant A for the Maxwell-Boltzmann distribution is given by $A = N/Z$.

    b   Show that the average energy per molecule is given by

$$\varepsilon_{av} = -\frac{\partial}{\partial \beta} \ln Z(\beta)$$

13-40 Show that the specific heat of a system (per molecule) can be expressed in terms of the partition function Z defined in Prob. 13-39 as follows:

$$C = T \frac{d^2(kT \ln Z)}{dT^2}$$

13-41 Suppose N electrons are placed in a one-dimensional box as discussed in Sec. 10-2.

    a   Assuming the electrons obey the exclusion principle, find the highest-energy state which is occupied at temperature $T = 0$.

    b   Find the Fermi energy at temperature $T = 0$.

    c   Find the average electron energy at temperature $T = 0$. The sum of the squares of the first N integers is $N(N + 1)(2N + 1)/6$. This may be useful.

13-42 Consider a fictitious quantum-mechanical system having equally spaced energy levels, 1 eV apart, starting with $E = 0$. Suppose three indistinguishable particles obeying the exclusion principle (one particle per level) and having a total energy of 12 eV, are placed in these levels.

    a   List the possible micro states of the system.

    b   Assuming all the micro states are equally likely, find the probability that the 0-eV state is occupied; the 2-eV state; the 4-eV state; the 6-eV state.

13-43 Using the Fermi-Dirac distribution, find the probability that a state is occupied if its energy is higher than ε_f by $0.1kT$, $1kT$, $2kT$, and $10kT$.

13-44 Show that for a system governed by the Fermi-Dirac distribution, the probability of occupation of a state with energy higher than ε_f by an amount $\Delta\varepsilon$ is equal to the probability that a state with energy lower than ε_f by the same amount is *unoccupied*.

PERSPECTIVE IV

The three preceding chapters have been concerned with applications of the basic principles of quantum mechanics to various systems of fundamental importance in the microscopic structure of matter. It was shown that the Schrödinger equation can be solved exactly for the hydrogen atom to yield the energy levels and wave functions for the single electron in this atom. Next it was shown how the same principles can be used for an approximate analysis of systems containing several electrons in an atom and for those containing several atoms in a molecule, bound by the interaction associated with the electron configurations of the atoms. Then we discussed the statistical methods that can be used for the analysis of a system consisting of a large number of identical components, which may be electrons, atoms, or molecules.

In the final three chapters we turn first to a discussion of matter in the solid state. In a solid there are strong interactions between the constituent atoms, and it is reasonable to think of a solid as essentially a molecule containing a very large number of atoms. In discussing solids, the central theme is the relation of macroscopic properties, including mechanical, thermal, electrical, and optical properties, to the microscopic structure of the material in terms of atomic and electronic configurations.

Because a solid ordinarily contains a very large number of atoms, a detailed analysis of such a system is much more difficult than for a simple system such as a hydrogen atom. Nevertheless, simple applications of the principles of quantum mechanics still lead to considerable insight into the behavior of solids. In all cases, it is found that the electron configurations in solids provide the key to the understanding and analysis of their macroscopic behavior.

Next we look inside the atomic nucleus, which we have treated up until now as a fixed, unchanging structure within each atom. Atomic nuclei are not rigid and unchangeable, as was once thought; there are reactions in which the internal structure of a nucleus is rearranged in a manner analogous to the rearrangement of atoms in molecules during chemical reactions. These so-called nuclear reactions were discovered much later than chemical reactions because of the much higher energies involved.

It is found that the interactions responsible for holding together the constituent parts of nuclei cannot be understood on the basis of known electromagnetic and gravitational interactions but that an interaction of a new and different character must be involved. As a result, there are some important differences between the internal structure of nuclei and the overall structure of atoms themselves, although it is believed that the same basic principles are applicable to both.

Finally, we bring this volume to a close with a brief discussion of what are believed to be the most basic building blocks of matter, the fundamental particles. Beginning with the few particles which constitute matter in its familiar forms, we then discuss the characteristics of the various unstable particles, many of which have been discovered only in the past 25 years. We examine various schemes for classifying these particles and their inter-actions and then conclude with some indication that there are still many unanswered questions in the area of fundamental particles.

The Solid State | 14

The concepts of quantum mechanics, particularly those of molecular binding and the associated electron distributions, are applied to a study of the behavior of systems consisting of a very large number of atoms or molecules bound in a solid structure. The structure of crystals is analyzed in terms of the kinds of bonds they contain, and the specific heats of these systems are discussed. The relation of thermal and electrical conductivity to electron motion and the electronic basis of paramagnetism are discussed. Finally, the band theory of solids is presented, along with applications to the properties of semiconductors and their uses in practical circuit devices.

14-1 STRUCTURE OF SOLIDS

The discussion of the structure and behavior of atoms and molecules in the three preceding chapters has treated an individual atom or molecule as an isolated system. This assumption is characteristic of the *gaseous* state of matter, in which ordinarily the average distance between molecules is very much greater than the dimensions of the molecules themselves. Then interactions between molecules can be neglected or at least are small enough to permit approximate treatment, such as the van der Waals corrections to the ideal-gas equation of state.

At ordinary temperature and pressure, however, the great majority of chemical elements and compounds are in the *solid* state. This is a condensed state of matter in which the separation between atoms is of the same order of magnitude as the dimensions of the electron cloud surrounding each nucleus. Thus atoms of a solid are *not* independent entities; interactions between atoms are of fundamental importance in determining the structure and properties of the material.

As observed in Sec. 6-1, solids frequently have an orderly arrangement of atoms comprising a repeated pattern which extends over many atoms. Any solid having such a recurring pattern is said to be *crystalline*, and the pattern itself is called the *crystal structure* of the solid. The high degree of orderliness in the structure of solids permits simplifications in calculations of properties of solids which would not be possible without this recurring pattern. This situation may be compared with the kinetic theory of gases, in which the complete *lack* of orderliness permits calculations based on a statistical description. The structure of liquids lies between these two extremes, having some correlation between the positions of atoms but no *long-range* order such as is found in crystalline solids.

The forces that bind atoms in crystalline solids in more or less fixed positions in the crystal lattice are exactly the same in nature as the forces responsible for molecular binding, namely, the electrical interaction of atomic electrons and nuclei. In fact, there is no essential difference between such a crystal and a large molecule. As in molecular binding, various types of bonding, such as ionic or covalent bonds, are found in crystals, depending on the electron configuration of the atoms involved. There is another type, the metallic bond, which has no direct analog in molecular structure but is usually the most important effect in metallic crystals.

The simplest crystal structure to understand is that of an *ionic* crystal. The most common examples are the structures of the *alkali halides* (compounds of an alkali metal with a halogen), of which the most familiar is ordinary salt, sodium chloride. X-ray diffraction experiments show that the crystal structure of salt is a cubic lattice, with the sodium and chlorine ions occupying alternate positions in the lattice, as shown in Fig. 14-1.

It is instructive to examine the energy relationships that make such a structure stable. We consider first a fictitious *one-dimensional* crystal lattice

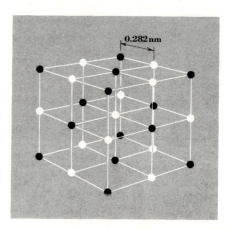

Fig. 14-1 Face-centered cubic crystal structure of sodium chloride. Black circles represent sodium ions; white circles, chlorine ions. This structure is called face-centered cubic (fcc) because eight sodium ions determine a cube, and there is an additional sodium ion at the center of each cube face. An identical position relationship holds for the chlorine ions.

0.282 nm

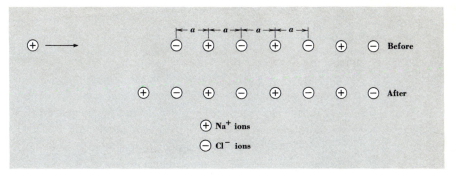

Fig. 14-2 Fictitious one-dimensional crystal lattice of sodium chloride, used to analyze the stability of the lattice. The change in energy resulting from adding a positive ion to the left end of the chain is calculated in the text.

consisting of a row of alternating sodium and chlorine ions with equal spacings, as shown in Fig. 14-2. We consider the change in potential energy of the system when one positive (sodium) ion is added to an end of the chain. The potential energy of this additional ion is defined as zero when it is very far from the chain. If the added ion is *positive*, its nearest neighbor is negative, and the attractive force results in an additional negative potential energy

$$V = -\frac{e^2}{4\pi\varepsilon_0}\frac{1}{a} \tag{14-1}$$

where a is the distance between adjacent ions, as in Fig. 14-2. The *second* atom in the chain, a *positive* ion, exerts a repulsive force on the added ion, with a corresponding *positive* potential energy

$$V = +\frac{e^2}{4\pi\varepsilon_0}\frac{1}{2a} \tag{14-2}$$

corresponding to its distance $(2a)$ from the added ion. Proceeding similarly down the line, we find that the *total* energy is

$$V = -\frac{e^2}{4\pi\varepsilon_0 a}(1 - \tfrac{1}{2} + \tfrac{1}{3} - \tfrac{1}{4} + \cdots) \tag{14-3}$$

If the chain is very long, we can approximate the quantity in parentheses as an *infinite* sum and evaluate it by reference to the power-series expansion for the function $\ln(1 + x)$, which is

$$\ln(1 + x) = x - \frac{x^2}{2} + \frac{x^3}{3} - \frac{x^4}{4} + \cdots \tag{14-4}$$

Evaluating this series for $x = 1$, we find that the quantity in parentheses is equal to ln 2, and the *total* interaction energy is

$$V = -\frac{e^2 \ln 2}{4\pi\varepsilon_0 a} \tag{14-5}$$

The fact that this quantity is negative indicates that the configuration with the added ion attached to the end of the chain is energetically more favorable (a state of lower energy) than the state in which it is separated. Generalizing, the state in which a large number of atoms are linked together in a chain has lower energy than the state in which they are all separated.

The same argument may be used to show that a series of such chains lying side by side with alternate ions adjacent has a lower energy than a state in which the same chains are separated by great distances. If there are several *planes* made of such rows of chains, the state in which these planes are stacked up with alternate ions adjacent has lower energy than the state where they are separated. Hence an extension of the simple chain argument shows that the three-dimensional crystal lattice is a state with lower energy than a state in which the same ions are all separated by great distances. When this energy difference is greater than the energy expended in creating the ions initially, the structure is stable.

As observed in Sec. 12-4, the electron configurations of the ions are both spherically symmetric filled-shell configurations, and the bonds are not *directional*. Thus the nature of the bond itself gives no information as to why the ions should fall into the *cubic* arrangement rather than other possible arrangements. The structure is determined by energy considerations; the atoms always tend to arrange themselves in a minimum-energy configuration whose details depend on the relative sizes of the ions. Each ion exerts attractive electrostatic forces on ions of opposite charge, and in the minimum-energy arrangement each ion is surrounded by several *nearest-neighbor* ions of opposite charge. The details of the arrangement are determined by the *number* of nearest neighbors that can be fitted around the smaller of the two ions with little enough overlap of wave functions to avoid violating the exclusion principle. In the present example, the Na^+ ion is considerably *smaller* than the Cl^- ion because its last filled shell is the $2p$ shell, while the Cl^- ion has filled $3s$ and $3p$ shells.

In visualizing ion arrangements, it is useful to think of each ion as a hard sphere whose radius approximates that of the electron charge cloud. One conceivable arrangement is for each sodium ion to be surrounded by four nearest-neighbor chlorine ions at the corners of a regular tetrahedron with the sodium ion at the center. If the radius of the chlorine ions is a, then a simple geometrical calculation (which is left as a problem) shows that the sodium ion can touch all four chlorine ions only if its radius r is at least equal to

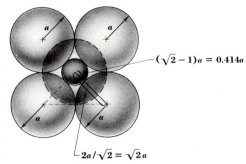

Fig. 14-3 A sphere (representing an ion in an ionic crystal) just touches six nearest neighbors, four with their centers in the same plane as the central sphere (the plane of the figure) and one each above and below, when its radius is 0.414 that of the neighbor spheres.

$$r = \left(\sqrt{3/2} - 1 \right) a = 0.225a \tag{14-6}$$

Another scheme, illustrated in Fig. 14-3, would place *six* nearest neighbors at the corners of an octahedron; in this configuration, the central ion can touch all its nearest neighbors only if its radius is at least

$$r = \left(\sqrt{2} - 1 \right) a = 0.414a \tag{14-7}$$

This leads to the face-centered cubic lattice of Fig. 14-1. Still another arrangement consists of *eight* nearest neighbors at the corners of a cube; the central ion can touch all eight if its radius is at least

$$r = \left(\sqrt{3} - 1 \right) a = 0.732a \tag{14-8}$$

This configuration leads to the *simple cubic* structure shown in Fig. 14-4.

The actual structure of sodium chloride as revealed by x-ray diffraction is the face-centered cubic lattice shown in Figs. 14-1 and 14-3, in which

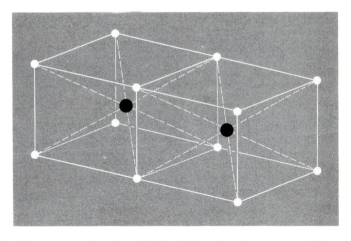

Fig. 14-4 Simple cubic structure of cesium chloride. Each cesium ion, represented by a black circle, has eight nearest-neighbor chlorine ions, represented by white circles. Ions of each type form a simple cubic lattice.

each ion has six nearest neighbors. The same situation is found in nearly all the other alkali halide crystals, and in all cases the reason is the small size of the alkali metal ion compared with the halogen ion. The only exceptions are the salts of cesium, whose ion is nearly the critical size given by Eq. (14-7). Thus the cesium ion can accommodate eight nearest neighbors rather than six, resulting in the simple cubic structure shown in Fig. 14-4. In CsF, the situation is just the reverse of that for NaCl; the F^- ion is considerably *smaller* than the Cs^+ ion, and again the structure is face-centered cubic.

Equation (14-5) can be used to estimate the binding energy of an ion in a crystal lattice. X-ray diffraction data show that the spacing between adjacent atoms in a crystal of NaCl is about 0.28 nm. The associated energy is

$$\frac{e^2 \ln 2}{4\pi\varepsilon_0 a} = \frac{(1.60 \times 10^{-19} \text{ C})^2 (9 \times 10^9 \text{ N} \cdot \text{m}^2/\text{C}^2)(0.693)}{2.8 \times 10^{-10} \text{ m}}$$
$$= 5.7 \times 10^{-19} \text{ J} = 3.6 \text{ eV} \tag{14-9}$$

This energy includes only the interaction of an ion with other ions along a single straight line in the lattice. The effects of other ions, though not negligible, are expected to be less than this because of their greater distance. Therefore as a rough guess we expect the binding energy of a single ion to be of the order of 5 eV.

This binding energy is related directly to the phenomenon of *melting*. At any temperature the ions have a statistical distribution of energy; the fraction having energies of 5 eV or above is, of course, an increasing function of temperature. The escape of these energetic ions is offset by ions in the liquid phase in contact with the crystal; these collide inelastically with it, losing energy and becoming bound to the lattice. The melting temperature is determined by the point at which these two competing processes proceed at equal rates, leading to a state of *phase equilibrium*. This equilibrium usually occurs at only one particular temperature, and so such solids usually have quite definite melting temperatures. A similar analysis can be made for boiling, and a relation between vapor pressure of a material and its temperature can be derived from statistical considerations.

In principle, ions in an ionic crystal can also be removed or displaced by an electric field, but the enormous field strength required is impossible to produce in practice. Thus under practical electric fields the ions are *not* displaced; correspondingly large fields would be required to remove individual electrons from ions because of the stability of the filled-shell configuration. Hence there are essentially no mobile charges in an ionic crystal, and the alkali halide crystals are *nonconductors* of electricity. But in a *molten* alkali halide the ions have considerable mobility, and molten alkali halides are good conductors of electricity. Similarly, an aqueous solution of an alkali halide is a good conductor, since the ions are separated from each other and can move readily through the solution.

In crystals having *covalent* bonds, unlike ionic crystals, the bonds are usually strongly directional in nature. As observed in Sec. 12-5, this directionality is associated with the shapes of the wave functions for electrons in the electron-pair covalent bonds. A simple example of a crystal formed by covalent bonding is the "diamond" structure, found in elements in group IV of the periodic table, including carbon, silicon, germanium, and tin. Each of these has four electrons in its outermost shell, and each tends to form four covalent bonds, one with each of four nearest neighbors. In the crystal structure of these elements, each atom has four nearest neighbors spaced symmetrically around it at the corners of a regular tetrahedron. Since all the electrons participate in the binding, none is particularly mobile, and we expect these materials to be poor conductors of electricity. This in fact is the case; the electrical properties of these materials classify them as semiconductors. The characteristics of semiconductors will be discussed in more detail in Sec. 14-6.

Covalent bonds are found in many solid organic compounds, where they play the same role as in organic molecules. A familiar example is polyethylene, in which long chains of hydrocarbon groups are held together by covalent bonds. Cross-links between chains are of a different type, to be discussed later.

An interesting difference in the behavior of ionic and covalent crystals is found in the dependence of the dielectric constant on frequency. As discussed in Sec. 6-4, the polarization of a dielectric material is in general frequency-dependent because of the inertial effects of the charged particles whose displacement provides the microscopic mechanism of polarization. In ionic crystals, motion of entire ions can contribute to the polarization but only at relatively low frequencies (e.g., less than 10^{12} Hz), because at higher frequencies the mass of an ion prevents any significant displacement in response to the rapidly varying electric field. Displacement of individual electrons is important as a mechanism of polarization at much higher frequencies, since the electron mass is much smaller than that of the ions. For example, the static dielectric constant of KCl is 4.7, while the dielectric constant at optical frequencies, given according to Eq. (6-16) by the square root of the index of refraction, is 2.1. Conversely, the dielectric constant of diamond, a covalent crystal, is 5.8 at both low frequencies and optical frequencies.

In *metallic* crystals a new feature appears, having no counterpart in molecular binding. In metallic crystals the valence electrons are not tightly bound to individual atoms; instead the electrons are better described as moving in the combined potential of an array of positive ions and hence are shared by the *entire crystal*. The reasons for this mobility of electrons will be discussed in more detail in Sec. 14-5; here we simply state that it exists and that it is chiefly responsible for the crystal structure of many metals. One may picture the crystal as an array of positive ions with the spaces between ions filled with a negatively charged fluid representing the total valence-electron distribution. This fluid, sometimes called the "electron gas," provides a useful model in discussing various physical properties of metallic crystals.

If enough electron gas can occupy the spaces between adjacent ions, the attraction of this gas for each ion can more than balance the repulsion between ions and lead to a state with lower potential energy than when the atoms of metal are separated. Thus there is reason to suspect that a stable solid structure may be possible. In addition, for reasons to be discussed in Sec. 14-5, the *kinetic* energies of the valence electrons are depressed by the binding to an extended array of ions rather than to individual ions. In some metals, particularly the transition metals with partially filled $3d$ shells, there is also some covalent binding involving $3d$ electrons as well as the above effects with the $4s$ valence electrons.

Metallic binding usually occurs only when the number of valence electrons is small, since when there are several valence electrons with overlapping wave functions, some are forced by the exclusion principle into higher energy states, making the metallic structure unstable. Thus the elements in groups I and II of the periodic table, and some in group III and the transition series, form metallic crystals. Elements in the middle groups (III, IV, and V) sometimes form metallic crystals, but in them covalent bonding becomes competitive. An interesting example is tin, which exists in two crystalline forms. Metallic (white) tin is stable above 13°C, while covalent (gray) tin, with its diamond crystal structure, is stable below 13°C.

In metallic crystals, electrons are shared not just between two neighbors but among *all* the atoms in the solid; valence-electron wave functions are no longer localized at individual atom sites. The bonding does not have the strongly directional character of covalent bonds, and as a result the atoms tend to come together to fill the available space as completely as possible. The crystal structure is thus determined by "close-packing" considerations.

It can be shown that when identical spheres are packed optimally into a certain volume, the fraction of the total volume occupied by the spheres is $\pi\sqrt{2}/6 = 0.74$. This ratio is called the *packing fraction*. The two arrangements which realize this optimum packing fraction are the face-centered cubic and the hexagonal close-packed lattices, both shown in Fig. 14-5. In both, each atom has 12 nearest neighbors. These are in fact the lattices found in most metallic solids. For comparison, we note that the packing fraction for the simple cubic lattice is $\pi/6 = 0.52$, for the body-centered cubic lattice $\pi\sqrt{3}/8 = 0.68$, and for the diamond lattice $\pi\sqrt{3}/16 = 0.34$.

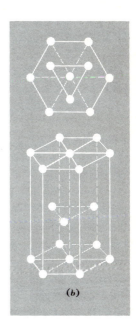

Fig. 14-5 (*a*) Face-centered cubic structure of a metallic element. Each atom has twelve nearest neighbors; for the atom in the center of the right face, there are four atoms at the corners of the face, and one each at the centers of the eight faces that adjoin this face at its edges. (*b*) Hexagonal close-packed structure. Again each atom has twelve nearest neighbors.

Two other bond types are found in solids. One of these, the *van der Waals force*, is associated with fluctuating electric-dipole moments in molecules. The resulting weak interaction is responsible for the structure of many organic solids and the solid phases of the inert gases. The other bond type is the *hydrogen bond*, in which a hydrogen atom in a molecule loses its electron to another atom, and the resulting proton is attracted to two molecules, forming a weak bond between them. In polyethylene and many other chain polymers, each chain is held together by covalent bonds, and hydrogen bonds form cross-links between chains.

The above discussion has regarded a crystal as a perfectly periodic structure. The concept of a "perfect crystal" is an abstraction; real crystals always have deviations from an ideal structure. One obvious reason is the fact that crystals have a finite extent; a crystal does not extend through all space but must have surfaces. The peculiarities of the electron configurations near the surface of a solid are responsible for phenomena such as contact potentials, rectifying surfaces, etc. Crystal lattices may also have *internal* defects such as *vacant* lattice sites where an atom is missing, *interstitial* atoms which are at positions other than normal lattice sites, and *impurity* atoms.

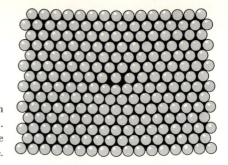

Fig. 14-6 Two-dimensional representation of one type of crystal-lattice dislocation. The pattern is seen best by viewing the page at a grazing angle.

There are also irregularities called *dislocations*, in which the periodic pattern of the crystal lattice is interrupted. A two-dimensional sketch illustrating a dislocation is shown in Fig. 14-6. Dislocations in metallic crystals have an important effect on their mechanical properties. The fact that some metals are *ductile* and can undergo considerable plastic deformation without fracture is due in large measure to the presence of dislocations which can move through the lattice during deformations.

The recurring structure of a crystal lattice can be used to analyze the behavior of its electrons and atoms and to understand the relationship between microscopic structure and such macroscopic properties as specific heats, thermal and electrical conductivities, elastic moduli, and electrical and magnetic properties. A detailed analysis of most of these properties requires the use of statistical techniques. The remainder of this chapter is concerned with understanding some of the macroscopic properties of crystalline solids on the basis of their microscopic structure.

In concluding this brief discussion, we remark that not all materials possessing the rigidity characteristic of solids have a definite crystal structure. A number of materials, most familiar of which is glass, exhibit a microscopic structure characterized by short-range correlations between atomic positions but without the long-range order characteristic of crystals. Such a structure is shown schematically in Fig. 14-7. These materials are said to be *amorphous*,

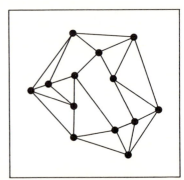

Fig. 14-7 Schematic diagram showing the arrangement of molecules in an amorphous solid. The circles represent molecules; the lines, the intermolecular forces. Intermolecular distances are expanded for clarity.

and their behavior exhibits important differences from that of crystals. They never have a definite melting point but rather undergo a continuous change of mechanical and other properties as the temperature is changed. Thus glass when heated gradually softens and becomes "tacky," rather than melting suddenly as do most metals. There is no phase transition, and no latent heat of fusion, associated with such a process. Thus amorphous solids are more closely related to very viscous liquids than to crystalline solids.

14-2 SPECIFIC HEATS

In this section we apply the above structural considerations, along with the statistical methods of Chap. 13, to the analysis of specific heats of solids. The rule of Dulong and Petit, an empirical rule based on measurement of specific heats of many solid elements, states that the molar specific heat of a solid element should *always* be about 25 J/mol · K. We shall see how this rule can be understood in terms of the microscopic basis of specific heat and under what circumstances departures from this rule should be expected.

In discussing the specific heats of *gases* in Sec. 13-5, we considered the contributions of translational, rotational, and vibrational motions; the specific heat of a *solid* material can be understood on a similar basis. In solids, atoms can vibrate about their equilibrium positions in the lattice. According to the equipartition theorem there should be, on an average, a kinetic energy $\frac{1}{2}kT$ per atom associated with motion in each of the three perpendicular directions, so that the average *total* kinetic energy per atom should be $\frac{3}{2}kT$. Furthermore, if the atoms are elastically bound by forces that obey Hooke's law, the motion is simple harmonic, and so the average *potential* energy is equal to the average kinetic energy.[1] Thus the average *total* energy per atom, including both kinetic and potential, should be $3kT$. The average energy per mole is $3RT$, and thus the molar specific heat should be

$$C = 3R = 3(8.314 \text{ J/mol} \cdot \text{K}) \cong 25 \text{ J/mol} \cdot \text{K} \qquad (14\text{-}10)$$

in agreement with the rule of Dulong and Petit.

Although this simple model accounts for the observed specific heats of solids in certain temperature ranges, it suffers from deficiencies similar to those of the corresponding theory for gases. It cannot account for the *temperature variation* of specific heats observed with many solids or for the fact that some measured specific heats are *larger* than predicted by the rule of Dulong and Petit. One source of these discrepancies is that the vibrational

[1] H. D. Young, "Fundamentals of Mechanics and Heat," 2d ed., sec. 19-5, McGraw-Hill Book Company, New York, 1974.

energy is *quantized*. The classical equipartition theorem holds only at temperatures sufficiently high so that kT is much larger than the spacing of adjacent energy levels; otherwise the average energy per atom is *less* than that predicted by the equipartition theorem.

The simplest model that takes this discreteness of vibrational energy into account assumes that each atom is elastically bound to its equilibrium position and executes simple harmonic motion with frequency ω about this equilibrium position. This motion can occur along any one of the three coordinate directions, and any superposition of such motions is also possible. The total energy is the same as that of three different oscillators with the same frequency moving in the three perpendicular coordinate directions. This is easily seen to be true in the classical case, where the total energy can be written

$$E = \tfrac{1}{2}m(v_x{}^2 + v_y{}^2 + v_z{}^2) + \tfrac{1}{2}k(x^2 + y^2 + z^2) \tag{14-11}$$

This can be separated into an energy associated with each of the three coordinate directions. A similar separation can be made in the quantum-mechanical treatment of the three-dimensional harmonic oscillator. Thus in this model the N atoms in a crystal are equivalent, as far as energy is concerned, to $3N$ harmonic oscillators, all with frequency ω.

Since each atom is bound to a definite crystal-lattice location, we regard the atoms as *distinguishable* particles; hence the Maxwell-Boltzmann distribution is the appropriate energy-distribution function. The number n_i of oscillators with energy ε_i is given, just as in Eq. (13-59), by

$$\begin{aligned} n_i &= Ae^{-\beta \varepsilon_i} \\ &= Ae^{-\beta(i+1/2)\varepsilon_0} \end{aligned} \tag{14-12}$$

where $\varepsilon_0 = \hbar\omega$, as previously, and the constant A is chosen to satisfy the condition

$$\sum_i n_i = 3N$$

We now see that this problem is really identical to that of the vibrational specific heat of a gas of diatomic molecules, discussed in Sec. 13-5, except that the number N is replaced by $3N$. Thus the average energy per atom is just three times that given by Eq. (13-71):

$$\varepsilon_{\text{av}} = \tfrac{3}{2}\varepsilon_0 \operatorname{ctnh} \frac{\varepsilon_0}{2kT} \tag{14-13}$$

The derivative of this quantity with respect to T is, as usual, the specific heat per atom. Replacing k by R gives the *molar* specific heat C; reference to Eq. (13-73) shows that this is

$$C = 3R \left[\frac{\varepsilon_0/2kT}{\sinh (\varepsilon_0/2kT)} \right]^2 \tag{14-14}$$

In the limit of large T, this approaches the value $3R$ predicted by the classical equipartition theorem, but at lower temperatures it deviates from this behavior in the same manner as shown in Fig. 13-6b.

The atoms *do not* actually vibrate independently with the same frequency; each vibrating atom exerts forces on its neighbors, and these forces *couple* the motions of adjacent atoms. A correct description of vibrational motion of atoms in a crystal lattice must take into account the fact that a lattice vibration is a *collective* phenomenon, involving *all* the atoms simultaneously. The motion can be described in terms of various *normal modes* which in general have different frequencies. More detailed analysis shows that for a crystal containing N atoms there are $3N$ normal modes with various frequencies and that the energy of each mode is quantized with the same energy levels as for a simple harmonic oscillator with the same frequency. The quanta of energy associated with normal-mode crystal-lattice vibrations are called *phonons*; there is a close analogy between these and *photons*, which are quanta of normal-mode electromagnetic-wave energy. The total energy can still be represented as the sum of energies of a large number of harmonic oscillators, but now with a *spectrum* of frequencies that depends on the lattice structure. This refinement permits a more precise calculation of lattice-vibration contributions to specific heats than does the single-frequency approximation.

We might also expect to find an additional temperature-dependent energy associated with *electron* energy levels, and a corresponding contribution to the specific heat. In *gases* the excitation of electron energy levels usually makes no noticeable contribution to specific heats at ordinary temperatures, since usually the energy levels are so much larger than kT that practically all the electrons are in the ground state. In the language of Sec. 13-5, the electronic degrees of freedom are "frozen out" at ordinary temperatures. The situation should be similar in ionic and covalent crystals, in which electrons are tightly bound in filled-shell ions or in shared-electron valence bonds. This prediction is borne out by experiment, which reveals no contribution to specific heats from electron excitation.

In *metallic* crystals the situation is somewhat different. As discussed in Sec. 14-1, the electrons in such a crystal behave in some respects like a gas of free or nearly free particles. Their energy levels are very closely spaced compared with kT at ordinary temperatures, unlike those of ionic or covalent crystals; hence electrons can gain or lose small amounts of energy readily. Thus we might expect each valence electron to have an average kinetic energy $\frac{3}{2}kT$ and contribute $\frac{3}{2}k$ to the specific heat. If there is one valence electron per atom, this means an additional specific heat of $\frac{3}{2}R$ per mole; if two, $3R$ per mole, and so on.

In fact, the measured values of specific heats of metals indicate that the contributions from electron energy are very much *smaller* than this. The resolution of this discrepancy provides an interesting application of the quantum-statistical methods developed in Sec. 13-6. We are dealing with electron energy states, and the appropriate distribution is not the Maxwell-Boltzmann but rather the Fermi-Dirac distribution, which takes into account the exclusion principle and the indistinguishability of identical particles.

The most striking consequence of the exclusion principle is that at absolute zero temperature the electrons do *not* all have zero energy, as the Maxwell-Boltzmann law would predict. Instead, they fill up the lowest available energy states, one electron in each state, up to a certain level ε_f called the *Fermi energy*. At $T = 0$ all states with energy less than ε_f are filled, and all those above ε_f are empty.

The crucial question in a specific-heat calculation is how the electron-energy distribution (and therefore the average electron energy) *changes* with temperature. This in turn depends critically on the magnitude of the Fermi energy. To understand the role of the Fermi energy, we suppose first that at ordinary temperatures ε_f is much *smaller* than kT. For example, at $T = 300$ K, kT has the value 0.0259 eV; let us suppose that $\varepsilon_f = 0.001$ eV. Then at 300 K the energy levels actually occupied are, on an average, much *higher* than those occupied at 0 K. That is, the electrons are distributed over many energy levels, the probability of occupation of any individual level is small, the exclusion principle becomes irrelevant, and the distribution approaches the classical Maxwell-Boltzmann distribution, with its associated average kinetic energy $\frac{3}{2}kT$.

Clearly, this does not happen; otherwise electron energy would make a large contribution to specific heats of metals. In actual metals the Fermi energy is typically of the order of 2 to 10 eV, an energy much *larger* than kT at ordinary temperatures. At ordinary temperatures most electron energies are much *larger* than kT and are determined almost entirely by the exclusion principle, hardly at all by the temperature. Correspondingly, the average *change* in electron energy per unit temperature change is small, and so the electron contribution to the specific heat is small.

The situation is shown graphically in Fig. 14-8, which shows the Fermi-Dirac distribution function at 0, 100, and 10,000 K corresponding to $\varepsilon_f = 5$ eV. As the figure shows, the function changes appreciably only in the vicinity of the Fermi energy (specifically, in a region within a few kT of the Fermi energy) as the temperature changes. But this energy range includes only a small fraction of the electrons; *most* of the electron energies do not change at all. Hence there is a correspondingly small contribution to specific heat.

This entire discussion can be made more quantitative. It would not be

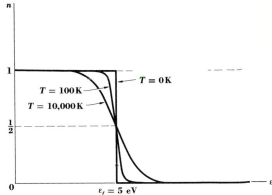

Fig. 14-8 Fermi-Dirac distribution corresponding to Fermi energy $\varepsilon_f = 5$ eV for several temperatures. The functions for different temperatures differ appreciably only in the small energy interval near ε_f.

appropriate to discuss all the details here, but we shall indicate how a more precise calculation can be made. First the degeneracy factor g in the Fermi-Dirac distribution must be found. Regarding electron energy ε as a continuous variable, we can find the number of quantum states in any energy interval $d\varepsilon$ by a calculation which is essentially a generalization to three dimensions of the particle-in-a-box problem of Sec. 10-2. Just as the energy levels for that problem depended on the size of the box, so in the three-dimensional analog they depend on the *volume* of the container. In the electron-gas model, which treats the electrons as free particles confined to the volume V of the crystal, the number of energy levels in the interval $d\varepsilon$ is found to be

$$g(\varepsilon)\, d\varepsilon = \frac{V}{2\pi^2}\left(\frac{2m}{\hbar^2}\right)^{3/2} \varepsilon^{1/2}\, d\varepsilon \qquad (14\text{-}15)$$

and the complete Fermi-Dirac function becomes

$$n(\varepsilon) = \frac{V}{2\pi^2}\left(\frac{2m}{\hbar^2}\right)^{3/2} \frac{\varepsilon^{1/2}}{1 + e^{(\varepsilon-\varepsilon_f)/kT}} \qquad (14\text{-}16)$$

We note that the degeneracy factor is proportional to $\varepsilon^{1/2}$ just as in the Maxwell-Boltzmann case, Eq. (13-47).

The Fermi energy ε_f is found by insisting that the integral of Eq. (14-16) over all energies be equal to the total number N of free electrons. At temperature $T = 0$ this is simple because the function in the denominator is unity for $\varepsilon < \varepsilon_f$ and infinite for $\varepsilon > \varepsilon_f$. Thus at $T = 0$ this integral becomes

$$N = \frac{V}{2\pi^2}\left(\frac{2m}{\hbar^2}\right)^{3/2} \int_0^{\varepsilon_f} \varepsilon^{1/2}\, d\varepsilon$$

$$= \frac{V}{3\pi^2}\left(\frac{2m}{\hbar^2}\right)^{3/2} \varepsilon_f^{3/2}$$

$$\varepsilon_f = \frac{\hbar^2}{2m}\left(\frac{3\pi^2 N}{V}\right)^{2/3} \qquad (14\text{-}17)$$

We note that ε_f depends on the number of valence electrons *per unit volume*, N/V, and is therefore independent of the dimensions of the crystal.

As a specific example, sodium has one valence electron per atom. The molecular mass is 23 g/mol and the density is 0.97 g/cm³. The number of *moles* per unit volume is

$$\frac{0.97 \text{ g/cm}^3}{23 \text{ g/mol}} = 0.0422 \text{ mol/cm}^3 = 4.22 \times 10^4 \text{ mol/m}^3$$

The number of atoms and of free electrons per unit volume is obtained by multiplying by Avogadro's number:

$$\frac{N}{V} = (6.02 \times 10^{23} \text{ atoms/mol})(4.22 \times 10^4 \text{ mol/m}^3)$$

$$= 25.4 \times 10^{27} \text{ atoms/m}^3$$

The Fermi energy, according to Eq. (14-17), is

$$\varepsilon_f = \frac{(1.05 \times 10^{-34} \text{ J} \cdot \text{s})^2}{2(9.11 \times 10^{-31} \text{ kg})}(3\pi^2 \times 25.4 \times 10^{27}/\text{m}^3)^{2/3}$$

$$= 5.04 \times 10^{-19} \text{ J} = 3.15 \text{ eV}$$

It is also easy to calculate the average electron energy at $T = 0$. The total electron energy E at *any* temperature is given by

$$E = \int_0^\infty \varepsilon n(\varepsilon)\, d\varepsilon \tag{14-18}$$

with $n(\varepsilon)$ given by Eq. (14-16). At $T = 0$ this becomes

$$E = \frac{V}{2\pi^2}\left(\frac{2m}{\hbar^2}\right)^{3/2} \int_0^{\varepsilon_f} \varepsilon^{3/2}\, d\varepsilon$$

$$= \frac{V}{5\pi^2}\left(\frac{2m}{\hbar^2}\right)^{3/2} \varepsilon_f^{5/2} \qquad \text{at } T = 0 \tag{14-19}$$

Comparing this with Eq. (14-17), we find

$$E = \tfrac{3}{5}N\varepsilon_f$$

or $\quad \varepsilon_{av} = \dfrac{E}{N} = \tfrac{3}{5}\varepsilon_f \qquad \text{at } T = 0 \tag{14-20}$

For the above example, $\varepsilon_{av} = 1.89$ eV. We note that in the *classical* kinetic theory of gases, where $\varepsilon_{av} = \tfrac{3}{2}kT$, this average energy would require a temperature of

$$T = \frac{2\varepsilon_{av}}{3k} = \frac{2(1.89 \text{ eV})(1.6 \times 10^{-19} \text{ J/eV})}{3(1.4 \times 10^{-23} \text{ J/K})} = 14{,}600 \text{ K}$$

Thus the average energy and the Fermi energy are much *larger* than kT at ordinary temperatures, and the electrons are very far from behaving according to the classical equipartition theorem.

The next step is to compute the specific heat associated with the temperature variation of electron energy. In principle this is done by computing the total energy using Eq. (14-18) and the distribution function of Eq. (14-16), dividing by N to obtain the energy per electron, and taking the derivative with respect to T. In practice this can be done only approximately; the integral cannot be evaluated in closed form, and the Fermi energy depends on temperature, decreasing with increasing temperature. We state without derivation the following approximate result. The average electron energy is given, when $kT \ll \varepsilon_f$, by

$$\varepsilon_{av} = \tfrac{3}{5}\varepsilon_f \left[1 + \frac{5\pi^2}{12}\left(\frac{kT}{\varepsilon_f}\right)^2 \right] \tag{14-21}$$

where the value of ε_f at $T = 0$ is used. The specific heat C per electron is the derivative of Eq. (14-21) with respect to T:

$$C = \frac{\pi^2}{3}\frac{kT}{\varepsilon_f}(\tfrac{3}{2}k) \tag{14-22}$$

Again using sodium as an example, we find at $T = 300$ K

$$kT = (300 \text{ K})(1.38 \times 10^{-23} \text{ J/K}) = 4.14 \times 10^{-21} \text{ J} = 0.0258 \text{ eV}$$

$$C = \frac{\pi^2}{3}\left(\frac{0.0258 \text{ eV}}{3.15 \text{ eV}}\right)(\tfrac{3}{2}k) = (0.0269)(\tfrac{3}{2}k)$$

which is less than 3 percent of the specific-heat contribution $\tfrac{3}{2}k$ to be expected if the electrons behaved like a classical Maxwell-Boltzmann gas. Since this is also small compared with the lattice part of the specific heat, it is usually observable only at high temperatures, where the lattice part becomes independent of T, and at very *low* temperatures, where the lattice part becomes proportional to T^3 and can be separated by data analysis from the electron contribution.

The above discussion has treated the electrons in a metal as free, with the corresponding degeneracy factor $g(\varepsilon)$ proportional to $\varepsilon^{1/2}$. In real metals the electrons are *not* free, but move in the periodically varying electric field of the positively charged ion cores in the lattice, and the degeneracy factor is more complicated. Calculation of degeneracy factors in real materials is part of the *band theory of solids*, to be discussed in Sec. 14-5.

14-3 CONDUCTIVITY

Analysis of the states of electrons in solids, so useful in understanding crystal structure, also provides the key to understanding electrical and thermal conductivity. A striking feature of *electrical* conductivity is the remarkably large range of magnitudes that occur. The conductivity of good conductors such as copper is larger than that of good insulators such as quartz by a factor of the order of 10^{20}. Most materials fall fairly near one or the other of these extremes, although there is an important class of materials called *semiconductors* whose conductivity is intermediate between those of good conductors and good insulators. Materials that are good *electrical* conductors are almost always good *thermal* conductors, and conversely.

The basic requirement for electrical conduction in solids is the presence of electric charges that are free to move from one region of the material to another under the influence of an electric field. In ionic and covalent crystals such mobile charges are not ordinarily available, since as we have seen in Sec. 14-1 the electrons in such materials are tightly bound to individual lattice sites. To remove a valence electron from its position requires several electron volts of energy—even more for inner electrons. For an electric field to do this much work on an electron in a distance comparable to lattice dimensions would require a field strength of the order of 10^{10} V/m, much larger than any available in the laboratory. Similarly, energies of thermal motion at ordinary temperatures are insufficient to liberate valence electrons to act as current carriers. Thus we expect ionic and covalent crystals to be insulators, and this prediction is borne out well by experiment.

In *metallic* crystals, on the other hand, the valence electrons are *not* tightly bound to individual lattice sites, and so they can move from one region of the crystal to another under the action of an electric field. To be sure, not *all* the valence electrons are free to move, even in the electron-gas model discussed in Sec. 14-2. To be accelerated by an electric field, an electron must be able to acquire small increments of energy from the field and correspondingly to make transitions to adjacent unoccupied energy states. For an electron in one of the lowest energy states in the Fermi-Dirac distribution this is *not* possible at ordinary temperatures because all the adjacent levels are already occupied and the exclusion principle prevents their being doubly occupied. The nearest vacant levels may be several electronvolts away, and this much energy is ordinarily not available. But electrons near the top of the distribution (with energies close to ε_f) *do* have nearby unoccupied levels available; it is these electrons that can be accelerated by the field and can thereby contribute to the electrical conductivity.

Electrical conductivity in metals can be discussed more quantitatively on the basis of a simple semiclassical model. We assume that the electrons that contribute to the conductivity (i.e., those with energies near ε_f) move about at random with a speed v determined by the relation $\frac{1}{2} mv^2 = \varepsilon_f$. An electron may collide with an atom in the lattice and rebound in a random direction. The average time between collisions is called the *mean free time*, denoted by τ. The average *distance* traveled between collisions, denoted by λ, is called the *mean free path*. These quantities are related by

$$\lambda = v\tau \tag{14-23}$$

For copper at 300 K, λ is the order of 10^{-8} m, τ the order of 10^{-14} s, and v the order of 10^6 m/s.

In the absence of an electric field, the electrons move in straight-line paths between collisions; the directions are random, and on the average there is no net drift of electrons in one direction or another. However, when an electric field $\mathbf{E}$ is applied, each electron experiences a force $\mathbf{F}$ of magnitude $F = eE$. The direction is opposite to that of $\mathbf{E}$ because the electron charge is negative. According to Newton's second law, each electron thus experiences a constant acceleration a between collisions, given by

$$F = eE = ma \tag{14-24}$$

The trajectories between collisions are then no longer straight lines but rather sections of parabolas, as shown in Fig. 14-9. During the interval τ between collisions an electron acquires an additional *drift velocity* $a\tau$ in the direction opposite to $\mathbf{E}$. Since the acceleration is constant, the *average* drift velocity v_d is one-half this, or $\frac{1}{2}a\tau$.

Using the expression for a from Eq. (14-24), we find

$$v_d = \frac{1}{2}a\tau = \frac{1}{2}\frac{eE}{m}\tau \tag{14-25}$$

 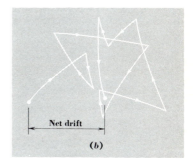

(a)   (b)

Fig. 14-9 Random electron motion in a metallic crystal. (*a*) In the absence of an electric field an electron moves in straight lines between collisions, the average velocity is zero, and there is no net drift. (*b*) When an electric field is applied, each path between collisions becomes parabolic, and there is an average drift velocity proportional to the applied field.

Fig. 14-10 Example of a specimen of material whose conductivity is to be calculated. The total charge emerging from an end in time Δt is equal to the amount of mobile charge contained in a section of specimen of length $v_d \Delta t$ and cross-section area A. This is equal to $e(N/V)Av_d \Delta t$.

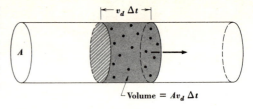

Volume $= Av_d \Delta t$

This drift velocity corresponds to a transport of charge from one region to another, and we may calculate the magnitude of the resulting current. This is most easily done with reference to a particular shape of specimen, as shown in Fig. 14-10. If the number of electrons participating in conduction is N, then the conduction electron density is N/V. In a time Δt the electrons drift a distance $v_d \Delta t$, and the number of electrons flowing through a given cross section of the specimen is $(N/V)Av_d \Delta t$. The total charge flow is this quantity multiplied by the charge e of each electron. Thus the charge passing any cross section *per unit time*, which is equal to the total *current*, is given by

$$i = e\frac{N}{V}Av_d$$

$$= \frac{e^2 E\tau}{2m}A\frac{N}{V} \tag{14-26}$$

Since E is proportional to the potential difference between the ends of the specimen, i is proportional to this potential difference, the familiar Ohm's law.

The *conductivity* is defined as the ratio $\sigma = j/E$, where j is the *current density*, or current per unit area, given in the present example by $j = i/A$. Dividing Eq. (14-26) by A, we find

$$j = \frac{e^2 E\tau(N/V)}{2m} \tag{14-27}$$

Finally, the electrical conductivity is given by

$$\sigma = \frac{e^2 \tau(N/V)}{2m} \tag{14-28}$$

As might be expected, σ is directly proportional to the density of current-carrying electrons, which, as explained earlier, are the electrons near the top of the Fermi distribution.

For most metals the conductivity is found to *decrease* with increasing temperature. In the classical model this can be understood on the basis that with increasing temperature the electrons move more rapidly, making more frequent collisions and decreasing the mean free time. In view of the Fermi-Dirac distribution of electron energies, however, this is not an adequate model. We have spoken rather glibly about collisions of electrons with the lattice, but a thorough analysis of the electron wave functions in the periodic potential energy of the lattice shows that electron wave functions whose periodicity is properly matched to that of the lattice can move through the lattice without undergoing collisions at all, so long as the lattice is perfect and free from defects. This effect is analogous to the passage of an alternating current through a series-resonant tuned circuit without any impedance when the frequency is equal to the resonant frequency of the circuit.

In view of this result, why do electrons not accelerate constantly and without limit, leading to an infinitely great conductivity? The reason is that no crystal lattice is really perfect. Even when there are no vacancies, interstitial atoms, dislocations, or other lattice imperfections, the perfect periodicity of the lattice is still disturbed by thermal motion of atoms in the lattice. This motion, as we have seen, is also chiefly responsible for the specific heats of solids.

Thus when an atom vibrates about its equilibrium position in the lattice, it becomes a target for electron collisions. In a semiclassical picture, the frequency of collisions is determined by the area of the target, which depends on the *amplitude* of the oscillation. An atom which moves a maximum distance A away from its equilibrium position presents a target area equal to the area of a circle of radius A, that is πA^2. Furthermore, A^2 is proportional to the total energy associated with vibration, which has been shown to be proportional to the absolute temperature T of the lattice. The mean free time between collisions should be inversely proportional to the collision cross section for each atom and thus inversely proportional also to T. Thus the conductivity of the material, given by Eq. (14-28), should also vary inversely with T.

The *temperature coefficient of conductivity* α is defined as the fractional change in conductivity per unit temperature change:

$$\alpha = \frac{1}{\sigma}\frac{d\sigma}{dT} \qquad (14\text{-}29)$$

If σ is proportional to $1/T$, we find simply that $\alpha = 1/T$. At ordinary temperatures, say $T = 300$ K, this gives $\alpha = 0.0033/\text{K}$. In fact, the measured values of α for many metals fall in the range 0.002 to 0.004, although there are some notable exceptions. This agreement with experiment is gratifying, but this crude model should not be taken too seriously.

Several additional remarks are in order. First, the *magnitude* of the drift velocity can be measured directly by a variety of means. The drift velocity is always extremely *small*, typically of the order of 0.001 to 0.1 m/s for electric fields of reasonable magnitude. This is to be compared with the speeds of random motion, which are typically of the order of 10^6 m/s. Thus the electron drift is a very small perturbation on the random motion.

Finally, the discussion of the distinction between conductors and insulators would seem to imply that the conductivity of insulators should be exactly zero. In fact, although conductivities are very small for good insulators, they are still measurable and are definitely *not* zero. The reason is that, although most of the valence electrons are tightly bound to individual atoms, a few fall in the high-energy tail of the statistical distribution, even at moderate temperatures, and therefore can break loose from their lattice sites and contribute to the conductivity. The number of electrons having sufficient energy is strongly temperature-dependent, and the increasing number N of carrier electrons with increasing T completely smothers the competing effect of increased electron scattering. Thus the conductivity of insulators almost invariably *increases* very rapidly with temperature; an increase of a factor of 2 over a $10°$ temperature rise is typical. This effect will be discussed in more detail in Sec. 14-5 in connection with the band theory of solids.

Thus the temperature dependence of electrical conductivity has quite different origins in conductors and insulators. In conductors, σ decreases with increasing T as a result of increased scattering of a nearly constant number of current-carrying electrons; in insulators, it increases with increasing T because of the increasing number of carriers. In this respect the behavior of insulators is similar to that of *semiconductors*, to be discussed in Sec. 14-6.

Although the discussion of this section has been confined thus far to *electrical* conductivity, a parallel discussion can be made for *thermal* conductivity, which involves a transport of energy rather than electric charge; in metals electron motion provides the basis for both. A material containing a significant density of mobile electrons can use them to transport energy from one region of the crystal to another if the average electron energy is different in the two regions. Macroscopically, the material conducts heat from a hot region to a colder region.

The thermal conductivity K measures the rate at which energy is transported from one region to another under a given temperature gradient. On the basis of our electron-gas model, this is expected to be proportional to the mean free path λ, to the average electron speed v, and to the electronic specific heat *per unit volume*, which measures the energy-carrying capacity of the free electrons. A more detailed calculation predicts that in this model K is given by

$$K = \frac{\lambda v C N}{3V} = \frac{v^2 \tau C N}{3V} \qquad (14\text{-}30)$$

where C is the specific heat per electron, given by Eq. (14-22).

As long ago as 1853, Wiedemann and Franz observed that for many common metals the ratio of thermal to electrical conductivity is equal to a constant times the absolute temperature. Thus it is of interest to compute the ratio K/σ for our electron-gas model. Combining Eqs. (14-28) and (14-30) and using Eq. (14-22) for the electronic specific heat, we find

$$\frac{K}{\sigma} = \frac{v^2 \tau C N}{3 V} \frac{2mV}{e^2 \tau N} = \frac{2mv^2}{3e^2} C = \frac{2mv^2}{3e^2} \frac{\pi k^2 T}{2\varepsilon_f}$$

The electrons participating in the conduction process are those with kinetic energies close to ε_f, so we set $\frac{1}{2}mv^2 = \varepsilon_f$, obtaining

$$\frac{K}{\sigma} = \frac{2\pi}{3} \frac{k^2}{e^2} T \tag{14-31}$$

This result reproduces the general form of the Wiedemann-Franz relation, and the numerical constant is found to be in qualitative agreement with experimental results, describing approximately the relation of K and σ for many metals at ordinary temperatures.

There is an additional mechanism for thermal conductivity, namely, lattice vibrations. Vibrations of a lattice in thermal equilibrium are characterized by standing waves in which there is no net transfer of energy in one direction or the other. Conversely, in a crystal that is *not* in thermal equilibrium the lattice vibrations correspond at least in part to traveling waves which originate in the hotter regions and propagate to the colder regions, transferring energy which is interpreted macroscopically as heat. In metals, this contribution to the thermal conductivity is usually much *smaller* than the electronic part, but in covalent and ionic crystals it is usually the principal mechanism for conduction of heat.

Finally, we mention briefly the phenomenon of *superconductivity*, in which some materials at sufficiently low temperatures undergo a phase transition to a state characterized by electrical resistance so small as to be totally unmeasurable. As an example, a current established in a superconductive ring persists undiminished for an indefinite period.

Figure 14-11 shows how the resistance of a specimen of tin falls in the vicinity of the superconducting-transition temperature $T_c = 3.72$ K. Over 20 elements and several hundred compounds and alloys exhibit superconductivity, with transition temperatures ranging from less than 1 K to about 20 K. Electromagnets with superconducting coils have been used to achieve magnetic fields of over 30 Wb/m; these are of great importance in research work and promise to have a variety of practical applications in electric-power generation, magnetic levitation for transportation systems, and other areas.

Although superconductivity was first observed in 1911, it has been understood theoretically only since 1957. There is no simple way to state

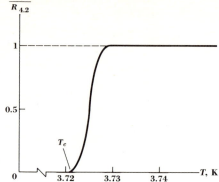

Fig. 14-11 Temperature variation of resistance of a specimen of tin as it approaches the critical temperature $T_c = 3.72$ K. The resistance is expressed as the ratio to the resistance at 4.2 K.

the basis of this understanding; we remark simply that it involves collective motion of *pairs* of electrons in the lattice, and so no independent-particle model such as our electron-gas model can deal with superconductivity.

14-4   MAGNETIC PROPERTIES

Magnetic properties of solids provide yet another example of the understanding of macroscopic phenomena that can be gained by considering the microscopic structure of matter. Most materials exhibit magnetic dipole moments, either spontaneously or when subjected to an externally produced magnetic field. This property is described quantitatively by the magnetic dipole moment per unit volume, called the *magnetization* of the material. Magnetization is a vector quantity; its direction is that of the magnetic moment, and it is usually denoted as **M**.

Magnetic moments in a material act as a *source* of magnetic-induction field **B**, just as do current distributions. Thus the total **B** field in a material is the sum of contributions from real current distributions either inside or outside the material and the contributions from the magnetization, which can also be described in terms of microscopic currents within atoms. It is customary in electrodynamics to introduce the auxiliary vector field **H** having the property that its sources are only *real* currents, not magnetization. The **H** field is defined by the equation

$$\mathbf{H} = \frac{\mathbf{B}}{\mu_0} - \mathbf{M} \tag{14-32}$$

Its role in magnetism is analogous to that of the electric-displacement vector **D**, whose sources are free charges but not polarization charges.

For some materials **M** is proportional to **B**. In this case Eq. (14-32) shows that **B** is also proportional to **H**, and so all three vectors are proportional. For historical reasons it is customary to represent the proportionality of **M** to the fields in terms of **H**, not **B**, and the *magnetic susceptibility* χ of a material is defined by

$$\mathbf{M} = \chi\mathbf{H} \tag{14-33}$$

Since **M** and **H** have the same units, χ is a *dimensionless* quantity. Equation (14-33) can also be expressed in terms of **M** and **B** with the help of Eq. (14-32); the result is

$$\mathbf{M} = \frac{\chi}{\mu_0(1 + \chi)}\mathbf{B} \tag{14-34}$$

When χ is much smaller than unity, this relation becomes approximately $\mathbf{M} = \chi\mathbf{B}/\mu_0$, from which we find approximately

$$\chi = \mu_0\frac{dM}{dB} \tag{14-35}$$

There are three principal types of magnetic behavior: diamagnetism, paramagnetism, and ferromagnetism. Of these, ferromagnetism is the most complicated from a theoretical point of view but is also of greatest practical importance. The classification is based on the origin of magnetic moments in materials and on their interactions.

In *diamagnetism* there are no permanent magnetic dipoles in the material, but a magnetic moment is *induced* by an external field. The origin of such a moment can be understood qualitatively by considering the motion of an electron in a **B** field. An electron with speed v which would move in a straight line in the absence of **B** moves in a circular or helical path when a field is applied. The resulting circulating charge is equivalent to a current loop, which has an associated magnetic moment. Analysis of the direction of the current shows that the direction of the induced magnetic moment is always *opposite* that of **B**, so that a diamagnetic material always has *negative* susceptibility. The above picture is naïve, of course, but a more rigorous treatment may be given, based on the changes in the quantum states of electrons in a molecule or solid which result from the magnetic force on the moving charges in the presence of a **B** field. Diamagnetic susceptibilities are always very small, typically of the order of -10^{-8} to -10^{-6}.

In *paramagnetism* the material contains permanent microscopic magnetic moments associated with electron spin or orbital electron motion, as discussed in Sec. 11-7. In this case the action of a **B** field is not to *create* magnetic moments where none existed before but rather to tend to *align* the permanent dipole moments with the field by means of the torque $\boldsymbol{\tau} = \boldsymbol{\mu} \times \mathbf{B}$ which a magnetic field **B** exerts on a magnetic moment $\boldsymbol{\mu}$. (In the following discussion care must be taken to distinguish between the magnetic moment $\boldsymbol{\mu}$ and the permeability of free space $\mu_0 = 4\pi \times 10^{-7}$ Wb/A $\cdot$ m.) The tendency of the microscopic dipoles to line up in the direction of the field under the action of this torque is partially offset by the effects of thermal motion tending to randomize the directions of the dipoles. Thus calculating the magnetization of a material becomes a *statistical* problem and, in fact, provides an interesting illustration of some of the statistical techniques developed in Chap. 13.

Because of the two competing effects just mentioned, it is to be expected that the susceptibility of a paramagnetic material will be temperature-dependent. At low temperatures, a relatively weak field should align most of the dipoles, since thermal motion will be insufficient to disturb this alignment when the interaction energy is large compared with kT. At higher temperatures a stronger field should be required to maintain the same degree of alignment, and so the susceptibility should *decrease* with increasing temperature. This temperature dependence is borne out by experiment as well as more detailed theoretical analysis and is in sharp contrast to diamagnetic susceptibilities, which are very nearly independent of temperature. Susceptibilities of many paramagnetic materials are found to be proportional to $1/T$, a result called the *Curie law*.

Paramagnetic behavior is expected to occur in any material whose electronic structure is characterized by partly filled shells, since then electrons can change their spin orientation without altering the electron configurations. Thus some of the transition metals, with their partly filled $3d$ shells, are paramagnetic. Conversely, in any material where pairing of electron spins is an essential element in the structure, the spin magnetic moments cannot change directions. For example, in ionic crystals whose ions have filled-shell electron configurations, each level is occupied by two electrons which are required by the exclusion principle to have opposite spins. Similarly, the electron-pair bonds in covalent crystals require pairs of electrons with opposite spins. Thus ionic and covalent crystals are expected to be diamagnetic but not paramagnetic, and this prediction is generally borne out by experiment. There are, however, some ionic crystals in which the ions are *not* filled-shell configurations, and there are corresponding spin and orbital magnetic moments that are free to change directions in a magnetic field. Such crystals are paramagnetic.

We now consider the simplest possible statistical calculation of paramagnetic susceptibility, assuming the magnetism is due entirely to unpaired electron spins, each having magnetic moment

$$\mu = \frac{e\hbar}{2m}$$

$$= 9.28 \times 10^{-24} \text{ J} \cdot \text{m}^2/\text{Wb} \tag{14-36}$$

(as discussed in Sec. 11-8), which must be oriented either parallel or anti-parallel to the magnetic field, corresponding to the two possible orientations of spin angular momentum. The interaction energy of a magnetic dipole with a **B** field is given by $-\boldsymbol{\mu} \cdot \mathbf{B}$. Thus a dipole parallel to the field has an energy $-\mu B$, while a dipole antiparallel to the field has energy $+\mu B$.

Now we consider N unpaired electrons in a volume V. For simplicity we neglect interactions between electrons. According to the Maxwell-Boltzmann distribution, the number of electrons in a given energy state E is

$$n = Ae^{-E/kT} \tag{14-37}$$

where A is a normalization constant. Denoting by n_+ and n_- the numbers of magnetic moments parallel and antiparallel to the field, respectively, we have

$$\begin{aligned} n_+ &= Ae^{\mu B/kT} \\ n_- &= Ae^{-\mu B/kT} \end{aligned} \tag{14-38}$$

with μ given by Eq. (14-36). The normalization constant A is determined by the requirement that the total number of spins is constant and equal to N; that is $n_+ + n_- = N$. Combining this equation with Eqs. (14-38) and rearranging, we find

$$A = \frac{N}{e^{\mu\beta/kT} + e^{-\mu\beta/kT}} = \frac{N}{2\cosh(\mu\beta/kT)} \tag{14-39}$$

The *total* magnetic moment in the direction of the field is

$$\mu(n_+ - n_-) = \frac{N\mu}{2}\frac{e^{\mu\beta/kT} - e^{-\mu\beta/kT}}{\cosh(\mu\beta/kT)}$$

$$= N\mu \tanh\frac{\mu B}{kT} \tag{14-40}$$

and finally the magnetization M is

$$M = \frac{N}{V}\mu \tanh\frac{\mu B}{kT} \tag{14-41}$$

A graph of this function is given in Fig. 14-12, which shows magnetization as a function of field. At sufficiently small values of B the magnetization is approximately proportional to B, but as B increases, M asymptotically approaches the value $(N/V)\mu$, corresponding to the state where *all* the electron magnetic moments are aligned with the field. This condition is called *saturation*. The small-field susceptibility, proportional to the initial slope of

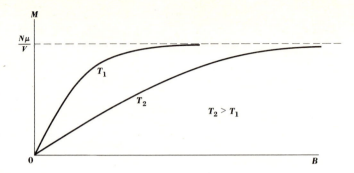

Fig. 14-12 Graph showing magnetization M as a function of the magnetic-induction field B. At small values of B the curve is approximately a straight line, but at larger values it bends over and approaches asymptotically the saturation value of M, when all the spin magnetic moments are aligned with B.

the curve, is given approximately by Eq. (14-35), which combined with Eq. (14-41) and evaluated at $B = 0$ gives

$$\chi = \frac{N}{V} \frac{\mu_0 \mu^2}{kT} \tag{14-42}$$

We note that χ is proportional to $1/T$, in agreement with Curie's law.

When the temperature is reduced, the initial slope of the curve (and therefore the susceptibility) is greater, as Eq. (14-41) shows, but the saturation magnetization is the same. It is instructive to look at some numerical magnitudes. Laboratory magnets can easily produce fields of the order of 1.0 Wb/m^2 (10,000 G). For such a field the interaction energy of the electron magnetic moment is

$$\mu B = \frac{e\hbar B}{2m}$$
$$= \frac{(1.60 \times 10^{-19} \text{ C})(1.05 \times 10^{-34} \text{ J} \cdot \text{s})(1 \text{ Wb/m}^2)}{2(9.11 \times 10^{-34} \text{ kg})}$$
$$= 0.927 \times 10^{-23} \text{ J}$$
$$= 0.58 \times 10^{-4} \text{ eV}$$

Since at ordinary temperatures $(T = 300 \text{ K})$ kT is about 0.026 eV, the interaction energy is much *smaller* than kT at these temperatures. Even with the strongest fields that can be produced with present-day technology, of the order of 30 Wb/m^2, the interaction energy is still less than 1 percent of kT at 300 K. These magnitudes correspond to the region of the curves in Fig. 14-12 very close to the origin; saturation cannot be achieved at ordinary temperatures even with the strongest fields available, and it is extremely difficult experimentally even to measure departures from straight proportionality of B and M. But at very *low* temperatures and very strong fields the interaction energy can become comparable to kT, and saturation effects *are* observed. This state of affairs is largely responsible for the great present-day interest in low-temperature magnetic properties of materials.

Equation (14-42) can be used to predict the magnitude of paramagnetic susceptibilities for typical materials. A typical density of atoms in a solid is 2×10^{28} atoms/m³. If each of these contributes one unpaired electron, then $N/V = 2 \times 10^{28}$. Inserting the other appropriate numerical values, we find

$$\chi = \frac{(2 \times 10^{28} \text{ m}^{-3})(4\pi \times 10^{-7} \text{ Wb/A} \cdot \text{m})(9.28 \times 10^{-24} \text{ J} \cdot \text{m}^2/\text{Wb})^2}{(1.38 \times 10^{-23} \text{ J/K})(300 \text{ K})}$$

$$= 5.2 \times 10^{-4}$$

Some materials exhibit paramagnetic susceptibilities of this order of magnitude, although many others have values *smaller* than this by a factor of the order of 10. In view of the rather primitive model we have used, neglecting all electron interactions except with the field, this is not surprising.

The behavior of *ferromagnetic* materials differs in several important respects from the other two types. Ferromagnetic materials exhibit very large susceptibilities, sometimes as large as 10^5, and at ordinary temperatures exhibit *saturation* at quite moderate fields, of the order of 0.1 to 2 Wb/m². Often there is a residual magnetization even after the external field is removed. The most common ferromagnetic materials are the transition metals iron, cobalt, and nickel, although there are a number of others, including a number of compounds and alloys containing these elements.

All these phenomena are related to the basic mechanism of ferromagnetism, which is a strong electron-electron interaction which tends to line up electron spins parallel to each other even in the absence of an external field. This is intrinsically a quantum-mechanical effect without a classical analog. It is analogous to the spin-dependent interaction energy in a diatomic molecule with a covalent bond, except that in the covalent bond the lowest-energy state is always one with antiparallel spins, whereas in ferromagnetic metals it is the state in which a large number of spins are parallel.

As a result of this interaction, small regions of the crystal called *magnetic domains* become spontaneously magnetized; each domain has a magnetic moment much larger than that of an individual electron. In the presence of an external field the total interaction energy of a domain with the field may be large compared with kT even at moderate fields, and the resulting reorientation of domains produces a large bulk magnetization. Roughly speaking, it is as though in Eq. (14-41) we divided N by a large numerical factor equal to the number of electrons in a domain and multiplied μ by the same factor. The effect is to increase the weak-field susceptibility by this factor and divide the field needed for saturation by the same factor.

The existence of residual magnetization is somewhat more subtle. It is associated with the fact that the magnetizing of a material by an external field is accomplished partly by changing the direction of magnetization of domains but also partly by movement of the domain boundaries. Because of lattice imperfections in polycrystalline specimens this motion is not entirely reversible, and when the field is removed, the material does not return to precisely the same state it was in before the field was applied. This effect is the basis of *hysteresis*.

From the above discussion it should be clear that ferromagnetism is intrinsically a collective phenomenon, in which interelectron interactions are of primary importance. Any model that treats electrons as independent, such as the electron-gas model of metals, is powerless to deal with ferromagnetism. However, for every ferromagnetic material there is a critical temperature called the *Curie point*, different for different materials, above which ferro-magnetic behavior disappears and the material becomes paramagnetic. This temperature is determined by the relative magnitude of kT and the interaction energy responsible for the spontaneous alignment. In the past 20 years a great deal of progress has been made in the theoretical analysis of ferromagnetism on the basis of statistical considerations and a detailed treatment of the electron-electron interactions in the material.

14-5 BAND THEORY OF SOLIDS

Electron states in solids play a central role in the analysis of the macroscopic properties of materials in terms of their microscopic structure, as the discussion of this chapter has shown. Detailed calculations of properties, especially those of a statistical nature, are often facilitated greatly by the concept of *energy bands*. We now introduce this concept and examine its relevance to some of the phenomena already discussed in this chapter.

When an atom is bound in a crystal lattice in close proximity to other atoms, the configurations of the valence electrons are altered significantly. The directional character of the wave functions is altered; instead of wave functions with definite total angular momentum, the electron energy states have mixtures of angular-momentum states because of the interactions with other atoms. When a valence electron is excited to an energy state higher than its ground state, the interactions with other atoms become even more important. Such an electron becomes less localized in the vicinity of a single nucleus and becomes more and more a property of the entire crystal lattice, with a correspondingly spreadout wave function.

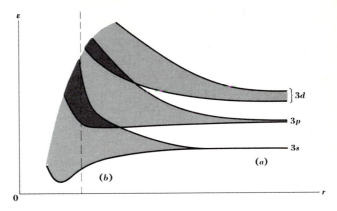

Fig. 14-13 Electron energy levels for sodium atoms in a crystal lattice, as a function of lattice spacing. (*a*) For large spacing the levels approach those of isolated atoms. (*b*) The bands become wider as lattice spacing decreases. The broken line shows the actual equilibrium lattice spacing. At this spacing, the bands overlap.

With the altered character of the wave functions, there are corresponding shifts in energy levels. If an isolated atom has an energy-level scheme as shown in Fig. 14-13*a*, then for N such atoms, far enough apart so that their interactions are negligible, each level can accommodate N times as many electrons as the exclusion principle would permit for an individual atom. When these atoms are brought together, some atomic levels shift in one direction, and some in another, because of interactions with other atoms; the energy levels for the N atoms become spread out over a range of energies, as shown in Fig. 14-13*b*. Since the number of atoms in a crystal is usually very large, this gives virtually a continuous distribution of energies over a certain range. This range of permitted energies is called an *energy band.* Just as an electron in an isolated atom can exist only in certain definite energy levels, an electron in a solid can exist only in certain definite regions of energy, or energy bands. The regions between bands, where no electron energy levels occur in a solid, are called *forbidden bands.*

In investigating the significance of energy bands, we consider again the matter of electrical conductivity. Suppose the band structure of a certain solid is such that in the ground state all the energy levels in a certain band are occupied by electrons and that the next higher band is entirely empty. This occurs in a covalent crystal when the valence electrons all participate in the crystal binding. The energy gap between bands may be several electronvolts, much larger than kT at ordinary temperatures, and practically no electrons can acquire enough energy to cross this gap and escape from a valence-bond state.

When an electric field is applied to the crystal, completely free electrons would accelerate in the direction of the electric-field force. They would not accelerate indefinitely because of collisions, but there would be an average drift in the direction of the electric-field force. But from a quantum-mechanical point of view, an electron must gain energy to be accelerated; this means that it must move from its original energy state in the band to a new energy. If all the energy levels in a given band are occupied, then according to the exclusion principle no additional electron can move into one of these levels. In this case, the only way such an electron can gain energy is to gain an amount at least equal to the separation between the full and empty bands. This would require an impossibly large electric field; hence such transitions do not ordinarily occur.

To put the matter another way: For an electron to be accelerated by an electric field, there must be empty states with energies close to that of its initial level, so that it can acquire energy in small increments under the action of the field. If no such adjacent levels are available, the acceleration does not take place, and the behavior of the material is characteristic of an insulator. Thus a material in which one band is completely full and the next higher band completely empty is expected to be an insulator. As a result of thermal motion, a few electrons may have enough energy to reach the higher band, but the conductivity of such materials is extremely small compared with that of metals.

On the other hand, when an energy band is *partially* filled with electrons, an electron in a state near the top of the filled portion of the band can easily acquire small increments of energy by moving to one of the unoccupied levels nearby; hence such electrons *can* be accelerated in the presence of an external field. Thus *materials having partially filled energy bands are electrical conductors*. This band structure is characteristic of metallic crystals.

Between these two extremes is another interesting possibility. Suppose one band is completely filled and the next higher one completely empty, but the forbidden region between the two bands is relatively small, say less than 1 eV. Then even at moderate temperatures a few electrons can make the jump from the lower band to the higher, where they have an abundance of nearby energy levels to which transitions can be made when an electric field is applied. The number of electrons in the upper band is strongly dependent on temperature, and so the electrical conductivity of such a material should increase sharply with temperature. This is also true for insulators, but the effect is much more readily observable if the energy gap is not too large compared with kT at ordinary temperatures. Materials exhibiting this behavior are called *semiconductors;* they will be discussed in more detail in Sec. 14-6.

Because of the importance of the full and empty bands in insulators and semiconductors in determining electrical conductivity, they are usually called the *valence band* and *conduction band,* respectively. When an electron makes a transition from a normally full band to a normally empty one, it contributes to the conductivity through its ability to move into adjacent levels in the nearly empty band. At the same time, it leaves an empty energy level in the valence band, and an electron in the valence band with energy close to that of the unoccupied level can make a transition to it, thereby also contributing to the electrical conductivity. This phenomenon is most readily described in terms of the transitions of the *unoccupied* state; one speaks of transitions of electrons in the conduction band and of *holes* (unoccupied states) in the valence band. In many respects, these unoccupied energy levels behave in a manner quite analogous to charged particles. Since they correspond to the absence of an electron, they have positive rather than negative charges. They can be characterized by an effective mass, corresponding to the response of their motion to an applied electric field.

If the preceding discussion of occupied and unoccupied states in various bands has seemed somewhat abstract, a homely illustration may help to clarify the situation. The full and empty bands in an insulator or a semiconductor are comparable to a two-level parking garage. When the first floor of the garage is completely filled with cars and the second completely empty, no motion can take place on either floor. But if one car is moved from the first floor to the second, then the second floor has many unoccupied spaces in which to move, and there is an empty space on the first floor which permits cars to move there as well. The two floors correspond to the valence and conduction bands in a solid.

Thus the concept of energy bands supplements the considerations of Sec. 14-3 in understanding the distinction between electrical properties of conductors and those of insulators. A similar analysis can be made for thermal conductivity, which involves the transport of *energy* rather than charge. The essential condition for electron mobility is the availability of unoccupied energy levels adjacent to the occupied ones, so that in interacting with an electric field (electrical conductivity) or exchanging energy through collisions (thermal conductivity) an electron can gain or lose energy in any required amount. Thus the metals, characterized by partially filled bands, are good electrical and thermal conductors, whereas nonmetals, characterized by filled bands, are poor conductors.

Here is a simple application of the band concept, together with some statistical considerations, to a calculation of the temperature dependence of electrical conductivity of a crystalline solid having a filled band separated by an energy gap from a normally empty band, as shown in Fig. 14-14. At very low temperatures there are *no* electrons in the empty band, but at any finite temperature a few electrons have enough energy to reach this band. The electron-energy distribution is given by the Fermi-Dirac distribution

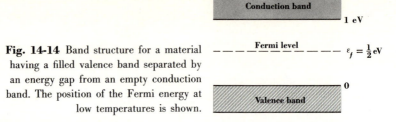

Fig. 14-14 Band structure for a material having a filled valence band separated by an energy gap from an empty conduction band. The position of the Fermi energy at low temperatures is shown.

function, and it is clear that at least at low temperatures the Fermi level lies somewhere in the forbidden region between bands. The conductivity is directly proportional to the number of electrons that have enough energy to reach the conduction band.

As a simple numerical example, let us suppose that the top of the valence band is at $\varepsilon = 0$, the Fermi level is at $\frac{1}{2}$ eV, and the beginning of the next allowed band is at 1 eV. At $T = 300$ K, kT is about 0.0259 eV, and the occupation index for a level near the bottom of the conduction band is approximately

$$n_i = \frac{1}{e^{(1\,\text{eV} - 1/2\,\text{eV})/0.0259\,\text{eV}} + 1} \cong e^{-19.30}$$

If the temperature is increased 10 K to 310 K, then $kT = 0.0267$ eV, and the occupation index is

$$n_i \cong e^{-18.72}$$

The *ratio* of the conductivity at $T = 310$ K to the value at 300 K is equal to the ratio of the two occupation indices:

$$\frac{\sigma_{310}}{\sigma_{300}} = \frac{n_{310}}{n_{300}} = \frac{e^{-18.72}}{e^{-19.30}} = e^{0.58}$$
$$= 1.78$$

That is, the conductivity nearly doubles with a 10° temperature rise. This effect is offset in part by the increased electron scattering at the higher temperature, as discussed in Sec. 14-3, but the increase in carrier density is by far the predominant effect. Thus, as already pointed out, the conductivity of insulators and semiconductors always increases rapidly with temperature, and the band theory of solids provides a useful picture of the mechanisms involved. It is possible to make more detailed calculations, taking into account the shift of the Fermi level with temperature, the degeneracy factor in the conduction band, and the temperature dependence of scattering; considerable progress has also been made in calculating the spacings of the energy bands themselves, and the degeneracy factors, on the basis of the electron configuration of the crystals. However, such calculations are beyond the scope of this book.

14-6   SEMICONDUCTORS

The semiconductors comprise the class of solids whose electrical properties are intermediate between the good metallic conductors and the good insulators. A few properties of semiconductors have already been mentioned, such as the temperature dependence of the electrical conductivity. The semiconductors are of considerable theoretical interest, inasmuch as they provide an interesting illustration of several of the principles discussed in this chapter. They are also of enormous practical interest, forming the basis for a wide variety of devices used in electronic circuitry, including diodes, transistors, photocells, and particle detectors.

The simplest semiconductors are elements in group IV of the periodic table: carbon, silicon, and germanium. These elements have several features in common; each has four valence electrons which in the solid state are used to form four covalent bonds, one with each of four nearest-neighbor atoms. In the resulting crystal structure, called the "diamond" structure, each atom lies at the center of a regular tetrahedron with four nearest neighbors at the corners.

Because of covalent bonding, the valence electrons are all fairly tightly bound to individual atoms; correspondingly, the band structure consists of a valence band completely filled at low temperatures, separated by an energy gap from a normally empty conduction band, as shown in Fig. 14-15. This description also fits many good insulators; the distinguishing feature of a semiconductor is that the energy gap separating the filled band from the empty one is relatively small, 1.1 eV in the case of silicon and only 0.7 eV for germanium. Thus these materials are insulators at low temperatures, but at higher temperatures increasing numbers of electrons are thermally excited to empty levels in the conduction band. Thus the conductivity is a rapidly *increasing* function of temperature. Conductivity resulting in this way from thermal excitation is called *intrinsic conductivity*, to distinguish it from another type of conductivity due to impurities, to be discussed later.

Electrons can also be excited from the conduction band to the valence band in other ways. One is by absorption of light with photon energies greater than that of the energy gap. Thus the conductivity of germanium is increased by illuminating it with light photons of energy greater than 0.7 eV; materials exhibiting this property are said to be *photoconductive*. Another mechanism is collisions of the electron with energetic charged particles. A high-energy proton or α particle passing through a crystal excites electrons from the

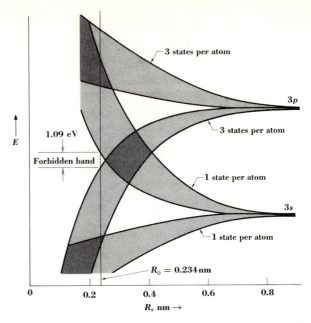

Fig. 14-15 Band structure of silicon crystal, as a function of interatomic spacing R of nearest neighbors. At the actual value R_0 the $3s$ and $3p$ bands have crossed, and there is an energy gap of 1.1 eV. The structure of the $4s$ and $4p$ bands of germanium is similar, but the energy gap is 0.72 eV.

valence to the conduction band, producing an increase in conductivity. Hence a semiconductor can be used as a detector of charged particles.

Some of the most interesting and useful properties of semiconductors are associated with the dramatic changes in conductivity produced by the presence of minute quantities of impurities. Suppose that an atom of arsenic finds its way into a germanium crystal. Arsenic lies in group V of the periodic table, adjacent to germanium, and has five valence electrons rather than four. When one of these electrons is removed, the configuration of the remaining electrons is very similar to that of germanium, being simply scaled down in size by the factor $^{32}/_{33}$ because the nuclear charge is $+33e$ instead of $+32e$. Thus an arsenic atom can masquerade in a crystal lattice as a germanium atom; four of the five valence electrons form covalent bonds with four germanium atoms, and the remaining electron is very loosely bound. Only a very small addition of energy, about 0.01 eV (much less than the energy gap between valence and conduction bands), is required to excite it into the conduction band; at ordinary temperatures, where $kT = 0.025$ eV, most of these extra electrons are in the conduction band, where their behavior is much like that of electrons in metals. Hence the conductivity of the material increases in direct proportion to the number of arsenic atoms present. Since at ordinary temperatures only a very small fraction of the valence electrons of germanium are in the conduction band, the presence of arsenic atoms, even to the extent of one part in 10^{10}, increases the conductivity drastically and is, in fact, the determining factor for conductivity.

The presence of these loosely bound electrons associated with the arsenic impurity atoms is represented in the energy-band scheme as a set of additional levels lying just below the bottom of the conduction band, as shown in Fig. 14-16a. Because electrons in these levels can readily be excited into the conduction band, they are called *donor levels,* and the arsenic atoms are called *donor impurities,* or *n*-type impurities; a semiconductor containing donor impurities is called an *n*-type semiconductor. Other group V elements such as phosphorus or antimony are also *n*-type impurities. The conductivity associated with *n*-type impurities is due entirely to electrons. Unlike the case of excitation of valence electrons of germanium, there is no corresponding motion of the holes left in the valence band, since the corresponding positive charges are associated with nuclei of impurity atoms and are not free to move.

The presence of an impurity atom with only three valence electrons has an analogous effect. Suppose we include some atoms of gallium, an element in group III, adjacent to germanium. Gallium tends to form four covalent bonds, one with each of four neighboring germanium atoms, but it lacks one electron for this. It can, however, steal an electron from a neighboring germanium atom to complete the four-bond crystal structure. When this theft is accomplished, one of the germanium atoms is left with a missing electron, or *hole.* Then, just as a donor electron is free to migrate in the conduction band, this hole in the valence band is also free to migrate. The resulting conductivity consists solely in the motion of holes, or regions of positive charge,

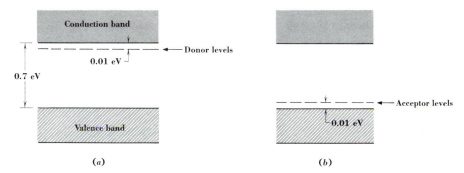

(a)   (b)

Fig. 14-16 (a) Band structure of germanium with donor impurities, showing the donor levels lying just below the conduction band. At $T = 0$ these levels are occupied, but with only a small addition of energy from thermal agitation the electrons are excited to the conduction band. (b) Band structure of germanium with acceptor impurities, showing the acceptor levels lying just above the valence band. Electrons excited to these levels leave holes in the valence band which contribute to conductivity.

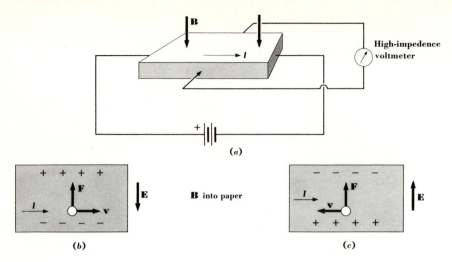

Fig. 14-17 (*a*) Apparatus for observing the Hall effect; (*b*) current carried by positive charges (holes); (*c*) current carried by negative charges (electrons) moving oppositely to the direction of conventional current flow *I*.

each corresponding to a missing electron; there is no contribution from the associated electron, which is bound to the impurity atom just as a vacancy is bound to an individual donor atom. An atom containing only three valence electrons is called an *acceptor* impurity. Correspondingly, a semiconductor containing such impurities is called a *p*-type semiconductor, indicating that the current is carried by positive "charges." Other elements in group III, such as boron, aluminum, and indium, are also acceptor impurities.

Ordinary measurements of electrical conductivity cannot distinguish between the various types of conductivity, intrinsic, *n*-type, and *p*-type, but the *Hall effect* may be used to determine whether the current is carried by positive or negative charges. This effect is produced by imposing a magnetic field perpendicular to the direction of current flow, as shown in Fig. 14-17*a*. We suppose first that the conductivity is due to the motion of positive charges, as shown in Fig. 14-17*b*. These charges move, on the average, in the direction of the current, and the magnetic field exerts, on an average, a force $q(\mathbf{v} \times \mathbf{B})$. The direction of this force, labeled **F** in the figure, is such as to tend to push the positive charges to one side in the sample. This transverse drift cannot continue indefinitely because charge accumulates on the sides, creating a transverse electric field just large enough to cancel the transverse magnetic-field force. Corresponding to this transverse electric field is a potential difference whose magnitude and sign may be measured.

Now suppose the current is carried by negative charges, which move in the direction opposite to that of conventional current flow, as shown in Fig. 14-17*c*. The signs of both q and $\mathbf{v}$ are reversed with respect to the positive-charge case, the direction of **F** is the same as before, and the transverse potential difference has the opposite polarity in this case. Thus the *sign* of the Hall-effect potential determines whether the conductivity is due to electrons or holes. More detailed measurements of the Hall effect may be used to obtain further information regarding the behavior of electrons and holes in semiconductors.

Semiconductor devices often use a crystal which has *n*-type impurities in some regions and *p*-type impurities in other regions. The most straightforward although not always the most practical way to make such a semiconductor crystal is to "grow" a crystal by pulling a small seed crystal very slowly out of a container of melted semiconductor. By varying the impurity concentration in the melt while the crystal is being grown, one can make a crystal containing alternate *n* and *p* regions. The boundary layer separating an *n* region from a *p* region is called a *p-n* junction; many of the interesting properties of semiconductor diodes, transistors, and other devices are determined by the properties of these junctions.

When a potential difference V is imposed between the terminals of a *p-n* junction and the current I is measured as a function of V, the result is similar to that shown in Fig. 14-18. This behavior is in striking contrast to that of ordinary conducting materials obeying Ohm's law, in which the current I is proportional to the potential difference V. Furthermore, the device conducts much more readily in one direction than in the other; it acts as a *rectifier*.

This directional characteristic of the device can be understood roughly

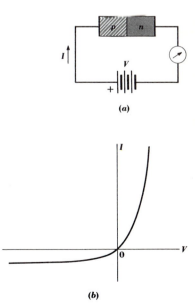

Fig. 14-18 (*a*) A semiconductor *p-n* junction in a circuit; (*b*) graph showing the asymmetric voltage-current relationship, in agreement with the theoretical prediction given by Eq. (14-43).

as follows: When the p region is at higher potential than the n region, the electric field is such as to cause holes in the p region to flow into the n region and electrons in the n region to flow into the p region. When the polarity is reversed, the fields are in such a direction as to tend to cause electrons to flow from the p to the n region and holes from the n to the p region. But at ordinary temperatures there are relatively few electrons in the p region and relatively few holes in the n region, only those contributed by thermal excitation of valence electrons. Thus the resulting current flow is much smaller.

A more detailed theoretical analysis of the action of a p-n junction takes into consideration the fact that in each region hole-electron pairs are constantly being generated by thermal excitation. These, along with the holes and electrons contributed by the acceptor and the donor impurity atoms, respectively, can *diffuse* from one region to the other. In an equilibrium state when no net current is flowing, the total diffusion current of holes and electrons across the junction is zero. When an external electric field is imposed, both the diffusion rate and the rate of thermal generation of holes and electrons are altered, and the net current flow is different from zero. For a simple p-n junction the relationship between current and applied voltage is given approximately by

$$I = I_0(e^{eV/kT} - 1) \tag{14-43}$$

where I_0 is a constant characteristic of the device. This equation is the function corresponding to the graph in Fig. 14-18b.

Other devices can be constructed from p-n junctions. A *transistor* is a sandwich containing at least two p-n junctions, in the configuration n-p-n or p-n-p. The simplest possible circuit employing such a device is shown in Fig. 14-19. The three regions are termed the *emitter*, the *base*, and the *collector*. In the absence of current in the emitter part of the circuit, relatively little current flows from collector to base, as with the simple p-n junction.

Fig. 14-19 An *n-p-n* transistor and associated circuit. With no voltage applied to the emitter, little current flows in the collector circuit. When a potential difference is applied between emitter and base, as shown, electrons travel from the emitter region to the base, and for sufficiently large collector voltage most of them continue into the collector. Thus a small amount of power into the emitter circuit can control a larger power in the collector circuit, and the device operates as an amplifier.

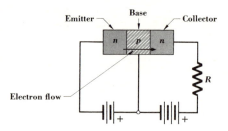

However, when a voltage between emitter and base is applied in the direction shown, the result is that some of the conduction electrons in the emitter travel into the base region, in which they come under the influence of the potential difference between base and collector and so pass on to the collector.

Thus a current in the emitter circuit is used to control a current in the collector circuit. Furthermore, the voltage source in the collector circuit may be considerably larger than that in the emitter circuit so that, although the currents are of comparable magnitudes, the *power* dissipated in the resistor *R* in the collector circuit may be considerably larger than the power input in the emitter circuit. Thus the device acts as a power amplifier. In other kinds of circuit connections, transistors can be used as voltage or current amplifiers as well.

The development of semiconductor devices in the past 25 years has brought sweeping changes to the field of electronic engineering. In many applications such as television, computers, and power-control devices, they have almost completely replaced vacuum tubes as a result of their smaller size, greater efficiency, reliability, and mechanical ruggedness. Of even greater importance, however, is the development in the past 10 years of *integrated circuits*.

An integrated circuit incorporates the functions of several electronic components, such as transistors, diodes, resistors, and capacitors, in a single device. This is accomplished by successively depositing on a small chip of silicon, typically a few millimeters on a side, layers of silicon dioxide (an insulator) and metals (which form *p-n* junctions or their equivalent with the silicon), and by etching appropriate patterns in each layer to form the required current paths, junctions, capacitors, and so on. Areas to be etched are defined by use of a photosensitive masking material, onto which the desired pattern is projected after optical reduction from an original drawing. By this technique, patterns with details as small as 0.001 mm can be made accurately and reproducibly. In the MOS (metal-oxide-semiconductor) chips presently used for pocket-size electronic calculators, the equivalent of several thousand transistors and associated circuit components are incorporated into a single chip. The degree of miniaturization thus accomplished promises to have even greater impact in the future in areas such as large-scale data processing systems.

Problems

14-1 In a simple cubic crystal lattice, each atom is at the center of a regular octahedron with six nearest neighbors at the corners. Show that in the "hard-sphere" model the central atom just touches six nearest-neighbor spheres of radius a if its radius is $(\sqrt{2} - 1)a$.

14-2   Show that, in a body-centered cubic crystal structure, a central sphere just touches each of eight nearest-neighbor spheres of radius a if its radius is $(\sqrt{3} - 1)a$.

14-3   Show that in a close-packed crystal structure an atom of radius a can accommodate twelve nearest neighbors of radius a if six are placed in a plane hexagonal arrangement around it, with three each above and below the plane. Show that all twelve neighbor spheres touch the central sphere in this arrangement, which is called the hexagonal close-packed structure.

14-4   Show that in a face-centered cubic lattice each atom has 12 nearest neighbors. This is most easily seen by considering the neighbors of an atom at a face-centered position.

14-5   From the data in Fig. 14-1 and the known atomic masses, determine the density of solid sodium chloride.

14-6   In the diamond crystal structure, determine the angle between two covalent bonds.

14-7   Show that the packing fraction for a simple cubic lattice of identical spheres is $\pi/6$.

14-8   The *Fermi temperature* T_f of a system is defined as $T_f = \varepsilon_f/k$. Find the Fermi temperature corresponding to $\varepsilon_f = 5$ eV.

14-9   Derive the electronic specific-heat formula, Eq. (14-22), from the expression for the average electron energy, Eq. (14-21).

14-10   For a metal with Fermi energy $\varepsilon_f = 5$ eV, find the root-mean-square speed of electrons with energy in the vicinity of ε_f.

14-11   In the discussion of lattice specific heats, leading to Eq. (14-14), find the approximate temperature, in terms of ε_0, at which the specific heat has half of its classical value $3R$. An approximate solution of the equation $\sinh x = \sqrt{2}\, x$ can be obtained from a table of values of hyperbolic functions.

14-12   The density of copper is about 8.9 g/cm^3 = 8.9 $\times$ 10^3 kg/m^3.
   a   Compute the number of atoms per unit volume.
   b   Assuming one valence electron per atom, compute the Fermi energy at $T = 0$.
   c   Compute the average electron kinetic energy at $T = 0$.
   d   At what temperature would an ideal-gas molecule have an energy equal to that of part (*c*)?

14-13   Repeat the calculation of the electronic specific heat in Sec. 14-2, for the case of *two* valence electrons per atom.

14-14 Considering N electrons in a box of volume V as a classical gas with molecular speeds governed by the Fermi-Dirac distribution, derive a relation between pressure P and volume V at temperature $T = 0$. The derivation proceeds exactly as in Sec. 13-1, up to and including Eq. (13-10), but the average molecular kinetic energy is given by Eq. (14-20), with the Fermi energy given by Eq. (14-17).

14-15 For any system consisting of N identical parts (molecules, atoms, or electrons) each with a set of energy levels ε_i with degeneracies g_i, governed by the Maxwell-Boltzmann distribution, the *partition function* is defined as

$$Z = \sum_i g_i e^{-\varepsilon_i / kT}$$

Show that the average energy ε_{av} is given by

$$\varepsilon_{av} = kT^2 \frac{\partial}{\partial T} \ln Z = -\frac{\partial}{\partial \beta} \ln Z$$

where $\beta = 1/kT$, and that the specific heat per part is

$$C = T \frac{\partial^2 (kT \ln Z)}{\partial T^2}$$

independent of the details of the energy levels or their degeneracies.

14-16 The density of copper is 8.9×10^3 kg/m³, and its electrical conductivity is 5.8×10^7 mho/m.

   a   Assuming one conduction electron per atom, compute the mean free time between collisions of electrons with the lattice.

   b   Assuming the electrons participating in the conduction process have average kinetic energies close to ε_f, find the electron speed and the mean free path.

14-17 Compare the predicted value of the temperature coefficient of conductivity given by Eq. (14-29) and the following paragraph with measured values listed in a handbook. Values usually listed are temperature coefficients of *resistivity;* show that this coefficient has the same magnitude as the quantity α defined in the text.

14-18 Check the validity of the Wiedemann-Franz law, Eq. (14-31), for three metals, using handbook values of K and σ.

14-19 Derive the relation between **M** and **B** given by Eq. (14-34), from Eqs. (14-32) and (14-33).

14-20 For the idealized paramagnetic solid of Sec. 14-4, what **B** field is required to produce magnetization within 1 percent of saturation at $T = 300$ K?

14-21 Metallic iron has about 7.4×10^{28} atoms per cubic meter. Suppose each iron atom has *two* unpaired spins and a total magnetic moment twice that given by Eq. (14-36), and that the spins do not interact. That is, suppose iron is paramagnetic instead of ferromagnetic.

   a Compute the magnetic susceptibility at $T = 300$ K.

   b Find the magnetic moment of a bar 1 by 1 by 10 cm in a magnetic field of 1.0 Wb/m^2.

   c Find the magnetic moment of the above bar if *all* the dipoles are parallel to the length of the bar, i.e., if it is magnetized to saturation.

   d In (*c*), suppose the bar is ferromagnetic and is magnetized to saturation in the absence of a field. Now it is placed in a field of 1.0 Wb/m^2 perpendicular to its axis. Find the torque exerted on the bar.

14-22 Consider the idealized paramagnetic substance discussed in Sec. 14-4.

   a Show that the total energy of interaction of the spins with the **B** field is

$$E = -N\mu B \tanh \frac{\mu B}{kT}$$

Show that at very low temperatures, where all the spins are aligned with the field, this becomes $E = -N\mu B$, but at high temperatures where the spin orientation is random, $E = 0$.

   b Find the specific heat C per electron, associated with this energy, if the field is held constant while the temperature changes. Find the limiting values of C at very low and very high temperatures.

   c Plot C as a function of T, or of the dimensionless variable $kT/\mu B$. Show that it has a sharp peak in the vicinity of $kT = \mu B$. Why should this be expected?

14-23 In the magnetization calculation preceding Eq. (14-41), show that the partition function for the system, as defined in Prob. 14-15, is given by

$$Z = 2 \cosh \frac{\mu B}{kT}$$

and that the magnetization is given by

$$M = \frac{N}{V} kT \frac{\partial}{\partial B} \ln Z$$

14-24 For a semiconductor with *n*-type impurities and a band scheme as shown in Fig. 14-16*a*, suppose the donor levels are 0.01 eV below the bottom of the conduction band. For relatively low temperatures and small impurity concentrations, the Fermi level is approximately the same energy as the donor levels. Explain why this should be so. At what temperature are one-half the electrons from the donor states excited to the conduction band? At what temperature are 99 percent in the conduction band?

14-25 Suppose a piece of very pure germanium is to be used as a photocell by making use of the increase in conductivity resulting from electron-hole pair generation by absorption of radiation. What is the longest wavelength radiation that can be detected? In what region of the spectrum does this radiation lie? Could a device be made sensitive to longer wavelengths by using a *p-n* junction instead?

14-26 What elements are suitable to use as impurities in silicon to make it an n-type semiconductor? A p-type?

14-27 As a very simple model, suppose a pure semiconductor crystal has N valence electrons and that their energy-band structure may be represented as N levels in the valence band, all with very nearly the same energy, and N more levels in the conduction band, also very close together but separated from the valence band by an energy V.

  a Show that for sufficiently low temperatures the Fermi energy is approximately halfway between these two narrow bands.

  b Find, in terms of V and other relevant quantities, the temperature at which 10^{-10} of the valence electrons are excited to the conduction band. Is there any temperature at which the populations in the two bands are equal? Explain.

14-28 For pure germanium, with the top of the valence band at $\varepsilon = 0$, the bottom of the conduction band at $\varepsilon = \varepsilon_c$, and the Fermi energy at $\varepsilon_f = \varepsilon_c/2$ (in the middle of the gap between valence and conduction bands), compute the density of conduction electrons at temperature T. The following procedure is suggested. The density of states in the conduction band can be taken to be that of an electron gas with kinetic energy $\varepsilon - \varepsilon_c$, in which case the distribution function becomes

$$n(\varepsilon) = \frac{V}{2\pi^2} \left(\frac{2m}{\hbar^2}\right)^{3/2} \frac{(\varepsilon - \varepsilon_c)^{1/2}}{1 + e^{(\varepsilon - \varepsilon_f)/kT}}$$

At ordinary temperatures, $\varepsilon - \varepsilon_f \gg kT$ for all states in the conduction band, so the term unity in the denominator can be dropped and this function integrated from ε_c to ε. What does the result tell you about the temperature dependence of the intrinsic conductivity of germanium?

14-29 Draw a circuit diagram similar to Fig. 14-19 but using a p-n-p transistor. Explain carefully the reasons for the polarities of the various voltage sources.

14-30 Semiconductor devices are intrinsically rather temperature-sensitive; for example, a p-n junction is not an effective rectifier above a certain temperature. Discuss how the maximum temperature limit depends on the relative concentrations of impurity current carriers and carriers resulting from thermal electron-hole generation.

The Atomic Nucleus | 15

In this chapter we discuss the structure and properties of the atomic nucleus. The most important properties of nuclei are introduced, and it is shown how some of them can be understood in terms of the structure of the nucleus. Not all nuclei are stable; several kinds of instability resulting in radioactivity and nuclear disintegration are discussed. Nuclei can also participate in a variety of reactions, in which the constituent parts are rearranged and new nuclei formed. These processes are analogous to the rearrangement of electrons and atoms in molecules in the course of chemical reactions. Two particular classes of reactions, fission and fusion, are of considerable practical importance. Some practical applications of radioactivity and the effects of radiation on living organisms are discussed.

15-1 PROPERTIES OF NUCLEI

In the discussion of atomic structure in the past several chapters the nucleus of the atom was usually represented as a *point,* containing most of the mass of the atom and a positive electric charge exactly equal in magnitude to the total negative charge of all the electrons in a neutral atom. In this chapter we shall discuss the properties and structure of the nucleus in more detail.

The basic building blocks of all nuclei are *protons* and *neutrons;* a variety of experimental evidence supporting this statement will be reviewed in this section and the next. The proton has a mass about 1836 times that of the electron and a positive electric charge equal in magnitude to that of the electron. The neutron is slightly more massive than the proton, about 1839 times the electron mass, and has no net electric charge. The generic term *nucleon* means either a proton or a neutron. A nucleus can be described by specifying the numbers of protons and neutrons it contains; the usual symbols are:

$Z =$ number of protons $=$ charge number
$N =$ number of neutrons $=$ neutron number
$A = Z + N =$ total number of nucleons $=$ mass number

Because the proton and neutron masses are nearly equal, the total mass of the nucleus is nearly proportional to A, hence the term *mass number*.

The most obvious physical property of a nucleus is its *size*. We have already discussed in Sec. 11-1 the experiments of Rutherford and his collaborators, which established in 1911 the fact that the atomic nucleus is much *smaller* than the overall dimensions of the atom. Rutherford established that the positive charge in the atomic nucleus is concentrated in a region no larger than 10^{-14} m in diameter, less than $\frac{1}{10,000}$ of the overall diameter of the atom; as far as the electronic structure of an *atom* is concerned, representing the nucleus as a point is a very good approximation. In later years many investigators have made other scattering experiments with α particles, protons, and electrons, to measure nuclear dimensions and charge configurations in more detail. Although the "surface" of a nucleus is not a sharply defined boundary, an approximate radius for each nucleus can be determined. The nuclear radius is found to vary smoothly with mass, as shown in Fig. 15-1, where nuclear radii determined from high-energy electron-scattering experiments are plotted as a function of the *nuclear mass number* A. The mass number is very nearly (but not exactly) equal to the mass of the nucleus expressed in *atomic mass units* (u) to be discussed later in this section.

The curve in Fig. 15-1 is described well by the empirical equation

$$r = r_0 A^{1/3} \qquad \text{with} \qquad r_0 = 1.2 \times 10^{-15} \text{ m} \tag{15-1}$$

This equation may be used to compute the volume V of a nucleus, and from that its density, which in terms of atomic mass units is approximately A/V. We find

$$V = \tfrac{4}{3}\pi r^3 = \tfrac{4}{3}\pi r_0^3 A$$
$$\frac{A}{V} = \frac{3}{4\pi r_0^3} \tag{15-2}$$

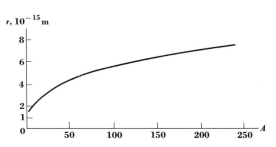

Fig. 15-1 Radii of nuclei, measured by electron-scattering experiments. The radius varies smoothly with nuclear mass number A. The nuclear volume is directly proportional to A, showing that the density of nuclear matter is nearly constant, independent of A.

The density is independent of A; *all nuclei have approximately the same density*. This observation is important in understanding the stability of nuclei, as will be shown later.

The fact that an atom with its normal complement of electrons is electrically neutral shows that the electric charge of the nucleus is an integer multiple of the electron charge magnitude e; it is usually denoted as Ze. Furthermore, since the electronic structure of an atom determines its chemical behavior, the identification of a nucleus as belonging to a particular element is determined by the nuclear charge. Thus the hydrogen nucleus has $Z = 1$, helium $Z = 2$, lithium $Z = 3$, and so on. Z is also equal to the number of electrons in a neutral atom and is therefore equal to the *atomic number* of an element, the number used to arrange the elements in sequence in the periodic table; in nuclear physics Z is also called the *charge number*.

As mentioned previously, the electrons in an atom account for only a small fraction of its total mass; most of the mass is associated with the nucleus. The total mass of a neutral atom can be determined from its *atomic mass*;[1] for example, the atomic mass of hydrogen is usually given as 1.008 g/mol, which means that 1 mol of hydrogen atoms has a total mass of 1.008 g. Now a *mole* of anything is N_0 atoms or molecules, where N_0 is Avogadro's number, equal to

$$N_0 = 6.022 \times 10^{23} \text{ molecules/mol} \tag{15-3}$$

Thus the mass of a hydrogen atom is

$$M_{\text{H}} = \frac{1.008 \text{ g/mol}}{6.022 \times 10^{23} \text{ molecules/mol}} = 1.674 \times 10^{-27} \text{ kg} \tag{15-4}$$

This value includes the mass of an electron, $m_e = 0.00091 \times 10^{-27}$ kg. Thus the mass of the hydrogen nucleus (a single proton) is

$$M_P = 1.673 \times 10^{-27} \text{ kg} \tag{15-5}$$

Nuclear masses are often most conveniently expressed in terms of the *atomic mass unit*, abbreviated u. By definition, an atomic mass unit is one-twelfth the mass of a neutral carbon atom (the nucleus plus six electrons). That is, by definition, the mass of one atom of the stable isotope of carbon is exactly 12 u. On this scale, the mass of a neutral hydrogen atom is 1.008 u. From the above discussion,

$$6.022 \times 10^{23} \text{ u} = 1 \text{ g} = 10^{-3} \text{ kg} \tag{15-6}$$

Atomic masses can be measured directly by means of an instrument

---

[1] The term *atomic weight* is sometimes used; since the fundamental physical quantity referred to is always *mass*, not weight, the term *atomic mass* is to be preferred. The latter term is used throughout this text

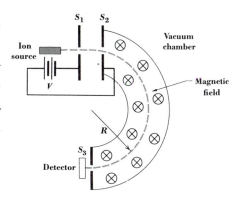

Fig. 15-2 A mass spectrometer of the type invented by Dempster about 1920. Ions created by electron bombardment are accelerated by the potential difference V and then pass through beam-defining slits S_1 and S_2 into a region of uniform magnetic field directed into the plane of the paper. Ions are detected by a photographic film or a sensitive electrometer at the detector position shown. The radius of curvature R of the ion trajectories can be measured directly.

called a *mass spectrometer;* a simple example is shown schematically in Fig. 15-2. Atoms of the element under study are partially ionized in an oven and then accelerated in the electric field between two electrodes S_1 and S_2 to a kinetic energy directly proportional to the accelerating voltage. They then travel into a region containing a uniform *magnetic* field, which exerts a force $q\mathbf{v} \times \mathbf{B}$, where q is the net charge of the ionized atom, $\mathbf{v}$ its velocity, and $\mathbf{B}$ the magnetic field. Under the action of this force, always perpendicular to $\mathbf{v}$, the ion describes a circular path with a radius R determined by the condition that the force, whose magnitude is qvB, is equal to the mass times the centripetal acceleration v^2/R.[1] That is,

$$qvB = \frac{mv^2}{R} \tag{15-7}$$

By appropriate design of the ion source one can obtain singly ionized atoms (i.e., atoms with one electron missing) so that the net charge of each atom is simply the electron charge e. The *speed* v of the ions emerging from the accelerating electrodes is determined by the energy relationship

$$\tfrac{1}{2}mv^2 = eV \tag{15-8}$$

where V is the potential difference. Combining this with Eq. (15-7), we find

$$m = \frac{B^2R^2e}{2V} \tag{15-9}$$

Thus by measuring the accelerating voltage, the magnetic field, and the radius of curvature of the path, one can measure the mass of the ion quite precisely.

All the masses of the light nuclei are found to be very nearly integer multiples of the mass of the proton. This fact was observed from chemical

---

[1] H. D. Young, "Fundamentals of Mechanics and Heat," 2d ed., sec. 8-5, McGraw-Hill Book Company, New York, 1974.

measurements many years before the mass spectrometer was developed and suggests strongly that protons are one of the fundamental building blocks of all nuclei. An apparent exception is chlorine, which from *chemical* observations appears to have an atomic mass of about 35.5 u. It is now known that chlorine as it exists in nature is a mixture of atoms with two kinds of nuclei, 75 percent having a mass of 35 u and the other 25 percent, 37 u. The electric charges of these two nuclei are equal, so that the electronic structure and chemical behavior of atoms containing them are very nearly identical.

Atoms containing two nuclei with the same nuclear charge number Z but different masses are called *isotopes* of an element. Two isotopes of a given element have the same positive charge in their nucleus and the same electronic structure but different masses. As we shall see in the next section, the two nuclei differ only in the number of *neutrons* they contain.

Two additional properties of nuclei which are of importance are *angular momentum* and *magnetic moment*. For electrons in atoms, these two quantities are closely related, and there is a similar relationship for nuclei. The mutual interactions among particles in a nucleus permit a relative motion analogous to the orbital motion of electrons in an atom; associated with this motion are angular momentum and, because of the circulating charge, also magnetic moment. In addition, protons and neutrons have an intrinsic or *spin* angular momentum and associated magnetic moment.

The earliest direct evidence for the existence of nuclear angular momentum and magnetic moment came from spectroscopy. Even before the origin of *fine structure* was understood on the basis of spin-orbit coupling (discussed in Sec. 11-8), it was observed that some lines exhibit still further splitting, known as *hyperfine* structure. A number of distinct effects are responsible for hyperfine structure; one of the important ones is interaction of electrons with the magnetic field of the nuclear magnetic moment leading to an interaction energy that depends on the relative orientations of nuclear spin, electron spin, and electron orbital angular momentum.

On the assumption that the nuclear angular momentum, like all other angular momenta, is *quantized,* the number of hyperfine energy levels into which a given level should be split by the hyperfine interaction is determined by the number of possible values of the component of nuclear angular momentum in a given direction. For example, hyperfine splitting of a level into five sublevels indicates an angular-momentum quantum number of 2, with corresponding components $\pm 2\hbar$, $\pm \hbar$, 0 in the direction of a specified axis. Furthermore, spectroscopic measurement of the *magnitude* of these energy shifts makes possible a determination of the *magnitude* of the magnetic moment of the nucleus.

Nuclear angular momentum has come to be called *nuclear spin*; this is something of a misnomer, inasmuch as it is made up of contributions from both spin angular momentum of particles and orbital angular momentum due to their motions with respect to each other. In order to account for hyperfine splitting due to nuclear spin, it is necessary to permit both integer and half-integer values of the nuclear angular-momentum quantum number, often denoted by I. Thus, certain nuclei have $I = \frac{3}{2}$, with possible components $\pm\frac{3}{2}$, $\pm\frac{1}{2}$ in a given direction, leading to a fourfold hyperfine splitting. All nuclei with *even* values of the mass number A are found to have *integer* nuclear spin, while all those with *odd* values of A have *half-integer* spins. This observation provides a valuable clue as to the constituents of nuclei, to be discussed in Sec. 15-2.

The ratio of magnetic moment to angular momentum is called the *gyromagnetic ratio*. For *orbital* motion of electrons, this ratio is $e/2m$, although for spin angular momentum and magnetic moment of the electron, it has very nearly twice this value. The gyromagnetic ratio of nuclei is conveniently expressed as

$$g\frac{e}{2M} \tag{15-10}$$

where g is a pure number, typically between 1 and 3, and M is the proton mass. Thus, while the spin angular momentum of a nucleus has the same order of magnitude as that for orbital motion of electrons, both being proportional to $\hbar$, the magnetic moments of nuclei are typically *smaller* than those associated with electron motion by the ratio of electron to proton masses, $m/M \cong \frac{1}{1836}$.

In 1946, two groups of physicists, working independently at Harvard and Stanford Universities, developed a method of measuring nuclear magnetic moments which is much more precise than the spectroscopic determinations outlined above. This method, called *nuclear magnetic resonance,* makes use of measurements of the frequency of *precession* of the nuclear angular momentum, analogous to the precession of a gyroscope, in a magnetic field.

15-2 NUCLEAR STRUCTURE

The nuclear properties outlined in Sec. 15-1 can be observed without any probing into the details of nuclear structure; we shall now examine this structure in more detail. What are the fundamental building blocks of nuclei? To experimenters in the early years of the present century, the fact that many nuclear masses are integer multiples of that of the hydrogen nucleus (a single proton) suggested that the total mass might be made up simply of the appropriate number of protons. For the heavier nuclei, this would lead to an electric charge greater than that actually observed, and so it was proposed to neutralize some of the proton charge by adding electrons to the nucleus. For example, the helium nucleus has a mass about four times that of the proton but a charge only twice as great; perhaps it contains four protons and two electrons. The fact that some radioactive nuclei emit electrons seemed to support this view.

Although this hypothesis appears attractive at first, there are several reasons why it cannot possibly be correct. One is that it is not possible to understand nuclear spins on this basis. Since both proton and electron have spin $\frac{1}{2}$, any nucleus with an even total number of particles (protons plus electrons) should have a spin that is an *integer* multiple of $\hbar$, whereas those with an odd number of particles should have half-integer spins. There are, in fact, many nuclei that do not follow this rule. The simplest example is deuterium, the isotope of hydrogen with mass number $A = 2$. If this nucleus consisted of two protons and an electron, it should have a spin of either $\frac{1}{2}$ or $\frac{3}{2}$; instead, its spin is found to be 1. Many other examples can be cited. Magnetic moments pose an even more serious problem. The electron magnetic moment is of the order of a thousand times greater than that of the proton; yet the magnitudes of the observed magnetic moments of nuclei are characteristic of that of the proton, not the electron, casting further doubt on the existence of electrons in the nucleus. Still other evidence might be cited.

About 1925 it was proposed that one of the nuclear building blocks might be a *neutral* particle (no electric charge) having a half-integer spin and a mass about equal to that of the proton. This particle, even before it was discovered experimentally, was named the *neutron*. The detection of a neutral particle posed serious experimental problems, inasmuch as none of the usual techniques for observing *charged* particles would work successfully with a particle having *no* charge. Such a particle would not be deflected by an electric or magnetic field, would not make its presence known by creating ions, and therefore would have no effect on photographic emulsions.

Finally in 1932 James Chadwick, one of Rutherford's associates, made a series of observations which could be interpreted as demonstrating the existence of the neutron. It had been discovered earlier that when a beryllium target is bombarded by α particles from a heavy radioactive element such as polonium, radiation is produced which does not consist of charged particles but penetrates matter more readily than any other radiation then known (α, β, or γ rays). This radiation in turn was observed to knock protons out of hydrogen-rich substances such as paraffin. Although it had originally been thought to consist of high-energy γ rays, Chadwick showed that a much more natural interpretation was that of a neutral particle with a mass approximately equal to the proton mass.

Further experiments confirmed Chadwick's hypothesis, and it was recognized that protons and neutrons are the fundamental building blocks of nuclei. The observed angular momentum of nuclei could then be understood on the assumption that the neutron spin is $\frac{1}{2}$. Deuterium, for example, was assumed to be a proton and a neutron bound together, so that a spin of 0 or 1 was to be expected. As pointed out above, the observed spin is 1.

The mass of the neutron is slightly greater than that of the proton; the two masses are, respectively,

$$M_N = 1.675 \times 10^{-27} \text{ kg} = 1.00866 \text{ u}$$
$$M_P = 1.673 \times 10^{-27} \text{ kg} = 1.00728 \text{ u}$$
(15-11)

As mentioned in Sec. 15-1, any nucleus is identified by the number of protons and neutrons it contains. The proton number Z is equal to the atomic number of the corresponding element, the neutron number is N, and these are related to the total number of nucleons A (the mass number) by

$$A = Z + N$$
(15-12)

The various nuclear species can also be identified by the notation $^A_Z X$, where X is the chemical symbol of the corresponding element. For example, the atomic number of chlorine is 17. The notation for the isotope of chlorine with mass number 35, corresponding to 17 protons and 18 neutrons, is $^{35}_{17}\text{Cl}$. This notation is redundant, inasmuch as the atomic number identifies the element. That is, the notation ^{35}Cl conveys the same information as does $^{35}_{17}\text{Cl}$. The subscript is often omitted.

We mentioned in Sec. 15-1 the existence of *isotopes*, various species of the same element, whose atoms have the same nuclear charge but different nuclear mass. Two isotopes of an element have nuclei with the same number of protons but different numbers of neutrons. For example, the nucleus of ^{35}Cl has 17 protons and 18 neutrons ($Z = 17$, $N = 18$, $A = 35$), while that of ^{37}Cl has 17 protons and 20 neutrons ($Z = 17$, $N = 20$, $A = 37$). Individual nuclear species, each identified by values of Z and N (or alternatively Z and A) are called *nuclides*.

The neutron, like the proton, has spin angular momentum $\hbar/2$. It also has a magnetic moment, with a direction *opposite* to that of the angular momentum and magnitude $-3.826(e/2M)$. Its gyromagnetic ratio, or g factor, is thus -3.826. It may not be immediately obvious how a particle with no electric charge can have a magnetic moment since in the cases considered thus far the two have been inseparable. The explanation is to be found in the internal structure of the neutron, which in some respects is not an indivisible particle. We defer further discussion of this matter to Chap. 16, where we shall discuss the nature of fundamental particles in more detail. Both protons and neutrons, like *all* particles having spin $\frac{1}{2}$, obey the Pauli exclusion principle.

The most immediate question concerning nuclear structure is what holds the constituents of a nucleus together. Protons, having like electric charges, repel each other. The observed radii of nuclei are less than 10^{-14} m. The amount of energy necessary to overcome the electrical repulsion and push two protons within 10^{-14} m of each other is

$$E = \frac{e^2}{4\pi\varepsilon_0 r} = \frac{(8.98 \times 10^9 \text{ N} \cdot \text{m}^2/\text{C}^2)(1.60 \times 10^{-19} \text{ C})^2}{10^{-14} \text{ m}}$$

$$= 2.30 \times 10^{-14} \text{ J}$$

$$= 1.44 \times 10^5 \text{ eV} \tag{15-13}$$

or about 10^4 times the ionization potential of the hydrogen atom. Yet despite this very strong electrical repulsion, protons are somehow bound together in a nucleus, along with neutrons. *Gravitational* attraction cannot account for the stability of nuclei; the gravitational attraction between two protons is *smaller* than their electrostatic repulsion by a factor of the order of 10^{-38}. Thus gravitational interactions are of no importance in the understanding of nuclear structure.

The forces responsible for the stability of nuclei are not of any familiar nature but instead are a manifestation of a new kind of force, which for lack of a better name is called the *nuclear force*. Not only must the nuclear force between two protons be much stronger than the electrical repulsion at short distances, but it must be a *short-range* force; otherwise protons would be attracted no matter how far apart they are. We might therefore expect that the potential energy due to the nuclear interaction should be proportional not to e^2/r, as in the case of the electrostatic force, but to a function which drops off more quickly with increasing r, such as

$$V(r) = -f^2 \frac{e^{-r/a}}{r} \tag{15-14}$$

where f is a constant characterizing the strength of the interaction, and a is a constant with units of length which describes the *range* of the interaction, that is, how rapidly it drops off with increasing r. Figure 15-3 illustrates the behavior of this function.

Equation (15-14) is not just a guess; it has some theoretical foundation. For the present, however, we regard it as an empirical description which helps to visualize the nature of nuclear forces. This potential-energy function is called the *Yukawa potential*, in honor of the Japanese theoretical physicist H. Yukawa, who first proposed such a potential-energy function in 1935 on the basis of a meson-exchange theory. We shall return to the Yukawa theory of nuclear forces in Sec. 16-3.

Experiments have shown that the potential energy associated with the attractive force between two nuclear particles is of the order of 10^7 eV and

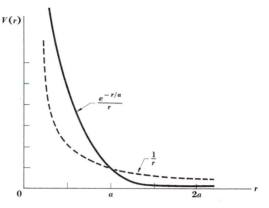

Fig. 15-3 Graph of the Yukawa potential function, given by Eq. (15-14), and, for comparison, a Coulomb ($1/r$) potential function having the same value at $r = a$. The Yukawa potential drops off much more rapidly with increasing r than the Coulomb potential.

is the same for neutron-neutron interactions as for proton-proton interactions. Thus the nuclear force is not directly connected with electric charge. Nuclear interaction energies are usually measured in *million electronvolts*, abbreviated MeV:

$$1 \text{ MeV} = 10^6 \text{ eV} \tag{15-15}$$

Another significant property of nuclear forces, not shared by more familiar forces such as electrical or gravitational interactions, is that of *saturation*. An individual nucleon does not interact simultaneously with an unlimited number of other nucleons but only with a small number. This is in contrast to electrical interactions, in which a given electric charge interacts with *all* other charges in its vicinity. Instead, the nuclear force seems to involve only interactions of an individual nucleon with at most three others. For example, the α particle, or helium nucleus, contains two protons and two neutrons in a stable structure with nucleon number $A = 4$. This structure, however, exerts very little attractive force toward an additional proton or neutron, and there is *no* stable nucleus with $A = 5$.

The fact that all nuclei have nearly the same *density*, as discussed in Sec. 15-1, provides additional evidence for the saturation of nuclear forces. If every nucleon in a nucleus attracted every other one, then in nuclei with large A the nucleons would be pulled closer together than in those with smaller A. The fact that this does *not* happen suggests that each nucleon interacts primarily with a few of its nearest neighbors.

Any discussion of the "size" of a nucleus must of course be approached cautiously; measured values of nuclear radii depend somewhat on the techniques used for the measurement. Nuclear radius, volume, and density are not precisely defined quantities, just as the diameter of an atom is not a precisely defined quantity. Nucleons are properly described in quantum-mechanical language by *wave functions;* when we say that a nucleus has a certain radius, we mean that the wave function describing its configuration is confined mostly within this radius, but the boundaries of a nucleus are not completely sharp.

Information concerning the interaction energies of nucleons can be obtained from precise measurements of nuclear masses. The simplest example is deuterium, the nucleus of the $A = 2$ isotope of hydrogen. This nucleus, the simplest of all nucleon bound states, contains one proton and one neutron and is called a *deuteron*. It might be thought that the mass of the deuteron would be simply the sum of proton and neutron masses,

$$M_P + M_N = 1.00728 \text{ u} + 1.00866 \text{ u} = 2.01594 \text{ u} \tag{15-16}$$

Instead, the observed value of the deuteron mass M_D is somewhat *less* than this, about 2.01356 u. On the basis of relativistic considerations, this result is to be expected, since the total *energy* of the system when the two particles are bound is less than when they are separated. The amount by which the mass of the deuteron is less than the sum of proton and neutron masses should be $1/c^2$ times the potential energy in the bound state. The magnitude of this energy is called the *binding energy*, abbreviated E_B. Thus we expect to find

$$E_B = (M_P + M_N - M_D)c^2 \tag{15-17}$$

In such calculations, a useful conversion factor is that a mass of 1 u is the equivalent of an energy of 931 MeV. Using this conversion factor, we find that the binding energy of the deuteron is

$$E_B = (0.00238 \text{ u})c^2 = 2.22 \text{ MeV} \tag{15-18}$$

This binding energy can also be measured directly by a technique analogous to that used in measuring ionization potentials of atoms: bombardment with high-energy particles or electromagnetic radiation. It is observed that the minimum energy necessary to dissociate the deuteron (in the frame of reference where the total momentum is zero) is 2.22 MeV, in agreement with the above calculation.

Similarly, the total binding energy E_B of a nucleus of mass M, having Z protons and N neutrons, is given in general by

$$E_B = (ZM_P + NM_N - M)c^2 \tag{15-19}$$

Thus a total binding energy can be computed for each nucleus. It is also of interest to calculate the binding energy *per nucleon*, $E_B/A = E_B/(Z + N)$ for various nuclei. Except for nuclei with very small A, this turns out to be approximately the same for all nuclei, about 8 MeV per nucleon. Figure 15-4 shows a graph of binding energy per nucleon as a function of the mass number A. This observation is further evidence of the fact that nuclear forces

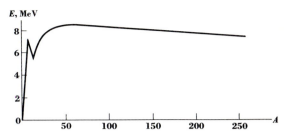

Fig. 15-4 Binding energy per nucleon, as a function of nucleon number. Except for very small values of A, the binding energy per nucleon is nearly independent of A. The "spike" at $A = 4$ shows the unusual stability of the α-particle structure.

exhibit saturation, in sharp contrast to the binding of electrons in atoms, where the average binding energy per electron increases sharply as the atomic number Z increases. The slight decrease of the binding energy per nucleon at large A is due chiefly to the increasing importance of the electrostatic repulsion of protons. This effect, which always tends to *decrease* the binding energy, is of longer range than the nuclear force and does not saturate; hence it becomes relatively more important at large A. In fact, electrostatic effects are primarily responsible for the fact that no nucleus with A greater than 209 is stable. Stability of nuclei will be discussed in the next section.

Nuclear masses are usually measured by mass spectrometer techniques, discussed in Sec. 15-1, capable of an accuracy of about one part in 10^7. The quantity usually measured is not the mass of the bare nucleus but the mass of a singly ionized *atom*. For this reason, values of nuclear masses found in tables are nearly always the masses of neutral atoms rather than bare nuclei. When these values are used in calculations, care must be taken to account for the differing numbers of electrons included in the tabulated nuclear masses. An additional complication is the binding energy of the atomic electrons. In light elements this is negligible; in hydrogen, for example, the ionization energy of 13.6 eV is equivalent to a mass of about 1.5×10^{-8} u. But in the most massive atoms the *total* electron binding energy is of the order of 1 MeV, equivalent to about 0.001 u; if a precise value for the mass of the bare nucleus is required, this binding energy must be taken into account.

The foregoing discussion has been a *phenomenological* approach to the properties of nuclei, a description of the most important elements of their characteristics and behavior which does not attempt to analyze the fundamental nature of nuclear interactions. Nuclear forces are not yet completely understood; all models that have achieved any success make use of additional unstable particles called *mesons*, which are created and destroyed by the protons and neutrons in a nucleus, in much the same way that photons are created and destroyed in transitions between electronic energy levels in atoms. The interaction between two nucleons can be described in terms of a game of catch in which the two particles toss mesons back and forth at each other. The meson-exchange theory of nuclear forces will be discussed in Sec. 16-3.

15-3   NUCLEAR STABILITY

Some nuclei are *stable*, while others are *unstable* in the sense that they spontaneously undergo transitions to configurations with two or more separated parts. Such a transition is often called a *decay*. An example of an unstable nucleus occurring in nature is uranium, $^{238}_{92}U$, which emits an α particle (^4_2He) to become $^{234}_{90}Th$. This is also unstable, and in fact is the second of a series of 14 successive decay products, the last of which is the stable nucleus $^{206}_{82}Pb$. Several other decay processes are also observed in nature, and these will be discussed shortly.

The stability or instability of a given nucleus is determined by the competition between the *attractive* nuclear force, with its negative potential energy, and the *repulsive* electrical interaction of the protons, with positive potential energy. For stability the total potential energy must be negative; the nucleus must have lower total energy than when all the nucleons are separated from each other. The binding energy is customarily defined as the negative of this potential energy. The binding energy of a stable nucleus must therefore be positive; otherwise it could spontaneously disintegrate into its component parts.

Although positive binding energy is a *necessary* condition for nuclear stability, it is not sufficient to *guarantee* stability; the total binding energy must also be greater than that of *any other* possible arrangement of its parts, whether completely separated or bound in other combinations. An equivalent statement is that for stability the mass of a nucleus must be less than the total mass of its constituents when arranged in *any other* combination. Thus the uranium nucleus cited above is unstable because the α particle and thorium nucleus to which it decays have lower total energy than the uranium nucleus. A nucleus with Z protons and N neutrons and mass $M(Z,N)$ is stable with respect to the emission of an α particle only if

$$M(Z,N) < M(Z-2, N-2) + M_\alpha \tag{15-20}$$

Alpha decay occurs only in heavy nuclei ($A > 209$). To understand why this should be, we recall that because of the saturating property of nuclear forces, the average binding energy per nucleon is nearly independent of A; the *total* attractive potential energy due to the nuclear force is approximately proportional to A. Conversely, however, the electrical repulsions of the particles continue to increase with Z. Since each proton repels *all* the other protons, the *total* electrostatic potential energy increases approximately as Z^2. Thus it is not surprising that as A and Z increase, a point is finally reached where the electrostatic repulsion with its longer range and lack of saturation overcomes the short-range saturating attractive nuclear forces. The critical point comes at $A = 209$; there are no known stable nuclei with mass numbers greater than this.

Why should an unstable nucleus emit an α particle? Why not individual protons or neutrons? Although there is no one-sentence answer to this question, the explanation is to be found in the peculiar stability of the α-particle structure, which in turn is directly related to characteristics of the nucleons and their interaction. Protons and neutrons individually obey the exclusion principle, in a manner analogous to the behavior of electrons in atoms. We may think of the nucleus in terms of a central-field approximation in which each nucleon moves under the influence of all the others. In this approximation there are single-nucleon energy levels analogous to the one-electron levels in atoms in the central-field approximation, discussed in Secs. 12-1 and 12-2. The exclusion principle permits two protons and two neutrons to occupy the lowest energy level, but a fifth nucleon would have to go into the next higher level. Hence the α particle is particularly stable (28 MeV binding energy), but there is *no* stable nucleus with $A = 5$.

Thus the exclusion principle favors pairs of protons and pairs of neutrons, each with opposite spins, and *pairs* of *pairs*, a pair of protons and a pair of neutrons occupying the same level. Emission of an α particle does not disturb this pairing, but emission of a single nucleon would; hence it is almost always more favorable energetically for a nucleus to emit an α particle than an individual nucleon.

Another mode of decay of unstable nuclei observed in nature is the emission of an electron or β particle. This may seem a little puzzling, especially since we have argued in Sec. 15-2 that there cannot be any electrons in the nucleus. The situation is analogous to the emission of photons by atoms in excited states; the atom does not *contain* photons, but it *creates* them during a transition from one energy state to a lower one. The analogous process for nucleons involves the transformation of a neutron into a proton, an electron, and a third particle with zero rest mass called a *neutrino* (symbol ν). Interactions such as this in which fundamental particles are created and destroyed will be discussed in greater detail in Chap. 16; for the present we simply remark that the reaction

$$n \rightarrow p + e^- + \nu \tag{15-21}$$

is energetically possible because the mass difference between neutron and proton (1.675×10^{-27} kg $- 1.673 \times 10^{-27}$ kg) is greater than the electron mass (0.0009×10^{-27} kg) and that it *does* occur.

Emission of electrons, usually called β decay, occurs when the ratio of neutrons to protons in a nucleus is not optimum for stability. For each

A there is an optimum value of N/Z for stability. If there were no electrical repulsion, the optimum ratio would be unity, corresponding to equal numbers of neutron pairs and proton pairs, occupying together the lowest available energy states. The Coulomb repulsion shifts the proton energies upward, with the result that the optimum N/Z increases from unity at small A to about 1.5 at $A = 208$. Figure 15-5 is a graph showing values of N for maximum stability, as a function of Z.

Thus a nucleus having too many neutrons for stability can adjust itself by emitting an electron; the residual or "daughter" nucleus has one less neutron and one more proton than the original one. Conversely, a nucleus is *stable* with respect to β decay only if

$$M(Z,N) < M(Z + 1, N - 1) + M_e \qquad (15\text{-}22)$$

For example, the nucleus $^{59}_{27}\text{Co}$ has $N/Z = 1.18$ and is stable, while $^{60}_{27}\text{Co}$ has $N/Z = 1.22$ and is unstable, undergoing β decay to the stable nucleus

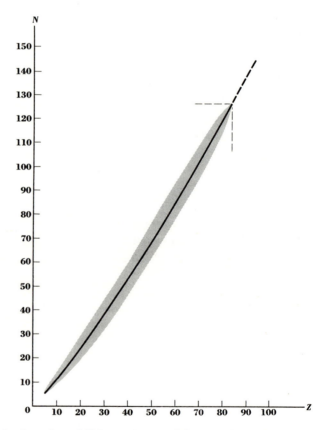

Fig. 15-5 Graph showing values of N for maximum stability, as a function of Z. All stable nuclei fall within the shaded area shown.

$^{60}_{28}$Ni, with $N/Z = 1.14$. It should also be noted that $^{60}_{27}$Co is an "odd-odd" nucleus containing both an unpaired neutron and an unpaired proton. Very few odd-odd nuclei are stable with respect to β decay.

Two variations on the β-decay theme occur with nuclei having *too few* neutrons for stability; these are emission of a *positron* and *capture* of an orbital electron by the nucleus. Both processes have the effect of increasing Z by unity and decreasing N by unity. They will be discussed in greater detail in Sec. 15-4. Finally, some nuclei, particularly those in the range $A > 230$, undergo *nuclear fission*, splitting into two fragments and sometimes a few free neutrons. Fission will be discussed in Sec. 15-8.

In summary, a nucleus is stable only if *all* the decay processes mentioned above are energetically impossible. A nucleus is unstable if it is too large ($A > 209$) or if its neutron-proton ratio is wrong. With a sufficiently precise table of nuclear masses, one can compute the various relevant binding energies and *predict* whether or not a given nucleus is stable. There are a few exceptional nuclei which on energy considerations ought to be unstable but which decay so slowly (e.g., a half-life of 10^{12} years) that they are in effect stable.

15-4 RADIOACTIVITY

A number of heavy elements have unstable nuclei; no nucleus with $Z \geq 84$ *or* $A \geq 210$ is stable. The most famous examples of unstable nuclei are uranium, thorium, and radium, although there are many others. The history of the investigation of radioactivity is an exciting tale with many of the characteristics of a good mystery story. It began in 1896 with the accidental discovery by Henri Becquerel that salts of uranium emit spontaneously a radiation with penetrating properties akin to those of x-rays, such as the ability to affect a photographic plate even when it is wrapped in black paper or thin sheets of metal. In the subsequent investigation of the phenomenon of radioactivity, many of the most famous physicists of the age were involved, including Becquerel himself, Roentgen (the discoverer of x-rays), Pierre and Marie Curie, Rutherford, and many others.

The emissions from radioactive nuclei were classified into three categories, which were labeled alpha, beta, and gamma (α, β, and γ) rays. By studying the deflections of these particles in electric and magnetic fields, it was shown that α rays consist of a stream of particles having a mass of 4 u and a charge of $+2e$. Subsequent work has shown conclusively that these particles are identical with the nuclei of helium atoms, $^4_2$He.

By similar techniques the β rays were identified as high-energy electrons. They have considerably greater penetrating ability than α particles and can pass through thin sheets of metal, whereas α particles are stopped even by a few centimeters of air at ordinary pressures. The nature of γ rays was in doubt for a considerable time; it was discovered that they are not deflected by electric or magnetic fields, so they cannot be charged particles. They are now known to be quanta of electromagnetic radiation, similar to x-rays but usually having higher energies. The penetrating ability of γ rays of energies typical of nuclear disintegrations is much greater than that of α or β rays with comparable energies. The reasons for the instability of nuclei having $A > 209$ have been discussed in Sec. 15-3. The mass number is nearly always decreased by emission of α particles rather than individual nucleons because the former is always more favorable energetically.

In *all* nuclei there is short-range correlation among the particles which can be described in terms of structures resembling α particles. On this basis, one may think of α emission in terms of motion of an α particle *within the nucleus* under the average influence of the other nucleons; associated with this interaction is a potential-energy function which varies with its distance r from the center of mass of the other nucleons in the general way shown in Fig. 15-6a. At sufficiently great distances r, where the nuclear force is no longer effective, the potential varies as $1/r$, characteristic of the electrostatic repulsion. But at sufficiently small r, when the nuclear forces become operative, the potential energy must *decrease*, corresponding to an attractive interaction; otherwise the α particle would not be bound even temporarily.

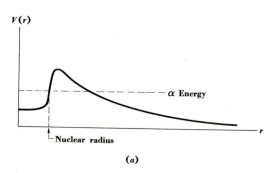

(a)

Fig. 15-6 (a) General form of the α-particle potential-energy function in a heavy unstable nucleus. Quantum mechanics predicts that there is a certain probability that the particle will be found outside the potential well, despite the fact that classical mechanics provides no way for it to escape from the well. (b) In a stable nucleus, the α-particle energy in the potential well is less than it is outside, and α emission is energetically impossible.

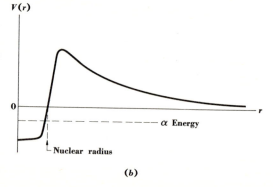

(b)

Assuming this generally plausible form for the interaction potential energy, we picture an α particle as trapped in the central potential well. In terms of classical mechanics, there is no way for it to escape from this well except by somehow acquiring enough additional energy to surmount the potential-energy barrier, which may be several megaelectronvolts, so there is no way to understand α emission on the basis of classical mechanics. Quantum mechanics, however, provides a natural explanation for α decay, and when the theory of α emission was first developed in 1928, it was regarded as an important confirmation of the newly born quantum mechanics. At a potential-energy barrier, beyond which the particle cannot pass according to classical mechanics, the wave function for the particle does not drop suddenly to zero but rather decreases asymptotically to zero. That is, there is some *penetration* of the wave function into regions which classically would have negative kinetic energy, just as in the situations discussed in Sec. 10-4.

Thus if the α-particle wave function is initially confined entirely within a potential well, there is a certain finite probability at any time that the particle will be found *outside* the well, despite the fact that classically there is no way for it to get out. This effect is called "tunneling"; the particle, in a manner of speaking, tunnels through the potential barrier rather than climbing over it. This general picture of α emission can be developed into a detailed theory, and α emission by nuclei is now quite well understood.

When a nucleus emits an α particle, the neutron number N and the charge number Z both decrease by 2, and the total nucleon number A decreases by 4. For example, a nucleus of radium, $^{226}_{88}\text{Ra}$, emits an α particle and becomes a nucleus of radon, $^{222}_{86}\text{Rn}$. This in turn emits another α particle and becomes a nucleus of polonium, $^{218}_{84}\text{Po}$. A different series contains, as one of its elements, actinium, $^{225}_{89}\text{Ac}$. This emits an α particle, decaying into francium, $^{221}_{87}\text{Fr}$, which decays into astatine, $^{217}_{85}\text{At}$, which decays into bismuth, $^{213}_{83}\text{Bi}$, and so on.

Because heavy nuclei always contain more neutrons than protons, each α decay *increases* the ratio N/Z. But because A decreases, a *smaller* value of N/Z would be required for stability. Thus it sometimes happens that after one or more α decays, the N/Z ratio is so far from optimum that β decay becomes energetically possible, either as an alternate decay mode or, if there is insufficient energy for α decay, as the *only* decay mode. In the above example, $^{213}_{83}\text{Bi}$ decays either by α emission to $^{209}_{81}\text{Tl}$ or by β emission to $^{213}_{84}\text{Po}$.

It has been mentioned in Sec. 15-3 that the basic process of β decay, the conversion of a neutron into a proton and an electron, is energetically possible because the neutron mass exceeds that of the proton by 0.00134 u, while the electron mass is only 0.00055 u. However, it was recognized as early as 1930 that a third particle must be produced in this process, for several reasons. In the first place, the proton, neutron, and electron all have spin $\frac{1}{2}$, so the total component of angular momentum of proton and electron in a given direction would have to be either zero or unity; since the neutron spin is $\frac{1}{2}$, angular-momentum conservation could not be satisfied.

The total kinetic energy of the decay products is determined by the mass difference, and the way this energy is divided between the proton and electron is determined by momentum conservation; if only two particles are emitted, both should have perfectly definite energies. Instead, the emerging electrons are found to have a *continuous spectrum* of energies; this is consistent with energy and momentum conservation only if a third particle is also emitted so that the total energy and momentum can be shared in a variety of ways by the three particles.

Thus the choice in 1930 was either to abandon three conservation laws (energy, momentum, and angular momentum) or to postulate the existence of an unseen neutral particle having spin $\frac{1}{2}$ and zero rest mass. Pauli christened this hypothetical particle the *neutrino*, and such was the faith of physicists in conservation laws that its existence has never been seriously doubted since that time, even though it was not directly observed experimentally until 1956. The energy-momentum relation for the neutrino is

$$E = pc \qquad (15\text{-}23)$$

just as for the (also massless) photon, although the two are quite different particles. We shall also see in Chap. 16 that there are actually several kinds of neutrinos, all massless and neutral spin $\frac{1}{2}$ particles but differing in the kinds of reactions in which they participate.

The production of γ rays (high-energy photons) during radioactive decay is not very surprising. Just as atoms have various energy levels corresponding to different electron configurations, nuclei also have various energy levels. When an unstable nucleus undergoes a radioactive disintegration, the residual nucleus may be left not in its ground state but in an excited state. It may then decay to the ground state with the emission of a photon. As we have seen, energies associated with nuclear interactions are typically of the order of several megaelectronvolts, in contrast to energies associated with atomic interactions, typically of the order of a few electronvolts. Thus energies of typical γ-ray photons are much larger than for visible light or x-rays.

We have referred briefly to the existence of radioactive decay *series*, in which a succession of decays occurs. Such decay series, as well as other nuclear reactions, are conveniently represented by means of a *Segre chart*, named for its inventor Emilio Segre, a collaborator of Fermi. Any nuclide is represented on this chart by a point whose coordinates are the proton number Z and the neutron number N. Nuclides having the same mass number $A = N + Z$ lie along diagonal lines oriented at $45°$.

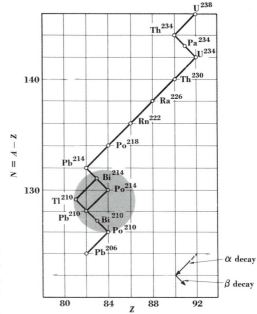

Fig. 15-7 Segre chart showing uranium $^{238}_{92}$U decay series, terminating with the stable nuclide $^{206}_{82}$Pb. Branching occurs at $^{214}_{83}$Bi, which has two alternate decay modes.

Figure 15-7 shows the uranium decay series as represented on a Segre chart. The first element in this particular series that occurs in nature is ^{238}U; the final member of the chain, that is, the only one that does not undergo further radioactive decay, is ^{206}Pb. An interesting feature is the branching at ^{214}Bi, which decays into ^{210}Pb by an α and a β decay which can occur in either order, as shown.

Three other decay series are known. Two of them, starting with thorium $^{232}_{90}$Th and uranium $^{235}_{92}$U, respectively, occur in nature; the other, starting with neptunium $^{237}_{93}$Np, begins with nuclei produced artificially in nuclear reactors, by means of processes to be discussed in Sec. 15-7. In most cases, α or β decay leaves the residual nucleus in an excited state rather than the ground state, and so α or β emission is often followed by γ emission.

Another interesting feature of the decay series illustrated in Fig. 15-7 is that it indicates the existence of *unstable* isotopes of nuclei which also have *stable* isotopes. For example, ^{206}Pb is stable, but ^{210}Pb and ^{214}Pb are unstable, containing four and eight more neutrons, respectively, than the stable isotope. This phenomenon occurs with *all* nuclei. For any given number of protons, there is a certain optimum number of neutrons for maximum stability. If there were no electrostatic effects, the most stable nuclei would be those with equal numbers of protons and neutrons, paired off into α-like structures. This actually occurs for the light elements, such as the stable nuclides $^{4}_{2}$He, $^{12}_{6}$C, $^{16}_{8}$O, $^{20}_{10}$Ne, $^{24}_{12}$Mg, $^{28}_{14}$Si, $^{32}_{16}$S, and $^{36}_{18}$Ar. An interesting exception is $^{8}_{4}$Be, which is *not* stable because it decays into two $^{4}_{2}$He nuclei!

With increasing A, the repulsive electrical interactions become relatively more important, and the most stable structure for a given Z contains a few *more* neutrons than protons. An example cited previously is the radioactive nuclide ^{60}Co, which contains one more neutron than the stable ^{59}Co and undergoes β decay into the stable nuclide ^{60}Ni.

Another example, and one which introduces a new feature, is the unstable nuclide ^{22}Na. The stable isotope of sodium has $A = 23$, so ^{22}Na has one neutron too *few*—a difficulty just the opposite of that of ^{60}Co. One is tempted to think that, if there were such a thing as a *positive electron,* this nucleus would emit one, decreasing Z and increasing N by one unit each, leading to ^{22}Ne, which is stable. As a matter of fact, positive electrons *do* exist; they were first discovered in cosmic rays in 1932 by the American physicist Carl Anderson. They do not have a permanent existence, since whenever a positive electron collides with an ordinary electron, both particles disappear and γ rays are produced. The properties of positive electrons will be discussed in more detail in Sec. 16-2. A nuclear disintegration in which a positive electron is produced is referred to as β^+ emission. Commonly, however, β *decay* is taken to mean emission of either an ordinary (negative) electron or a positive electron, also called *positron.*

An interesting variation of the β-decay process occurs with nuclei having too few neutrons for stability but insufficient energy to make β^+ emission possible. In some such cases it is energetically possible for a nucleus to *capture* an orbital electron from one of the inner shells, transforming a proton in the nucleus into a neutron according to the scheme

$$p + e^- \rightarrow n + \nu \tag{15-24}$$

Usually the residual nucleus is in an excited state, and one or more γ photons are emitted in addition to the neutrino. Because electrons in the K shell, being closest to the nucleus, are most likely to be captured, this decay mode is called K *capture;* the more general term *orbital-electron capture* is also used. An example of this process is

$$^7_4\text{Be} + e^- \rightarrow ^7_3\text{Li} + \gamma + \nu$$

If a K electron is absorbed by the Be nucleus, the result is an Li atom with the proper number of electrons, but in a K x-ray energy state.

15-5 DECAY RATES

It is of interest to examine the *rates* at which nuclear decay processes take place. Energies involved in nuclear interactions are so large compared with those associated with thermal agitation, photons of visible light, chemical binding, and other ordinary influences, that decay rates are nearly independent of environment. If at times t there are N radioactive nuclei, then the number of decays occurring in a short time interval following this time, say Δt, is expected to be proportional to N and to the time interval. That is,

$$\Delta N = -\lambda N \, \Delta t \tag{15-25}$$

or, in the limit as Δt approaches zero,

$$\frac{dN}{dt} = -\lambda N \tag{15-26}$$

where λ is a constant characteristic of the decay process for a given nuclide, called the *decay constant* for the process.

If there are N_0 nuclei at time $t = 0$, the number $N(t)$ at any later time t can be found by integrating this differential equation. This is most easily accomplished by separating variables and integrating both sides directly, as follows:

$$\int_{N_0}^{N} \frac{dN}{N} = \int_{0}^{t} - \lambda \, dt$$

$$\ln \frac{N}{N_0} = -\lambda t$$

$$N = N_0 e^{-\lambda t} \tag{15-27}$$

On both sides of the first equation, the lower limits represent the initial values of N and t, respectively, and the upper limits the final values. The number of nuclei surviving at time t decreases exponentially from the initial value N_0 and asymptotically approaches zero after a very long time.

The decay rate of a nucleus can also be characterized by the *half-life* $T_{1/2}$, defined as the time required for the number of nuclei to decrease by a factor of 2. To obtain the relationship of $T_{1/2}$ to the decay constant λ, we observe that the time $T_{1/2}$ at which the number of nuclei has decayed to $\frac{1}{2}N_0$ is given by

$$\tfrac{1}{2}N_0 = N_0 e^{-\lambda T_{1/2}} \tag{15-28}$$

from which we find

$$T_{1/2} = \frac{\ln 2}{\lambda} = \frac{0.693}{\lambda} \tag{15-29}$$

Half-lives observed for decay processes cover an extremely wide range, from the shortest time intervals that can be measured in the laboratory (of the order of 10^{-11} s) to at least 10^{15} years.

The actual number of disintegrations per unit time, given in Eq. (15-26) as λN, is called the *activity* of the specimen. For historical reasons, it is customary to measure activity in a unit called the *curie,* defined to be 3.70×10^{10} disintegrations per second. This is approximately equal to the activity of one gram of radium $^{226}_{88}\text{Ra}$.

If the residual or "daughter" nucleus is stable, the number N_2 of daughter nuclei at time t is equal to the number of parent nuclei that have decayed; denoting the number of parent nuclei now by N_1, we have

$$N_2(t) = N_0(1 - e^{-\lambda t}) \tag{15-30}$$

As we have seen, however, the daughter nuclei may also be unstable. If so, the time rate of change of N_2 is the rate at which they are produced by decaying parents, *less* the rate at which they decay. Letting the decay constants of parent and daughter be λ_1 and λ_2, respectively, we have

$$\frac{dN_2}{dt} = +\lambda_1 N_1 - \lambda_2 N_2 \tag{15-31}$$

If $N_2 = 0$ at time $t = 0$ and N_1 is given by Eq. (15-27), this equation can be integrated; the details are left as a problem.

If the half-life of the parent is much *greater* than that of the daughter, then after a time long compared to the half-life of the daughter a steady state is reached, in which the daughter nuclei decay at the same rate as they are produced. In that case N_2 is constant, and Eq. (15-31) becomes

$$\lambda_1 N_1 = \lambda_2 N_2 \tag{15-32}$$

which may be rewritten with the help of Eq. (15-29) as

$$\frac{N_1}{T_{1(1/2)}} = \frac{N_2}{T_{2(1/2)}} \tag{15-33}$$

This relation describes any two members of a radioactive decay series, provided the system has not been disturbed (by chemical removal of some members or other disruption) for a time much longer than any of the daughter half-lives. It can be used, for example, to predict the relative abundance in a rock sample of two members of the decay chain shown in Fig. 15-7. For example, the half-life of ^{226}Ra is 1600 years $= 5.0 \times 10^{10}$ s, while that of ^{222}Rn is 3.8 d $= 3.3 \times 10^5$ s. Thus a sample containing 10^{-6} mol (about 0.25 mg) of radium should contain

$$\frac{3.3 \times 10^5 \text{ s}}{5.0 \times 10^{10} \text{ s}} 10^{-6} = 6.6 \times 10^{-12} \text{ mol}$$

of radon, provided of course that no radon has escaped since the rock was formed.

An interesting application of radioactivity is the dating of archaeological specimens by measuring their content of a radioactive isotope of carbon, ^{14}C. This unstable isotope, with a half-life of 5568 years, is produced in the atmosphere by bombardment of ^{14}N nuclei by cosmic rays. Living plants and animals which obtain their carbon from carbon dioxide in the atmosphere contain ^{14}C in the same proportion as it is found in the atmosphere. When the organism dies, the intake of ^{14}C stops, and the ^{14}C that has already been deposited decays, with a half-life of 5568 years. Thus by measuring the relative concentrations of ^{14}C and ^{12}C in the remains of a once-living organism, one can deduce how long ago it died. Similar techniques with other isotopes are used in dating rock formations.

15-6 INSTRUMENTS OF NUCLEAR PHYSICS

In this section we survey briefly some of the instruments used for research in nuclear and high-energy physics. These fall generally into two categories: devices for *observing* particles and measuring their properties, and instruments for accelerating charged particles to very high energies for use in collision experiments. The first category can be subdivided into techniques which simply *detect* the presence of a particle and perhaps measure its energy, and those which permit observation of *trajectories* of particles.

Most particle detectors depend for their operation on the fact that when charged particles or photons pass through matter, they can excite or ionize atoms in the material. For example, when an α particle passes through air, the electrical interaction of its charge with electrons in the oxygen and nitrogen atoms creates positive ions and free electrons. The resulting increase in conductivity can be measured; this is in fact the basic principle of the *ionization chamber*, to be discussed below.

Historically speaking, the earliest particle detector was photographic emulsion. Photographic plates were responsible for the discovery of both x-rays and radioactivity in the last decade of the nineteenth century. A photographic emulsion consists of a suspension of a silver halide in a gel, which is dried after preparation. The silver halides have the property that when exposed to any kind of ionizing radiation, either photons or charged particles of sufficiently high energies, the molecules are excited to metastable states; this makes them susceptible to a chemical reaction in which the silver ions are reduced by a developing solution to metallic silver, which because of its colloidal form appears black. This process is used in ordinary black-and-white photography.

When a charged particle passes through an emulsion, it loses energy along the way, leaving a track which, when developed, shows as a black line along the trajectory of the particle. Furthermore, the density of the line depends on the *rate* at which the particle is losing energy, which in turn depends on its speed and charge. Rapidly moving particles lose less energy per unit path length because there is less time for interaction with any individual electron. Thus tracks in emulsions provide information about not only the trajectory of the particle but also its speed and therefore its energy. Even more information can be obtained if, during the passage of the particle through the emulsion, a magnetic field is imposed. When a particle with mass m and charge q moves with a speed v perpendicular to a uniform magnetic field B, the field exerts a force perpendicular to the direction of the velocity, resulting in a circular trajectory whose radius R is given by

$$R = \frac{mv}{qB} \tag{15-34}$$

if the speed v is nonrelativistic, or

$$R = \frac{mv}{qB \sqrt{1 - v^2/c^2}} \tag{15-35}$$

if v is in the relativistic range. Thus if the charge of the particle is known, measurements of the track can be used to determine both its energy and momentum and thus its mass.

More recent devices for observing trajectories include the cloud chamber, the bubble chamber, and the spark chamber. The cloud chamber uses a vapor which can be *supercooled,* that is, cooled below the temperature at which it would ordinarily liquefy. Condensation of a vapor always involves a phenomenon called *nucleation,* associated with the fact that a droplet of liquid must attain a certain critical size to be thermodynamically stable. The formation of droplets out of the vapor phase is facilitated by the presence of irregularities such as dust particles or ions, which serve as *nucleation centers*. Thus, when a charged particle passes through a supercooled vapor, it provides along its path a series of nucleation centers, around which the vapor begins to condense. Visually, the effect is of a thin cloudy streak in an otherwise transparent vapor. As with photographic emulsions, a magnetic field can be used to produce curvature of the paths, and the energy and momentum of the particle can be measured. Stereoscopic photography can be used to record a three-dimensional picture of the trajectory.

A related device is the *bubble chamber,* invented in 1952. This uses a superheated liquid, usually liquid hydrogen or propane, rather than a supercooled vapor. The passage of a charged particle through the liquid creates nucleation centers which become small bubbles of vapor; hence the particle produces a track of vapor bubbles in an otherwise transparent liquid. The matter in a bubble chamber is ordinarily much more dense than that in a cloud chamber, and collisions are much more likely; for this and other reasons, bubble chambers have largely supplanted cloud chambers. A typical bubble chamber is shown in Fig. 15-8.

(a)

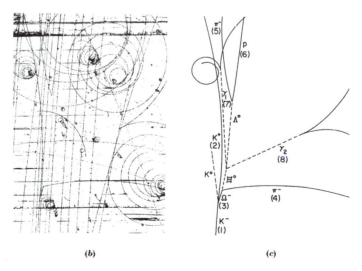

(b)   (c)

Fig. 15-8 (a) A hydrogen bubble chamber. (b) Photograph made with this bubble chamber. Several particle trajectories can be seen. (c) Diagram identifying some of the trajectories in the photograph. Broken lines show trajectories of neutral particles, which leave no tracks.

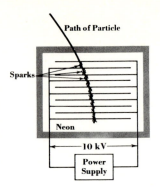

Fig. 15-9 Schematic diagram of a spark chamber. Charged particle creates ions along its path, initiating spark discharges as shown. In practice the high-voltage power supply is energized by passage of a particle of interest through a detector, to prevent recording of events of no interest.

A *spark chamber* consists of a series of parallel conducting plates, typically thin metal foil, spaced a few millimeters apart, with a potential difference of the order of 10^4 V between adjacent plates, as shown in Fig. 15-9. The entire device is immersed in an inert gas such as neon. The passage of a charged particle through the device creates ions along the path, initiating spark discharges between plates along the path. The resulting spark pattern can then be photographed. The spark chamber has the advantage that the application of the high voltage can be triggered by a signal from a counter detecting an incoming particle, ensuring that the event recorded is one of interest and not the result of a stray or unwanted particle entering the chamber. The location of the track cannot be determined as precisely as with the bubble chamber, however.

Among the devices used for detecting particles and measuring their energy precisely are scintillation detectors, ionization detectors, and semiconductor detectors. *Scintillation* is the emission of visible light by a material when an ionizing particle passes through it. Various materials, when bombarded by charged particles or high-energy electromagnetic photons, absorb energy through excitation of electronic energy levels and subsequently reradiate this energy as visible light. The phenomenon is similar to *fluorescence,* in which a material exposed to ultraviolet radiation emits visible light of a color that is nearly independent of the wavelength of the initial radiation. In the early twentieth century, thin sheets were coated with zinc sulfide and used to detect beams of x-rays, α particles, and other radiation. A particle striking the screen induces a faint flash of light at the point of impact. Present-day scintillation counters typically use a transparent crystal, often an alkali halide or one of various organic materials, in conjunction with a vacuum phototube or a similar but much more sensitive device called a *photomultiplier,* both of which operate on the principle of the photoelectric effect discussed in Chap. 8. These are used to generate an electrical pulse to activate counting circuits. Scintillation counters are used both with γ photons and with charged particles.

Another class of detectors makes more direct use of the ionizing property of energetic charged particles. These devices had their genesis with the observation that a charged electroscope placed near a radioactive material gradually becomes discharged; α and β particles produce ions in the surrounding air, increasing its conductivity and permitting the electroscope charge to leak off. A common ionization detector is the Geiger-Müller tube, shown in Fig. 15-10. Two electrodes are sealed in a glass tube containing any one of various gases under low pressure, and a potential difference is applied between the electrodes, not large enough to initiate a glow discharge. A charged particle passing through creates ions, which are accelerated under the action of the potential difference. Some ions acquire enough kinetic energy so that further ionization is produced by collision. The result is an avalanche, in which many more ions are produced than those from the original charged particle. Because of the electrode configuration, the electric field is more intense near the central wire electrode than elsewhere; the avalanche occurs only close to this electrode, and so the discharge does not continue indefinitely. Again, the result is an electrical pulse in the external circuit, which can be used to trigger any of various electronic devices that count pulses. There are many variations on this basic theme, some of which are constructed in such a way that they can also be used to measure particle energies.

More recently, Geiger counters have been largely supplanted by solid-state devices. The use of semiconductors as photocells was mentioned in Sec. 14-6. Similarly, semiconductor devices may be used as detectors of radiation, and by proper design it is possible to produce avalanche effects exactly analogous to those in the Geiger counter. Because of their versatility, reliability, and mechanical ruggedness, solid-state particle detectors are widely used in nuclear and high-energy physics.

All the devices described above depend for their operation on the *charge* of the particle being observed, and hence none is directly useful for detecting *neutral* particles, such as neutrons or neutrinos. Neutrons are most commonly detected by means of a nuclear reaction in which the neutron is absorbed by a nucleus, which then emits a charged particle. An example is boron ($^{10}_{5}B$),

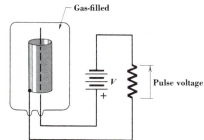

Fig. 15-10 Schematic diagram of a Geiger tube. If the voltage V is sufficiently large, a charged particle which creates ions in the gas between the electrodes initiates an ion avalanche that results in a pulse of current in the circuit, nearly independent of the initial amount of ionization.

which absorbs a neutron and emits an α particle, according to the reaction

$$^{10}_{5}\text{B} + n \rightarrow \, ^{4}_{2}\text{He} + \, ^{7}_{3}\text{Li} \tag{15-36}$$

or, in a shorthand notation often used, $^{10}\text{B}(n,\alpha)^{7}\text{Li}$. The charged particles that result can be detected by any of the means outlined above. Detecting *neutrinos* is much more difficult, since they interact only very weakly with other particles. To observe their very unlikely collisions with other particles, it is necessary to build scintillation counters of heroic dimensions, several meters on a side.

In the early days of nuclear physics, experiments involving collisions of particles with nuclei always used particles emitted by naturally radioactive nuclei. These sources, however, imposed a severe limitation on the variety of experiments that could be performed; energies available from nuclear disintegrations are typically 1 to 5 MeV. Various devices have been developed which accelerate charged particles to energies much *larger* than any available from natural radioactivity and which can be controlled precisely. In some of these machines, the particles are simply accelerated in a straight line; in others they are accelerated in a circle or other closed path.

In the former category, the class of machines known as *linear accelerators*, the original model was an ordinary x-ray tube, described in Sec. 8-3. Electrons are accelerated by a large potential difference, producing x-rays when they strike the target anode. These high-energy electrons can also be used for various kinds of collision experiments. By a simple modification, such a machine can be made to accelerate protons, α particles, or other charged particles. All that needs to be added is a source of ions, which in the case of hydrogen might be a source of hydrogen gas with an electric arc to ionize it. Since an α particle has twice the charge of a proton, accelerating an α particle through a potential difference of 50 kV produces an α-particle energy of 100 keV. Even so, the energy is limited by the maximum dc potential difference that can be developed. For reasons associated with the technology of rectifiers, dielectric breakdown problems, and so on, this is usually limited to the order of $1 \text{ MV} = 10^6 \text{ V}$.

A variation of the linear accelerator which permits much larger maximum energy is shown schematically in Fig. 15-11. The accelerating electrodes are tubes, and alternate electrodes are connected to the two poles of an alternating potential difference, as shown. The potential differences and therefore the fields appear in the gaps between electrodes, and so these are the regions where acceleration occurs. It is possible to arrange the polarities so that a particle is accelerated in the first gap and then, while it is within the second electrode, the polarity is reversed so that it is accelerated *again* at the second gap. With proper timing of the reversals of polarity, the particle can be given an additional push at each gap. Thus, if the accelerating potential is 100 kV

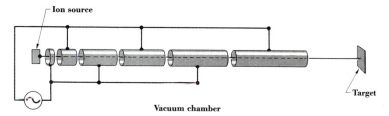

Fig. 15-11 A linear accelerator. The alternating-voltage source reverses polarity in synchronism with the passage of bursts of particles through successive electrodes, so that they are accelerated at each gap. The entire electrode configuration and ion source are enclosed in a vacuum chamber to prevent collision of particles with air molecules.

and there are 10 gaps, the total energy is 1 MeV. One practical way of achieving the synchronization is to make the potential difference a periodically varying function, often simply sinusoidal, and to adjust the electrode spacing so that the particle spends equal times in successive electrodes.

The *Stanford Linear Accelerator* (SLAC) operates on a modified version of this scheme and is the largest such machine built thus far. Electrons are accelerated to an energy of 20 GeV (20×10^9 eV) in a tube 10 cm in diameter and about 3 km long. There are 240 stages of acceleration; the accelerating frequency, produced by klystron oscillators, is about 2.8×10^9 Hz. The electron beam is very intense, about 10^{14} electrons per second.

The *cyclotron*, invented by Lawrence in 1932, uses a uniform magnetic field to make a charged particle move in a *circular* path, as shown in Fig. 15-12. The radius R of the path is given by $R = mv/qB$, so the *angular velocity*

$$\omega = \frac{v}{R} = \frac{qB}{m} \tag{15-37}$$

is independent of radius. A vacuum chamber between the magnet poles

Fig. 15-12 Schematic diagram of a cyclotron. The accelerating electric field which appears across the gap between the dees is periodically reversed by the alternating-voltage source, in synchronism with the charged particles moving in arcs of circles. As they gain energy, the particles spiral outward until they reach the outer edge of the magnetic field, when they fly off at tangents. The dees are enclosed in a vacuum chamber, not shown.

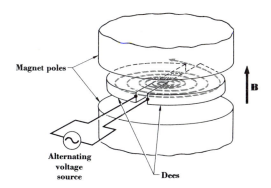

encloses two D-shaped electrodes, called *dees*. An accelerating potential is applied between them, and the polarity is reversed twice each cycle. Each time a particle arrives at the gap between the dees, it is accelerated and moves into a segment of a circular orbit of slightly larger radius than previously, acquiring an added energy equal to the potential difference between the dees.

Cyclotrons have been built which accelerate protons to about 20 MeV. The fundamental energy limitation is a relativistic effect. Relativistically, the momentum of a particle is given not simply by mv but by

$$p = \frac{mv}{\sqrt{1 - v^2/c^2}} \tag{15-38}$$

The orbit radius becomes

$$R = \frac{mv}{qB\sqrt{1 - v^2/c^2}} \tag{15-39}$$

and the angular velocity

$$\omega = \frac{v}{R} = \frac{qB}{m}\sqrt{1 - \frac{v^2}{c^2}} \tag{15-40}$$

Thus ω is no longer constant but *decreases* as the particle energy increases, and the frequency of the oscillator supplying the potential difference to the dees must be decreased in synchronism with the motion of the particles. This frequency variation is carried out in a cyclic manner, so that the particles are accelerated in bursts rather than continuously. A machine having this modification is called a *synchrocyclotron;* the largest such machine accelerates protons to an energy of about 700 MeV.

For larger energies it would be necessary to make an electromagnet so huge as to be prohibitively expensive. Another type of accelerator has been developed in which the *radius* of the orbit is constant but the magnetic field is increased as the particle speeds increase. Thus the magnetic field is required only in a ring-shaped region, not over an entire disk as in the cyclotron. Correspondingly, the vacuum chamber can be a doughnut-shaped enclosure. Such a machine is called a *synchrotron*. The magnetic field and the accelerating electric field are varied periodically to keep pace with a certain group of particles (usually protons), so that the particles are again accelerated in bunches rather than continuously.

The first two synchrotrons built in the United States were the Bevatron (6.2 GeV) at the University of California in Berkeley and the Cosmotron (3.0 GeV) at Brookhaven National Laboratory (Fig. 15-13). The two highest-energy synchrotrons now in operation are at the Enrico Fermi National Laboratory near Batavia, Illinois (200 to 500 GeV), and at Serpukhov, near Moscow, U.S.S.R. (76 GeV). The former employs an accelerating ring 2 km in diameter

Fig. 15-13 Part of the 33-GeV alternating-gradient synchrotron (AGS) at Brookhaven National Laboratory on Long Island, New York. (Photo courtesy of Brookhaven National Laboratory.)

and cost about \$400 million to build. The technology is at hand for building even higher-energy (and higher-cost) machines, but there are serious questions concerning allocation of national resources which make it unlikely that a larger machine will be built in the near future. At any rate, this is a far cry from the early days of nuclear physics, when an expenditure of \$1000 in Rutherford's laboratory was a huge investment!

It is perhaps not completely clear from the above discussion why such high energies are of interest, especially since the total binding energy of the largest nucleus is of the order of 2 GeV. The chief interest centers around investigation of the nature and interactions of fundamental particles, to be discussed in Chap. 16.

15-7 NUCLEAR REACTIONS

A nuclear reaction is any encounter between nuclei or between a nucleus and a particle that results in a rearrangement of their constituent parts. The term *reaction* is used in the same sense as in chemical reactions, in which molecules of two substances are changed into molecules of other substances by rearrangement of their constituent parts (atoms). The same notations are used in both cases. For example, if nucleus A is bombarded by an α particle, resulting in the formation of a new nucleus B and a proton, the reaction is symbolized by the equation

$$A + \alpha \rightarrow B + p \qquad (15\text{-}41)$$

or, in an abbreviated notation, $A(\alpha,p)B$. Various notations are used for labeling particles:

$$
\begin{aligned}
&\text{Proton} = p = {}_1^1 p \\
&\text{Neutron} = n = {}_0^1 n \\
&\text{Alpha} = \alpha = {}_2^4 \text{He} \\
&\text{Electron} = \beta^- = {}_{-1}^0 e \\
&\text{Positron} = \beta^+ = {}_1^0 e
\end{aligned}
\qquad (15\text{-}42)
$$

There are several *conservation laws* which are believed to be obeyed universally in all nuclear reactions. Some are identical with corresponding principles of classical mechanics and electrodynamics; others are unique to nuclear physics. In the former category are conservation of energy (including energies associated with mass), momentum, angular momentum, and electric charge. In the latter category is the conservation of the number of nucleons. No reactions are observed in which a proton disappears unless a neutron appears, and conversely.

Reactions are classified as *exothermic* or *endothermic,* according to whether the final total kinetic energy is greater than or less than the initial total kinetic energy. Just as an exothermic chemical reaction is one that evolves heat, an exothermic nuclear reaction is one that "evolves" kinetic energy. An *increase* in total kinetic energy must be accompanied by a corresponding *decrease* in total rest mass. If M_1 is the *total* initial mass of all reacting particles, M_2 the total final mass, T_1 the initial total kinetic energy, and T_2 the final total kinetic energy, then conservation of energy requires that

$$T_1 + M_1 c^2 = T_2 + M_2 c^2 \qquad (15\text{-}43)$$

Any endothermic reaction always requires a certain minimum initial kinetic energy, called the *threshold energy,* for the reaction to occur. As a simple example, we consider the reaction

$$
{}_3^6 \text{Li} + {}_2^4 \text{He} \rightarrow {}_4^9 \text{Be} + {}_1^1 p \qquad (15\text{-}44)
$$

produced by bombarding a lithium target with α particles. Reference to a table of nuclear masses shows that the total mass on the left side is

$$6.01513 \text{ u} + 4.00260 \text{ u} = 10.01773 \text{ u}$$

while that on the right side is

$$9.01219 \text{ u} + 1.00782 \text{ u} = 10.02001 \text{ u}$$

Thus the final mass is greater than the initial mass by 0.00228 u. Using the conversion factor $(1 \text{ u})c^2 = 931$ MeV, we find that the energy equivalent of this mass is 2.12 MeV. Thus the total *initial* kinetic energy must be greater than the total final kinetic energy by about 2.1 MeV.

It would *not* be correct to conclude that this reaction can be produced by bombarding a lithium target with α particles of any energy greater than 2.12 MeV. The reason is a fundamental one and merits further discussion. The problem is that the α particle cannot give up *all* its kinetic energy in the collision, for then all the final particles would be at rest after the collision, and conservation of *momentum* would be violated. In order to conserve momentum, there must be some residual kinetic energy after the collision; thus the initial α-particle energy must be considerably *greater* than 2.12 MeV.

It is instructive to calculate in detail the relationship between the minimum kinetic energy T for the reaction and the energy Q (in the present example, 2.12 MeV) obtained from the mass difference. This calculation is greatly facilitated by the use of the *center-of-mass coordinate system*, a frame of reference which moves with respect to the laboratory so that the total momentum in this system is zero. In the center-of-mass system the kinetic energy after the collision *can* be zero, and in fact the minimum initial energy corresponds to the case when both final particles are produced with zero kinetic energy. Their common final velocity with respect to the *laboratory* frame of reference is then equal to the velocity of the center-of-mass system with respect to the laboratory.

We now proceed with the details. For simplicity we use nonrelativistic mechanics; the kinetic energy of each particle in the present example is much smaller than its rest energy. We let m_1 be the mass of the bombarding particle and m_2 that of the target particle, and let their initial speeds *relative to the center of mass* be v_1 and v_2, respectively. Since m_2 is stationary in the laboratory coordinate system, the center-of-mass velocity relative to the laboratory has magnitude v_2, both before and after the collision, and the initial speed of m_1 in the laboratory system is $v_1 + v_2$. The situation is illustrated in Fig. 15-14.

The threshold situation, viewed in the center-of-mass system, occurs when the total initial kinetic energy is just Q, so that the two particles collide head on, leaving two new particles with no appreciable kinetic energy. Thus

$$Q = \tfrac{1}{2}m_1 v_1^2 + \tfrac{1}{2}m_2 v_2^2 \tag{15-45}$$

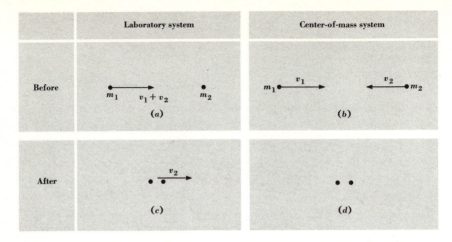

Fig. 15-14 (a) Bombarding particle m_1 and target particle m_2 as seen in the laboratory
coordinate system. (b) Particles as seen in the center-of-mass coordinate system. (c)
Motion of particles with common velocity after the collision, as seen in the laboratory
coordinate system. (d) In the center-of-mass coordinate system, both final particles are at
rest after the collision.

Also, the total momentum is zero at all times, by definition of the center-of-mass coordinate system, and so

$$m_1 v_1 = m_2 v_2 \tag{15-46}$$

In the laboratory system the bombarding particle's speed is $v_1 + v_2$, and its
kinetic energy T is

$$T = \tfrac{1}{2} m_1 (v_1 + v_2)^2 \tag{15-47}$$

We may now use Eq. (15-46) to eliminate v_2 from Eqs. (15-45) and (15-47):

$$Q = \tfrac{1}{2} m_1 \left(1 + \frac{m_1}{m_2}\right) v_1^2 \tag{15-48}$$

$$T = \tfrac{1}{2} m_1 \left(1 + \frac{m_1}{m_2}\right)^2 v_1^2 \tag{15-49}$$

Finally, combining these two equations, we find

$$T = \left(1 + \frac{m_1}{m_2}\right) Q \tag{15-50}$$

which shows that the threshold kinetic energy T of the bombarding particle
in the laboratory coordinate system must always be *greater* than the threshold
energy Q in the center-of-mass system, by a factor depending on the ratio
of the masses.

A similar calculation shows that for *any* bombarding particle energy T_0 (measured in the laboratory system), the total kinetic energy T_C in the center-of-mass system is given by

$$T_C = \frac{m_2}{m_1 + m_2} T_0 \qquad (15\text{-}51)$$

That is, only a fraction $m_2/(m_1 + m_2)$ of the bombarding energy is "available" for the reaction. If the target particle is much more massive than the bombarding particle ($m_2 \gg m_1$), this fraction is nearly unity, but for a proton-proton collision it is $\frac{1}{2}$.

In the previous example, Eq. (15-44), the mass of the bombarding particle is approximately $m_1 = 4\text{ u}$, and that of the target particle, lithium, is $m_2 = 6\text{ u}$. Thus we have approximately

$$T = (1 + \tfrac{4}{6})(2.12\text{ MeV}) = 3.53\text{ MeV} \qquad (15\text{-}52)$$

as the minimum α-particle energy for the reaction.

In these calculations we have used nonrelativistic dynamics, on the basis that the kinetic energy of each particle is small compared with mc^2 for that particle. At higher energies relativistic dynamics must be used, and the energy relations are somewhat more complex than Eqs. (15-50) and (15-51). In the *extreme-relativistic* range, where the energies are much *larger* than the total rest-mass energy, they become simple again! Examples of relativistic and extreme-relativistic calculations will be given in Chap. 16 in connection with fundamental-particle interactions.

An interesting class of nuclear reactions is involved in *neutron activation analysis,* in which a specimen to be analyzed is bombarded with slow neutrons. Some nuclei absorb neutrons, becoming excited states of stable nuclides, or in some cases β emitters. In either case, the resulting β and/or γ radiation is different for each element, just as each element has a characteristic optical spectrum. Measurement of the energy and intensity of the radiation permits determination of the concentration of each element. Concentrations as small as one part in 10^9, much too small for conventional chemical analysis, can be measured with precision.

In experiments involving nuclear collisions and reactions, the probability of occurrence of a reaction is conveniently expressed in terms of a *cross section* for the reaction, which is simply the effective target area presented by each target nucleus to the bombarding particle. The cross section, denoted by σ, is defined by specifying that, when a target nucleus is placed in a *beam* of bombarding particles containing N particles per unit area perpendicular to the direction of the beam, the number of events (collisions, reactions, or whatever is being described) *per target nucleus* is given by $N\sigma$.

As a simple example, suppose that in the reaction described by Eq.

(15-41) a beam of α particles containing 10^{10} particles/cm^2 impinges on a target of area 1 cm^2, containing 10^{16} target nuclei, and that 10^2 reactions are found to occur. The probability for any one α particle to undergo a reaction is then $10^2/10^{10} = 10^{-8}$. The probability for any one α particle to undergo a reaction with a *particular* target nucleus is $10^{-8}/10^{16} = 10^{-24}$. Thus the effective target area *per nucleus* is smaller than the total target area (1 cm^2) by 10^{-24} and the cross section for the reaction is therefore $\sigma = 10^{-24}$ cm$^2 = 10^{-28}$ m^2.

Since nuclear dimensions are typically of the order of 10^{-15} to 10^{-14} m, it is not surprising that cross sections for nuclear reactions are often of the same order of magnitude as cross-section areas of nuclei themselves. It is convenient to introduce a unit of area called the *barn,* defined by

$$1 \text{ b} = 10^{-24} \text{ cm}^2 = 10^{-28} \text{ m}^2 \qquad (15\text{-}53)$$

Reaction cross sections are not necessarily related directly to the actual geometrical cross section of the nuclei participating in the reaction. For example, the cross section for the reaction

$$^9\text{Be} + p \rightarrow {}^6\text{Li} + \alpha \qquad \text{or} \qquad {}^9\text{Be}(p,\alpha) \, {}^6\text{Li} \qquad (15\text{-}54)$$

for 0.1-MeV protons is 5×10^{-5} b, while the cross section for the neutron-capture reaction in which a cadmium nucleus absorbs a slow neutron is of the order of 3000 b. A nucleus can have a reaction cross section much *larger* than its geometrical cross section because of the spatial extension of the wave functions describing particles. The wavelength of a slow neutron is much *larger* than nuclear dimensions, and the neutron cannot be described as a point interacting with a nucleus.

In many cases a particular combination of target nucleus and bombarding particle can participate in a variety of reactions, each leading to a different set of final particles and nuclei. In such cases, there is a different cross section for each reaction, and each cross section depends on the bombarding energy. In addition, the concept of cross section can be extended to provide a more detailed description of the characteristics of a reaction. For the above example, it is of interest to describe the *directions* of the emergent α particles relative to the direction of the incident proton beam; some directions are more likely than others. This behavior is conveniently described by a *differential cross section,* defined as the cross section $d\sigma$ per unit solid angle $d\Omega$ of emergent particle direction, denoted by $d\sigma/d\Omega$. It is usually a function of emergent angle, bombarding particle energy, and spin orientation of bombarding and target particles.

Measurements of cross sections for nuclear reactions, as well as cross sections for various elastic scattering processes, have played an extremely important role in research in nuclear physics and in fact have provided the great preponderance of evidence on which present understanding of nuclear structure is based.

15-8 FISSION AND FUSION

We now discuss briefly two classes of nuclear reactions which, although not different in principle from those considered in the previous section, are important enough to be given special attention.

Nuclear fission, as the name implies, is a reaction in which a nucleus splits into two smaller nuclei. Fission is most commonly observed with heavy radioactive elements which can also undergo other forms of radioactive disintegration. It is customary to distinguish between *spontaneous fission,* in which a nucleus spontaneously divides without any external stimulus, and *induced fission,* in which the fission is a result of absorption of another particle, usually a neutron. The most familiar element that undergoes spontaneous fission is uranium ($^{235}_{92}U$). There are many possible fission reactions; usually the products are two smaller nuclei called *fission fragments* and a few free neutrons; an example of a spontaneous fission is

$$^{235}_{92}U \rightarrow {}^{140}_{56}Ba + {}^{93}_{36}Kr + 2n \tag{15-55}$$

Fission of heavy nuclei is energetically possible because, as Fig. 15-4 shows, the binding energy per nucleon is less in heavy nuclei than in those of moderate size, say $A = 100$ or so, because of the electrical repulsion of protons. Thus a heavy nucleus can achieve a state of lower total energy (greater total binding energy) by dividing into two smaller pieces. There are usually competing processes, particularly α and β decay; for most unstable nuclei these are the predominant mechanisms for achieving stable structures. In some others induced fission resulting from neutron absorption is possible but the absorption cross section is very small. However, ^{235}U is one of several nuclides in which both spontaneous and induced fission are important modes of decay.

Investigation of the various nuclear masses involved shows that fission is energetically most favorable when the two fragments are of unequal size. Figure 15-15 shows the distribution of fission-fragment mass numbers from induced fission of ^{235}U with thermal neutrons. There is a strong peak in the vicinity of $A = 95$ and another around $A = 140$, and the curve is symmetric around $A = 235/2$. (Why?)

The neutron-proton ratio of stable nuclei increases with mass. Thus when a heavy nucleus divides in two, the fragments always have too many neutrons for stability. The situation is adjusted by the liberation of free neutrons at the time of fission and by subsequent β decays of the fission fragments, in

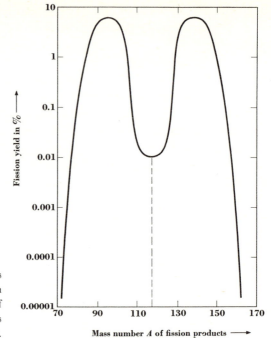

Fig. 15-15 Graph showing the mass distribution of fission fragments from fission of ^{235}U induced by absorption of thermal neutrons. The vertical scale is logarithmic.

which Z increases and N decreases until a stable configuration is reached. In the fission described by Eq. (15-55), each fission fragment undergoes several successive β decays following fission. In *induced fission*, the fission reaction is triggered by absorption of another particle, usually a neutron; in other respects it is similar to spontaneous fission.

An interesting feature of fission reactions is that neutrons from fission of one nucleus can in turn trigger the fission of other nuclei. On the average, each fission of a ^{235}U nucleus produces about 2.5 neutrons. Thus, if sufficient numbers of these neutrons can be made to induce further fission, a self-sustaining *chain reaction* can occur. The first successful chain reaction was produced in 1942 by Fermi and his collaborators at the University of Chicago.

Not all the neutrons are able to produce further fission; some escape from the region where the uranium nuclei are contained, and others participate in other reactions. The cross section for neutron absorption followed by fission is much larger with slow neutrons ($<$0.1 eV) than with energetic neutrons; ordinarily a controlled chain reaction is possible only when some means is provided to slow down the neutrons by collision with other nuclei before they are absorbed by uranium nuclei. This slowing down is the function of the *moderator* material in a nuclear reactor.

Such chain reactions are an important practical source of energy. The average kinetic energy of the fragments from a single nuclear fission is of the order of 200 MeV; energies of combustion of ordinary fuel such as coal or gasoline are typically of the order of 10 eV per molecule. On an "energy per unit mass" basis, fission of uranium produces about 10^7 times as much energy as burning of ordinary fuels. Fission chain reactions are also used in bombs, but perhaps the less said about them, the better.

An interesting by-product is the development of new elements with $Z > 92$, the *transuranic* elements. Here is an example: ^{235}U is a relatively rare isotope of uranium; the common isotope is ^{238}U, which is not readily fissionable. But if some ^{238}U is included in a reactor in which ^{235}U is undergoing fission, some of the ^{238}U nuclei absorb neutrons, becoming ^{239}U. This in turn undergoes β decay, forming a new nucleus with charge number $Z = 93$, which does not occur in nature. This new element has been named *neptunium*. It in turn β-decays into an element with $Z = 94$, *plutonium*. This series of reactions is represented symbolically as

$$^{238}_{92}\text{U} + {}^1_0 n \rightarrow {}^{239}_{92}\text{U}$$
$$^{238}_{92}\text{U} \rightarrow {}^{239}_{93}\text{Np} + \beta^- + \nu \tag{15-56}$$
$$^{239}_{93}\text{Np} \rightarrow {}^{239}_{94}\text{Pu} + \beta^- + \nu$$

Plutonium, $^{239}_{94}$Pu, is fissionable, so the effect of this series of reactions is to convert the nonfissionable ^{238}U into a fissionable material which then serves as further fuel for the reactor. In such a reactor, called a *breeder reactor*, it is actually possible to produce more new fuel than is consumed.

Variations on this theme have provided a large number of additional elements which do not occur in nature. Examination of the products of chain reactions in nuclear reactors has revealed the existence of elements with atomic numbers up to 104. Another amusing sidelight is the fulfillment of the alchemists' dream of transmutation of the elements. In one experiment, it was necessary to convey an extremely corrosive solution through a pipe in the presence of a high neutron flux. To avoid corrosion, the pipe was lined on the inside with gold. Alas, the gold, $^{197}_{79}$Au, absorbed neutrons and β-decayed into mercury, $^{198}_{80}$Hg, which was promptly eaten away by the solution. Such are the dreams of the philosophers!

The detailed mechanism of nuclear fission can be understood at least qualitatively on the basis of the *liquid-drop model*, which is also relevant for other nuclear phenomena. This model makes use of the close analogy between the binding of nucleons in a nucleus by their short-range attractive nuclear forces and the binding of molecules in a liquid by short-range attractive forces, both mainly with nearest neighbors. In both cases there are "surface-tension" effects resulting from the fact that particles near the surface of the structure are pulled toward its center by the asymmetric distribution of neighbors.

In the absence of any disturbing influence, a drop of water is spherical; this configuration minimizes the surface-to-volume ratio and therefore the energy associated with surface tension. Similarly, heavy nuclei would be spherical if it were not for the disturbing effect of the electrical repulsion of protons. In all cases, the spherical configuration is an equilibrium state, but it may sometimes be an *unstable* equilibrium. If an external influence, such as an incoming neutron, distorts the nucleus more than a certain critical amount from its equilibrium shape, the resulting electrical forces may tend to distort it further, to the point where it breaks in two.

A slightly more sophisticated point of view is that when the nuclear surface is disturbed by some outside influence, the result is a *wave* on the surface, which increases the probability that two sections of the nucleus can separate far enough so that their electrical repulsion can overcome the nuclear attraction and push them completely apart, resulting in fission.

The inverse of fission is *nuclear fusion*, in which two light nuclei combine to form a single heavier one. Fusion reactions are exothermic only for light nuclei. A simple example is

$$\,^2_1\text{H} + \,^2_1\text{H} \rightarrow \,^4_2\text{He} + Q \tag{15-57}$$

The total mass of the two deuterium atoms is 4.02820 u, while that of the helium atom is 4.00260 u; thus the reaction is exothermic by 0.02560 u, or about 23.8 MeV.

For fusion to occur, the two nuclei must be brought together within the range of the nuclear force, of the order of 10^{-15} m. For this to occur, the repulsive Coulomb force must be overcome; the potential energy associated with Coulomb repulsion of two charges of magnitude e at a separation of 10^{-15} m is about 1.4 MeV, and this is therefore the order of magnitude of the threshold energy (in the center-of-mass system) for fusion in the above example. One conceivable way of producing fusion reactions is somehow to make deuterium gas very hot, so that a sizable fraction of the atoms in the high-energy tail of the Maxwell-Boltzmann distribution have energies of the order of 1 MeV. The required temperature is in the range 10^6 to 10^8 K.

Because of the very high temperatures involved, fusion reactions are also called *thermonuclear* reactions. The first man-made thermonuclear reaction occurred in the hydrogen bomb; intensive efforts are currently under way to develop controlled thermonuclear reactions that can be used for the generation of power in a manner similar to the fission reactors currently in use. Deuterium (^2_1H), one of the likely "fuel" materials for such a thermonuclear reactor, occurs on the earth in much greater abundance than any of the fissionable heavy elements, such as uranium, and hence potentially constitutes an energy source of enormous abundance. Among the reactions under study are:

$$\mathrm{^2_1H} + \mathrm{^2_1H} \rightarrow \mathrm{^3_1H} + \mathrm{^1_1H} + 4\,\mathrm{MeV}$$

$$\mathrm{^2_1H} + \mathrm{^3_1H} \rightarrow \mathrm{^4_2He} + \mathrm{^1_0}n + 17.6\,\mathrm{MeV}$$

$$\mathrm{^2_1H} + \mathrm{^2_1H} \rightarrow \mathrm{^3_2He} + \mathrm{^1_0}n + 3.3\,\mathrm{MeV} \qquad (15\text{-}58)$$

$$\mathrm{^2_1H} + \mathrm{^3_2He} \rightarrow \mathrm{^4_2He} + \mathrm{^1_1H} + 18.3\,\mathrm{MeV}$$

Fusion reactions are the source of the energy liberated in stars. The following reactions occur in the sun and similar stars:

$$\mathrm{^1_1H} + \mathrm{^1_1H} \rightarrow \mathrm{^2_1H} + \mathrm{_{+1}^{0}}e + \nu$$

$$\mathrm{^1_1H} + \mathrm{^2_1H} \rightarrow \mathrm{^3_2He} + \gamma$$

$$\mathrm{^3_2He} + \mathrm{^3_2He} \rightarrow \mathrm{^4_2He} + \mathrm{^1_1H} + \mathrm{^1_1H}$$

The net effect of these three reactions is to fuse four protons into an α particle, two positrons, and two neutrinos. About 25 MeV of energy is released for each α particle produced. If the protons in turn originate in β decay of neutrons, one can picture the universe as having originated as a vast swarm of neutrons, from which β decays and fusion reactions led to the evolution of the various nuclides and electrons and thus to atoms of the various elements.

15-9   RADIATION AND LIFE

The interaction of radiation with living tissue is a topic of ever-expanding interest. We here construe radiation to include α, β, and γ emission from radioactive nuclei as well as x-rays, high-energy particles from accelerators, and cosmic rays. Any radiation with energy of more than a few electronvolts has the ability to change the structure of tissue by breaking chemical bonds and creating ions. The sunburn produced by the ultraviolet component of sunlight is a familiar example; similar burns are produced by x-rays.

Various schemes are used to measure exposure of an organism to radiation. For x-rays, a widely used unit is the *roentgen*, abbreviated R, defined as that amount of exposure which creates $\frac{1}{3} \times 10^{-9}$ C of ions (of either sign) when passing through 1 cm^3 of dry air at 0°C and 1 atm. Since on the average about 35 eV is required to produce an ion pair in air, one can compute the corresponding energy input, and it turns out that 1 R corresponds to energy absorption of about 1.2×10^{-8} J/cm^3 or about 0.012 J/m^3. For 200-kV x-rays, 500 R causes reddening of the skin, and 700 R over the entire body causes death in about 50 percent of humans.

The roentgen measures radiation *exposure*, not actual absorption; the latter is best characterized by the *energy* absorbed from the radiation per unit mass of absorber; by definition *one rad* is the absorbed radiation corresponding to 0.01 J/kg of absorbed energy. Even this is not a complete description, since equal energies of different radiations have different effects, so a correction factor for each radiation (α, β, γ, x-ray, etc.) and energy range is introduced; this is called the *relative biological effectiveness* (RBE). It is used in connection with another unit of absorption or "dose" called the *rem* (roentgen equivalent mammal); the relation of this to the rad is

$$\text{Dose (in rem)} = \text{RBE} \times \text{dose (in rads)}$$

For medium-energy x-rays, RBE is about unity; for fission neutrons it is about 10, and for 1-MeV α particles about 25. Because various radiations produce widely varying effects in different tissues, radiation dosimetry is not an exact science.

For man, exposure to cosmic rays and radioactivity in soil and rocks amounts to about 0.1 rem per year. A dose of 400 rem in a short time causes death in 50 percent of humans. One widely accepted standard is that a person working with radiation can receive no more than 5 rem per year without incurring health hazards. For comparison, a single chest x-ray typically involves a dose of about 0.1 rem, comparable to the annual "natural" dose mentioned above.

Radiation has many useful applications in medicine, in both diagnosis and therapy. The use of x-rays to examine bone fractures and tooth decay is familiar, and abnormalities of the digestive tract can be photographed following ingestion of materials (typically barium salts) that are opaque to the radiation being used. Some of the common *therapeutic* applications of radiation result from the fact that some tumors absorb radiation more strongly than the surrounding tissue and hence can be selectively destroyed by appropriate radiation. This is particularly useful if the tumor cannot be removed surgically or if the disease has become generalized by metastasis to many sites in the body. These applications often involve massive doses which can have serious side effects and considerable risk, but if the alternative is certain death, this risk may be justified.

A widely used source is cobalt, $^{60}_{27}\text{Co}$, an unstable nuclide prepared by bombarding the stable isotope $^{59}_{27}\text{Co}$ with neutrons in a nuclear reactor; neutron absorption leads to the odd-odd nuclide $^{60}_{27}\text{Co}$, which decays by β and γ emission with a half-life of about 5 years and maximum γ energy of about 1.3 MeV. Such sources, having relatively short half-lives, can be made much more intense than those using naturally radioactive elements. They do not emit α particles, which are usually not wanted, and the β particles are easily stopped by thin metal sheets.

Among the more subtle effects of radiation is the possibility of alteration of genes, causing genetic mutations, the effects of which may become apparent only after several generations. To some scientists this phenomenon, as yet incompletely understood, suggests much more stringent limitations on exposure of humans to radiation than those presently used. This is a hotly debated topic, and there has been considerable hysteria in the popular press concerning such questions as the radiation hazards of nuclear power plants. It is certainly true that radiation emission from such plants is *not* zero, but to evaluate the resulting hazards in a meaningful way, one must compare them with the alternatives. The health hazards of coal smoke are severe and well-documented, and even the *radiation hazards* from the radioactive materials in coal are believed to be considerably greater than from corresponding nuclear plants. A very serious problem that remains unsolved is the long-term storage of radioactive waste materials from reactors.

Finally, we mention briefly the use of radioisotope tracer techniques, which have found very wide applications in medicine as well as in a variety of other areas in chemistry, molecular physics, and metallurgy. Because unstable nuclei have the same *charge* as stable nuclei of the same element, the electronic structure and therefore the *chemical* behavior is the same for both

A familiar example is the use of iodine, $^{131}_{53}I$, to measure thyroid function. Nearly all the iodine ingested by humans is concentrated in the thyroid, and the body does not distinguish between $^{131}_{53}I$, a β and γ emitter, and the stable isotope $^{127}_{53}I$. The patient is fed a minute measured quantity of ^{131}I, and the speed with which it is concentrated in the thyroid, a measure of the level of thyroid activity, is measured by observing the level of γ radiation from the thyroid. The half-life of $^{131}_{53}I$ is about 8 d, so there are no long-lasting radiation hazards.

Hundreds of other examples might be cited. Piston ring wear can be measured by incorporating radioactive iron in the rings and looking for the corresponding emissions in the oil. Radioactive "tags" on pesticide molecules can be used to follow their progress through food chains; laundry detergent manufacturers test the effectiveness of their products by incorporating radio-isotopes into the dirt and testing for residue after laundering. The list of such applications grows daily.

Thus radioactivity is a two-edged sword, posing definite threats to health and safety and yet providing a wide variety of tools for the benefit of mankind, including diagnosis and treatment of disease, analytical tools in a wide variety of applications, and even the direct effects of radiation, such as strengthening of polymers by cross-linking, sterilizing of surgical tools and foods, and dispersion of unwanted static electricity by ionization of the surrounding air.

Problems

15-1 Compute the approximate density of nuclear matter, and compare your result with typical densities of ordinary solid materials.

15-2 *a* Find the mass of the electron, in u, to three significant figures.

    b Find the energy equivalent of the electron mass, in megaelectronvolts.

15-3 For what value of the mass number A is the nuclear radius half that of the $^{238}_{92}$U nucleus? What stable nuclide has this mass number?

15-4 Is the nuclear electric charge *density* greater for light nuclei or heavy nuclei? Explain.

15-5 A mass spectrometer of the Dempster type is used to separate the two isotopes ^{235}U and ^{238}U. The radius of curvature of the particles is to be approximately 1 m, and the accelerating potential difference is 10^4 V. Assuming the ions are singly ionized, what magnetic field B is needed?

15-6 A mass spectrometer of the type shown in Fig. 15-2 is to be used to measure masses of isotopes of iron. If the magnetic field is to be $B = 0.1$ Wb/m^2, approximately what accelerating voltage V should be used?

15-7 In a magnetic field $B = 10$ Wb/m^2, what frequency is necessary for nuclear magnetic resonance with protons?

15-8 Using the Bohr model of the hydrogen atom, find the magnetic field at the position of the nucleus resulting from the "current" associated with the moving charge. From this, together with the magnetic moment of the proton, calculate approximately the magnitude of the hyperfine splitting of energy levels resulting from the interaction of the nuclear magnetic moment with this field.

15-9 The atomic mass of $^{12}_{6}$C is 12.000000 u and that of $^{13}_{6}$C is 13.003354 u. Find the energy required to remove a neutron from $^{13}_{6}$C, in megaelectronvolts.

15-10 The mass of a neutral $^{12}_{6}$C atom, including six electrons, is precisely 12.000000 u, by definition. Find the mass of the $^{12}_{6}$C *nucleus*, to six significant figures.

15-11 In Prob. 15-10, estimate the order of magnitude of the total binding energy of the electrons in the atom. Express your result in atomic mass units; is it significant in computing the above mass difference?

15-12 The mass of the neutral $^{3}_{1}$H atom is 3.016050 u, and that of the neutral $^{3}_{2}$He atom is 3.016030 u.

    a Calculate the mass of each bare nucleus, in atomic mass units.

    b Show that $^{3}_{1}$H is unstable against β decay.

    c Assuming this mass difference is due to the neutron-proton mass difference and to Coulomb repulsion of the protons in $^{3}_{2}$He, and treating the protons as classical point particles, find the distance between them.

15-13 Suppose the total electric charge Q in a nucleus is uniformly distributed through the volume of a sphere of radius R, where $Q = Ze$ and $R = r_0 A^{1/3}$.

    a Show that the total electrostatic energy U is given by

$$U = \frac{1}{4\pi\epsilon_0} \cdot \frac{3Q^2}{5R}$$

    b   Use this result to predict the mass difference between the nuclides $^{13}_{6}C$ and $^{13}_{7}N$, assuming the difference is due entirely to electrostatic energy.

15-14 The mass of the α particle, without electrons, is 4.00151 u. Find the total binding energy (in megaelectronvolts) and the binding energy per nucleon.

15-15 How much electrical potential energy (in megaelectronvolts) is required to add a proton to a nucleus with $Z = 91$ and $A = 234$?

15-16 Discuss the possibility of existence of electrons in the nucleus on the basis of the uncertainty principle. For example, for an electron to be localized in a region of nuclear dimensions, how much momentum must it have? How much energy? How does this energy compare with nuclear binding energies? (Cf. Prob. 9-21.)

15-17 The total binding energy of $^{35}_{17}Cl$ is 289 MeV.
    a   What is the binding energy per nucleon?
    b   Find the mass of the nuclide in atomic mass units, to five significant figures.

15-18 Derive an expression for the *force* corresponding to the Yukawa potential function, Eq. (15-14). If $a = 10^{-15}$ m and $f^2/a = 10$ MeV, at what distance is this force equal in magnitude to the Coulomb repulsion of two protons?

15-19 When ^{226}Ra undergoes α decay, it leads to ^{222}Rn. The masses, including all electrons in each atom, are 226.0254 and 222.0163 u, respectively. What is the maximum-energy α particle that can be emitted?

15-20 Sodium, ^{22}Na, undergoes β^+ decay to the stable isotope ^{22}Ne. The masses of the neutral atoms are 21.99444 and 21.99138 u, respectively. Find the energy of the β^+ on the assumption that it accounts for the entire energy difference. Is this assumption realistic?

15-21 A carbon specimen from a certain archaeological find was found to contain 0.20 as much ^{14}C per unit mass of ^{12}C as currently living organic matter. What is the approximate age of the specimen?

15-22 The radioactive isotope ^{90}Sr has a half-life of 25 years.
    a   What is the decay constant?
    b   After what time has 99 percent of the original amount decayed?

15-23 Nuclei that undergo α decay usually emit α particles with definite energy or at most a discrete spectrum of energies, while β-decay energy spectra are often continuous. Why?

15-24 The radioactive isotope of potassium, $^{40}_{19}K$, occurs with an abundance of about 0.01 percent relative to the common, stable isotope $^{39}_{19}K$, and its half-life is 1.3×10^9 years. Assuming that these two isotopes were produced with equal abundance at the time of formation of the elements, calculate the age of the universe.

15-25 The nuclide $^{60}_{27}Co$, widely used in radiation therapy, has a half-life of 5.3 years. What mass of ^{60}Co is needed for an activity of 1 mCi (millicurie)?

15-26 The activity of a certain specimen of a radioactive element decreases by a factor of 10 in 2 h. Find the decay constant and the half-life.

15-27 The thorium decay series found in nature begins with $^{232}_{90}$Th and ends with $^{208}_{82}$Pb after the following sequence of decays:

$$\alpha,\ \beta,\ \beta,\ \alpha,\ \alpha,\ \alpha,\ \alpha,\ \beta,\ \beta,\ \alpha$$

Draw a Segre chart similar to that in Fig. 15-7 for this decay series.

15-28 A radioactive decay series found in nature begins with $^{235}_{92}$U and ends with $^{207}_{82}$Pb. How many α and how many β decays occur in the series?

15-29 If the neutron at rest could decay to a proton and an electron, *without* a neutrino, find the kinetic energies of proton and electron. Hint: The proton energy is *non*relativistic, but the electron energy is relativistic.

15-30 Combine Eqs. (15-27) and (15-31) and solve the resulting differential equation.

15-31 A certain Van de Graaff generator develops a potential difference of 1 million V. If it is used to accelerate α particles, what energy do the particles have?

15-32 In a cyclotron, the maximum energy attainable is determined by the magnetic field B and the radius R of the vacuum chamber between the poles of the magnet. If the field is $B = 2$ Wb/m^2, what radius is necessary for 10-MeV protons? What frequency should the oscillator which supplies the alternating potential difference to the dees have?

15-33 The cyclotron in Prob. 15-32 is to be modified to accelerate α particles.
   a   What is the maximum-energy α particle that can be obtained?
   b   What frequency should the oscillator have?

15-34 A certain synchrocyclotron accelerates protons to 450 MeV. The magnetic field is 2.0 Wb/m^2. Find the maximum and minimum oscillator frequencies.

15-35 A β-ray spectrometer is an instrument similar in design to a mass spectrometer but used to measure energies of β-decay electrons. Calculate the radius of curvature of the path of a 1-MeV electron in a magnetic field $B = 0.1$ Wb/m^2. Is it necessary to use relativistic dynamics to compute this radius? Explain.

15-36 The reaction $^{16}_{8}$O $+\ n \rightarrow\ ^{13}_{6}$C $+\ ^{4}_{2}$He is endothermic by 2.20 MeV. If a target of $^{16}_{8}$O is bombarded by neutrons, what minimum neutron energy is necessary for the reaction to occur?

15-37 The radioactive isotope of cobalt, $^{60}_{27}$Co, is produced by irradiating the stable isotope $^{59}_{27}$Co with thermal neutrons in a reactor. The cross section for neutron absorption is about 20 b. A sheet of ^{59}Co with a total mass of 0.010 kg is placed in a reactor where the neutron flux is 10^{16} neutrons/m^2 · s for a period of 10 h. How many ^{60}Co nuclei are produced? (The half-life is sufficiently long so that the decay during irradiation is negligible.)

15-38 In photodisintegration of deuterons, a deuteron absorbs a γ-ray photon and splits into a proton and a neutron. The deuteron binding energy is about 2.23 MeV. What minimum energy must the photon have?

15-39 Consider the hypothetical fusion reaction

$${}^3\text{H} + {}^6\text{Li} \rightarrow {}^9\text{Be} + Q$$

The masses, including atomic electrons, are 3.01605, 6.01513, and 9.01219 u, respectively. Calculate the energy liberated in this reaction, and energy per unit mass of fuel consumed.

15-40 A fusion reaction which is believed to be of importance in some stars is the fusion of three α particles to form a ${}^{12}_{6}\text{C}$ nucleus. The masses of the corresponding neutral atoms are 4.002604 and 12.000000 u, respectively. How much energy is released in each fusion?

15-41 A target of ${}^3_1\text{H}$ nuclei (also called *tritons*) is bombarded with protons, leading to the reaction

$${}^1_1\text{H} + {}^3_1\text{H} \rightarrow {}^2_2\text{H} + {}^2_2\text{H}$$

The masses of the corresponding neutral atoms are 1.007825, 2.014102, and 3.016050 u. What is the minimum proton energy needed for this reaction?

15-42 The annual energy consumption in the United States is of the order of 10^{20} J.
   a   In the first reaction of Eqs. (15-58), what mass of deuterium must fuse to produce this much energy?
   b   What mass of uranium ${}^{235}\text{U}$ must undergo fission to produce this much energy?

Fundamental Particles | 16

The study of fundamental particles embodies the most recent attempts to understand the constitution of all matter in terms of a few basic building blocks. The development of the *atomic* view of matter is reviewed, and then it is shown how a relativistic theory of the electron leads to a model in which particles can be created and destroyed. This in turn opens the door to an understanding of nuclear forces in terms of the exchange of unstable particles between nucleons. Particles having the necessary properties have been observed in cosmic radiation and in laboratory experiments with high-energy accelerators. The quest for the understanding of these particles has also led to the discovery of still other particles, known as "strange particles." The symmetry and conservation laws introduced in an attempt to classify and understand the interactions of these new particles are discussed, and finally a few areas of current research in the theory of fundamental particles are reviewed.

16-1 ATOMIC VIEW OF MATTER

The idea that matter as we know it is composed of certain irreducible and indivisible building blocks is at least 2500 years old and has stimulated imagination and research activity over the years. The word *atomic* is derived from two Greek words meaning *not divisible;* the proposal that fundamental units exist and are the basis of all matter was advanced by the Greek philosophers Leucippus and Democritus in about 400 B.C.

The emergence of chemistry as an exact science in the early nineteenth century brought with it the concept of *atoms* of the various chemical elements; each element was supposed to be made up of many identical and indivisible atoms, and the combining of elements in definite proportions to form compounds was to be understood on the basis of atoms of various elements combining to form *molecules*, the fundamental units of the compound. Toward the end of the nineteenth century it became clear that atoms are in fact *not* indivisible, but are made up of still smaller units, at least some of which are electrically charged, and that in some circumstances they can be partially taken apart.

The first such smaller unit to be identified was the *electron;* its existence was suspected as early as 1870 and was established conclusively by the fundamental experiments of J. J. Thomson in 1897. By the mid-1930s the existence and most important properties of the *proton, neutron,* and *positron* had been put on an equally firm footing, and it was widely believed that these four fundamental particles formed the basis for all matter.

In the rapid development of physical theory which took place in the 1920s and early 1930s, the newly discovered principles of quantum mechanics were applied to these particles in an effort to understand phenomena related to atomic and molecular structure, such as energy levels, specific heats, and so on. By 1930, it appeared that the problems of *atomic* physics were essentially solved, inasmuch as the new quantum mechanics was believed to provide all the necessary principles.

With respect to the structure of the *nucleus,* however, the problems were far from solved. In fact, in 1930 virtually nothing was known about the details of nuclear structure. It was known that the dimensions of nuclei are smaller by a factor of 10^5 than those of atoms and that energies associated with interactions of nuclear particles are larger by the same factor, but there was virtually no understanding of the nature of the interaction by which nuclear particles are held together.

More generally, the nature of fundamental particles was only partially understood. *Classical* physics provides only two basic interactions, electromagnetic and gravitational. The stability of nuclei suggests the existence of another strong interaction between nuclear particles. Does this third kind of interaction complete the list, or are there still others? What about the *masses* of the particles? Why should there be two particles, one charged and one neutral, with approximately equal masses, and a third with opposite charge and much *smaller* mass? Should a complete theory be able to *predict* these masses? What is the status of the *photon,* the quantum of electromagnetic radiation? Should it be classified as a fundamental particle? If so, how can one understand the fact that photons can be created and destroyed in atomic processes, while the other particles seem to have a permanent existence?

In summary, while the main features of *atomic* structure were reasonably well understood by 1930, the corresponding problems of *nuclear* structure had just begun to be investigated, and there was not even the beginning of a comprehensive theory of fundamental particles. In short, the problem of atomic structure in 1900 has its counterparts in the problems of nuclear structure in 1930 and of the properties and interactions of fundamental particles in the 1970s. Some of the questions raised in the preceding paragraphs have been answered fairly completely by subsequent investigations; others remain only partially answered or completely unanswered. Thus the discussion of fundamental particles and their interactions takes us to one of the present-day frontiers in theoretical physics.

16-2   RELATIVISTIC ELECTRON THEORY

The relativistic theory of the electron has been very successful in the analysis of purely *electromagnetic* interactions of particles, where the nuclear force need not be considered. Development of this theory began in 1928 when the English theoretical physicist P. A. M. Dirac derived a relativistic generalization of the Schrödinger equation. To understand the need for such a generalization, we recall that in developing the Schrödinger equation in Chaps. 9 and 10, we used the relationship $E = p^2/2m$ for the kinetic energy E and the momentum p of a particle of mass m. This is valid only when the speed is much smaller than c and the energies involved are all much smaller than mc^2. Just as classical newtonian mechanics is a special case of relativistic mechanics, so quantum mechanics as expressed by the Schrödinger equation is a special case of a more general formulation based on relativistic considerations. This generalization is just what the Dirac equation provides.

Although this equation and its solutions cannot be developed in detail here, we can discuss some of its most important general features. Dirac found that the requirements that the equation be compatible with relativity and that in the nonrelativistic limit it should reduce to the Schrödinger equation for a particle with spin $\frac{1}{2}$, were sufficient to specify *uniquely* the form of the equation. Even more important, when interactions with an electromagnetic field are included, the form of the interaction term in the equation is also specified uniquely by requirements of relativistic invariance.

One of the most significant features of this interaction is that part of it can be identified as the interaction of a magnetic dipole with a magnetic field, with magnetic moment μ related to the spin angular momentum S by

$$\mu = \frac{e}{m}S = \frac{e\hbar}{2m} \qquad (16\text{-}1)$$

Thus the gyromagnetic ratio for the intrinsic magnetic moment is e/m, rather than $e/2m$ as for orbital motion of charged particles. This conclusion, we recall, is also suggested by the analysis of fine structure in atomic spectra, discussed in Sec. 11-8. But in the Dirac equation the magnetic moment of the electron comes out *automatically*, without having to be introduced as an additional assumption. The Dirac equation thus synthesizes in one body of theory the various assumptions that led to the original Schrödinger equation, the concept of electron spin, and the different gyromagnetic ratios for spin and orbital magnetic moments.

An equally significant result from the Dirac equation concerns energy levels of electrons. For a free particle without interactions there are solutions of the equation corresponding to all energies greater than mc^2. This is to be expected, since the *rest* energy of the particle is mc^2. But the equation also permits solutions having *negative* energies, less than $-mc^2$, as shown in Fig. 16-1. It was not clear at first what physical significance, if any, these negative energy levels had, yet neither was it clear how one could justify simply ignoring them. Worse yet, there seemed to be nothing to prevent a particle in a *positive* energy state from making a transition to a *negative* energy state by emitting a photon of energy greater than $2mc^2$; this made the stable existence of electrons difficult to understand.

To circumvent this difficulty Dirac proposed an ingenious but somewhat artificial scheme. He supposed that what we call *vacuum* actually corresponds to a state in which *all* the negative energy levels are filled and all the positive energy levels are empty. In this case, an additional electron in a positive energy level cannot make a transition to a negative energy level, since the latter levels are already filled and the exclusion principle prevents their being occupied by more than one electron each. Electrons in the negative energy states would not be observable in any ordinary low-energy interaction because *all* the negative energy levels are occupied. To be observed, a negative-energy electron must interact with its surroundings, altering its state in the process. But if there are no nearby unoccupied states available, its state cannot change unless an energy of at least $2mc^2$ is available; otherwise it is unobservable. Clearly this proposal requires a rather drastic revision of the concept of what empty space is.

If this picture is correct, what physical meaning has a situation in which one of the normally filled negative energy states is empty? Dirac proposed

Fig. 16-1 Energy levels for a free particle, as predicted by the Dirac equation. An electron can have any energy greater than mc^2. Transitions from positive to negative energy states are prevented by assuming that what is called "vacuum" is actually a state in which all the negative energy levels are occupied and the positive levels all empty. Thus the exclusion principle prevents transitions to negative energy levels.

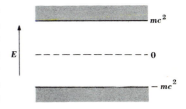

that this "hole," the absence of a negative charge, should be physically observed as a positively charged particle. Attempts were made to show that the observed mass of such a particle might be different from that of an electron, so that conceivably it might be identified as a proton. Then in 1932 C. D. Anderson, using a cloud chamber to investigate cosmic-ray particles, observed a particle which appeared to have the same mass as that of the electron but a positive charge, as indicated by opposite deflection in a magnetic field. Subsequent investigation disclosed that this particle, which was soon christened the *positron*, was identical to the electron in all its properties except that its charge was *positive* and its magnetic moment and angular momentum were in the *same* direction rather than opposite directions, as for a negatively charged particle. Furthermore, it was soon established that electron-positron pairs are *created* in collisions involving high-energy cosmic-ray particles. This process is illustrated by the cloud-chamber photograph of Fig. 16-2.

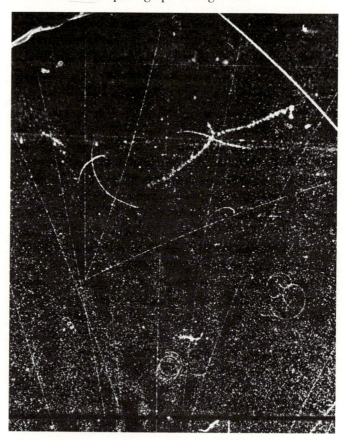

Fig. 16-2 Photograph of cloud-chamber tracks produced by a cosmic-ray shower. Several electron-positron pairs, forming V-shaped tracks, are produced by one original high-energy particle. (Photo courtesy of Brookhaven National Laboratory.)

This creation, called *pair production,* can be understood on the basis of the Dirac theory as a transition in which an electron in a negative energy state gains enough energy (at least $2mc^2$) to reach a positive energy state in which it becomes physically observable, leaving a hole in the negative energy states that is observed as a positively charged particle or positron. Conversely, when a positron collides with an electron, both particles disappear and a corresponding amount of electromagnetic energy appears, usually as two or three γ photons with total energy $2mc^2$. This process is called *annihilation* of positrons.

Although Dirac's original theory was formulated in terms of energy levels for electrons, it was soon recognized that it could be reformulated to put electrons and positrons on an equally fundamental basis and eliminate the necessity for filling all the negative energy states. Conceptually, this amounts simply to saying that if filled negative energy states are unobservable, and only holes in these states are observable, then it is physically more realistic to describe the state of the system directly in terms of the numbers of electrons and positrons.

Thus in the reformulated Dirac theory the *state* of a system is described in terms of the *numbers* of electrons and positrons in various energy, momentum, and angular-momentum states. Not only are transitions in states of individual particles permitted, but allowance is also made for processes in which the *number* of particles changes, corresponding to production or annihilation of electron-positron pairs. The relativistic electron theory is intrinsically a *many-particle* theory; no longer is it possible to speak of a system which can be said with certainty to contain only one particle.

This is a major departure from Schrödinger quantum mechanics; yet in a sense it is a welcome departure, since it tends to put electrons and photons on a similar footing. Photons are created and destroyed in various kinds of atomic processes; we have noted various similarities in behavior of electron and photon, particularly their dual wave-particle nature, and it seems natural that they should also share the ability to be created or destroyed. One fundamental difference is that, whereas photons are created and destroyed singly, electrons and positrons must be created or destroyed only in *pairs* in order to satisfy conservation of electric charge. Thus the complementary nature of electrons and positrons is described by saying that one is the *antiparticle* of the other. In Sec. 16-4 we shall cite several other examples of antiparticles.

Electrons and positrons obey the exclusion principle, whereas photons do not. There is nothing to prevent an electromagnetic field from containing a large number of photons of the same energy, momentum, and polarization, and in fact the limiting case, where there are very many photons present and quantum effects can be ignored, is simply classical wave optics, described by the Maxwell electromagnetic field equations. There is *no* corresponding "classical limit" for electrons and positrons, since each possible state can accommodate only one particle.

In this unified theory of electrons and the electromagnetic field, a *state* of a system is described by the number of electrons, positrons, and photons with each of the various possible energies and momenta. Similarly, a *transition* from one state to another is described in terms of the *creation* or *destruction* of any of these particles. When an electron with momentum $\mathbf{p}_1$ is scattered during an electromagnetic interaction and emerges with momentum $\mathbf{p}_2$, we can say that an electron with momentum $\mathbf{p}_1$ is destroyed and one with $\mathbf{p}_2$ is created. Similarly, if this process involves electromagnetic waves, we speak of the emission or absorption of a photon of a certain energy and momentum.

It is convenient to represent electron-photon interactions by means of schematic space-time diagrams or graphs in which one axis is a space coordinate for each particle; the other is time. These are known as *Feynman diagrams*, in honor of Richard P. Feynman, who introduced them in 1949 and has made many of the most important contributions to the understanding of electron-photon interactions (including demonstrating the usefulness of these graphs). In such a diagram, an electron is represented by a solid line and a photon by a broken line.

Several elementary Feynman diagrams are shown in Fig. 16-3. Figure 16-3*b* shows that a collision of two electrons (either positive or negative) can be described in terms of exchange of a photon, which acts as the mechanism for transfer of energy and momentum from one particle to another. Thus the interaction is described not as a *force* but as the emission and absorption of an intermediary particle. The situation is analogous to that of two basketball players exerting a repulsive force on each other by tossing a ball back and forth. For the *attractive* interaction of an electron and a positron, we may think of the players as alternately snatching the ball away from each other.

In Fig. 16-3, each corner, or *vertex*, includes two electron lines and one photon line, corresponding to an electron emitting or absorbing a photon. But such a process violates the classical principles of conservation of momentum and energy; this can be seen by considering an electron at rest. When it emits a photon, it must recoil in the opposite direction in order to conserve momentum; but then both the photon and the electron have energy, and so energy conservation has been violated. The resolution of this apparent paradox is the fact that, according to the uncertainty principle (Sec. 9-4), a state which lasts for a time interval Δt must have an uncertainty ΔE in its energy, given by

$$\Delta E \, \Delta t \geq \hbar \tag{16-2}$$

Thus a transition in which an electron emits or absorbs a photon is possible,

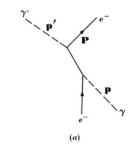

(a)

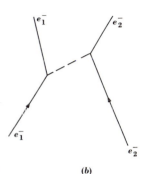

(b)

Fig. 16-3 Three simple Feynman diagrams. In each, solid lines represent electrons or positrons, and broken lines, photons. The diagrams are schematic; no attempt is made to relate directions of lines with particle speeds. (a) Compton scattering. An electron at rest absorbs a photon with momentum **p,** leading to a virtual intermediate state. Then the electron emits a photon with momentum **p′**; the final electron momentum is **P.** (b) Electron-electron scattering by exchange of a virtual photon. (c) Electron-positron annihilation, with production of two photons.

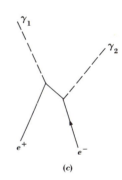

(c)

provided the resulting state lasts a sufficiently short time so that Eq. (16-2) permits the necessary uncertainty in energy. In the diagrams in Fig. 16-3, the intermediate states of the system during a transition are not states of well-defined energy, but if the initial and final states both last a long time, their energies must be well defined, and in fact must be equal.

Particles that exist temporarily in states which violate the classical energy principle but are permitted by the uncertainty principle are called *virtual* particles, to emphasize their transitory nature. A state in which such particles are present is called a *virtual state*. In Fig. 16-3b, the photon exchanged in the electron-electron scattering diagram is a *virtual photon*.

The theory described briefly above is called *quantum electrodynamics*.

Since its initial development starting in about 1949 it has become one of the most highly developed of all physical theories; in problems where only electromagnetic interactions are present, its predictions agree with experimental observations with an accuracy sometimes as great as one part in 10^9. In this sense, there is reason to believe that our understanding of the interaction of electrons with the electromagnetic field is nearly complete. But there are also electromagnetic interactions with other particles whose behavior is not nearly so well understood. Some of them will be discussed in the next sections.

16-3 MESONS AND NUCLEAR FORCES

We return now to the interactions of *nuclear* particles. In 1930 virtually nothing was known about this interaction. Observations of the dimensions and binding energies of nuclei indicated that, unlike electromagnetic forces, the nuclear force has a very short range, of the order of 1.5×10^{-15} m, but within this range it is of the order of a hundred times as strong as the electrical repulsion between two protons at corresponding distances. It was proposed that the interaction between two nucleons could be described by a potential-energy function having the general form

$$V(r) = -f^2 \frac{e^{-r/a}}{r} \tag{16-3}$$

or something similar. Aside from this very general picture, however, information about the nuclear force was mostly negative. It was certainly *not* electromagnetic or gravitational in nature. Its behavior was unlike that of any other known interaction. In short, the nuclear force was a mystery.

In 1935, the Japanese physicist H. Yukawa made a bold hypothesis. Suppose that nucleons can emit and absorb some kind of particle, in a manner similar to the emission and absorption of photons by atomic electrons. This game of catch with particles would be accompanied by transfer of energy and momentum, resulting in an interaction between the two nucleons. In 1935 no direct experimental evidence for the existence of such a particle had been found, so Yukawa's proposal was a radical and speculative one. But just as with de Broglie's wave hypothesis 10 years earlier, it was clear that a radical idea was needed, and Yukawa's suggestion was taken seriously and carefully explored.

Just as with the emission of a photon by an electron, the emission of an intermediary particle by a nucleon is forbidden by classical energy and momentum conservation, but again we are saved by the uncertainty principle; roughly speaking, a transition that violates energy conservation by an amount ΔE is possible, so long as the resulting virtual state lasts a sufficiently short time $\Delta t = \hbar/\Delta E$. This consideration can be used to estimate the *mass* such a particle must have. In the particle-exchange picture of nuclear forces, the *range R* of the force must be related to the distance the virtual particle can travel during the time Δt of its temporary existence. Since the speed of the particle can never be greater than c, the range can be at most

$$R = c \, \Delta t \tag{16-4}$$

Furthermore, the uncertainty in energy ΔE of the state necessary for such a particle to be produced must be at least as great as mc^2, where m is the mass of the particle. Combining this and Eq. (16-4) with the fundamental uncertainty relation, Eq. (16-2), we find that the mass of the particle should be of the order of

$$m = \frac{\hbar}{Rc} = \frac{1.0 \times 10^{-34} \text{ J} \cdot \text{s}}{(1.5 \times 10^{-15} \text{ m})(3.0 \times 10^8 \text{ m/s})} = 2.3 \times 10^{-28} \text{ kg} \tag{16-5}$$

or about 250 times the electron mass.

Accordingly, Yukawa postulated the existence of an unstable particle with a mass between 200 and 300 times that of the electron, which can be emitted or absorbed by a nucleon. In proton-neutron interactions, the particles can be either neutral or charged. For example, a proton may emit a positively charged particle, becoming a neutron. This particle is then absorbed by the neutron, which then becomes a proton, leaving one proton and one neutron as in the initial state. These particles were soon given the name *mesotrons*, from the Greek word *mesos*, meaning "middle," referring to the fact that their masses are intermediate between those of the electron and the nucleons. This name has since been shortened to *meson*.

In 1937, 2 years after Yukawa's hypothesis, charged particles with masses of about 200 times the electron mass were discovered in cloud-chamber track analysis, and it was immediately suspected that they were the particles Yukawa had predicted. They exhibited some very puzzling behavior, however. Because of the role these particles supposedly play in the nuclear interaction, they themselves should have strong interactions with nuclei. That is, the cross section for *scattering* of a meson by a nucleus should be much larger than if only the electromagnetic interaction were present. It turned out, however, that these particles behaved exactly as though their interaction with the nucleus was entirely electromagnetic; there was no indication of a strong "nuclear-force" interaction. Thus the initial excitement was followed immediately by a period of confusion and frustration. The meson was supposed to be the nuclear glue; yet it appeared not to interact with nuclei at all!

No appreciable progress was made in the solution of this mystery until 10 years later, when in 1947 *another* family of mesons was discovered. These mesons are somewhat heavier than the first, having masses of about 270 times

Table 16-1 Properties of Mesons

Particle	Charge	Mass, m_e	Spin	Decay products	Mean life, s
π^+	$+$	273	0	$\mu^+ + \nu$	2.6×10^{-8}
π^-	$-$	273	0	$\mu^- + \nu$	2.6×10^{-8}
π^0	0	264	0	$\gamma + \gamma$	0.8×10^{-16}
μ^+	$+$	207	$\frac{1}{2}$	$e^+ + \nu + \bar{\nu}$	2.2×10^{-6}
μ^-	$-$	207	$\frac{1}{2}$	$e^- + \nu + \bar{\nu}$	2.2×10^{-6}

the electron mass, and scattering experiments show that they *do* interact very strongly with nucleons. The strongly interacting particles discovered in 1947 are called π mesons or *pions,* while the weakly interacting particles discovered 10 years earlier are called μ mesons or *muons.*

Further investigation of the mesons, mostly with cloud chambers and photographic emulsions, revealed various additional features. There are three kinds of pions, with positive, negative, and zero charge, and two kinds of muons, positively and negatively charged. In each case, the charge has the same magnitude as the electron charge. The masses are shown in Table 16-1, which also shows that pions have zero spin (and therefore no intrinsic magnetic moment) while muons have spin $\frac{1}{2}$.

All the mesons are *unstable;* each decays spontaneously into other particles. Experiment shows that a charged pion always (with the exception of the very rare event $\pi^\pm \rightarrow e^\pm + \nu$) decays into a muon with the same charge; furthermore, if the pion is initially at rest, the resulting muon always has the same energy. Energy and momentum conservation require that at least one additional particle must be produced, but since it is not observed in cloud-chamber tracks, it must be neutral. The fact that the muon always has the same energy shows that there is *only* one additional particle, since if there were two or more, they could share the energy and momentum in various ways and the muons would be observed to have a *spectrum* of energies. Angular-momentum conservation shows that the neutral particle has spin $\frac{1}{2}$; energy and momentum relations show that it has zero rest mass, and so it is assumed to be a neutrino. Thus the decay scheme of the charged pions is represented as

$$\pi^\pm \rightarrow \mu^\pm + \nu \tag{16-6}$$

The *lifetime,* or average time between production and decay, is about 2.6×10^{-8} s, as shown in Table 16-1. It is now known that the neutrino associated with π decay is not the same as that associated with β decay, and that there are two kinds of neutrinos. We return to this point in Sec. 16-5.

The neutral pion, which cannot decay into a muon because of charge conservation, decays very rapidly into two γ photons, represented symbolically as

$$\pi^0 \rightarrow \gamma + \gamma \tag{16-7}$$

or (very rarely) into $e^+ + e^- + \gamma$.

The muons always decay into electrons with a continuous spectrum of energy, showing that at least two neutral particles are produced in each decay. It has been established that the decay process is

$$\mu^\pm \rightarrow e^\pm + \nu + \bar{\nu} \tag{16-8}$$

where $\nu + \bar{\nu}$ represents a neutrino-antineutrino pair. The lifetime for this process is 2.2×10^{-6} s.

Because of the role of pions in nuclear interactions, it is possible to *produce* π mesons in the laboratory in sufficiently energetic nucleon collisions. Artificial pion production was first accomplished in 1948, using protons accelerated in the synchrocyclotron of the University of California (Berkeley). The energy equivalent of the mass of the charged pions is

$$\begin{aligned} m_\pi c^2 &= (273)(9.11 \times 10^{-31} \text{ kg})(3.00 \times 10^8 \text{ m/s})^2 \\ &= 2.24 \times 10^{-11} \text{ J} \\ &= 140 \text{ MeV} \end{aligned} \tag{16-9}$$

The bombarding particle must have *more* energy than this, for reasons discussed in Sec. 15-7. The proton cannot give up *all* its kinetic energy in a collision; otherwise all the particles would be at rest after the collision, violating conservation of momentum. The minimum energy for the bombarding particle is the energy required to produce a pion in a state in which the bombarding particle, the target particle, and the pion all move off with a common velocity. Then in the center-of-mass coordinate system the bombarding particle and the target particle approach each other with zero total momentum, leaving all three particles at rest after the collision.

It is instructive to calculate the energy required for pion production in a collision between two protons, one from a high-energy accelerator such as a synchrotron, the other in a stationary target such as liquid hydrogen. Because of the large energies involved, it is necessary to use relativistic dynamics; the energy E and momentum p of a particle of mass m are related by

$$E^2 = (mc^2)^2 + (pc)^2 \tag{16-10}$$

For a system which initially contains two protons of mass M, one with momentum p and the other at rest, the *total* energy is

$$E = Mc^2 + \sqrt{(Mc^2)^2 + (pc)^2} \tag{16-11}$$

which may be rewritten

$$E^2 = 2EMc^2 + p^2c^2 \tag{16-12}$$

After the collision, if the bombarding particle has the *minimum* energy needed for pion production, all three particles move off with a common final velocity, so that the energy-momentum relation is exactly the same as for a single particle of total mass $2M + m$, where m is the pion mass. The *total* energy and momentum are the same as before the collision. Thus we have

$$E^2 = (2M + m)^2c^4 + p^2c^2 \tag{16-13}$$

Comparing this with Eq. (16-12), we find

$$2EMc^2 = (2M + m)^2c^4$$

$$E = 2Mc^2 + 2mc^2 + \frac{m^2}{2M}c^2 \tag{16-14}$$

The first term represents the *rest* energy of the two protons, and the remaining two terms are the kinetic energy of the bombarding proton. Thus for pion production this energy must be somewhat larger than twice the rest energy mc^2 of the pion; the threshold energy is about 290 MeV. By 1952, there were several machines capable of accelerating protons to these energies, and it became possible to produce pions in the laboratory. There ensued an intensive investigation of the properties of these particles as well as the muons produced in their decay. The precision of the numerical values in Table 16-1 results from experiments with artificially produced pions.

In addition to their contributions to the understanding of nucleon-nucleon interactions, pions also are helpful in understanding properties of individual nucleons. One problem is the magnetic moment of the proton, which, if it behaved in accordance with the Dirac equation, should have a gyromagnetic ratio e/M, as discussed in Sec. 16-2. Instead, the measured value is found to be $2.79\ e/M$. Moreover, the neutron, which has no charge and therefore according to the Dirac theory ought to have *no* magnetic moment, has a magnetic moment corresponding to a gyromagnetic ratio of $-1.91\ e/M$. Both these anomalous magnetic moments can be interpreted as the effects of virtual pions emitted and reabsorbed by single nucleons. Some of these pions are charged, and the currents associated with their motion lead to additional interactions with a magnetic field, which appears as an additional magnetic moment.

With the construction of machines of higher and higher energies, several new phenomena have appeared. Scattering of pions by nucleons is found to be strongly dependent on energy, suggesting a *resonance* phenomenon, akin to the strong scattering of light by atoms at frequencies close to excitation energies of the atoms. Another phenomenon which occurs at sufficiently high energy is *multiple* production of mesons in a single collision. A great deal of experimental effort has gone into attempts to understand in detail the properties and behavior of pions.

These efforts have been accompanied by corresponding efforts at constructing a *theoretical* foundation for the description of mesons. Most of them employ concepts similar to those used in the Dirac theory of the electron, describing interactions in terms of the creation and destruction of various kinds of particles, in the language of quantum field theory. Considerable progress has been made in the understanding of the theoretical basis of the behavior of these particles but the theory can by no means be regarded as complete at the present time. In addition to the difficulties of describing the properties of the mesons themselves, there are related problems associated with the existence of still other particles, to be discussed in the following section.

16-4 HIGH-ENERGY PHYSICS

The discovery of pions in 1947 and their laboratory production starting in 1950 cleared up at least partially the paradox of the muon, which evidently was not the particle predicted by Yukawa, and clearly established the essential role of pions in nucleon-nucleon interactions. One might have hoped that this discovery completed the list of the elementary particles, but that was not to be. Even in 1950 evidence had been found in cosmic-ray phenomena of still other particles, and higher-energy accelerators began to be planned, to produce and study these particles in the laboratory. Thus began the era of *high-energy physics*.

To understand the need for higher-energy particle accelerators, let us consider again the energy and momentum relations in collisions. In the discussion of pion production in Sec. 16-3, we noted that not all the energy of the incident bombarding proton is "available" for pion production; the pion rest energy is 140 MeV, but the proton must have at least 290 MeV of kinetic energy for pion production. The energy available for particle production is the total energy *in the center-of-mass system*, in which the total momentum is zero; only in that system can all the final particles be at rest. Thus it is worthwhile to derive a general relation between the energy in the laboratory system and that in the center-of-mass system. Because of the energies involved, it is essential to use relativistic energy-momentum relations in this derivation.

We consider the collision of an incident particle of mass m with a stationary target particle of mass M. Let the total energy (rest and kinetic) of the incident particle be E. We wish to find the total energy E_c of both particles in the center-of-mass system. The calculation is facilitated by using a general relation of relativistic mechanics. The energy and momentum of a single particle are different when measured in different frames of reference, but the quantity $(mc^2)^2 = E^2 - p^2c^2$ is the same in all systems because the rest mass is *invariant*. Similarly, it can be shown that for a *system* of particles the quantity

$$\mu^2 = (\Sigma E)^2 - (\Sigma \mathbf{p})^2 c^2 \tag{16-15}$$

is the same in all coordinate systems. We can therefore evaluate this quantity for our two-particle collision, in the laboratory and center-of-mass systems, and equate the results.

In the center-of-mass system $\Sigma \mathbf{p} = \mathbf{0}$, by definition, so we have simply

$$\mu^2 = E_c{}^2 \tag{16-16}$$

where E_c is the total energy in the center-of-mass system, the quantity we wish to find. In the laboratory the total energy is $E + Mc^2$, and the total momentum is simply the momentum p of mass m, given by $E^2 = (mc^2)^2 + p^2c^2$. Thus in the laboratory

$$\mu^2 = (E + Mc^2)^2 - [E^2 - (mc^2)^2] \tag{16-17}$$

Now equating Eqs. (16-16) and (16-17) and simplifying, we obtain

$$\begin{aligned} E_c{}^2 &= (E + Mc^2)^2 - E^2 + (mc^2)^2 \\ &= 2Mc^2E + (Mc^2)^2 + (mc^2)^2 \end{aligned} \tag{16-18}$$

To illustrate the application of this result, we consider again the threshold energy for pion production in a proton-proton collision, discussed in Sec. 16-3. Let the proton mass be m and that of the pion m'. Then E_c must be at least equal to $(2m + m')c^2$. Inserting this in the left side of Eq. (16-18) and $M = m$ in the right side, we obtain

$$[(2m + m')c^2]^2 = 2mc^2E + (mc^2)^2 + (mc^2)^2 \tag{16-19}$$

Solving for E and simplifying, we find

$$E = mc^2 + 2m'c^2 + \frac{m'^2}{2m}c^2 \tag{16-20}$$

Recalling that E is the *total* energy of the bombarding particle in the laboratory, we see that the first term is its rest energy and the remaining two are its kinetic energy; this agrees with Eq. (16-14), although different symbols are used.

As a second example, we consider the production of a proton-antiproton pair in a proton-proton collision. At threshold energy the final state consists of three protons and an antiproton at rest in the center-of-mass system, with $E_c = 4mc^2$. According to Eq. (16-18), the minimum total energy of the bombarding proton is given by

$$(4mc^2)^2 = 2mc^2E + 2(mc^2)^2$$
$$E = 7mc^2 \tag{16-21}$$

For the proton, $mc^2 = 938$ MeV. Subtracting off the rest energy, we find that a kinetic energy in the laboratory of $6mc^2$ or about 5.6 GeV is required for production of a proton-antiproton pair. The first accelerator with this capacity was the Berkeley Bevatron, a proton synchrotron, which went into operation in 1954 with maximum energy of 6.4 GeV. Antiprotons were observed in this laboratory the following year.

Equation (16-18) also illustrates a kind of law of diminishing returns for high-energy collisions. At high energies the available center-of-mass energy becomes much *less* than the laboratory energy. In the extreme-relativistic limit, when the kinetic energies are much larger than the rest energies, this equation becomes approximately

$$E_c = \sqrt{2Mc^2E} \tag{16-22}$$

For example, if M is the proton mass, a laboratory kinetic energy of 10 GeV gives $E_c = 4.3$ GeV, while 100 GeV gives $E_c = 13.6$ GeV, only a threefold increase in center-of-mass energy for a tenfold increase in laboratory energy.

This fundamental limitation can be circumvented by *colliding beam* experiments in which there is no stationary target but in which protons circulate in opposite directions in two rings and can collide in the region where the rings intersect. An example is the ISR (intersecting storage rings) installation in the CERN laboratory in Geneva, Switzerland, where two proton beams of energy up to 28 GeV collide. In this case the laboratory system *is* the center-of-mass system, and $E_c = 56$ GeV. To achieve this value of E_c with a stationary target would require a beam energy of about 1670 GeV!

The motivation toward higher and higher center-of-mass energies is manifold; more and more thresholds for multiple particle production come into reach, and studying interactions at a variety of energies gives theoreticians more detailed data to test theories describing the nature of these interactions. An important example is the production of *strange particles,* to be discussed in the next section.

16-5   STRANGE PARTICLES

The years since 1950 have witnessed a proliferation of new fundamental particles, presenting some unusual and seemingly paradoxical features which are still only partially understood. New and higher-energy particle accelerators have played an essential role in this exploration; a few examples are the 33-GeV Alternating-Gradient Synchrotron (AGS) at Brookhaven National Laboratory (1961), the 70-GeV proton synchrotron at Serpukhov, U.S.S.R. (1967), and the 500-GeV proton synchrotron at the Enrico Fermi National Laboratory, Batavia, Illinois (1972).

All the new particles share with the π and μ mesons the property that they are *unstable;* each decays into stable particles, sometimes by several successive decay processes. The new particles can be classified in various ways. In this section we confine our attention to classification in terms of mass and decay products; in Sec. 16-7 we shall examine more fundamental classification schemes.

The first new particles, or *strange* particles, as they are called, are the K mesons, or *kaons.* Their masses are about 970 electron masses. Positive, negative, and neutral K mesons have been observed. They exhibit a variety of decay modes, a few of which are the following:

$$
\begin{aligned}
K^+ &\rightarrow \pi^+ + \pi^+ + \pi^- \\
K^+ &\rightarrow \pi^+ + \pi^0 + \pi^0 \\
K^+ &\rightarrow \pi^+ + \pi^0 \\
K^+ &\rightarrow \mu^+ + \pi^0 + \nu \\
K^0 &\rightarrow \pi^+ + \pi^- \\
K^0 &\rightarrow \pi^\pm + \mu^\mp + \nu \\
K^0 &\rightarrow \pi^\pm + e^\mp + \nu
\end{aligned}
\tag{16-23}
$$

The lifetimes of the K mesons can be determined from their tracks in cloud chambers or photographic emulsion, except for the neutral K^0, which leaves no track and whose path must be inferred by the appearance of its decay products at certain points. The lifetime for the K^+ is of the order of 10^{-8} s and for the K^0 of the order of 10^{-10} s. The K mesons all have spin zero. Corresponding to K^+ and K^0 are two antiparticles, $\overline{K^-}$ and $\overline{K^0}$.

An interesting property exhibited by K mesons is that they interact strongly with nucleons, as shown by the scattering of K mesons by nucleons. This property is similar to that of pions and indicates that K mesons play a significant role in nucleon interactions. That is, heavy-meson exchange effects can produce interactions of the same sort as pion exchange. Since the K mesons have considerably greater masses, the corresponding interactions are of shorter range, but within the range they may be of considerable strength.

Closely associated with the K mesons is a second class of strange particles which have masses *greater* than those of the nucleons and are therefore called *hyperons.* The first hyperon to be observed is a particle which has been labeled Λ^0, having a mass of about 2181 electron masses (compared with about 1840 for nucleons). It has a mean life of about 2.5×10^{-10} s and decays as follows:

$$\Lambda^0 \to p + \pi^-$$
$$\Lambda^0 \to n + \pi^0 \tag{16-24}$$

The total mass of the two decay particles is considerably *less* than that of the Λ^0; the remainder appears as kinetic energy.

Another type of hyperons, the Σ particles, occur as positive, negative, or neutral particles, all having masses of approximately 2340 electron masses. The usual decay schemes for the Σ particles are

$$\Sigma^+ \to p + \pi^0$$
$$\Sigma^+ \to n + \pi^+$$
$$\Sigma^0 \to \Lambda^0 + \gamma \tag{16-25}$$
$$\Sigma^- \to n + \pi^-$$

The lifetimes for Σ^+ and Σ^- are of the order of 10^{-10} s. A third class of hyperons, still more massive than the nucleons, is the Ξ particles, having a mass of about 2580 electron masses and observed to decay according to the scheme

$$\Xi^0 \to \Lambda^0 + \pi^0$$
$$\Xi^- \to \Lambda^0 + \pi^-$$

Finally, there are the η^0 mesons at 1070 electron masses and the Ω^- hyperon at 3280. All the hyperons have spin $\frac{1}{2}$ except for the Ω^-, which is believed to have spin $\frac{3}{2}$, and all the heavy mesons have spin zero.

In addition to the heavy mesons and hyperons, other new particles have been discovered. Two of them, the antiproton and antineutron, were anticipated as long ago as 1935. We recall that the Dirac equation for the electron predicts the existence of both positive and negative electrons, with the same mass and magnitude of charge, and both with spin $\frac{1}{2}$. Since the proton is also known to have spin $\frac{1}{2}$, might not there be a corresponding *antiparticle*, having the same mass as the proton but a negative charge? If this analogy between electrons and protons is valid, it ought to be possible to produce proton-antiproton pairs in sufficiently high-energy collisions. Since the proton is nearly 2000 times as massive as the electron, much higher energies are necessary. The antiproton was sought for many years in cosmic rays, but without success. Finally, in 1955, antiprotons were produced in nucleon collisions, using 6-GeV protons from the Bevatron at the University of California at Berkeley. As expected, an antiproton and a proton annihilate when they collide, just as in the case of positrons and electrons. The products of annihilation, however, are usually different. Because of the strong nucleon-meson interactions, the annihilation of a proton and antiproton is most likely to lead to several pions.

Not long after the discovery of the antiproton, the existence of the *antineutron* was established. It is perhaps not obvious what one means by the "antiparticle" of a particle having no charge. One important attribute of the antineutron is a gyromagnetic ratio of opposite sign to that of the neutron; of even greater significance is the fact that antiprotons and antineutrons are produced and destroyed only as part of a *pair* interaction. Just as it is impossible to create or destroy a single electron (+ or −), it is also impossible to create or destroy a single nucleon or antinucleon. Creation or destruction invariably involves a nucleon-antinucleon *pair*. This phenomenon is related to a new conservation law to be discussed in the next section.

Each of the hyperons mentioned above has an associated antiparticle. There is an anti-Λ^0, denoted as $\overline{\Lambda^0}$, three anti-Σ's (+, −, and neutral), and two anti-Ξ's (+ and neutral). Each antiparticle is produced only in association with a nucleon or hyperon and annihilates similarly.

A significant feature in the behavior of heavy mesons is that on the one hand they are produced copiously in high-energy nucleon-nucleon or pion-nucleon collisions, indicating a strong interaction with nucleons, while on the other hand kaons, once produced, appear to be scattered rather weakly with nucleons; the latter observation, together with the relatively long lifetime of the kaons, suggests a much weaker interaction with nucleons.

Part of the key to this puzzle came with the discovery of the phenomenon of *associated production;* bubble-chamber records of proton-proton or pion-proton collisions in which kaons are created show that in each such collision a Λ or Σ hyperon is also produced. This suggests that two different interactions are involved, a strong one in which a heavy meson and a hyperon are produced *together,* and a weaker one in which a heavy meson decays with *no* corresponding hyperon involvement. As we shall see in the next section, these interactions are tied directly to a new *conservation law,* which is obeyed in the production mechanism but violated during decay.

A quick check over the above list shows that the total number of elementary particles (and antiparticles) discussed thus far is up to about 30. In the next section we shall describe some of the attempts to find orderly relationships among them.

16-6 CLASSES OF INTERACTIONS

In preceding sections we have described *interactions* between particles in terms of *creation* and *destruction* of particles. The nuclear "force" representing the interaction between two nucleons was described in terms of the creation of a meson by one nucleon and its absorption by the other. This description is analogous to describing the electromagnetic interaction of two charged particles in terms of the emission of a photon by one particle and its absorption by the other. In this description, it is also clear that the *strength* of a given interaction is determined by the likelihood of emission and absorption of the particles responsible for the interaction. The fact that within its range the nuclear force between two protons is much stronger than the electromagnetic interaction indicates that at least at short distances the likelihood of emission and absorption of mesons by the nucleons is much greater than for photons.

As pointed out in Sec. 16-3, particles associated with interactions, such as mesons and photons, are *virtual* particles; their emission and absorption would violate energy conservation, except that the virtual states in which they are created live for a sufficiently short time so that the uncertainty principle permits the required uncertainty in energy. Such particles cannot be observed directly unless they are given enough additional energy so that the state can live an indefinitely long time without violating energy conservation. A rough calculation shows that pions exchanged between nucleons have lifetimes of the order of 10^{-24} s, while pions observed in the laboratory have lifetimes of the order of 10^{-8} s. In the latter case, the lifetime is determined not by the close proximity of the particles but by the probability of spontaneous decay. This probability in turn is governed by the likelihood of destruction of one particle and the associated creation of others, just as in the processes determining the interactions between particles.

We are thus led to the conclusion that the very same processes responsible for *interactions* between particles are responsible also for the *production* and *decay* of particles. Furthermore, particles that interact very strongly should have relatively short lifetimes, and particles that interact weakly should have correspondingly longer lifetimes. For example, the free π^0 meson decays according to the scheme

$$\pi^0 \to \gamma + \gamma \tag{16-26}$$

with a lifetime of the order of 10^{-16} s, while the decay of the free neutron occurs according to

$$n \to p + e^- + \bar{\nu} \tag{16-27}$$

with a lifetime of the order of 15 min, longer than that for the π^0 by a factor of 10^{19}. Thus the interaction corresponding to the β decay of the neutron must be very much *weaker* than that corresponding to the decay of the π^0 meson.

The electromagnetic interaction between two particles of charge e is proportional to e^2. It is often convenient to express this interaction strength in terms of the dimensionless quantity

$$\frac{e^2}{4\pi\varepsilon_0 \hbar c} = \frac{(1.60 \times 10^{-19}\ \text{C})^2 (8.99 \times 10^9\ \text{m/F})}{(1.05 \times 10^{-34}\ \text{J} \cdot \text{s})(3.00 \times 10^8\ \text{m/s})} = \frac{1}{137} \tag{16-28}$$

Stated in other terms, the probability of absorption or emission of a photon by a particle with charge e is proportional to e, so the strength of an interaction involving both emission and absorption must be proportional to e^2. The corresponding parameter for the strength of meson-nucleon interactions is usually called g, and the quantity $g^2/\hbar c$, analogous to Eq. (16-28), is found experimentally to have values of the order of 1 to 10, depending on the details of the particular theory used. This again corresponds to the observation that, within their range, *nuclear* interactions between two protons are *stronger* by a factor of the order of 100 than their *electromagnetic* interactions.

Thus there is evidence for at least four different classes of interactions: the *strong* interactions (the interactions of mesons with nucleons), the *electromagnetic* interactions, the *weak* interactions associated with β decay, and the still weaker *gravitational* interactions, which are believed to be of no consequence in particle interactions. Not all particles participate in *all* these interactions. Particles having strong interactions, including all the mesons, nucleons, and hyperons and their antiparticles, are collectively called *hadrons*. Electrons, muons, and neutrinos, all spin-$\frac{1}{2}$ particles with *no* strong interactions, are collectively called *leptons*.

An additional observation is that particles having zero or integer spin are created and absorbed *singly*; this category includes photons and the various mesons. Conversely, all particles having half-integer spin are created and destroyed in *pairs*. This phenomenon has already been mentioned for the production of electron-positron pairs. Correspondingly, an antiproton can be produced only in combination with a proton or neutron. For example, the reactions

$$
\begin{aligned}
p + \pi^- &\to p + n + \bar{n} \\
p + n &\to p + n + \bar{p} + p \\
p + \bar{n} &\to \pi^0 + \pi^0 + \pi^+ + \pi^+ + \pi^-
\end{aligned}
\tag{16-29}
$$

are possible and are observed, but reactions such as

$$
\begin{aligned}
p + n &\to p + n + n \\
n &\to \pi^+ + e^- + \gamma \\
p + n &\to n + \pi^+ + \pi^0
\end{aligned}
\tag{16-30}
$$

are *not* observed, although they do not violate the classical conservation laws of energy, momentum, angular momentum, or charge. This observation is important in connection with the following classification of interactions.

16-7 SYMMETRY AND CONSERVATION LAWS

In this section we discuss schemes for *classifying* the fundamental particles and their interactions and for relating the interactions to various *conservation principles.* This area represents a branch of theoretical physics in which understanding is still incomplete; some of the following discussion is necessarily more empirical than fundamental, and it is sometimes necessary to make ad hoc assumptions regarding the behavior of particles. In this sense, particle physics at the present time is in much the same state as the Bohr theory of the hydrogen atom, which in 1915 provided a partially successful representation of the energy levels of the atom but no real fundamental understanding of the nature of its structure.

Four of the conservation laws for fundamental-particle interactions are taken directly from classical physics. These are conservation of energy, momentum, angular momentum, and electric charge. Every process taking place within an *isolated system,* that is, a system that does not interact with its surroundings, obeys these four conservation laws, no matter what kind of particles or interactions are involved. No exceptions to this general statement have been discovered experimentally.

Each of these four conservation principles is related to a *symmetry* of the physical system. This is most readily seen for angular momentum. The total angular momentum of an *isolated* system is constant because no external torques act on this system. If there were such a torque, it would have to be associated with a particular direction in space. The absence of torque indicates that insofar as the system is concerned, any orientation in space is equivalent to any other. This fact is expressed succinctly by saying that the system and the mathematical language used to describe it are invariant with respect to rotations of the space coordinates. If there were some external agency, such as an external magnetic field, which would give preference to some particular direction, all directions could no longer be said to be equivalent; correspondingly it would no longer be true that the total angular momentum is constant. Thus the *conservation* of angular momentum for an isolated system is directly related to the *symmetry* property of invariance under space rotations.

In precisely the same way it can be shown that conservation of *momentum* for an isolated system is directly related to invariance of the system under *translation* from one point in space to another, or a transformation of coordinates involving a translation of the coordinate axes. Conservation of energy can be shown to be related similarly to invariance under a translation of the *time* scale, and conservation of electric charge to the property of the electromagnetic potentials called *gauge invariance.* So it is with all the other conservation laws to be mentioned; each is associated with a certain symmetry. In some cases the description of this symmetry is somewhat more subtle than in the cases just mentioned, but such a symmetry exists for every conservation law.

There are two other universal conservation laws which have no analog in classical physics. They are the conservation of the *baryon* number and the *lepton* number. Lepton and baryon are generic names for two distinct classes of spin-$\frac{1}{2}$ particles. The *baryons* all have masses equal to that of nucleons or larger; this class includes nucleons, Λ, Σ, Ξ, and Ω hyperons, and their corresponding antiparticles. *Leptons* are the light particles with spin $\frac{1}{2}$, including electrons, neutrinos, and muons. These two conservation laws are related to the above observation that spin-$\frac{1}{2}$ particles are created and destroyed only in pairs.

The principle of conservation of baryon number states that in any interaction the number of baryons minus the number of antibaryons is constant. For example, the reactions

$$\Sigma^+ + \bar{p} \rightarrow \pi^+ + \pi^- + \pi^0$$
$$\Lambda^0 \rightarrow n + \pi^0$$

are permitted by this principle, but the reactions

$$n \rightarrow \pi^- + e^+ + \nu$$
$$\pi^- + p \rightarrow n + n$$

are forbidden. Similarly, the reactions

$$\mu^+ \rightarrow e^+ + \nu + \bar{\nu}$$
$$\pi^0 \rightarrow e^+ + e^-$$

obey the law of conservation of leptons, but the reactions

$$\pi^+ \rightarrow \pi^0 + e^+$$
$$p + \pi^- \rightarrow p + e^- + \gamma$$

do not, and they do not occur. Like the four classical conservation principles mentioned above, the principles of conservation of baryons and of leptons are believed to be *universal* conservation laws; no exceptions have been discovered.

We now come to a group of conservation laws which are different from those of classical physics, inasmuch as they are obeyed in some interactions and not in others. The first is *isotopic spin,* often called *isospin,* a concept devised originally to express the fact that the observed strong interactions between nucleons are *charge-independent,* in that the nuclear interaction between two protons is exactly the same as that between two neutrons. We cannot describe the isospin formalism in detail, but the basic idea is to introduce a fictitious three-dimensional space, not related to the actual physical space in which the particles move, and in this space a vector quantity τ called isospin, which is quantized according to the same rules as angular momentum. That is, the quantum number describing the total isospin of a particle must be zero or an integer or half integer. Correspondingly, the z (or 3) component of isospin τ_3 can take integer or half-integer values, respectively. Furthermore, we assert that τ_3 for a particle is directly related to the *charge* of the particle.

Thus the three π mesons are described as three states of a single particle, having total isospin of one unit, with a component in the 3-direction of 1, 0, or -1, corresponding to the three possible charges, $+1$, 0, and -1, of the pion. The charge Q of the pion, in units of e, is given simply by $Q = \tau_3$. Similarly, the nucleon has isospin $\frac{1}{2}$, with the proton state represented by $\tau_3 = +\frac{1}{2}$ and the neutron state by $\tau_3 = -\frac{1}{2}$. Thus the nucleon charge is given by $Q = \tau_3 + \frac{1}{2}$.

We see that conservation of the total 3-component of isospin is equivalent to the conservation of electric charge. Conservation of the other components or of the magnitude of τ may not seem to have any direct physical significance, but it has been found that all the strong interactions among the various hadrons (mesons and baryons) occur in such a way that the *magnitude* of the total isospin is *also* conserved. Thus the observed charge independence of nuclear forces is equivalent to *conservation of isospin,* which in turn is equivalent to the *symmetry* of the interaction with respect to rotations, not in real physical space but in isospin space.

The most remarkable feature of this new conservation principle is that it is *not* universal. Conservation of isospin is a property only of the strong interactions, not of the electromagnetic or weak interactions. Thus this is the first example of the use of a conservation principle to classify interactions.

Next we consider the principle of conservation of *strangeness*, born in an attempt to understand the properties of the strange particles, the heavy mesons and hyperons. We recall that the associated production of these particles is characteristic of a strong-interaction process, while the decay of the individual particles seems more characteristic of a weak interaction, suggesting a conservation law that is obeyed in the production process but violated in the weaker decay process.

These considerations suggest a new quantum number S, called, for the lack of a better term, *strangeness.* Values of this quantum number for all the known particles were assigned as follows: All particles except the heavy mesons and hyperons have a strangeness number $S = 0$. The Λ and Σ hyperons have $S = -1$, and the mesons K^+ and K^0 have $S = +1$. The Ξ particles have $S = -2$. Correspondingly the antihyperons $\bar{\Lambda}$ and $\bar{\Sigma}$ have $S = +1$, and $\bar{\Xi}$ has $+2$, and the mesons K^- and $\bar{K^0}$ have -1.

With this scheme, the production and decay of the strange particles can be understood at least qualitatively on the assumption that the *production* process for strange particles is a *strong* interaction, of strength comparable to that of the pion-nucleon interaction, in which strangeness is *conserved.*

For example, in the reaction

$$p + p \rightarrow K^+ \rightarrow \Sigma^-$$

the *total* strangeness on each side is zero. Furthermore according to this theory, the interactions by which these particles decay are *not* subject to this conservation law, so that in a decay process the total strangeness need not be conserved. An example is

$$\Sigma^- \rightarrow n + \pi^-$$

Finally, we mention the principle of conservation of *parity*. The basic idea is the following: Suppose for a given experiment we make two sets of apparatus, one of which is precisely the mirror image of the other. According to the principle of conservation of parity, the results of any experiment performed with one set of apparatus will be exactly the mirror image of the results with the other set of apparatus. This conservation law is associated with symmetry with respect to *reflections* of the physical system, just as angular-momentum conservation is associated with *rotational* symmetry.

For many years this principle seemed so obvious and self-evident as not to require experimental testing; there is certainly no evidence in *classical* mechanics or electrodynamics to suggest a violation of it. Furthermore, none of the phenomena of atomic physics or even the strong interactions of nuclear particles suggest a violation of this principle. But by 1956 a number of phenomena had been observed in connection with the decay of heavy mesons which were difficult to understand within the framework of theories that included conservation of parity in their description of the weak interactions responsible for the decay. Thus it seemed desirable to design new experiments to test directly whether or not parity is conserved in the weak interactions.

Several experiments to test conservation of parity directly were suggested by T. D. Lee and C. N. Yang of Columbia University. The first such experiment was performed in 1956 at Columbia by C. S. Wu; it involved the angular distribution of β particles emitted by radioactive nuclei whose spins were aligned by a magnetic field. To everyone's surprise, this experiment revealed that in the weak β-decay interaction parity is *not* conserved. This discovery represented the overthrow of a seemingly obvious and long-cherished principle. The theory of the weak interactions is now reasonably well established, and it is recognized that parity is *not* conserved in *any* weak interactions, although it *is* conserved in strong and electromagnetic interactions.

The discovery of nonconservation of parity in weak interactions has led to reexamination of two other principles, the invariance of physical theory under *time reversal* (changing t to $-t$ everywhere in the formulation) and *charge conjugation*, the operation of replacing every particle by its antiparticle. Denoting the parity, time reversal, and charge conjugation operations by P, T, and C, respectively, we note that P invariance is violated in weak interactions; later investigation revealed that C invariance is also violated, although nature does appear to be at least approximately invariant under the combined operation CP. There are theoretical reasons for believing that *every* physical theory must be invariant under the combined operation CPT. Thus violation of CP would also imply a violation of T, and indeed there is now some evidence of T violation in some decay processes, notably the decay $K^0 \to \pi + \pi$.

We now summarize briefly the properties of the three classes of interactions discussed. A fundamental event in an *electromagnetic* interaction always involves three particles, one of which is a photon. Photons interact directly only with particles having electric charge. A Feynman diagram describing a fundamental electromagnetic interaction always contains three lines meeting at a point, as shown in Fig. 16-4b. One of these is a photon; the other two are charged particles. Electromagnetic interactions obey all the universal conservation laws discussed above and also conservation of parity and strangeness, but *not* conservation of isospin. A fundamental *strong* interaction process always involves two baryons and one meson. These processes are believed to obey *all* the conservation laws discussed above, including isospin, strangeness, and parity.

The weak interactions, as contrasted with the other two, always involve

(a)

(b)

Fig. 16-4 Diagrammatic representation of strong, electromagnetic, and weak interactions. (*a*) Strong-interaction vertex, corresponding to the creation or destruction of a meson (broken line) by a baryon (solid line). (*b*) Electromagnetic interaction, corresponding to the creation or absorption of a photon (broken line) by a charged particle which may be a lepton, meson, or baryon. (*c*) Weak interaction, in which four spin-$\frac{1}{2}$ particles are involved.

(c)

four different particles of spin $\frac{1}{2}$. These are the interactions responsible for β decay, the decay of muons, and indirectly the decay of charged pions. All these processes can be described in terms of a four-particle interaction. For example, the decay of the π^+ meson into a μ^+ meson and a neutrino can be understood as a two-stage process in which the π^+ meson first creates a virtual nucleon-antinucleon pair, via the strong interaction; this undergoes a transition via the weak interaction to a μ^+ meson and a neutrino. This process is shown by the Feynman diagram of Fig. 16-5a. The weak interactions may or may not conserve strangeness and *do not* conserve parity.

The observed production and decay processes for all the fundamental particles can be understood on the basis of combinations of these three fundamental interactions. Several examples of processes involving combinations of two or more interactions are illustrated in Fig. 16-5. In all these examples, the concept of virtual intermediate states plays an essential role.

The weak interaction always involves at least one neutrino, and it is now known that there are actually *two* kinds of neutrinos, one involved with electrons and the other with muons. Thus the neutrino in the process

$$n \rightarrow p + e^- + \nu$$

is not the same particle as in

$$\pi^+ \rightarrow \mu^+ + \nu$$

and the notations ν_e and ν_μ are used to distinguish them. The definitive test of the two-neutrino hypothesis was made at Brookhaven National Laboratory in 1963, and the existence of two kinds of neutrinos is now firmly established. Each kind has a corresponding antineutrino, $\bar{\nu}_e$ and $\bar{\nu}_\mu$. In the above discussion

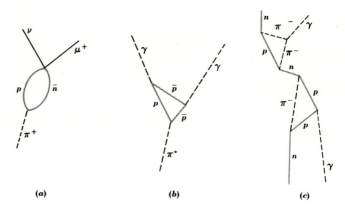

(a)   (b)   (c)

Fig. 16-5 Several diagrams showing reactions which combine two or more fundamental interactions of the types shown in Fig. 16-4. (a) $\pi^+ \rightarrow \mu^+$ decay; (b) π^0 decay; (c) scattering of γ by neutron.

we have not distinguished between neutrino and antineutrino; in the usual convention, the particle on the right side of the neutron-decay reaction above is actually an antineutrino and should be denoted as $\bar{\nu}_e$.

The above discussion may be summarized as follows: First, particles are classified and characterized by means of several quantum numbers, including spin σ, isospin and its 3-component (τ and τ_3), baryon number B, and strangeness S. These also determine the particle's charge Q, which (in units of e) is given by

$$Q = \tau_3 + \frac{B}{2} + \frac{S}{2} \tag{16-31}$$

For some purposes it is convenient to introduce a quantity called *hypercharge* Y, defined as

$$Y = B + S \tag{16-32}$$

The two numbers Y and B thus convey the same information as S and B. In this notation Eq. (16-31) becomes

$$Q = \tau_3 + \frac{Y}{2} \tag{16-33}$$

Each of these quantum numbers corresponds to a physical quantity, and conservation of that quantity corresponds to invariance of the system with respect to a specific symmetry operation. The characteristics of some of the fundamental particles are summarized in Table 16-2.

Second, interactions are classified according to which conservation laws they obey and which not, or equivalently what symmetries they possess or do not. Table 16-3 summarizes this characterization. The fundamental event in the strong interaction is the emission or absorption of a meson by a baryon; particles that participate in strong interactions are collectively called *hadrons*. The fundamental event in the electromagnetic interaction is the emission or absorption of a photon by any charged particle, and for the weak interaction the fundamental event is an interaction involving four particles of half-integer spin.

Finally, the classical conservation laws of energy, momentum, angular momentum, and charge are believed to be obeyed in *all* interactions.

The search for conservation laws and associated symmetry properties in the interactions of fundamental particles has led to a certain degree of understanding of the roles of these various processes in the structure of matter. Furthermore, the symmetry properties provide a very important guide in the formulation of detailed theories to describe the interactions. Just as the principle of relativistic invariance, together with the requirement of spin $\frac{1}{2}$,

Table 16-2   Properties of Fundamental Particles

Name	Symbol	Charge	Spin	m_e	MeV	Lifetime, s	τ	S	B	Y
				Mass						
Photon	γ	0	1	0	0	stable	0	0	0	0
Neutrino	ν_e, ν_μ	0	$\frac{1}{2}$	0	0	stable	0	0	0	0
Electron	e^-	-1	$\frac{1}{2}$	1	0.511	stable	0	0	0	0
Muon	μ^-	-1	$\frac{1}{2}$	207	105	2.20×10^{-6}	0	0	0	0
Pion	π^+	$+1$	0	273	140	2.60×10^{-8}	1	0	0	0
	π^0	0	0	264	135	0.8×10^{-16}	1	0	0	0
Kaon	K^+	$+1$	0	965	493	1.24×10^{-8}	$\frac{1}{2}$	$+1$	0	$+1$
	K^0	0	0	975	498	0.86×10^{-10}	$\frac{1}{2}$	$+1$	0	$+1$
Eta	η^0	0	0	1074	549	0.25×10^{-18}	0	0	0	0
Proton	p	$+1$	$\frac{1}{2}$	1836	938	stable	$\frac{1}{2}$	0	1	1
Neutron	n	0	$\frac{1}{2}$	1839	940	0.93×10^3	$\frac{1}{2}$	0	1	1
Lambda	Λ^0	0	$\frac{1}{2}$	2182	1116	2.5×10^{-10}	0	-1	1	0
Sigma	Σ^+	$+1$	$\frac{1}{2}$	2328	1189	0.80×10^{-10}	1	-1	1	0
	Σ^0	0	$\frac{1}{2}$	2333	1192	$< 10^{-14}$	1	-1	1	0
	Σ^-	-1	$\frac{1}{2}$	2343	1197	1.49×10^{-10}	1	-1	1	0
Xi	Ξ^0	0	$\frac{1}{2}$	2572	1315	3.0×10^{-10}	$\frac{1}{2}$	-2	1	-1
	Ξ^-	-1	$\frac{1}{2}$	2585	1321	1.66×10^{-10}	$\frac{1}{2}$	-2	1	-1
Omega	Ω^-	-1	$\frac{3}{2}$?	3280	1672	1.3×10^{-10}?	0	-3	1	-2

led to the formulation of the Dirac equation, so the requirements of the various conservation laws and their associated symmetries lead directly to the permissible mathematical formulations of the fundamental-particle interactions. It has not yet been possible to use symmetry properties to predict *uniquely* what the form of the detailed theory should be; some choices still have to be made empirically. Some physicists hope that, with the discovery of new

Table 16-3   Classification of Interactions

Conserved quantity	Strong	Electromagnetic	Weak
Isospin	yes	no	no
Strangeness	yes	yes	no
Parity	yes	yes	no
Charge conjugation	yes	yes	no

The following quantities are conserved in *all* interactions:

energy	charge
momentum	baryon number
angular momentum	lepton number

phenomena and new associated conservation laws, perhaps we shall eventually be led to a unique theory. This, however, is purely conjecture at the present time.

16-8 FRONTIERS

Lest the reader should receive the erroneous impression that the problems of fundamental-particle physics are now essentially solved, we bring this volume to a close with a brief mention of some of the unsolved fundamental problems.

In the years since 1955 still other particles have been discovered, including additional short-lived mesons more massive than the K mesons, as well as heavier hyperons. These particles are usually described not as independent entities but rather as excited states of some other system. The situation may be compared with atomic physics. In the usual point of view, a hydrogen atom does not cease to be a hydrogen atom when it is excited by absorption of a photon to an energy level above the $n = 1$ ground state. But if the details of the atom's structure were not known, we might perfectly well call it a different atom; it certainly has different mechanical properties, including energy-mass and angular momentum, from the usual hydrogen atom, and it is *unstable,* decaying spontaneously into an ordinary hydrogen atom and a photon. Perhaps some of the new unstable particles have a similar status.

As an example of this viewpoint, we consider the scattering of π^+ by protons. The scattering cross section goes through a prominent maximum at pion kinetic energy of about 195 MeV, corresponding to *total* center-of-mass energy of about 1236 MeV. We can call this a *resonance* in the scattering process, we can call it a new unstable particle with spin $\frac{3}{2}$ and mass 1236 MeV, or we can call it an excited state of the proton. Such a "particle" decays via strong interaction with a lifetime of the order of 10^{-24} s; nevertheless, the usual viewpoint at present is that such a state has just as much right to be called a fundamental particle as, for example, the Σ^+, which also can be considered an excited nucleon but which decays via *weak* interaction with a much longer lifetime. Whether we refer to such states as *particles,* as *resonances,* or as *excited states* is principally a matter of taste.

The analogy with excited states of atomic systems suggests an appealing hypothesis: Suppose the familiar particles are *not* the most fundamental particles, but are instead combinations of other even more fundamental particles, in bound states with various states of excitation. The most promising such scheme to date, proposed by Gell-Mann in 1964, includes three particles called *quarks,* labeled $\boldsymbol{p}$, $\boldsymbol{n}$, and $\boldsymbol{\lambda}$, each having its antiparticle. Their properties are outlined in Table 16-4.

It turns out that all mesons can be represented as bound states of a

Table 16-4 Properties of Quarks

		p	n	λ
Isospin	τ	$\frac{1}{2}$	$\frac{1}{2}$	0
	τ_3	$\frac{1}{2}$	$-\frac{1}{2}$	0
Charge	Q	$\frac{2}{3}$	$-\frac{1}{3}$	$-\frac{1}{3}$
Baryon number	B	$\frac{1}{3}$	$\frac{1}{3}$	$\frac{1}{3}$
Strangeness	S	0	0	-1
Hypercharge	Y	$\frac{1}{3}$	$\frac{1}{3}$	$-\frac{2}{3}$

Each antiquark ($\bar{p}$, $\bar{n}$, $\bar{\lambda}$) has the same τ as the corresponding quark, but all other values have opposite sign.

quark-antiquark pair. For example,

$$\pi^+ = p\bar{n}$$
$$K^+ = p\bar{\lambda}$$

Similarly, all known baryons can be represented as combinations of *three* quarks; examples are

$$\text{proton} = ppn$$
$$\Sigma^+ = pp\lambda$$

In this scheme there appears to be nothing in nature corresponding to a two-quark or two-quark-plus-antiquark combination, although no one knows why not.

The symmetry properties represented by these sets of combinations, or *multiplets*, as they are called, are best represented in the language of group theory; the appropriate group of transformations, which we cannot discuss here, is referred to as SU(3). This model has been developed into a more detailed theory which can be used to predict the masses of the various particles, and considerable progress has been made in this area.

Many questions remain. Do quarks really exist as independent entities, or are they just a mathematical scheme? If they do exist, why have they not been observed? One hypothesis is that they are extremely massive (perhaps 50 GeV) but in combination have correspondingly large binding energies so as to account for the observed masses of particles. More elaborate quark models have been proposed. One scheme has several sets of quarks with different values of a quantum number called *color;* another introduces a fourth quark distinguished from the other three by a different value of a quantum number called *charm.* In late 1974 two new particles were discovered with rest energies of about 3.1 GeV and 3.7 GeV. These can be interpreted as combinations of charmed and uncharmed quarks. Experiments now under way promise to provide significant new information concerning the existence of quarks and related questions.

The concept of charm also offers some hope for understanding of the muon, which remains something of a puzzle. It behaves very much like a fat electron; it has no strong interactions and does not fit into the original quark model. Charmed quarks make it possible to treat leptons (electrons, muons, and neutrinos) on the same basis as hadrons (strongly interacting particles), but this theoretical proposal must still be regarded as somewhat speculative.

We have hardly mentioned cosmological questions. What is the origin of cosmic rays? What events occur in remote regions of space to produce particles with a million times as much energy as have been produced in the laboratory? Do some parts of the universe contain antimatter made of antiprotons, antineutrons, and positrons? If so, it has been proposed in jest that we solve our pollution and energy problems by importing antigarbage, annihilating it with our garbage, and generating vast amounts of useful energy!

More seriously, what relevance does the composition of matter in remote regions of the universe have for the understanding of matter as we know it? What relation do these questions have to the *gravitational interaction,* much weaker than any of the three interactions described above and believed to be of no significance in fundamental-particle interactions, yet clearly of primary importance in governing the large-scale structure of the universe? Current theories of gravitational interactions employ non-euclidean geometries to represent the manifestations of gravitational fields; might such considerations be relevant to the behavior of fundamental particles?

In short, physicists are not running out of new areas to explore. For every phenomenon that is analyzed and understood, new ones clamor for attention. It seems very unlikely that man will ever know everything there is to be known about the world in which he lives. Nevertheless, the quest for new knowledge and understanding proceeds on an ever-expanding frontier. And this inquiry into the properties and behavior of the physical world, which we call *physics,* continues and will continue to be one of the most exciting adventures of the human mind.

Problems

16-1 In the energy-level scheme shown in Fig. 16-1, where would the energy levels for an electron in a hydrogen atom lie?

16-2 An electron and a positron annihilate, with the emission of two photons. Find the energy of each, in megaelectronvolts, assuming the two particles were initially at rest. What is the photon wavelength?

16-3 An electron and a positron annihilate with the emission of *three* photons. Show that the photons can have various energies in various events, within a certain range. Find the minimum and maximum photon energies.

16-4 Find the energy threshold for electron-positron pair production in a proton-proton collision, with one proton initially at rest.

16-5 Draw a Feynman diagram which represents photon-photon scattering, i.e., the collision of two photons. Hint: One photon produces a virtual electron-positron pair; one of these absorbs the other photon; a photon is emitted, and then the pair annihilate.

16-6 Is it possible for an electron and a positron to annihilate and produce only one photon? Explain.

16-7 Use the uncertainty principle to estimate the maximum lifetime of a virtual pion emitted as described in Sec. 16-3.

16-8 Suppose a virtual pion is emitted with total energy $2mc^2$, where m is the pion mass.
  a What is the particle's speed?
  b What is the particle's lifetime?
  c How far can the particle travel during its lifetime?

16-9 In Prob. 16-8 suppose the particle is a K meson instead of a pion. Answer the same questions for this particle, and compare the range of the nuclear force mediated by the kaon with that of the pion.

16-10 A neutral pion with kinetic energy 140 MeV decays in flight. If one γ is emitted in the direction of flight and the other in the opposite direction, find the energy of each γ.

16-11 A π^+ meson decays at rest. Find the kinetic energies of the resulting μ^+ meson and neutrino.

16-12 Find the energy of each of the two γ photons resulting from decay of a π^0 meson at rest.

16-13 If a muon at rest decays into two neutrinos emitted in the same direction and an electron in the opposite direction, find the energy of the electron. Extreme-relativistic approximations may be used. (Why?)

16-14 Find the threshold energy for two-meson production, e.g., for the reaction

$$p + p \rightarrow p + p + \pi^0 + \pi^0$$

with one proton initially at rest.

16-15 Find the threshold energy for the reaction

$$\pi^- + p \rightarrow K^+ + \Sigma^-$$

if the proton is initially at rest.

16-16 Find the threshold energy for the reaction

$$p + p \rightarrow \Sigma^+ + K^0 + p$$

assuming one proton is initially at rest.

16-17 The threshold energy for production of $\overline{K^-}$ meons in a proton-pion collision is considerably higher than for K^+ mesons. Explain, on the basis of conservation of baryon number and strangeness.

16-18 A K^+ meson decays at rest into two pions. Find the kinetic energy of each pion. For simplicity, assume they have equal masses.

16-19 A Λ^0 hyperon at rest decays to a proton and a π^-. Find the total kinetic energy of the decay products. What fraction of the energy is carried off by each particle?

16-20 Construct a diagram in which hypercharge Y is plotted on the vertical axis and the 3-component of isospin τ_3 on the horizontal axis of a coordinate system.
    a   Plot the positions of the quarks and antiquarks on this diagram.
    b   Plot the positions of all the possible quark-antiquark pairs, and identify the corresponding particles.

16-21 Find the combination of three quarks corresponding to:
    a   neutron
    b $\overline{\Sigma^+}$
    c Ω^-
    d Λ^0

APPENDIX A
THE INTERNATIONAL SYSTEM OF UNITS

The Système International d'Unités, abbreviated SI, is the system developed by the General Conference on Weights and Measures and adopted by nearly all the industrial nations of the world. It is based on the MKSA (meter-kilogram-second-ampere) system.

Quantity	Name of unit	Symbol	Equivalent unit
SI Base Units			
Length	meter	m	
Mass	kilogram	kg	
Time	second	s	
Electric current	ampere	A	
Thermodynamic temperature	kelvin	K	
Luminous intensity	candela	cd	
Amount of substance	mole	mol	
SI Derived Units			
Area	square meter	m^2	
Volume	cubic meter	m^3	
Frequency	hertz	Hz	s^{-1}
Mass density (density)	kilogram per cubic meter	kg/m^3	
Speed, velocity	meter per second	m/s	
Angular velocity	radian per second	rad/s	
Acceleration	meter per second squared	m/s^2	
Angular acceleration	radian per second squared	rad/s^2	
Force	newton	N	$kg \cdot m/s^2$
Pressure (mechanical stress)	pascal	Pa	N/m^2
Kinematic viscosity	square meter per second	m^2/s	
Dynamic viscosity	newton second per square meter	$N \cdot s/m^2$	
Work, energy, quantity of heat	joule	J	$N \cdot m$
Power	watt	W	J/s
Quantity of electricity	coulomb	C	$A \cdot s$
Potential difference, electromotive force	volt	V	W/A
Electric field strength	volt per meter	V/m	
Electric resistance	ohm	Ω	V/A
Capacitance	farad	F	$A \cdot s/V$
Magnetic flux	weber	Wb	$V \cdot s$
Inductance	henry	H	$V \cdot s/A$
Magnetic flux density	tesla	T	Wb/m^2

Quantity	Name of unit	Symbol	Equivalent unit
Magnetic field strength	ampere per meter	A/m	
Magnetomotive force	ampere	A	
Luminous flux	lumen	lm	cd · sr
Luminance	candela per square meter	cd/m^2	
Illuminance	lux	lx	lm/m^2
Wave number	1 per meter	m^{-1}	
Entropy	joule per kelvin	J/K	
Specific heat capacity	joule per kilogram kelvin	J/kg · K	
Thermal conductivity	watt per meter kelvin	W/m · K	
Radiant intensity	watt per steradian	W/sr	
Activity (of a radio-active source)	1 per second	s^{-1}	

In general, names of units which are derived from proper names are *not* capitalized (e.g., the coulomb and the newton), but the abbreviations are usually capital letters (e.g., C and N).

SI Prefixes

The names of multiples and submultiples of SI units are formed by using the following prefixes:

Factor by which unit is multiplied	Prefix	Symbol
10^{12}	tera	T
10^9	giga	G
10^6	mega	M
10^3	kilo	k
10^2	hecto	h
10	deka	da
10^{-1}	deci	d
10^{-2}	centi	c
10^{-3}	milli	m
10^{-6}	micro	μ
10^{-9}	nano	n
10^{-12}	pico	p
10^{-15}	femto	f
10^{-18}	atto	a

APPENDIX B
PHYSICAL CONSTANTS

Fundamental Physical Constants

Name	Symbol	Value
Speed of light	c	2.998×10^8 m/s
Charge of electron	e	1.602×10^{-19} C
Mass of electron	m	9.109×10^{-31} kg
Mass of neutron	m_n	1.675×10^{-27} kg
Mass of proton	m_p	1.673×10^{-27} kg
Planck's constant	h	6.626×10^{-34} J $\cdot$ s
	$\hbar$	1.055×10^{-34} J $\cdot$ s
Permittivity of free space	ε_0	8.854×10^{-12} F/m
Permeability of free space	μ_0	$4\pi \times 10^{-7}$ Wb/A $\cdot$ m
Boltzmann's constant	k	1.380×10^{-23} J/K
Gas constant	R	8.314 J/mol $\cdot$ K
Avogadro's number	N_0	6.022×10^{23} molecules/mol
Mechanical equivalent of heat	J	4.186 J/cal
Gravitational constant	G	6.672×10^{-11} N $\cdot$ m^2/kg^2

Other Useful Constants

Name	Symbol	Value
Planck's constant	h	4.136×10^{-15} eV $\cdot$ s
Boltzmann's constant	k	8.617×10^{-5} eV/K
Coulomb constant	$e^2/4\pi\epsilon_0$	14.42 eV $\cdot$ Å $= 1.442$ eV $\cdot$ nm
Electron rest energy	mc^2	0.5110 MeV
Proton rest energy	$M_p c^2$	938.3 MeV
Energy equivalent of 1 u	Mc^2	931.5 MeV
Electron magnetic moment	$\mu = e\hbar/2m$	0.9273×10^{-23} J $\cdot$ m^2/Wb
Bohr radius	$a = 4\pi\epsilon_0\hbar^2/me^2$	0.5292×10^{-10} m
Electron Compton wavelength	$\lambda_c = h/mc$	2.426×10^{-12} m
Fine-structure constant	$\alpha = e^2/4\pi\epsilon_0\hbar c$	$1/137.0$
Classical electron radius	$r_e = e^2/4\pi\epsilon_0 mc^2$	2.818×10^{-15} m
Rydberg constant	R_∞	1.097×10^{-7} m

Conversion Factors

1 eV $= 1.602 \times 10^{-19}$ J

1 Å $= 10^{-10}$ m $= 10^{-1}$ nm

1 u $= 1.661 \times 10^{-27}$ kg $\leftrightarrow 931.5$ MeV

APPENDIX C
GROUP VELOCITY

A wave packet is constructed from a superposition of sinusoidal waves of the form $e^{i(kx-\omega t)}$; the most general superposition is written

$$\Psi(x,t) = \int_{-\infty}^{\infty} A(k)e^{i(kx-\omega t)}\,dk \tag{C-1}$$

where the function $A(k)$ specifies the distribution of wave numbers to be used. We consider only wave packets formed by superposing sinusoidal waves with values of k in the vicinity of a central value k_0, in which case the function $A(k)$ is sharply peaked at $k = k_0$, dropping off toward zero on both sides. The angular frequency ω is a function of k. If all sinusoidal waves have the same wave speed u, then $\omega = uk$, and the speed of the wave packet is also u. In general, however, the ratio $\omega/k = u$ is different for different values of k, and so ω is a more complicated function of k. We now calculate the velocity of the envelope of the resulting wave packet, usually called the *group velocity* of the packet.

The key to the calculation is the observation that since $A(k)$ differs significantly from zero only near k_0 it is legitimate to expand the function $\omega(k)$ in a Taylor series about the point $k = k_0$, as follows:

$$\omega(k) = \omega(k_0) + \left(\frac{d\omega}{dk}\right)_{k_0}(k-k_0) + \frac{1}{2!}\left(\frac{d^2\omega}{dk^2}\right)_{k_0}(k-k_0)^2 + \cdots \tag{C-2}$$

In the spirit of this approximation, we retain only the first two terms of the series. Using the abbreviation $\omega(k_0) = \omega_0$, we obtain

$$\omega = \omega_0 + \left(\frac{d\omega}{dk}\right)_{k_0}(k-k_0) \tag{C-3}$$

We now introduce Eq. (C-3) into the exponent of Eq. (C-1) and make a series of rearrangements, adding and subtracting ik_0x, as follows:

$$
\begin{aligned}
kx - \omega t &= kx - \omega_0 t - \left(\frac{d\omega}{dk}\right)_{k_0}(k-k_0)t \\
&= (k-k_0)x + k_0 x - \omega_0 t - \left(\frac{d\omega}{dk}\right)_{k_0}(k-k_0)t \\
&= k_0 x - \omega_0 t + (k-k_0)\left[x - \left(\frac{d\omega}{dk}\right)_{k_0}t\right]
\end{aligned}
\tag{C-4}
$$

The exponential function in Eq. (C-1) can now be written

$$e^{i(kx-\omega t)} = e^{i(k_0 x-\omega_0 t)}e^{i(k-k_0)[x-(d\omega/dk)_{k_0}t]} \tag{C-5}$$

The first factor is independent of k and may be taken outside the integral. Equation (C-1) then becomes

$$\Psi(x,t) = e^{i(k_0 x-\omega_0 t)} \int_{-\infty}^{\infty} A(k)e^{i(k-k_0)[x-(d\omega/dt)_{k_0}t]}dk \tag{C-6}$$

The factor preceding the integral is a sinusoidal wave with the central wave number k_0 and corresponding frequency ω_0. The integral represents the envelope function, whose speed of propagation is to be identified with the group velocity of the wave packet. The form of Eq. (C-6) shows that the envelope is a superposition of waves each of which contains x and t in the combination

$$x - \left(\frac{d\omega}{dk}\right)_{k_0} t$$

Thus each of these waves, and therefore their superposition, moves with a speed v given by

$$v = \left(\frac{d\omega}{dk}\right)_{k_0} \tag{C-7}$$

which establishes this expression as the group velocity of the wave packet.

APPENDIX D
EVALUATION OF WAVE-PACKET INTEGRAL

The wave function $\psi(x)$ corresponding to the wave-number distribution function $A(k) = Ae^{-a^2(k-k_0)^2}$ is given by the integral

$$\psi(x) = \int_{-\infty}^{\infty} Ae^{-a^2(k-k_0)^2}e^{ikx} \, dk \tag{D-1}$$

To evaluate this integral, we first introduce the change of variable $K = k - k_0$ to obtain

$$\psi(x) = \int_{-\infty}^{\infty} Ae^{-a^2K^2}e^{i(k_0+K)x} \, dK$$

$$= Ae^{ik_0x} \int_{-\infty}^{\infty} e^{-(a^2K^2 - iKx)} \, dK \tag{D-2}$$

We now complete the square in the exponent in the integrand by adding and subtracting the quantity $x^2/4a^2$, as follows:

$$a^2K^2 - iKx = a^2K^2 - iKx - \frac{x^2}{4a^2} + \frac{x^2}{4a^2}$$

$$= \left(aK - i\frac{x}{2a}\right)^2 + \frac{x^2}{4a^2}$$

$$= a^2\left(K - i\frac{x}{2a^2}\right)^2 + \frac{x^2}{4a^2} \tag{D-3}$$

Introducing this expression into Eq. (D-2) yields

$$\psi(x) = Ae^{ik_0x} \int_{-\infty}^{\infty} e^{-a^2(K-ix/2a^2)^2}e^{-x^2/4a^2} \, dK$$

$$= Ae^{ik_0x}e^{-x^2/4a^2} \int_{-\infty}^{\infty} e^{-a^2(K-ix/2a^2)^2} \, dK \tag{D-4}$$

Equation (D-4) is simplified by the further substitution $y = K - x/2a^2$, which puts it in the form

$$\psi(x) = Ae^{ik_0x}e^{-x^2/4a^2} \int_{-\infty}^{\infty} e^{-a^2y^2} \, dy \tag{D-5}$$

By a bit of mathematical trickery or by inspection of a table of definite integrals, it can be shown that this last integral has the value $\sqrt{\pi}/a$ Thus we finally obtain

$$\psi(x) = \frac{\sqrt{\pi}\,A}{a} e^{ik_0x}e^{-x^2/4a^2} \tag{D-6}$$

APPENDIX E   PERIODIC TABLE OF THE ELEMENTS

The number above the symbol of each element is its atomic mass, and that below is its atomic number. The elements whose atomic masses are given in parentheses do not occur in nature, but have been prepared artificially in nuclear reactions. The atomic mass in such a case is the mass number of the most long-lived radioactive isotope of the element.

Period	Group I	Group II											Group III	Group IV	Group V	Group VI	Group VII	Group VIII
1	1.00 H 1																	4.00 He 2
2	6.94 Li 3	9.01 Be 4											10.81 B 5	12.01 C 6	14.01 N 7	16.00 O 8	19.00 F 9	20.18 Ne 10
3	22.99 Na 11	24.31 Mg 12											26.98 Al 13	28.09 Si 14	30.98 P 15	32.07 S 16	35.46 Cl 17	39.94 Ar 18
4	39.10 K 19	40.08 Ca 20	44.96 Sc 21	47.90 Ti 22	50.94 V 23	52.00 Cr 24	54.94 Mn 25	55.85 Fe 26	58.93 Co 27	58.71 Ni 28	63.54 Cu 29	65.37 Zn 30	69.72 Ga 31	72.59 Ge 32	74.92 As 33	78.96 Se 34	79.91 Br 35	83.8 Kr 36
5	85.47 Rb 37	87.66 Sr 38	88.91 Y 39	91.22 Zr 40	92.91 Nb 41	95.94 Mo 42	(99) Tc 43	101.1 Ru 44	102.91 Rh 45	106.4 Pd 46	107.87 Ag 47	112.40 Cd 48	114.82 In 49	118.69 Sn 50	121.75 Sb 51	127.60 Te 52	126.90 I 53	131.30 Xe 54
6	132.91 Cs 55	137.34 Ba 56	* 57–71	178.49 Hf 72	180.95 Ta 73	183.85 W 74	186.2 Re 75	190.2 Os 76	192.2 Ir 77	195.09 Pt 78	197.0 Au 79	200.59 Hg 80	204.37 Tl 81	207.19 Pb 82	208.98 Bi 83	(210) Po 84	(210) At 85	222 Rn 86
7	(223) Fr 87	226.05 Ra 88	† 89–103															

* Rare earths

138.91 La 57	140.12 Ce 58	140.91 Pr 59	144.24 Nd 60	(145) Pm 61	150.35 Sm 62	152.0 Eu 63	157.25 Gd 64	158.92 Tb 65	162.50 Dy 66	164.92 Ho 67	167.26 Er 68	168.93 Tm 69	173.04 Yb 70	174.97 Lu 71

† Actinides

227 Ac 89	232.04 Th 90	231 Pa 91	238.03 U 92	(237) Np 93	(242) Pu 94	(243) Am 95	(247) Cm 96	(249) Bk 97	(251) Cf 98	(254) Es 99	(253) Fm 100	(256) Md 101	(254) No 102	(257) Lw 103

APPENDIX F
ATOMIC ELECTRON CONFIGURATIONS

	K	L		M			N				O				P			Q
	1s	2s	2p	3s	3p	3d	4s	4p	4d	4f	5s	5p	5d	5f	6s	6p	6d	7s
1 H	1																	
2 He	2																	
3 Li	2	1																
4 Be	2	2																
5 B	2	2	1															
6 C	2	2	2															
7 N	2	2	3															
8 O	2	2	4															
9 F	2	2	5															
10 Ne	2	2	6															
11 Na	2	2	6	1														
12 Mg	2	2	6	2														
13 Al	2	2	6	2	1													
14 Si	2	2	6	2	2													
15 P	2	2	6	2	3													
16 S	2	2	6	2	4													
17 Cl	2	2	6	2	5													
18 Ar	2	2	6	2	6													
19 K	2	2	6	2	6		1											
20 Ca	2	2	6	2	6		2											
21 Sc	2	2	6	2	6	1	2											
22 Ti	2	2	6	2	6	2	2											
23 V	2	2	6	2	6	3	2											
24 Cr	2	2	6	2	6	5	1											
25 Mn	2	2	6	2	6	5	2											
26 Fe	2	2	6	2	6	6	2											
27 Co	2	2	6	2	6	7	2											
28 Ni	2	2	6	2	6	8	2											
29 Cu	2	2	6	2	6	10	1											
30 Zn	2	2	6	2	6	10	2											
31 Ga	2	2	6	2	6	10	2	1										
32 Ge	2	2	6	2	6	10	2	2										
33 As	2	2	6	2	6	10	2	3										
34 Se	2	2	6	2	6	10	2	4										
35 Br	2	2	6	2	6	10	2	5										
36 Kr	2	2	6	2	6	10	2	6										
37 Rb	2	2	6	2	6	10	2	6			1							
38 Sr	2	2	6	2	6	10	2	6			2							
39 Y	2	2	6	2	6	10	2	6	1		2							
40 Zr	2	2	6	2	6	10	2	6	2		2							
41 Nb	2	2	6	2	6	10	2	6	4		1							
42 Mo	2	2	6	2	6	10	2	6	5		1							
43 Tc	2	2	6	2	6	10	2	6	5		2							
44 Ru	2	2	6	2	6	10	2	6	7		1							
45 Rh	2	2	6	2	6	10	2	6	8		1							
46 Pd	2	2	6	2	6	10	2	6	10									
47 Ag	2	2	6	2	6	10	2	6	10		1							
48 Cd	2	2	6	2	6	10	2	6	10		2							
49 In	2	2	6	2	6	10	2	6	10		2	1						
50 Sn	2	2	6	2	6	10	2	6	10		2	2						
51 Sb	2	2	6	2	6	10	2	6	10		2	3						
52 Te	2	2	6	2	6	10	2	6	10		2	4						

	K	L		M			N				O				P			Q
	1s	2s	2p	3s	3p	3d	4s	4p	4d	4f	5s	5p	5d	5f	6s	6p	6d	7s
53 I	2	2	6	2	6	10	2	6	10		2	5						
54 Xe	2	2	6	2	6	10	2	6	10		2	6						
55 Cs	2	2	6	2	6	10	2	6	10		2	6			1			
56 Ba	2	2	6	2	6	10	2	6	10		2	6			2			
57 La	2	2	6	2	6	10	2	6	10		2	6	1		2			
58 Ce	2	2	6	2	6	10	2	6	10	2	2	6			2			
59 Pr	2	2	6	2	6	10	2	6	10	3	2	6			2			
60 Nd	2	2	6	2	6	10	2	6	10	4	2	6			2			
61 Pm	2	2	6	2	6	10	2	6	10	5	2	6			2			
62 Sm	2	2	6	2	6	10	2	6	10	6	2	6			2			
63 Eu	2	2	6	2	6	10	2	6	10	7	2	6			2			
64 Gd	2	2	6	2	6	10	2	6	10	7	2	6	1		2			
65 Tb	2	2	6	2	6	10	2	6	10	9	2	6			2			
66 Dy	2	2	6	2	6	10	2	6	10	10	2	6			2			
67 Ho	2	2	6	2	6	10	2	6	10	11	2	6			2			
68 Er	2	2	6	2	6	10	2	6	10	12	2	6			2			
69 Tm	2	2	6	2	6	10	2	6	10	13	2	6			2			
70 Yb	2	2	6	2	6	10	2	6	10	14	2	6			2			
71 Lu	2	2	6	2	6	10	2	6	10	14	2	6	1		2			
72 Hf	2	2	6	2	6	10	2	6	10	14	2	6	2		2			
73 Ta	2	2	6	2	6	10	2	6	10	14	2	6	3		2			
74 W	2	2	6	2	6	10	2	6	10	14	2	6	4		2			
75 Re	2	2	6	2	6	10	2	6	10	14	2	6	5		2			
76 Os	2	2	6	2	6	10	2	6	10	14	2	6	6		2			
77 Ir	2	2	6	2	6	10	2	6	10	14	2	6	7		2			
78 Pt	2	2	6	2	6	10	2	6	10	14	2	6	9		1			
79 Au	2	2	6	2	6	10	2	6	10	14	2	6	10		1			
80 Hg	2	2	6	2	6	10	2	6	10	14	2	6	10		2			
81 Tl	2	2	6	2	6	10	2	6	10	14	2	6	10		2	1		
82 Pb	2	2	6	2	6	10	2	6	10	14	2	6	10		2	2		
83 Bi	2	2	6	2	6	10	2	6	10	14	2	6	10		2	3		
84 Po	2	2	6	2	6	10	2	6	10	14	2	6	10		2	4		
85 At	2	2	6	2	6	10	2	6	10	14	2	6	10		2	5		
86 Rn	2	2	6	2	6	10	2	6	10	14	2	6	10		2	6		
87 Fr	2	2	6	2	6	10	2	6	10	14	2	6	10		2	6		1
88 Ra	2	2	6	2	6	10	2	6	10	14	2	6	10		2	6		2
89 Ac	2	2	6	2	6	10	2	6	10	14	2	6	10		2	6	1	2
90 Th	2	2	6	2	6	10	2	6	10	14	2	6	10		2	6	2	2
91 Pa	2	2	6	2	6	10	2	6	10	14	2	6	10	2	2	6	1	2
92 U	2	2	6	2	6	10	2	6	10	14	2	6	10	3	2	6	1	2
93 Np	2	2	6	2	6	10	2	6	10	14	2	6	10	4	2	6	1	2
94 Pu	2	2	6	2	6	10	2	6	10	14	2	6	10	5	2	6	1	2
95 Am	2	2	6	2	6	10	2	6	10	14	2	6	10	6	2	6	1	2
96 Cm	2	2	6	2	6	10	2	6	10	14	2	6	10	7	2	6	1	2
97 Bk	2	2	6	2	6	10	2	6	10	14	2	6	10	8	2	6	1	2
98 Cf	2	2	6	2	6	10	2	6	10	14	2	6	10	10	2	6		2
99 Es	2	2	6	2	6	10	2	6	10	14	2	6	10	11	2	6		2
100 Fm	2	2	6	2	6	10	2	6	10	14	2	6	10	12	2	6		2
101 Md	2	2	6	2	6	10	2	6	10	14	2	6	10	13	2	6		2
102 No	2	2	6	2	6	10	2	6	10	14	2	6	10	14	2	6		2
103 Lw	2	2	6	2	6	10	2	6	10	14	2	6	10	14	2	6	1	2

APPENDIX G
STIRLING'S APPROXIMATION

Following is a demonstration of Stirling's formula, valid for large integers N:

$$\ln N! \cong N \ln N - N \tag{G-1}$$

By definition

$$N! = N(N-1)(N-2) \cdots (3)(2)(1) \tag{G-2}$$

and so

$$\ln N! = \ln 1 + \ln 2 + \ln 3 + \cdots \\ + \ln (N-2) + \ln (N-1) + \ln N \tag{G3}$$

Figure G-1 is a plot of $\ln x$ as a function of x. In the figure, $\ln 2$ is simply the rectangular area shown between $x = 1$ and $x = 2$, $\ln 3$ that between $x = 2$ and $x = 3$, and so on. Of course, $\ln 1 = 0$. Thus $\ln 3!$ is the sum of the rectangular areas between $x = 1$ and $x = 3$, and in general $\ln N!$ is the sum of the rectangular areas between $x = 1$ and $x = N$.

This area may be approximated as

$$\int_1^N \ln x \, dx$$

which is less than $\ln N!$ because it does not include the shaded three-cornered areas between the curve and the top of each rectangle. But for very large N this omitted area becomes negligibly small compared with the *total* area, and the *fractional error* in the approximation becomes very small. Thus we have

$$\ln N! \cong \int_1^N \ln x \, dx$$

$$= \left[x \ln x - x \right]_1^N = N \ln N - N - 1 \tag{G-4}$$

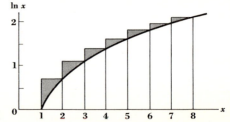

Figure G-1

Since the three-cornered areas have a magnitude of the order of unity, omitting the term -1 improves the approximation somewhat, and we obtain

$$\ln N! \cong N \ln N - N \qquad \text{(G-5)}$$

which is the form of Stirling's approximation used in Chap. 13.

A somewhat more precise approximation[1] is given by

$$\ln N! = (N + \tfrac{1}{2}) \ln N - N + \ln (2\pi)^{1/2} \qquad \text{(G-6)}$$

This added precision is never needed in statistical mechanics, for which Eq. (G-5) is always sufficient.

---

[1] See, for example, R. Courant, "Differential and Integral Calculus," vol. I, p. 361, Interscience Publishers, Inc., New York, 1937.

Answers to Odd-Numbered Problems

Chapter 1

1-1 (a) 4.33×10^{-8} s

(b) 10.4 m

1-3 Bolt at rear appears to come first.

1-5 2.60×10^8 m/s

1-7 (a) 2.00×10^8 m/s

(b) 3.72×10^{-7} s

(c) 74.5 m

(d) 2.00×10^8 m/s

1-9 0.943×10^{-7} s

1-11 86.6 m

1-13 $x = \dfrac{x' + ut'}{\sqrt{1 - u^2/c^2}}$

$y = y'$
$z = z'$

$t = \dfrac{t' + ux'/c^2}{\sqrt{1 - u^2/c^2}}$

1-15 $x' = \sqrt{(\Delta x)^2 - (c\,\Delta t)^2}$; yes

1-19 $23.4°$

Chapter 2

2-1 (a) 0.50%

(b) 43.6%

2-3 no

2-5 2.60×10^8 m/s; 63% too large

2-15 (a) 5.72×10^{11} J

(b) 6.29×10^4 kg

2-17 (a) $\omega = qB/m$

(b) $\omega = qBc^2/E$

(c) 20×10^6 r/s

Chapter 3

3-1 (a) up 5 m/s for 0.02 s, then down 5 m/s for 0.02 s

(b) up 1 m/s for 0.1 s, then down 1 m/s for 0.1 s

3-3 (b) 5 m/s, + x direction

(c) $y(x,t) = \dfrac{0.10}{4 + (2x + 10t)^2}$

3-5 (a) $-kuA \cos k(x - ut)$

(b) $kA \cos k(x - ut)$

3-7 (b) 1.0 m

3-9 100 m/s

3-11 $y(x,t) =$ (0.1 m) sin $2\pi\,[(0.5\text{ m}^{-1})x - (5\text{ s}^{-1})t]$, 10 m/s

3-13 There is no net transverse force to cause acceleration.

3-15 $F_y = 0.1\pi\ F \cos (10\pi\text{ s}^{-1})t$

3-17 20 m/s, 10 m, 0.5 s, 2 Hz, $\pi/5$ m^{-1}, 4π s^{-1}

3-19 (a) 20 m

(b) increase by $\sqrt{2}$

3-23 250 W, 0.04 s, 10 J

3-25 (b) $(1 + k)/(1 - k)$

3-27 $f = nu/4L$, $n = 1, 3, 5, \ldots$

3-29 5.44 m

3-31 increase by factor of 4

3-35 (a) 103.1 Hz

(b) 97.1 Hz

3-39 $f' = f(u - v)/(u + v)$

3-41 $f' = f(u - v_0)/(u - v_s)$

Chapter 4

4-1 (a) 300 m

(b) 3 m

4-3 $B = \frac{1}{2}\mu\varepsilon\omega\, rE_0 \sin \omega t$

4-5 $f = 1.05 \times 10^{18}$ Hz; $90°$

(Classical electrodynamics is not really applicable at this frequency.)

4-7 (a) 3.3×10^{-12} T

(b) very much smaller (factor of 10^{-8})

4-11 0.0173 V/m, 5.77×10^{-11} T

4-13 1.56×10^{-14} kg/m^{2}s

4-17 3.33×10^{-6} N; no

4-19 $E = 3 \times 10^4$ V/m

4-21 S/u^2

4-23 1.58

4-25 $I_r = I_0 \left(\dfrac{\sqrt{\varepsilon_1/\mu_1} - \sqrt{\varepsilon_2/\mu_2}}{\sqrt{\varepsilon_1/\mu_1} + \sqrt{\varepsilon_2/\mu_2}} \right)^2$

$I_t = I_0 \dfrac{4\sqrt{\varepsilon_1/\mu_1}\,\sqrt{\varepsilon_2/\mu_2}}{(\sqrt{\varepsilon_1/\mu_1} + \sqrt{\varepsilon_2/\mu_2})^2}$

4-27 (a) plane-polarized along axis of first filter; plane-polarized along axis of second filter

(b) $\sqrt{2}(\mu/\varepsilon)^{1/4}(I_0/2)^{1/2}$, $I_0/2$; $\sqrt{2}(\mu/\varepsilon)^{1/4}(I_0/4)^{1/2}$, $I_0/4$

4-29 plane-polarized perpendicular to grid wires

4-33 Use a quarter-wave plate with axes at $45°$ to desired direction of plane polarization; use two quarter-wave plates with corresponding axes aligned, or one half-wave plate.

4-35 $B_y = (E_0/c) \cos (kx - \omega t)$

$B_z = (E_0/c) \sin (kx - \omega t)$

4-37 (a) right (looking backward)

(b) E_1 right-circular plus $(E_2 - E_1)$ in z plane, or E_2 right-circular plus $(E_1 - E_2)$ in y plane

Chapter 5

5-3 x axis: $E_y = E_z$

$= \dfrac{p_0\omega^2}{4\pi\varepsilon u^2}\dfrac{\cos (kx - \omega t)}{x}$

(plane-polarized at $45°$ to y and z axes)

y axis: $E_z =$

$\dfrac{p_0\omega^2}{4\pi\varepsilon u^2}\dfrac{\cos (ky - \omega t)}{y}$

(plane-polarized in z direction)

z axis: $E_y =$

$\dfrac{p_0\omega^2}{4\pi\varepsilon u^2}\dfrac{\cos (kz - \omega t)}{z}$

(plane-polarized in y direction)

5-5 1.73×10^{-5} W

5-7 $2E_0$, $1.85E_0$, $1.41E_0$, $0.765E_0$, 0

5-15 i, -1, $-i$, 1

5-17 (b) $I = 2I_0[1 + \cos (\pi + \pi \sin \theta)]$

5-19 no interference pattern because polarizations are perpendicular

5-21 0.376 m

5-23 $I = I_0 \dfrac{\sin^2 (2\pi \sin \theta)}{\sin^2 (\frac{1}{2}\pi \sin \theta)}$

5-25 $\lambda = 1000 \text{ nm}/n$ $(n = 1, 2, 3, \ldots)$ Only 500 nm is in the visible region.

5-27 $I = I_0 \dfrac{\sin^2 [N\pi(1 + \sin \theta)/4]}{\sin^2 [\pi(1 + \sin \theta)/4]}$

5-29 162 nm

5-31 0.188 mm; dark

5-33 (a) dark

    (b) bright: r_n
$$= [(n - \tfrac{1}{2})\lambda R - (n - \tfrac{1}{2})^2\lambda^2/4]^{1/2}$$
$$\cong [(n - \tfrac{1}{2})\lambda R]^{1/2}$$
dark: r_n
$$= (n\lambda R - n^2\lambda^2/4)^{1/2}$$
$$\cong (n\lambda R)^{1/2}$$
$(R = 30 \text{ cm}, \lambda = 600 \text{ nm},$ so $\lambda \ll R)$

Chapter 6

6-1 14.5°, 30°, 48.6°

6-3 8.6°, 17.5°, 26.7°, 36.9°, 48.6°, 64.2°

6-5 (a) 2.17 g/cm^3
    (b) 0.0979 nm,
        0.0979/2 nm, . . .

6-7 5 cm

6-11 0.25×10^{-3} mm

6-13 (a) 7
    (b) 2.5×10^{-3} r
    (c) $(2/\pi)^2 = 0.405$

6-15 (a) 3.05 cm
    (b) 3.66 cm

6-17 larger in each dimension, and farther from hologram, by factor 6/5; different color

6-19 Each bright spot is smeared into a color spectrum, resulting in superposed images in various colors, with blue images smaller than red.

6-21 Increasing thermal agitation decreases the extent of polarization in a given field.

6-23 $K_E = 1 - \dfrac{Ne^2}{\varepsilon_0 m\omega^2}$

6-25 Blue light is scattered more than red light; if there were no scattering, the sky would be black.

Chapter 7

7-1 6.67 ft

7-5 36 in, bottom edge 33 in above floor

7-9 (a) 10 cm in front of mirror, 1 cm, inverted, real
    (b) 20 cm behind mirror, 5 cm, erect, virtual

7-13 (a) 0.5 cm, 10 cm to left, erect, virtual
    (b) 1.0 cm, 5 cm to left, erect, virtual

7-15 (a) 30 cm to right, 1.5 cm, inverted, real
    (b) 15 cm to left, 3 cm, erect, virtual

7-17 Object appears with actual size, at actual location.

7-19 Beam is focused to a line parallel to cylinder axis at a distance $n_2 R/(n_2 - n_1)$ from surface. If this distance is negative, virtual focus and diverging cylindrical wave.

7-23 (a) -3.33 cm

(b) 2.5 cm to left, 0.25 cm, erect, virtual

7-29 (a) 5 cm

(b) $375\times$

7-31 (a) 2.93 in

(b) 3 in

7-33 (a) 6 cm

(b) $5\times$ (or $\frac{1}{5}\times$)

7-35 (a) 25 cm in front of mirror

(b) $25\times$

7-37 800 lines/mm

7-39 minimum aperture about 6 mm (f:8)

Chapter 8

8-1 3×10^{20}; 5×10^6 m

8-3 1.24×10^{-12} m, 2.42×10^{20} Hz, 1000 times larger

8-5 (a) 1.33 MeV

(b) 7084 m/s

(c) no

8-7 1 eV, 6.4×10^{-34} J · s

8-9 Wavelength shifts are too small (order of 1 part in 10^6) to be easily observable.

8-11 7.09×10^{-13} m, gamma ray

8-13 because of definition of potential energy; $V(r)$ is zero at infinity and negative at all finite distances.

8-15 1.03 eV, 3.10 eV (4.13 eV)

8-17 10.2 eV, 0.05% correction

8-19 3.85 m/s

8-21 5.29×10^{-11} m, 2.19×10^6 m/s, 4.13×10^{16} s^{-1}, 1.054×10^{-34} kg · m^2/s

8-23 energies larger by factor of 4, radii smaller by factor of 2

8-27 (a) 6.11×10^3 T

(b) 6.51×10^6 T

8-29 21.8 mm; actual area is less; heat is also lost by conduction

8-31 483 nm, blue-green part of visible spectrum

Chapter 9

9-1 8.67×10^{-12} m; smaller by the order of 10^{-5}

9-3 (a) 0.0388 eV

(b) 1.45×10^{-10} m

9-5 4.42×10^{-34} m; no

9-9 0.1 to 1 eV

9-11 $u = c \sqrt{1 + \mu^2/k^2}$, $v = c/\sqrt{1 + \mu^2/k^2}$

9-13 $2Ae^{ik_0x} (\sin ax)/x$, $(2A/x) \sin ax$

9-17 5×10^{-10} m, no

9-19 6×10^{23} kg · m/s

9-21 approximate values: 1.0×10^{-19} kg m/s; 2 MeV, 200 MeV; 1.44 MeV

9-23 5×10^{-24} s, 1.4×10^{-15} m

Chapter 10

10-1 0.10

10-3 $\frac{1}{2} + 1/\pi = 0.818$

10-5 8.19 MeV

10-7 $(2/L) \sin^2 (n\pi x/L)$

10-15 $\hbar^{1/2}/(mk)^{1/4}$

Chapter 11

11-1 5490 eV, 0.055%

11-3 32.5 MeV

11-5 $\frac{1}{2}(2\pi a^3)^{1/2}$

11-7 121 nm, 102 nm, 97.1 nm, ultraviolet

11-9 1.05×10^5 K

11-11 (a) -0.00136 eV, 0.529×10^{-6} m

(b) 2.76×10^{-5} eV, 6.68×10^{9} Hz, 4.49 cm, microwave

11-13 (a) 0.265×10^{-10} m

(b) 54.4 eV

(c) Brackett (ending at $n = 4$), also last line of Paschen $(4 \rightarrow 3)$

11-19 It is correct.

11-25 (a) $7\omega_0/2$, $5\omega_0/2$, $\omega_0 = (k/m)^{1/2}$ (angular frequencies)

(b) ω_0

(c) ω_0

11-27 (a) 1.85×10^{-23} J

(b) $\pm 1.16 \times 10^{-4}$ eV, 0.661 eV (0.0175%)

(c) 0, ± 0.328 nm

11-31 9.27×10^{-24} J/T ("one Bohr magneton"), three, original level and original $\pm 5.79 \times 10^{-5}$ eV

Chapter 12

12-5 Terms in the sums represent numbers of electrons in successive filled subshells.

12-7 cesium; differences in screening by electrons in inner shells

12-9 xenon; smallest ionization potential because of screening effects

12-11 1.51 eV; 5.1 eV; the $3s$ electron is not completely shielded from nucleus by inner electrons.

12-13 (a) $r > a$: $E = e/4\pi\varepsilon_0 r^2$, $V = e/4\pi\varepsilon_0 r$

$r < a$: $E = (e/4\pi\varepsilon_0)(3/r^2 - 2r/a^3)$, $V = (e/4\pi\varepsilon_0)(3/r - 3/a - r^2/a^3)$

12-15 22,860 eV, 4165 eV, 0.067 nm

12-17 9910 eV

12-21 1.44×10^{-10} m, if Cl^- ions are on opposite sides of Mg^{2+}

12-25 $r_n = \dfrac{4\pi\varepsilon_0 n^2 \hbar^2}{(3\sqrt{3} - 1)me^2}$

$E_n = -\left(\dfrac{3\sqrt{3} - 1}{2}\right)^2 \left(\dfrac{e^2}{4\pi\varepsilon_0}\right)^2 \dfrac{m}{n^2\hbar^2}$

12-27 (a) 3.48 μm

(b) 483 N/m

12-31 1.18×10^{-21} J, 168 μm; twice as large, (the $l = 1$ to $l = 0$ transition in H_2 does not ordinarily occur, for reasons discussed in Prob. 12-19).

Chapter 13

13-1 1.25 kg/m^3

13-3 7.09×10^{7} N/m^2, or 700 atm; no; intermolecular forces become significant

13-5 3.4 m/s, 4.29 m/s

13-7 3.97×10^{23}

13-9 (a) Nmv^2/d, Nmv^2/Ad

(b) $k/2m$ (per unit mass)

(c) $p = NkT/Ad$

13-11 (a) 478 m/s

(b) 1352 m/s

(c) 79.0 m/s

13-13 2.4×10^{6}

13-15 0.087; no; shape of curve is independent of T

13-17 0.023

13-19 H and He molecules have higher molecular speeds and diffuse through leaks faster than heavier molecules.

13-21 $(2kT/m)^{1/2}$

13-23 no; for air, $v_{rms} = 0.1$ c at about 10^{12} K; yes, higher for larger m

13-27 11,610 K

13-29 2.48 cal/g · C°; larger by factor of 2 to 100

13-31 three translational and three rotational degrees of freedom ($3R$ total) plus partly frozen vibrational degrees ($0.78 R$)

13-33 (a) 5.34×10^{-46} kg · m^2
 (b) 20

13-35 0.336

13-41 (a) $n_{max} = N/2$, $E_{max} = (1/2m)(\pi\hbar/L)^2 (N/2)^2$
 (b) $E_f = (1/2m)(\pi\hbar/L)^2 (N/2)^2$
 (c) $(1/12m)(\pi\hbar/L)^2 (N/2 + 1)(N + 1) \cong (1/m)(\pi\hbar/L)^2 (N^2/24)$ if N large

13-43 0.475, 0.269, 0.119, 4.54×10^{-5}

Chapter 14

14-5 2.18 g/cm^3

14-11 $0.335 \, \varepsilon_0/k$

14-17 0.002 to 0.006 K^{-1} for many common metals

14-21 (a) 3.87×10^{-3}
 (b) 0.0307 J/T
 (c) 13.7 J/T
 (d) 13.7 N · m

14-25 1770 nm; near infrared; yes

14-27 (b) $0.0217 \, V/k$; populations are nearly equal when $kT \gg V$, but material has vaporized at this temperature

Chapter 15

15-1 2.3×10^{17} kg/m^3, larger by 10^{14}

15-3 39; $^{30}_{14}$Si

15-5 0.22 T

15-7 21.3 MHz

15-9 4.95 MeV

15-11 1000 eV, 10^{-6} u; marginal

15-13 0.00423 u

15-15 17.7 MeV

15-17 (a) 8.26 MeV
 (b) 34.969 u

15-19 6.05 MeV

15-21 12,900 yr

15-23 In beta decay the electron shares the energy with a neutrino.

15-25 0.89 μg

15-29 892 eV, 0.782 MeV (Electron gets about 99.9% of the energy.)

15-31 2 MeV

15-33 (a) 10 MeV
 (b) 15.2 MHz

15-35 0.474 m; yes, 1 MeV is greater than mc^2 for electron

15-37 7.34×10^{16}

15-39 17.7 MeV or 2.83×10^{-12} J, 1.88×10^{14} J/kg (compared to 3×10^7 J/kg for coal)

15-41 5.38 MeV in lab system

Chapter 16

16-1 Just below mc^2; for ground state, $mc^2 - 13.6$ eV

16-3   zero, 0.511 MeV

16-7 5×10^{-24} s

16-9   (a) 2.60×10^8 m/s

      (b) 0.66×10^{-24} s

      (c) 0.17×10^{-15} m

      (K range is shorter than π by ratio of masses)

16-11   muon: 4.12 MeV; neutrino: 29.8 MeV

16-13   52.8 MeV; much larger than mc^2 for electron

16-15   905 MeV

16-17   To conserve both S and B, either two K's or a baryon-antibaryon pair must be produced.

16-19   37.7 MeV; proton, 14.3%; pion, 85.7%

16-21   (a) ppn

      (b) $\overline{nn}\,\overline{\lambda}$

      (c) $n\lambda\lambda$

      (d) $pn\lambda$

Index

Index